Handbook of Research on Advancing Cybersecurity for Digital Transformation

Kamaljeet Sandhu
University of New England, Australia

A volume in the Advances in Information Security,
Privacy, and Ethics (AISPE) Book Series

Published in the United States of America by
IGI Global
Information Science Reference (an imprint of IGI Global)
701 E. Chocolate Avenue
Hershey PA, USA 17033
Tel: 717-533-8845
Fax: 717-533-8661
E-mail: cust@igi-global.com
Web site: http://www.igi-global.com

Library of Congress Cataloging-in-Publication Data

Names: Sandhu, Kamaljeet, 1970- editor.
Title: Handbook of research on advancing cybersecurity for digital transformation /
   Kamaljeet Sandhu, editor.
Description: Hershey, PA : Information Science Reference, an imprint of IGI
   Global, 2021. | Includes bibliographical references and index. |
   Summary: "This book offers a variety of perspectives on issues,
   problems, and innovative solutions and strategies that are linked to
   cybersecurity and its an impact on private and public organizations,
   government institutions, and consumers interacting on digital data"--
   Provided by publisher.
Identifiers: LCCN 2020048929 (print) | LCCN 2020048930 (ebook) | ISBN
   9781799869757 (hardcover) | ISBN 9781799869764 (ebook)
Subjects: LCSH: Computer security. | Computer networks--Security measures.
Classification: LCC QA76.9.A25 A379 2021 (print) | LCC QA76.9.A25 (ebook)
   | DDC 005.8--dc23
LC record available at https://lccn.loc.gov/2020048929
LC ebook record available at https://lccn.loc.gov/2020048930

This book is published in the IGI Global book series Advances in Information Security, Privacy, and Ethics (AISPE) (ISSN: 1948-9730; eISSN: 1948-9749)

British Cataloguing in Publication Data
A Cataloguing in Publication record for this book is available from the British Library.

All work contributed to this book is new, previously-unpublished material. The views expressed in this book are those of the authors, but not necessarily of the publisher.

For electronic access to this publication, please contact: eresources@igi-global.com.

Advances in Information Security, Privacy, and Ethics (AISPE) Book Series

Manish Gupta
State University of New York, USA

ISSN:1948-9730
EISSN:1948-9749

MISSION

As digital technologies become more pervasive in everyday life and the Internet is utilized in ever in-creasing ways by both private and public entities, concern over digital threats becomes more prevalent.

The **Advances in Information Security, Privacy, & Ethics (AISPE) Book Series** provides cutting-edge research on the protection and misuse of information and technology across various industries and settings. Comprised of scholarly research on topics such as identity management, cryptography, system security, authentication, and data protection, this book series is ideal for reference by IT professionals, academicians, and upper-level students.

COVERAGE

- Privacy-Enhancing Technologies
- Network Security Services
- Telecommunications Regulations
- Device Fingerprinting
- Access Control
- Security Classifications
- Privacy Issues of Social Networking
- Electronic Mail Security
- Tracking Cookies
- Cyberethics

IGI Global is currently accepting manuscripts for publication within this series. To submit a pro-posal for a volume in this series, please contact our Acquisition Editors at Acquisitions@igi-global.com or visit: http://www.igi-global.com/publish/.

Titles in this Series

For a list of additional titles in this series, please visit: www.igi-global.com/book-series

701 East Chocolate Avenue, Hershey, PA 17033, USA
Tel: 717-533-8845 x100 • Fax: 717-533-8661
E-Mail: cust@igi-global.com • www.igi-global.com

I dedicate this book to the memory of my mother and father.

Editorial Advisory Board

List of Contributors

Table of Contents

Detailed Table of Contents

Chapter 1

 Kamaljeet Sandhu, University of New England, Australia

Advancing cybersecurity for digital transformation provides opportunities and challenges. Many enterprises are accelerating the digital transformation to reach their customers, suppliers, and other parties over the internet; at the same time cybersecurity has become a serious concern. Cyberattacks have exponentially increased globally. While digital transformation makes the business process more efficient and effective, and increased cyberattacks pose obstacles, threats, and risks on the way. Cyberattacks consist of different types such as political, financial, accessing private and confidential information, ransomware, identity theft, destruction to essential infrastructure and public utilities such as energy, water, telecommunication, transportation, health, and others. This chapter presents case analysis from recent cyberattacks to show the scale, size, and type of impacts within and outside the enterprise. Newer technologies to counter cyberattacks are introduced such as quantum computing, nanotechnologies, artificial intelligence, blockchain that have the capabilities to eliminate cyberattacks.

Chapter 2

 Joni A. Amorim, Universidade Estadual de Campinas (UNICAMP), Brazil
 Jose-Macario de Siqueira Rocha, Universitat de València, Spain
 Teresa Magal-Royo, Universitat Politécnica de València (UPV), Spain

Information security is increasingly necessary between citizens and public services. In a nearby environment, such as cities, there are digital services and infrastructures that help improve our quality of life. Secure access to services must be regulated and offer trust to the user. Initiatives like the Regulation from European Union, (EU) N° 910/2014 of the European Parliament and the Council intend to favour solutions for problems like interoperability and cybersecurity. In this chapter, two European countries are considered so that implementations of the electronic identification, authentication, and trust services are presented and discussed. The main contribution is a description of relevant European projects, a first step necessary to propel further research on this topic. The chapter also presents the current challenges for the consolidation of the technology used and for the adaptation of the electronic services offered by public administration bodies to citizens.

True to its nickname 'cyber nation', the country of Israel is seen as a kind of role model in terms of intelligence and defence capabilities by many countries. The present study aims to provide a comprehensive but far from a complete picture of the cyber defence ecosystem of Israel, a country with more than 430 start-ups and unicorns valued at billions of US dollars. The authors outline the major incidents of the recent period, as well as current challenges and threats. The purpose of the chapter is to introduce good practices and cooperation for opportunities to policymakers and cybersecurity experts as well.

Cybersecurity is a critical consideration for all users of electronic health records (EHR), particularly for patients. With the advent of Healthcare 4.0, which is based on the internet of things (IoT) and sensors, cyber resilience has become a key requirement in ensuring the protection of patient data across devices. Blockchain offers crypto-enforced security, data immutability, and smart contracts-based business logic features to all the users in the network. This study explores how blockchain can be a single digital option that can address both the cybersecurity and cyber resilience needs of EHR. The effective use lens is adopted to analyze how blockchain can be leveraged to meet cybersecurity needs while the novel use lens is adopted to analyze how blockchain can be leveraged to address cyber resilience needs originating from IoT. Based on the analysis, this study proposes two Hyperledger-based security models that contribute to individual privacy and information security needs.

The main aim of embracing evolutionary digital e-health technologies such as 'My Health Records' is to transform and empower the patients to control their health records, access, choose the right healthcare provider and suitable treatment, when required. It has been a challenge for the healthcare practitioners, hospital staff, as well as patients to accept, embrace, and adopt transformative digital e-health technologies and manage their healthcare records amidst concerns of slow adoption by the patient due to data privacy and cybersecurity issues. Australia, since COVID-19, has stressed the importance of secure online connectivity for the government, business, and the consumers. It is essential that My Health Record platform is cyber-safe, and user-friendly so that consumers feel conformable, safe and secure regarding their personal health records. This chapter discussed the challenges of embracing e-health digital technologies and assurance of advancing cybersecurity of online My Health Record, which will transform e-health provision and empower patients and healthcare providers.

As the pace of changes in the digital world is increasing exponentially, the appeal to shift from traditional platforms to digital ones is increasing as well. Accomplishing digital transformation objectives is impossible without information security considerations. Business leaders should rethink information security challenges associated with digital transformation and consider solutions to seize existing opportunities. When it comes to information security, human beings play a critical role. Raising users' awareness is a meaningful approach to avoid or neutralize the likelihood of unwanted security consequences that may occur during transforming a system digitally. This chapter will discuss cybersecurity and information security awareness and examine how digital transformation will be affected by implementing information security awareness. This chapter will discuss the digital transformation advantages and serious challenges associated with cybersecurity, how to enhance cybersecurity, and the role of information security awareness to mitigate cybersecurity risks.

Internet of things (IoT) has revolutionized digital transformation and is present in every sector including transportation, energy, retail, healthcare, agriculture, etc. While stepping into the new digital transformation, these sectors must contemplate the risks involved. The new wave of cyberattacks against IoT is posing a severe impediment in adopting this leading-edge technology. Artificial intelligence (AI) is playing a key role in preventing and mitigating some of the effects of these cyberattacks. This chapter discusses different types of threats and attacks against IoT devices and how AI is enabling the detection and prevention of these cyberattacks. It also presents some challenges faced by AI-enabled detection and prevention and provides some solutions and recommendations to these challenges. The authors believe that this chapter provides a favorable basis for the readers who intend to know more about AI-enabled technologies to detect and prevent cyberattacks against IoT and the motivation to advance the current research in this area.

Cyber security threatens vital elements of enterprises such as network, information, application, operational, sustainability, education, and trade secret. Digital transformation and widespread use of IoT caused by the pandemic reveal the importance of cybersecurity vulnerabilities. This study is prepared by a systematic review method for cybersecurity. The inspiration of this chapter is the cyberattacks that threaten the global economy and enterprises and the effects of cybercrime on management and strategy. The cybersecurity problem, which continues to increase with the pandemic in the manufacturing and service sector, is current and becoming a serious threat. This study reveals strategy development against cybersecurity threats; sustainability elements in management; measures to be taken against cybercrime, cyberattack, and cyberterrorism; and organizational and business culture management in digital transformation.

Chapter 9

Digital banking allows banks to make their new products more readily available, as they can package them with their essential software that has implications for cybersecurity. Internet presence also allows banks to extend their geographical reach without overbearing costs. In Pakistan, most internet offerings currently used by banks are more based on information than transactions; therefore, the issues for cybersecurity have gained high interest. The offerings on the websites by banks generally seem like electronic brochures. As they mainly offer company events, product information, along with a list of services rendered. Pakistan has various barriers to e-commerce, such as relatively few internet users, inadequate infrastructure (i.e., frequent power failures, fewer phone lines), and lack of cybersecurity for online transactions being hacked. The Government of Pakistan is rigorously working on these areas to overcome respective problems and progress in this sphere. This research focuses on the challenges for e-banking and e-commerce in Pakistan and issues relating to cybersecurity.

Chapter 10

The financial sector across the globe ensures sustainable growth in the economy by mobilizing investments, funds, and savings. This chapter attempts to comprehend the current state of cybersecurity within the financial services industry worldwide. The chapter explores the different aspects of global cyber-attacks in financial sectors to elucidate the salient problems, issues, threats, safeguards, and solutions. As technology is progressing, highly technology-savvy criminals are becoming a new threat in the cybercrime space. The entire industry needs an intense transformation to create innovative, state-of-the-art information, and an up-to-date architecture of cybersecurity that is capable of confronting the continuous tides of cyber-attacks and data breaches on an everyday basis. The use of security tools like proxy servers, firewalls, multi-layered email strategy, virus security software, and effective governance strategies are necessary to protect financial sectors from cyber threats and attacks.

Chapter 11

Digital transformation has revolutionized human life but also brought many cybersecurity challenges for users and enterprises. The major threats that affect computers and communication systems by damaging devices and stealing sensitive information are malicious attacks. Traditional anti-virus software fails to detect advanced kind of malware. Current research focuses on developing machine learning techniques for malware detection to respond in a timely manner. Many systems have been evolved and improved to distinguish the malware based on analysis behavior. The analysis behavior is considered a robust technique to detect, analyze, and classify malware, categorized into two models: a static and dynamic analysis. Both types of previous analysis have advantages and limitations. Therefore, the hybrid method combines the strength of static and dynamic analyses. This chapter conducted a systematic literature review (SLR) to summarize and analyze the quality of published studies in malware detection using machine learning techniques and hybrid analysis that range from 2016 to 2021.

Romil Rawat, Shri Vaishnav Vidyapeeth Vishwavidyalaya, India
Vinod Mahor, IPS College of Technology and Management, Gwalior, India
Anjali Rawat, Independent Researcher, India
Bhagwati Garg, Union Bank of India, Gwalior, India
Shrikant Telang, Shri Vaishnav Vidyapeeth Vishwavidyalaya, India

The heterogeneous digital arena emerged as the open depiction for malicious activities, and cyber criminals and terrorists are targeting the cyber depiction for controlling its operation. In the dark web (DW), diverse illegal hacking communities are using the sensing-chip webnet to transfer their bots for tracking the user activity so that criminal activities could be accomplished like money laundering, pornography, child trafficking, drug trafficking, arms and ammunition trafficking, where professionals could also be hired and contracted for generating flood infringement and ransomware infringement.

Shahid Alam, Adana Alparsalan Turkes Science and Technology University, Turkey

As corporations are stepping into the new digital transformation age and adopting leading-edge technologies such as cloud, mobile, and big data, it becomes crucial for them to contemplate the risks and rewards of this adoption. At the same time, the new wave of malware attacks is posing a severe impediment in implementing these technologies. This chapter discusses some of the complications, challenges, and issues plaguing current malware analysis and detection techniques. Some of the key challenges discussed are automation, native code, obfuscations, morphing, and anti-reverse engineering. Solutions and recommendations are provided to solve some of these challenges. To stimulate further research in this thriving area, the authors highlight some promising future research directions. The authors believe that this chapter provides an auspicious basis for future researchers who intend to know more about the evolution of malware and will act as a motivation for enhancing the current and developing the new techniques for malware analysis and detection.

Tansif ur Rehman, University of Karachi, Pakistan

In this technological era, almost all renowned banks have equipped themselves with the latest technology significantly pertinent to enhance their services and have provided e-banking facilities to their customers. Nevertheless, cybersecurity has been the focus of many organizations. Banks are offering more facilities to facilitate their customers with ease and convenience regarding e-banking. However, in Pakistan this is not the case. As people still refrain from using e-banking in Pakistan because of various issues, the e-banking sector has exponentially grown in the last decade. It has more chances of growth as enterprises such as banks still encourage clients to carry out e-transactions, like utility bill payments, access to account information, and money transfer. During this process, cybercriminals attempt to steal customer data and hack their online sessions. With regards to e-banking fraud, digitization has caused a revolution. Cybercriminals have employed various tools to steal crucial information through identity theft, trojans, viruses, and phishing.

Chapter 15

In this chapter, the author bases his research project on his authentic mixed multidisciplinary applied mathematical model for transformation projects. His mathematical model, named the applied holistic mathematical model for projects (AHMM4P), is supported by a tree-based heuristics structure. The AHMM4P is similar to the human empirical decision-making process and is applicable to any type of project; it is aimed to support the evolution of organisational, national, or enterprise transformation initiatives. The AHMM4P can be used for the development of the cybersecurity subsystems, enterprise information systems, and their decision-making systems, based on artificial intelligence, data sciences, enterprise architecture, big data, deep learning, and machine learning. The author attempts to prove that an AHMM4P-based action research approach can unify the currently frequently-used siloed MLI4P and DLI4P trends.

Chapter 16

Cybersecurity in Europe as the rest of the world has been legislated for only 20 years. Numerous governmental institutions such as councils offer electronic services through their recently created electronic offices. In all of them, the volume of citizens who register temporarily or permanently to request online services related to the processing of documents and services with the government has increased significantly since the pandemic. Confinement has forced users to request numerous online services where authentication is one of the most relevant aspects to access safely and securely. European Union through the Connecting Europe Mechanism, CEF projects of the European Health Executive Agency, and Digital HaDEA has allowed numerous institutions to connect through the eIDAS created to establish trust in electronic transactions between individuals, organizations, and government entities across European member states.

Jonika Lamba, The NorthCap University, Gurugram, India
Esha Jain, The NorthCap University, Gurugram, India

Cybersecurity is not just about fortification of data. It has wide implications such as maintaining safety, privacy, integrity, and trust of the patients in the healthcare sector. This study methodically reviews the need for cybersecurity amid digital transformation with the help of emerging technologies and focuses on the application and incorporation of blockchain and the internet of things (IoT) to ensure cybersecurity in the well-being of the business. It was found in the study that worldwide, advanced technology has been used in managing the flow of data and information, India should focus on maintaining the same IT-enabled infrastructure to reduce causalities in the nation and on the other hand improve administration, privacy, and security in the hospital sector. Depending on the network system, resource allocation, and mobile devices, there is a need to prioritize the resources and efforts in the era of digitalization.

Tansif ur Rehman, University of Karachi, Pakistan

The practice of protecting computers, websites, mobile devices, electronic services, networks, and digital data from malicious attacks is known as cybersecurity. Since political, military, private, financial, and medical institutions collect, process, and maintain massive volumes of data on computers and other devices, cybersecurity is critical. Sensitive data, such as intellectual property, financial data, personal records, or other forms of data, can make up a large amount of the data. Improper access or disclosure to that data can have profound implications. Technology has undoubtedly made a significant change in every aspect of life in Pakistan, whether it is a financial or non-financial sphere. Technology's usage is thoroughly utilized by banks worldwide. They have started adopting it frequently because of the immense need to achieve goals and satisfy customer needs more efficiently. Almost all leading banks have now provided e-commerce facilities. Over time, more and more services and facilities are offered to bank customers conveniently via e-commerce products.

Preface

Cybersecurity has become a serious issue for enterprises, government institutions, and largely for people interacting with digital online systems. Cyberattacks have increased exponentially and cybersecurity has also been a major concern for business leaders. Despite increased investments in safety measures and security controls, cyber-attacks keep continuing, and losses and cost keeps rising. As many individuals and enterprise activities (e.g., finance, banking, health, utilities, and many others) continue to grow and conducted in the digital space, new vulnerabilities have arisen which have led to cybersecurity threats in the digital transformation. The nature, source, reasons, and sophistication for cyberattacks are not clearly understood, and many times invisible cyber attackers are never traced or can never be found.

Cyberattacks can only be known once the attack and the destruction have already taken place long after the attackers have left. Sometimes cyberattacks are not discovered as snooping software (or hackers) that maliciously works and hidden within the systems without being found for many years. It is unknown how many such malicious programs are silently running without being discovered. Cybersecurity for computer systems has increasingly become important because the government, military, corporate, financial, critical infrastructure, and medical organizations rely heavily on digital network systems, which process and store large volumes of data on computer devices that are exchanged on the internet, and they are vulnerable to "continuous" cyberattacks, and in recent times have been a target. As cybersecurity has become a global concern, it needs to be clearly understood, and innovative solutions are required.

The primary aim of this book is to study deeper into issues, problems, and innovative solutions and strategies that are interlinked to cybersecurity. Cybersecurity is having an impact on consumers for interacting with digital data. An increasing number of cyberattacks, on computer systems and networks, unauthorized access to data, identity theft, phishing, malware, spam emails, and many other forms of cyberattacks on the digital platform to interrupt or destroy normal business process has led to implementing effective cybersecurity measures which are challenging as there are more number of devices and systems that can become a target and face cyberattacks which can impact computers, systems, and users at the same time. This book provides important knowledge that can impact on improving the cybersecurity which can add value in terms of innovation to solving cybersecurity threats.

Researchers have presented chapters that go deep inside critical issues that have been magnified and studied through research lens for cybersecurity, and data dissected to make meaningful sense of such cyberattacks. This book will also seek to advance new knowledge of senior managers, decision-makers, policymakers, and senior technical experts on how to better manage cybersecurity strategically within and outside the enterprise and make preparations for cybersecurity attacks. As cybersecurity has become a global concern it needs to be clearly understood in an international context and as the recent cyberattacks on enterprises such as Microsoft have shown that cybersecurity affects all of us including private, public, and not for profit enterprises, government institutions, and people interacting with digital online systems internationally.

The advancement in research leading to innovations for computer technology and systems can solve many problems associated with cybersecurity weaknesses. For example, advancement in artificial intelligence, blockchain, are increasingly being used to monitor large-scale IoT systems in which the computer systems and technologies autonomously communicate with each other, through face, voice, fingerprints, multi-factor authentication, and other digital user-id are automatically matched in nano seconds and unauthorized users and cyber attackers blocked from accessing the systems. Quantum computing is revolutionizing the next generation of innovative computers that will be very difficult or impossible to cyberattacks as the codes running on quantum computers will be extremely complex to hack by humans. Advancement in the field of nano computers suggests that the nanotechnology for computers will be minuscule in size (computing devices will be made less than 5 nanometres, compared to a single human hair which is approximately 80,000 nanometres), meaning it will be invisible to the human eye and can only be viewed through high powered electron microscopes. Such new and modern developments have the capabilities to eliminate cyberattacks as it will be unproductive for the attackers as the new technologies and systems will become increasingly difficult and complex to manipulate and the financial or other motivations of the attackers will no longer be economical to the time and effort devoted.

ORGANIZATION OF THE BOOK

A brief description of each of the chapters follows:

Chapter 1

Advancing cybersecurity for digital transformation provides opportunities and challenges. Many enterprises are accelerating the digital transformation to reach their customers, suppliers, and other parties over the internet, at the same time cybersecurity has become a serious concern. Cyberattacks have exponentially increased globally. While digital transformation makes the business process more efficient, cyberattacks pose obstacles on the way. Cyberattacks consist of different types such as political, financial, accessing private and confidential information, ransomware, identity theft, destruction to essential infrastructure and public utilities such as energy, water, telecommunication, transportation, health, and others. The chapter presents case analysis from recent cyberattacks to show the scale, size, and type of impacts. Newer technologies to counter cyberattacks are introduced such as quantum computing, nanotechnologies, artificial intelligence, blockchain that have the capabilities to eliminate cyberattacks.

Chapter 2

Information security transaction in the world is increasingly necessary within the communication between citizens and the public services. In a nearby environment, such as cities, there are digital services and infrastructures that help improve our quality of life. Secure access to services must be regulated and offer trust to the user. Initiatives like the Regulation from European Union, (EU) N° 910/2014 of the European Parliament and the Council intend to favour solutions for problems like interoperability and cybersecurity. In this chapter, two European countries are considered so that implementations of the electronic identification, authentication and trust services are presented and discussed. The main contribution is description of relevant European projects, a first step necessary to propel further research on this topic. The chapter also presents the current challenges for the consolidation of the technology used and for the adaptation of the electronic services offered by public administration bodies to citizens.

Chapter 3

True to its nickname 'cyber nation', the country of Israel is seen as a kind of role model in terms of intelligence and defence capabilities by many countries. The present study aims to provide a comprehensive but far from a complete picture of the cyber defence ecosystem of Israel, a country with more than 430 start-ups and unicorns valued at billions of US dollars. The authors outline the major incidents of the recent period, as well as current challenges and threats. The purpose of the article is to introduce good practices and cooperation for opportunities to policymakers and cybersecurity experts as well.

Chapter 4

Cybersecurity is a critical consideration for all users of Electronic Health Records (EHR), particularly for patients. With the advent of Healthcare 4.0, which is based on the Internet of Things (IoT) and sensors, cyber resilience has become a key requirement in ensuring the protection of patient data across devices. Blockchain offers crypto-enforced security, data immutability, and smart contracts-based business logic features to all the users in the network. This study explores how Blockchain can be a single digital option that can address both the cybersecurity and cyber resilience needs of EHR. The effective use lens is adopted to analyze how Blockchain can be leveraged to meet cybersecurity needs while the novel use lens is adopted to analyze how Blockchain can be leveraged to address cyber resilience needs originating from IoT. Based on the analysis, this study proposes two Hyperledger based security models that contribute to individual privacy and information security needs.

Chapter 5

The main aim of embracing evolutionary digital e-health technologies such as 'My Health Records' is to transform and empower the patients to control their health records, access, choose the right healthcare provider and suitable treatment, when required. It has been a challenge for the healthcare practitioners, hospital staff as well as patients to accept, embrace and adopt transformative digital e-health technologies and manage their healthcare records amidst concerns of slow adoption by the patient due to data privacy and cybersecurity issues. Australia, since COVID-19 has stressed the importance of secure online connectivity for the government, business and the consumers. It is essential that My health Record platform is cyber-safe and user-friendly so that consumers feel conformable, safe, and secure regarding their personal health records. This chapter discussed the challenges of embracing e-health digital technologies and assurance of advancing cybersecurity of online My Health Record', which will transform e-health provision and empower patients and the healthcare providers.

Chapter 6

As the pace of changes in the digital world is increasing exponentially, the appeal to shift from traditional platforms to digital ones is increasing as well. Accomplishing digital transformation objectives is impossible without information security considerations. Business leaders should rethink information security challenges associated with digital transformation and consider solutions to seize existing opportunities. When it comes to information security, human beings play a critical role. Raising users' awareness is a meaningful approach to avoid or neutralize the likelihood of unwanted security consequences that may occur during transforming a system digitally. This book chapter will discuss cybersecurity and information security awareness and examines how digital transformation will be affected by implementing information security awareness. This book chapter will discuss the digital transformation advantages and serious challenges associated with cybersecurity, how to enhance cybersecurity, and the role of information security awareness to mitigate cybersecurity risks.

Chapter 7

Internet of things (IoT) has revolutionized digital transformation and is present in every sector including transportation, energy, retail, healthcare, agriculture, etc. While stepping into the new digital transformation these sectors must contemplate, the risks involved. The new wave of cyberattacks against IoT is posing a severe impediment in adopting this leading-edge technology. Artificial intelligence (AI) is playing a key role in preventing and mitigating some of the effects of these cyberattacks. This chapter discusses different types of threats and attacks against IoT devices and how AI is enabling the detection and prevention of these cyberattacks. It also presents some challenges faced by AI-enabled detection and prevention and provides some solutions and recommendations to these challenges. The authors believe that this chapter provides a favorable basis for the readers who intend to know more about AI-enabled technologies to detect and prevent cyberattacks against IoT, and the motivation to advance the current research in this area.

Chapter 8

Cyber Security threatens vital elements of enterprises such as network, information, application, operational, sustainability, education, and trade secret. Digital transformation and widespread use of IoT caused by the pandemic reveal the importance of cybersecurity vulnerabilities. This study is prepared by a systematic review method for cybersecurity. The inspiration of this chapter is the cyberattacks that threaten the global economy and enterprises, and the effects of cybercrime on management and strategy. The cybersecurity problem, which continues to increase with the pandemic in the manufacturing and service sector, is current and becoming a serious threat. This study reveals strategy development against cybersecurity threats, sustainability elements in management, measures to be taken against cybercrime, cyberattack, and cyberterrorism, organizational and the business culture management in digital transformation.

Chapter 9

Digital banking allows banks to make their new products more readily available, as they can package them with their essential software that has implications for cybersecurity. Internet presence also allows banks to extend their geographical reach without overbearing costs. In Pakistan, most internet offerings currently by banks are more based on information than transactions, therefore the issues for cybersecurity have gained high interest. The offerings on the websites by banks generally seem like electronic brochures. As they mainly offer company events, product information, along with a list of services rendered. Pakistan has various barriers to e-commerce, such as relatively few internet users, inadequate infrastructure (i.e., frequent power failures, fewer phone lines), and lack of cybersecurity for online transactions being hacked. The Government of Pakistan is rigorously working on these areas to overcome respective problems and progress in this sphere. This research focuses on the challenges for e-banking and e-commerce in Pakistan and issues relating to cybersecurity.

Chapter 10

The financial sector across the globe ensures sustainable growth in the economy by mobilizing investments, funds, and savings. This chapter attempts to comprehend and understand the current state of cybersecurity within the financial services industry worldwide. The chapter explores the different aspects of global cyber-attacks in financial sectors to elucidate the salient problems, issues, threats, safeguards & solutions. As technology is progressing, highly technology-savvy criminals are becoming a new threat in the cybercrime space. The entire industry needs an intense transformation to create innovative, state-of-the-art information and an up-to-date architecture of cybersecurity that is capable of confronting the continuous tides of cyber-attacks and data breaches on an everyday basis. The use of security tools like proxy servers, firewalls, Multi-layered email strategy, virus security software, and effective governance strategies are necessary to protect financial sectors from cyber threats and attacks.

Chapter 11

Digital transformation has revolutionized human life but also brought many cybersecurity challenges for users and enterprises. The major threats that affect computers and communication systems by damaging devices and stealing sensitive information are malicious attacks. Traditional anti-virus software fails to detect advanced kind of malware. Current research focuses on developing machine learning techniques for malware detection to respond in a timely manner. Many systems have been evolved and improved to distinguish the malware based on analysis behavior. The analysis behavior is considered a robust technique to detect, analyze, and classify malware, categorized into two models: a static and dynamic analysis. Both types of previous analysis have advantages and limitations. Therefore, the hybrid method combines the strength of static and dynamic analyses. This chapter conducted a systematic literature review (SLR) to summarize and analyze the quality of published studies in malware detection using machine learning techniques and hybrid analysis that range from 2016 to 2021.

Chapter 12

The heterogeneous digital arena emerged as the open depiction for malicious activities and cybernated criminals and terrorist are targeting the cybernated depiction for controlling its operation. At dark web(DW) depiction diverse illegal hacking communities are using the sensing-chip webnet to transfer their bots for tracking the user activity so that criminal activities could be accomplished like money laundering, pornography, child trafficking, drug trafficking, arm and ammunition trafficking, where professionals could also be hired and contracted for generating flood infringement, and ransomware infringement.

Chapter 13

As corporations are stepping into the new digital transformation age and adopting leading-edge technologies such as cloud, mobile, and big data, it becomes crucial for them to contemplate the risks and rewards of this adoption. At the same time, the new wave of malware attacks is posing a severe impediment in implementing these technologies. This chapter discusses some of the complications, challenges, and issues plaguing current malware analysis and detection techniques. Some of the key challenges discussed are automation, native code, obfuscations, morphing, and anti-reverse engineering. Solutions and recommendations are provided to solve some of these challenges. To stimulate further research in this thriving area, the authors highlight some promising future research directions. The authors believe that this chapter provides, an auspicious basis for future researchers who intend to know more about the evolution of malware, and will act as a motivation for enhancing the current and developing the new techniques for malware analysis and detection.

Chapter 14

In this technological era, almost all renowned banks have equipped themselves with the latest technology significantly pertinent to enhance their services and have provided e-banking facilities to their customers. Nevertheless, cybersecurity has been the focus of many organizations. Banks are offering more and more facilities to facilitate their customers with ease and convenience regarding e-banking. However, in Pakistan, this is not the case. As people still refrain from using e-banking in Pakistan because of various issues. The e-banking sector has exponentially grown in the last decade. It has more chances of growth as enterprises such as banks still encourage clients to carry out e-transactions, like utility bill payments, access to account information, and money transfer. During this process, cybercriminals attempt to steal customer's data and hack their online sessions. With regards to e-banking fraud, digitization has caused a revolution. Cybercriminals have employed various tools to steal crucial information through identity theft, trojans, viruses, and phishing.

Chapter 15

In this chapter, the author bases his research project on his authentic mixed multidisciplinary applied mathematical model for transformation projects. His mathematical model, named the Applied Holistic Mathematical Model for Projects (AHMM4P), which is supported by a tree-based heuristics structure. The AHMM4P is similar to the human empirical decision-making process and is applicable to any type of project; it is aimed to support the evolution of organisational, national or enterprise transformation initiatives. The AHMM4P can be used for the development of the cybersecurity subsystems, enterprise information systems, and their decision-making systems, based on Artificial Intelligence, Data Sciences, Enterprise Architecture, Big Data, Deep Learning, and Machine Learning. The author attempts to prove that an AHMM4P-based Action Research approach can unify the currently frequently used siloed MLI4P and DLI4P trends.

Chapter 16

Cybersecurity in Europe as the rest of the world has been legislated for only 20 years. Numerous governmental institutions such as councils offers electronic services through their recently created electronic offices. In all of them, the volume of citizens who register temporarily or permanently to request online services related to the processing of documents and services with the government has increased significantly since the pandemic. Confinement have forced users to request numerous online services where authentication is one of the most relevant aspects to access safely and securely. European Union through the Connecting Europe Mechanism, CEF projects of the European Health Executive Agency and Digital HaDEA, has allowed numerous institutions to connect through the eIDAS created to establish trust in electronic transactions between individuals, organizations and government entities across European Member States.

Chapter 17

Cybersecurity is not just about fortification of data it has wide implications such as maintaining safety, privacy, integrity, and trust of the patients in the healthcare sector. This study methodically reviews the need for cybersecurity amid digital transformation with the help of emerging technologies and focuses on the application and incorporation of blockchain and the Internet of Things (IoT) to ensure cybersecurity in the well-being of the business. It was found in the study that worldwide, advanced technology has been used in managing the flow of data and information, India should focus on maintaining the same IT-enabled infrastructure to reduce causalities in the nation and on the other hand improve administration, privacy, and security in the hospital sector. Depending on the network system, resource allocation, and mobile devices, there is a need to prioritize the resources and efforts in the era of digitalization.

Chapter 18

The practice of protecting computers, websites, mobile devices, electronic services, networks, and digital data from malicious attacks is known as cybersecurity. Since political, military, private, financial, and medical institutions collect, process, and maintain massive volumes of data on computers and other devices, cybersecurity is critical. Sensitive data, such as intellectual property, financial data, personal records, or other forms of data, can make up a large amount of the data. Improper access or disclosure to that data can have profound implications. Technology has undoubtedly made a significant change in every aspect of life in Pakistan, whether it is a financial or non-financial sphere. Technology's usage is thoroughly utilized by banks worldwide. They have started adopting it frequently because of the immense need to achieve goals and satisfy customer's needs more efficiently. Almost all leading banks have now provided e-commerce facilities. Over time, more and more services and facilities are offered to bank customers conveniently via e-commerce products.

Kamaljeet Sandhu
University of New England, Australia

Acknowledgment

I would like to acknowledge the help and contribution of all people, more specifically, to the authors and reviewers that took part in the review process. Without their support, this book would not have become a reality. All the authors have made valuable contribution by making many revisions to their chapters, presenting their interesting research to the readers of this book.

Reviewers provided continuous and important feedbacks to the authors for improvements in their chapters, coherence, and content presentation of chapters. I would like to personally thank all the authors and reviewers who have worked very hard to complete this book successfully. At every step we worked together as a highly coordinated and focused team.

In this journey we became very good and close colleagues, and this book has brought us all together from different parts of the world, and we have a valuable working relationship and I look forward to working with this great team again in another interesting book project to come soon. I would like to personally thank the staff at IGI-Global, development editors, who have provided the highest level of service and have been very helpful and supportive in this research at each stage of the book development process, without their persistent help this publication would not have been possible.

I would like to thank my family, including my father and mother who passed away leaving beautiful memories and the importance for higher education and new learning that was ingrained in my very early life and which later was built into my ability to provide this advanced scholarly work to the advancement of new scientific knowledge. This book is a tribute to my dear mum for all her love, support, belief, kindness, and trust, that I have received which transformed me into an author for scholarly research. I would not have achieved this book success without it. I also like to thank Jasper (my king charles spaniel puppy) for all the love, kisses, and support that I have received on writing this book. I also wish to thank Professor Brian Corbitt (RMIT University Melbourne, Australia), my research mentor and colleague, without him I would not have been here today writing this book.

Kamaljeet Sandhu
University of New England, Australia

Chapter 1
Advancing Cybersecurity for Digital Transformation:
Opportunities and Challenges

Kamaljeet Sandhu
https://orcid.org/0000-0003-4624-6834
University of New England, Australia

ABSTRACT

Advancing cybersecurity for digital transformation provides opportunities and challenges. Many enterprises are accelerating the digital transformation to reach their customers, suppliers, and other parties over the internet; at the same time cybersecurity has become a serious concern. Cyberattacks have exponentially increased globally. While digital transformation makes the business process more efficient and effective, and increased cyberattacks pose obstacles, threats, and risks on the way. Cyberattacks consist of different types such as political, financial, accessing private and confidential information, ransomware, identity theft, destruction to essential infrastructure and public utilities such as energy, water, telecommunication, transportation, health, and others. This chapter presents case analysis from recent cyberattacks to show the scale, size, and type of impacts within and outside the enterprise. Newer technologies to counter cyberattacks are introduced such as quantum computing, nanotechnologies, artificial intelligence, blockchain that have the capabilities to eliminate cyberattacks.

INTRODUCTION

In recent times, cybersecurity has become a global challenge for many enterprises wanting to transform digital business activities. Since the beginning of the pandemic, the FBI has seen a fourfold increase in cybersecurity complaints, whereas the global losses from cybercrime exceeded $1 trillion in 2020 (Gurinaviciute 2021). And the loss figures keeps increasing. In a study conducted by IBM (2021), the data reported that internal and external threats account for 51%, which involve malicious attacks, 25% that involve IT/business process failures, and 24%, which are due to human error. As more and more activities during Covid-19 pandemic are shifting over the digital platform providing newer business

DOI: 10.4018/978-1-7998-6975-7.ch001

opportunities, at the same time the risks, threats and challenges associated with cybersecurity for the enterprise has exponentially increased to the highest levels. Though the enterprise and government institutions have considered seriously implementing cybersecurity solutions, they fall short of addressing the core problems of keeping the cyberspace safe (ACSC 2021) because of the dispersed nature of the internet. The nature and the global scope of cybersecurity attacks makes it difficult to secure the cyberspace, which is used by billions of people and the digital devices, which makes it a massive market for the cyberattackers. The cybersecurity threats and attacks can be categorised as human, and machine created. Cisco (2021) defines cybersecurity as the practice of protecting systems, networks, and programs from digital attacks from cybercriminals.

These cyberattacks are usually aimed at accessing, changing, manipulating, or destroying sensitive information; extorting money from users; or interrupting normal business processes. Implementing effective cybersecurity measures is particularly challenging today because there are more devices than people, and attackers are becoming more innovative in their business. There can be number of motivations for the cyberattacks such as political, financial, accessing private and confidential information, identity theft, cryptocurrency theft, destruction to essential infrastructure and public utilities such as energy, water, telecommunication, transportation, and others such as manufacturing, banking, and hospitals which are critical sources for providing important services to the society and often the victims (e.g., people, computer systems, and enterprises) of such cyberattacks are affected on a vast scale. The modus operandi of cyber attackers is to either completely (or partially) shut down or do maximum damage to gain control of the computer systems which can then lead to achieving their objectives. One of the important characteristics of cyber attackers is that they are highly skilled in breaking into computer systems, by identifying and studying the weaknesses of those systems either through software codes, operating systems, or through other weaknesses in computer networks (e.g., wireless networks). Once they have found and studied the weakness, they exploit the system by gaining access to control and stealing sensitive confidential information or by infecting the system through malicious programs that can inflict heavy damages.

As hackers grow more sophisticated in their business, securing the IT infrastructure has become more and more complex. The human created threats such as a hacker stealing vast array of confidential data, getting to access to peoples personal & financial records, conducting illegal activities, and selling sharing unauthorised data. Whereas the machine created threats are more serious and rapid and deeply destructive and have the capability of infecting machines globally at a speed unimaginable, such as malicious software's unknowingly and without user's permission installed through accessing malicious emails and websites, which then are virally distributed over a vast global network doing destruction activities to millions of digital devices on the way and to the hardware, software, networks, and to the worldwide web. In order to safeguard and keep vulnerabilities at minimum, enterprises need a multi-layered approach to server security with visibility into each of these layers: hardware, firmware, hypervisor, and the operating system (IBM 2021). Recent cyberattacks have shown operating systems such as Microsoft Windows are more vulnerable because of its weaknesses in software codes. Many users are still using the Windows legacy systems, and large numbers of computers globally having the legacy systems and are more easily attacked as the software upgrades have not been completed, and some older versions of the Windows software are no longer supported for upgrades by Microsoft which means the users are left by themselves.

For example, ransomware attack, in which the malicious software locks the user's digital device till the ransom is paid. Claughton and Beilharz (2021) reported that global meat processing company JBS

Foods has confirmed that it paid the equivalent of $US11 million to a criminal gang to end a five-day cyberattack that halted its operations around the world, including Australia. The company said it paid the money to mitigate any unforeseen issues related to the attack and ensure no data was exfiltrated. The decision had to be made to prevent any potential risk for their customers. A statement from the company highlights the FBI's assessment that the gang is "one of the most specialised and sophisticated cyber-criminal groups in the world". The ransom was paid in Bitcoin. Similarly, there are other cyberattacks such as phishing, malware, social engineering, which can have a deeper destructive impact on digital devices, people, and the digital enterprises. These cyberattacks are far reaching and go beyond borders and continents and are capable of bringing down the entire global internet network and the worldwide web and destroying large numbers of web servers on their way. The next section seeks to identify main elements from case 1 and 2 that can have wider impact from cyberattacks.

CASE ANALYSIS

The purpose of case analysis is to examine issues deeply and study the real-life problem in a logical and informed manner that can then provide a clearer picture of research problem. The following section seeks to analyse data from different case analysis to find the impacts of cyberattacks within and outside the enterprise.

Case 1

On May 7, 2021, in a serious cyberattack on Colonial Pipeline, which is an American oil pipeline system that originates in Houston, Texas, and provides gasoline and jet fuel to the Southeastern USA, came under a ransomware cyberattack that affected their computerized equipment managing the pipeline. Kumar and Sanicola (2021) reported that gas stations from Florida to Virginia began running dry and prices at the pump rose, as the shutdown of the biggest U.S. fuel pipeline by hackers extended into a fifth day and sparked panic buying by motorists that lead to fuel supply at gas stations running out and leaving many motorists without fuel. Colonial Pipeline reported that it shut down the pipeline as a precaution due to a concern that the hackers might have obtained sensitive information allowing them to carry out further attacks on vulnerable parts of the pipeline. It was also found that attackers also stole nearly 100 gigabytes of data and threatened to release it on the internet if the ransom was not paid. It was reported that within hours after the attack the company paid a ransom of nearly 75 Bitcoins ($5 million) to the hackers in exchange for a decryption tool which proved so slow that Colonial's own backups were used to bring the system back online ("Colonial Pipeline cyber attack," 2021). The Colonial Pipeline case demonstrates that the nature and seriousness of such a cyberattack can have widespread impact on people, the economy, and on the resources of an enterprise, and lead to a shutdown of an entire (or part) of a computer system, and to give in to the ransom demands of cyber attackers.

Case 2

Jibilian (2020) reported that SolarWinds, a major US information technology firm, was the subject of a cyberattack that spread to its clients and went undetected for months, Foreign hackers, were able to use the hack to spy on private companies like the elite cybersecurity firm FireEye and on other government institutions. Hackers secretly broke into Texas-based SolarWind's systems and added malicious code into the company's software system. The system, called "Orion," is widely used by companies to manage IT resources. SolarWinds has 33,000 customers that use Orion. SolarWinds unwittingly sent out software updates to its customers that included the hacked code. The code created a backdoor to customer's information technology systems, which hackers then used to install even more malware that helped them spy on companies and organisations. The SolarWinds case shows that even the computer systems of an IT company are not safe from hackers and is vulnerable to widescale (or part) being infected by malware that can quickly spread across the systems and also lead to impacting other systems within and outside the firm including its customers, suppliers, and to other enterprises, and sometimes such malicious malware may go undetected for long periods of time. This raises an important question: How many malwares and other malicious software's are still operating without being identified? The answer is unknown.

In today's connected societies, everyone benefits from advanced cyberdefense programs. At an individual level, a cybersecurity attack can result in everything from identity theft, to extortion attempts, to the loss of important data like family photos. Everyone relies on critical infrastructure like power plants, hospitals, and financial service companies. Securing these critical IT infrastructure and other enterprise information systems is essential to keeping our society functioning.

Case 3

Bajak et al (2021) recently reported that Microsoft servers were hacked globally. It was reported that the victims of a massive global hack of Microsoft email server software — estimated in the tens of thousands by cybersecurity responders — hustled to shore up infected systems and try to diminish chances that intruders might steal data or hobble their networks. Victims run the spectrum of organizations that run email servers, from mom-and-pop retailers to law firms, municipal governments, healthcare providers, and manufacturers. The authors found that many were infected and have skeleton IT staff and can't afford an emergency cybersecurity response — not to mention the complications of the pandemic. Fixing the problem isn't as simple as clicking an update button on a computer screen. It requires upgrading an organization's entire so-called "Active Directory," which catalogues email users and their respective privileges. The impact was far reaching and global and deeply cyber destructive in nature. This demonstrates that preparations for cybersecurity 'before and after' the cyberattacks requires enormous preparations and resources including financial and nonfinancial, and as well as complete upgrades, and total overhaul of the IT infrastructure.

Case 4

Akhtar (2021) in a published article claims that SolarWinds hackers were able to spy on federal agencies like the Department of Homeland Security and Treasury Department. In the same article, Kelvin Coleman, the executive director at the National Cyber Security Alliance, said security experts are still unsure of the hackers' motivations, and whether the incident may have been a "test run" for a larger attack – which makes protecting user accounts with quality passwords and multi-factor authentication imperative. Coleman said the Microsoft attack has received relatively less media attention due to the victims being small- to mid-size organizations and local governments, but that still leaves systems and personal information vulnerable. The attack also differs from others because hackers did not need to interact with victims to get access to their information, said Ben Read, the senior manager for Cyber Espionage Analysis in FireEye's Intelligence unit. Unlike a phishing scam, which relies on users clicking into a link with malware, the Exchange Server attack gave hackers more control.

Case 5

Paquet-Clouston et al. (2019) explains that ransomware attacks have eclipsed many other cybercrime threats and have become the dominant concern for law enforcement and security professionals in many nations. The growing numbers of ransomware attacks globally is a serious concern and is not restricted to one country or a particular geographic region. Ransomware is a class of malicious software that, when installed on a computer, prevents a user from accessing the device—usually through unbreakable encryption—until a ransom is paid to the attacker. Often the control of the device is overtaken by the attackers. The authors suggest that in this type of attack, cybercriminals do not profit from the resale of stolen information on underground markets, but from the value victims assign to their locked data and their willingness to pay a fee to regain access to them which is in he form of a key or a password to unlock the system. Till the time when the ransom is not paid, the user is unable to access the device which is locked. To that extent, the business model of ransomware seems conducive to more favourable monetizing opportunities than other forms of cybercrimes, due to its scalable potential and the removal of intermediaries.

Case 6

Cybercriminal's access dark net or darknet which is an overlay network within the Internet that can only be accessed with specific software, configurations, or authorization, and often uses a unique customized communication protocol ("Darknet", 2021). Two typical darknet types are social networks (usually used for file hosting with a peer-to-peer connection), and anonymity proxy networks such as Tor via an anonymized series of connections. Similarly, cybercriminals access a darknet market which is a commercial website on the dark web that operates via darknets such as Tor or I2P ("Darknet market", 2021). They function primarily as black markets, selling or brokering transactions involving drugs, cyber-arms, weapons, counterfeit currency, stolen credit card details, forged documents, unlicensed pharmaceuticals, steroids, and other illicit goods as well as the sale of legal products. To facilitate and offer their services for illegal activities on the internet, cyberattackers have been networking and flourishing over the internet and making it difficult to track the cyber criminals and their activities for planning future attacks (Mirea et al. 2019). The webservers used by cybercriminals which are often ghost webservers which are extremely difficult to track, monitor, and to be shut down. The IP addresses are impossible to identify and locate.

Case 7

Canner (2021) reported that a compilation file of stolen and leaked passwords, dubbed RockYou2021, recently appeared on a hacker forum. The author explains that an anonymous forum poster uploaded a 100GB TXT file containing 8.4 billion entries of passwords. Given that only 4.7 billion people are online across the world, the perpetrators may have multiple passwords for millions if not billions of users. The RockYou2021 compilation file may be the stepping stone hackers are looking for to begin mass credential stuffing or more targeted credentials cyberattacks. Since so many people were potentially affected, businesses should begin alerting employees to the danger and mandating password changes across all accounts. Additionally, enterprises should begin (if they haven't already) implementing multifactor authentication (MFA) and other critical identity management protections. The report raises serious questions about web servers not be being one hundred percent safe for password storage and protection.

The summary of important findings from the above case analysis suggests that the interaction (dealings and blackmailing) for ransomware is directly between the attacker and the user, and the financial ransom terms of the attack is fully controlled by the attackers (Seselja 2021). The user's business can be brought to a halt and the users having to give in to the attacker's terms and conditions for the ransom and there may not be any other way out. This may cause considerable loss to the users in terms of business loss and as well high financial losses for the ransom paid to the attackers. Another area of concern is noticeably after the ransomware attack, in which the user has make considerable assessments and investments in modernising to safeguard the IT systems, for putting safeguards so that such an attack is not repeated again. There may be loss of trust and confidence from customers and suppliers towards the enterprise IT systems and embarrassment as well due to negative publicity and loss of confidence in the enterprise and its digital system.

MAIN FOCUS OF THE CHAPTER

The main focus of the chapter is on the serious impacts that cyberattacks can have on an enterprise. Broeders (2021) argues that there is some variation in different reports as to what the grey zone consists of, but Fig. 1 captures its main ingredients. The lower impact/risk actions in the grey zone are generally tools of deception or information tools, like 'honeypots' that are embedded in the defender's network and which lure in attackers with fake attractive data, so their behaviour and methods can be studied. In the first instance it not clear and often unknown the desires and motives for the hackers to break into the systems. Many of these are legitimate cyber security measures that companies do in house or hire private cyber security companies to do for them. Sharing information and various techniques to thwart, detect and deflect attackers such as tar pits, honeypots, denial and deception techniques and hunting actively engage attackers, but on the home turf of the defender's network. These techniques are high end, but relatively common. Towards the end of the 'light grey' zone is beaconing, where measures start to operate on the network of the attacker and/or transit networks and send information back to the home network. Nevertheless, the threats and attacks posed by the hackers is an early indication of the vulnerability of systems and its weaknesses that the hackers tend to exploit. Knowing or not knowing the weaknesses of the systems that are at risk creates bigger problems as the enterprise may not be aware that their cybersecurity has been breached. Finding out cybersecurity has been breached is one thing, and finding a solution to fix that from not happening again, is an entirely different thing, which is a long and lengthy process of repairing the digital system from inside out.

Luck (2019) suggests that internal cyberattacks (cyber-attacks which occur from within an organization) pose a serious threat to an organization's security. One tool that an enterprise can employ to help them detect such threats is the internal cyber-sting. An internal cyber-sting involves an organization enticing its members into performing a (controlled) internal cyber-attack in order to apprehend them. However, there is (rightly) considerable moral consternation about employing such a tool; for it is deceitful and undermines trust. It may also provide directions to the weaker spots of the systems that the hackers seem to exploit. This is not one hundred percent bullet proof strategy as one systems interacts with vast numbers of other systems, inside and outside the enterprise.

Figure 1. The continuum between defensive and offensive cyber operations

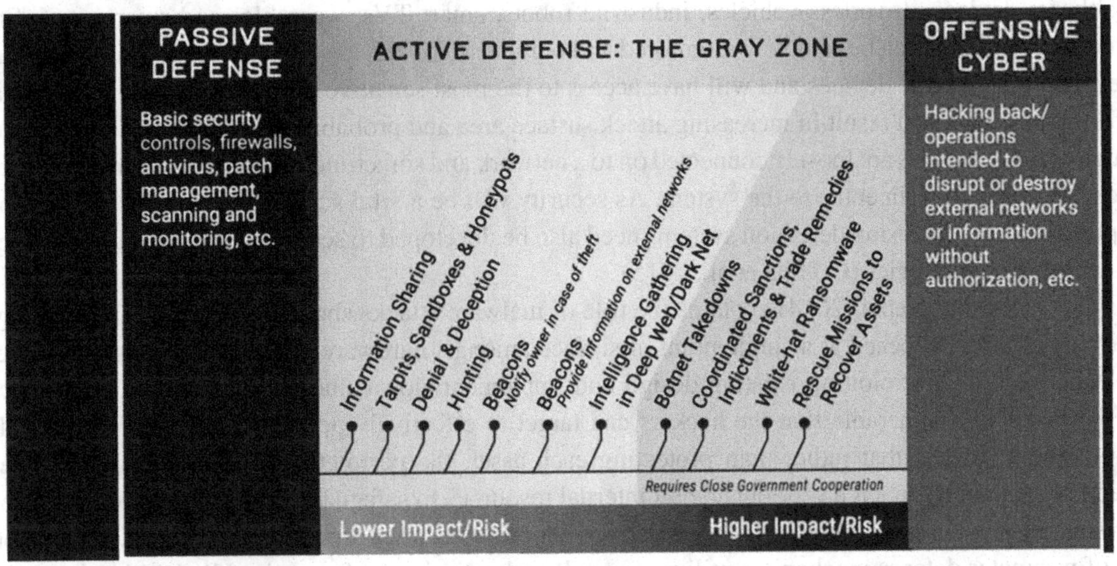

the continuum between defensive and offensive cyber operations.
Source: Centre for Cyber and Homeland Security [9, p. 10]

Arnold (2014) explains that cybersecurity experts today identify four kinds of primary threat to the financial sector. First, sophisticated cyber actors –usually states –use espionage to steal intellectual capital and data from banks and destabilize them. Second, banks can be targeted for systemic disruption by a range of cyber actors who view them as symbols of Western capitalism or have reason to threaten the financial system. Third, "hacktivists" take advantage of vulnerabilities to break into banks' IT networks, usually in order to gain publicity for their cause. Finally, organized criminal organizations and cyber fraudsters have shifted from stealing money through traditional bank heists to using other means (online, telephone, card fraud) that are harder to detect (Ravich 2015).

Romanosky (2016) report four types of cyber events: data breaches (unauthorized disclosure of personal information), security incidents (malicious attacks directed at a company), privacy violations (alleged violation of consumer privacy), and phishing/skimming incidents (individual financial crimes). Of all cyber incidents from the dataset, they found that data breaches are by far the most common, dwarfing rates of all other cyber events. Beyond name and address, also found that credit card numbers and medical information were the most commonly compromised pieces of information. And incidents caused by malicious actions (as opposed to accidental or unintentional activities) have remained relatively constant at around 60% of all incidents. Further, of the almost 1700 resulting legal actions, over 50% continue to be private civil actions brought in federal courts, with only 17% being criminal actions. The author has presented some very interesting data which suggests that the numbers of criminal actions recorded were small (17%) which may indicate that the criminal actions for breaching cybersecurity may need revisiting and newer laws brought in to punish the actions of the offenders.

Khraisat & Alazab (2021) demonstrate that new technologies are more vulnerable to cybersecurity attacks. New technologies such as Internet of Things (IoT) are interconnected systems of devices that facilitate seamless information exchange between physical devices. These devices could be medical and healthcare devices, driverless vehicles, industrial robots, smart TVs, wearables and smart city infrastructures; and they can be remotely monitored and regulated. IoT devices are expected to become more prevalent than mobile devices and will have access to the most sensitive information, such as personal information. This will result in increasing attack surface area and probabilities of attacks will increase. Much of these devices are loosely connected on to a network and sometimes unmonitored through which hackers can easily gain entry to the system. As security will be a vital supporting element of most IoT applications, IoT intrusion detection systems need also be developed to secure communications enabled by such IoT technologies (Granjal et al., 2015).

Jang-Jaccard & Nepal (2014) explains the role of malware attacks shown in figure 2. Traditionally, malware attacks happened at a single point of surface amongst hardware equipment's, software pieces or at network level exploiting existing design and implementation vulnerabilities at each layer. Each of the layers are vulnerable that the hackers can target to effectively penetrate and launch an attack. The authors suggest that rather than protecting each asset, the perimeter defense strategy has been used predominantly to put a wall outside all internal resources to safeguard everything inside from any unwanted intrusion from outside. This provides bullet proof security around the perimeter. The majority of perimeter defense mechanism utilizes firewall and anti-virus software installed within intrusion prevention/detection systems.

Any traffic coming from outside is intercepted and examined to ensure there is no malware penetrating into the inside resources. General acceptance of this perimeter defense model has occurred because it is far easier and seemingly less costly to secure one perimeter than it is to secure a large volume of applications or a large number of internal networks. To give more defined access to certain internal resources, the access control mechanisms have been used in conjunction with the perimeter defense mechanism. On top of perimeter defense and access control, accountability is added to identify or punish for any misbehaviors, as represented in figure 2. The authors argue that the combined efforts of perimeter defense strategy have been found to be increasingly ineffective as the advancement and sophistication of malware improves. Ever evolving malware always seems to find loopholes to bypass the perimeter defense altogether which is an indication for further improvement.

Ablon (2018) reported that attackers, or cyber threat actors, can be grouped by their set of goals, motivation, and capabilities. Four groups of note are: cyberterrorists, hacktivists, state-sponsored actors, and cybercriminals. It is important to understand the full environment of threat actors, as they are of greatest concern to businesses and the government. A brief overview of these four types of cyber threat actors, is shown in table 1. The author notes that the motivation and techniques are the key drivers for the attackers to operate.

Ablon (2018) provides detailed characteristics, techniques, and targets of cyber threat actors shown in table 1 which is compared to Jang-Jaccard, & Nepal (2014) study showing common attacks in the hardware, software and network layers presented in table 2 which represents the platform for launching cyberattacks from a digital space by cyberhacker to effectively penetrate through multiple techniques expanding the reach and widening the scope of their attacks. The compounding effects of such a cyberattack is powerful, deeply destructive, and far reaching.

Figure 2. Vulnerabilities and defense strategies in existing systems
Source: Jang-Jaccard, J., & Nepal, S. (2014)

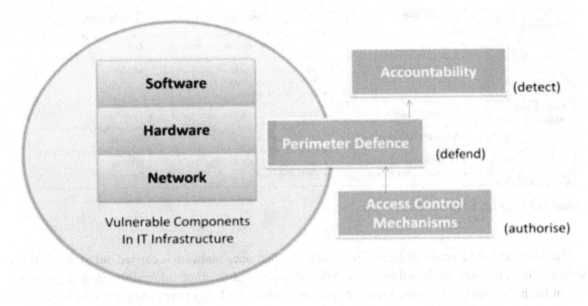

Table 1. Characteristics, Techniques, and Targets of Cyber Threat Actors

Cyber Threat Actors	Description	Motivator	Technique	Types of Targets	Use of Stolen Data
Cyberterrorists (theoretical)	Extremist groups or nonstate actors using cyber techniques to intimidate, coerce, or influence an audience; force a political change; cause fear or physical harm	Gain support for and deter opposition to a cause; carry out dictates of an ideology	Cause kinetic damage: destroy or disrupt critical infrastructure or systems; loss of life	Determined by actors' ideology	Disrupt critical infrastructure via cyberattack; Change prescription or allergy information, switch or delete medical record; further a campaign on a particular target
Hacktivists	Bring awareness to a cause (political, economic, social); exercise free speech (e.g., "lulz")	Ideological activism; disruption of services or access	Steal and leak sensitive, proprietary, or classified information; conduct DDoS on websites or services	No one type of target	Gather personal information of a specific target; publicize a breach to highlight how vulnerable a particular organization is
State-sponsored actors	Receive direction, funding, or technical assistance from nation-states; highly sophisticated and often use the most-sophisticated methods (e.g., zero-day vulnerabilities); targeted and persistent	Advance interests of their nation-state; further political agenda	Conduct intelligence, surveillance, reconnaissance, espionage; employ watering-hole attacks; exfiltrate data (e.g., intellectual property); degrade or destroy technical components; conduct targeted attacks	Other nation-states, defense contractors, technology sector, and critical infrastructure; (rare) banks or cryptocurrency wallets	Build profiles of possible targets for follow-on targeting, exploitation, or espionage campaigns; use personal, financial, or medical information as leverage to gain other types of intelligence
Cybercriminals	Access personal, financial, or health data to monetize it	Financial gain; power	Use crimeware (e.g., exploit kits, "script-kiddy" tools); rely on already known vulnerabilities, phishing, and spearphishing; smash-and-grab	Data repositories (e.g., banks, retail companies, health care) that can be monetized; cryptocurrency wallets	Use credentials (username/password combinations) and harvest contact lists for phishing attacks; exploit password reuse; conduct identity theft, tax, or medical fraud

Source: Ablon (2018)

Table 2. Common attacks and examples of countermeasures in existing system

	Hardware	Software	Network
Common attacks	• Hardware Trojan • Illegal clones • Side channel attacks (i.e. snooping hardware signals)	• Software programming bugs (e.g. memory management, user input validation, race conditions, user access privileges, etc.) • Software design bugs • Deployment errors	• Networking protocol attacks • Network monitoring and sniffing
Examples of countermeasures	• Tamper-Resistant Hardware (e.g. TPM) • Trusted Computing Base (TCB) • Hardware watermarking • Hardware obfuscation	• Secure coding practice (e.g. type checking, runtime error, program transformation, etc.) • Code obfuscation • Secure design and development • Formal methods	• Firewall • Intrusion prevention and detection • Virtual Private Network (VPN) • Encryption

Source: Jang-Jaccard, J., & Nepal, S. (2014)

The authors (Jang-Jaccard, & Nepal 2014) suggests that once malware is carried out to the victim's system, cyber criminals could utilize many different aspects of existing vulnerabilities in the victim's system further to use them in their criminal activities which can lead to exploiting the existing vulnerabilities in hardware, software, and network systems and contaminating other the system fully (or in parts) whereby the control is taken over by the hackers to use the system for their advantages.

SOLUTIONS AND RECOMMENDATIONS

Cybersecurity principles play an important role in safeguarding cybersecurity (ACSC 2021). An important element for maintaining a robust cybersecurity is to train employees in cybersecurity safeguards. In this process an enterprise can offer mandatory cybersecurity education programs, quizzes, seminars, workshops and training sessions that the employees can undertake. It's a good idea to have a professional trainer(s) (inhouse or from outside) to work on such programs in consultation with the IT Department. Such cybersecurity programs should focus on the core risks and challenges that involves human computer interaction for cybersecurity. For example, regularly changing passwords and having distinct username and user-id, identifying scam emails, monitoring and deleting spam emails and malicious emails such as phishing, directing the user to download content linked to malicious software, and multi-factor authentication (ACSC 2021). Multi-factor authentication is a digital identification process in which a digital device of a user is provided access to a website or application only after successfully presenting two or more pieces of evidence to an authentication mechanism, which can be a unique code sent to a smart phone or to the registered email account and identified by a login password. Many enterprises including Microsoft, Google, Yahoo, major banks, and other enterprises have adopted this practice. This has considerably reduced the unauthorized entry into the system; however, it has not eliminated hackers into exploring newer ways from breaking into the system.

The recent Colonial Pipeline attack in which cyberattackers gained access to "one" password only, to gain entry into a legacy VPN system which lacked the capabilities for multifactor authentication. Kelly and Resnick-Ault (2021) reported that the head of Colonial Pipeline told US senators that hackers who launched cyberattack against the company were able to get into the system by stealing a single password.

Colonial Pipeline Chief Executive Joseph Blount told a US Senate committee that the attack occurred using a legacy Virtual Private Network (VPN) system that did not have multifactor authentication in place. That means it could be accessed through a password without a second step such as a text message, a common security safeguard in more recent software. This demonstrates the vulnerability of the legacy systems providing an easy way for the cyberattackers to gain entry into the system and that can have serious impacts from cyberattacks. In another article Browne (2021) disclosed that U.S. law enforcement officials had said they had seized $2.3 million in bitcoin ransom paid to DarkSide, the cybercriminal gang behind a crippling cyberattack on Colonial Pipeline. DarkSide, which reportedly received $90 million in bitcoin ransom payments before shutting down, operated a so-called "ransomware as a service" business model, where hackers develop and market ransomware tools and sell them to affiliates who then carry out attacks. This suggests that there is a vast growing global market for cyberattacks operated by cybercriminal activities which are being formed as business service models and then franchised to other cybercriminals.

Installing, regularly updating, and using software's that are authentic and registered with the software vendors, and regularly update antivirus and antispyware software on every digital device accessed from the enterprise by the people. Computer auditors and systems administrators should regularly inspect the system to check for viruses that may have made their way into the system and run security audits for compliance obligations (IBM 2021). In such situations detect and eliminate the virus such as trojan horse, and other forms of malware swiftly found and eliminated before the whole system is infected and implement measures to protect against launching widespread advanced cyberattacks (IBM 2021). Using a firewall, VPN (virtual private network), for accessing Internet connection, and a dedicated Intranet in which only the employees can have a dedicated access to sensitive data/files.

Such a system should be protected by unique username and password and multi-factor authentications having face, voice, and fingerprint of the users. Making strong and complex passwords for users' login to the system, consisting through a combination of different numbers, containing words in upper and lower cases, and using special characters, that will make it difficult for the hackers to guess, and user should regularly change and update passwords that would make it difficult for the hackers to access. Downloading and installing latest software updates and patches from registered sites only for the operating systems such as Microsoft windows, Apple mac, Google android, as soon as the applications become available.

Making backup copies of important sensitive data and information on servers that are highly sensitive and making them secured by having strong encryption (256 bits). Such encryption should regularly be tested and checked for performance from within and outside the enterprise to make sure its functionality safeguard features are one hundred percent guaranteed and no intruder can break into the system (ACSC 2021). Often such a task is performed by a qualified, experienced, and registered computer auditor, and every node of a computer system is checked and rechecked and tested for weaknesses and errors that a hacker can exploit to gain access into the system. This exercise should be conducted regularly to check cybersecurity processes and safeguards.

Controlling physical access to digital devices and network components from multiple logins and blocking unauthorised users to access the device and the network. Often such details of unauthorised login and wrong username and password and network details are recorded in log files, which should be investigated by the systems administrator and the IT team of the enterprise. Securing the Wi-Fi networks and open networks should be encrypted, and sensitive data monitored. Wi-Fi network of an enterprise should always be secured and authenticated before use login with a strong encryption key and hidden from general public access. Virtual private network (VPN) can add another layer of security that will provide secure communications.

Limiting the access of employee to sensitive data and information which they do not require and providing extra layers of software security for restricting highly sensitive digital data of an enterprise and limiting or at the best restricting the authority to install software by employees (ACSC 2021). Use of social media should either be restricted, limited, or provided through another web server not connected with the main system. Emails should be scanned for viruses using antivirus software, and the email web servers separated from the main system to avoid the spread of dangerous viruses coming via emails. Regular updates of antirust to scan emails for malicious attachments, spam, and phishing emails, before they can infect and spread to vast numbers of computers.

FUTURE RESEARCH DIRECTIONS

The future researchers should focus on opportunities to advancing cybersecurity for digital transformation by integrating into the fast-changing digital environment. More investments in quantum computing for cybersecurity. Quantum computing is the future generation of computers and many enterprises such as Google, Microsoft, IBM, and others have been researching, and developing, quantum computing capabilities that are much more superior compared to present day computers. Quantum computers and their data will be difficult to hack as the systems and technology are complex and having complicated codes which is beyond the capability of hackers and attackers. IBM designed quantum computers to solve complex problems that today's most powerful supercomputers cannot solve, and never will (IBM 2021). Quantum computers can greatly benefit research in the areas of health to find cures for cancer, alzheimer's, parkinson, and many other chronic diseases.

Major upgrades to operating systems such as Windows, Mac, Android, to close the weak spots of the operating systems that hackers can exploit to launch cyberattacks. Microsoft, Goggle, and Apple are required to do more together as many of the cyberattacks launched are from these operating systems. More robust operating systems developed to make it difficult and complex and unproductive to launch cyberattacks and provide deterrence. Enterprises should engage in higher levels of communications with customers, local government institutions, and international governments on cybersecurity and work collectively to counter the cybersecurity attacks and threats. Setting up a sole cybersecurity ministry/ division within the government to strategically manage cybersecurity risks seriously, before and after the cyberattacks. Clear guidelines, policies, and best practices identified and communicated.

The nature, motivations, source and origin of such cyberattacks needs to be studied deeply for finding innovative solutions to be implemented. Advanced cyber intelligence gathering that can prepare ahead of an imminent cyberattacks. Microsoft operating systems Windows, Google operating system Android, and Apple operating systems Mac, develop advanced tools for stopping cybercrime. Social media and cybersecurity threats need to be taken seriously by these organisations, especially from smart phones and other mobile devices such as tablets. Antivirus software should target malicious malwares and take them out before it spreads and infects across vast numbers of computers operating system globally.

Future research should focus on opportunities for implementing cybersecurity core courses for children's early in schools and at the university levels. A core unit for cybersecurity made mandatory for all programs at the university before students can graduate. Both technical and nontechnical skills included in the course curriculum. This will provide valuable skills to students to learn and manage cybersecurity risks, assessments, threats and attacks. These skills will also be valuable for future employers when students gain employment and will also lead to closing the gap and shortages for cybersecurity professionals in the IT industry. Research suggests that there are very high shortages for highly paid jobs of skilled cybersecurity professionals internationally.

Cybersecurity should be promoted to females (and also males) in schools and universities as a long-term career and profession and incentives provided. For example, mothers can be provided with opportunities to take jobs in cybersecurity and use their skills by working from home, as much of the work can be done offsite and from one's home as well and same time taking care of their children and families and being in the workforce. Flexible employment arrangements (e.g., flexible hours, working offsite or from home, and others) both for female and males can be provided to entice people to take cybersecurity jobs. Governments and enterprises provide more places for apprenticeship in cybersecurity, for young people in schools and universities, to train in managing cyber risks, threats, and attacks. People these days are proficient in using computers at schools and universities and have knowledge to progress in cybersecurity. Such apprentice training can provide induvial with valuable skills that they can use with employers, and as well as closing the shortages of cybersecurity professionals and which can also benefit the IT industry.

Future studies need to find innovative ways for encrypting data, by adopting techniques that makes it difficult, complicated, and unproductive (financial & nonfinancial) for hackers, thus directly targeting their motivation for not launching cyberattacks. Studies from multidisciplinary fields such as psychology, computer science and software engineering should focus on eliminating the motivations of hackers. Such studies and their important findings will be very useful to understand why cyberattacks are taking place and the reasons for their increase. Understanding hacker's psychology, their motivation for launching such a cyberattack is an important area that needs investigation.

Enterprises and governments institutions should separate the main system from the ordinary and placing buffers between more important and sensitive systems. Setting up dummy systems within the buffer systems to fool and mislead hackers by redirecting to more complex systems and provide discouragement. Data over the cloud made safe and secure to use. Hacking the hackers by launching counter cyberattacks from multiple different points is another area of future study to provide deterrence to the hackers. Mobile networks such as 5g and Wi-Fi should provide bullet proof cybersecurity and the data across wireless networks made difficult to intercept. Many cyberattacks are taking place through intercepting data on unsecured networks. Networks should be made highly secured. Web servers should increase their security to the highest levels to detect and block unauthorised access and intrusions.

CONCLUSION

Cybersecurity is an important area that has received serious attention globally from consumers, private and public enterprises, and government institutions, and all are being affected through cyberattacks and threats, hacking, unauthorised access to data, malware, ransomware, spam and phishing, destructive viruses, ATM cash outs, cryptomining, identity theft, cyber scams, social engineering, DDoS attacks, cloud computing vulnerabilities, corporate security challenges, and many others which have accounted to losses and increased cost. As reported earlier in the chapter the cost exceeded $1 trillion in 2020 (Gurinaviciute 2021). Cyber threats are getting more complicated, sophisticated, effective, and in present times the increasing levels of remote work and dependence on digital devices. Though the scale and proportion of such damage is known in terms of dollar cost, little has been achieved in stopping cyber-attacks, and it continues to increase many folds and spreading globally over the internet. Anyone with internet access are the target of cybercrime. Over the last few years, the number of computing devices especially mobile devices such as smart phones, tablets etc, have increased exponentially, so have the cyberattacks, as it has become very easy for cyberattackers to reach vast numbers of people globally.

Research suggests that cyberattackers are getting more innovative in their attacks and targeting people who have very little or no knowledge of cybersecurity attacks, especially elderly people, children, and females, by sending emails of enticing offers which are too good to be true, or requesting user-id to reset passwords for internet banking, asking to provide personal information for identity theft, and many others. Large proportions of cyberattacks are communicated through emails. More and more people are becoming victims of such cyberattacks. Research suggests that increasing numbers of enterprises (e.g., banking) are now communicating with their customers through mobile apps on safe platform, which are based on multifactor authentication and data is encrypted, and the customer and the enterprise have confirmation of the registered device. Though emails have been an effective communication tool for many years, due to being used as a tool for increased cyberattacks in recent times, their usage is being discouraged. Another reason is that the user personal information and privacy can be compromised if that information gets to the hackers for using in cyberattacks.

The next generation of modern computers (e.g., quantum computers offering cryptographic security) have to make Internet secure and devices can autonomously identify user-ids through face, voice, eye, and fingerprint recognitions, such technologies are being increasing used for internet banking using smartphones from Samsung, Apple, and many others. Newer technologies such as Blockchain adoption by enterprises have made significant improvement, only a small proportion of business has migrated to blockchain technology. Large numbers of businesses still rely on the legacy systems for conducting their core business activities which are vulnerable to massive cyberattacks. Taking out the legacy system and replacing with a modern system is a challenge and very costly exercise involving migration of large volumes of data without being lost and requires expertise of highly trained IT professionals. This is an area that needs massive overhaul of the IT engine of an enterprise and requires large investments in modern upgrades of hardware, software, and networks that will then match today's modern enterprise systems. But the work in this area has been extremely slow, which has provided a fertile ground to the hackers to launch cyberattacks due to the legacy system being inadequate to meet the challenges of cybersecurity.

REFERENCES

Ablon, L. (2018). *Data Thieves: The Motivations of Cyber Threat Actors and Their Use and Monetization of Stolen Data*. The RAND Corporation. Retrieved from: https://www.rand.org/content/dam/rand/pubs/testimonies/CT400/CT490/RAND_CT490.pdf

ACSC. (2021). *Australian Cyber Security Centre. The cyber security principles*. Retrieved from: https://www.cyber.gov.au/acsc/view-all-content/guidance/cyber-security-principles

Akhtar, A. (2021). The Microsoft Exchange hack shows attackers are working 'smarter, not harder,' experts say. *Business Insider Australia*. Retrieved from: https://www.businessinsider.com.au/microsoft-exchange-server-hack-why-cyberattack-matters-2021-3?r=US&IR=T

Arnold, M. (2014). Banks Face Rising Threat from Cybercrime. *Financial Times*. Retrieved from: http://www.ft.com/intl/cms/s/0/5fd20f60-4d67-11e4-8f75-00144feab7de.html#axzz3FOFcGxgh

Bajak, F., Tucker, E., & O'Brien, M. (2021). Chinese Hackers Blamed for Massive Microsoft Server Hack. *The Diplomat*. Retrieved from: https://thediplomat.com/2021/03/chinese-hackers-blamed-for-massive-microsoft-server-hack/

Broeders, D. (2021). Private active cyber defense and (international) cyber security—pushing the line? *Journal of Cybersecurity, 7*(1). doi:10.1093/cybsec/tyab010

Browne, R. (2021). Bitcoin falls after U.S. seizes most of Colonial ransom. *CNBC Tech*. Retrieved from: https://www.cnbc.com/amp/2021/06/08/bitcoin-btc-price-slides-as-us-seizes-most-of-colonial-ransom.html

Callinan, R. (2021). UnitingCare cyber attack claimed by notorious ransom gang REvil/Sodin. *ABC News*. Retrieved from: https://mobile.abc.net.au/news/2021-05-06/qld-uniting-care-hack-revil-revealed/100118590

Canner, B. (2021). RockYou2021 is Largest Password Leak at 8.4 Billion Entries. *Solutions Review*. Retrieved from: https://solutionsreview.com/identity-management/rockyou2021-is-largest-password-leak-at-8-4-billion-entries/

Claughton, D., & Beilharz, N. (2021). JBS Foods pays $14.2 million ransom to end cyber attack on its global operations. *ABC Rural*. Retrieved from: https://www.abc.net.au/news/rural/2021-06-10/jbs-foods-pays-14million-ransom-cyber-attack/100204240

Colonial Pipeline cyber attack. (2021, June 5). In *Wikipedia*. Retrieved from: https://en.wikipedia.org/wiki/Colonial_Pipeline_cyber_attack

Darknet. (2021, June 8). In *Wikipedia*. Retrieved from: https://en.wikipedia.org/wiki/Darknet

Darknet market. (2021, June 8). In *Wikipedia*. Retrieved from: https://en.wikipedia.org/wiki/Darknet_market

Granjal, J., Monteiro, E., & Silva, J. S. (2015). Security for the internet of things: a survey of existing protocols and open research issues. *IEEE Communications Survey Tutor, 17*(3), 1294–1312. Retrieved from: https://ieeexplore.ieee.org/document/7005393

Gurinaviciute, J. (2021). 5 biggest cybersecurity threats: How hackers utilize remote work and human error to steal corporate data. *Security*. Retrieved from: https://www.securitymagazine.com/articles/94506-5-biggest-cybersecurity-threats

IBM. (2021). *Today's chief security challenges*. Retrieved from: https://www.ibm.com/it-infrastructure/us-en/resources/power/it-security-challenges/

IBM. (2021). *What is quantum computing?* Retrieved from: https://www.ibm.com/quantum-computing/what-is-quantum-computing/

Jang-Jaccard, J., & Nepal, S. (2014). A survey of emerging threats in cybersecurity. *Journal of Computer and System Sciences, 80*(5), 973-993. doi:10.1016/j.jcss.2014.02.005

Kelly, S., & Resnick-Ault, J. (2021). One password allowed hackers to disrupt Colonial Pipeline, CEO tells senators. "Not a Colonial123-type password. *IT News*. Retrieved from: https://www.itnews.com.au/news/one-password-allowed-hackers-to-disrupt-colonial-pipeline-ceo-tells-senators-565

Khraisat, A., & Alazab, A. (2021). A critical review of intrusion detection systems in the internet of things: Techniques, deployment strategy, validation strategy, attacks, public datasets and challenges. *Cybersecurity*, *4*(1), 18. doi:10.118642400-021-00077-7

Kumar, D., & Sanicola, L. (2021). Pipeline outage causes U.S. gasoline supply crunch, panic buying. *Reuters*. Retrieved from: https://www.reuters.com/business/energy/us-fuel-supplies-tighten-energy-pipeline-outage-enters-fifth-day-2021-05-11/

Luck, M. (2019). Entrapment behind the firewall: the ethics of internal cyber-sting. *Australasian Journal of Information Systems, 23*. Retrieved from: https://journal.acs.org.au/index.php/ajis/article/view/1886/843

Mirea, M., Wang, V., & Jung, J. (2019). The not so dark side of the darknet: A qualitative study. *Security Journal*, *32*(2), 102–118. doi:10.105741284-018-0150-5

Paquet-Clouston, M., Haslhofer, B., & Dupont, B. (2019). Ransomware payments in the Bitcoin ecosystem. *Journal of Cybersecurity*, *5*(1), tyz003. Advance online publication. doi:10.1093/cybsec/tyz003

Ravich, S. (2015). *Cyber-Enabled Economic Warfare: An Evolving Challenge*. Hudson Institute. Retrieved from: http://prognoz.eurasian-defence.ru/sites/default/files/source/2015.08cyberenabledeconomicwarfareanevolvingchallenge.pd

Romanosky, S. (2016, December). Examining the costs and causes of cyber incidents. *Journal of Cybersecurity*, *2*(2), 121–135. doi:10.1093/cybsec/tyw001

Seselja, E. (2021). *Cyber attack shuts down global meat processing giant JBS*. ABC Radio Brisbane.

ADDITIONAL READING

Baker, P. (2020). Beyond the hype: Digital Economy. Retrieved from: https://www.tradeeconomics.com/beyond-the-hype-digital-economy/

Bavin, E. (2021). Scam warning: Millions targeted as Google and Microsoft exploited. Yahoo Finance. Retrieved from: https://au.finance.yahoo.com/news/scam-warning-millions-targeted-google-microsoft-exploited-000942194.html

Brown, N. (2021). Top cybersecurity official warns of more ransomware attack after JBS hacking. Retrieved from: https://amp.news.com.au/technology/online/hacking/top-cybersecurity-official-warns-of-more-ransomware-attack-after-jbs-hacking/news-story/32eaadab27da4f47b60879d8b2178d7c

Digitalnation (2021). Digital transformation best practice for Australian businesses. What is zero trust cybersecurity? Retrieved from: https://www.itnews.com.au/digitalnation/what-is-zero-trust-cybersecurity-560887

KEY TERMS AND DEFINITIONS

Cyberattack: A cyberattack is an digital destruction launched by cybercriminals using one or more computers and other digital devices against a single or multiple computers or networks.

Cybercrime: Cybercrime is the use of a computer device or an online network to commit digital crimes and destruction such as fraud, online image abuse, identity theft or threats and intimidation, which are unethical in nature, and such illegal activities can result in loss, damages, destruction to users and their computing devices.

Cybersecurity: Cybersecurity is the practice of protecting and securing the IT systems, networks both wireless and wired, and software programs and hardware from digital attacks.

Hackers: A computer hacker is a computer expert who uses their technical knowledge in systems and technologies to achieve a goal such as making unauthorised entry or overcome an obstacle by breaking into a software, within a computerized system by non-standard and unethical ways.

Chapter 2
Cybersecurity in Europe:
Digital Identification, Authentication, and Trust Services

Joni A. Amorim
https://orcid.org/0000-0002-9837-9519
Universidade Estadual de Campinas (UNICAMP), Brazil

Jose-Macario de Siqueira Rocha
Universitat de València, Spain

Teresa Magal-Royo
https://orcid.org/0000-0002-7640-6264
Universitat Politécnica de València (UPV), Spain

ABSTRACT

Information security is increasingly necessary between citizens and public services. In a nearby environment, such as cities, there are digital services and infrastructures that help improve our quality of life. Secure access to services must be regulated and offer trust to the user. Initiatives like the Regulation from European Union, (EU) N° 910/2014 of the European Parliament and the Council intend to favour solutions for problems like interoperability and cybersecurity. In this chapter, two European countries are considered so that implementations of the electronic identification, authentication, and trust services are presented and discussed. The main contribution is a description of relevant European projects, a first step necessary to propel further research on this topic. The chapter also presents the current challenges for the consolidation of the technology used and for the adaptation of the electronic services offered by public administration bodies to citizens.

DOI: 10.4018/978-1-7998-6975-7.ch002

INTRODUCTION

According to the Netherlands Environmental Assessment Agency, PBL (2016), the European Union has more than 800 cities with more than 50,000 inhabitants. Europe is considered to be highly urbanized, with different types of regions: monocentric, dispersed, linear and polycentric urban regions. These many regions in Europe are now undergoing a digital transformation since cities are starting to use smart technologies. Smart Cities represent the future of urban development in a world where daily activities depend more and more on different kinds of technologies like the Internet of Things, (IoT) and Artificial Intelligence, (AI). A more interconnected world demands improved electronic services that enable interactions between businesses, citizens and public authorities. The increased interconnection suggests new cyber risks in connection with technologies like IoT (Kalkan & Rasmussen, 2020), AI (Hintze, 2016). Pedersen & Tjørnehøj suggest: *"...e-government lacks theoretical models that can increase our understanding of the relationship between the external environment and e-government investments and how these investments pay off by renewing public sector* capabilities", (Pedersen & Tjørnehøj, 2018).

Authors also advocate that the reduction of operating costs together with a high level of integration of processes are essential if the intent is to provide efficient services for citizens. Pedersen & Tjørnehøj listed five main characteristics of transformational governments as being (i) citizen centricity, (ii) single points of contact, (iii) flexible service delivery, (iv) integration, and (v) reengineering and optimization. All this process needs a progressive digital transformation of the society including citizens. According to Vial, this transition may be understood as: *"...a process where digital technologies create disruptions triggering strategic responses from organizations that seek to alter their value creation paths while managing the structural changes and organizational barriers that affect the positive and negative outcomes of this process" (Vial, 2019).*

The inherent complexity associated to definitions like this one suggests different research agendas that may be easily related to cybersecurity, privacy, trust, cyberresilience, etc...

Seppänen et al. (2018), the failure to manage digital services architecture in a city *"...leads into problems in interoperability and holistic development that are the requirements for a fluid digital transformation of governments"*. In this way, it is essential to determine the components of the government organization to understand their synergy so that their actions would be aligned to the objectives of each specific organization. On the other hand, it is also essential to consider how organizations would interact with each other and with stakeholders as well while taking into consideration factors like cyber security and privacy.

This context suggests electronic identification (eID) and electronic trust services (eTS) as being enablers of interactions between businesses, citizens and public authorities as suggested by recent regulations from the European Union. The Regulation 910 from the European Parliament and the Council (EPC, 2014). National electronic identification schemes should be interoperable while following a framework consisting of characteristics like common operational security standards, rules of procedure and a reference to a minimum set of person identification data uniquely representing a natural or legal person. This same regulation also implies that cooperation between the states members should involve information exchange experience and good practices.

Since 2000, electronic services managed by the public institutions of the Member States of the European Union are adapting to the new society times in terms of creating cross-border and efficient digital services for their citizens (Al-Hujran et al., 2015). Due to a large amount of digital information and electronic transactions that are currently managed within the context of Smart Cities, the identification of citizens is a fundamental pillar to optimize the use and exploitation of online services (Goodchild, 2007). In this regard, national platforms have been developed throughout Europe in recent years, thanks to initiatives supported by the European Union for all member countries like Cl@ve initiative in Spain and the autenticação.gov initiative in Portugal.

The European Commission also recognizes the importance of the use and interoperability of these national platforms for the identification of citizens and has promoted legal and technical initiatives. To this end, it has been developing specific legislation, highlighting Regulation (EU) No 910/2014 (eIDAS Regulation) of the European Parliament and Council, of July 23, 2014, on electronic identification and trust services for electronic transactions in the internal market (EPC, 2014). At the same time, the Connecting Europe Facility (CEF) Telecom financing line was approved as a key financing instrument to promote growth, employment, and competitiveness through investment in infrastructure directed at the European level. CEF supports the development of trans-European networks of high performance, sustainable and efficiently interconnected in the fields of transport, energy and digital services. Investments in projects managed by the CEF seek to improve and resolve deficiencies in energy, transport and the digital network in Europe (European Commission, 2019a). The European Commission has allocated until the end of 2019 about € 340K distributed among the 492 projects of the CEF Telecom program, of which 53 projects with a total € 26.4K correspond to the specific CEF eID program (INEA, 2019a).

Through this European solution, the electronic services of public entities connected to the national node eIDAS outsource the identification process of European citizens to accomplish with the eIDAS Regulation.

Authentication systems capable of being controlled by institutions in a common and transnational way are the only system to ensure universal and controlled access to the services of European institutions. Taking into account the identification systems of each country, the protocols promoted by the European Union must be recognized as the best option for secure access to electronic services established by any European institution that needs citizen-oriented services throughout Europe.

This technology criteria unification was the fundamental basis for the development of the eIDAS nodes of Spain and Portugal connected to the national electronic identification platforms of citizens presented in the chapter.

The chapter presents an introduction with a theoretical framework about the policy related to cybersecurity created by European Commission and its state members through the last two decades, a section related to the context of the eIDAS Regulation and the electronic trust services (eTS) associated with CEF support and finally a section dedicated to recent initiatives carried out in two European countries such as Spain and Portugal. The current limitations of the eIDAS nodes are presented and analyzed and finally there is a description of the future steps that central governments and public entities must follow to connect their electronic services in compliance within eIDAS Regulation and electronic security frameworks.

Background

There are many different definitions for Smart City, with terms that sometimes are considered synonyms: future city, eco city, intelligent city, sustainable city, compact city, liveable city, digital city, innovative city, green city, (Eremia et al., 2017). The authors mention the ISO 37120:2014 named "Sustainable Development of Communities-Indicators for City Services and Quality of Life" (ISO, 2014) as an example of a set of indicators that may be used as reference by city managers, researchers, and so on. Seventeen control point has defined to verify the efficiency of a city management. These indicators are; economy, education, energy, environment, finance, fire and emergency response, governance, health, recreation, safety, shelter, solid waste, telecommunication and innovation, transportation, urban planning, wastewater, and water management and sanitation.

Standardized indicators may be used in many ways but in special for comparisons between different urban areas also. The overmentioned standard ISO 37120 (ISO, 2014) was revised in 2018 (ISO, 2018) while a new standard was created, in this case ISO 37122:2019 named "Sustainable cities and communities-Indicators for Smart Cities". According to ISO (2019), the new document may be useful "to implement Smart City policies, programs and projects", for example, while facilitating innovation and growth in the social and digital interaction. This new standard defines a Smart City as: *"... a city that increases the pace at which it provides social, economic and environmental sustainability outcomes and responds to challenges such as climate change, rapid population growth, and political and economic instability by fundamentally improving how it engages society, applies collaborative leadership methods, works across disciplines and city systems, and uses data information and modern technologies to deliver better services and quality of life to those in the city (residents, businesses, visitors), now and for the foreseeable future, without unfair disadvantage of others or degradation of the natural environment"* (ISO, 2019).

It is also believed that *"information technology and communications (IT&C) is essential in the Smart City while data security is critical,* (Eremia et al., 2017). Examples of indicators presented in the new standard (ISO, 2019) follows. For Telecommunication, indicators would be: (i) Percentage of the city population with access to sufficiently fast broadband, (ii) Percentage of city area under a white zone/ dead spot/not covered by telecommunication connectivity and (iii) Percentage of the city area covered by municipally provided Internet connectivity. For Recreation, main indicator would be the percentage of public recreation services that can be booked online while for Safety, main indicator would be the Percentage of the city area covered by digital surveillance camera. These indicators might suggest how essential IT&C is.

The use of digital communication services in a Smart City would depend heavily on cyber security since the access to images from digital surveillance cameras, for example, should be strictly controlled in most situations. Nowadays, face recognition is a well-known developed technology that may use images to identify citizens in a city; this kind of identification brings benefits but if misused it may also create different problems for the local population since facial recognition may have different vulnerabilities (Zizi, 2019). Therefore, it is possible to argue that use of new technologies for identification, like facial recognition, demands regulations. In the case of the European Union, the regulations would have to guarantee an agreement between the many countries involved so that ethical guidelines would regulate the corresponding market of smart products appropriately for the benefit of citizens living in Smart Cities.

According to PWC (2019), the total value of the global Smart City market projected to exceed US$1 trillion by 2020 and US$2.5 trillion by 2025. The same report indicates main challenges in the implementation of Smart Cities is security: (i) complex and massive attacks (cyber terrorism) due to interrelated critical areas; (ii) large-scale ramifications of an attack (iii) shared responsibility for securing the city. Another challenge is policy, (i) lack of IoT standards, (ii) legislation and policies, (iii) embedded or rigid public sector processes, (iv) and (vii) slow government procedures and reaction times. In the other hand, citizens would represent an additional challenge like the lack of confidence in using and benefiting from Smart City services, citizen participation and privacy concerns and inclusivity and socioeconomic consequences.

Part of the many challenges demand policy regulations oriented to users Part of the many challenges demand policy regulations oriented to users' recommendations for decision makers. A report created by Smart Cities Information System platform named. The making of a Smart City, recommends as a policy that European Commission encourage to member states to give more prominence to the deployment of Smart City solutions in their national strategies for the use of EU funds, (SCIS, 2017).

This policy would certainly affect the corresponding market of smart products. Another recommended policy from the same report is presented as follows: "expectations on the projects have to be in line with the inherent characteristics of research and development, such as their complexity, their often-weak returns to investment, unexpected complications during implementation". This policy would facilitate the understanding of the complexity of managing collaborative projects which may involve companies, universities and the government in the search for new solutions to relevant problems being considered.

There is an important issue about how effective policy recommendations are in social context now. Despite that, policies may represent the best way to shape the society of the next few years or decades. Cathelat (2019) believes that there exists a broad range of choices that may affect cities, which it will have the chance to develop in a variety of different ways. According to the author, old laws and regulations seem outdated and new rules must be devised taking account the Electronic Identification, Authentication and Trust Services issues. A good example of necessary regulation refers to cities that would require anonymity of consolidated data in collective data in all their services. However, many user-oriented services need an acceptable security level that allows trust in the system and that governments ensure the controlled privacy of a citizen's data. More and more, massive digital attacks on public institutions have shown that an essential service can collapse due to lack of access to the most basic data in the time of COVID-19. Also, data commercial exploitation from citizens needs an urgent study because this should be regulated through international mechanisms.

Cybersecurity From the European Framework

Information and communication technologies, ICT, become the keystone of economic growth in the EU and in the world. There is a critical resource on which all economic sectors depend because digital environments enable economies to function in key sectors such as finance, healthcare, energy, and transportation. The report created by the EU in 2006 named Strategy for a Secure Information Society in Europe was pioneer to point out the concept of cybersecurity (Commission of the European Communities, 2006).

In 2013, the European Commission and the EU High Representative for Foreign Affairs and Security Policy presented a joint Communication to the European Parliament, the Council, the European Economic and Social Committee, and the Committee of the Regions entitled Cybersecurity Strategy of the European Union: An open, protected and safe cyberspace, (European Commission, 2013).

According to the report, the Cybersecurity Strategy, due to the complexity of the problem, the solution cannot consist of a centralized European supervision. National administrations are the ones in the best position to organize prevention and response activities to cyber incidents and attacks, as well as to establish contacts and networks with the private sector and citizens through established legal frameworks and procedures. For this reason, the European Union, in the field of cybersecurity, was articulated in five strategic priorities that have been followed by the European Agency for Network and Information Security (ENISA) created in 2004:

- Achieving cyber resilience.
- Drastically reducing cybercrime
- Developing cyberdefence policy and capabilities related to the Common Security and Defence Policy (CSDP)
- Develop the industrial and technological resources for cybersecurity
- Establish a coherent international cyberspace policy for the European Union and promote core EU values.

Nowadays, the Digital Europe program is a central element of the Commission's comprehensive response to the challenge of digital transformation, which is part of the proposed Multiannual Financial Framework (MFF) for 2021-2027. Its objective is to offer an instrument adapted to the operational requirements of capacity building in the areas identified by the European Council, and to exploit the synergies between them. Therefore, it will focus on strengthening Europe's capabilities in high-performance computing, artificial intelligence, cybersecurity and advanced digital skills and ensuring their wide use in the economy and society. Future objectives will focus on aspects such as high-performance computing, artificial intelligence, cybersecurity and trust, advanced digital skills and the best use of digital capabilities and interoperability in e-government applications.

eIDAS Regulation in Europe

eIDAS (electronic IDentification, Authentication and trust Services) is an European Union regulation on electronic identification and trust services for electronic transactions in the European Single Market. One of the main objectives of the eIDAS regulation is that a public service offered to national citizens via the Internet with an electronic identification system must also recognize the electronic identifications of European citizens of other Member States. This promotes the free movement of people and goods in Europe across borders by facilitating access to electronic services offered to citizens regardless of whether they are national or from another Member State (European Commission, 2019c).

The eIDAS Regulation aims to promote interoperability between the Member States to facilitate the establishment of legal certainty, trust, and security in electronic transactions, (Zaccaria et al., 2019). This regulation entered into force on July 1, 2016, and through the European Agreement (Commission Implementing Decision) No. 2015/296, the eIDAS Cooperation Network was created to facilitate cooperation between the Member States (European Commission, 2019b).

The implementation of the eIDAS Regulation is carried out considering the agreements of the European Commission (INEA, 2019b) establishing the interoperability framework (Commission Implementing Regulation 2015/1501), defining the technical specifications and minimum procedures for the levels of electronic identification assurance (Commission Implementing Regulation 2015/1502) and the procedures for the notification of national citizen identification schemes (Commission Implementing Decision 2015/1984).

This regulation contemplates both the recognition of the actors involved, including the providers of electronic services, as well as the legal bases to provide legal validity of electronic transactions. It also allows citizens to use their country's electronic identification schemes to access the public services offered in the other Member States, and thus encourage Europe to use the eIDAS network as a direct interoperability solution between national nodes.

Both the eIDAS Regulation and the eIDAS network were developed taking into account the results of some previous projects and initiatives that seek a European solution for the mutual recognition of citizens of different Member States. These projects include the project called Secure idenTity acrOss boRders linked, (STORK) with the aim of developing a cross-border electronic identification system piloted by about 20 Member States (Leitold, 2011). Through this project, Proxy services known as Pan-European Proxy Service (PEPS) were created. Both the documentation generated by this project and the collaboration between the representatives of the different participating Member States were essential for the preparation of the eIDAS Regulation and the implementation of the portal corresponding to the CEF eID Building Block (Ribeiro et al., 2018). Services provided through this portal include the update of the standard solution known as CORE Platform for eIDAS nodes, the coordination of the eIDAS Cooperation Network to support interoperability between nodes and the dissemination of the concept of identification of European citizens through the eIDAS network. All these European initiatives show both the importance and the short-term obligation of public electronic services to allow the identification of European citizens.

SOLUTIONS AND RECOMMENDATIONS

The Cl@ve Initiative in Spain

Considering the results of the European STORK project, from the beginning, the Government of Spain established that the Cl@ve system should also facilitate the identification of European citizens. Through STORK, Spain operated for some years a PEPS electronic identification node, contemplating access to foreign citizens to the electronic services included in the project. Therefore, the option to identify European citizens through the STPS project PEPS was included in the first version of Cl@ve.

With the publication of the eIDAS Regulation in 2014, the Spanish government decided to implement and operate its own eIDAS node connected to Cl@ve to comply with the technical specifications derived from said European Regulation. This change also necessitated the migration of electronic services previously connected to the PEPS node of the STORK project.

The government of Spain approved in 2014 the creation of the Cl@ve system - https://clave.gob.es/, aimed at unifying and simplifying citizens' electronic access to public services (Gobierno de España, 2019). In 2015, it established the necessary technical requirements for the system, including the scope of application, the purpose of the system, guarantee levels, accession procedures, among others (Gobierno de España, 2015). Cl@ve is the national platform used by the electronic headquarters of both local and regional public administrations to outsource the process of electronic user identification. Through this system, citizens can identify themselves in any connected electronic service without using different registers, users, passwords or certificates, (see Figure 1).

The first version of the Spanish eIDAS node was managed between 2014 and 2016 thanks to two Actions co-financed by the European Commission through the eID call of the CEF Telecom program called Setting up of an eIDAS compliant PEPS in Spain (2014-EN -IM-0009) and Operation of the Spanish Pan-European Proxy Services for the first years (2014-ES-IM-0010).

Electronic services in Spain, through Cl@ve, also allow access to current identification systems through DNI-e and electronic certificate, and there is also the possibility3 of making signatures with personal digital certificates kept in remote servers on official documents such as the declaration of income, application for Social Security certificates, etc. It is, therefore, a common platform for identification, authentication and electronic signature.

Several eIDAS node projects has been implemented in several cities. In 2016, Action 2015-ES-IA-0087 (Connecting public services to the Spanish eIDAS node) (INEA, 2015) was initiated, through which the Government of Spain made various adjustments to its eIDAS node and facilitated the connection and interoperability with electronic services through the new version 2.0 of the Cl@ve system taking into account the different electronic identifications existing in the Member States. Through this Action, the eIDAS node was prepared for exhaustive use by any Spanish public institution and the electronic services of the Ministry of Defense, the Government of Navarra and the municipalities of Valencia, Ibiza, Gandia, Estepona, and Castellón were connected.

Figure 1. Cl@ve Website
Source: Spanish goverment, 2020

In 2018, the eID4Spain action (2018-ES-IA-0039, Connecting Regional and Local Administrations to the Spanish eIDAS node) was initiated through which the Junta de Extremadura, the city council of Rivas, Madrid and the councils of Valencia and Ciudad Real connected its electronic services to the Spanish eIDAS node (Universitat de València, 2018). In 2019 the European Commission approved the eID4Spain-19 project (2019-ES-IA0040), through which the Andalusian Health Service (SAS) and the Valladolid Provincial will connect their electronic services to the eIDAS node through Cl@ve 2.0.

All these European actions and projects include the performance of various interoperability and compliance tests identifying citizens of other Member States and have served to demonstrate the efficiency of the Spanish eIDAS node following European guidelines. They have also served to promote its use by consolidating the digital identification service of European citizens through Cl@ve.

In fact, electronic services of Spanish public institutions are already connected to Cl@ve for the identification of Spanish citizens, so they only need to make specific adjustments on the connection to version 2.0 of Cl@ve for to be able to use the European citizen's identification service through the eIDAS node. In this way, the efforts of public entities concentrate on adjusting electronic services to consider their use by citizens of other countries with an identification code and personal data structured in different formats than those used in Spain.

The Autenticação.gov Initiative in Portugal

The Government of Portugal uses the Autenticação.gov system associated with the *"Cartão Cidadão"*(Portuguese citizen card) as a solution for the secure identification of a citizen in electronic operations following European guidelines (Gobierno de Portugal, 2019). This smart card must be activated by the citizen before its first use by acquiring a PIN code, it can be managed through a specific application and integrates into a single document the identification of social security, health user and the taxpayer.

This system coexists with the system called *digital key in motion*, which is a public identification service through an SMS registered and associated with the Identity card.

With the arrival of the eIDAS Regulation and the CEF eID program, the Portuguese government has also developed its own eIDAS node so that European citizens can use the electronic services offered by the public administration and so that Portuguese citizens can use the electronic services offered in the other states members, (see Figure 2).

Nowadays the Agency for Administrative Modernization (AMA) is responsible for the electronic services associated with the eIDAS node in several smart cities in National Institutions. In 2016, AMA coordinated the CEF Action 2016-EU-IA-0066 eIDAS2Business called Making private businesses benefit from eIDAS whose main objective was to verify and establish the connection between the Portuguese eIDAS node and the electronic services provided by the AMA to all citizens and EU companies that use their national eID (INEA, 2016).

In 2017, Action 2017-PT-IA-0044 called Development of an eIDAS - open NCP Connector for cross border eHealth was initiated, focused on the development of an eID connector that linked the National Contact Point for eHealth based on the OpenNCP framework (NCPeH) and the eIDAS node (INEA, 2017). This reference implementation was transferable to all national institutional scenarios of the eIDAS with the national NCPeH allowing secure access to Cross-border eHealth Information Services, (CBeHIS), such as digital access to medical records and the prescription service of Medicines of a user.

Figure 2. AUTENTICAÇÃO.GOV Website
Source: Portugal goverment, 2020

In 2018, the PT-eIDAS (Authentication and eSignature in Portuguese services) project began, with code 2018-PT-IA-0045, focused on the connection between the Portuguese eIDAS node and various electronic services in the justice and culture, allowing the identification of European users in the Portal of Justice of Portugal and in the Portal of the General Inspection of Cultural Activities (IGAC) (INEA, 2018).

As can be seen through the aforementioned projects, the Portuguese government is promoting relevant projects that exploit the network of eIDAS nodes for the identification of European citizens, demonstrating the transversality of electronic services in Portugal and Europe.

FUTURE RESEARCH DIRECTIONS

In the future, the eIDAS network will promote the efficiency in interoperability between national nodes using previously notified data schemas between them. In addition, Europe has the challenge to create a secure environment from national platforms are not attacked by cyberattacks that could endanger the confidential information of users and be exposed to the digital world.

Although the European Commission provides a standard solution for the implementation of the eIDAS node, each member state faces four important challenges: (i) the implementation and operability of the eIDAS node according to the needs of national and regional institutions; (ii) implement and publicize the connection tool available to public and private institutions so that they can use the services of the eIDAS node; and (iii) establish the connection and maintain interoperability with the eIDAS nodes of the other countries; (iv) Detection and monitoring of possible national and international cyberattacks. Overcoming these four challenges that are linked to each other will allow in the future a comprehensive citizen identification system in all member states of the European Union, promoting both interoperability between eIDAS nodes and between electronic services and their national eID platform.

The creation of the eIDAS nodes of Portugal and Spain have followed the principle of offering the European citizens identification service through the national eID platform, which simplifies the various identification methods to a centralized connection for the electronic services they want Identify both national and European citizens. In addition, both governments have collaborated efficiently to establish interoperability between their eIDAS nodes and perform the tests corresponding to the European projects identified in this chapter.

The interoperability connection through eiDAS node for an european citizen to an electronic delivered system with a public institution established as follows (see Figure 3):

However, Spain Government and most of the other Member States still do not offer the eIDAS Node service to private entities, limiting their use to public entities. In addition, currently, only six eIDAS nodes from other Member States (Germany, Belgium, Estonia, Italy, Luxembourg, and Portugal) are interoperating in production with the Spanish node, so only a small part of European citizens can currently use the Spanish electronic services already available.

Figure 3. e-government services connection through eiDAS node for european citizens
Source: Universitat Politécnica de Valencia, 2020

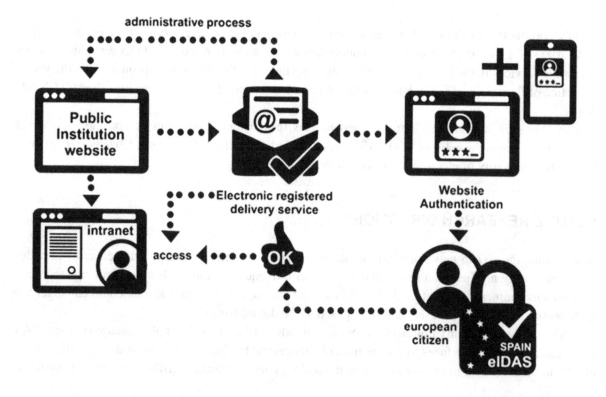

In relation to interoperability among all European nodes, the current status in each country disseminated by the eIDAS Cooperation Network (INEA, 2019c) and the results obtained so far corresponding to the actions and initiatives presented in this article regarding implementation and the use of the eIDAS nodes of Portugal and Spain show the following five obstacles to the consolidation of the eIDAS network, (INEA, 2019c) (see Figure 4).

- eIDAS nodes have not yet been able to connect in production with the majority of the other nodes of other Member States, noting that some Member States have not yet completed the implementation of their national node.
- Until the end of 2019, less than half of the countries of the European Union have notified their national schemes.
- The structure of citizen identification codes varies considerably between the Member States and different identification documents like passport number and tax number coexist; identifications in some countries are not unique codes nor do they last over time, which complicates automation in the unequivocal electronic identification of a citizen through these codes.
- eIDAS network does not contemplate the signing of electronic documents: a large part of the public services requires a citizen to sign a document or their request, but the identification of citizens through the eIDAS node does not include any tools for signing documents, so the European citizen needs in these cases to use an additional electronic certificate to access the electronic service.
- Most Member States have not yet allowed access to the services of the eIDAS node by private entities and are waiting for the specific procedures for the provision of this service to be regulated and defined: despite the intention of the eIDAS Regulation to promote a single digital market, the obligation for the Member States is to include the identification of European citizens in public services, so neither Spain nor the majority of the other Member States are offering access to the private sector.

CONCLUSION

According to Markopoulou et al. (2019), a global perspective is relevant since cybersecurity is a critical field of global regulatory interest. The authors also believe that cybersecurity, unlike data protection, essentially does not grant any rights to individuals. The chapter present two initiatives coordinated by the European Commission and the governments of Spain and Portugal that have demonstrated the high degree of commitment of public entities to adapt electronic identification platforms according to the guidelines of the eIDAS Regulation. Both *Cl@ve* in Spain and *autenticação.gov* in Portugal are connected to the national eIDAS node to facilitate access to the citizen identification service through the eIDAS network.

However, there are several obstacles to the consolidation of the eIDAS network, highlighting the lack of operability among several national nodes and the refusal of several Member States to offer access to the private sector until specific procedures are regulated and established. Despite the fact that the potential of the eIDAS network has not yet been efficiently exploited, as production interoperability between national nodes increases, the eIDAS network as a whole will be consolidated, strengthening the connection with new electronic services and finally reaching the impact Expected among citizens. According to Massachusetts Institute of Technology, MIT Sloane Management Review, an electronic journal specialized on technological change: *"...governments have a very important role to play in mitigating the adverse short-term impacts on people since the ones that are negatively affected by automation tend to be against the changes that, in the end, benefit most of the society".* (MIT SMR, 2020)

Figure 4. eIDAS Future Challenges
Source: ENISA, 2020

Considering that time is necessary for new technological solutions to be properly valued by the majority of citizens living in Smart Cities, new policies and new legislation turn to be essential for the expected transformation to happen with minimal turbulence. In this way, it is expected that initiatives like the ones focused on electronic identification, authentication and trust services might have positive influence with minimal negative disruptions on people lives. In this work, projects from different countries were presented and discussed so that new venues for research may be drawn.

The main contribution of this chapter are examples success results obtain of relevant European projects promoting by CEF to consolidate and promote the use of eIDAS in e-government environments, a first step necessary to further research on this topic. However, it is necessary to create international mechanisms against massive data cyberattacks that can affect public institutions and digital services in a smart city where trust must be created in the use of data provided by citizens to the system.

The chapter also presents the current challenges for the consolidation of the technology used by the eIDAS network and for the adaptation of the electronic services offered by public bodies to citizens. In this way, the findings presented here extend the current knowledge on how Member States of the European Union are cooperating with regard to the security and interoperability of the electronic identification schemes necessary for an efficient use of Information and Communications Technologies (ICTs) in the infrastructure of urban areas in a smart city.

Future work might also include the strategies communicate and concern to citizens the necessity of presenting this type of communications with the municipality services for technological changes from the security that public administrations must offer in the storage of sensitive information of the citizen, for example with fiscal data, medical data, location data, etc ... that protect your privacy from the law.

According to Pervane and Gu (2019), city administrations should start to assess how well their communities are positioned for the coming technological changes. In this way, a better understanding of the characteristics of the current workforce would suggest gaps to be filled in different ways, which might include public-private partnerships in different projects toward the development of Smart Cities.

Bélanger and Carter (2008) argument that citizen confidence in government and technology is imperative to the wide-spread adoption of e-government. On the other hand, Gracia and Ariño (2015) noticed a worldwide reduction on citizen trust in the public administration, it also suggests that there is still a scarcity of works analyzing what are the effects of e-government introduction. In this context, future work on the development of Smart Cities should consider the different perceived effects of the introduction of e-government in terms of trust, risk and cybersecurity for the digital transformation of urban areas.

ACKNOWLEDGMENT

This research was supported by European Health and Digital Executive Agency – HaDEA within the framework program Connecting Europe Facility (CEF) Telecom and developed in the project named Connecting Public Administrations to the Spanish eIDAS Node, eID4Spain-19. [Action N°: 2019-ES-IA-0040].

REFERENCES

Al-Hujran, O., Al-Debei, M. M., Chatfield, A., & Migdadi, M. (2015). The imperative of influencing citizen attitude toward e-government adoption and use. *Computers in Human Behavior*, *53*, 189–203. doi:10.1016/j.chb.2015.06.025

Bélanger, F., & Carter, L. (2008). Trust and risk in e-government adoption. *The Journal of Strategic Information Systems*, *17*(2), 165–176. doi:10.1016/j.jsis.2007.12.002

Cathelat, B. (2019). *Smart Cities - Shaping the Society of 2030*. Global Sociology Study Report. NET-EXPLO, Observatory. Paris, France. United Nations Educational, Scientific and Cultural Organization (UNESCO). Retrieved from: https://unesdoc.unesco.org/ark:/48223/pf0000367762.locale=es

Commission of the European Communities. (2006). *A strategy for a Secure Information Society – "Dialogue, partnership and empowerment"*. Retrieved from: https://ec.europa.eu/information_society/doc/com2006251.pdf

Eremia, M., Toma, L., & Sanduleac, M. (2017). The Smart City Concept in the 21st Century. *Procedia Engineering, 181,* 12–19. doi:10.1016/j.proeng.2017.02.357

European Commission. (2013). *Cybersecurity Strategy of the European Union: An Open, Safe and Secure Cyberspace.* Retrieved from: https://eeas.europa.eu/archives/docs/policies/eu-cyber-security/cybsec_comm_en.pdf

European Commission. (2019a). *Connecting Europe Facility in Telecom*. Retrieved from: https://ec.europa.eu/digital-single-market/en/connecting-europe-facility

European Commission. (2019b). *eIDAS cooperation network portal.* Retrieved from: https://ec.europa.eu/cefdigital/wiki/display/EIDCOOPNET/eIDAS+Cooperation+Network

European Commission. (2019c). *What are the benefits of eID?* Retrieved from: https://ec.europa.eu/cefdigital/wiki/display/CEFDIGITAL/Benefits+of+eID

European Parliament Council. (2014). Regulation (EU) N° 910/2014 of the European Parliament and of the Council of 23 July 2014 on electronic identification and trust services for electronic transactions in the internal market and repealing Directive 1999/93/EC. *Official Journal of the European Union.* L 257/73. European Legislation Identifier (ELI) Retrieved from: https://eur-lex.europa.eu/legal-content/EN/TXT/PDF/?uri=CELEX:32014R0910&from=EN

Gobierno de España. (2015). *BOE-A-2015-14215.* Resolución de 14 de diciembre de 2015, de la Dirección de Tecnologías de la Información y las Comunicaciones, por la que se establecen las prescripciones técnicas necesarias para el desarrollo y aplicación del sistema Cl@ve. Retrieved from: https://www.boe.es/eli/es/res/2015/12/14/(3)/con

Gobierno de España. (2019). *Portal Cl@ve.* Retrieved from: https://clave.gob.es

Goodchild, M. (2007). Citizens as sensors: The world of volunteered geography. *GeoJournal, 69*(4), 211–221. doi:10.100710708-007-9111-y

Governo de Portugal. (2019). *Sistema Autenticação.gov.* Retrieved from: https://www.autenticacao.gov.pt

Gracia, D. B., & Ariño, L. C. (2015). Rebuilding public trust in government administrations through e-government actions. *Revista Española de Investigación de Market, 19*(1), 1–11. doi:10.1016/j.reimke.2014.07.001

Hintze, A. (2016). Understanding the Four Types of Artificial Intelligence. *Government Technology.* Retrieved from: https://www.govtech.com/computing/Understanding-the-Four-Types-of-Artificial-Intelligence.html

Innovation and Networks Executive Agency. (2015). *Connecting public services to the Spanish eIDAS node.* Retrieved from: https://ec.europa.eu/inea/en/connecting-europe-facility/cef-telecom/2015-es-ia-0087

Innovation and Networks Executive Agency. (2016). *eIDAS2Business: Making private businesses benefit from eIDAS*. Retrieved from: https://ec.europa.eu/inea/en/connecting-europe-facility/cef-telecom/2016-eu-ia-0066

Innovation and Networks Executive Agency. IEA (2017). *Development of an eIDAS – openNCP Connector for cross border eHealth*. Retrieved from: https://ec.europa.eu/inea/en/connecting-europe-facility/cef-telecom/2017-eu-ia-0044

Innovation and Networks Executive Agency. (2018). *Authentication and eSignature in Portuguese services*. Retrieved from: https://ec.europa.eu/inea/en/connecting-europe-facility/cef-telecom/2018-pt-ia-0045

Innovation and Networks Executive Agency. (2019a). *CEF Telecom 2019 Report*. Retrieved from: https://ec.europa.eu/inea/sites/inea/files/cefpub/cef-telecom-brochure-2019-final_web.pdf

Innovation and Networks Executive Agency. (2019b). *Trust Services and Electronic identification*. Retrieved from: https://ec.europa.eu/digital-single-market/en/trust-services-and-eid

Innovation and Networks Executive Agency. (2019c). *eID Documentation*: Country overview Retrieved from: https://ec.europa.eu/cefdigital/wiki/display/CEFDIGITAL/Country+overview

International Organization for Standardization. (2014). *ISO 37120:2014: Sustainable development of communities- Indicators for city services and quality of life*. International Organization for Standardization. Retrieved from: https://www.iso.org/standard/62436.html

International Organization for Standardization. (2018). *ISO 37120:2018: Sustainable Cities and Communities-Indicators for City Services and Quality of Life*. Retrieved from: https://www.iso.org/standard/68498.html

International Organization for Standardization. (2019). *ISO 37122:2019: Sustainable Cities and Communities — Indicators for Smart Cities*. Retrieved from: https://www.iso.org/standard/69050.html

Kalkan, K., & Rasmussen, K. (2020). TruSD: Trust framework for service discovery among IoT devices. *Computer Networks*, *178*(4).

Leitold, H. (2011). Challenges of eID Interoperability: The STORK Project. In S. Fischer-Hübner, P. Duquenoy, M. Hansen, R. Leenes, & G. Zhang (Eds.), *Privacy and Identity Management for Life. Privacy and Identity 2010. IFIP Advances in Information and Communication Technology, 352*. Springer. doi:10.1007/978-3-642-20769-3_12

Markopoulou, D., Papakonstantinou, V., & Hert, P. (2019). The new EU cybersecurity framework: The NIS Directive, ENISA's role and the General Data Protection Regulation. *Computer Law & Security Review*, *35*(6), 105336. Advance online publication. doi:10.1016/j.clsr.2019.06.007

Massachusetts Institute of Technology. (2020). Can We Escape the Technology Trap? Carl Frey interview by Paul Michelman. *MIT Sloan Management Review's Three Big Points podcast*. Massachusetts Institute of Technology. Retrieved from: https://sloanreview.mit.edu/audio/can-we-escape-the-technology-trap/

Netherlands Environmental Assessment Agency. (2016) *Cities in Europe: Facts and figures on cities and urban areas*. PBL Publishers. Retrieved from: https://ec.europa.eu/futurium/en/system/files/ged/pbl_2016_cities_in_europe_23231.pdf

Pedersen, K., & Tjørnehøj, G. (2018). Successful E-government Transformation: Pressure, Support, Capabilities and the Freedom to use them. *The Electronic Journal of E-Government, 16*(2), 168–184.

Pervane, T., & Gu, K. (2019). How Cities Should Prepare for Artificial Intelligence. Frontiers. August 07, 2019. Massachusetts Institute of Technology. *MIT Sloane Management Review*. Retrieved from: https://sloanreview.mit.edu/article/how-cities-should-prepare-for-artificial-intelligence/

PricewaterhouseCoopers. (2019). *Creating the smart cities of the future: A three-tier development model for digital transformation of citizen services*. PricewaterhouseCoopers. Retrieved from: https://www.pwc.com/gx/en/sustainability/assets/creating-the-smart-cities-of-the-future.pdf

Ribeiro, C., Leitold, H., Esposito, S., & Mitzam, D. (2018). STORK: A real, heterogeneous, large-scale eID management system. *International Journal of Information Security, 17*(5), 569–585. doi:10.100710207-017-0385-x

Seppänen, V., Penttinen, K., & Pulkkinen, M. (2018). Key Issues in Enterprise Architecture Adoption in the Public Sector. *The Electronic. Journal of E-Government, 16*(1), 46–58.

Smart Cities Information System. (2017). *The making of a smart city: Policy recommendations for decision makers at local regional, national and EU levels*. Smart Cities Information System. Retrieved from: https://smartcities-infosystem.eu/library/publications

Universitat de València. (2018). *Connecting Regional and Local Administrations to Spanish eIDAS Node (eID4Spain)*. Retrieved from: https://lmtgroup.eu/eid4spain/

Vial, G. (2019). Understanding digital transformation: A review and a research agenda. *The Journal of Strategic Information Systems, 28*(2), 118–144. doi:10.1016/j.jsis.2019.01.003

Zaccaria, A., Schmidt-Kessel, M., Schulze, R., & Gambino, A. M. (2019). *EU eIDAS Regulation: Regulation (EU) 910/2014 on electronic identification and trust services for electronic transactions in the internal market*. Beck C.H. Publisher.

Zizi, M. (2019). The Flaws and Dangers of Facial Recognition. *Security Today*. Retrieved from: https://securitytoday.com/articles/2019/03/01/the-flaws-and-dangers-of-facial-recognition.aspx

ADDITIONAL READING

Alzoubi, O. M. (2019) The Digital Disruption: The Past, Present, and Future of Digitalization and Its Impact on The World We Live In. Independently published.

Carreira, P., Amaral, V., & Vangheluwe, H. (2021) Foundations of Multi-Paradigm Modelling for Cyber-Physical Systems. Springer International Publishing.

Colombo, P., & Ferrari, E. (2019). Access control technologies for Big Data management systems: Literature review and future trends. *Cybersecurity, 2*(3), 3. Advance online publication. doi:10.118642400-018-0020-9

Council of the European Union. (2018). European Union Cyber Defence Policy Framework, update Retrieved from: https://data.consilium.europa.eu/doc/document/ST-14413-2018-INIT/en/pdf

European Commission. (2021). eIDAS-Node version 2.5. Retrieved from: https://ec.europa.eu/cefdigital/wiki/display/CEFDIGITAL/eIDAS-Node+version+2.5

European Union Agency for Cybersecurity. ENISA (2020). ENISA programming document 2020–2022 Retrieved from: https://www.enisa.europa.eu/publications/corporate-documents/enisa-programming-document-202020132022

Eurosmart, (2020). Implementation of the eIDAS nodes: State of play. Retrieved from: https://www.eurosmart.com/wp-content/uploads/2020/09/Eurosmart_study_eIDAS_nodes_interconnection_final.pdf

Franke, T., & Zoubir, M. (2020). Technology for the People? Humanity as a Compass for the Digital Transformation. *Wirtschaftsdienst (Hamburg, Germany)*, *100*(S1), 1004–1011. doi:10.100710273-020-2609-3

Hodson, C. J. (2019). *Cyber Risk Management: Prioritize Threats, Identify Vulnerabilities and Apply Controls*. Kogan Page.

Miyaji, A., & Mimoto, T. (2021). *Security Infrastructure Technology for Integrated Utilization of Big Data: Applied to the Living Safety and Medical Fields*. Springer.

Robert, H. J., Linda, L., & David, R. (2019). *EDGE: Value-Driven Digital Transformation*. Addison-Wesley Professional.

United Union. (2003). Creation of a global culture of cybersecurity: resolution / adopted by the General Assembly. Retrieved from: https://digitallibrary.un.org/record/482184

Yildiz, M. (2019) *Architecting Digital Transformation: 12-step Architectural Leadership Method*. S.T.E.P.S. Australia. ASIN B07YB961YH.

KEY TERMS AND DEFINITIONS

eID Building Block: The electronic identity (eID) building block helps public administrations and private online service providers to easily extend the use of their online services to citizens from other EU Member States. It allows cross-border authentication, in a secure, reliable and trusted way, by making existing national electronic identification systems.

Electronic Authentication: The electronic process of establishing confidence in user identities presented to an information system. The process of proving an individual is a claimed identity. Authentication is the first element of the AAA services concept, which includes Authentication, Authorization, and Accounting. Authentication occurs after the initial step of identification (i.e. claiming an identity). Authentication is accomplished by providing one or more authentication factors—Type 1: something you know (e.g. password, PIN, or combination), Type 2: something you have (e.g. smart card, RSA SecureID FOB, or USB drive), and Type 3: something you are (e.g. biometrics—fingerprint, iris scan, retina scan, hand geometry, signature verification, voice recognition, and keystroke dynamics).

Electronic Authorization: The security mechanism determining and enforcing what authenticated users are authorized to do within a computer system. The dominant forms of authorization are DAC, MAC and RBAC. DAC (Discretionary Access Control) manages access using ACL (Access Control Lists) on each resource object where users are listed along with the permissions or privileges granted or denied them. MAC (Mandatory Access Control) manages access using labels of classification or clearance on both subjects and objects, and only those subjects with equal or superior clearance are allowed to access resources. RBAC (Role Based Access Control) manages access using labels of a job role that has been granted the permissions and privileges needed to accomplish a specific job or role.

Electronic Identification (eID): Digital solution for proof of identity of citizens or organizations. They can be used to view to access benefits or services provided by government authorities, banks, or other companies, for mobile payments, etc.

Electronic Services: Services that use information and communication technologies.

Internet of Things: the network of physical objects that are embedded with sensors, software, and other technologies for the purpose of connecting and exchanging data with other devices and systems.

Interoperability: The ability of computer systems to exchange and make use of data or information. Means the possibility for spatial data sets to be combined, and for services to interact, without repetitive manual intervention, in such a way that the result is coherent and the added value of the data sets and services is enhanced.

Public Administration: A state, regional, or local authority governed by public law or an association formed by one or several such authorities or a private entity mandated by at least one of those authorities or associations to provide public services, when acting under such a mandate.

Public Authority: Any government or other public administration, including public advisory bodies, at national, regional, or local level; any natural or legal person performing public administrative functions under national law, including specific duties.

Smart City: An urban area that uses electronics to collect and interoperate data; a municipality that uses technologies based on electronics to improve operational efficiency, to share data with the public and to improve services.

Chapter 3
The Advancing Cybersecurity Ecosystem of Israel:
An Overview of Current Challenges and Opportunities in the Early 2020s

Szabolcs Szolnoki

iD https://orcid.org/0000-0001-6253-3628

John von Neumann University, Kecskemét, Hungary

Árpád Ferenc Papp-Váry

John von Neumann University, Kecskemét, Hungary

ABSTRACT

True to its nickname 'cyber nation', the country of Israel is seen as a kind of role model in terms of intelligence and defence capabilities by many countries. The present study aims to provide a comprehensive but far from a complete picture of the cyber defence ecosystem of Israel, a country with more than 430 start-ups and unicorns valued at billions of US dollars. The authors outline the major incidents of the recent period, as well as current challenges and threats. The purpose of the chapter is to introduce good practices and cooperation for opportunities to policymakers and cybersecurity experts as well.

INTRODUCTION: THE ADVANCING ECOSYSTEM OF THE 'CYBER NATION'

The modern and independent State of Israel celebrated the seventieth anniversary of its proclamation of independence in 2018. Besides this landmark anniversary, the remarkable development of Israel's image in the past decade was also a cause for celebration. Nowadays, many people around the world consider Israel as a start-up nation, the stronghold of innovation, research and development and risk capital, and the home of outstanding researchers.

Israel is increasingly referred to as a 'Cyber Nation' as the country not only excels in defending its own cyberspace, but also 'exports' its capabilities. There is conscious country image building behind

DOI: 10.4018/978-1-7998-6975-7.ch003

the brand name, which is not surprising as its aims are primarily economic, and their purpose is to develop competitiveness, for example, through the development of export (Papp-Váry, 2019). Government support for the cyber security industry has been present from the beginning with programmes such as Kidma[1] and Masad[2], which provide assistance for the sector's start-ups and facilitate a healthy competition between them. In addition, the government has partnered with the army, universities and the private sector. (Israel Cyber Alliance, 2021)

The cyber ecosystem boasts more than 430 companies, from listed large enterprises to start-up garage companies across the country. Their total value exceeds US$ 3.5 billion, representing about 5 percent of the global cyber security market. (Israel Cyber Alliance, 2021)

The most important current challenge is the shortage of manpower in the high-tech industry, which is also causing difficulties for government, academic and corporate actors in cyber security. In addition, considering all market participants, the fastest growing, innovative start-ups are threatened by the multinational companies' local research, development and innovation centres, enticing programmers and engineers with significantly higher salaries and extremely attractive fringe benefit packages. The average annual salary in the sector is NIS 275,714[3] (approximately USD 84 thousand). (Payscale, 2021) According to a 2019 survey by IVC Research Center, at least 800 highly skilled employees were needed in the sector employing approximately 20,500 people at the time of the study. (Solomon, 2019)

The list of challenges also includes the constant and intense threat not only in the physical space but also in cyberspace. Nevertheless, the country's reputation does not deter offensive political or economic rivals – on the contrary, the cyber cold war between Israel and Iran (which has been steadily intensifying for nearly a decade) has become more and more spectacular, making headlines in the world press with further attacks in 2020. From the beginning of the early 2010s, Iran started to invest significant financial resources in the development of its capabilities, both in technologies and training. Within a noticeably short period of time the country became a first-tier cyber power and a real threat to the top players of this game – the United States, Russia, China, and Israel according to cybersecurity experts and politicians. (Martins, 2018)

According to a recent report by US information security company F5 Labs, Israel became the number one target for hackers between July and October 2020, preceding the United States, India, Russia, Turkey and the Czech Republic. (Nocamels, 2020)

Of course, cybercrime in Israel is not limited to incidents against critical and government infrastructures initiated from abroad, either. The citizens' vigilance is also regularly tested by compatriot digital bandits – and inattention comes at a high price. In social engineering – that is, psychological manipulation and deception – they take advantage of the fact that in many cases people are the weakest link, and it is worth stealing login IDs and passwords from users rather than attacking IT systems directly. Fraudulent SMS messages based on URL (Uniform Resource Locator)[4] abbreviations are extremely common in Israel. We can get acquainted with the details of the method in a book by Krisztián Fehér – its point is to use misleading text in order to persuade the recipient to click on a link to an unidentifiable website (Fehér 2018). In November 2020, mobile phone subscribers received thousands of SMS messages with the message "Your account has been blocked, Please re-confirm your identity via this link". A joint operation by the cyber security unit of the police and the Israeli National Cyber Directorate (INCD) led to the arrest of two criminals, who reportedly sent thousands of SMS messages on behalf of banks and credit card companies, stealing hundreds of thousands of shekels from deceived citizens using their online banking passwords and Two-Factor Authentication Codes. (Israel National Cyber Directorate, 2020/3)

According to police reports, 8,377 cyber incidents were investigated in 2020, most of which were in connection with identity theft and document forgery. According to a document acquired by the newspaper Israel Hayom, only 75 persons (50 officers and 25 soldiers and volunteers in national service) are serving in the Lahav 433 unit of the Israel Police. The office is also known as the Israeli FBI, integrating five different crime investigation units.[5] Critics say that headcount is critically low to successfully investigate so many cases. (The Jerusalem Post, 2020/2). Nevertheless, the authors do not agree with the camp of critics, being aware of the close collaboration between Lahav 433 and its partners, and the outstanding process automation and technological capabilities of investigating the dark web[6], social media, instant messaging applications, internet forums and other platforms.

It has led to numerous debates and criticism that the implementation of the national cyber defence strategy launched in 2010 has not yet been able to be completed due to the freezing of the adoption process of the cyber law two years ago. The national agencies (notably the Israel National Cyber Directorate) are forced to operate within the framework of the hybrid interventionist-cooperative cyber policy approved by the government in 2015 until the legislation enters into force, thus empowering the agencies to operate effectively.

Regulatory and policy challenges also include the uncertainties about the expected finalization of the Israeli Cyber Defense Methodology 2.0 document and the availability of the budget required for implementation. Although they published an outline of the concept for social consultation only recently, in December 2020, parliamentary elections were held in March 2021 for the fourth time in two years, and the political crisis also results in delays in an area where both the regulatory environment and infrastructure need to be kept up to date – and this requires authorized decision-makers and a budget. Based on the near-final results announced on 25 March, no candidate has a clear path to a coalition, and continued instability can lead to another election.

BACKGROUND: CHALLENGES IN THE PROTECTION OF CRITICAL INFRASTRUCTURES AND RECENT ATTACKS

Although Israel's natural conditions are not particularly favourable, the state is considered one of the most developed countries in the Middle East in economic and industrial terms. In his book, Tim Marshall derives that the physical realities that underpin economic and political relations hold states captive to geography, but with the development of technology, the possibility of an advancement has opened up. (Marshall, 2016) This was recognized by the leadership of the Jewish state very early on – thanks to the government programmes, it permeates the productivity and development of almost every sector, moving innovation, science, and technology forward. At the same time, large-scale digitalization also provides threats and an attack surface for their enemies, and their intensive research and development activities intensify industrial espionage. According to the head of the National Cyber Directorate, two-thirds of the 8,500 suspicious incidents identified in 2019 were unsuccessful attacks on critical infrastructures.

Attacks on Water Management

The protection of critical infrastructure (CIP) was identified as a high priority task at an early stage. In 2002, Israel implemented a legal and regulatory model for CIP and the ecosystem approach was soon solidified by the organic cooperation of the public, security, academic and private sectors. From the early 2010s, Israel has been considered as one of the most advanced countries regarding cyber defense capabilities alongside Sweden and Finland. The Special Resolution B/84 – which was the result of the National Security Council's efforts and government decisions – opened an era of national civilian cyber security policy. The measures led to the creation of a centralized national Critical Infrastructure Protection policy which was quite unique even in the developed world at that time. (Tabansky, 2013)

Today in Israel, one of the most important infrastructures that need protection is water utility, as the climate with poor rainfall forced them to use innovative solutions to cover the large-scale freshwater consumption for residential, industrial and agricultural purposes. 86 percent of the generated wastewater is recycled, mainly for agricultural irrigation, and seawater is treated in several desalination plants. The Sorek facility near Tel Aviv is the largest desalination plant in the world in terms of capacity (with an annual capacity of 151.4 billion litres). With the help of these plants, the country struggling with water scarcity has become an exporter of drinking water.

In April 2020, as part of the cyber cold war between Israel and Iran, the Persian state targeted Israel's water supplies, that is, control centres of rural water pumps, reservoirs and aqueducts. They had access to wastewater treatment and systems controlling the addition of chlorine and other chemicals. Apart from minor damage to valves and control systems, the operation did not cause significant technical, operational failure or water supply interruption, because the intrusion attempt was detected early, and they were able to prevent it. Hackers thought to belong to the cyber force of the Islamic Revolutionary Guard Corps of Iran launched the attack from servers in the United States and Europe. According to expert opinions, the manipulation of Israeli devices was carried out by modifying the code of Stuxnet. The damage was probably deliberately limited, as the competition between the two countries in the virtual space can be interpreted as a kind of cyber cold war – it can often be interpreted as a survey of power relations and a demonstration of force. It is extremely easy, even by accident, to cause damage that could serve as a casus belli and trigger a traditional backlash, which does not serve the interest of either party – for the time being.

Threats to the Energy Sector

In addition to water supply, the electricity network is also constantly in the crosshairs. In a statement issued in January 2020, Minister of Energy Yuval Steinitz said that Israel's energy infrastructure recently had to defend itself against a number of serious cyber-attacks. He mentioned as an example an attempt to paralyse and take over a power plant, which was detected and neutralized in time. (Ackerman, 2020) Yosi Shneck, a representative of the state-owned utility company Israel Electric Corporation (IEC), confirmed the minister's statements in a press release, acknowledging that although the incident was detected, it was not directed against IEC's plant. IEC supplies about 70 percent of the country's electricity, and the remaining 30 percent comes from smaller private competitors. IEC director Yiftah Ron-Tal reported that the state utility faces an average of 11,000 suspected cyberattacks per second, making it one of the most targeted companies in the world. (Reuters, 2020) In 2018, the head of the company reported staggering numbers similar to those of today – in a presentation given at an international conference, he said that 191 million attacks against the IEC (an average of 15 million a month) were registered in 2017. (Arkin, 2018)

IBM's announcement on malicious software developments by hackers backed by the Iranian state can also be related to the statement issued in January. The ZeroCleare data destruction malware was created by the groups xHunt and APT34, and it was used in cyberattacks against companies in the Middle East energy sector. IBM's report (IBM Security, 2020) did not specify the companies that were attacked by ZeroCleare. The National Cybersecurity Authority of Saudi Arabia has already identified a more advanced version of ZeroCleare. On 29 December 2019, the Dustman data wiping malware attacked BAPCO, an oil company of Bahrain, and the incident was partially successful.

Information Security Challenges for Healthcare Institutions and Vaccine Developing Research Institutes

Taking advantage of the coronavirus pandemic, the healthcare sector has become one of the key targets worldwide. According to the Check Point cyber security company, health care facilities in Israel were subject to an unprecedented number of attacks between November 2020 and January 2021. This represents a 25 percent increase from last year's data, compared to a 45 percent increase globally. An average of 620 cyberattacks per week hit health care facilities globally, compared to an average of 813 attacks per week in the Jewish state.

In a conference in May 2020, an official of the Israeli Health Ministry announced the inauguration of a "cyber defence shield" for the country's healthcare sector, developed in cooperation with FireEye. (Margit, 2020) There are no news of the system's deployment, but the sophisticated cyberattack that hit FireEye in December 2020 raises doubts and further questions. They stole so-called Red Team Tools[7] solutions used by the company to test the security of the clients' IT systems. According to their statement (Koi, 2020), state-supported organized cybercriminals (a so-called APT group[8]) may be behind the action.

Vaccine developing and licensing organizations have become a target in Israel just like anywhere in the world. Following the attack in May 2020, a television channel reported (without indication of source) that the hackers' aim was not to steal information, but to sabotage research processes. (The Times of Israel, 2020) The Israeli COVID-19 vaccine called BriLife is being developed at a governmental laboratory called Israel Institute of Biological Research (IIBR), established in 1952 as part of the Israel Defence Forces' Science Corps, and later became a civilian organisation. (The Israel Institute of Biological Research, 2021)

Insurance Industry – Blackmail and Customer Data Leakage

In December 2020, an attack by the Black Shadow hacker group against the Shirbit insurance company caused a great furor. Cybercriminals demanded that the company send them 50 bitcoins – a ransom of US\$ 961,110 at the time of the incident – within 24 hours, stating that if the money was received, the stolen data would not be disclosed and sold. Black Shadow warned Shirbit that if they do not pay, the ransom will rise to 100 bitcoins, and after another 24 hours to 200 bitcoins, then they will put the obtained confidential information on sale, gradually leaking the data. Shortly after the message was published, the hacking group released files containing the identity cards and other sensitive data of the insurance company's customers as threatening evidence. Although Shirbit hired a negotiation expert, after several rounds of negotiations and large amounts of intermittently leaked corporate and customer data, the victim company announced that it would not yield to blackmail, and it did not intend to meet Black Shadow's payment claim. Following the incident, the Israeli National Cyber Directorate (INCD) called on Shirbit customers to replace their ID cards and driver's licenses, as leaked documents could be misused by cybercriminals to their detriment. (Bob, 2020/1)

The incident against the insurance company was not unique, but unlike the other cases, it caused serious damage. In November alone, a total of 141 Israeli companies were hit by a blackmail virus attack and 137 were attacked in October. 14 percent of the targeted companies operate in the high-tech sector and 7 percent work in the insurance sector. A further 11.5 percent of the attacks affected government offices and 5.6 percent affected the health sector. (Bob, 2020/1)

Looking back at the findings of a research conducted in 2016, it can be stated that the costs of cyber incidents are much higher today thanks to the flood of ransomware in remote working and the spread of fake news during COVID-19 times. According to an article written five years ago, the cost of cyber incidents for most firms was less than US$ 200k, and the estimated representation of firm revenues was only 0.4%. It means that other losses, for example bad debt, theft or corruption were considered as more severe threats. In addition, a consumer survey-based research showed that the majority of respondents (77%) were very satisfied with the response to data breaches at their companies. (Romanosky, 2016)

Logistics, Import Sector, Manufacturing – Attacks on the Supply Chain and Defense Against Them

In December 2020, the hacking of the servers of the software company Amital Data enabled an attack on about 40 of its customers, affecting the largest companies in the logistics and import sector in Israel. The hackers managed to infiltrate the servers of dozens of companies, and thus also enter the country's supply chain. The attacked companies are among the largest, and such an attack may severely disrupt the country's supply of basic goods. Stolen information can also be of strategic value to hostile states. Although the infiltration was successful, the attackers did not request a ransom, which raises suspicions that the target was strategically to explore Israel's critical infrastructure. In connection with the hacking of Amital, it was revealed that there were another 15-20 attacks against logistics companies that were not their customers but were other participants in the logistics and supply sector. The attackers developed a systematic plan to map companies and obtain their data. The full list of parties concerned is still unknown, but Amital's customer base includes companies that are involved in the trade of confidentially sold products, including military equipment. (Orbach-Hazani, 2020)

Due to the significant threat, in January 2021, the Manufacturers Association of Israel (MAI) announced that it would establish an independent cyber security centre under its direction to deal with attacks on and against its members. In the future, MAI (the umbrella organization of industry players) will seek to protect the Israeli industrial and business sectors through information and awareness-raising campaigns, as well as services such as real-time IT support in the management of cyberattacks. They invited recognized and experienced Israeli high-tech and cyber defence experts to join the newly formed defence unit, including Refael Franco, former deputy director of the Israel National Cyber Directorate (INCD), who will be the head of the centre. (Big News Network, 2021)

Higher Education, IT Protection of Intellectual Property

There is also a number of functions associated with Israel's universities that belong to critical infrastructures. This includes physical and information technology equipment, that is, networks, services and devices whose collapse or destruction could have serious consequences in terms of the health, protection, security and economic well-being of citizens and the efficient functioning of governments. (Országos Katasztrófavédelmi Főigazgatóság, 2021) Among these are, for example, university hospitals, but thanks to the cooperation between the military and the academia, sensitive information and confidential research results also appear in university IT systems, thus making them an attractive target.

The latest cyber incident also mentioned in the press was the January 2021 breaking into the servers of Ben-Gurion University in Southern Israel. The case was discovered as part of a routine investigation conducted jointly by the University and the Israel National Cyber Directorate (INCD). What makes it especially interesting is that Ben-Gurion University is located in the city of Beer-Sheva, a centre for the development of military force and cyber capabilities, and the activities of the higher education institution are also related to the defence industry in many ways. (Dombe, 2021)

The threat to Israeli education and knowledge centres is such that a computer security incident response team (a so-called CERT[9]) was set up by higher education institutions and research institutes in close collaboration with the government's CERT and the market players of the industry. As part of its efforts to improve data security in Israeli higher education institutions, the Inter-University Computation Center[10] also created a test environment called the National Cyber Testbed, involving emerging and veteran information security companies. (IUCC, 2021)

Threats to the Defense Industry

At the end of December 2020, hackers from the Pay2Key group linked to Iran released a database to prove that they had hacked into the servers of ELTA Systems, a subsidiary of Israel Aerospace Industries (IAI). Pay2Key boasted about unauthorized data collection in connection with individuals such as Camila Edry, head of cyber projects development at ELTA, or Esti Peshin, general manager of the Cyber Division at IAI. (Shulman, 2020)

IAI is the country's largest aerospace and defence company, specializing in the development and manufacturing of state-of-the-art weapons and defence systems for all branches of the military, as well as cyber security and internal security. Its subsidiary ELTA is one of the leading players in defence electronics, developing, manufacturing and selling radars, early warning systems, communication and intelligence technologies, electronic warfare technologies and cyber security products to domestic and international (predominantly governmental) customers.

Pay2Key's malwares were used in blackmail attacks against several Israeli companies late last year, including the servers of Intel-owned Habana Labs. It is not yet clear whether the Persian state supported the action. Some Israeli cyber security experts say that Pay2Key is not officially affiliated with the Iranian regime but is operated by hackers who are based in Iran or use the Persian language. Some believe that their actions are purely financially motivated and do not serve espionage or strategic purposes. During the investigation to identify the attackers, they followed the path of the bitcoins extorted by blackmail to a cryptocurrency exchange in Iran. (Kahan, 2020) Other sources including the Israeli cyber security company ClearSky say that Pay2Key can be linked to Iran's Fox Kitten APT group, a detailed report of which had been released before the incident against ELTA Systems. According to ClearSky, the attack on Amital Data and major Israeli logistics companies was also Pay2Key's action. (Clearsky Cyber Security Ltd., 2020)

Cyber Cold War Between the Jewish and Persian States

The cyber cold war between Israel and Iran has been getting more intense and more spectacular for nearly a decade. The parties are uncertain and skating on thin ice – improper non-kinetic operations can easily lead to kinetic cyber and cause direct or indirect physical damage, injury or death. Studies in the past clearly pointed out the crucial importance and necessity of regulating cyber warfare and creating the new norms of jus in bello in the digital space. (Wang, 2014)

Secrecy is only one choice among many strategic options today, and the clashes of Israel and Iran became intense and open, coming out of the shadows and sending each other messages via public channels – for example, statements saying that Israel would do everything to prevent Iran from obtaining a nuclear weapon. (Ram, Israel, Baram 2020)

On 9 May 2020, it made headlines in the world press with another incident – the terminal at the Shahid Rajaee port in southern Iran was paralysed, and cargo transport was suspended for ten days as a result of the intrusion. The incident is considered an Israeli response to the aforementioned action by the Persian state in April, which targeted water supplies to disrupt the Israeli critical infrastructure – attacking the control centres of pumps, reservoirs and aqueducts in rural waterworks. (Haaretz, 2020/1)

Attack and counterattack between the two sides is not uncommon. In his book, Amael Cattaruza recalls that cyber operations are already an integral part of military doctrine, and while we have not heard of many cases in the private sector yet, Donald Trump's government already had ideas that caused a stir, such as the application of the practice called 'hack back'. Legitimate self-defence would entitle companies to hack back, thus they could launch a counterattack against those suspected of causing an incident against them. (Cattaruza, 2020)

Although the incident when an Iranian navy ship was hit by a missile during a military exercise in the Gulf of Oman on 10 May was reported as an accident involving 'friendly fire', killing 19 sailors and injuring 15 others, some suspect that the launch unit was compromised as another event in the cyber warfare. (Marcus, 2020)

On 21 May, an Iranian-backed group calling itself 'Hackers of Savior' changed the content of thousands of Israeli websites as part of a successful attack on uPress, one of Israel's largest hosting providers. Among other interventions, the homepages were replaced with messages announcing the fall of the Jewish state in Hebrew and English[11], seeking permission to access the visitors' webcams through the browsers. It is not yet clear whether the databases of the hosting provider were hacked. The vulnerability was caused by a plugin in WordPress, a free open-source content management system. According to experts, these vulnerabilities had already been discovered and analysed on Iranian social media sites prior to the attack, and this is interpreted as part of the triggering antecedents and preparations. (Paganini, 2020)

The most recent incident happened on the 11th of April 2011: there was a blackout in Iran's underground Natanz atomic facility on the same day when U.S. Defense Secretary Lloyd Austin landed in Israel for talks with Prime Minister Benjamin Netanyahu and Defense Minister Benny Gantz. Teheran described the event as nuclear terrorism. According to Israeli public broadcaster Kan, the Jewish state may have been behind the incident; however, no one has claimed responsibility for any of the attacks. One day before the blackout, Iran announced the launch of a chain of 164 IR-6 centrifuges at the plant and the testing of the IR-9 centrifuge which is able to enrich uranium 50 times faster than the first generation IR-1. (Gambrell, Zion, 2021)

The Impact of the Normalized Relationship Between Israel and the United Arab Emirates on Cyber Cooperation

Simultaneously with the normalization of relations between the United Arab Emirates and Israel, industry experts and economic analysts predict an explosive expansion of scientific and technological cooperation.

At the same time, this rapprochement has sparked a series of cyberattacks on the Gulf state, according to a statement by Mohamed Hamad al-Kuwaiti, the head of government cyber security, who highlighted malicious incidents that have become particularly spectacular in the financial sector. (Haaretz, 2020/2)

Immediately after the announcement of the peace agreement, a number of new joint projects were launched, with a focus on, but not limited to the fight against the COVID-19 coronavirus pandemic. The expected areas of cooperation are info-communication, insurance and financial technologies, agricultural innovation, medical technologies, venture capital investments, food industry, desalination and water management. (Lyngaas, 2020)

Of course, not all recent announcements are related to unprecedented partnerships. We had already seen many examples of successful collaborations before the normalization of relations. There is a significant dominance of Israeli cyber security companies with a representative or distributor in the Arab country, such as Cybereason, CheckPoint, CyberArk, and InSights. Other high-tech companies have also been successful in the Emirates in the past, including Cato Networks, an Israeli cloud services company that operates a server farm in Dubai. The admission of these companies to market of the Arab state before the peace agreement also confirms the existence of trust and willingness to cooperate with Israel. (Alexander, 2020)

The abolition of the boycott against Israel allows companies in the two states to openly build relationships in the business, financial, tourism, technology, research, energy, and science sectors. The memorandum of understanding signed to facilitate business transactions also contributes to technology investments. A joint committee will be set up in its framework to support financial and investment cooperation, reduce barriers and create incentives. One of the specified aims of the tripartite agreement with the United States is to promote cooperation in research and development and set up a common innovation fund. Israel primarily considers the Arab country as a wealthy target market hungry for new technologies. (Kabir, 2020)

The authors of the study believe that the Cybertech Global UAE-Dubai conference in April 2021 will be considered as a historic milestone in the cooperation of the two countries and its impact will not be limited to cybersecurity communities. Firstly, during the midst of the COVID-19 pandemic, organizers were able to host an in-person event with the participation of prominent experts and industry leaders from more than 10 countries, including the United States, the United Kingdom, India, Japan, and Germany. (Cybertech group, 2021) Secondly, the event delivered an incredibly special political and cultural message: on the eve of Holocaust Remembrance Day, a memorial service was held as part of the Cybertech Conference on Dubai soil, in a Muslim country in the Persian Gulf, a place that until a few months ago was considered out of the reach for most Israeli citizens. (Israel Defense, 2021) At the same event on 05 April, Director General Yigal Unna representing the Israel National Cyber Directorate welcomed the initiation of UAE Government's Head of Cyber Security, H.E. Dr. Mohammed Al-Kuwaiti, and agreed to hold a joint cybersecurity exercise. (Kogosowski, 2021) The rapprochement of the two countries in turn facilitates the solidification of the two adversary blocks in the region lead by Saudi Arabia and Iran. The Sunni-Shiite Tension joined by the Jewish state results in clashes indirectly and directly both in the physical and digital space. The present situation between Saudi Arabia and Iran is described as a cyber cold war. It is true that less risk is involved in a cyber attack than in a kinetic attack, but even so, a casus belli which justifies war from the side of a state can easily be provoked by a cyber incident causing excessive damage. (Easttom, Butler, 2021).

DIGITAL TRANSFORMATION CAUSED ISRAEL'S MAIN SECURITY CHALLENGES IN THE EARLY 2020'S

Parliamentary Elections

In the United States, election systems are already included in the list of critical infrastructure, while in Israel, election agencies receive special assistance from the national cyber defense authority, but they do not receive the same kind of oversight as other critical infrastructures. (Bob, 2020/2)

Since parliamentary elections were planned to be held in Israel for the fourth time in two years, State Comptroller and Ombudsman of Israel Matanyahu Englman (The State Comptroller and Ombudsman of Israel, 2019) has announced that his office will comprehensively review the ability of the Central Electoral Commission (CEC) to face the threat of a potential cyberattack. Englman's office was working to review the CEC's computer systems, its activities in the past three rounds of elections, and assess its ability to handle an external cyberattack, to allow a democratic voting procedure and rule out the possibility of external intervention. (Joffre, 2020) The investigation was successful, at least no reference was made in the press to any successful cyber incidents related to the legislative elections on 23 March 2021. The digital support infrastructure of paper-ballot-based election systems can also be threatened by serious cyber incidents, and their protection deserves high priority with significant financial and human investment. The authors of this study agree with researchers who have a clear answer to the question: why do not we vote online? The unquestionable convenience for many voters is negligible compared to the amount of possible fatal flaws of internet-based or blockchain-based voting. The technology itself introduces new security concerns because of its decentralized nature which can cause inefficiencies. (Park, Specter, Narula, Rivest, 2021)

The Lack of Cyber Law

On 20 June 2018, the Prime Minister's Office published the draft Cyber Security and National Cyber Directorate Bill on the website of the Ministry of Justice. The bill is also serving as the basis for the establishment of the Israeli National Cyber Directorate (INCD). Although there was agreement on the importance of its adoption, the wording of the draft received much criticism, and the process froze due to the political crisis. The entry into force of the legislation would be the final step in the implementation of the cyber security strategy launched in 2010, with the establishment of a national authority and the provision of powers to ensure its fully functional operation.

Examples include, but are not limited to:

INCD staff could get authorization to obtain and collect any information and documents related to cyber security and the performance of their duties,

they could enter non-residential buildings and seize assets,

in the case of residential properties, they could enter by court order or with the consent of the owner,

they could issue binding instructions to public and private service providers to prevent, detect and respond to cyberattacks, they could apply for a judicial warrant for sampling purposes, authorizing computer actions – in emergency circumstances, however, the head of the INCD could authorize this without a judicial warrant for a period not exceeding 24 hours (with a court review performed later),

high-risk organizations that are high priority in terms of national security and national economy may be under the direct control of the INCD from an information security point of view, while in the case of low-risk organizations and sectors, INCD may require them to report regularly, also enhancing cyber security with soft techniques, such as training and recommendations. (Cahane, 2018)

The Israel National Cyber Directorate (INCD) was created by an Amendment to the Law for the Regulation of Security in Public Bodies, passed on 27 December 2018. (Levush, 2019) It unified the Israeli National Cyber Bureau and the National Cyber Security Authority, allowing for the provision of temporary tasks until the adoption of the act on cyber protection and the National Cyber Directorate. The mission, tasks and powers of the INCD are therefore not yet regulated by a separate legislative act.

Therefore professional and political debates often mention the lack of the above-mentioned law in connection with the country's cyber vulnerabilities – it would provide the authority to define cyber security standards for the private sector, which companies should adhere to and which should be enforced in certain cases. It would also serve as the basis for immediate intervention by the national authority without a court order in case of incident management.

In May 2019, a report by then-state comptroller and ombudsman[12] Joseph Shapira criticized the government because the process to adopt the law addressing the regulation of cyber defense standards in the private sector was frozen. According to the report, the lack of the law is clearly an obstacle to the capacity of INCD and other actors in state cyber security, making it difficult to protect the country's critical infrastructure. Although the INCD (under the authority of the Prime Minister's Office) agreed that adopting the law as soon as possible was important, it defended the government's decision, highlighting innovative practices that would replace the legislation in the period leading up to the adoption of the law. Both INCD itself and the ministries in cooperation with it created such regulations – for example, the Ministry of Environmental Protection defined cyber defence standards for companies handling hazardous waste. (Bob, 2020/3)

They also voiced criticism not only over the bill, but also over the delay in its adoption. Critical points include possible conflicts with law enforcement authorities regarding their competences and the performance of their tasks, the lack of access to information on transparency processes by the parliament and citizens, constitutional concerns, and unsettled relations with the law on the security of public bodies.

For the second year in a row, the adoption of the law has not moved from its pre-frozen state, which was not helped by the dissolution of the Knesset on 23 December 2020 and the elections held in March 2021 – for the fourth time in two years. The 'hybrid interventionist-cooperative' cyber policy approved by the government in 2015 has been pursued in the transition period since 2018. This approach allows the INCD to involve the private sector in its protection measures in a direct and creative way, in order to protect the country more effectively. In a practice conducted with the consent of the Attorney General, they do not collect personal information until they have a specific legal basis for it and obtain the consent of the person concerned. In some cases, an organization may also give its consent on behalf of an individual. According to INCD's senior legal adviser, they managed to develop model contracts which were accepted by the other party each time during ad hoc agreements, and authority access to the other party's IT system was also granted within that framework.

The discussions involve several questions about what should happen when an organization does not show willingness to cooperate. Perhaps one of the most difficult questions is where we can find the point (if there is one) where the authority may intervene without consent in the case of a threat, even on a national scale. The second contentious issue is that of accountability. Can the representative of an organization be questioned or even prosecuted if he/she refuses to cooperate, thereby endangering the country's cyber ecosystem?

The INCD plans to split its relations with the private sector into two levels following the adoption of the law. In the first round, they request information from organizations and provide guidance on how to handle cyber events. The resolution of an incident can be jeopardized by a delay of a few hours or even a few minutes, but according to INCD's senior legal adviser, legitimate intervention can be ensured by setting up a panel of judges with specialized expertise, available at any time.

The creation of legislation authorizing national cyber defence organizations to intervene immediately in the event of large-scale incidents that are dangerous to the entire national economy could also promote pilot projects such as the digital vaccination called 'lighthouse'. As part of this, government authorities are working with telecommunications and leading technology companies to enable them to immunize the public with 'virtual vaccines' and facilitate the effective isolation of already infected devices, preventing further spread. (The Jerusalem Post, 2020/1)

Recommendations and the Israeli Cyber Defense Methodology 2.0

In addition to binding laws, soft instruments such as recommendations are constantly being developed in Israel. On 15 December 2020, the Israel National Cyber Directorate (INCD) issued a draft concept called Israeli Cyber Defense Methodology 2.0 – stakeholders can deliver their opinion in writing, and several video conferences are planned as part of the consultation process. The document significantly exceeds version 1.0 published in 2017, also providing economic actors with good practices and important and practical knowledge for the development of their own organizational information security strategy. However, the adoption of the final version and the implementation of its measures are jeopardized by the political crisis and the lack of a budget. The appropriate level of applying the recommended measures will be sought through the creation of organization-specific chapters. Of course, there are key players who receive even more personalized support, developing their information security systems together with INCD due to their strategic and national economic importance. (Israel National Cyber Directorate, 2020/1)

In addition to organizational-level recommendations, the state cyber security agency also publishes regulatory and technical guidelines focusing on various sub-areas. Examples include a collection of best practices in mobile device management[13] that was published in January 2021, more relevant than ever due to teleworking and the coronavirus pandemic. They also publish studies specifically tailored to CISO[14] jobs, that is, for information security managers – topics include, but are not limited to hardening (Israel National Cyber Directorate, 2019), conducting cyber security exercises within the organization, or even IoT[15]-based recommendations for firefighting systems and fire alarms. (Israel National Cyber Directorate, 2021)

Shortage of Professionals in the Cyber Security Sector

The country's population of just nine million people, its strict immigration policy and the issuance of worker's visas pose a serious challenge to all parties interested in the training and employment of highly skilled workforce. In addition, the industries of research and development, innovation and high-tech require that the production of human resources have a potential for renewal to keep pace with the dynamic changes in these sectors.

In his book Geopillanat ("Geomoment"), Norbert Csizmadia derives the three-level development classification used in the annual competitiveness reports of the World Economic Forum: factor-driven economy, efficiency-driven economy, innovation-driven economy. (Csizmadia, 2016) Israel is in the last, most advanced stage according to this classification system. One of its characteristics is that it considers humans and their communities to be the most important value, and its evaluation of data also creates the conclusion that people's ability to innovate and adapt is the most important economic resource.

The shortage of professionals is indicated by the fact that in July 2019 there were 18,500 vacancies in the high-tech scene according to a research by Startup Nation Central. (Israel Innovation Authority - Startup Nation Central, 2019) About 50 percent of those working in the technology industry work for a start-up company, while another 50 percent are employed in large enterprise R&D centres. Among the market participants, the fastest growing, innovative garage companies are threatened by the research, development and innovation development centres of multinational companies in Israel, which attract talented programmers, engineers and business developers with significantly higher salaries and extremely attractive fringe benefit packages.

The average annual salary in the cyber security sector is NIS 275,714 (approximately HUF 25,000,000). According to a 2019 survey by the IVC Research Center, cyber firms employing approximately 20,500 people at the time of the study need at least an additional 800 highly skilled employees. 4,500 of the total number of employees work in the R&D centres of foreign companies in Israel, and 5,900 people are employed in the public sector. The statistics do not include the number of cyber experts working for defence companies. The employment rate in the sector showed an annual growth of 12 percent between 2015 and 2018. (Solomon, 2019)

The primary and most important issuer remains higher education, but in some areas, such as cyber defence, other school-based and non-school-based education programs and institutions are also prominent – these include non-profit organizations and the military. The system of secondary school education and non-school education in general also play a significant role, as well as the ecosystem approach and the close cooperation of stakeholders.

In their study A High-School Program in Computer Science, Gal-Ezer, Beeri, Harel, and Yehuda follow a chronological order to demonstrate that there is a significant tradition of computer science education in Israel. It was introduced as a secondary school subject in the mid-1970s, although it is also true that it was not yet a full-fledged, recognized scientific subject like physics, biology, or chemistry. (Gal-Ezer, Beeri, Harel, Yehudai, 2018) Nowadays, preparation and early recognition of talent begins at a very young age. There are also kindergartens that organize computer skills development and robotics classes. Equipping children with cyber capabilities has become a kind of national mission. The aim of the training programs is to prepare them for careers in military intelligence, defence agencies, high-tech industry, or academia. Students in several Israeli schools are now starting to study the basics of programming as early as in fourth grade, while talented 10th graders study encryption and the prevention of malicious intrusions in after-school classes.

There are also many other school and post-school programmes for young people; the subject of these programmes is not cyber security, but some closely related field. These also operate with great success in the areas of computing, robotics, artificial intelligence, space industry, and the so-called STEM[16] disciplines in general. These are backed by state, non-profit and corporate actors alike, based on their clearly visible interests. An excellent example of this is the 5x2 project by Intel, which encourages Israeli secondary school students to take the highest level of the matriculation exam in mathematics. 6,000 Intel employees are helping them with this as a volunteer, along with the programme itself with an ample budget of 20 million shekels (approximately US$ 6 million) over the past four years. (Intel, 2019)

The shortage of labour and the success of early training are well illustrated by the fact that 61 of the 234 students who graduated from the so-called Magshimim programme organized by the Rashi Foundation in 2017 had already worked in paid jobs in the high-tech industry before graduating from secondary school and starting their compulsory military service. In addition, their average hourly wage is twice the minimum wage, and they get the average earnings of adult workers when they are employed on a full-time basis in the months of school holidays. (Leichman, 2018)

As military service is mandatory for most Israeli Jewish young people (both boys and girls) after secondary school, the Israeli Defense Forces (IDF[17]) is also becoming interested, benefiting from investing in young talent. Graduates from two cyber-training programmes become soldiers of the internationally recognized intelligence unit called Unit 8200, which specializes in intercepting digital communication and intelligence activities related to hostile states in the Middle East. Many former members of the Unit are eventually embarking on careers in the high-tech and cyber security industries, with the most successful companies founded by Unit 8200 veterans. (Estrin, 2018) In his book in search of the secret to Israel's high-tech business success, Osnat Lautman describes how the former soldiers of the special unit become start-up entrepreneurs and maintain a close relationship with each other (also called the 'safety net' among them). They take great advantage of these informal and formal connections in both politics and business. (Lautman, 2015) The phenomenon described is fully in line with several laws mentioned in the book The Formula by Albert-László Barabási, especially number three, which suggests that aptitude coupled with past successes leads to future successes, and if the former is accompanied by social influence, success knows no limits. (Barabási, 2018)

The IDF considers both the preparation of young people entering the military and the support of employment opportunities for veterans as an investment. As a result of that motivation, they launched Cyber4s, a six-month training programme for the cyber security training of Israeli soldiers leaving the military. In the framework of the programme, ex-soldiers who have previously served in high-profile combat units in non-technological positions are trained for junior positions in the cyber industry. The initiative also helps participants and the companies employing them to address the labour market challenges posed by the coronavirus pandemic. (Solomon, 2020)

The aim of Shabak, Israel's internal security service is to protect the country from espionage and terrorism. True to its motto, 'the unseen shield' is a user and developer of the most advanced intelligence and response technology tools. The detection and prevention of espionage within the national borders, the maintenance of the personal security of public and political leaders, the fight against terrorism, and the protection of strategic state assets require the highest level of cyber defence capabilities. Accordingly, the Technology and Cyber Division is constantly striving to recruit the best experts. At the time of writing this study, the internal security service has more than sixty job vacancies, mostly in developer and technology project manager positions. (Shabak, 2020)

Many market participants – the so-called 'code schools' – offer courses that, once completed, make available junior positions in the high-tech sector and even cyber security companies. Examples include the Israel Tech Challenge (ITC), which offers training modules inspired by the IDF's 8200 elite unit. Large companies such as Intel, Apple, Samsung, Dell, or HP are involved in the development of the curriculum. Labour shortages and the interest of these companies allow for a unique funding model for

4-5 months of learning: it is free for the students until they find a suitable, well-paying job. This means that they only have to pay tuition fees are if they already earn more than a certain amount in their new job. (Secret Tel-Aviv, 2018)

SOLUTIONS AND RECOMMENDATIONS

The present article identified four major challenges in the advancing Israeli cyber-ecosystem. Based on their research and findings, the authors hereby share the recommendations they have drafted:

- In Israel, one in ten high-tech workers are employed in the cyber industry, and 800 new positions are opened every year. The demand is not met and shortage is incessant. (Schulman, 2021)
  - Using international best practices, continue to organize and develop technical cybersecurity trainings for the youth, minorities and women.
  - Foster the training and placement of experienced IT personnel to cybersecurity, and work out models for their replacement by outsourcing solutions, process innovation and workforce training.
  - Provide tax benefits – social contribution allowance for the trainers and employers of cyber security personnel, since their work contributes to the protection of national economy and national data assets regardless of whether they work in a corporate or government environment.
- Cyber-peacekeeping is a new way to prevent and manage extensive cyberattacks. Peacekeeping has proved its effectiveness in physical space, and with some adjustments it could be implemented in the digital space. (Dorn, Webb, 2019)
  - Consider the initiation and participation in an international platform which is made up of sovereign nation-states and has its own code of ethics and procedures to tackle cyber challenges that can have fatal consequences by observation, monitoring and reporting, as well as by creating a buffer zone. (Robinson, Janicke, Maglaras, 2018) Setting up a new organization could be more advantageous than integrating the initiative to an existing international organization which may be divisive for certain actors.
- The necessity of the adoption of the Israeli cyber law was not questioned, however the wording of the draft received much criticism, and the process froze due to the political crisis. To reach the final step in the implementation of the cyber security strategy launched in 2010 and to provide a transparent framework, procrastination should not be tolerated anymore. An urgent review and adoption of legislation is essential right after the formation of government.
- Strengthen system approach allowing the government and the infrastructure operators to prioritize resilience measures (Florin, Sachs, 2019). Strengthen both technical and organizational resilience and keep the balance between Critical Infrastructure Protection (CIP) and Critical Infrastructure Resilience (CIR) (Trifunovic, 2020). Furthermore, increase the number of physical sensors detecting and possibly preventing accidents by overriding the signals of deceived digital systems.
- In the name of hardening and making reconnaissance more difficult, strive to use self-developed robust software with unique code instead of globally well-known providers, whenever it is possible. Even if tech giants' solutions might seem convenient and cost-effective, they are in the focus of politically or economically motivated malignant groups exploiting vulnerabilities especially zero days which are the most valuable demanded for nation state or state-sponsored groups. This

could help avoid involvement in global cyber incidents such as the Solarwinds or the Microsoft Exchange hack, because if one or a few companies dominate the software market, they offer a single point of attack. It is always difficult to confidentially attribute attackers. Even so, the Solarwinds hack is said to be initiated by Russia (Akhtar, 2021), and the Microsoft Exchange breach is attributed to Chinese cyber spies targeting U.S. think tanks, but it dropped its leash and compromised hundreds of thousands of organizations. (Bajak, Tucker, O'Brien, 2021)

FUTURE RESEARCH DIRECTIONS

The aim of the present article is to provide an overview on the current challenges and opportunities of the Israeli cyber ecosystem. Due to length constraints and the nature of this paper, only the highest priority challenges have been highlighted and each of them deserves a separate in depth-analysis. The authors hope that the study will inspire experts and scholars to conduct research using their findings and the questions raised. Based on the current article, a priority order has been set up by the authors, and their first thorough research will be related to the technical cyber education of the youth – students under the age of 18 years. The purpose of the future research is to identify Israeli best practices and challenges in addition to draft policy recommendations both for Israel and countries which would like to implement advanced educational methodologies and materials.

CONCLUSION

2020 will surely become a part of history as an incredibly significant year with painful memories. There is no country and sector that is not surrounded and strangled by the virus. As a result of the consequences of the pandemic, Israel has suffered enormous damage just like the whole world and is still suffering damage at the time of writing the study.

Cybercriminals and other malicious attackers always find the vulnerabilities that they can use to make profit or cause harm. This is justified by information security expert Krisztián Fehér, who makes it clear that computer technology is inherently vulnerable due to its structure, thus a combination of two solutions can achieve the desired results in protection – the first element is the so-called system hardening (i.e. making intrusion too cumbersome for malicious actors) and the second element is achieving a high degree of user awareness. (Fehér, 2016) Thus security is a myth – even in a country where extensive cyber defence education begins at a young age, the engine for economy is high-tech, and vigilance and suspicion are imprinted in people's instincts. This should not mean discredit or loss of reputation for us but should serve as a warning instead. The methods of hackers and APT groups are becoming more sophisticated, and our lives will only get even more complicated and faster, making it harder to detect a scam.

In addition to its advanced cyber-immunity, Israel faces several challenges as the article has outlined. However, the country has handled them well, and only suffered a few wounds even in extremely serious incidents. Nevertheless, it produced five so-called unicorns, that is, cyber defence companies worth US$ 1 billion in 2020. A total of US$ 2.9 billion in investment landed at market players in the sector involving more than 100 transactions, and the cyber industry generated US$ 6.85 billion for the national economy through exports. These numbers have resulted in that 33 percent of all cyber unicorns in the world are Israeli companies in early 2021, and 31 percent of investments worldwide went to the start-ups and scale-up businesses of the cyber nation. (Israel National Cyber Directorate, 2020/2)

Appropriate digitalization and the stability of the IT infrastructure is vital for the operation of a country's social, political and economic system. This has been an extremely important issue during the COVID-19 pandemic, when the staff of companies and state bodies was forced to work in home office or at various locations. The stable digital system of a nation also contributes to the brand and communication of the country – both domestically and internationally. Israel's robust cyber and physical security system and its self-protection against cybercrime and digital intrusions suggest that the country has a massive IT background that supports its strong social and economic backbone. As a conclusion: the outstanding business performance of the Israeli cyber sector and its defence capabilities have passed the test despite the pressure on them. The increase in investments at the Israeli cyber sector reached more than 70% during the coronavirus-plagued last year and more unicorns will probably be born soon. Startups in the sector raised US$ 1.5 billion in 17 separate deals in the first quarter of 2021. Two sub-sectors are expected to grow rapidly: Cyber Services and SME's (small and medium-sized enterprises). There will be an increased demand for cyber-service models among small and medium-sized companies, since they often do not have security teams and are becoming more and more popular targets. (Vidal, 2021) The Startup Nation is also becoming a Scaleup Nation – entrepreneurs are not hungry for early exits anymore; they build large companies and target large markets, such as the cloud security market, which will be worth about US$ 11 billion within three years. (Martin, 2021)

2021 will certainly not be a quieter year than the previous one, and the best strategy is probably to strengthen international cooperation and exchange best practices. Furthermore, moving from protection to resilience and generating innovative and unique solutions will be the keys to better, improving, but far from perfect security.

This research received no specific grant from any funding agency in the public, commercial, or not-for-profit sectors.

REFERENCES

Ackerman, G. (2020). *Israel Power Plants Have Fended Off Cyber Attacks, Minister Says.* Bloomberg. Retrieved from https://www.bloomberg.com/news/articles/2020-01-29/israel-power-plants-have-fended-off-cyber-attacks-minister-says

Akhtar, A. (2021) *The Microsoft Exchange hack shows attackers are working 'smarter, not harder,' experts say.* Business Insider. Retrieved from https://www.businessinsider.com.au/microsoft-exchange-server-hack-why-cyberattack-matters-2021-3?r=US&IR=T

Alexander, K. (2020). *Israeli-Gulf cyber cooperation.* Modern Diplomacy. Retrieved from https://moderndiplomacy.eu/2020/12/23/israeli-gulf-cyber-cooperation/

Arkin, D. (2018). *The world needs multi-layered, multi-dimensional cybersecurity systems.* Israel Defense. Retrieved from https://www.israeldefense.co.il/en/node/32887

Bajak, F., Tucker, E., & O'Brien, M. (2021). *Chinese Hackers Blamed for Massive Microsoft Server Hack.* The Diplomat. Retrieved from https://thediplomat.com/2021/03/chinese-hackers-blamed-for-massive-microsoft-server-hack/

Barabási, A. L. (2018). A képlet [The Formula]. *Libri*.

Big News Network. (2021). *Israeli manufacturers launch cybersecurity HQ following rise in attacks.* Retrieved from https://www.bignewsnetwork.com/news/267448715/israeli-manufacturers-launch-cybersecurity-hq-following-rise-in-attacks

Bob, Y. J. (2020). *Cyber authority to victims post-Shirbit hack: Get new identity cards.* The Jerusalem Post. Retrieved from https://www.jpost.com/breaking-news/shirbit-hackers-to-leak-more-documents-by-9-am-if-money-not-received-651276

Bob, Y. J. (2020). *NSA, Israeli, UK cyber chiefs confront new hacker threats in corona era.* The Jerusalem Post. Retrieved from https://www.jpost.com/jpost-tech/nsa-israeli-uk-cyber-chiefs-confront-new-hacker-threats-in-corona-era-639475

Bob, Y. J. (2020). *With no cyber law, can gov't stop Shirbit-style cyberattacks?* The Jerusalem Post. Retrieved from https://www.jpost.com/israel-news/cyber-lawyer-to-post-law-needs-amending-to-bolster-cybersecurity-650949

Cahane, A. (2018). *The New Israeli Cyber Draft Bill – A Preliminary Overview.* The Federmann Cyber Security Research Center. Retrieved from https://csrcl.huji.ac.il/news/new-israeli-cyber-law-draft-bill#_ftn1

Cattaruza, A. (2020). *A digitális adatok geopolitikája ("Geopolitics of Digital Data").* Pallas Athéné Könyvkiadó.

ClearSky Cyber Security Ltd. (2020). *Pay2Kitten - Pay2Key Ransomware – A New Campaign by Fox Kitten.* Retrieved from https://www.clearskysec.com/wp-content/uploads/2020/12/Pay2Kitten.pdf

Csizmadia N. (2016). *Geopillanat* [Geomoment]. L'Harmattan Kiadó.

Cybertech Group. (2021). *Cybertech Global UAE-Dubai Conference agenda.* Retrieved from https://www.cybertechconference.com/program

Defense, I. (2021). *Cybertech Dubai: An exciting Holocaust Remembrance Day ceremony was held during the conference.* Retrieved from https://www.israeldefense.co.il/node/49233

Dombe, A. R. (2021). *Servers of Ben Gurion University breached.* Israel Defense. Retrieved from https://www.israeldefense.co.il/en/node/47630

Dorn, A. W., & Webb, S. (2019). Cyberpeacekeeping: New Ways to Prevent and Manage Cyberattacks. *International Journal of Cyber Warfare & Terrorism, 9*(1), 19–30. doi:10.4018/IJCWT.2019010102

Easttom, C., & Butler, W. (2021). The Iran-Saudi Cyber Conflict. *International Journal of Cyber Warfare & Terrorism, 11*(2), 29–42. doi:10.4018/IJCWT.2021040103

Estrin, D. (2018). *In Israel, teaching kids cyber skills is a national mission.* The Times of Israel. Retrieved from https://www.timesofisrael.com/in-israel-teaching-kids-cyber-skills-is-a-national-mission/

Fehér, K. (2016). *Kezdő hackerek kézikönyve [The Handbook of Novice Hackers].* BBS-INFO Kiadó.

Fehér, K. (2018). *Hacker-technikák [Hacker Techniques].* BBS-INFO Kiadó.

Florin, M. V., & Sachs, R. (2019). *Critical Infrastructure Resilience - Lessons from Insurance*. Retrieved from https://www.researchgate.net/publication/339271660_Critical_Infrastructure_Resilience_-_Lessons_from_Insurance

Gal-Ezer, J., Beeri, C., Harel, D., & Yehudai, A. (2018). *A High-School Program in Computer Science*. The Open University of Israel. Retrieved from https://www.openu.ac.il/personal_sites/download/galezer/high-school-program.pdf

Gambrell, J., & Zion, I. B. (2021). *Iran calls Natanz atomic site blackout 'nuclear terrorism'*. AP News. Retrieved from https://apnews.com/article/middle-east-iran-358384f03b1ef6b65f4264bf9a59a458

Haaretz. (2020a). *Iran Says One of Two 'Large Scale' Cyber Attacks Targets Country's Ports*. Retrieved from https://www.haaretz.com/israel-news/tech-news/iran-says-one-of-two-cyber-attacks-targets-country-s-ports-1.9239908

Haaretz. (2020b). *UAE Hit With Cyberattacks in Response to Ties With Israel, Official Says*. Retrieved from https://www.haaretz.com/israel-news/tech-news/uae-hit-with-cyberattacks-in-wake-of-israel-deal-official-says-1.9351738

IBM Security. (2020). *New Destructive Wiper "ZeroCleare" Targets Energy Sector in the Middle East*. Retrieved from https://www.ibm.com/downloads/cas/OAJ4VZNJ

Intel. (2019). *Intel in Israel*. Retrieved from https://www.intel.com/content/www/us/en/corporate-responsibility/intel-in-israel.html

Israel Cyber Alliance. (2021). *Cyber security is Israel*. Retrieved from https://israelcyberalliance.com/cyber-security-in-israel-2/

Israel Innovation Authority - Startup Nation Central. (2019). *High Tech Human Capital Report 2019*. Retrieved from https://www.startupnationcentral.org/wp-content/uploads/2020/02/Start-Up-Nation-Centrals-High-Tech-Human-Capital-Report-2019-2.pdf

Israel National Cyber Directorate. (2019). *Best Practices Hardening Computer Systems*. Retrieved from https://www.gov.il/BlobFolder/generalpage/hardingcomputersystem/en/hardening.pdf

Israel National Cyber Directorate. (2020). *Draft public address on improvements and additions to defense theory*. Retrieved from https://www.gov.il/he/departments/publications/Call_for_bids/tohag_draft

Israel National Cyber Directorate. (2020). *The Israeli cyber industry continues to grow: record fundraising in 2020*. Retrieved from https://www.gov.il/en/departments/news/2020ind

Israel National Cyber Directorate. (2020). *The Israeli Police Cyber Unit arrested suspects of stealing hundreds of thousands of ILS from Israeli citizens*. Retrieved from https://www.gov.il/en/departments/news/accounttakeover

Israel National Cyber Directorate. (2021). *Cyber protection for the organization*. Retrieved from https://www.gov.il/he/departments/topics/organization_cyber_protection

IUCC. (2021). *Inter-University Computation Center Cyber & Data Security Services*. Retrieved from https://www.iucc.ac.il/en/infrastructuretechnologies/cyber/

Joffre, T. (2020). *State comptroller to review preparedness for cyberattack on elections.* The Jerusalem Post. Retrieved from https://www.jpost.com/israel-news/state-comptroller-to-review-preparedness-for-cyberattack-on-elections-651380

Kabir, O. (2020). *UAE views Israel as a strategic cybersecurity partner, says head of national cyber authority.* Calcalist. Retrieved from https://www.calcalistech.com/ctech/articles/0,7340,L-3874096,00.html

Kahan, R. (2020). *Pay2Key hackers claim they breached IAI servers.* Calcalist. Retrieved from https://www.calcalistech.com/ctech/articles/0,7340,L-3883010,00.html

Kogosowski, M. (2021). *UAE cyber security head calls for joint exercise with Israel.* Israel Defense. Retrieved from https://www.israeldefense.co.il/en/node/49182

Koi, T. (2020). *Kiberfegyvereket loptak el a FireEye-től* [Cyberweapons stolen from FireEye]. HWSW. Retrieved from https://www.hwsw.hu/hirek/62656/fireeye-red-team-betores-hacker-kiberbiztonsag.html

Lautman, O. (2015). *Israeli Business Culture.* Academic Press.

Leichman, A. K. (2018). *The Israeli high-school kids earning high-tech salaries.* Israel21C. Retrieved from https://www.israel21c.org/the-israeli-high-school-kids-earning-high-tech-salaries/

Levush, R. (2019). *Israel: Knesset Passes Amendment Law Recognizing Role of National Cyber Directorate in Protecting Cyberspace.* The Library of Congress. Retrieved from https://www.loc.gov/law/foreign-news/article/israel-knesset-passes-amendment-law-recognizing-role-of-national-cyber-directorate-in-protecting-cyberspace/

Lyngaas, S. (2020). *Israel, UAE say they're allies in cyberspace. They have plenty of tech power to draw upon.* CyberScoop. Retrieved from https://www.cyberscoop.com/israel-uae-cybersecurity-deal-tech-firms/

Marcus, J. (2020). *Iran navy 'friendly fire' incident kills 19 sailors in Gulf of Oman.* BBC. Retrieved from https://www.bbc.com/news/world-middle-east-52612511

Margit, M. (2020). *Israel to launch 'Cyber Defense Shield' for health sector.* The Jerusalem Post. Retrieved from https://www.jpost.com/israel-news/israel-to-launch-cyber-defense-shield-for-health-sector-627304

Marshall, T. (2016). *A földrajz fogságában ("Prisoners of Geography").* Park Könyvkiadó.

Martin, N. (2021). *Israeli entrepreneurs have starting building larger companies.* Israel Hayom. Retrieved from https://www.israelhayom.com/2021/04/04/israeli-cyber-startups-ride-covid-wave-with-no-sign-of-stopping/

Martins, R. P. (2018). Punching Above Their Digital Weight: Why Iran is Developing Cyberwarfare Capabilities Far Beyond Expectations. *International Journal of Cyber Warfare & Terrorism, 8*(2), 32–46. doi:10.4018/IJCWT.2018040103

Nocamels. (2020). *Israel Is Number 1 Target For Hackers And Cybercriminals – Report.* Retrieved from https://nocamels.com/2020/12/israel-target-hackers-cybersecurity-cybercriminals/

Orbach, M., & Hazani, G. (2020). *Israel's supply chain targeted in massive cyberattack.* Calcalist. Retrieved from https://www.calcalistech.com/ctech/articles/0,7340,L-3881337,00.html

Országos Katasztrófavédelemi Főigazgatóság. (2021). *A kritikus infrastruktúra* [The Critical Infrastructure]. Retrieved from https://regi.katasztrofavedelem.hu/index2.php?pageid=lrl_index

Paganini, P. (2020). *Tens of thousands Israeli websites defaced.* Security Affairs. Retrieved from https://securityaffairs.co/wordpress/103570/hacktivism/israeli-websites-defaced.html

Papp-Váry, Á. (2019). *Országmárkázás [Country branding]* (Vol. 41). Akadémiai Kiadó.

Park S., Specter M.A., Narula N., Rivest R. (2021). Going from bad to worse: from Internet voting to blockchain voting. *J. Cybersecur., 7.*

Paycale. (2021). *Salary for Skill in Israel: Cyber Security.* Retrieved from https://www.payscale.com/research/IL/Skill=Cyber_Security/Salary/Page-4

Ram, Y., Israel, I., & Baram, G. (2020). Cyberwar Between Iran and Israel Out in the Open. Yuval Ne'eman Workshop for Science, Technology and Security at Tel Aviv University.

Reuters. (2020). *Israel says it thwarted serious cyberattack on power station.* Retrieved from https://www.reuters.com/article/us-israel-cyber-powerstation/israel-says-it-thwarted-serious-cyber-attack-on-power-station-idUSKBN1ZS1SU

Robinson, M., Jones, K., Janicke, H., & Maglaras, L. (2018). An Introduction to Cyber Peacekeeping. *Journal of Network and Computer Applications, 114,* 70–87. Advance online publication. doi:10.1016/j.jnca.2018.04.010

Romanosky, S. (2016). Examining the costs and causes of cyber incidents. *Journal of Cybersecurity, 2,* tyw001. Advance online publication. doi:10.1093/cybsec/tyw001

Schulman, S. (2021). *The best for cyber: How much do you earn in the hottest professions in the field?* Calcalist. Retrieved from https://www.calcalist.co.il/internet/articles/0,7340,L-3902412,00.html

Sebastien G., Anderhalden D. (2020). *Insurability of Critical Infrastructures.* . doi:10.1007/978-3-030-41826-7_3

Secret Tel Aviv. (2018). *Best Coding And Tech Schools In English In Tel Aviv.* Retrieved from https://www.secrettelaviv.com/magazine/blog/useful-info/best-coding-schools-in-english-in-tel-aviv

Shabak. (2020). *Career in the Shin Bet.* Retrieved from https://www.shabak.gov.il/career/jobs/Pages/TechnologicalUnits.aspx?pk_campaign=quiz&pk_kwd=klali-3001#cbpf=*

Shulman, E. (2020). *Iranian Hackers Test Israeli Cyber Mettle.* Mishpacha. Retrieved from https://mishpacha.com/iranian-hackers-test-israeli-cyber-mettle/

Solomon, S. (2019). *Israel cybersecurity sector hamstrung by shortage of labor, report says.* The Times of Israel. Retrieved from https://www.timesofisrael.com/israel-cybersecurity-sector-hamstrung-by-shortage-of-labor-report-says/

Solomon, S. (2020). *Program arms discharged fighters with cyberskills, wins IDF Chief of Staff award.* The Times of Israel. Retrieved from https://www.timesofisrael.com/progam-arms-discharged-fighters-with-cyberskills-wins-idf-chief-of-staff-award/

Tabansky, L. (2013). Critical Infrastructure Protection: Evolution of Israeli Policy. *International Journal of Cyber Warfare & Terrorism, 3*(3), 80–87. doi:10.4018/ijcwt.2013070106

The Israel Institute for Biological Research. (2021). Retrieved from https://iibr.gov.il/Pages/Who-We-are.aspx

The Jerusalem Post. (2020). *Israel must use Intelligence to mitigate cyber attacks: official.* Retrieved from https://www.jpost.com/cybertech/israel-must-use-intelligence-to-mitigate-cyber-attacks-senior-official-632012

The Jerusalem Post. (2020). *Israel Police reports a staggering 8,377 cyberattacks for 2020.* Retrieved from https://www.jpost.com/jpost-tech/israel-police-reports-a-staggering-8377-cyberattacks-for-2020-653378

The State Comptroller and Ombudsman of Israel. (2019). *Matanyahu Englman. State Comptroller and Ombudsman of the State of Israel* Retrieved from https://www.mevaker.gov.il/En/About/mevakrim/Pages/Englman.aspx

The Times of Israel. (2020). *Israeli vaccine research centers reportedly among sites targeted by hackers.* Retrieved from https://www.timesofisrael.com/israeli-vaccine-research-centers-reportedly-among-sites-targeted-by-hackers/

Trifunovic, D. (2020). *Elements of Critical Infrastructure Resilience. National security and the future.* Retrieved from https://www.researchgate.net/publication/347514909_Elements_of_Critical_Infrastructure_Resilience doi:10.37458/nstf.20.1-2.6

Vidal, E. (2021). *Israel's 2021 Cyber landscape: Which sector will the new unicorns emerge from?* Calcalistech. Retrieved from https://www.calcalistech.com/ctech/articles/0,7340,L-3892650,00.html

Wang, Q. (2014). Applicability of Jus in Bello in Cyber Space: Dilemmas and Challenges. *International Journal of Cyber Warfare & Terrorism, 4*(3), 43–62. doi:10.4018/ijcwt.2014070104

ADDITIONAL READING

Cohen, M., Freilich, C., & Siboni, G. (2016). Israel and Cyberspace: Unique Threat and Response. *International Studies Perspectives, 17*, 307–321. doi:10.1093/isp/ekv023

Frei, J. (2020) *Israel's National Cybersecurity and Cyberdefense Posture Policy and Organizations.* Retrieved from https://css.ethz.ch/content/dam/ethz/special-interest/gess/cis/center-for-securities-studies/pdfs/Cyber-Reports-2020-09-Israel.pdf

Garnett, H., & James, T. (2020). Cyber Elections in the Digital Age: Threats and Opportunities of Technology for Electoral Integrity. Election Law Journal: Rules. *Politics & Policy, 19*(2), 111–126. Advance online publication. doi:10.1089/elj.2020.0633

Housen-Couriel, D. (2018) *National Cyber Security Organisation: ISRAEL.* Retrieved from https://ccdcoe.org/uploads/2018/10/IL_NCSO_final.pdf

Keupp, M. (2020). *The Security of Critical Infrastructures.* Springer. doi:10.1007/978-3-030-41826-7

KEY TERMS AND DEFINITIONS

Botnet: A botnet is a network of infected IT devices that can be used by a botnet host for multiple types of damage. The purpose of using infected workstations is primarily to send unsolicited mail, launch Denial-of-Service (DoS) attacks, or even steal sensitive (such as banking) data.

Cyber Attribution: The process investigations to attribute the incident to specific threat actors in order to gain a complete picture of the attack, and to help ensure the attackers are brought to justice.

Denial-of-Service: Denial-of-service (DoS) attacks are electronic attacks that can load systems, services, or networks to such an extent that the affected system, service, or network may become inaccessible. This can be achieved on the one hand by paralyzing the systems and on the other hand by increasing the network traffic, as a result of which the legitimate data traffic does not reach the target system. A DoS attack can come from a single system or even a group of systems. The latter case is called Distributed Denial of Service (DDoS) attack.

Malware: Software that is capable of copying itself while running an infected program. Depending on their prevalence, they can be viruses that infect files (such as macro viruses, executable infectious files, etc.) or viruses that infect the boot sector required to boot systems.

Phishing: A phishing website is a site that presents itself as the official site of a known organization or company and attempts to obtain personal information, typically user IDs, passwords, and credit card information. Scammers often try to get users to click on the link in the message, which leads them to a phishing page by sending unsolicited emails and instant messages. If users follow the instructions there, they can become victims.

Ransomware: Blackmail (ransomware) is malicious software designed to "take hostage" in some way the data stored on users' IT devices, which it makes available again only upon payment of a ransom.

Spam: All bulk unsolicited messages sent electronically. These are most often created by so-called infected computers and distributed through robotic networks. The most common form is commercial e-mail sent to many addresses, promoting products or services that in many cases do not even exist. Spamming can take place through a variety of channels, such as SMS, instant messaging applications, social media, or voice messaging.

ENDNOTES

[1] Advancement of Cyber Defense R&D was a program launched in 2013, which supported the RDI projects of the industry with 80 million new Israeli shekels. Driven by its success, Kidma 2.0 had an even bigger budget of 100 million shekels in 2015.

[2] Dual Cyber R&D was a program to support national and defence cyber technologies with a budget of 10 million shekels between 2012-2013.

[3] New Israeli shekel

[4] A standardized address for certain resources (such as texts and images) on the Internet.

[5] The name of the units: Serious and International Crime Unit, National Economic Crimes Unit, National Car Theft Unit, National Fraud Squad, Gidonim Unit for intelligence gathering and special operations

[6] The non-indexed, non-searchable layer of the Internet, with encrypted connection and data traffic passing through repeaters around the world, so the user can remain anonymous.

7   They use these tools to simulate attackers trying to infiltrate the systems of their clients – thus discovering vulnerable, weak points and gaps in the shield.

8   Advanced Persistent Threat.

9   Computer Security Incident Response Team

10 IUUC – Inter-University Computation Center

11 For example, 'The countdown of Israel destruction has begun since a long time ago'.

12 This officer performs audits and reports on the activities of ministries, municipalities and various public sector organizations to ensure that they operate in accordance with legal regulations and the principles of good governance, integrity and efficiency.

13 Mobile Device Management – MDM and Enterprise mobility management – EMM.

14 Chief Information Security Officer – CISO

15 Internet of Things

16 Science, Technology, Engineering, and Mathematics

17 Israeli Defense Forces

Chapter 4
Cyber Security and Cyber Resilience for the Australian E-Health Records:
A Blockchain Solution

Nagarajan Venkatachalam
iD https://orcid.org/0000-0002-5545-0549
Queensland University of Technology, Australia

Peadar O'Connor
Queensland University of Technology, Australia

Shailesh Palekar
Queensland University of Technology, Australia

ABSTRACT

Cybersecurity is a critical consideration for all users of electronic health records (EHR), particularly for patients. With the advent of Healthcare 4.0, which is based on the internet of things (IoT) and sensors, cyber resilience has become a key requirement in ensuring the protection of patient data across devices. Blockchain offers crypto-enforced security, data immutability, and smart contracts-based business logic features to all the users in the network. This study explores how blockchain can be a single digital option that can address both the cybersecurity and cyber resilience needs of EHR. The effective use lens is adopted to analyze how blockchain can be leveraged to meet cybersecurity needs while the novel use lens is adopted to analyze how blockchain can be leveraged to address cyber resilience needs originating from IoT. Based on the analysis, this study proposes two Hyperledger-based security models that contribute to individual privacy and information security needs.

DOI: 10.4018/978-1-7998-6975-7.ch004

INTRODUCTION

Electronic Health Records (EHRs) have been widely adopted for exchanging health information between stakeholders (hospitals, labs, insurance companies, government, and patients) in health systems (Del Fiol et al. 2020; Fragidis and Chatzoglou 2018). However, most EHRs still use the traditional client-server architecture for storing and exchanging data. Hence, with client-server-based controls, any errors in controlling data confidentiality, integrity, and accessibility (CIA) can result in significant loss of privacy and increase security threats to all stakeholders whereby the data become vulnerable to cyberattacks and other intruders (Tanwar et al. 2020). In Australia, the lack of adequate investments in cyber-security protocols and security solutions in health systems, use of old legacy computing systems by hospitals, lack of health-management training in cyber security, and the lack of mandatory reporting of cyberattacks are key reasons that make health systems vulnerable (Offner et al. 2020).

On the other hand, health care is transitioning toward Healthcare 4.0, which involves rapid and disruptive technological changes for aligning with Industry 4.0 initiatives. These include building cyber-physical systems and interoperability, and cyber-security solutions. Big data, cloud computing, and Internet of Things (IoT) are identified as the three digital pillars supporting Healthcare 4.0 transformations (Aceto et al. 2020) wherein the key objectives are (i) the continuous, simple, and bi-directional exchange of information; and (ii) accurate monitoring of health conditions and intake of medicines. Personalized health care, telepathology, telemedicine, disease monitoring, and assisted living are core areas of health and economic constraints addressed by the three pillars (Aceto et al. 2020). However, high-impact risks, such as (i) security concerns related to sensitive information and the digital devices storing the information; (ii) compromising privacy and ethical issues relating to ownership, dissemination, and sharing of information; and (iii) poor monitoring of information and system use, highlight serious concerns about the massive drive toward Healthcare 4.0 (Aceto et al. 2020). Based on the abovementioned dynamics, it is imperative that protecting the privacy and security of individual health records and health-related data, as well as securing the bi-directional exchange of information, are critical for realizing the benefits offered by EHR and Healthcare 4.0. For example, a recent survey on the security requirements for IoT-based healthcare systems identified cyber security and cyber resilience as key requirements that need to be addressed for developing and adopting new digital solutions (Nasiri et al. 2019). Based on the above, this study proposes a blockchain-enabled solution to address both requirements.

Blockchain offers an immutable audit trail of data and provides a consistent view for all network participants. The early success of blockchain, with the first disruptive innovation called Bitcoin (Nakamoto 2008), has evolved significantly toward frameworks such as Ethereum and Hyperledger. The power of these blockchain tools enables the enforcement of crypto security and reliable data exchanges between participants. Strategic management scholars refer to blockchain as a "foundational institutional technology" (Davidson et al. 2018), as it represents a digital-transaction ledger containing value exchanges between two peers. Blockchain also guarantees asset ownership for all individuals in the network through intelligent and trusted consensus protocols (Catalini 2017; Pilkington 2016) without the need for traditional centralized governance structures. Hence, this technology has been applied to improving information storage and distribution in supply chains, the finance sector, and other professional services, such as health care. In the health industry, ongoing studies have investigated how blockchain can be leveraged to address the needs of Healthcare 4.0 (Angraal et al. 2017; Griggs et al. 2018); (Gupta et al. 2019; Tanwar et al. 2020). These studies have highlighted the urgent need for developing robust and reliable digital infrastructures to address serious flaws and deficiencies in cyber-security and cyber-resilience protocols. To address the abovementioned security needs, this study undertakes a comprehensive review of blockchain case studies in health services. Further, it addresses two key research questions:

1. How can blockchain be leveraged to address the cyber-security needs of EHRs?
2. How can blockchain be leveraged to address the cyber-resilience needs of EHRs?

This chapter is organized as follows. First, we review literature that examines the concepts of cyber security and cyber resilience, privacy implications in EHRs, and the effective and novel use of cyber security and cyber resilience. Next, we explore Healthcare 4.0, including the changing industry landscape based on the integration of IoT and wearable devices with cloud and big-data services. Further, we examine how blockchain technology works, and how it can provide a secure solution for recording EHRs using Hyperledger Fabric. This is followed by an assessment of the solution for cyber-security and cyber-resilience tenets. Finally, future research areas and the study's conclusion are presented.

LITERATURE REVIEW

Cyber Security and Cyber Resilience

The CIA triad is often referred to when defining information security (IS), as it forms a simple model that can be applied to other domains beyond the information technology (IT) industry. However, it limits the security aspects when dealing with digital information in cyberspace (Warkentin & Orgeron, 2020, p. 3). Nasiri et al. (2019) show that the CIA triad model can be utilized for (i) protection of information, including authentication (i.e., validating who is accessing the information); (ii) authorization (i.e., controlling access to the information); (iii) non-repudiation (i.e., proving who took what action); and (iv) data freshness (i.e., ensuring access to all information). Combined with the CIA triad, these additional tenets are frequently used as pillars that define cyber security (Geusebroek, 2012, p. 25). However, cyber-security models often focus on control of access to information and ignore the complexity of modern IT infrastructures, such as cloud services and the IoT. For example, a business owner deploying IoT may not often know the location of information and the devices storing it, or how access to such devices and information can be obtained. Thus, increased complexity opens new pathways for potential attacks that can affect the operability of information systems and devices. Researchers have urgently called for a secure, scalable, and immutable solution for health data, particularly in the wake of a multitude of information system attacks in the health sector, including the WannaCry availability compromise of the National Health Service in the UK, and the Medijack integrity attacks that infected networked medical devices (Stamatellis et al., 2020, p. 2).

To understand cloud- and IoT-compromised vectors, Nasiri et al. (2019) state that new tenets are required to maintain reliability (how information sources can be made more reliable), configurability (how components can be changed without compromising the information system), autonomy (whether the components are self-healing, self-optimizing, and self-protecting), adaptability (how elements can be repurposed as demands change), repairability (how elements can detect faults and correct them), safety (where a compromised element can potentially cause physical harm), survivability (where the system can continue operating when some of the elements are compromised), and performability (where the information system can still meet the needs, even if some parts of its system are compromised). The collection of these tenets used in combination with cyber-security tenets is referred to as cyber resilience. This definition relating to IoT also fits well with Harman et al.'s (2019, p. 1) interpretation of cyber resilience, which relates to how quickly an organization can restore its services after an attack.

Blockchain for E-Health

Blockchain is a digital representation of a utility based on the seven layers of the Open-System Interconnection model. It is a network-wide distributed database (*Data layer*), where the data are replicated across a set of nodes connected by a peer-to-peer network (*Network layer*; (Pilkington 2016). The network is customizable through a communication messaging protocol (*Transport layer*) that uses cryptography (*Session layer*) for protecting user identities and guarantees the transactions data (*Presentation* and *Application layers*) associated with the asset value of all participating members (Glaser 2017). Due to this integrated combination, blockchain offers security, privacy, transparency, reliability, access flexibility, and decentralization of transactional data stored in the chain for all participants in the network (Seebacher and Schüritz 2017; Tapscott and Tapscott 2017; Yaga et al. 2019).

Health and technology scholars have explored how blockchain can be leveraged for tele-surgery (Gupta et al. 2019), remote and automated patient monitoring (Griggs et al. 2018), and e-health data storage and distribution (Tanwar et al. 2020). However, these studies assume that cryptography methods inherent in blockchain automatically provide the necessary CIA triad needs. This study posits that such assumptions need to be evaluated and validated. Hence, the first research question is posed to address this need.

Gajek et al. (2020) explore how air-gapped devices can be compromised by the Stuxnet attack through the use of USB drives containing compromised firmware updates. This type of attack can produce serious issues if applied to health-related life-saving devices, and can be further amplified if elements are networked together. Additionally, Gajek et al. (2020) argue that blockchain can offer an intelligent solution where a digital twin of the firmware can be recorded in the ledger, thereby allowing the device to remotely and automatically validate the new firmware while ensuring the integrity of the firmware and avoiding any security compromises. A similar concept is explored by Harman et al. (2019) in which backups of data are hashed, and the hashes are stored on a blockchain solution, providing irrefutable proof of whether or not the stored backup has been tampered with. Such an application can be applied to e-health through the recording of EHRs.

Effective Use of Blockchain for CIA Compliance

Effective use is defined as using the system in a way that helps its users to attain the goals for using the system (Burton-Jones and Grange 2013). For example, a network of affordances of information systems and IT artifacts can enable a hospital to achieve its goals with EHRs and realize specific benefits (Burton-Jones and Volkoff 2017). Though a system may offer many features, the user can leverage those that they specifically need. This helps in achieving system benefits by using the system within their routines more effectively. This study illustrates how blockchain can be used to address CIA compliance for all EHR users. Further, it postulates that protecting the privacy affordance of EHR users (e.g., doctors, patients, hospitals, labs, insurance companies) is necessary to maximize the usage of EHR in healthcare. In this context, since effective use can be the enabler for actualizing a specific affordance (Burton-Jones and Volkoff 2017), this study adopts the effective-use lens to illustrate how privacy of individual affordance can be realized and protected through the efficient use of blockchain.

Novel Use of Blockchain for Cyber Resilience

The novel-use lens is an effective way to analyze how users can:

- Take advantage of previously used features for accomplishing additional tasks.
- Engage features that were not previously accessed.
- Use features and extensions of a specific technology (Bagayogo et al. 2014).

Novel use is also referred to as the enhanced use of IT wherein the analysis focuses on the use of technology after implementation. Scholars have elaborated on how novel use can leverage the fit between digital technologies characteristics and specific users' needs for particular tasks (Beaudry et al. 2020). In this study, the novel use of blockchain (as the IT) is analyzed through blockchain features to scrutinize cyber-resilience needs. Novel use of IT can also disrupt and transform entire work processes by enabling conditions that allow users to realize the full potential of new technology innovations (Bagayogo et al. 2014). This study illustrates how IS needs for protecting data in Healthcare 4.0 can be realized through the novel use of blockchain. Considering the Healthcare 4.0 and IoT-based IS needs, it proposes a solution through the novel use of blockchain to address the IS needs of Healthcare 4.0 data.

ELECTRONIC HEALTH RECORDS: THE QUESTION OF INDIVIDUAL PRIVACY

Although the benefits of EHRs are numerous (Kierkegaard, 2011, p. 503), privacy remains a key concern for both the subjects and stakeholders of the records. Privacy refers to personal information stored in information systems and is defined by the Australian Privacy Act of 1988 as "information or an opinion about an identified individual, or an individual who is reasonably identifiable" (Privacy Act 1988, p. 25). Simply put, it refers to information that defines who someone is. EHRs contain sensitive and private data related to a user's (e.g., patient's) physical and mental health, medications, treatments, and even religious beliefs. Therefore, protection of data privacy and compliance with standards are of paramount importance, as users of such records place trust in such systems. The document AS ISO 279911:2011, published by Standards Australia, highlights the need for cyber-security tenets to be applied to secure the information contained in EHRs (Standards Australia, 2011, p. 5). It further states that such systems should be resilient in facing attacks, failures, and disasters. This can be difficult to control and manage in simple air-gapped computer networks where the risk of breaching privacy remains high, given that many individuals interact with the data. The risk of breaching privacy expands considerably when information is moved into networked cloud and IoT environments (Nasiri et al., 2019).

Industry 4.0, Healthcare 4.0, and a Secured Collaboration Quest

The IoT, along with Internet of Services (IoS) and physical systems connected in cyberspace, are generally considered key components of the Industry 4.0 concept (Thuemmler & Ba, 2017). These empower industries to evolve by providing customized solutions to specific user and client scenarios. As the concept extends into healthcare, it has triggered a new phase known as Healthcare 4.0, wherein individual health information is directly connected to autonomous IoT systems (Thuemmler & Ba, 2017, pp. 30–31). For example, Al-Odat et al. (2018) show through IoT architecture how insulin pumps can track patient measurements and upload data to cloud storage, which helps medical practitioners to remotely monitor the patient's health. This big data can also be used for providing insights into conducting large-scale medical studies. As the volume of data increases, so does the complexity of collecting, processing, and storing the information (Klonoff, 2017, p. 647). New computing methods (e.g., fog, edge computing) help in analyzing voluminous data. Cisco has forecast that, by the end of 2021, there could be an estimated 700 million edge-hosted containers (Cisco, 2020, p. 4). The increased complexity and diversity of networks make the security of elements and the information carried and stored within them crucial.

Individual Privacy Questions?

Assessing how data should be treated by various IoT devices is complex. In this context, the IS CIA triad helps in assessing the data interaction points. For example, it can help in understanding (i) how data can be stored so that only authorized users can access it, thereby keeping the data private; (ii) how data can be accessed; (iii) how medical practitioners can know that it is complete; and (iv) whether or not the data have been accessed by other individuals. Depending on the specificity of the data collected, and how it is collected, ethical and legislative protocols are required to answer the above questions.

Long-Term Quest: Clinical Notes for Collaborative Health Care

In addition to the data-volume issues of big data, EHRs are designed to address two distinct needs. First, they serve as a means to capture the patient's narrative as useful data with the clinical notes from general practitioners, specialist physicians, and nurses. Second, they are historical and legal references related to research, management, and quality assurance (Bansler et al. 2016). The clinical notes about a patient in EHRs constitute the working document that records the core narrative of medical care, which unfolds over time (Hobbs 2003). Hence, EHRs should be designed to enable collaboration between primary health care providers to address the individual patient's health care over a period of time. Despite the benefits gained from the historical analysis of EHR data, many questions persist, for example, how can medical narratives be stored in EHRs (note: this problem is compounded by the individual privacy questions identified in the earlier section)?

IoT, Cloud, and Big Data: Information Security Challenges

With IoT devices, the data collected can be accessed and stored on numerous Internet-connected devices, and each element can be questioned (for assessment) from an IS perspective. For example, if the data are collected on a fog computing device, will the device owner have access to the data? How can one determine whether the stored data file is the latest version of those data? When can an IoT-enabled device, such as a cardiac defibrillator, take remedial action on a patient's condition (Klonoff, 2017, p. 650)? Based on the above, it is critical to record (i) a command provided to the device, (ii) who provided the command, and (iii) the data associated with the decision. In other words, the system needs to be auditable such that accountability is maintained, the data trail is immutable, and the reputability of events is clear. Conversely, if the records are intended for big-data analysis, then they must be deanonymized so that the privacy of the patient is retained even if the data are in use.

BLOCKCHAIN FOR ELECTRONIC HEALTH RECORDS

This study positions blockchain as a faithful representation for (i) protecting individual privacy and (ii) ensuring the IS of transactional exchanges and the value of assets stored in the blockchain.

Effective Use of Blockchain for Protecting Individual Privacy

The Bitcoin blockchain solution has demonstrated that irrefutable data records can be stored publicly while typically maintaining users' privacy. However, Henry et al. (2018, pp. 38–39) highlight that it is possible to heuristically link users to transactions. Other blockchain models offer increased privacy, such as the Hawk model proposed by Kosba et al. (2016), which uses smart contracts to obfuscate the data stored within the public Ethereum blockchain, or the Sony educational solution that protects data on the IBM blockchain cloud utilizing a private Hyperledger Fabric solution (Grech & Camilleri, 2017, p. 59). Adlam and Haskins (2018) highlight how a permissioned blockchain, such as Hyperledger Fabric, can store EHRs in a distributed blockchain, allow access to medical practitioners at multiple hospitals, and contribute to the data using protected channels built into the blockchain architecture.

What Is Blockchain and How Does It Work?

The generally accepted classification of blockchain is an immutable decentralized digital ledger distributed to a group of networked peer nodes. The ledger is made up of a chain of blocks, with each block containing verifiable data, and a linkage that proves the block is in sequence and accurate. How the data are distributed among networked peers depends on the mechanism developed for chain implementations, which is called a "consensus mechanism." The information stored in the blocks and the consensus mechanism vary across implementations and the type of blockchain (e.g., public/permission-less, private/permissioned).

The public Bitcoin block architecture described by Nakamoto (2008) is summarized in Figure 1. It contains a group of transaction records between two entities, plus a SHA-256 cryptographic hash of each transaction (Nakamoto, 2008). The block also contains a header containing a cryptographic hash of the transaction hashes (known as a Merkle root hash), which proves the integrity of the block. The header also includes a hash of the previous block in the chain and an integer (called a nonce), which is calculated by the mathematical algorithm defined by the consensus mechanism (Nakamoto, 2008, p. 3; Grech & Camilleri, 2017, pp. 121–122).

As new blocks are created and distributed among network peers, the peers need to validate that the new block is suitable to be added to the chain. This is achieved using the aforementioned consensus mechanism. There are three common methods of achieving consensus: (i) proof of work (PoW), (ii) proof of stake (PoS), and (iii) proof of authority (PoA; Parisi, 2020; Ma & Fang, 2020, pp. 21–22; Grech & Camilleri, 2017, p. 127).

Public and permission-less blockchain solutions, such as Bitcoin and Ethereum, use a PoW consensus mechanism (Parisi, 2020). These chains have an indefinite number of peers in the network, can be accessed by anyone, and have no central authority. The open nature of the network presents a challenge in determining whether or not a new block should be added to the chain. The PoW mechanism requires the peer creating the new block to perform a complex mathematical task. The effort of calculation is deemed as suitable proof that the block proposal can be assessed by other peers in the network. Additionally, the

PoW mathematical challenge defined by the architecture becomes more complex as the chain grows. If a peer faces a conflict in assessing multiple blocks, then the block with the greater challenge is considered the superior block by the peer (Nakamoto, 2008, p. 3; Grech & Camilleri, 2017, pp. 121–122). The complexity of this permission-less configuration has several drawbacks, including an increasing cost to write the chain, a limit on how quickly data can be written to the chain, and that anyone can read the data stored on the chain (addressed by a permissioned blockchain solution).

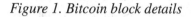
Figure 1. Bitcoin block details

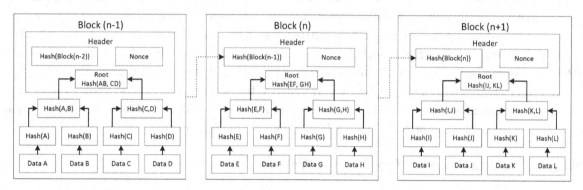

The PoS mechanism can be used in permission-less blockchain solutions (Ma & Fang, 2020, pp. 21–22; Grech & Camilleri, 2017, p. 127). In the PoS option, stakeholders of the network are trusted proportionally, based on their commitment and investment in the network and validated by their digital certificates (Parisi, 2020; Grech & Camilleri, 2017, p. 127).

Permissioned blockchains, such as Hyperledger, create an authority to govern what and how blocks can be added to the chain. They are often referred to as "private blockchains" managed by a single organization, or "consortium blockchains" managed by a group of consenting organizations (Parisi, 2020). The authority is defined by the participating organizations that use digital certificates to prove that the peer proposing the block has the requisite authority. This mechanism is referred to as PoA and allows for faster processing of blocks at a consistent cost to the peers. Permissioned chain solutions usually restrict access to the data stored on the chain, which can assist in protecting the privacy of the data, although some privacy can be achieved on public blockchains using techniques such as smart contracts.

A few blockchain models include the ability to execute a set of code stored on-chain, such as Ethereum's smart contracts (Parisi, 2020). The code can be customized to user needs and is written specifically for the chain technology, the data being stored, and the users' needs. For example, the smart contract code can only be written to commit transaction data after two parities meet their defined prerequisites (Chen et al., 2018, p. 31). Alternatively, the code can be crafted to add additional layers of encryption and privacy to the data per the previously discussed proposal by Kosba et al. (2016).

Since the implementation in Bitcoin, many blockchain digital ledger models and implementation solutions have been proposed and implemented with varying levels of success, each with its own strengths and weaknesses. When considering blockchain as a solution for EHRs, the privacy of the data recorded is of paramount importance.

SOLUTIONS AND RECOMMENDATIONS

Novel Use of Blockchain for Protecting Information Security

A Permissioned Blockchain EHR Solution

Blockchain may be an ideal solution for protecting EHRs collected and stored in IoT networks. It also addresses many concerns raised by the cyber-security and cyber-resilience tenets. Hyperledger Fabric is a permissioned blockchain model released by the Linux Foundation that can be configured with various security and consensus modules. A well-configured model can store patient data privately while providing the ability to manage access to a wide range of clients using a combination of attribute-based access controls (ABAC), well-defined roles in the membership service provider (MSP) service module, and use of private state databases within the blockchain ledger.

Hyperledger Fabric can have multiple channels defined within the peer network, wherein organizations can communicate with each other and share digital ledgers. However, the channels keep the data independent from others that may utilize the same peers and networks (Hyperledger Fabric, 2020). Channel separations allow for multiple solutions to be implemented on the same platform and peer network without sharing data between the solutions or clients. Figure 2 shows how two health authorities can create their own ledger solutions on a common network while storing their EHR on peers without sharing them with other authorities. Separating the data into different channels increases the overhead managing the network across multiple channels. Additionally, the solution does not easily permit the sharing of data within the ledger with other clients. Although the solution maintains confidentiality of the patient data by restricting access to the managed private channels, it limits the availability and integrity tenets, as the data are not available to those off chain or those that are not authorized, and the data cannot be easily verified by others.

Figure 2. Hyperledger Fabric channel separation (adapted from Hyperledger Fabric, 2020)

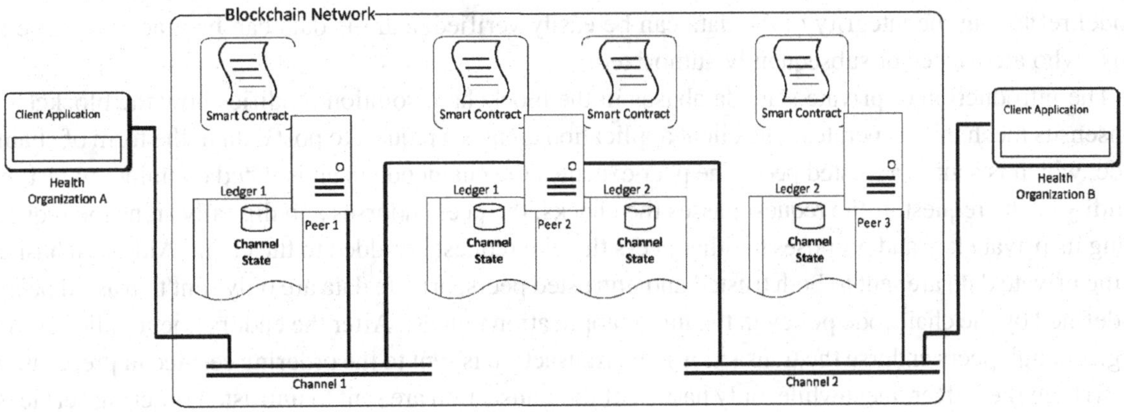

The private data-collection feature of Hyperledger Fabric offers an alternative solution, whereby private state databases can be created within digital ledgers. Figure 3 highlights how different organizations can share a common channel, although private data are distributed only to trusted peers.

Figure 3. Hyperledger Fabric private state ledgers (Hyperledger Fabric, 2020)

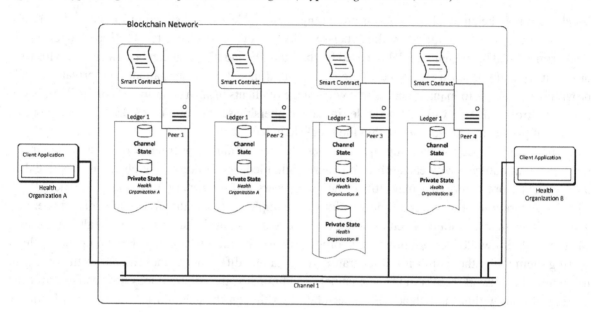

Digital signatures (or hashes) of the private data are created and distributed to both trusted and untrusted peers in the common channel-state databases, as shown in Figure 4. Where required, discrete records of private data can be shared with untrusted peers and clients. Because all peers in the network have a copy of the digital signature of the records, the shared private data can be easily verified by hashing the supplied data and comparing them with the record in the common channel-state database. This model reflecting the integrity of the data can be easily verified, and the data can be made available to those who are trusted or subsequently authorized.

The introduction of private state databases in the blockchain solution modifies how the blockchain consensus mechanism operates. The client application creates a request to post data in the form of chaincode, which is sent to a trusted peer. The peer executes the chaincode in an isolated container to test the validity of the request. If the request passes the checks, the peer endorses and digitally signs the request using its private key and proposes to other peers that the request be added to the chain. Although hashes of the private data are sent to both trusted and untrusted peers, private data are only sent to trusted peers, as defined by the chaincode policy in the initial application request. After the endorsement policy is met (e.g., enough peers endorse the transaction), the transaction is sent to the ordering service in preparation for writing the ledger; meanwhile, only hashes of the transaction are sent to untrusted ordering services. When the ordering service is complete, the hash sets are sent to all peers in the network for validation, and are subsequently written to the channel-state databases for every peer in the channel. The private data are distributed to any trusted peer that does not yet have a copy of the data, and each of the peers commit the records to the private state database within the ledger. This solution maintains the confidentiality of the patient data, as only authorized clients, services, and peers have access to the actual data.

Figure 4. Private data collection for Health Organization A (adapted from Hyperledger Fabric, 2020)

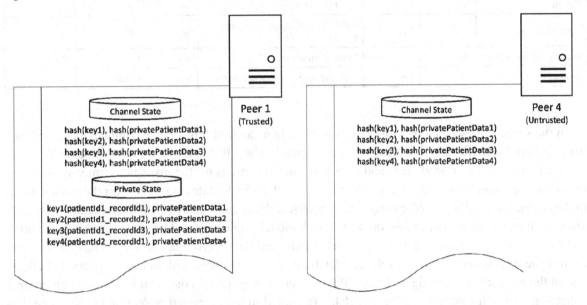

Suitable access controls underpin the privacy of the described blockchain solution. Two primary factors provide this control, namely, the MSP and the configuration of the ABACs. The MSP stores the public keys of peers and defines what elements and actions are permitted within the network (Hyperledger Fabric, 2020). It can define roles for the permissions a particular actor has within the network or on a particular node. For example, the MSP can store the trusted peers in a particular organization or a client that is a member of an organization. ABACs can enhance the MSP to define permissions in a more granular manner for each organization and for elements within the blockchain network.

Let us now look at how a combination of an MSP and ABACs can assist with managing permissions of EHRs for a patient undergoing treatment at a hospital. In this context, we define four roles: patient, doctor, the hospital practice administrator, and a health insurance company. The doctor (treating the patient), or other medical practitioners involved in the patient's treatment, can create a new EHR for the patient. They should be able to read all of the patient's past and current EHRs, as governed by the MSP. Likewise, patients should be able to read their own EHRs from previous and current treatments, but only those records requiring a *patientId* attribute control. A hospital practice administrator should be able to read a patient's EHR for treatment at the practice, but only those records requiring a *practiceId* attribute control. A health insurance company can review the specific treatment records as part of a patient claim, should the patient consent to disclosing the records, but only those requiring *patientId*, *practiceId*, and *treatmentId* attribute controls for sharing specific private data. These roles, access rights, and permissions are summarized in Table 1.

Table 1. Example of an MSP and ABACs for an EHR for patient treatment in a hospital

Role	MSP Access Control		Read Conditions	Access Control by Attribute		
	Create Records	Read Records		*patientId*	*practiceId*	*treatmentId*
Patient	No	Yes	Limit to own records, full history	Yes	No	No
Treating Doctor	Yes	Yes	Full history of any patient being treated	No	No	No
Practice Administrator	No	Yes	Limit to current treatment	No	Yes	No
Insurance Company	No	Yes	Selective based on patient consent	Yes	Yes	Yes

In the scenario described in Table 1, it is implied that the health insurance company is treated as a trusted client for EHRs, and that the data are protected by the ABAC privileges. An alternate solution is to create additional untrusted peers and establish data collections for the insurance company, meaning the insurance company would not have direct access to the private state data, except for the hashes stored in the common-state ledger. When required, the private data can be shared with the insurance company via several mechanisms, depending on the network model implemented. Off-chain data sharing allows a client to export the private data via external means, and the receiver can verify the hash of the data against the data stored in the control-state database, which is shared with untrusted peers and clients within the network (Hyperledger Fabric, 2020). Alternatively, private data can be shared with another collection within the network, where the data are copied to the untrusted collection private state data (Hyperledger Fabric, 2020). Again, the private data copied can be validated using the hash data stored in the common-state ledger. This solution carries less risk of losing the shared private data, as it is shared only within the blockchain network.

Given the Hyperledger Fabric configuration proposed in Figures 3 and 4, and with the MSP and ABACs proposed in Table 1, the key question is: How does the model address the cyber-security and resiliency tenets namely confidentiality, integrity, availability, authorization, non-repudiation, configurability, autonomy, adaptability, repairability, safety, survivability and performability? Next, we elaborate on how these tenets are addressed by the solution.

Confidentiality is achieved by protecting data in a permissioned blockchain ledger, with encrypted private state databases, clearly defined roles and access attributes, and managed by the owning organization. The data can be stored in privately managed networks or cloud services so the appropriate level of controls can be enacted on the private state databases to provide much-needed confidentiality of the EHR.

Integrity is enacted with multiple layers of data hashing within the blockchain, providing certainty that the data are correctly recorded, and that shared hashes of private data are validated by others if they should be shared. The integrity of the solution is inherent in the design of blockchain, whereby the whole chain can be verified at any time, in its entirety, as the header of each block includes a hash of the previous block.

Availability is achieved through the use of multiple peers that store the data so that any single peer failure will not affect the availability of the data. As each trusted node contains a full copy of the private state databases, and each untrusted node contains a copy of the entire hash ledger, availability can be extended as much as desired by adding more trusted and untrusted nodes in the network, and selecting high-reliability services, such as cloud data storage solutions. This means that the EHR can be made available practically anywhere, at any time, if it is provided enough capacity.

Authorization is ensured through the use of digital certificate infrastructure to certify each actor and network element with protection built in via the MSP. The consortium holds the responsibility for defining who may have access to the system in the MSP and can define record-level permissions through the use of well-designed ABACs. Using the model proposed, each patient, doctor, or other actor must first prove who they are and then be assessed on what rights they have for each EHR.

Non-repudiation relates to the idea that blockchain ledgers are immutable through the use of multi-stage data hashing and peer sharing, ensuring that the EHR history is accurately reflected. Put simply, once the record is entered in the database, it cannot be changed without this change being noticed, as the hash on the blockchain will not match the record in the private state database.

Configurability means that the model is highly configurable to the environment, where elements, actors, services and access controls can be set up as required, and altered during operation by the network administrators, with the consensus of those forming the network. This means that, as the medical industry and user demand evolves, so can the solution. New types of records and data sources can be added at a later time if the primary solution is well designed. For example, should a new type of wearable monitor be created with custom data requirements, a new private state database can be established and linked to the channel-state database, as the channel state will only record the hash of the new database records being incorporated.

Autonomy means that the network is designed to continue operating even if a number of peers are under attack, compromised, or otherwise faulty. By harnessing reputable cloud service providers, each node of the solution can be designed to withstand a large range of issues before they are compromised.

Adaptability indicates that elements can be added, changed, and removed without impacting the basic operations of the network. This can apply to the entire node elements of the network or the individual components.

Repairability means that the Fabric modules implemented can change based on the consensus mechanisms, the level of encryption, and the level of fault tolerance permitted during the acceptance of new data blocks.

Safety is protected in that optional safety features can be accounted for in the chaincode, if required.

Survivability and performability are achieved if the minimum number of trusted peers are operational in the network (as defined by the MSP and chaincode).

There are many ways in which blockchain digital ledger technologies can be implemented for EHRs. For example, the above solution can be enhanced with the use of in-hospital IoT smart-monitoring devices. If the devices are configured with the suitable digital certificates, authorizations, and network connections, then the *patientId* can be input into the devices, and the monitoring data can be automatically sent to the blockchain as new EHR data.

Guo et al. (2019) propose a different model wherein smart health devices can cryptographically communicate and store data at edge nodes, while a Hyperledger Fabric blockchain facilitates access to the data while logging access requests. Protection of the data is enforced by the edge node using ABACs. This is only accessible if the correct decryption key and data address are supplied in a one-time, self-destructing uniform resource locator provided by smart contracts built into the blockchain. Such a system can provide non-repudiation and auditability access to the data, control who and how the data are accessed, and guarantee the freshness of the data.

FUTURE RESEARCH DIRECTIONS

Patient data analysis in EHRs has been growing over the past few decades. However, the adoption and use of new and emergent information technologies to analyze and manage the data vastly differ between developed and developing countries. There are three distinct areas where scholars can extend their research and investigations.

First, this study introduced cyber-security and resilience models based on blockchain use that cater to the challenges posed to the IoS and the IoT. Future investigators can evaluate and validate these models as well as identify new factors that need to be added to handle the hyper-dynamic volatility of IoT-enabled health care in Healthcare 4.0.

Second, current designs of EHRs are proving to be a challenge in enabling collaboration between physicians and specialists for recording and tracking clinical notes data. This arises due to the complexity of processes related to storing and sharing relevant data and individuals' privacy considerations. Though this study provides a model to address this gap, future work could investigate how collaboration-related problems and scans can be addressed by standardizing data stored in blockchain.

Third, as the adoption and implementation of EHRs vary extensively between developed and developing countries, privacy and security considerations of EHR data also fluctuate based on capital funding and other government-related priorities. Scholars can investigate how blockchain-based EHRs can address the needs of developing countries, such as India and Brazil.

In addition, more research is required to analyze how diverse data sources can be secured, and how consistent levels of security are achieved across systems before a universal solution is attained and adopted.

CONCLUSION

IS is a constantly evolving requirement for systems adopted by public and private enterprises and entities. As the complexity of network elements and the volume of data increase, so do the requirements for protecting the data. EHRs can provide revolutionary improvements in patient care and medical research, as the healthcare industry evolves toward Healthcare 4.0. However, technological advances should not compromise patient privacy and data security to achieve their intended outcomes. Therefore, any solution must focus on and mandate the core privacy and IS principles as intrinsic pillars of the design.

A suitable private/consortium blockchain-implementation model with ABACs can address the cyber-security CIA tenets demanded by IS protocols by separating patient records into managed private state databases, while recording irreversible hashes of the records in a common channel-state blockchain. Such a solution can also manage access at the data-record level to address authorization issues, with non-repudiation built into the core design of blockchain. Additionally, the solution can help tackle cyber-resiliency issues, such as survivability, reliability, maintainability, and adaptability, which are particularly useful as the realm of EHRs evolve rapidly with new IoT services and security demands.

REFERENCES

Aceto, G., Persico, V., & Pescapé, A. (2020). Industry 4.0 and health: Internet of Things, big data, and cloud computing for Healthcare 4.0. *Journal of Industrial Information Integration, 18*, 100129. doi:10.1016/j.jii.2020.100129

Adlam, R., & Haskins, B. (2019). A permissioned blockchain approach to the authorization process in electronic health records. In *2019 International Multidisciplinary Information Technology and Engineering Conference (IMITEC)*, (pp. 1-8). IEEE 10.1109/IMITEC45504.2019.9015927

Al-Odat, Z. A., Srinivasan, S. K., Al-qtiemat, E., Dubasi, M. A. L., & Shuja, S. (2018). *Iot-based secure embedded scheme for insulin pump data acquisition and monitoring.* arXiv preprint arXiv:1812.02357.

Angraal, S., Krumholz, H. M., & Schulz, W. L. (2017). Blockchain technology: Applications in health care. *Circulation: Cardiovascular Quality and Outcomes, 10*(9), e003800. doi:10.1161/CIRCOUTCOMES.117.003800 PMID:28912202

Bagayogo, F. F., Lapointe, L., & Bassellier, G. (2014). Enhanced use of IT: A new perspective on post-adoption. *Journal of the Association for Information Systems, 15*(7), 3. doi:10.17705/1jais.00367

Bansler, J. P., Havn, E. C., Schmidt, K., Mønsted, T., Petersen, H. H., & Svendsen, J. H. (2016). Cooperative epistemic work in medical practice: An analysis of physicians' clinical notes. *Computer Supported Cooperative Work, 25*(6), 503–546. doi:10.100710606-016-9261-x

Beaudry, A., Vaghefi, I., Bagayogo, F., & Lapointe, L. (2020). Impact of IT user behavior: Observations through a new lens. *Communications of the Association for Information Systems, 46*(1), 15. doi:10.17705/1CAIS.04615

Burton-Jones, A., & Grange, C. (2013). From use to effective use: A representation theory perspective. *Information Systems Research, 24*(3), 632–658. doi:10.1287/isre.1120.0444

Burton-Jones, A., & Volkoff, O. (2017). How can we develop contextualized theories of effective use? A demonstration in the context of community-care electronic health records. *Information Systems Research, 28*(3), 468–489. doi:10.1287/isre.2017.0702

Catalini, C. (2017). How blockchain technology will impact the digital economy. *Blockchains Smart Contracts Internet Things, 4*, 2292-2303. https://ide.mit.edu/sites/default/files/publications/IDE%20Research%20Paper_v0517.pdf

Chen, L., Xu, L., Gao, Z., Lu, Y., & Shi, W. (2018). Tyranny of the majority: On the (im)possibility of correctness of smart contracts. *IEEE Security and Privacy, 16*(4), 30–37. doi:10.1109/MSP.2018.3111240

Cisco. (2020). *2020 Global Network Trends Report.* https://www.cisco.com/c/m/en_us/solutions/enterprise-networks/networking-report.html

Davidson, S., De Filippi, P., & Potts, J. (2018). Blockchains and the economic institutions of capitalism. *Journal of Institutional Economics, 14*(4), 639–658. doi:10.1017/S1744137417000200

Del Fiol, G., Kohlmann, W., Bradshaw, R. L., Weir, C. R., Flynn, M., Hess, R., Schiffman, J. D., Nanjo, C., & Kawamoto, K. (2020). Standards-based clinical decision support platform to manage patients who meet guideline-based criteria for genetic evaluation of familial cancer. *JCO Clinical Cancer Informatics, 4*(4), 1–9. doi:10.1200/CCI.19.00120 PMID:31951474

Fragidis, L. L., & Chatzoglou, P. D. (2018). Implementation of a nationwide electronic health record (EHR). *International Journal of Health Care Quality Assurance, 31*(2), 116–130. doi:10.1108/IJHC-QA-09-2016-0136 PMID:29504871

Gajek, S., Lees, M., & Jansen, C. (2020). IIoT and cyber-resilience: Could blockchain have thwarted the Stuxnet attack? *AI & Society*. Advance online publication. doi:10.100700146-020-01023-w

Geusebroek, J. (2012). *Cyber Risk Governance-Towards a framework for managing cyber related risks from an integrated IT governance perspective* (Master's thesis). Institute of Information and Computing Sciencem, Utrecht University.

Glaser, F. (2017). *Pervasive decentralisation of digital infrastructures: A framework for blockchain enabled system and use case analysis*. doi:10.24251/HICSS.2017.186

Grech, A., & Camilleri, A. F. (2017). *Blockchain in education*. Publications Office of the European Union. doi:10.2760/60649

Griggs, K. N., Ossipova, O., Kohlios, C. P., Baccarini, A. N., Howson, E. A., & Hayajneh, T. (2018). Healthcare blockchain system using smart contracts for secure automated remote patient monitoring. *Journal of Medical Systems, 42*(7), 130. doi:10.100710916-018-0982-x PMID:29876661

Guo, H., Li, W., Nejad, M., & Shen, C. C. (2019, July). Access control for electronic health records with hybrid blockchain-edge architecture. In *2019 IEEE International Conference on Blockchain (Blockchain)* (pp. 44-51). IEEE. 10.1109/Blockchain.2019.00015

Gupta, R., Tanwar, S., Tyagi, S., Kumar, N., Obaidat, M. S., & Sadoun, B. (2019). Habits: Blockchain-based telesurgery framework for Healthcare 4.0. *2019 International Conference on Computer, Information and Telecommunication Systems (CITS)*, 1–5. 10.1109/CITS.2019.8862127

Harman, T., Mahadevan, P., Mukherjee, K., Chandrashekar, P., Venkiteswaran, S., & Mukherjea, S. (2019). Cyber resiliency automation using blockchain. *2019 IEEE International Conference on Cloud Computing in Emerging Markets (CCEM)*, 51–54. 10.1109/CCEM48484.2019.00011

Henry, R., Herzberg, A., & Kate, A. (2018). Blockchain access privacy: Challenges and directions. *IEEE Security and Privacy, 16*(4), 38–45. doi:10.1109/MSP.2018.3111245

Hobbs, P. (2003). The Use of Evidentiality in Physicians' Progress Notes. *Discourse Studies, 5*(4), 451-478.

Hyperledger Fabric. (2020a). *Blockchain network, 2.2*. https://hyperledger-fabric.readthedocs.io/en/release-2.2/network/network.html

Hyperledger Fabric. (2020b). *Membership Service Provider, 2.2*. https://hyperledger-fabric.readthedocs.io/en/release-2.2/membership/membership.html

Hyperledger Fabric. (2020c). *Private Data, 2.2.* https://hyperledger-fabric.readthedocs.io/en/release-2.2/private-data/private-data.html#what-is-a-private-data-collection

Kierkegaard, P. (2011). Electronic health record: Wiring Europe's healthcare. *Computer Law & Security Review, 27*(5), 503–515. doi:10.1016/j.clsr.2011.07.013

Klonoff, D. (2017). Fog computing and edge computing architectures for processing data from diabetes devices connected to the medical Internet of Things. *Journal of Diabetes Science and Technology, 11*(4), 647–652. doi:10.1177/1932296817717007 PMID:28745086

Ma, Y., & Fang, Y. (2020). Current status, issues, and challenges of blockchain applications in education. *International Journal of Emerging Technologies in Learning, 15*(12), 20–31. doi:10.3991/ijet.v15i12.13797

Nakamoto, S. (2008). Bitcoin: A peer-to-peer electronic cash system. *Bitcoin.* https://bitcoin.org/bitcoin.pdf

Nasiri, S., Sadoughi, F., Tadayon, M. H., & Dehnad, A. (2019). Security requirements of Internet of Things-based healthcare system: A survey study. *Acta Informatica Medica, 27*(4), 253. doi:10.5455/aim.2019.27.253-258 PMID:32055092

Offner, K., Sitnikova, E., Joiner, K., & MacIntyre, C. (2020). Towards understanding cybersecurity capability in Australian healthcare organisations: A systematic review of recent trends, threats and mitigation. *Intelligence and National Security, 35*(4), 556–585. doi:10.1080/02684527.2020.1752459

Parisi, A. (2020). *Securing blockchain networks like Ethereum and Hyperledger Fabric* (1st ed.). Packt Publishing.

Pilkington, M. (2016). Blockchain technology: Principles and applications. In F. X. Olleros & M. Zhegu (Eds.), *Research handbook on digital transformations* (pp. 1–39). Edward Elgar. doi:10.4337/9781784717766.00019

Privacy Act. 1988 (Cth) part ii.6 (Austl.). (1988). https://www.legislation.gov.au/Details/C2014C00076

Seebacher, S., & Schüritz, R. (2017). Blockchain technology as an enabler of service systems: A structured literature review. *International Conference on Exploring Services Science*, 12–23. https://link.springer.com/chapter/10.1007/978-3-319-56925-3_2

Stamatellis, C., Papadopoulos, P., Pitropakis, N., Katsikas, S., & Buchanan, W. (2020). A privacy-preserving healthcare framework using Hyperledger Fabric. *Sensors (Basel), 20*(22), 1–14. doi:10.339020226587 PMID:33218022

Standards Australia. (2011). *Information security management in health using ISO/IEC 27002 (AS ISO 27799-2011).* Techstreet Enterprise.

Tanwar, S., Parekh, K., & Evans, R. (2020). Blockchain-based electronic healthcare record system for Healthcare 4.0 applications. *Journal of Information Security and Applications, 50*, 102407. doi:10.1016/j.jisa.2019.102407

Tapscott, D., & Tapscott, A. (2017). How blockchain will change organizations. *MIT Sloan Management Review, 58*(2), 10.

Thuemmler, C., & Bai, C. (2017). Health 4.0: Application of industry 4.0 design principles in future asthma management. In C. Thuemmler & C. Bai (Eds.), *Health 4.0: How virtualization and big data are revolutionizing healthcare* (pp. 23–37). Springer International Publishing. doi:10.1007/978-3-319-47617-9_2

Warkentin, M., & Orgeron, C. (2020). Using the security triad to assess blockchain technology in public sector applications. *International Journal of Information Management, 52*, 1–8. doi:10.1016/j.ijinfomgt.2020.102090

Yaga, D., Mell, P., Roby, N., & Scarfone, K. (2019). *Blockchain technology overview*. doi:10.6028/NIST.IR.8202

Chapter 5
My Health Record and Emerging Cybersecurity Challenges in the Australian Digital Environment

Anita Medhekar

https://orcid.org/0000-0002-6791-4056

Central Queensland University, Australia

ABSTRACT

The main aim of embracing evolutionary digital e-health technologies such as 'My Health Records' is to transform and empower the patients to control their health records, access, choose the right healthcare provider and suitable treatment, when required. It has been a challenge for the healthcare practitioners, hospital staff, as well as patients to accept, embrace, and adopt transformative digital e-health technologies and manage their healthcare records amidst concerns of slow adoption by the patient due to data privacy and cybersecurity issues. Australia, since COVID-19, has stressed the importance of secure online connectivity for the government, business, and the consumers. It is essential that My Health Record platform is cyber-safe, and user-friendly so that consumers feel conformable, safe and secure regarding their personal health records. This chapter discussed the challenges of embracing e-health digital technologies and assurance of advancing cybersecurity of online My Health Record, which will transform e-health provision and empower patients and healthcare providers.

INTRODUCTION

In the 21st century, developed countries such as Australia, has adopted digital transformation of healthcare records or e-health revolution for advancing cybersecurity, by implementing My Health Records to empower patients, and improve healthcare practice for clinicians and medical professionals, and provide positive experience to consumers at large. It has been a challenge for the healthcare practitioners, hospital staff as well as patients to accept, embrace, advance, and adopt digital e-health technologies and manage their healthcare records amidst concerns of slow adoption by the patient due to data privacy, security,

DOI: 10.4018/978-1-7998-6975-7.ch005

security of technical devices, user authentication, and Cybersecurity issues (Chandrakar, 2021; Coventry & Branley, 2018; Office of Australian Information Commissioner, 2021a; OAIC, 2021b; Pandey & Litoriya, 2020; Tanwar, Tyagi, & Kumar 2019). The main aim of advancing and embracing innovative digital e-health technologies such as health informatics and 'My health Records' is to transform and empower the patients to control their health records, choose the right healthcare provider and suitable treatment, without compromising the safety, privacy and security of private health data. Further, adoption of e-health records, helps in digitizing, maintaining and storing e-health records, and introduces ease of communication between the various healthcare departments through electronic data interchange for sharing information between the patient and the healthcare providers (Baldwin et al., 2017; Bhuyan et al., 2020; Kim & Johnston, 2002; Medhekar & Nguyen, 2020; Queensland Health, 2017; Sittig, 2002).

Given that the e-health revolution is driven by innovators of healthcare technologies, entrepreneurs, medical professionals, healthcare providers and government policy makers to bring about a transformative change in healthcare ecosystems. It is essential that e-health innovation such as My health Record platform is cyber-safe and user-friendly so that consumers as patients feel comfortable, safe, and secure regarding protection of their personal health-care records and diagnostic reports by the hospitals cloud system (Tanwar et al., 2019). Assurance of cybersecurity related to My Health Record' will help to change the patient experience and empower them to embrace e-health digital technologies and empower the patients to manage their own health records with positive healthcare experience and digitally transform health care delivery (Bhuyan et al., 2016; Coventry & Branley, 2018; Medhekar & Nguyen, 2020; Medhekar, 2021). On the 26th of November 2018, the Australian parliament passed the My Health Records amendment bill to protect the privacy of the people using the digital e-health system to meet the multi-layered privacy and cybersecurity standards and to protect the electronic health records system from malicious attacks from online hackers and cyber-criminals (Australian Digital Health Agency {ADHA}, 2019; Aunger, 2020). Since COVID-19 pandemic on one hand governments, business and consumers are increasingly depending on online delivery of business, goods and services; on the other hand cyber criminals are busy attacking the internet cloud information systems from all over the world, stealing money, identities, and sensitive finance, government, business, defense data, research facilities and healthcare data for ransom or stealing patient privacy (Bhuyan et al., 2020; Department of Home Affairs, 2020; Sharma & Purohit, 2018; William, Chaturvedi, & Chakravarthy, 2020).

My health records can only be accessed by the patient and the healthcare provider involved in treating patients, and registered with My Health Record System Operator, who are allowed by law to access patients My Health Record (Wood et al., 2013). For example, patients GP, specialist physician/surgeon, pharmacies for prescription medicine, pathology, hospitals, and allied healthcare professionals. The Queensland health has identified four key roles for digital technologies or e-health system. **(i)** *Promoting wellbeing* by thorough healthy behaviour to improving health of Queenslanders. **(ii)** *Delivering healthcare* by emphasizing access, equity, and quality in healthcare delivery for all. **(iii)** *Connecting healthcare* by tackling funding, policy, and delivery barriers, to make the health system work better for consumers and communities. **(iv)** *Pursuing innovation* by developing evidence-based models that work, promoting research and translating it into better healthcare practice (Queensland Health, 2017). Therefore, patient's healthcare data privacy and two- factor based user authentication is essential for data security, from cyber-attacks as it hinders patient care at all levels (Bhuyan et al., 2020; Chandrakar, 2021; Ehrenfeld, 2017; Jalali & Kaiser, 2018). According to William et al. (2020) in COVID-19 period cyber threats have increased fivefold and by the end of 2021, "cybersecurity threats are estimated to cost the world US $6 trillion" and healthcare organisations and health industry as a whole need to protect the sensitive health research and patient data from cyber-crimes. Healthcare organisations pay huge fines to department of justice for cybercrime related patients personal data breaches.

According to Harman et al. (2012) there are three major ethical requirements for electronic health records of the patients (i) privacy and confidentiality, (ii) security, and (iii) data integrity and availability for patient and providers use. Further, the global healthcare emergent COVID-19 pandemic, has also raised concerns of cybersecurity challenges, where the cyber-criminals are targeting healthcare providers, pharmaceuticals companies, medical research, academics, and government health departments to collect personal information, health related intellectual property which aligns with countries national security priorities (Aunger, 2020; William et al., 2020). According to HIPPA Journal (2019) USA, reported that in 2019, more than 500 healthcare data breaches took place from department of health and human services office, with an increase of 196% from 2018 breaches, where healthcare records of 12.55% of US population was exposed, disclosed or stolen by cybercrime attacks.

Digital transformation of the healthcare system records, and diagnostic reports has its benefits and opportunities of digitisation of health reports and records, for longitudinal studies, research, ease of communication between health departments and patient's history. However, it has to face many costs or challenges for keeping confidential private health records safe from cyber-threats and cyber-attacks from hackers, who could misuse the data for a ransom. Literature review also indicates publications on healthcare transformation to digitization of health reports and cybersecurity of digital health/e-health reports and My Health Records ' of healthcare organisations is relatively an emerging new area of research globally and in Australia (Jalali et al., 2019; Tanwar et al., 2019).

The key objective of this chapter is to explore the importance and significance of cybersecurity of e-health records and my health records of the patients. This chapter is structured as follows. The first introductory section of the chapter introduces the growing importance and significance of digital or e-health adoption and Cybersecurity concerns in Australia. Section two provides the literature review on e-health related My Health Record and Cybersecurity risk assessment and management. Section three discusses the example of Australia in adopting e-health strategies such as My Health Records and related Cybersecurity concerns. Section four discusses the challenges of my health records from cybersecurity threats, recommendations to improve cybersecurity of healthcare records, and policy implications proposing a *My Health Record and Cybersecurity Empowerment Model,* which can be empirically tested in the future with the proposed hypothesis. This is followed by future research directions to advance the knowledge in the field Cybersecurity of electronic My Health Records and conclusion.

Background: Literature Review

Medical records of the patients were traditionally paper, or file based with the doctor, in a legible handwriting. These medical records were in control of the hospital and the doctors who used for patient's treatment, clinical research, administrative and financial reason. Paper based records also had limitations in terms of storage and security (Harman, Flite, & Bond, 2012). Patients as well kept the information related to prescription medicines, x-ray, and reports of diagnostic tests. According to Greenlalgh et al. (2010) as we move from information-age to industrial-age, adoption of 'My Health Record' is a move from specialists-driven to patient-driven self-managed care, with an interactive digital platform of communication between the patient and the healthcare provider which is patient-centered care at all levels.

Since health informatics systems and digital e-health was introduced, patient data related to visits, prescriptions, diagnostic test results, treatment was electronically saved on healthcare providers super computers, and was easily accessed by the treating doctor and further there was electronic data interchange between the clinic and the diagnostic centers, which made it easy for healthcare decision making based on documentation of the patient's treatment.

Online My Health Record System was launched in Australia in 2018, where the consumers had the choice to opt-in or opt-out, as the history and treatment of patient is available on My Health Record system (ADHA, 2019), which could be susceptible to cyber-crime or cyber-attack hindering patient care (Bogle, 2018; Coventry & Branley, 2018; Ehrenfeld, 2017). A study by Torrens and Walker (2017) found that females were more likely to register and use the online My Health Records than males. Moreover, middle-aged males, older females and adolescents of both sexes had lowest registration and uptake of My Health Record due to digital literacy and online security concerns. Therefore, cybersecurity, safety, and privacy of patient's personal health records, is of concern to the patients as consumers, medical professionals, health informatics managers, and government healthcare system.

My Health Record

My Health Record is defined by ADHA (2019), as an online summary of key health information of the patients, which can be recorded and tracked over time in a safe online environment. These electronic health records can be viewed in a secure online environment from anywhere in the world and can be accessed on any device with an internet connection. When a patient visits a doctor, or is in an emergency, unable to talk, healthcare providers can access the information related to patients' allergies, prescription medicine, health history, medical conditions, medical images and pathology diagnostic tests results to provide appropriate treatment for getting the best outcomes for the patient. Healthcare providers and doctors can access patient's important health care information if they cannot talk under anesthetic, to know about patient's prescription medicine, allergies, family history of diseases, pathology and radiology tests results and medical condition for diagnosis and treatment plan (ADHA, 2019).

My Health Record system was originally called as the personally administered electronic health record (PCEHR), of the Australian citizens, which was launched by the Australian Government nationwide in July 2012, with an opt-in or opt-out model provided by National E-Health Transition Authority. By the end of 2012, nearly 2.6 million (11%) had registered, and since March 2016, it was relaunched as 'My Health Record' an opt-out model operated by Digital Health Agency (Department of Health, 2016). My health record is covered by four key regulatory acts introduced by the Australian Commonwealth Government for administration related to use, privacy and regulation of 'My Health Records' system. **(i)** *Healthcare Identifier Act 2010,* **(ii)** *My Health Record Act 2012',* **(iii)** *My Health Record Regulations 2012, and* **(iv)** *My Health Record Rule 2016, and Privacy Act 1988* to provide access, identify the user, privacy and confidentiality of patient records, and the rules governing the electronic health records (Australian Government, 2016a; Commonwealth of Australia, 2012 & 2015). In 2019, Amendment to the Privacy Act 1988 was passed by the Morrison Government to tighten the cybersecurity. In 2020, the Morrison government introduced the 2020- Cyber Security Strategy, replacing the 2016-Cyber Security Strategy which has been a catalyst for change, launching a series of government and private sector activities and responses to cyber-security and cyber-crime challenges (Department of Home Affairs, 2020).

The Australian national participation rate for uptake of My Health Record as at 28th of July 2019, reported by the Australian Government was 90.1 percent. This is the rate of people who chose not to opt-out as a percentage of those who meet the eligibility criteria for Medicare (Australian Government, 2019). State wise participation rate and uptake of My Health Records across Australia is as follows: Northern

Territory (93.6%), Queensland (91.2%), Western Australia (90.4%), Tasmania (90.3), New South Wales (90.2%), South Australia (89.3%), Victoria (89.3), and Australian Capital Territory (86.7%). Overall an approximate number of 16,400 healthcare provider organisations have registered with My Health Record (Australian Government, 2019). The number and types of health care providers organisation registered are as follows: General Practice Organisations (7,240), Pharmacies (4770), Other Categories of healthcare providers Including Allied Health (2960), Public Hospitals and Health Services (832), Aged Care Residential Services (239), Private Hospitals and Clinics (190), Pathology and Diagnostic Imaging Clinics (119) Services (Australian Government, 2019).

Electronic health reports on My Health Record, shares confidential patient information with all healthcare staff involved in treating a patient at all levels of care. It helps to improve the flow of information between the Doctor-GP, the specialists and the patients. This may also help to improve patient treatment outcomes. Patients can choose to share the information with their healthcare providers, manage My Health Records by deleting or adding information, choosing privacy and security settings by adding personal notes regarding allergies, care-plan, set access control to restrict access to who can and cannot see your health information, review healthcare information that doctors can see and set-up e-mail and SMS notification. This helps to provide detail picture of health history, diagnosis, and treatment plan (ADHA, 2019). Concerns have been raised by the public regarding cybersecurity of personal data on My Health Record since the one and a half million Singaporean nationals, including the prime ministers my health personal records were hacked in July 2018 as reported by the British Broadcasting Corporation (BBC, 2010). Therefore protecting the privacy and security of patients My Health Record from misuse, cyber-attack, and cyber-crimes is crucial.

Cybersecurity

Cybersecurity is defined by Merriam-Webster dictionary as "measure taken to protect a computer or computer system on the internet against unauthorized access or attack". Cybersecurity of patients online 'My Health Records' which is an electronic record of patient's meetings with the general practitioner, specialist, nursing staff, results of diagnostic reports, blood tests, x-ray, allergies, prescription medicine records at one central place. These sensitive health records stored in cloud can be accessed on demand by the medical practitioner and the patients with access to internet, on any device, anytime, anywhere in the world. It helps to keep check on our health over our lifetime (Regola & Chawla, 2013; Varadharajan, 2018). Electronic health records therefore can be accessed and viewed by many stakeholders at the same time, using various information technology and electronic tools in a timely manner to improve patient treatment outcomes. However, the rich healthcare information of the organisations and sensitive patient data is susceptible to cyber security breaches of patient privacy and safety and for financial gains by the hackers (Conaty-Buck, 2017; Perakslis, 2020; Rowe, Lunt, & Ekstrom, 2011).

These personal e-health or 'My health Records' are managed by the patients to restrict access to some, or all health records stored. However, in an emergency the doctor can override the safeguard to access information to provide the best care to the patient. This also requires everyone to have access to internet connection, smart phones, and laptop. Two studies- Zurita and Nøhr (2004) in New Zealand and Chhanabhai and Holt (2007) in Denmark, found that patients were concerned about the privacy, safety, and security of their personal e-health records from cyber-attackers. Fernández-Alemán, Carrión Señor, Lozoya and Toval (2013) conducted a systematic review of literature around security of e-health record, and concluded from 49 articles that, security and privacy of patient's electronic health records and regulation around security and privacy policy is a concern given that countries are moving away from paper-based to online integrated electronic health records.

According to Kelly (2020), healthcare sector in Australia reported in 2018 the highest incidence of health data security breaches, because Australia does not have US-Style mandatory security standards and regulations for the protection of private electronic health information. The costs to the patient in terms of loss of trust in organisations in protecting their privacy and safety of sensitive personal health data, including the healthcare organisations of cybersecurity breaches are enormous. Conaty-Buck (2017) has summarized the costs of cybersecurity breaches to United States electronic healthcare records systems, in terms of fines, and the average cost of breach per record is US $380. For example **(i)** Advocate health care had four stolen laptops, and data of 4 million patients was breached, and had to incur a fine of US $5.55 million. **(ii)** Anthem in Indiana state paid fine of US $115 million, as 80 million patients' private data was breached containing social security, birthdates, names, address, e-mail, employment, and income information. **(iii)** Alaska department of health and social services was fined 1.7 million due to stolen USB drive containing patient's personal health information. **(iv)** New York, Presbyterian hospital and Columbia University was fined 4.8 Million, because a physician left data insecure in an attempt to deactivate a personal computer. **(v)** Oregon Health and Science University was fined US $ 2.7 million for cyber security breaches of 7000 patient's health records from stolen laptops and data stored in an unapproved and insure google cloud system.

Therefore patients are concerned about the safety and privacy of their e-health records in terms of who has access and permission to use their personal health records and for what purposes as justified by a study conducted by Atienza et al. (2015). Consumers as patients are concerned about unauthorized access, control, misuse and sharing of their confidential health data with healthcare providers in a trustworthy manner. Further, a quantitative survey in Queensland by Gajanayake and Sahama (2014), where they surveyed 750 Australian participants, up to the age of 65. These participants had opted out and not used My Health Records due to the lack of trust in the e-health system, perceived risk of cybersecurity issues, involved in using and sharing the online health record system, and privacy and confidentiality breaches by healthcare providers and users of their personal health records.

Moreover, technologies developed by Australia Cyber–Security Engineering Research Centre can be used to protect the personal health records data by encryption and at the same time allow the users that is the patients and the healthcare providers to access the data, and the administrator of the cloud can have access to data only if provided by the patient (Pavithra & Chandrasekaran, 2021; Regola & Chawla, 2013; Zhou, Varadharajan, & Gopinath, 2016). The global patients or medical travelers also have to exchange medical data and diagnostic health reports via shared cloud storage provided by the international hospitals treating foreign patients which is password protected, before they travel abroad for surgery. Patients therefore have to have internet knowledge regarding uploading files, reports and security identification (Medhekar & Wong, 2020). Further, Varadharajan (2018) also mentions about the literacy of the users of my health records that is the patients and provider's literacy and healthcare stakeholders, capability and competency in setting preferences and strong privacy controls by default, to protect the data from cyberattack.

Further, a qualitative pilot study by Kerai, Wood, and Martin (2014), where they interviewed 80 senior citizens in Australia to know their perspective on usage of electronic health record. Kerai et al. (2014) study found that due to lack of knowledge of online usage of My Health Records, 84% of the participants were not ready to take on the responsibility of using the system and preferred their general practitioner's medical practice to manage their health records. Furthermore, from clinician's perspective, an Australian study with 26 clinicians from three large hospitals found that hospital clinician staff were not trained to use and understand the information and regulation related to privacy and security implementation effectively and identify confidential and sensitive private information of the patients. This resulted in suboptimal patient safety, security of patient private data, and healthcare outcomes (Fernando & Dawson, 2009). Therefore, cyber-attackers can demand ransom from hospitals, resulting in appointments being cancelled, delayed surgeries impacting the total healthcare system- as it happened in 2017 in United Kingdom, putting the patients in life and death situation (Bogle, 2018).

Various articles have discussed the application and benefits of innovative and transformative blockchain technology in bio-medical and healthcare industry for security, privacy of patient information, transparency, and integrating consumers health records and efficient access by the users – healthcare providers and the patients (Kuo, Kim, & Ohno-Machado, 2017; Krawiec & White 2016; Schumacher, 2017; Tanwar Parekh & Evans, 2020; Zhang et al., 2018). In terms of innovation in cybersecurity systems, Pandey and Litoriya (2020), provide a conceptualized ecosystem of blockchain technology in digital healthcare design in their research and suggest that a centralised system of keeping health records is more vulnerable and easy single point of contact for cyber-crime and failure of communication. Whereas a complex decentralized and innovative blockchain technology is computationally expensive using cryptographic algorithms, with multiple coordinator nodes, which can maintain communication, if one fails, or is hacked. In the age of data insecurity, decentralized blockchain technology distribution system is therefore more reliable in providing patient centered care in terms of security, transparency, privacy, safety and inter-operationality of patient's e-healthcare data in the healthcare system, which is continuously updated and securely stored.

Qualitative research by Jalali and Kaiser (2018), where they interviewed 19 participants such as hospitals chief medical officers, and hospital cyber security officers and cyber security experts to understand hospitals cybersecurity capabilities to protect hospital and patient's data from cyber-crime. They found that the risk of cyber-attack in the hospital comes from end point complexity and internal hospital users/stakeholder's alignment. Therefore cybersecurity capabilities-gap can be closed if all hospitals not only devote equitable mount of resources to enhance and upgrade the entire healthcare industry cybersecurity infrastructure to protect e-health records from cyber-crime, but also reduce end point complexity and improve internal hospital users/stakeholder's alignment of hospitals and patient's healthcare data from cyber-attackers.

Given the cybersecurity issues since COVID-19 has come to the forefront of all countries including the Australian government's overall security strategy, on the 6th of August 2020, the Australian Government released the Australia's Cyber Security Strategy-2020. The strategy aims to invest Aus $1.67 billion over the 10 years to create a cyber-secure and safe online environment for the Australian citizens, businesses and the three levels of government. Australia's Cyber Security Strategy-2020 was a consultative process, face-to-face, workshops, roundtables and bilateral meetings. It is to be implemented through actions taken by the Australian government, business and the community to ensure and protect the essential services of all Australians, by upgrading the security and resilience of critical cyber security online infrastructure facilities of national significance (Department of Home Affairs, 2020). **(i)** Governments action to strengthen the protection of Australians, businesses and critical infrastructure from the most sophisticated threats. **(ii)** Businesses action to secure their products and services and protect their customers from known cyber vulnerabilities. **(iii)** Community action to practice secure online behaviours and make informed purchasing decisions (Department of Home Affairs, 2020).

Cybersecurity- AustrAlia My Health Records

My Health Records shares information with patents and physician/clinicians, which also engages patients in managing their healthcare issues and records related to sickness, diagnostic results x-rays, and prescribed medications. It is essential that patients have e-health literacy in the use of internet and eHealth record portals to engage and manage their online health records to improve self-management of healthcare (Baldwin et al., 2017; Coughlin et al., 2018; Greenlee, 2021). Medical imaging devices for example ultra-sound, CT-scan and MRI machines have also gone through digital transformation and innovation and link digital images and reports of diagnostic tests of the patients with My Health Records and can be obtained from computer desktop. Therefore, digital imaging technology should be built with cybersecurity firewalls in place, as diagnostic reports are also faced with cyber-threats from cyber-attackers' who may steal private sensitive patient data for a ransom. These attacks can range from insider threats, data breaches, e-mail scams, phishing attacks, ransomware and distributed denial of service attack (Greenlee, 2021; Langer, 2017; Nigrin, 2014).

A mixed methods study in England by Greenlalgh et al. (2010) found that patients perceived online Health- Space neither useful nor easy to use to self-manage their health records. Policy makers according to their study hoped that adopting HealthSpace will empower patients, lower NHS costs, provide better quality of data, personalize healthcare, and improve patient health literacy. Australian study found that, protection of private data, ease of use of e-Health records, lack of interest and lack of integration of health records with the existing health systems, privacy and security of personal information of the patent is critical for the health consumer and healthcare professionals (Andrews et al., 2014; Lehnbom, McLachlan, & Brien, 2012).

Findings from Australian Commission on Safety and Quality in Health Care {ACSQHC}, commissioned report by Shaw, Hines, and Kielly-Carroll (2017) identified five key areas of digital health interventions: (**i**) electronic patient portals, (**ii**) Electronic patient reminders on mobile phone technologies, (**iii**) information-sharing by electronic discharge summaries, (**iv**)computerized provider order entry and electronic prescription, and (**v**) clinical decision support systems. Given these high levels of e-health and digital intervention, it is essential to build trust, for safety and security to protect patients e-health data from cyber-crime and online-hackers, better planning by healthcare organizations and government health departments is required to prevent cyber breaches.

Bhuyan et al. (2020), have identified seven types of health organisation related cyber-attacks and motivation of cyber-criminals behind these attacks. (**i**) *Denial-of-Services* (DoS), which is prevent access by shutting down the entire network of healthcare organizations for example 2014 Boston's children's hospitals DoS attack, disrupting network of various healthcare organizations sharing information. (**ii**) *Privilege Escalation Attacks* are vertical and horizontal to have access to highest level of information, compromising patient's safety. (**iii**) *Eavesdropping Attack* or man in the middle (MITM), when communication is intercepted by a third party compromising the integrity of the healthcare data communicated, by gaining access to patients' confidential information for blackmail. (**iv**) *Cryptographic Attack*, to decrypt encrypted information which can be understood by the sender and the receiver. (**v**) *Structured Query Language (SQL)* can be exploited by the hackers to alter the information of the patients in the database, affecting availability, integrity and authenticity of the healthcare information stored in hospital information system. (**vi**) *Malware or malicious software attack* .The examples of *Malware/ malicious software* are *Virus, Trojans, spyware, ransomware, Phishing, and worms.* They are designed to harm the computer system without the knowledge of the user and infect virus on other computer systems through user activation, by deleting and corrupting files and stored data. For example in 2017, malware attack shut down the Medical Centre at Erie country New York.

There are many benefits of adopting e-health technologies to the clinicians as well as to empower the patients to manage their own health records. However, there are also many challenges in terms of internet health literacy, and key stakeholders' responsibility in ensuring privacy and Cybersecurity of patient's personal health history and data (ADHA, 2019; Russo et al., 2016; Sittig, Belmont, & Singh, 2018). According to Davidson (2019), My Health Record failed to manage cybersecurity and privacy risk audit. Literature review indicates publications on Cybersecurity of My Health Records from cyber criminals is relatively an emerging new area of research. The Vision of Cyber Security Strategy-2020 is to provide "A more secure online world for Australians, their businesses and the essential services upon which we all depend". This cybersecurity is to be delivered by complementary action taken by the government, businesses and community to protect accessing of sensitive defense, health, research, information and data for financial gains, dark-web crimes, exploitation of children and vulnerable people, and other crime by cyber-criminals and hackers. The next section summaries challenges of cybersecurity and provides few recommendations to deal with the issues related to cybersecurity of My Health Records (Department of Home Affairs, 2020).

SOLUTIONS AND RECOMMENDATIONS

Emerging Cybersecurity Challenges

Medical practice is increasingly depending on information systems and becoming information-intensive using various applications for doctors' appointments to medical alerts and notification including, My Health Records. Information Systems managers, Cybersecurity managers, healthcare providers and patients face many challenges of securing sensitive private healthcare records from misuse by cyber-criminals.

1. *Technological and Digital Competency:* General practitioners, physicians, nurses and specialist surgeons need to have skills and expertise in clinical practice as well as be technologically competent. Therefore, continuous information systems skilling and training is requited to be able to use the information system and various electronic health records and applications.
2. *Back-up Digitized Health Records:* Digitized personal health records are prone to cyber-crime and security issues. It is essential, that digitized health records are backed-up in more than one place to prevent loss of healthcare records and data required for treatment and medical research.
3. *Cybersecurity and Privacy:* With increasing digitization of health records and automation of health-related appointments and applications the downside is the cybersecurity and privacy issues related with the My Health Records of the patients.
4. *Medical Imaging Devices and Cybersecurity: M*edical imaging devices have improved patient care and healthcare outcomes. However, medical imaging technology and equipment such as CT-scan and MRI machines need to have built-in innovative cybersecurity alerts, multi-layered protection, and firewalls to protect the personals sensitive healthcare and medical-imaging data from cyber-threats, e-mail scams and phishing attacks.
5. *My Health Record User Literacy, training and Empowerment:* The stakeholders and users of My Health Records, are continuously updated by the user and cyber security policy which empowers

them to keep or delete and provide access to their personal health records such as general practitioners. Therefor consumers have to be aware of the definitions of the following terms and how cyber-crime hackers attack the internet devices using various tools: such as **(i)** *Virus* which infects software and reproduces copies when it is opened; **(ii)** *Worm* infects software and spreads without the user taking any actions. **(iii)** *Trojan* contains malware, which acts when downloaded and opened. **(iv)** *Ransom-ware*, allows the users to access their system or encrypts files until a ransom has been paid. (v) *Rootkits* hide malware from antivirus detection and removal programs. (vi) *Keystroke* logger program records user keystrokes, to acquire passwords. (vii) *Adware* produces a code which automatically download malware.

6. *Public-Private- Partnerships (PPPs)*: Challenge of partnerships between the key stakeholder's government, regulators, healthcare organisations, community, individuals for cybersecurity regulation, planning and implementation are required to prevent health organisations cyber-breaches of sensitive healthcare data.

RECOMMENDATIONS

The following recommendations in dealing with the issues, controversies, or problems presented in the preceding section can be made related to cybersecurity of My Health Records.

1. *Cybersecurity Alarm:* In case of cybercrime or hacking of the personal healthcare records, the information system to check cyber -crime thoroughly, should have a built-in system for alerting the user via a firewall alarm, so that all systems automatically close down to protect the data from cybercrime, prevent data manipulation, and preserve sensitive health records along with backup facilities.

2. *Alerts for Health Data Entry Errors:* It is important that health data entry by the healthcare professionals is correct when it is shared through electronic data interchange (EDI) system between different healthcare departments such as doctors' clinics, hospital, diagnostic clinics, rehab centers and aged-care institutions and health systems for accurate data integrity at all levels. Cyber-attack alerts set in place can warn any suspicious cyber-criminal attack.

3. *Software Menu Choices:* Various items related to drop down menu choices available in the software have to be increased, so clinicians can make an appropriate choice of the problem as per the diagnosis, so that the original health data is preserved and there are no system errors due to incorrect choice made in a hurry from the drop-down menu.

4. *Innovative Data System:* Continuous innovation and improvement in the e-health data systems and cyber-security software will result in security of e-health records, better healthcare outcomes, greater efficiency in healthcare delivery and more effective research into e-healthcare and digital health.

5. *Digital Health Partnerships:* Australian Digital Health Authority could seek global partnerships in order to engage with Global Digital Health, for implementing and ensuring cybersecurity and safety of patient's e-health records, including cyber-security related education and training.

6. *Cybersecurity Training:* Consumers, clinicians, health-care professional staff and administrators need to go through online education and security training of usage and protection related to cyber security of healthcare data. Regular upgrade training and alerts should be made available to the

users, confirmation with a tick that the information or training has been completed, with a small quiz, before we access or log-on to My Health Records platform for cybersecurity education and training.

7. *Re-Engineering Healthcare Cybersecurity:* National government should invest to continuously re-engineer and improve e-health cybersecurity. Funds should be allocated for cybersecurity education provided by cybersecurity experts and professionals. It is also essential to have updated innovation and technological improvement to protect healthcare data from cyber-threat and hackers. Hospitals and healthcare clinics are at greater risk due to shortage of funds allocated to keep up-to-date with the latest cyber-security technology, software upgrade and training.

8. *Cybersecurity Awareness Culture:* Healthcare professionals and workers at the clinics, diagnostic centers, hospitals, aged-care institutions, need to embed a culture of awareness of cybersecurity of healthcare reports, data and medical imaging records with the aim to protect patient privacy, prevent cyber-crime, preserve records, and back-up healthcare reports and records.

9. *Cybersecurity Awareness and Education:* Consumers as users of My Health Records, online banking, shopping, and using other internet applications and cloud storage, should build cyber-security awareness as part of their daily life when using internet applications, and acquire online cyber-security awareness education and information related to cybersecurity, antivirus software program and protecting their data from unauthorized access and cyber- crime. Most of the government health departments, provide cybersecurity related resources for individuals and use by the professionals in organizations. Various tips and steps for cybersecurity awareness of My Health Records are necessary to follow as suggested by Conaty-Buck (2017) as it is everyone's business to be aware of cybercrime and be safe. Such as: choosing a secure password, not opening and therefore deleting e-mails and attachments from unknown people, using data encryptions for all internet connected devices, downloading security updates, educate oneself and others, reporting any suspicious e-mails to organisations information technology (IT) department, and while accessing resources "Stop, Think and Connect" steps to be followed, to be safe and secure from cyber-crime.

10. *Adoption of Blockchain Technology in Healthcare:* Sharing peer-to-peer healthcare related data between pharmaceuticals industry, healthcare providers and hospitals, health insurance providers and consumers in a secure manner, without the fear of breach can be done by adopting blockchain technology. It can save healthcare sector millions of dollars in costs related to cybercrime data breaches in operations, IT costs, support services, and personnel. Blockchain technology can help the health sector in recording accurately each and every medical and cash transaction, storing and securely data sharing, and transfer between devices and healthcare providers, thus ensuring cybersecurity and preventing sensitive data breaches. It also helps to find right patients for medical trials for the pharmaceutical companies and enhances healthcare related supply chain operations management (Tanwar et al., 2019).

The following hypothesis is proposed for future research on My Health Record Cybersecurity survey based on Figure-1.

H-1: *Technological and Digital Competency will positively improve My Health Record Cybersecurity Empowerment.*

H-2: *Cybersecurity Awareness Culture will positively improve My Health Record Cybersecurity Empowerment.*

H-3: *Cybersecurity Training will positively improve My Health Record Cybersecurity Empowerment.*

H-4: *Cybersecurity Alarm Recognition will positively improve My Health Record Cybersecurity Empowerment.*

H-5: *My Health Record Cybersecurity Stakeholder Communication will positively improve My Health Record Cybersecurity Empowerment.*

H-6: *My Health Record Cybersecurity Digital Health Partnerships will enhance and positively improve My Health Record Cybersecurity Empowerment.*

Figure-1 provides a model for My Health Record and Cybersecurity, which can be tested via qualitative interviews with the stakeholders and quantitative survey for future research. Figure-1 illustrates that My Health Records cybersecurity depends on the six dimensions such as **(i)** Technological and Digital Competency, **(ii)** Cybersecurity Awareness Culture, **(iii)** Cybersecurity Training, **(iv)** Cybersecurity Alarm Recognition, **(v)** MHR-Cybersecurity Stakeholder Communication, and **(vi)** MHR- Cybersecurity Digital Health Partnerships between the regulators, three levels of government, businesses, and the community.

Figure 1. My Health Record and Cybersecurity Empowerment Model
Source: Developed for this Chapter

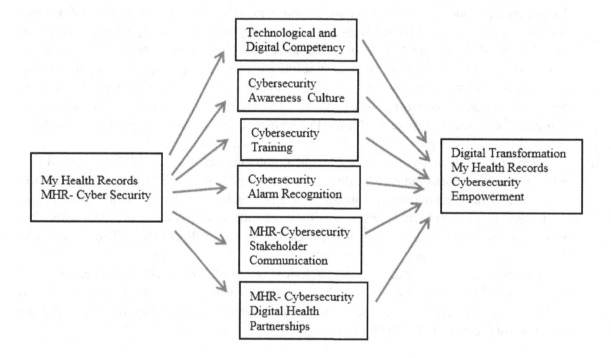

FUTURE RESEARCH DIRECTIONS

Given the reliance of consumers, business and governments on internet technology and its devices such computers, iPad and mobile phones including various applications, safety and cybersecurity of personal, business and government data is a very challenging issue. All the sectors such as My Health Records, banking, finance, defense, education, businesses corporations, tax office, including governments have gone through digital transformation in context of the use of the internet for online business transactions and cloud computing data storage. The use of internet and various applications has increased since March 2020 pandemic and increasingly businesses and retails sector have shown online presence to sell goods and services to reach out to their customers during lockdown and keep their business afloat. Similarly various health, general practitioners, education and legal consulting services are also relying heavily on the internet and communication technologies, various applications and cloud storage to share documents with the customers. The future and emerging trends is all about cybersecurity of internet transactions, sensitive documents, personal data of health records, and data storage. Future research opportunities can focus on conducting one to one interview with Step-1: the key stakeholders'- users of My Health Record system from the health sector such as health informatics, information technology maintenance staff responsible for Cybersecurity, information health-care providers, doctors, nurses, and administrators. Step-2 one to one interview with consumers as stakeholders and users of My Health Records. Step 3: Applying the Conceptual Model of My Health Record and the proposed hypothesis, by developing the items to operationalize the cybersecurity constructs related to My Health Record and conducting an online survey.

CONCLUSION

The chapter covers consumer's personal health data on 'My Health Record' related cybersecurity issues and challenges in Australia. Many Australians have opted out of My Health Record, due to concerns related to Cybersecurity issues personal and sensitive health data related privacy, confidentiality on the internet and possibility of cyber-criminals hacking the personal health information of millions of citizens. Cybersecurity is on the agenda of all the governments since 2020, COVID -19 year, given the changing geo-political environment to protect the strategic government data, business data and individual citizens My Health Records, finance and other personal data with tax and social security systems.

This chapter covered increasing adoption of digital e-health technologies such as health informatics and 'My Health Records' to transform and empower the patients to control their health records, have access choose the right healthcare provider and suitable treatment, when required. It has been a challenge for the healthcare practitioners, hospital staff as well as patients to accept, embrace and adopt transformative digital e-health technologies and manage their healthcare records amidst concerns of slow adoption by the patient due to data privacy and cybersecurity issues. This chapter discussed the challenges of embracing e-health digital technologies and assurance of advancing cybersecurity of individuals My Health Record', which will transform e-health provision and experience for patients and the healthcare providers. It is time to continually re-engineer and upgrade cybersecurity firewalls and technology with the aim to meet patients and health sectors needs to protect patient privacy and confidential healthcare data and medical images from cyber-crime. Professional staff of information technology and cybercrime division along with healthcare professionals, government, regulators, businesses and community should work in partnership to protect health information without sacrificing and compromising patient's data privacy and security, and strengthen cyber security at all levels.

REFERENCES

Andrews, L., Gajanayake, R., & Sahama, T. (2014). The Australian general public's perceptions of having a personally controlled electronic health record. *International Journal of Medical Informatics, 83*(12), 889–900. doi:10.1016/j.ijmedinf.2014.08.002 PMID:25200198

Atienza, A. A., Zarcadoolas, C., Vaughon, W., Hughes, P., Patel, V., Chou, W.-Y., & Pritts, J. (2015). Consumer Attitudes and Perceptions on mHealth Privacy and Security: Findings from a Mixed-Methods Study. *Journal of Health Communication, 20*(6), 673–679. doi:10.1080/10810730.2015.1018560 PMID:25868685

Aunger, C. (2020). *It's Time to Re-engineer Healthcare Cybersecurity. Forbes Technology Council.* Available from www.forbes.com/sites/forbestechcouncil/2020/08/05/its-time-to-re-engineer-health-care-cybersecurity/?sh=e74c6f412784

Australian Digital Health Agency (ADHA). (2019). *My Health Record.* Available from https://www.myhealthrecord.gov.au/for-you-your-family/what-is-my-health-record

Australian Government. (2016). *MyHRCs Rule 2016.* Available from https://www.legislation.gov.au/Details/F2016C00607

Australian Government. (2019). *My Health Record Statistics.* Available from https://www.myhealthrecord.gov.au/sites/default/files/my_health_record_dashboard_-_28_july_2019.pdf?v=1565831963

Baldwin, J. L., Singh, H., Sittig, D. F., & Giardina, T. D. (2017). Patient portals and health apps: Pitfalls, promises, and what one might learn from the other. *Health Care, 5*(3), 81–85. PMID:27720139

Bhuyan, S. S., Bailey-DeLeeuw, S., Wyant, D. K., & Chang, C. F. (2016). Too Much or Too Little? How Much Control Should Patients Have Over EHR Data? *Journal of Medical Systems, 40*(7), 174. doi:10.100710916-016-0533-2 PMID:27272134

Bhuyan, S. S., Kabir, U. Y., Escarino, J. M., Ector, K., Palakodeti, S., ... Dobalian, A. (2020). Transforming Healthcare Cybersecurity from Reactive to Proactive: Current Status and Future Recommendations. *Journal of Medical Systems, 44*(98), 98. Advance online publication. doi:10.100710916-019-1507-y PMID:32239357

Bogle, A. (2018). *Healthcare data a growing target for hackers, cybersecurity experts warn.* Available from https://www.abc.net.au/news/science/2018-04-18/healthcare-target-for-hackers-experts-warn/9663304

Chandrakar, P. (2021). A Secure Remote User Authentication Protocol for Healthcare Monitoring Using Wireless Medical Sensor Networks. In *Research Anthology on Telemedicine Efficacy* (pp. 549–572). Adoption, and Impact on Healthcare Delivery. www.igi-global.com/chapter/a-secure-remote-user-authentication-protocol-for-healthcaremonitoring-using-wireless-medical-sensor-networks/

Commonwealth of Australia. (2012). *MyHRCs Act 2012 (Australia).* Available from https://www.legislation.gov.au/Series/C2012A00063

Commonwealth of Australia. (2015). *MyHRCs Regulation 2012 (Australia)*. Available from https://www. legislation.gov.au/Details/F2016C00093

Conaty-Buck, S. (2017). Cyber security and healthcare records. Tips for ensuring patient safety and privacy. *American Nurse Today, 12*(9), 62–65.

Coventry, L., & Branley, D. (2018). Cybersecurity in healthcare: A narrative review of trends, threats and ways forward. *Maturitas, 113*, 48–52. doi:10.1016/j.maturitas.2018.04.008 PMID:29903648

Davidson, H. (2019). My Health Record failed to manage cybersecurity and privacy risk- audit finds. *The Guardian.* Available from https://www.theguardian.com/australia-news/2019/nov/25/my-health-record-failed-to-manage-cybersecurity-and-privacy-risks-audit-finds

Department of Health. (2016, March). MyHRC *Stastics*. Canberra: Australian Government. Available from https://myhealthrecord.gov.au/internet/mhr/publishing.nsf/

Department of Home Affairs. (2020). *Australia's Cyber Security Strategy*. Available from https://www. homeaffairs.gov.au/about-us/our-portfolios/cyber-security/strategy

Ehrenfeld, J. M. (2017). WannaCry, Cybersecurity and Health Information Technology: A time to act. *Journal of Medical Systems, 41*(7), 104. doi:10.100710916-017-0752-1 PMID:28540616

Fernández-Alemán, J. L., Carrión Señor, I., Lozoya, P. L. O., & Toval, A. (2013). Security and privacy in electronic health records: A systematic literature review. *Journal of Biomedical Informatics, 46*(3), 541–562. doi:10.1016/j.jbi.2012.12.003 PMID:23305810

Fernando, J., & Dawson, L. (2009). The health information system security threat lifecycle: An informatics theory. *International Journal of Medical Informatics, 78*(12), 815–826. doi:10.1016/j.ijmedinf.2009.08.006 PMID:19783203

Greenlalgh, T., Hinder, S., Stramere, K., Bratan, T., & Russell, J. (2010). Adoption, non-adoption, and abandonment of a personal electronic health record: Case study of HealthSpace. *Biomedical Journal, 341*, c5814. doi:10.1136/bmj.c581 PMID:21081595

Greenlee, M. (2021). *Cybersecurity for Healthcare: Addressing Medical Image Privacy*. Available from https://securityintelligence.com/articles/cybersecurity-for-healthcare-problems-and-solutions/

Harman, L. B., Flite, C. A., & Bond, K. (2012). Electronic Health Records: Privacy, Confidentiality, and Security. *AMA Journal of Ethics, 14*(9), 712–719. doi:10.1001/virtualmentor.2012.14.9.stas1-1209 PMID:23351350

HIPPA Journal. (2019). *2019 Healthcare Data Breach Report*. Available from https://www.hipaajournal. com/2019-healthcare-data-breach-report/

Jalali, M. S., & Kaiser, J. P. (2018). Cybersecurity in Hospitals: A Systematic, Organizational Perspective. *Journal of Medical Internet Research, 20*(5), e10059. doi:10.2196/10059 PMID:29807882

Jalali, M. S., Razak, S., Gordon, W., Perakslis, E., & Madnick, S. (2019). Health care and cybersecurity: Bibliometric analysis of the literature. *Journal of Medical Internet Research*, *21*(2), e12644. doi:10.2196/12644 PMID:30767908

Kelly, J. M. (2020). Australia would benefit from US-Style health Information Security regulation. *The Journal of Law and Technology*, *1*(2), 1–24.

Kerai, P., Wood, P., & Martin, M. (2014). A pilot study on the views of elderly regional Australians of personally controlled electronic health records. *International Journal of Medical Informatics*, *83*(3), 201–209. doi:10.1016/j.ijmedinf.2013.12.001 PMID:24382474

Kim, M. I., & Johnston, K. B. (2002). Personal Health Records: Evaluation of Functionality and Utility. *Journal of the American Medical Informatics Association: JAMIA*, *9*(2), 171–180. doi:10.1197/jamia. M0978 PMID:11861632

Krawiec, R., & White, M. (2016). *Blockchain: Opportunities for health care*. Available from: https://www2.deloitte.com/content/dam/Deloitte/us/Documents/public-sector/us-blockchainopportunities-for-health-care.pdf

Kuo, T. T., Kim, H. E., & Ohno-Machado, L. (2017). Blockchain distributed ledger technologies for biomedical and health care applications. *Journal of the American Medical Informatics Association: JAMIA*, *24*(6), 1211–1220. doi:10.1093/jamia/ocx068 PMID:29016974

Langer, G. (2017). Cybersecurity Issues in Healthcare Information Technology. *Journal of Digital Imaging*, *30*(1), 117–125. doi:10.100710278-016-9913-x PMID:27730416

Lehnbom, E. C., McLachlan, A., & Brien, J. A. (2012). A qualitative study of Australians' opinions about personally controlled electronic health records. *Studies in Health Technology and Informatics*, *178*, 105–110. PMID:22797027

Medhekar, A. (2021). Digital Health Innovation Enhancing Patient Experience in Medical Travel. In *Research Anthology on Telemedicine Efficacy, Adoption, and Impact on Healthcare Delivery. Edition1* (pp. 199–223). IGI Global. doi:10.4018/978-1-7998-8052-3.ch011

Medhekar, A., & Nguyen, J. (2020). My Digital Healthcare Record: Innovation, Challenge and Patient Empowerment. In K. Sandhu (Ed.), *Opportunities and Challenges in Digital Healthcare Innovation* (pp. 131–150). IGI Global., doi:10.4018/978-1-7998-3274-4.ch008

Medhekar, A., & Wong, H. (2020). Medical Travellers' Perspective on Factors Affecting Medical Tourism to India. *Asia Pacific Journal of Tourism Research*, *25*(12), 1295–1310. doi:10.1080/10941665.2 020.1837893

Merriam-Webster. (2021). *Cybersecurity*. Available from https://www.merriam-webster.com/dictionary/cybersecurity

Nazi, K. M., Hogan, T. P., Wagner, T. H., McInnes, D. K., Smith, B. M., Haggstorm, D., Chumbler, N. R., Gifford, A. L., Charters, K. G., Saleem, J. J., Weingardt, K. R., Fischetti, L. F., & Weaver, F. M. (2010). Embracing a Health Services Research Perspective on Personal Health Records: Lessons Learned from the VA My HealtheVet System. *Journal of General Internal Medicine*, *25*(1), 62–67. doi:10.100711606-009-1114-6 PMID:20077154

Nigrin, D. J. (2014). When "Hacktivists" Target Your Hospital. *The New England Journal of Medicine*, *371*(5), 393–395. doi:10.1056/NEJMp1407326 PMID:25075830

OAIC. (2021b). *Tips to protect My Health Record*. Available from https://www.oaic.gov.au/privacy/health-information/my-health-record/tips-to-protect-your-my-health-record/

Office of Australian Information Commissioner (OAIC). (2021a). *Health Information Privacy*. Available from https://www.oaic.gov.au/privacy/health-information/

Pandey, P., & Litoriya, R. (2020). Securing and authenticating healthcare records through blockchain technology. *Cryptologia*, *44*(4), 341–356. doi:10.1080/01611194.2019.1706060

Pavithra, V., & Chandrasekaran, J. (2021). Developing Security Solutions for Telemedicine Applications: Medical Image Encryption and Watermarking. In *Research Anthology on Telemedicine Efficacy, Adoption, and Impact on Healthcare Delivery* (pp. 612-631). Retrieved from www.igi-global.com/chapter/developing-security-solutions-for-telemedicineapplications/

Perakslis, E. D. (2014). Cybersecurity in Health Care. *The New England Journal of Medicine*, *371*(5), 395–397. doi:10.1056/NEJMp1404358 PMID:25075831

Queensland Health. (2017). *Digital Health Strategic Vision for Queensland 2026*. Retrieved from https://www.health.qld.gov.au/__data/assets/pdf_file/0016/645010/digital-health-strat-vision.pdf

Regola, N., & Chawla, N. V. (2013). Storing and Using Health Data in a Virtual Private Cloud. *Journal of Medical Internet Research*, *15*(3), e63. doi:10.2196/jmir.2076 PMID:23485880

Rowe, D. C., Lunt, B. M., & Ekstrom, J. J. (2011). *The Role of Cyber-Security in Information Technology Education*. SIGITE'11, West Point, NY, USA. .2047628 doi:10.1145/2047594

Russo, E., Sittig, D. F., Murphy, D. R., & Singh, H. (2018). Challenges in patient safety improvement research in the era of electronic health records. *Health Care*, *4*(4), 285–290. PMID:27473472

Schumacher, A. (2017). *Reinventing healthcare: Towards a global, blockchain-based precision medicine ecosystem*. Available from: https://www.researchgate.net/publication/317936859_Blockchain_Healthcare_-_2017_Strategy_Guide

Sharma, R., & Purohit, M. (2018). Emerging Cyber Threats and the Challenges Associated with them. *International Research. Journal of Engineering Technology*, *5*(2). https://www.irjet.net/archives/V5/i2/IRJET-V5I2127.pdf

Shaw, T., Hines, M., & Kielly-Carroll, C. (2017). *Impact of Digital Health on the Safety and Quality of Health Care*. Sydney: ACSQHC. Available from https://www.safetyandquality.gov.au/

Sittig, D. F. (2002). Personal health records on the internet: A snapshot of the pioneers at the end of the 20th Century. *International Journal of Medical Informatics*, *65*(1), 1–6. doi:10.1016/S1386-5056(01)00215-5 PMID:11904243

Sittig, D. F., Belmont, E., & Singh, H. (2018). Improving the safety of health information technology requires shared responsibility: It is time we all step up. *Health Care*, *6*(1), 7–12. PMID:28716376

Tanwar, S., Parekh, K., & Evans, R. (2020). Blockchain-based electronic healthcare record system for healthcare 4.0 applications. *Journal of Information Security and Applications*, *50*, 102407. Advance online publication. doi:10.1016/j.jisa.2019.102407

Tanwar, S., Tyagi, S., & Kumar, N. (2019). Security and Privacy of Electronic Health Records. London, UK: The Institution of Engineering and Technology.

Varadharajan, V. (2018). *Cybersecurity and privacy issues surrounding My health records.* Retrieved from https://www.newcastle.edu.au/newsroom/research-and-innovation/my-health-record

William, C. M., Chaturvedi, R., & Chakravarthy, K. (2020). Cybersecurity Risks in a Pandemic. *Journal of Medical Internet Research*, *22*(9), e23692. doi:10.2196/23692 PMID:32897869

Wood, S., Schwartz, E., Tuepker, A., Pres, N. A., Nazi, K. M., Turvery, C., & Nichol, W. P. (2013). Patient Experiences with Full Electronic Access to Health Records and Clinical Notes Through the My HealtheVet Personal Health Record Pilot: Qualitative Study. *Journal of Medical Internet Research*, *15*(3), e65. doi:10.2196/jmir.2356 PMID:23535584

Zhang, P., Schmidt, D., White, J., & Lenz, G. (2018). Blockchain technology use cases in healthcare. In *Advances in Computers*. Elsevier.

Zhou, L., Varadharajan, V., & Gopinath, K. (2016). A Secure Role-Based Cloud Storage System for Encrypted Patient-Centric Health Records. *The Computer Journal*, *59*(11), 1593–1611. doi:10.1093/comjnl/bxw019

ADDITIONAL READING

Al-Muhtadi, J., Shahzad, B., Saleem, K., Jmeel, W., & Orgun, M. A. (2017). Cybersecurity and privacy issues for socially integrated mobile healthcare applications operating in a multi-cloud environment. *Health Informatics Journal*, *25*(2), 315–329. doi:10.1177/1460458217706184 PMID:28480788

Amatayakul, M. K. (2012). *Electronic Health Records: A Practical Guide for Professionals and Organizations* (5th ed.). American Health Information Management Association.

Ayala, L. (2016). *A Guide to Detection and Prevention.* Springer. Available from https://link.springer.com/content/pdf/10.1007/978-1-4842-2155-6.pdf

Bray, K., & Mihm, U. (2019). M*y Health Record- what you need to know- stay in or opt out.* Retrieved from https://www.choice.com.au/health-and-body/health-practitioners/online-health-advice/articles/my-health-record-and-what-you-need-to-know

Burke, W., Oseni, T., Jolfraei, A., & Gongal, I. (2019). Cybersecurity Indexes for eHealth. *Proceedings of the Australasian Computer Science Week Multiconference*. Article No. 17, 1-18 10.1145/3290688.3290721

Clauson, K., Breeden, E., Davidson, C., & Mackey, T. (2018). Leveraging Blockchain Technology to Enhance Supply Chain Management in Healthcare. *Blockchain in Healthcare Today*, *10*. Advance online publication. doi:10.30953/bhty.v1.20

Coventry, L., & Branley, D. (2018). Cybersecurity in healthcare: A narrative review of trends, threats and ways forward. *Maturitas*, *113*, 48–52. doi:10.1016/j.maturitas.2018.04.008 PMID:29903648

Offner, K. L., Sitnikova, E., Joiner, K., & MacIntyre, C. R. (2020). Towards understanding cybersecurity capability in Australian healthcare organisations: A systematic review of recent trends, threats and mitigation. *Intelligence and National Security*, *35*(4), 556–585. doi:10.1080/02684527.2020.1752459

Webb, T., & Dayal, S. (2017). Building the wall: Addressing cybersecurity risks in medical devices in the U.S.A. and Australia. *Computer Law & Security Review*, *33*(4), 559–563. doi:10.1016/j.clsr.2017.05.004

Wirth, A. (2020). Cyberinsights: COVID-19 and What It Means for Cybersecurity. *Biomedical Instrumentation & Technology*, *54*(3), 216–219. Advance online publication. doi:10.2345/0899-8205-54.3.216 PMID:32442003

KEY TERMS AND DEFINITIONS

Blockchain Technology: Blockchain technology is defined as an effective technology of chain of transactions or datasets, chained together by a cryptographic signature, stored in a shared ledger and supported by a network of connected nodes or processes, which are continuously updated, and data synced. Blockchain technology can help to prevent data breaches in the healthcare industry, as it is a secure method of recording, storing, sharing, and updating sensitive data of the patients.

Confidentiality: Personal health records of the patients, must be protected from being misused by those who are not concerned with it. The information of the patient must be released only with patient's formal consent and authorized medical persons have access to the information for clinical treatment or research purposes.

Cybersecurity Risk: Measures taken by an organsiation such as banks, hospitals, universities, schools, businesses, governments, and individuals to protect their own computer or computer systems in an organsiation as a whole from internet hackers, malwares or cyber-attacks.

Digital Health Technology: Digital health technology also known as e-health technology is convergence of digital technologies and internet with healthcare records and reports, mobile-phones, apps, tablets and computer vis the internet to improve people's health and maximise impact. Digital health helps to enhance efficiency in healthcare service delivery for effective and positive healthcare outcomes, providing personalized and precise healthcare plan.

Digital Transformation: Digital transformation is the process of using internet based digital technologies to create, improve and transform existing business processes that is re-engineering and innovating digital health technology applications continuously. This will not only manage risk from cyber-threat but also improve consumer use experience and value by the patients and the healthcare providers, to meet changing healthcare needs of the consumers, hospitals and healthcare organisations efficiency.

Healthcare Data Integrity: Data integrity related to accuracy of healthcare data. Due to electronic data interchange and exchange of information between the diagnostic clinics and general practitioners, clinicians or relevant medical professionals between healthcare organisations, data can be changed or tampered with as it moves between healthcare organisations, resulting in poor documentation integrity and errors in medical records.

Information Security: Information security can be defined as preserving and protecting patient's data in terms of confidentiality, integrity, and availability of patients' personal health information data by the hospital, healthcare providers, healthcare professionals such as doctors, clinicians, physicians, nurses and allied healthcare staff. The back-up of electronic data is essential in case of cyber-attack.

My Health Record: My Health Record is a personal health record and summary of individuals key health information in an electronic or digital format on a patient portal. Patients can maintain, manage and provide access to their personal health information to healthcare providers such as their doctor or hospital regarding medication, allergies and diagnostic tests results. This e-health information is private, and protected, in a secure confidential online digital environment.

Chapter 6
Advancement of Cybersecurity and Information Security Awareness to Facilitate Digital Transformation:
Opportunities and Challenges

Hamed Taherdoost

https://orcid.org/0000-0002-6503-6739

Department of Arts, Communications and Social Sciences, University Canada West, Vancouver, Canada

Mitra Madanchian

Research and Development Department (Research Club), Hamta Business Corporation, Canada

Mona Ebrahimi

Research and Development Department (Research Club), Hamta Business Corporation, Canada

ABSTRACT

As the pace of changes in the digital world is increasing exponentially, the appeal to shift from traditional platforms to digital ones is increasing as well. Accomplishing digital transformation objectives is impossible without information security considerations. Business leaders should rethink information security challenges associated with digital transformation and consider solutions to seize existing opportunities. When it comes to information security, human beings play a critical role. Raising users' awareness is a meaningful approach to avoid or neutralize the likelihood of unwanted security consequences that may occur during transforming a system digitally. This chapter will discuss cybersecurity and information security awareness and examine how digital transformation will be affected by implementing information security awareness. This chapter will discuss the digital transformation advantages and serious challenges associated with cybersecurity, how to enhance cybersecurity, and the role of information security awareness to mitigate cybersecurity risks.

DOI: 10.4018/978-1-7998-6975-7.ch006

INTRODUCTION

Digital transformation is revolutionizing most businesses. Today, it is of significant importance for businesses to prioritize investment in digital transformation to stay successful in the competition. Recent changes in contemporary business have provided organizations with a valuable opportunity to leave their traditional manual processes and move toward digital technologies (Ted Saarikko, Ulrika H. Westergren, & Blomquist, 2020). Digital transformation is a necessity of today's digital age and one of the most recent manifestations of recent technological changes in the business environment. The impact of digitalization in operating, delivering value to customers, and providing a clear vision for the business in the competitive digital world of today is not negligible. The prevalent advent of powerful new technological devices with abundant opportunities that they provide for both people and organizations, signals the definite need for organizations to transform their business to digital platforms (Verhoef et al., 2021). It is also important to note that, digital transformation is not just the matter of shifting to digital technologies (Henriette, Feki, & Boughzala, 2015), it is about changing mindset, and alignment of attitude, strategy, people, resources and leadership (Goran, LaBerge, & Srinivasan, 2017). During recent years, digital transformation is recognized as an ecosystem and societal challenge and necessity (Gong & Ribiere, 2020), and thus, it has attracted the attention of researchers and practitioners to identify implications of digital transformation, its benefits, shortcomings and consequences (Zaoui & Souissi, 2020).

The world is gone digital and in this digital age that systems are growing in size and complexity, the scope of potential vulnerabilities has broadened as well. The revolution of internet technology and fundamental changes caused as a result of digital developments have increased electronic data transfer and the number of online transactions. Cyberattacks and unauthorized access to valuable data are respected as one of the top-ranked threats that any business may face through digital transformation. Since the amount of data transferred through digital platforms is increased, the likelihood to face data loss and cybercrime incidents is also increased dramatically (Aloul, 2012). Today, a great number of businesses rely on information including financial data, customers' profile data, legal data, and market and competition data (Taherdoost, 2020b). There are always possibilities to happen unwanted security incidents within systems that are dependent on information (Diesch, Pfaffa, & Krcmar, 2020). Thus, the vulnerability of information assets due to unpredictable attacks through a range of variable stealthy techniques by cybercriminals is considerable. Based on a report presented by the World Economic Forum (Vina, 2016), the cost of cybercrime is a staggering US$445 billion annually. Therefore, companies make attempts to minimize risks by paying prior attention to information security risks (Banfield, 2016). The information security program is one definite forward-thinking solution to address the risk of valuable data loss. Cybersecurity includes all of the information technology and data in the technological platform.

As the security of systems is a chain of different elements, achieving cybersecurity objectives is impractical without bearing in mind other influencing factors (Domínguez, Ramaswamy, Martinez, & Cleal, 2010). Human behavior is generally known as the greatest threat to cybersecurity (Crossler et al.,2013). During recent years that the Internet and technology usage has been growing exponentially, attackers have also adopted smarter techniques to exploit end-users' trust that steal their valuable information for their benefit. Based on prior research, "it is estimated that more than 6m stolen credentials are leaked every day, either free or sold on as lists" (Fortson, 2017). Thus, people who are constantly under threat while using any technological and internet-based platform to reveal their personal information are considered as one of the top reasons for data loss. To mitigate the information security issues related to humans as the main source (Banfield, 2016), users' awareness about information security should be increased through organized training. Information security awareness aims to train end-users about their possible risk-taking behavior and how their unintentional ignorance about information security concerns can leave negative impacts on the organization as a whole.

Rapid development in technology and the Internet has provided an opportunity for businesses to reach a greater audience, facilitate their processes and lower their costs by implementing digital transformation. Today, digital transformation is not an optional opportunity for businesses but it is a must to remain in the market and stay attractive from the consumers'' perspective. The fundamental shifts caused by digital transformation have made access to data more convenient and even broader. Consequently, the amount of data transfer by the Internet users has exploded globally (Ögˇütçü, Testik, & Chouseinoglou, 2016). Despite all advantages of the digital transformation, it has also risen several challenges. More data and information are moved, stored, processed, carried, and copied in digital media. These pieces of data may be disclosed and become subject to illegal collection, theft, and cybercrime. Therefore, cybersecurity is one of the major challenges of digital transformation. Organizations develop lots of software and hardware protection methods to achieve higher information security purposes, but they will be all useless if the critical role of human beings is ignored. Information security mitigates the possibility of data loss through the digital transformation process by regarding users as critical components to protect data and valuable information (Ögˇütçü et al., 2016). The development of information security awareness in turn, plays an integral role to accelerate and alleviate digital transformation due to its dependency on the credibility of a system and its crucial impact on decreasing users' resistance to change. Information security plays a critical role particularly because of its direct correlation with the experience of the end-user.

DIGITAL TRANSFORMATION

Digital transformation simply refers to integrating various technologies into all areas of daily lives. This includes transferring processes and activities to digital formats as far as possible (Scholl, 2018). Digital transformation, technically, is a comprehensive term defined as "a change in all job and income creation strategies, application of a flexible management model standing against the competition, quickly meeting changing demands, a process of reinventing a business to digitize operations and formulate extended supply chain relationships; functional use of internet in design, manufacturing, marketing, selling, presenting and is data-based management model" (Schallmo, Williams, & Boardman, 2018).

The introduction of digital technologies and constant changes in the digital economy is associated with creating new values for both customers and employees (ULAS, 2019). Digital transformation is recognized to shift paradigms, rearrange technologies, processes and business models to increase the capabilities of businesses and improve their processes. Thus, the likelihood to meet digital age requirements, and improvement in efficiency and effectiveness of internal and external operations can be increased significantly through leveraging digital approaches (GregoryVial, 2019; Taherdoost & Madanchian, 2020).

Implementing Digital Transformation

As digital transformation is associated with paradigm-shifts and significant time and money investments, prior guidance and preparation are necessary for its implementation. The result of implementing digital transformation in organizations will be felt by all stakeholders; however, understanding visible changes made by digital transformation depends on the motivation of stakeholders to involve in the implementation process.

Top- managers or owners play an integral role in digital transformation implementation. They should lead to analyze and identify current weaknesses and challenges in operations as well as understanding changing customer expectations and existing opportunities (Matarazzo, Penco, Profumo, & Quaglia, 2021). Thus, they can detect gaps and set realistic goals. The establishment of a learning culture is also essential in the implementation process since employees should be constantly educated to achieve proper knowledge about unprecedented changes in the competitive market and understand the future technological changes (ULAS, 2019). Collaboration with other organizations with the same specification, benchmarks and asking for consultation services from companies that have expertise in this field is also highly recommended (Taherdoost, Sahibuddin, & Jalaliyoon, 2015).

As gaps are detected and goals are set, a roadmap should be designed to summarize objectives, time, quality, and cost limitations. The roadmap prevents businesses from misconduct through the whole process (Daniel, Christopher, & Luke, 2018).

One determining factor in the successful implementation of digital transformation is the acceptance and involvement of employees in the process. Therefore, creating a transparent environment with high awareness about realistic deliverables of digital transformation should be regarded as a must in organizations (Pelletier & Cloutier, 2019).

Digital Transformation Advantages

As most aspects of our daily lives are covered by digital technologies, new opportunities are provided for businesses to interact with their stakeholders. Today, rapidly growing businesses are using the pillars of digital transformation and consumers have found thousands of channels to access effortlessly dozens of products and services while experiencing a fast and easy customer journey through the touchscreen of their digital devices (Verhoef et al., 2019).

Digital transformation helps businesses to reach a greater audience, create a competitive advantage, decrease costs, store and process data and eventually stand ahead in the market among other competitors (Ibarra, Igartua, & Ganzarain, 2018). Regardless of adding remarkable value to businesses, digital transformation also brings benefits for the whole society and economy. Economic growth, more employment opportunities, more effective communication systems, and a greater level of well-being are expected as predicted advantages of digital transformation (Galindo-Martín, Castaño-Martínez, & Méndez-Picazo, 2019; Taherdoost & Hassan, 2020).

The Importance of Digital Transformation

The prevalence of new digital technologies has revolutionized the customers' behavior, business processes, and the competition in the market (Verhoef et al., 2019). In a market that most consumers are heavily reliant on their digital applications, traditional business rules do not create value anymore. Businesses need to leverage their technologies in order to be attractive to their existing and potential customers. Today, costly manual mechanisms are replaced with robots and virtual assistants that decrease the operational expenses significantly and optimize outputs by simplifying processes (Verhoef et al., 2019).

On the other hand, the customers' taste and purchase behavior is changed too. Customers, as a result of the digital revolution, have shifted their purchases to online stores with the aid of their smart devices.

They have become also more alert about recent trends and changes in the market due to the help of search engines and social media platforms (Verhoef et al., 2019). Thus, adopting the new digital norm of the world instead of insisting on traditional business rules can push businesses towards being accepted in the competitive market, otherwise, they may seem unattractive from the consumers' viewpoint. Digital transformation has turned into an international topic of crucial importance for all businesses and firms (Krugera & Kearney, 2006; Zaoui & Souissi, 2020).

Digital Transformation Requirements

Embracing the necessity to implement digital information in an organization, businesses need to analyze and identify their current technology status, potentials, opportunities and infrastructures to fill the gaps and develop in the future (Saarikko, Westergren, & Blomquist, 2020). It is of significant importance for businesses to realize technologies that are relevant to their core organizational processes and market success. Organizations should then concentrate on the development of the most determining technologies that will promote the future of their business. Their business strategies and business model will be inevitably changed following the digital transformation requirements and necessities (Taherdoost, Keshavarzsaleh, Wang, 2016).

The Difference Between Digital Transformation and Digitization

Digital transformation should not be mistaken with digitization and digitalization. In the digital age that information is dominant, digitization, digitalization and digital transformation terms are often used interchangeably; however, there are significant differences among these terms (Saarikko et al., 2020). Digitization is defined as "the technical process of converting analog signals to digital signals" (Tilson, Lyytinen, & Sørensen, 2010). While the word digitalization refers to "the sociotechnical process of leveraging digitized products or systems to develop new organizational procedures, business models, or commercial offerings" (McAfee & Brynjolfsson, 2017). In other words, digitization helps to understand what technology is and what its capabilities are, while digitalization helps to connect this technology to its relevant implementation fields.

Digital transformation; however, includes a broader definition and goes beyond digitization and digitalization. Digital transformation is about the application of digital technologies and making shifts in the business model, organizational processes and tasks. Through the digital transformation process, the whole company and its value creation process will be affected positively (Verhoef et al., 2021).

Phases of Digital Transformation

Digitization, digitalization and digital transformation may indeed be differentiated from each other but they are not segregated originally. It has consented in the digital transformation literature that in most of the cases digitization and digitalization are both certain prerequisites of digital transformation and are essentially required in the first phase of the digital transformation process (Parviainen, Tihinen, Kääriäinen, & Teppola, 2017). Implementation of digital transformation is impossible without understanding the function of digital technologies and their relevance to existing processes.

Digital Transformation Process

Digital transformation is not limited just to focusing on updates in hardware and software. The process of digital transformation includes "a change in all job and income creation strategies, application of a flexible management model standing against the competition, quickly meeting changing demands, a process of reinventing a business to digitize operations and formulate extended supply chain relationships; functional use of internet in design, manufacturing, marketing, selling, presenting and is data-based management model" (Daniel et al., 2018). The digital transformation process is more profound than simply changing technological devices (Henriette, Feki, & Boughzala, 2016). It affects strategic decisions, organizational entities, the public and employees are all transformed, and business models and business practices are reshaped based on new digitally-based paradigms (ULAS, 2019).

Obstacles of Implementing Digital Transformation

Digital transformation is driven by strategy not solely by technological devices (Kane, Doug Palmer, Anh Nguyen Phillips, Kiron, & Buckley, 2015). Indeed, digital technologies do not add value and convenience to systems automatically (Saarikko et al., 2020). Companies embrace several serious barriers and challenges in this process. Implementing digital transformation usually comes along with several obstacles. This reveals the fact that businesses need to improve their competencies in order to experience a successful digital transformation and benefit from existing opportunities (Bygstad & Øvrelid, 2021).

Obstacles that organization following digital transformation purposes need to consider include budget deficiencies, possible resistance against technological changes, lack of knowledge to understand internet technologies, inadequate information about digital standards, and problems in internet connection, unqualified staff, being unaware of future benefits of digital transformation, lack of competencies, data security, and concerns about privacy (ULAS, 2019).

One of the main obstacles that organizations face in their way through digital transformation is a potential threat that puts valuable data at risk (Taherdoost, 2017).

Digital transformation simplifies data storage, data process, and data transfer. An abundant amount of data flows in digital platforms, thus, the protection of this data may cause the digital transformation with serious difficulties (Jones, Hutcheson, & Camba, 2021).

Cyber Security and Digital Transformation

Regardless of all necessary requirements of digital transformation, including software and hardware development, to achieve digital transformation, one fundamental issue to consider is cybersecurity. As more new digital technologies are introduced, cybersecurity threats and the possibility of being at the risk of data loss are increasing continuously too (Taherdoost, 2016).

Organizations should take care of information security and ensure the security of every person who is involved in the digital-based processes. When people use different digital and online platforms, they are often under the pressure to reveal their private information. Most importantly, their credentials are asked as an obligation in case of signing to a website or digital application. This shared information provides an opportunity for cybercriminals to exploit users' data as the target of cybercrimes. Thus, any kind of failure in protecting data may disappoint users to maintain their usage, leads to significant data loss for organizations, and subsequently brings along long-term negative consequences (Taherdoost, 2020a).

CYBER SECURITY

What is Cybersecurity?

Cybersecurity is defined as "The protection of information against unauthorized disclosure, transfer, modification, or destruction whether accidental or intentional" (Federal Standard 1037C, 1997). Based on another definition information security is "an official organizational program with the goal of training users about the potential threats to an organization's information and how to avoid and behave in these situations" (Banfield, 2016). As it is recognized from the definitions, cybersecurity and information security terms are almost used interchangeably.

Various information risks associated with the worldwide increase in information technology, electronic data, mobile device usage, that mainly lead to increasing hackers' motivation to attack information and cybercrimes and finally financial and reputational consequences for businesses and their customers can be addressed by principles and policies of information security. Cybersecurity is also highlighted because people are recognized as key elements of information systems, and human beings do not always act in the most secure and appropriate manner (Aytes & Connolly, 2004).

Cybersecurity Process

Information security is a process. It is not recognized as a single feature. Information security should be planned from the initiation and cover all organizational processes and structures. It is a process collaborated with people, the information technology landscape and infrastructure in order to create a secure integration within internal and external business operations that is confidential for all users to simply rely on it (Scholl, 2018). The current information security status and requirements of organizations should be recognized and understood by decision-makers (Taherdoost, 2018). If there are gaps, they should be improved to respond to current and future cybersecurity issues and if there are no controls, possible policies and procedures should be set in order to protect the organizational information. However, the cybersecurity process is not limited solely to implementation, it should be maintained and measured periodically. Periodic feedback and controls aid to cover possible gaps and address cybersecurity concerns.

Cybersecurity Goals

Every cybersecurity strategy aims to achieve several goals. Based on general information security goals that are defined in the Figure.1, information systems should be protected to ensure that information cannot be accessed by any unauthorized user, data is properly processed and managed in a system that decision-makers can rely on it for critical business decisions, authorized users can reach different kinds of services based on the level of their of accessibility, information is authentic, users are recognized and verified to access information and systems function properly because of their acceptable quality.

The Importance of Cybersecurity

Recent developments in the prevalence of the Internet and technology have increased its usage significantly for different purposes. As a considerable amount of transactions are led online, data transfer is increased as well.

Figure 1. Information Security Goals (Scholl, 2018)

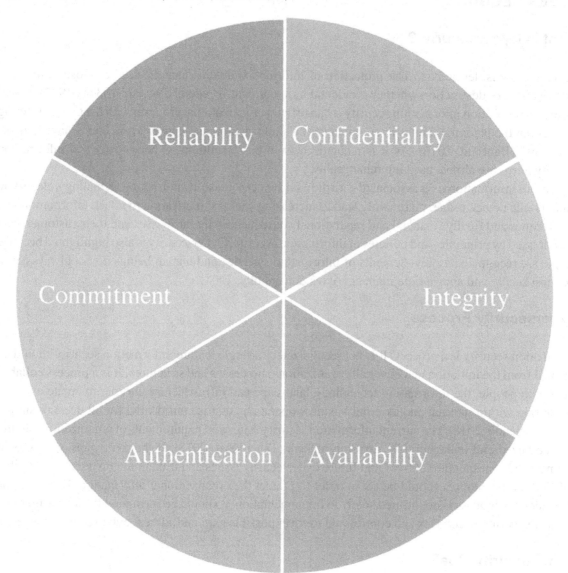

Many businesses and organizations regardless of their size are dependent on data transfer and on-line transactions to stay in today's competitive market (Knapp, Marshall, Rainer, & Morrow, 2006). Prevalent transactions of data through wireless networks have increased data challenges and threats. Consequently, data loss is considered as one of the major factors to loss of revenue and reputation in organizations (Banfield, 2016). The revolution of the Internet and data explosion has brought many threats to personal and organizational data. Different pieces of data can be subject to cyber threats and bring along significant losses.

In addition, different users' connections with various levels of accessibility, investment in keeping data secure, and senior managers' approach through the importance of the data can increase the risk of data loss significantly (Banfield, 2016). It is estimated that the economic impact of security breaches is relatively half a trillion dollars globally (Ponemon-Institute, 2018). Thus, information security is an obligation to keep information and the underlying technology secure against cyber threats for organizations that are affected by overshadowing reliance on computer networks.

How to Enhance Cybersecurity?

Computers and technologies are tools in systems and human beings are the users of these tools. The critical role of people is sometimes forgotten and large amounts of money are invested on technological controls. However, effective ways to enhance information security are through both technology and human beings (Domínguez et al., 2010). It is sometimes

Organizations need to focus on strong technical security devices like network access controls, firewalls, e-mail filtering and even more possible opportunities. On the other hand, they should implement standards, procedures, policies, and guides to ensure that people who configure, install and implement technological tools and information security systems.

Since human behavior is a determining factor besides technology, ignoring its impacts can result in threats for enterprises in complying with regulations, and losing reputation (Domínguez et al., 2010). Information security cognitive campaigns and training sessions can be effective contemporary to technological developments in order to achieve information security goals. A higher level of knowledge and understanding increases the likelihood to respond effectively to cybersecurity principles significantly (Trim & Lee, 2019).

Information Security Culture

The impact of controls will be destroyed if people pillars for the success of information security systems do not use them. Employees of organizations can abuse or circumvent information security controls by ignoring security procedures and policies (Krunger & Kearney, 2006). Thus, instilling a cybersecurity culture in which people understand the importance of information security and engage in cybersecurity practices is essential for organizations.

In a positive security environment in which individuals are positively changed to understand security policies and participate actively in implementing information security procedures within the organization, there will be a common insight into information security structures and procedures. This common insight through information security leads to coordinated information security interactions in an organization and subsequently enhances effective information security (EirikAlbrechtsen & JanHovden, 2010).

The Role of Human in Information Security

Technical controls are necessary elements to protect information but the determining role of people who are users of systems is often underestimated and remained as the weakest line in the organizational defense (Boss, 2007; EirikAlbrechtsen & JanHovden, 2010). Users are considered as the biggest threat factors for information security that are prone to cause cybersecurity incidents regularly by their intentional or unintentional risk-taking behavior (Crossler et al., 2013). A combination of individuals' risky behaviors can facilitate future possibilities to harm systems through cybersecurity attacks and theft of confidential data. Risk-taking behaviors such as surfing on unsecured web pages, toxics usage of mobile phones, unsecure data practices, and handling information carelessly can lead to significant data loss and subsequently put the organization at the harm of financial and reputation loss (Stanton, Stam, Mastrangelo, & Jolton, 2005).

Learning Information Security

The growing importance of cybersecurity in systems and its positive correlation with organizational culture raises the importance to motivate and train technology users to protect themselves against cyber-attacks. As the frequency of security incidents happened by individuals increases, the role of an appropriate educational approach in order to mitigate the disclosure or destruction of information increased as well (Mamonov & Benbunan-Fich, 2018). Abundant research on the components of information security in different systems have revealed that weakness in every component of the information security chain can cripple the effectiveness of all others (Desman, 2003). It is impossible to push information security policies to people. The success of information security requires in-depth understanding, learning principles, acquiring skills, and using the obtained knowledge (Domínguez et al., 2010). Otherwise, end-users are prone to simply disregard security policies and procedures and consequently leave the organization at security risk (Boss, 2007).

A well-built information security learning curve includes three key areas (Peltier, 2005). The first pillar is increasing awareness of the audience to aid them to realize the importance and functions of the security within a system and subsequently become motivated to apply security principles. Users should be then trained based on organized training sessions to learn the proper usage of required tools. The third element in the learning process is education. Education refers to the required time in-depth dedicated to alleviate security risk and support the tools (Domínguez et al., 2010).

Information Security Program Success Factors

It is stated that although technological devices and methods may perform effectively in their respective ways to protect the information, a great number of information losses are not basically caused by faulty technology or lack of technology but they are made because of the faulty users' behavior (Im & Baskerville, 2005; Mitnick & Simon, 2002; Orshesky, 2003).

According to cybersecurity professionals, two factors that play an integral role in the success of information security implementation are the support of the senior manager and users' awareness about information security (Knapp, Marshall, Morrow, & Rainer, 2006). The key to having a successful cybersecurity program in an organization is the ability to translate its principals into business terms and provide recognizable relation to business processes. The possibility to regard information security policies will be raised remarkably in case of understanding its impact on core business processes of an organization and even final revenue (Ravenel, 2007). The effectiveness of information security is strongly dependent on integrity, confidentiality, and availability of information, as factors that ensure the success of information security within an organization in the long run (Domínguez et al., 2010; Peltier, 2005).

Information Security Implementation

Different technological controls, security policies, procedures, and guidelines should be implemented and improved in organizations in order to mitigate security issues and protect organizational information. The information security implementation process is not free from challenges. Lack of importance given to implementing security awareness is one of the major challenges organizations face today. To maintain integrity, confidentiality, and availability of the information as main objectives of cybersecurity programs, awareness of individuals who are operating in systems should be increased as well as developing technological infrastructure. Some companies invest an exorbitant amount of money and devote a lot of time and effort to establish technical controls in order to protect information; however, implementation of information security will not be successful if end-users are left unaware. Thus, in the implementation process, increasing awareness of the people about their critical role in protecting or placing privileged information at high-security risk through training of great importance (Im & Baskerville, 2005; Mitnick & Simon, 2002; Orshesky, 2003).

Effective implementation of information security is highly dependent on deploying a combination of relevant technical and procedural controls to mitigate risks of information loss (Krunger & Kearney, 2006). In most information-based organizations, top-manager is responsible for security policy guidelines and procedures and the information security department is in charge of instilling policies within the organization, updating policies and increasing employees' understanding about possible hazards. The information security department also plays an integral role in finding security gaps and providing technical solutions that contribute to effective information security (Banfield, 2016).

The overall success and assurance of cybersecurity is the responsibility of senior managers. Not only top-managers need to be alert about challenges associated with possible cyber-attacks (Trim & Lee, 2019), but also they are in charge of familiarizing employees of the organization about the importance of cybersecurity implementation and provide them with clear guidance. The support and understanding of senior managers about information security promote general organizational knowledge and vision about the role of cybersecurity within an organization (Takeuchi & Nonaka, 1995). Senior managers' role in terms of leadership and authority in the establishment of information security is controversial (Mudrack, 2007).Senior managers should perform actively to increase users' awareness about information security and change their attitude in order to successfully implement information security (Trim & Lee, 2019).

The critical issue in cybersecurity is not just about the development of advanced technological devices and appropriate infrastructure, it is also about how it is implemented and managed within an organization in order to maximize its positive impacts (Cascio & Montealegre, 2016). Organizations in order to implement information security need to change attitudes of their employees, suppliers, and contractors as well as developing technological devices and placing detailed security policies and procedures. The supportive approach of top-management also is considered as a must to achieve information security objectives and implement cybersecurity programs fast.

INFORMATION SECURITY AWARENESS

Information security awareness is defined as "a formal process for educating end-users about computer security and organizational security practice" (Banfield, 2016).Based on the definition of information security awareness by the Information Security Forum (Forum, 2003), "information security awareness is the degree or extent to which every member of staff understands the importance of information security, the levels of information security appropriate to the organization, their individual security responsibilities, and acts accordingly".

Information security awareness that is usually overlooked in organizational security programs maintains to create a positive-behavior security environment in which information security implementation is more likely to perform effectively (Krunger & Kearney, 2006).

It is estimated that around 50 - 70% of cybersecurity incidents in organizations happen as a result of human misuse of digital platforms (Kranz & Haeussinger, 2013). Employees' defense against cybersecurity attacks is regarded as the weakest line in organizational defense due to various reasons that are directly related to employees' behaviors (Siponen, 2000). Hence, employees' understanding of the factors that influence the protection of data and may lead to cybersecurity crimes is recognized remarkably important. Information security awareness is the process of educating end-users about existing security threats and making them aware of ways to avoid the organization's vulnerability to cyberattacks.

Information Security Awareness Advantages

Deployment of information security awareness that brings along more employees' attention to security policies and behavior can make organizations more resilient to cyberattacks and less vulnerable to data loss (RuthShillair et al., 2015). Since poor individuals' security behavior and low commitment and motivation to follow security policies increase threats (Safa et al., 2015) and damage organizational reputation, information security awareness plays a deterrence role to prevent hackers and cybercriminals from deploying various schemes and trap individuals to abuse sensitive data and information (Trim & Lee, 2019).

Regarding the importance of awareness and behavior among all kinds of users, cyberspace can provide numerous business opportunities for organizations. Reducing the possibility of data breach through information security awareness programs leads to a significant decrease in direct or indirect misuses of information from employees ranging from intentional harms and naïve staff mistakes (Kranz & Haeussinger, 2013).

The Importance/Role of Information Security Awareness

As organizations continue to expand their use of advanced technologies and operate through cyberspace, hackers attempt to penetrate systems by targeting the weakest security line, that is often the human being, increases dramatically (Katz, 2006). Organizations tend to assign their annual budget for the development of technological and digital solutions in order to safeguard information security; however, breaks into organizational information by targeting unconscious users that can result in irreparable security losses and incidents are ignored (AIRC, 2008; Symantec, 2009).

Based on a study conducted to realize obstacles in information security, it has been demonstrated that lack of security awareness by end-users is known as one of the top barriers to effective information security (Young, 2004). It is stated that attackers normally target those users who neglect security practices due to their lack of information security awareness (Ramalingam, Khan, & Mohammed, 2016). Users' negligence and unawareness are mainly considered as root causes for possible negative impacts of a security breach or failure (Krunger & Kearney, 2006).

Information security protocol could not perform effectively without providing adequate training for employees and showing them how to follow security policies, procedures, and tools (Peltier, 2005). Thus, making changes in individuals' behavior and attitude and providing them with direct and indirect training sessions through investments in information security awareness programs is fundamentally required for accomplishment to effective implementation of information security in today's digital age.

Information Security Awareness Goals

The main goal of deploying information security awareness is the establishment of an information security culture throughout the organizations in which users understand the consequences of their security misbehaviors. Information security awareness aims to help employees understand organizational vulnerabilities, security threats, and risks. It emphasizes protection policies like password protection and helping individuals understand their responsibility in case of password disclosure and information loss (Domínguez et al., 2010). Effective information security awareness programs eventually lead to a positive security environment in organizations in which all members are motivated to respect information security procedures and are entirely aware of possibilities of cyberattacks and harms.

Information security awareness was initially designed and implemented to play a deterrent role (Goodhue & Straub, 1991). Today, it is known as a state of mind and attitude that should be renewed periodically for users (Johnston, Warkentin, McBride, & Carter, 2017). Users should be reminded constantly about fast changes of technologies and new possibilities of cybersecurity issues to stay aware (Clarke, Stewart, & Lacey, 2012).

Information Security Awareness Success Factors

Information security awareness is not a one-time feature, but it is a dynamic process (Krunger & Kearney, 2006). As the market changes continuously and digital technologies develop day in day out, it gets even more difficult to maintain up-to-date information security awareness programs. The success of increasing users' awareness should be measured and assessed continually in certain periods of time. The assessment validates the users' understanding and knowledge about security awareness. To keep the users motivated and justified about any kind of changes and recent incidents in information security, managers need to receive feedback and analyze weak areas to use as inputs of security awareness programs. The more real inputs are entered to security awareness programs, the better it works (Domínguez et al., 2010).

It is stated that another key factor in awareness is the message that is delivered to users. It is important to keep the message consistent and relevant but vary the delivery mechanism. Repetition and clearance of the message will keep the audience interested and focused on security principles at the same time (Krunger & Kearney, 2006).

A rewarding approach, both tangible and intangible, is also recognized as an effective way to encourage employees to respect information security policies and procedures. The importance of rewarding is highlighted mainly because of the reason that dictating employees in an authoritative manner to respect information security policies does not work (Modic & Anderson, 2014). The attention and motivation of employees play a critical role in the success of information security awareness, thus, rewarding those users who act in manners on compliance with security policies can positively affect performing information security practices (Bulgurcu, Cavusoglu, & Benbasat, 2010).

INFORMATION SECURITY AWARENESS AND DIGITAL TRANSFORMATION

Social behavior is mainly changing due to digital transformation. Numerous technical and digital developments are designed and implemented in different organizations to facilitate processes and increase internet-based access to information. As more amount of data is transferred through various technological devices, the risk of abusing data by cybercriminals and attackers increases as well. The predicted solution to mitigate the significant threats and hazards associated with organized cybercrimes and data abuse is implementing information security. Information security should be considered as a must for all challenges ahead as a consequence of using a computer or mobile devices that perform digitally. Information security is indeed a necessity in all organizations but it cannot be achieved in an authoritative manner. In addition, since information security is beyond development in technical devices and digital infrastructure, a remarkable change in behavior and awareness of users plays a critical role in the successful implementation of information security (Scholl, 2018).

Information security and information security awareness are integrated elements to protect all types of information through digitally-based systems. Digital transformation has affected almost all areas of our lives in an increasingly rapid manner. Transforming digitally under the well-known slogan "Digitalization for All", comes with unlimited users' internet access and subsequently excessive data transfer. That is where information security awareness comes into play. A trained workforce is even more effective than technological developments. That is the reason why cybercriminals typically employ their tricks to target unaware users. Thus, training employees to understand appropriate security behaviors is essential is the key ingredient for a successful digital transformation.

CONCLUSION

New digital technologies have revolutionized the world of business, business processes, the shape of the competition in the market and eventually the customers' behavior. Traditional business platforms do not create value for the new generation customers since they are highly reliant on their digital devices. Thus, digital transformation is considered a topic of crucial importance for all businesses and subsequently, decision-makers and business leaders are seeking ways to facilitate the process of digital transformation. There are challenges and barriers in implementing the digital transformation process that may affect the whole transformation positively or negatively. The potential risk of data loss is one of the main concerns through implementing digital transformation. Information security and the matter of educating end-users about information security and organizational security practices is considered as one of the key areas that businesses need to embrace in the advancement of this process.

Organizational security policy can be violated broadly by end-users' security misbehavior which will lead to organizational assets loss. Intentional or unintentional misbehavior of users who neglect to follow security policy and get involved in information protection activities will result in a significant financial and reputational loss for organizations (Whitman & Mattord, 2011). The critical role of information security awareness is increasingly highlighted in the digital transformation process since data is an inseparable asset of every digital transformation. Digital transformation is integrated with information security and information security is integrated with information security awareness. Information security awareness to increase users' understanding and awareness about potential information security risks and threats, aims to protect data through the digital transformation process regardless of the types and origins of data or whether they are stored in computers or any other digital devices(Scholl, 2018). Digital transformation affects all the processes of collecting, storing, processing and transferring diverse information and large amounts of data. Information security awareness is a certain response to the challenges ahead of digital transformation.

SOLUTIONS AND RECOMMENDATIONS FOR FUTURE RESEARCH DIRECTIONS

The technological transformation is a must that accompanies the advent of the digital world or the network society. This book chapter argues that cybersecurity awareness has certain implications for digital transformation and plays an integral role to facilitate and expedite the process of digital transformation. However, we have not assessed any framework that can contribute to the efficient and effective achievement of digital transformation objectives through linking it to cybersecurity awareness principles. Thus, apart from the aforementioned challenges and opportunities in the process of digital transformation, it is also worth pointing out that the approaches presented in this book chapter may be further developed, by adopting a new framework.

REFERENCES

AIRC. (2008). *Attack Intelligence Research Center Annual Threat Report: 2008 Overview and 2009 Predictions*. Attack Intelligence Research Center, Alladin Knowledge Systems. Available online at http://www.aladdin.com/pdf/airc/ AIRC-Annual-Threat-Report2008.pdf

Albrechtsen, E., & Hovden, J. (2010). Improving information security awareness and behaviour through dialogue, participation and collective reflection. An intervention study. *Computers & Security, 29*(4), 432–445. doi:10.1016/j.cose.2009.12.005

Aloul, F. A. (2012). The Need for Effective Information Security Awareness. *Journal of Advances in Information Technology, 3*(3), 176–183. doi:10.4304/jait.3.3.176-183

Aytes, K., & Connolly, T. (2004). Computer Security and Risky Computing Practices: A Rational Choice Perspective. *Journal of Organizational and End User Computing, 16*(3), 22–40. doi:10.4018/joeuc.2004070102

Banfield, J. M. (2016). *A study of information security awareness program effectiveness in predicting end-user security behavior* (Master Thesis). Eastern Michigan University.

Boss, S. R. (2007). *Control, perceived risk and information security precautions: external and internal motivations for security behavior* (PhD Thesis). University of Pittsburgh.

Bulgurcu, B., Cavusoglu, H., & Benbasat, I. (2010). Information security policy compliance: An empirical study of rationality-based beliefs and information security awareness. *Management Information Systems Quarterly, 34*(3), 523–548. doi:10.2307/25750690

Bygstad, B., & Øvrelid, E. (2021). Managing two-speed innovation for digital transformation. *Procedia Computer Science*, *181*, 119–126. doi:10.1016/j.procs.2021.01.111

Cascio, W. F., & Montealegre, R. (2016). How technology is changing work and organizations. *Annual Review of Organizational Psychology and Organizational Behavior*, *3*(1), 349–375. doi:10.1146/annurev-orgpsych-041015-062352

Clarke, N., Stewart, G., & Lacey, D. (2012). Death by a thousand facts. *Information Management & Computer Security*, *20*(1), 29–38. doi:10.1108/09685221211219182

Daniel, S., Christopher, W., & Luke, B. (2018). Digital Transformation of Business Models-Best Practice, Enabler, and Roadmap. *International Journal of Innovation Management*, *21*(8), 1–13.

Desman, M. B. (2003). The Ten Commandments of Information Security Awareness Training. *Information Systems Security*, *11*(6), 39–44. doi:10.1201/1086/43324.11.6.20030101/40430.7

Diesch, R., Pfaffa, M., & Krcmar, H. (2020). A Comprehensive Model of Information Security Factors for Decision-Makers. *Computers & Security*, *92*, 1–21. doi:10.1016/j.cose.2020.101747

Domínguez, C. M. F., Ramaswamy, M., Martinez, E. M., & Cleal, M. G. (2010). A Framework For Information Security Awareness Programs. *Issues in Information Systems*, *6*(1), 402–409.

Fortson, D. (2017, Apr. 2). 90% of all attempts logins are by cyber-hackers. The Sunday Times, p. 5.

Forum, I. S. (2003). *The standard of good practice for the information security*. Information Security Forum.

Galindo-Martín, M., Castaño-Martínez, M., & Méndez-Picazo, M. (2019). Digital transformation, digital dividends and entrepreneurship: A quantitative analysis. *Journal of Business Research*, *101*, 522–527. doi:10.1016/j.jbusres.2018.12.014

Gong, C., & Ribiere, V. (2020). Developing a unified definition of digital transformation. *Technovation*.

Goodhue, D. L., & Straub, D. W. (1991). Security concerns of system users: A study of perceptions of the adequacy of security. *Information & Management*, *20*(1), 13–27. doi:10.1016/0378-7206(91)90024-V

Goran, J., LaBerge, L., & Srinivasan, R. (2017). Culture for a digital age. *The McKinsey Quarterly*.

Henriette, E., Feki, M., & Boughzala, I. (2015). The shape of digital transformation: a systematic literature review. *Ninth Mediterranean Conference on Information Systems (MCIS)*, 1-13.

Henriette, E., Feki, M., & Boughzala, I. (2016). *Digital transformation challenges*. Paper presented at the Mediterranean Conference on Information Systems (MCIS), Samos, Greece.

Ibarra, D., Igartua, J. I., & Ganzarain, J. (2018). *Engineering Digital Transformation*. Springer.

Im, G. P., & Baskerville, R. L. (2005). A longitudinal study of information system threat categories: The enduring problem of human error. *ACM SIGMIS Database: the DATABASE for Advances in Information Systems*, *36*(4), 68–79. doi:10.1145/1104004.1104010

Johnston, A. C., Warkentin, M., McBride, M., & Carter, L. (2017). Dispositional and situational factors: Influences on information security policy violations. *European Journal of Information Systems*, *25*(3), 231–251. doi:10.1057/ejis.2015.15

Jones, M. D., Hutcheson, S., & Camba, J. D. (2021). Past, present, and future barriers to digital transformation in manufacturing: A review. *Journal of Manufacturing Systems*. Advance online publication. doi:10.1016/j.jmsy.2021.03.006

Kane, Palmer, Phillips, Kiron, & Buckley. (2015). Strategy, Not Technology, Drives Digital Transformation. MIT Sloan Management Review and Deloitte University Press.

Katz, F. H. (2006). The effect of a university information security survey on instruction methods in information security. *Proceedings of the 2nd annual conference on Information security curriculum development*, 43-48.

Knapp, K. J., Marshall, T. E., Morrow, D. W., & Rainer, R. K. (2006). The Top Information Security Issues Facing Organizations: What Can Government Do to Help? *Information System Security*, *15*(4), 51–58. doi:10.1201/1086.1065898X/46353.15.4.20060901/95124.6

Kranz, J., & Haeussinger, F. (2013). Information security awareness: its antecedents and mediating effects on security compliant behavior. *International Conference on Information Systems*, 1-16.

Krunger, H. A., & Kearney, W. D. (2006). A prototype of assessing information security awareness. *Computers & Security*, *25*(4), 289–296. doi:10.1016/j.cose.2006.02.008

Mamonov, S., & Benbunan-Fich, R. (2018). The impact of information security threat awareness on privacy-protective behaviors. *Computers in Human Behavior*, *83*, 32–44. doi:10.1016/j.chb.2018.01.028

Matarazzo, M., Penco, L., Profumo, G., & Quaglia, R. (2021). Digital transformation and customer value creation in Made in Italy SMEs: A dynamic capabilities perspective. *Journal of Business Research*, *123*, 642–656. doi:10.1016/j.jbusres.2020.10.033

McAfee, A., & Brynjolfsson, E. (2017). *Machine, Platform, Crowd: Harnessing Our Digital Future* (1st ed.). Kindle Edition.

Mitnick, K., & Simon, W. (2002). *The Art of Deception: Controlling the Human Element of Security*. Wiley Publishing, Inc.

Modic, D., & Anderson, R. (2014). Reading this may harm your computer: The psychology of malware warnings. *Computers in Human Behavior*, *41*, 71–79. doi:10.1016/j.chb.2014.09.014

Mudrack, P. (2007). *Individual personality factors that affect normative beliefs about the rightness of corporate social responsibility*. Academic Press.

Öğütçü, G., Testik, Ö. M., & Chouseinoglou, O. (2016). Analysis of personal information security behavior and awareness. *Computers & Security*, *56*, 83–93. doi:10.1016/j.cose.2015.10.002

Orshesky, C. M. (2003). Beyond technology – The human factor in business systems. *The Journal of Business Strategy*, *24*(4), 43–47. doi:10.1108/02756660310494872

Parviainen, P., Tihinen, M., Kääriäinen, J., & Teppola, S. (2017). Tackling the digitalization challenge: How to benefit from digitalization in practice. *International Journal of Information Systems and Project Management*, *5*, 63–77.

Pelletier, C., & Cloutier, L. M. (2019). *Challenges of Digital Transformation in SMEs: Exploration of IT-Related Perceptions in a Service Ecosystem. Hawaii International Conference on System Sciences, Maui*, HI. 10.24251/HICSS.2019.597

Peltier, T. R. (2005). Implementing an Information Security Awareness Program. *Information Systems Security, 14*(2), 37–49. doi:10.1201/1086/45241.14.2.20050501/88292.6

Ponemon-Institute. (2018). *Cost of a Data Breach Study: Global Overview*. IBM Security and Ponemon Institute.

Ramalingam, R., Khan, S., & Mohammed, S. (2016). The need for effective information security awareness practices in Oman higher educational institutions. *Symposium on Communication, Information Technology and Biotechnology: Current Trends and Future Scope, Sur College of Applied Sciences, Ministry of Higher Education, Sultanate of Oman*, 1-6.

Ravenel, J. P. (2007). Effective operational security metrics. *The EDP Audit, Control, and Security Newsletter, 34*(6), 11–20.

Saarikko, T., Westergren, U. H., & Blomquist, T. (2020). Digital transformation: Five recommendations for the digitally conscious firm. *Business Horizons, 63*(6), 825–839. doi:10.1016/j.bushor.2020.07.005

Saarikko, T., Westergren, U. H., & Blomquist, T. (2020). Digital transformation: Five recommendations for the digitally conscious firm. *Business Horizons, 63*(6), 825–839. doi:10.1016/j.bushor.2020.07.005

Safa, N. S., Sookhak, M., Von Solms, R., Furnell, S., Ghani, N. A., & Herawan, T. (2015). Information security conscious care behaviour formation in organizations. *Computers & Security, 53*, 65–78. doi:10.1016/j.cose.2015.05.012

Schallmo, D., Williams, C. A., & Boardman, L. (2018). Digital Transformation of Business Models-Best Practices, Enablers and Roadmap. *International Journal of Innovation Management, 21*(8), 1–17.

Scholl, M. C. (2018). *Awareness in Information Security. 12th International Multi-Conference on Society*. Cybernetics and Informatics.

Shillair, R., Cotten, S., Tsai, H.-Y. S., Alhabash, S., LaRose, R., & Rifon, N. (2015). *Online safety begins with you and me: Convincing Internet users to protect themselves*. Academic Press.

Siponen, M. (2000). A conceptual foundation for organizational information security awareness. *Information Management & Computer Security, 8*(1), 31–41. doi:10.1108/09685220010371394

Symantec. (2009). *Symantec Internet Security Threat Report: Trends for 2008*. Symantec Corporation. Retrieved from http://eval.symantec.com/mktginfo/enterprise/white_papers/bwhitepaper_exec_summary_internet_security_threat_report_xiv_04-2009.en-us.pdf

Taherdoost, H. (2016). *Electronic Service Technology; Concepts, Applications and Security* (1st ed.). OmniScriptum.

Taherdoost, H. (2018). Development of an adoption model to assess user acceptance of e-service technology: E-Service Technology Acceptance Model. *Behaviour & Information Technology, 37*(2), 173–197. doi:10.1080/0144929X.2018.1427793

Taherdoost, H. (2020a). Electronic Service Quality Measurement (eSQM); Development of a Survey Instrument to Measure the Quality of E-Service. *International Journal of Intelligent Engineering Informatics*, *7*(6), 491–528. doi:10.1504/IJIEI.2019.104559

Taherdoost, H. (2020b). Evaluation of Customer Satisfaction in Digital Environment; Development of Survey Instrument. In K. Sandhu (Ed.), *Digital Transformation and Innovative Services for Business and Learning* (pp. 195–222). IGI Global. doi:10.4018/978-1-7998-5175-2.ch011

Taherdoost, H., & Hassan, A. (2020). Development of An E-Service Quality Model (eSQM) to Assess the Quality of E-Service. In R. C. Ho (Ed.), *Strategies and Tools for Managing Connected Customers* (pp. 177–207). IGI Global. doi:10.4018/978-1-5225-9697-4.ch011

Taherdoost, H., & Madanchian, M. (2020). Developing and Validating a Theoretical Model to Evaluate Customer Satisfaction of E-Services. In K. Sandhu (Ed.), *Digital Innovations for Customer Engagement, Management and Organizational Improvement* (pp. 46–65). IGI Global. doi:10.4018/978-1-7998-5171-4.ch003

Taherdoost, H., Sahibuddin, S., & Jalaliyoon, N. (2015). A Review Paper on E-Service; Technology Concepts. *Procedia Technology*, *19*, 1067–1074. doi:10.1016/j.protcy.2015.02.152

Takeuchi, H., & Nonaka, I. (1995). *The knowledge-creating company: How Japanese companies create the dynamics of innovation.* Oxford University Press.

Tilson, D., Lyytinen, K., & Sørensen, C. (2010). Digital Infrastructures: The Missing IS Research Agenda. *Information Systems Research*, *21*(4), 748–759. doi:10.1287/isre.1100.0318

Trim, P. R. J., & Lee, Y.-i. (2019). The role of B2B marketers in increasing cyber security awareness and influencing behavioural change. *Industrial Marketing Management*, *83*, 224–238. doi:10.1016/j.indmarman.2019.04.003

Ulas, D. (2019). Digital Transformation Process and SMEs. *Procedia Computer Science*, *158*, 662–671. doi:10.1016/j.procs.2019.09.101

Verhoef, P. C., Broekhuizen, T., Bart, Y., Bhattacharya, A., Dong, J. Q., Fabian, N., & Haenlein, M. (2019). Digital transformation: A multidisciplinary reflection and research agenda. *Journal of Business Research*, *122*, 889–901. doi:10.1016/j.jbusres.2019.09.022

Vial, G. (2019). Understanding digital transformation: A review and a research agenda. *The Journal of Strategic Information Systems*, *28*(2), 118–144. doi:10.1016/j.jsis.2019.01.003

Vina, G. (2016). *Patients in limbo after cyber attack.* Retrieved from https://www.ft.com/content/1292d25c-a12a-11e6-891e-abe238dee8e2

Whitman, M., & Mattord, H. (2011). *Principles of information security.* Nelson Education.

Young, E. (2004). *Global Information Security Survey 2004.* Ernst & Young.

Zaoui, F., & Souissi, N. (2020). Roadmap for digital transformation: A literature review. *Procedia Computer Science*, *175*, 621–628. doi:10.1016/j.procs.2020.07.090

Chapter 7
Advancing Artificial Intelligence–Enabled Cybersecurity for the Internet of Things

Alper Kamil Demir

Adana Alparsalan Turkes Science and Technology University, Turkey

Shahid Alam

(iD) https://orcid.org/0000-0002-4080-8042

Adana Alparsalan Turkes Science and Technology University, Turkey

ABSTRACT

Internet of things (IoT) has revolutionized digital transformation and is present in every sector including transportation, energy, retail, healthcare, agriculture, etc. While stepping into the new digital transformation, these sectors must contemplate the risks involved. The new wave of cyberattacks against IoT is posing a severe impediment in adopting this leading-edge technology. Artificial intelligence (AI) is playing a key role in preventing and mitigating some of the effects of these cyberattacks. This chapter discusses different types of threats and attacks against IoT devices and how AI is enabling the detection and prevention of these cyberattacks. It also presents some challenges faced by AI-enabled detection and prevention and provides some solutions and recommendations to these challenges. The authors believe that this chapter provides a favorable basis for the readers who intend to know more about AI-enabled technologies to detect and prevent cyberattacks against IoT and the motivation to advance the current research in this area.

DOI: 10.4018/978-1-7998-6975-7.ch007

INTRODUCTION

Internet of Things (IoT) is another technical revolution whose time has also most definitely come (Atzori et al., 2010). Internet of Things (IoT) is the interconnection of heterogeneous smart devices through the Internet with diverse application areas such as smart home, car, cities, healthcare, wearables, retail, grid, agriculture, and the industry as shown in Figure 1. Gartner, a global research and advisory firm, forecasts that the IoT market will grow to 5.8 billion endpoints in the year 2020, a 21% increase from the previous year. Most of the enterprises have already started embracing IoT as a way of expediting the digital transformation initiatives. The essence of IoT will give all companies a new norm of digitizing business models. The IoT will enable a smooth integration of business processes through digitization. However, one of the main challenges plaguing a successful deployment of IoT is Cybersecurity. In IoT, not all of the Things that form an IoT network have adequately tested for cyberattacks. As a result, the entire system is threatened.

Cybercrime is increasing, and cybersecurity is ultimately evolving. This evolution is calling for innovation in the field of cybersecurity defense. This phenomenon is becoming more vital due to the boost on the Internet and diversified devices that constitute the IoT. The contemporary world of digital transformation is bringing challenges to the cybersecurity of the IoT environment. A cyberthreat is a threat that involves a computer or a computer network. Vulnerabilities in computers bring about cyberthreats. Vulnerabilities are due to weakness in the design, implementation, operation, or control of computers and computer networks. Because of the exploitable vulnerabilities, cyber hackers attack computing systems of individuals or cooperation. As a result, we need to defend these computing systems against cyberattacks.

Figure 1. Internet of Things: the big picture

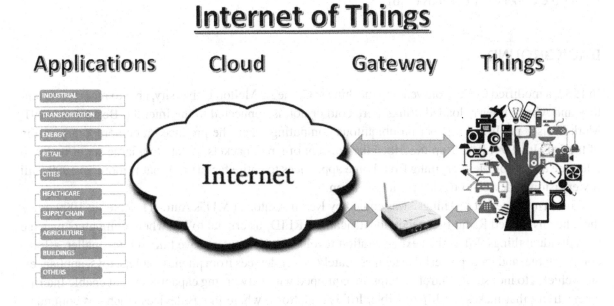

Until recent decades, traditional defense mechanisms are deployed to protect the computing facilities. However, history showed that traditional defense mechanisms are not adequate anymore as hackers become more sophisticated and plentiful. Thus, the Artificial Intelligence (AI) might be the only way to keep pace. Artificial intelligence (AI) is currently being implemented into information systems across all industries. A vast amount of data is being produced regularly by IoT devices. The data produced by IoT devices is far more than any traditional method that can process or make use of in a productive way. As a result, the IoT environment is progressively challenging cybersecurity professionals to secure without hindering IoT functions. Fortunately, AI is a solution. The IoT obligates AI. AI is a key cybersecurity weapon in the IoT era. In this work, we introduce how AI enables cybersecurity for IoT.

Around the 1990s, because of low speed, the use of the Internet was very limited where the Internet connectivity was only diffused into the enterprise and consumer market. Around the 2000s, the Internet brought up many applications in our lives. By 2010, Internet connectivity propagated into the enterprise, consumer, and industrial products to provide access to all kinds of data and information from the sensor and to actuator devices that form the concept of IoT. The evolution of the IoT from "Internet of the Content" to "Internet of Things" is depicted in Figure 2. Nevertheless, today, these IoT devices are still only "Things" on the Internet, as they require human interaction and monitoring through applications. The future is promising. IoTs responding to how we want everything to act and operating ubiquitously behind the scenes. For sure, life is going to be amazing.

AI is a field of computer science addressing to automate computing problems that require human intelligence (Aishath et al., 2019). The AI tries to construct artificially learning and acting agents by researching living creatures existing in nature. In other sophisticated words, it aims to create agents that have high cognitive functions like sensing, learning, thinking, associating, reasoning, problem-solving, communicating, inferring, and decision-making capabilities. If general AI is to be accomplished, it might also lead to superintelligence. Since both AI and IoT lie on a large amount of data, it is one of the best fits for the Cybersecurity needs of IoT.

BACKGROUND

In 1982, a modified CoCa-Cola vending machine at Carnegie Mellon University, able to report its inventory and whether newly loaded drinks were cold or not, is connected to the Internet. Besides, in 1991, Mark Weiser published a paper on ubiquitous computing where he produced a contemporary vision of the IoT. In 1994, Reza Raji described the concept of small packets of data to a large set of nodes to integrate and automate everything from home appliances to entire factories. What is more, in 1999, Bill Joy envisioned device-to-device communication.

The term, "Internet of Things" was coined by Kevin Ashton at MIT's Auto-ID Center in 1999. Back then, he envisioned Radio Frequency Identification (RFID) as crucial to IoT where computers manage all individual things. IoT is the next generation revolution. Computers have turned into smaller, affordable, portable, and more powerful machines. Lately, many devices from phones, tablets, toys, appliances, and vehicles to industrial control systems are equipped with networking capabilities that enable Internet connectivity that makes the IoT possible. IoT is a platform where things/devices/machines communicate with each other over the Internet. The things consist of various types of sensors and actuators and conveniently share the information.

Figure 2. Evolution of Internet of Things
source: *(Zeadally, 2020)*

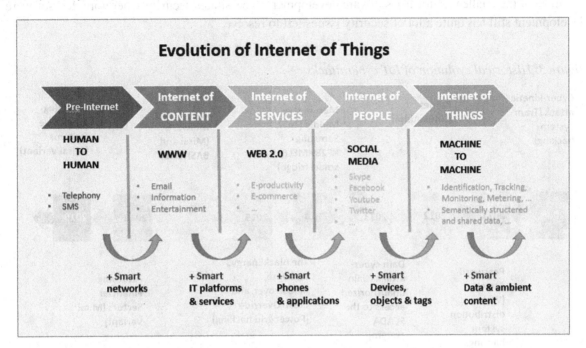

IoT software development is a minefield. The market needs high-quality, scalable, robust, secure, and user-friendly solutions. First and foremost, developers need to choose IoT devices with that they will work. As we already know, IoT devices are resource-limited and far less powerful. By that, developers pick the corresponding IoT operating system (OS). IoT software should fit in the capabilities of the IoT device and OS. IoT gateways are located between the Things and the Cloud. Thus, IoT gateways are the key connectivity to all the components. Serial port, Bluetooth, Wi-Fi, and LoRaWAN are among different connectivity protocols. As a result, developers need to select the IoT gateways that meet IoT application requirements.

Safe, private, and credible communication is necessary by default. IoT frameworks, used in IoT software, should provide connectivity, security, scalability, easy integration, and usability. Figure 3 depicts the historical evolution of IoT cyberattacks, and it is expected that the number of cyberattacks on IoTs will continue to grow. Therefore, cybersecurity is a colossal challenge for IoT software developers working on IoT projects. Quality assurance is another keen issue of IoT software. After all, IoT devices are used not only for generally insensitive values such as temperature control in warehouses but also for delicate values such as insulin pumps in healthcare. A very tiny issue can turn out to be deadly. As a result, testing should be eminently thorough.

Since, in an IoT application, every Thing may talk to each other, the workflow is complex and the amount of data is huge. Therefore, IoT software should be designed as simple as possible. Moreover, the user-friendliness of IoT software is much more important than that of traditional software. Last, but not least, IoT software should consider cross-platform deployment. An IoT ecosystem might include Things with different hardware architecture, protocols, and operating systems. Therefore, reputable organizations, i.e., IETF and IEEE, have come up with the open standards and architecture models for cross-platform deployments. The bottom line is that IoT software is distinct from traditional software, and most of the challenges for IoT software development necessitates security. Therefore, IoT software development still has quite a lot of security issues left to resolve.

Figure 3. Historical evolution of IoT cyberattacks

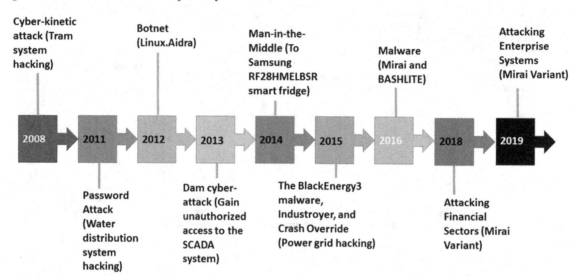

The study of formal reasoning began with philosophers and mathematicians in antiquity (Buchanan, 2005). Alan Turing's Theory of Computation, suggesting that a machine by leveraging symbols as simple as 0 and 1, could simulate any conceivable act of mathematical deduction. The theory was led by the study of mathematical logic. AI was founded as an academic discipline in 1955. The field of AI research was born as a workshop at Dartmouth College in 1956. John McCarthy coined the term "Artificial Intelligence" (McCorduck et al., 1977).

AI is concerned with how machines can think or act correctly, given what they know (Russel & Norvig, 2002). Turing tests sets the standard on machine intelligence (Turing, 1956). According to the Turing test, a computer, behind the scenes and communication with a human is said to have artificial intelligence when the human cannot differentiate whether the responses come from a computer or a human. AI incorporates computing areas such as natural language processing, knowledge representation, logic, automated reasoning, machine learning, mathematics, and game theory (Zeadally, 2020).

Artificial intelligence (AI) is intelligence demonstrated by machines, unlike the natural intelligence displayed by humans and animals. AI is the field of study of Intelligent Agents. Agents perceive their environment and take proper actions to maximize the chance of successfully achieving their goals. AI describes the machines that imitate cognitive functions that human's accomplice with the human mind such as learning and problem-solving.

AI offers various opportunities in cybersecurity such as Intelligent Agents, Computational Intelligence, Artificial Neural Networks (ANN), Artificial Immune Systems, Machine Learning (ML), Genetic Algorithms, Data Mining, Pattern Recognition, Fuzzy Logic, Expert Systems, and Heuristic Methods (Dilek et al., 2015). AI systems are generally both scalable and effective. Furthermore, AI systems can exceed human capabilities.

AI-ENABLED CYBERSECURITY DETECTION AND PREVENTION MECHANISMS

The ubiquitous nature of IoT makes them more susceptible to cyberattacks. IoT is a collection of devices networked together to provide different services. If one of them is compromised in an IoT network the others also become vulnerable. Therefore, securing all the devices is vital for the security of the network. Due to the increase in the use of IoTs, the cyberattacks against these devices have significantly increased. This section first discusses the different types of threats and attacks against IoT devices used in various sectors, and then AI-enabled detection and prevention mechanisms to stop some of these Cyberattacks (Latif et al., 2020; Vu et al., 2020; Boukerche & Coutinho, 2020; Zeadally & Tsikerdekis, 2020; Tahsien et al., 2020; Liang et al., 2019a; Farivar et al., 2019; Wang et al., 2019; Xiao et al., 2018; Restuccia et al., 2018).

Types of Threats and Attacks against IoT in Various Sector

Here we discuss some of the major types of threats and attacks against IoTs in various sectors with examples from real-life cyberattacks. We are not going to cover all the sectors, but only a few important ones.

Type of Threats and Attacks

Botnet: Several internet devices (including computers, smartphones, and IoTs) connected and running one or more bots is called a botnet (the network of bots). A bot is a software application that runs automated tasks, such as web crawling etc., over the internet. A botnet is controlled through a command and control (C&C) software. Botnets are increasingly rented by cybercriminals to perform different malicious tasks. Some of the tasks performed by botnets are, DDoS (distributed denial of service) attacks, send spam, allow the user to access the device and its connections, and steal data, etc. Mirai, a real-life malware that created around 380000 IoT bots, primarily targeted online consumer devices mostly with DDoS attacks. The two popular botnet models are client-server and peer-to-peer. In a client-server model, the individual clients request services and resources from a centralized server. In a peer-to-peer model interconnected devices share resources among each other without the use of a centralized server. A botnet diagram illustrating a DDoS attack is shown in *Figure* 4. Following are a set of steps on how a botnet is created and used for malicious purposes. ML methods are successfully applied to the Botnet detection problem (Shafiq et al., 2020).

- A malware is launched that starts infecting the bots (internet devices)
- The infected device (bot) connects to the C&C server. The botmaster (a cybercriminal who owns the botnet) through the C&C server controls the bots.
- The botmaster uses the bots to perform malicious actions, such as stealing online credentials, renting the botnet for DDoS or spam attacks, etc.

Distributed Denial-of-Service Attack (DDoS): A denial of service (DoS) is an attack that renders a service unavailable. The main reason for unavailability is the overuse of the infrastructure that runs the service. A DDoS attack is launched by many systems (e.g., bots) attacking one target. This is usually accomplished using bots. Each bot requests the same service at the same time flooding the target system with so many requests, that the system either fails or slows down its operations. Because of the system failing or slowing down, affects the company's reputation and business. The customer may decide to switch the company due to fear of security loss or the unavailability of the service. An example of a DDoS attack is shown in Figure 1. Mirai is a real-life example of this kind of attack. Another attack using a malware Bashlite, specially designed for the ARM version of Linux, was able to hack the CCTV cameras in different shopping centers and turned them into a large botnet for launching a DDoS attack. The target of the DDoS attack was a large cloud service provider, serving millions of users worldwide.

Figure 4. An example of a DDoS attack carried out by an IoT botnet

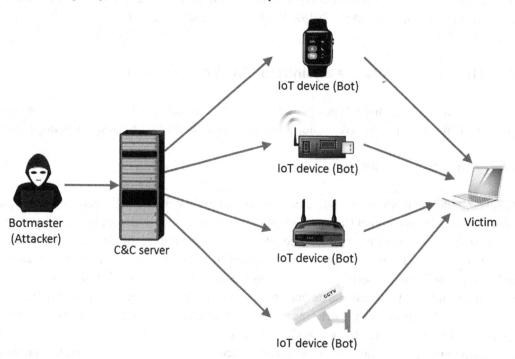

Malware: Malware is malicious software that carries out malicious activities, such as stealing passwords, setting up a back door, etc. Antimalware software is used to detect, neutralize, and mitigates the effect of malware. Different traditional classification of malware is viruses, worms, trojans, ransomware, spyware, and rootkits, etc. During the digital transformation, malware has evolved into a complex and reusable piece of software. Malware writers use different techniques to hide malware, such as obfuscations. These techniques obscure the code and make it difficult to understand, analyze, and detect malware embedded in the code. Using similar techniques malware writers can easily create copies (variants) of the original malware, which are not detectable. With the recent advancements in the IoT devices such as more CPU power and memory, these devices are prone to more sophisticated malware attacks. Because of their limited energy resources, running a complete malware detector on these devices is quite challenging. In general, IoT malware is used to perform DDoS attacks, scanning open ports of IoT services such as FTP, SSH, and Telnet, and brute-force attack to gain access to IoT devices.

Man-in-the-Middle (MITM) Attack: MITM attack uses different techniques to intercept communication between two IoT devices. After interrupting the communication, the attacker can act as a proxy. The attacker creates a new connection and now the communication between the two devices goes through the new connection. An example of a MITM attack is shown in *Figure* 5. IoT devices are often maintenance-free with low interaction. Therefore, the end-users of these IoT devices are not aware of possible attacks. A major reason for a MITM attack on IoTs is their insecure defaults, such as simple default usernames (admin) and passwords (admin), lack of security updates, and open access to management systems via the Internet, etc. An MITM attack is usually combined with other attacks. MITM attacks are often targeted at individuals and hence remain undiscovered. Only large-scale attacks become public, others remain hidden to preserve the targeted company's image.

Figure 5. An example of a man-in-the middle (MITM) attack

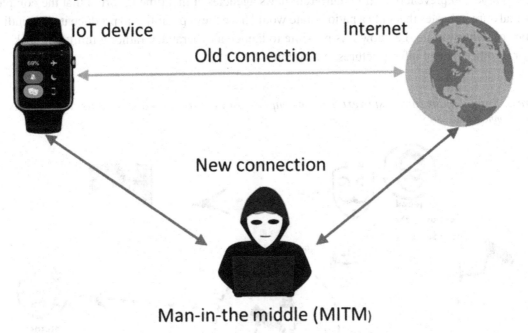

Password Attack: Open Web Access Security Project (OWASP) listed weak, guessable, or hard-coded passwords as one of the top ten IoT vulnerabilities. This makes it easy for an attacker to gain access to an IoT device to deploy large-scale botnets and other malware. IoT devices do not have human operators to instigate password change, so it is very difficult to manage passwords for these devices. Recently a list of credentials (each device's IP address, and username and password for Telnet) for more than 500K servers, home routers, and other IoT devices were leaked on a popular hacker's forum. This demonstrates the inherent insecurity of different protocols used by smart IoT devices to connect to the Internet. Not only the device users and smart homes but also the enterprises are at risk because of these insecure IoT devices.

Data Transfer and Storage: The protection of IoT data is very crucial to the security of IoT applications. Some of the requirements for delivering data securely from and to IoT devices are: Securing access to the data; verifying the source and integrity of the data; and use of strong encryption methodologies from data creation to consumption. Providing an update mechanism, for firmware updates etc, is very important. Some of the common mistakes in update mechanisms are: lack of firmware validation; updates without encryption in transit; and failure to provide notification of security changes due to updates. If the personal information stored on the device is stored insecurely then the privacy of the user can be leaked.

Real-Life Examples of Cyberattacks

Industrial Control Systems: Stuxnet, malware, and the world's first digital weapon was discovered in 2010. Stuxnet targets SCADA (supervisory control and data acquisition) systems, as shown in Figure 6, and is known to have damaged nuclear power plants in different countries. Its specific target is PLC (programmable logic controller), which is used to control machinery and industrial processes including nuclear centrifuges. Targeting industrial control systems, it infected over 200,000 computers. It used a rootkit to hide and prevent detection. Different news agencies at that time reported that the complexity of the malware indicates that only a nation-state would have the capabilities to produce it. This indicated the start of cyberwarfare, i.e., now it is possible to launch a cyberattack rather a military attack on the nuclear or other critical infrastructures of a country.

Figure 6. Spread of Stuxnet to subvert Seimens supervisory control and data acquisition systems
Source: (Connell et al., 2013)

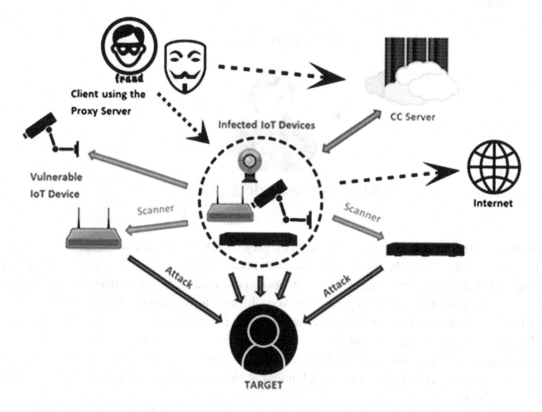

Smart Homes and Cities: Mirai, one of the most popular IoT malware first found in 2016, targets various IoT devices (such as IP cameras and home routers) with a distributed denial of service (DDoS) attack. Devices infected by Mirai continuously scan the internet for other IoTs. When found they log into them using a table of common factory default usernames and passwords. This is how Mirai spreads quickly through a network of IoT. The infected device continues to function normally but with sluggishness and increased use of the bandwidth. A Mirai-based bot DDOS attack detected by Fortinet, a security company, is shown in Figure 7. The IoT devices were turned into proxy servers, which were then sold to other cybercriminals.

Figure 7. Mirai-based bot DDOS attack, turning IoT devices into proxy servers
Source: (Manuel et al., 2018).

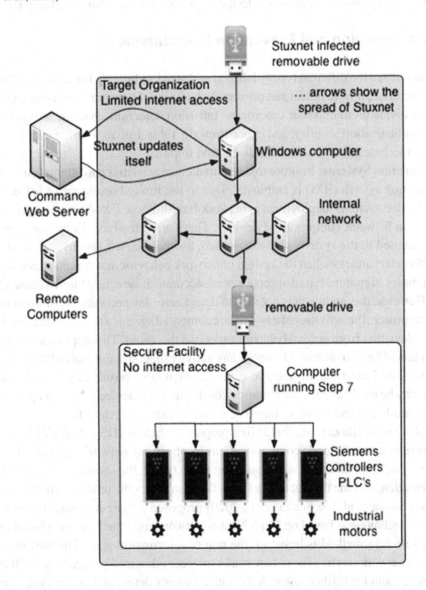

Intelligent Transport Systems: In 2016, the San Francisco transportation agency was hit by a crypto-ransomware attack. The attackers managed to infect and take over more than 2000 computers operating San Francisco's transport system. As a result, the agency allowed free rides to all the riders until the system was fixed.

Smart Power Grids: In the 2016 Ukraine power grid shutdown, the attackers were able to take offline various substations leaving more than 230,000 residents in the dark. This attack was carefully planned over many months by some skilled and stealthy strategists. They were able to overwrite the firmware on various critical devices leaving them unresponsive to any remote commands and operations. It took many months to make the power grid station fully operational. The malicious software responsible for the attack was spread through phishing emails via a Word document attachment. When clicked and given permission, a malicious program called BlackEnergy3 infected the computers and opened a backdoor to the attackers. This intrusion led the attackers to the SCADA networks that controlled the grid.

Cyberattacks, Detection and Prevention Mechanisms

So far, we have discussed the different types of threats and attacks plaguing IoT devices. Now the question arises, how to defend i.e., how to detect and prevent such attacks. There are various mechanisms used for this purpose. We divide them into four categories: Intrusion detection systems, access and authentication controls, communication security, and cyber-firewall. Table 1 gives a summarized comparison and analysis of these mechanisms and a detailed discussion follows.

Intrusion Detection Systems: In-order to detect malicious activities and attempts in an IoT paradigm an intrusion detection system (IDS) is employed. Due to the limited resources of IoT devices, most of the intrusion detection systems' deployment is network-based. These IDSs' active response system halts any communication between compromised devices. There are three basic detection approaches based on the mechanism used in the system: signature-based, anomaly-based, and hybrid. In signature-based approaches, IDSs detect attacks when the system or network behavior matches an attack signature stored in the IDSs' databases. signature-based approaches are accurate at detecting known threats and are easier to understand. However, this approach is not able to detect zero-day and variants of known attacks. In an anomaly-based approach, the activities of a system are compared against a normal behavior. It generates an alert whenever a deviation from normal behavior exceeds a threshold. This approach can detect zero-day attacks and variants of known attacks. However, any activity that does not match the normal behavior is tagged as an intrusion. Therefore, this method generates high false-positive rates. It also uses statistical techniques that may be too heavy for the resource constrained IoT devices. Hybrid approaches use concepts from signature-based and anomaly-based detection to maximize the advantages and minimize the disadvantages. Raza et al. (Raza et al., 2013) first proposed a hybrid IDS called SVELTE for IoTs. This IDS monitors inconsistencies in node communications by observing network topology. The IDS consists of three modules. The first gathers information about the network, the second is responsible for analysis and intrusion detection, and the third acts as a firewall which filters the unwanted traffic to reach the IoT devices. Recently Souza et al. (de Souza et al., 2020) proposed a fog computing-based IDS to protect IoT networks. The technique is based on Deep Neural Networks and the k-Nearest Neighbor algorithm. Their attributes selection method is based on the rate of information gain. The attributes are selected from the captured network traffic. These two works indicate advanced progress in the IDS techniques, but still, they leave room for further research. IDS mechanisms detect and prevent only limited attacks, therefore, relying on them is not sufficient to provide effective security to IoT devices and networks.

There exist ML and DL based IDS mechanisms presented in (Daim et al., 2020; Latif et al., 2020; da Costa et al., 2019; Hasan et al., 2019; Alrashdi et al., 2019; Liang et al., 2019b; Abeshu & Chilamkurti, 2018; Androcec & Vrcek, 2018).

Table 1. Comparison and analysis of different mechanisms for detecting and preventing IoT cyberattacks

Research Work	Mechanism	Techniques Used	Description
Raza et al., 2013	Intrusion detection system	Routing protocol destination-oriented directed acyclic graph	Monitors inconsistencies in IoT's node communications by observing network topology. Provides real-time intrusion detection in IoTs.
Souza et al., 2020	Intrusion detection system	Fog computing Deep neural networks K-nearest neighbor	Attributes are captured from the IoT's network traffic and are selected based on the rate of information gain.
Kim & Lee, 2017	Authentication & authorization controls	Edge computing	Provides authorization for locally registered IoT devices while managing trust relationships with others globally.
Fang et al., 2020	Authentication & authorization controls	Machine learning	Establishes a secure connection between transceivers in large-scale IoT networks.
Kim et al., 2020	Authentication & authorization controls	Edge computing	The approach is based on secure migration, which allows an IoT device to migrate to a trusted edge computer when its authorization service fails or becomes unavailable.
Gauhar et al., 2020	Authentication & authorization controls	Blockchain	Performs permission delegation and access control for both internal and external user/IoT devices.
Misra et al., 2011	Communication security	Learning automata	Performs IoT's DDOS detection by limiting the number of service requests.
Ahmed et al., 2017	Communication security	Software defined networking Machine learning	Performs IoT's traffic analysis in real-time and detect and prevent malicious flows.
Sagirlar et al., 2017	Communication security	Image processing Convolutional neural network	Recognizes different IoT's DDOS malicious behaviors and uses lightweight classification for detection.
Javaidet al., 2018	Communication security	Blockchain	Facilitates secure communication between the IoT devices and the distributed servers.
Sari, 2019	Cyber Firewall	Artificial intelligence	Captures IoT's TCP/IP packets and filters them based on security policies written in a high-level programming language. It uses AI to learn from previous attacks and prevent new attack variants.

Authentication and Authorization Controls: To address different threats and attacks against IoT devices and networks, authentication and authorization techniques are typically adopted. However, such mechanisms are a challenge for resource constrained IoT devices. Recently there are some efforts to address this concern. Establishing trust among IoT devices is a challenging task. There are two basic ways to achieve this. One is using a centralized authority, and the other is to use distributed trusted fellows. Each has its advantages and disadvantages. Failure of the centralized authority results in failure of the whole system but is simpler to implement and consumes fewer resources. Distributed trust schemes avoid the problem of centralized authority but are difficult to implement and manage and consume more resources. To maximize the advantages and minimize the disadvantage of both these schemes Kim et al. (Kim & Lee, 2017) proposed a hybrid scheme that uses a locally centralized and globally distributed infrastructure. The scheme provides authorization for locally registered IoT devices while managing trust relationships with others globally. Fang et al. (Fang et al., 2020) leverage artificial intelligence (AI) for enhancing the security of IoT devices. They developed a lightweight authentication approach by exploring machine learning at the base station. Then a holistic authentication and authorization approach is proposed, where online machine learning and trust management are adopted for achieving adaptive access control. The new AI-enabled approaches establish a secure connection between transceivers in large-scale IoT networks. Kim et al. (Kim et al., 2020) propose a resilient authentication and authorization framework to enhance the availability of IoT services under DDoS attacks. They use edge computing to accomplish this. The approach is based on secure migration, which allows an IoT device to migrate to a trusted edge computer when its authorization service fails or becomes unavailable. Ali et al. (Gauhar et al., 2020) present a decentralized blockchain-based cross-domain authentication and authorization framework for IoT. They also propose a hierarchy of contracts that perform permission delegation and access control for both internal and external user/IoT devices.

Communication Security: Distributed denial of service (DDoS) is one of the most well-known attacks over IoT networks. DDoS interrupts and blocks genuine users/devices' communication with the IoTs. Generally, this is accomplished by flooding the targeted host either using botnets (in most of the cases) or some other mechanisms. Here we present some of the different defense mechanisms against DDoS attacks.

- **Learning Automata** (Misra et al., 2011): This approach uses three phases. (i) DDoS detection – If the number of service request surpass a certain limit (threshold) an alert is issued. (ii) Attacker identification – In this phase, the attacking device is identified. (iii) DDoS defense – All the incoming packets from the attacking device are discarded if it fails to be legitimate.
- **Software-Defined Networking** (Ahmed et al., 2017): To control the propagation of DDoS attacks reaching the endpoints the concept of software-defined networking (SDN) based infrastructure is used. SDN can dynamically manipulate the traffic flows or packets flowing in the network. This allows traffic analysis to be performed in real-time using machine learning algorithms, and hence the detection and prevention of malicious flows.
- **Detecting IoT Malware Botnets** (Sagirlar et al., 2017): A lightweight technique for detecting DDoS malware is proposed especially for IoT networks. Image processing is used to recognize and analyze different malware behaviors. For a lightweight classification CNN (convolutional neural network) is used. Cloud is used for deeper analysis as the IoTs lack resources.
- **Blockchain** (Javaidet et. al., 2018): In this system, blockchains are used for self-executable computer programs called smart contracts. A smart contract facilitates secure communication between the IoT devices and the distributed servers. The use of blockchains enables a transparent and decentralized approach for storing data across all the networks.

Cyber-Firewall: Cyber-Firewall is a security system that monitors the incoming and outgoing traffic of a network based on some specified security rules. It acts as a barrier between a trusted and an untrusted network, such as the IoT network. Traditional cyber-firewalls provide conventional security solutions that do not cope with sophisticated cyberattacks. We present here a system called *Seddulbahir* (Sari, 2019) which provides lightweight, unified, and AI-oriented firewall-as-a-service technology to defend against IoT cyberattacks. It provides support to deal with IoT threats and vulnerabilities, specifically IoT-powered cyberattacks. Seddulbahir system is a cyber-firewall that captures TCP/IP packets and filters them based on security policies written in a high-level programming language. The system also manipulates live traffic streams and has the capability of dropping, creating, and injecting packets. It uses AI to learn from previous attacks and prevent new attack variants. Some of the features of this system are discussed as follows. **On-the-fly advanced packet modification** – This feature allows the system to automatically disinfect a set of compromised IoT nodes. This also enables the system to drop any malicious activities or connection requests that violate a country's cybersecurity policy. **Advanced packet inspection** – The system has an interactive mode that enables it to inspect specific packets and their contents, such as flags, ports, and checksums, etc. **AI security engine** – To deal with the new variants of existing attacks, an AI module is used which uses previous attacks' data for feature extraction. This feature information is used by the classification and clustering algorithm to update the security rules. **Logging and alerting** – The system logs the complete network including suspicious activities. The alerts are generated, and both the logs and alerts are visualized for experts' review.

ISSUES AND CHALLENGES

Creation of a Solid AI Model of acceptable behavior: One of the main issues is that it might be difficult to create a solid AI model of acceptable behavior. As a result, numerous false alarms might be triggered by anomalous behavior. Besides, currently, the speed of AI models is slow. Customized hardware or parallel computing methods are needed. Moreover, the development and deployment of online learning AI systems are hard and complex to design. The other challenges might be listed as:

Availability of Cybersecurity-Related IoT Datasets: Cybersecurity related IoT data sets are few and biased. Although the same dataset is used for evaluation, the sample extraction methods are different. The evaluation methods are not uniform. Most of the studies are on the accuracy of the experiments. Hence, the results are one-sided. Multi-criteria evaluation research relies on different metrics or a combination of metrics. Therefore, the research results cannot be compared with each other. Most of the research is carried in the labs. Deployment efficiency is not being considered adequately. This leads to problems in the actual IoT network. Fine-tuning the algorithms require many experiments resulting in poor interoperability. In addition, confidentiality and user privacy restrictions cause many datasets internal where the datasets cannot be shared with the public. The companies commonly evade sharing their protected data because of these issues.

Many datasets may lack specific statistical characteristics. As the companies avoid sharing their datasets, researchers are obliged to generate datasets for training and testing purposes in the simulated or closed experimental environments that may miss full coverage. Such uncomprehensive datasets result in a semantic gap between the result and their application. Datasets generated in such environments may perform well with a certain experimental environment, but it may not perform suitable with other datasets. Moreover, the datasets may show different performances with the same experiment.

The training datasets must be comprehensive and diverse (Al-Garadi et al., 2020). In particular, it is very hard to extract or generate a realistic and high-quality dataset. AI learning algorithms require high-quality datasets for training accurately. The used dataset needs to contain various possible attack types. The model knowledge of the learning methods is generated according to the used dataset where it needs to contain information that reflects all of the strategies. As IoT systems produce large volumes of data, maintaining the quality of the dataset remains a challenge.

It is crucial to assemble a hybrid dataset using various major datasets. As any dataset is limited in size, several datasets can be merged to create a large-scale dataset. However, it is not straightforward to assemble such datasets because each dataset might have different characteristics of IoT cyber traffic.

Imbalanced Dataset: Cyber attackers do not wish to be exposed. Cyberattacks are usually run randomly in short periods of time. As a result, the cyberattack data leads to a very low amount to train the learning algorithms. This phenomenon is known as an imbalanced dataset problem. Particularly, the imbalanced dataset states that the percentage of cyberattack traffic compared to the normal traffic in the whole dataset is very tiny. IoT cybersecurity techniques suffer from the severely imbalanced dataset. An imbalanced dataset problem may result in different outcomes compared to models trained with the full dataset.

Proper Feature Extraction and Selection: As we already know, training ML and DL algorithms also depend upon selected features. As a result, one of the very first consideration is to choose proper features from the IoT network traffic dataset. Usually, IoT network traffic is obtained during a long period from many IoT devices with different sampling frequencies. These results with high-dimensional datasets. Therefore, it is compelling to extract discerning features. Extracting and selecting proper features is a harder task for a high-dimensional IoT dataset.

Augmentation of IoT Security Data to Improve the Learning Algorithm Performance: Collecting a large set of the dataset for ML and DL is rather difficult in the domain of data security in IoT systems (Al-Garadi et al., 2020). Naturally, when ML and DL algorithms are trained with richer data, more accurate results are obtained. Hence, obtaining substantial amounts of data in the IoT domain is desirable.

Computational Complexity: IoT devices are resource-constrained devices. Many AI-based cybersecurity schemes are computationally intensive. They necessitate a large number of training data. The feature extraction process of these schemes is very complicated. Therefore, it is very challenging to design simple algorithms for these resource-constrained devices.

Inability to Maintain Cybersecurity Autonomously: Security systems are not yet fully autonomous although there have been huge advances in adapting AI techniques to cybersecurity. Security systems are not yet able to absolutely replace human decisions. Still, there exist some tasks needing human intervention.

Complicated IoT Network Topology: Investigating IoT network topology is a complex challenge because IoT network topologies can be very complicated.

Learning to Secure IoT With Low-Quality Data: In general, DL methods are for high-quality data (Al-Garadi et al., 2020; Zhang et al., 2018). As IoT systems are composed of heterogeneous connected devices and generate large-scale streaming, the data has the possibility of high-noise and can be corrupted. As a result, effective DL methods, that can handle and learn from low-quality data, needs to be used because obtaining high-quality data might be practically infeasible. This requires multi-modal and effective DL models.

SOLUTIONS AND RECOMMENDATIONS

Machine Learning

Deep Learning (DL) is part of a broader family of machine learning methods based on Artificial Neural Networks (ANN) with representation learning. Deep Neural Networks, Deep Belief Networks, Recurrent Neural Networks, and Convolutional Neural Networks are among DNN architectures applied to computational problems. DNN has shown promising results comparable to, and in some cases, surpassing human expert performance (Koroniotis et al., 2020). The "deep" in DL comes from the use of multiple layers in the artificial network. For example, attack detection by the use of DL in the cyberspace could be a resilient mechanism to small mutations or novel attacks because of its high-level feature extraction capability (Ahmed & Askar, 2021; Al-Garadi et al., 2020; Alotaibi & Alotaibi, 2020; Velliangiri & Kasaraneni, 2020; Diro et al., 2018;). DL architectures have the self-taught and compression capabilities. These are key mechanisms for hidden pattern discovery from the training data so that attacks are discriminated from benign traffic. Like ML, DL is a powerful method for data exploration to learn about normal and abnormal states according to how IoT devices behave in an IoT network. Specifically, In (Yavuz, 2018), the use of DL based routing attack detection for IoT environments is investigated. In addition, comprehensive development of new intelligent and autonomous DL-based Intrusion Detection and Classification System is proposed in (Abu Al-Haija & Zein-Sabatto, 2020).

Supervised learning requires a vast amount of labeled data. Collecting a great deal of data is very expensive. As a result, the future deep learning methods are expected to be unsupervised, more human-like. Semi-supervised learning is another option with a large amount of unlabeled data. It is essential to emphasize that DL is not applicable to be used in every application domain. DL may be used in domains with large-scale data, complex-non-linear hypotheses with many features, and high-order polynomial terms. ML might suffice for linear problems with small amounts of data. Low computational supervised learning techniques, such as distributed Frank-Wolfe (Xiao et al., 2017), can be applied to IoT cybersecurity systems to improve spoofing resistance.

Transfer Learning (TL) is a machine learning problem that targets storing knowledge achieved while solving one problem and administering it to a distinct but related problem. Simply, knowledge gained while learning to recognize cats could be apply when trying to recognize dogs. TL bears some roots to the history of psychological literature on transfer learning. TL can enhance reinforcement learning, from the practical point of view, as it leverages previously learned tasks for the learning of new tasks. Currently, application of TL is not a vastly explored area. However, we believe that it needs a concrete attention. The work in (Vu, 2020) proposes a novel deep transfer learning (DTL) approach based on AutoEncoder (AE) to enable further applications of machine learning in IoT attack detection.

Federated/Distributed Learning (FL) is a machine learning method that trains a learning algorithm across multiple decentralized devices (nodes) holding a local dataset. The nodes are able to coordinate themselves to obtain the global model. The major advantage is that FL prevents single point of failures because the model update are exchanged only between interconnected nodes. However, a specific network topology might change the performance of the learning process. The research has demonstrated that, such as, distributed attack detection can better expose cyberattacks than centralized algorithms (Diro et al., 2018). This is due to the sharing of parameters that can avoid local minima in training. The work on FL has already been emerging. There do not exists much work on it. The research presented in (Regan, 2020) proposes a federated-based approach that employs a deep autoencoder to detect botnet attacks using on-device traffic data. The suggested federated learning solution will be able to consider the privacy and security of data by providing that the data of the device is not moved off the network edge.

Deep Reinforcement Learning (DRL) uses reinforcement learning (RL) and deep learning to create adequate algorithms. DRL was proposed in (Mnih et al., 2015; Mnih et al., 2013). RL is a process in which an agent learns to make decisions through trial and error. This problem often modeled mathematically as a Markov Decision Process (MDP). In most of practical decision-making problems, the states of the MDP are high-dimensional. Traditional RL algorithms cannot solve these states. RL has been applied in securing IoT technology in various domains (Uprety, & Rawat, 2020). Consequently, DRL incorporate deep learning to solve such MDP problems. DRL has opened encouraging directions of research in a range of Cybersecurity domains. DRL is forecasted to become one of the most promising cybersecurity paradigms in the near future (Blanco et al., 2018; Anderson et al., 2018). Although DRL is not explored in the context of cybersecurity of IoT networks, we believe that it is worth to explore it, and research results are yet to come for IoT networks.

Edge Computing

Many AI-based cybersecurity schemes are computationally intensive and may not be suitable for an individual IoT device. Edge computing provides a solution by enabling distributed computing for IoTs. It brings computation and data closer to the IoT device where it is needed to improve response times and bandwidth. However, one challenge of edge computing is potentially heavy load of computation. Several solutions exist that tries to improve the computational capabilities. The research in (Wang et al., 2018) proposed EdgeFlow for offloading data in edge computing. This approach distributes the tasks evenly to individual edge devices, hence preventing any single device from being overwhelmed with computational tasks. By integrating edge computing with IoTs (Yuan and Li, 2018), now IoT devices can process large amount of computation. This is possible because of the reinforced trust between these devices. In (Chen et al., 2018) the authors propose a scheme to adopt many small cell base stations (SBS) for edge computing. SBS are effective in data reception and subsequent service computing. This feature improves the IoTs computing efficacy. The work carried out in (Chao et al., 2021) proposes an edge-based network security mechanism for IoT devices that reduces the computational burden while still ensuring security.

FUTURE RESEARCH DIRECTIONS

AI, IoT, and Cybersecurity need more consideration in the digital transformation era. As human involvement has limitations, and in some cases, it is not possible at all, more intelligent solutions need to be deployed against cyberattacks in a timely manner. AI algorithms are computationally expensive as they are evolutionary by nature. Hence, developing fast algorithms for AI solutions should be an active research area. The amount of traffic will naturally increase as the number of IoT devices increases. Therefore, quick data analysis will be necessary. Consequently, high-end computing platforms will be needed to analyze the vast amount of data and traffic.

More advanced AI techniques will be needed, planned, and require further research. With AI, it is possible to design automated knowledge management methodologies for the cybersecurity of IoT. A considerable amount of research is needed to be done so that trustworthy and deployable intelligent system, that can manage the distributed infrastructure of IoT, can be designed and constructed.

Hybrid Augmented Intelligence

A hybrid combination of AI technologies will provide more effective solutions. At this technological stage, a strong interdependence between AI systems and human factors is necessary for augmenting the maturity of cybersecurity. Furthermore, a holistic view is required. An expert cybersecurity analysist becoming part of the AI process to facilitate and enhance the decision-making process is referred to as hybrid augmented intelligence. This human-AI collaboration (Cichocki and Kuleshov, 2021) in comparison to a system that only utilizes either an AI process or human expert can significantly increase the performance of a system.

Data Augmentation

Data augmentation is one of the alternative means to obtain IoT security data. The limited IoT data is expanded by generating new samples from existing ones. The new augmented IoT data is utilized to generate new samples from the existing IoT security samples. Thus, data augmentation will help to increase the available dataset. The key challenge in data augmentation is that new IoT security data samples need to preserve the appropriate data distribution for each class. Thus, the development of suitable augmentation methods are open to research and needs more investigation to improve the classification accuracy of learning methods.

Tiny Machine Learning

To secure an IoT system, the traditional high-end security solutions are not suitable, as IoT devices are of low storage capacity and less processing power. Moreover, the IoT devices are connected for longer time periods without human intervention. This raises a need to develop smart security solutions which are light weight, distributed and have a high longevity of service. Tiny Machine Learning (TinyML), the latest IoT software technology, about making the computation at the edge more predictable and cheaper. TinyML is to some extent about how to best implement ML in ultra-low power systems. TinyML is the intersection of ML and IoT. The field is emerging discipline that has potential to revolutionize many industries (Sanzhez-Iborra et. Al., 2020; Soro, 2020). TinyML will open to new opportunities to the new types of edge services and applications that do not rely on cloud processing. It will be built on distributed edge inference and autonomous reasoning.

Lightweight Encryption

Encryption is an effective countermeasure. IoT is now required to administer encryption to IoT devices in environments with disparate restrictions. Lightweight Encryption (LE) is a technology that is researched and developed to respond to this problem. LE is a sub-field of encryption that is meant for the collection of resource limited IoT devices. Lightweight encryption is indicated for using less memory, computing resources, and energy to provide security solutions to resource-constrained IoT devices (Abbas & Al-

Shargabi, 2020; Aziz & Singh 2019; Usman, et al., 2017). There is a need to do more research in this area, and also explore more options such as edge and fog computing for offloading security functions.

CONCLUSION

AI has become an indispensable technology in the cybersecurity area. In the latest research, AI techniques have demonstrated their promise in combating future cybersecurity threats. Recently proposed AI-based cybersecurity solutions for IoT largely focused on machine learning techniques involving the use of intelligent agents. Intelligent agents act as humans whose task is to detect and prevent IoT computing facilities against cyberattacks. Compared to conventional cybersecurity solutions, AI is more flexible, adaptable, and robust.

In this work, we discussed AI enabled cybersecurity for IoT in terms of how advances in technologies are transforming the digital information age where cyberattacks can be launched, detected, and mitigated. The rapid development of AI has had a lot of decisive impact on the cybersecurity needs of IoT. As the technology of AI evolves, the technology of cyberattacks changes correspondingly. Additional promising technologies are currently being researched in the domain of AI enabled cybersecurity for IoT in the digital transformation age.

The study of hybrid models has been becoming popular in recent years. By rationally combining different algorithms, better metrics are being defined, and results are being obtained. The methods handling a large amount of data without human involvement is emerging. The research and number of researchers are increasing year by year.

Some industry experts agree that entire reliance on AI would be a dull mistake. They believe that human touch is imperative, and a hybrid system between AI and human is necessary. We believe that AI's role in cybersecurity will increase continuously. We are excited about many of these developments. However, until now, we need to keep in mind that neither AI nor people alone have proven overall success in cybersecurity.

REFERENCES

Abbas Fadhil Al-Husainy, M., & Al-Shargabi, B. (2020). Secure and Lightweight Encryption Model for IoT Surveillance Camera. *International Journal of Advanced Trends in Computer Science and Engineering, 9*(2), 1840–1847. doi:10.30534/ijatcse/2020/143922020

Abeshu, A., & Chilamkurti, N. (2018). Deep learning: The frontier for distributed attack detection in fog-to-things computing. *IEEE Communications Magazine, 56*(2), 169–175. doi:10.1109/MCOM.2018.1700332

Abu Al-Haija, Q., & Zein-Sabatto, S. (2020). An Efficient Deep-Learning-Based Detection and Classification System for Cyber-Attacks in IoT Communication Networks. *Electronics (Basel), 9*(12), 2152. doi:10.3390/electronics9122152

Abusnaina, A., Khormali, A., Alasmary, H., Park, J., Anwar, A., & Mohaisen, A. (2019, July). Adversarial learning attacks on graph-based IoT malware detection systems. *2019 IEEE 39th International Conference on Distributed Computing Systems (ICDCS),* 1296-1305. 10.1109/ICDCS.2019.00130

Ahmed, K. D., & Askar, S. (2021). Deep Learning Models for Cyber Security in IoT Networks: A Review. *International Journal of Science and Business, 5*(3), 61–70.

Ahmed, M. E., & Kim, H. (2017, April). DDoS attack mitigation in Internet of Things using software defined networking. In *2017 IEEE third international conference on big data computing service and applications (BigDataService)* (pp. 271-276). IEEE. 10.1109/BigDataService.2017.41

Aishath Murshida, A., Chaithra, B. K., Nishmitha, B., Raghavendra, S., & Mahesh Prasanna, K. (2019). Survey on Artificial Intelligence. *International Journal on Computer Science and Engineering, 7*(5), 1778–1790.

Al-Garadi, M. A., Mohamed, A., Al-Ali, A., Du, X., Ali, I., & Guizani, M. (2020). A survey of machine and deep learning methods for internet of things (IoT) security. *IEEE Communications Surveys and Tutorials, 22*(3), 1646–1685. doi:10.1109/COMST.2020.2988293

Alotaibi, B., & Alotaibi, M. (2020). A Stacked Deep Learning Approach for IoT Cyberattack Detection. *Journal of Sensors, 2020*, 1–10. doi:10.1155/2020/8828591

Alrashdi, I., Alqazzaz, A., Aloufi, E., Alharthi, R., Zohdy, M., & Ming, H. (2019, January). Ad-iot: Anomaly detection of iot cyberattacks in smart city using machine learning. In *2019 IEEE 9th Annual Computing and Communication Workshop and Conference (CCWC)* (pp. 0305-0310). IEEE.

Anderson, H. S., Kharkar, A., Filar, B., Evans, D., & Roth, P. (2018). Learning to evade static PE machine learning malware models via reinforcement learning. arXiv preprint arXiv:1801.08917.

Andročec, D., & Vrček, N. (2018, January). Machine learning for the Internet of things security: A systematic review. *The 13th International Conference on Software Technologies.* 10.5220/0006841205970604

Atzori, L., Iera, A., & Morabito, G. (2010). The internet of things: A survey. *Computer Networks, 54*(15), 2787–2805. doi:10.1016/j.comnet.2010.05.010

Aziz, A., & Singh, K. (2019). Lightweight security scheme for Internet of Things. *Wireless Personal Communications, 104*(2), 577–593. doi:10.100711277-018-6035-4

Blanco, R., Cilla, J. J., Briongos, S., Malagón, P., & Moya, J. M. (2018, November). Applying cost-sensitive classifiers with reinforcement learning to IDS. In *International Conference on Intelligent Data Engineering and Automated Learning* (pp. 531-538). Springer. 10.1007/978-3-030-03493-1_55

Boukerche, A., & Coutinho, R. W. (2020). Design Guidelines for Machine Learning-based Cybersecurity in Internet of Things. *IEEE Network.*

Buchanan, B. G. (2005). A (very) brief history of artificial intelligence. *AI Magazine, 26*(4), 53–53.

Chao, H. C., Wu, H. T., & Tseng, F. H. (2021). AIS Meets IoT: A Network Security Mechanism of Sustainable Marine Resource Based on Edge Computing. *Sustainability, 13*(6), 3048. doi:10.3390u13063048

Chen, L., Zhou, S., & Xu, J. (2018). Computation peer offloading for energy-constrained mobile edge computing in small-cell networks. *IEEE/ACM Transactions on Networking, 26*(4), 1619–1632. doi:10.1109/TNET.2018.2841758

Cichocki, A., & Kuleshov, A. P. (2021). Future trends for human-ai collaboration: A comprehensive taxonomy of ai/agi using multiple intelligences and learning styles. *Computational Intelligence and Neuroscience*.

Connell, A., Palko, T., & Yasar, H. (2013, November). Cerebro: A platform for collaborative incident response and investigation. In 2013 IEEE international conference on technologies for homeland security (HST) (pp. 241-245). IEEE. doi:10.1109/THS.2013.6699007

Da Costa, K. A., Papa, J. P., Lisboa, C. O., Munoz, R., & de Albuquerque, V. H. C. (2019). Internet of Things: A survey on machine learning-based intrusion detection approaches. *Computer Networks*, *151*, 147–157. doi:10.1016/j.comnet.2019.01.023

Daim, T., Lai, K. K., Yalcin, H., Alsoubie, F., & Kumar, V. (2020). Forecasting technological positioning through technology knowledge redundancy: Patent citation analysis of IoT, cybersecurity, and Blockchain. *Technological Forecasting and Social Change*, *161*, 120329. doi:10.1016/j.techfore.2020.120329

De Souza, C. A., Westphall, C. B., Machado, R. B., Sobral, J. B. M., & dos Santos Vieira, G. (2020). Hybrid approach to intrusion detection in fog-based IoT environments. *Computer Networks*, *180*, 107417. doi:10.1016/j.comnet.2020.107417

Dilek, S., Çakır, H., & Aydın, M. (2015). Applications of artificial intelligence techniques to combating cyber crimes: A review. *International Journal of Artificial Intelligence & Applications*, *6*(1), 21–39. doi:10.5121/ijaia.2015.6102

Diro, A. A., & Chilamkurti, N. (2018). Distributed attack detection scheme using deep learning approach for Internet of Things. *Future Generation Computer Systems*, *82*, 761–768. doi:10.1016/j.future.2017.08.043

Fang, H., Qi, A., & Wang, X. (2020). Fast Authentication and Progressive Authorization in Large-Scale IoT: How to Leverage AI for Security Enhancement. *IEEE Network*, *34*(3), 24–29. doi:10.1109/MNET.011.1900276

Farivar, F., Haghighi, M. S., Jolfaei, A., & Alazab, M. (2019). Artificial Intelligence for Detection, Estimation, and Compensation of Malicious Attacks in Nonlinear Cyber-Physical Systems and Industrial IoT. *IEEE Transactions on Industrial Informatics*, *16*(4), 2716–2725. doi:10.1109/TII.2019.2956474

Gauhar, A., Ahmad, N., Cao, Y., Khan, S., Cruickshank, H., Qazi, E. A., & Ali, A. (2020). xDBAuth: Blockchain Based Cross Domain Authentication and Authorization Framework for Internet of Things. *IEEE Access: Practical Innovations, Open Solutions*, *8*, 58800–58816. doi:10.1109/ACCESS.2020.2982542

Gupta, G. P., & Kulariya, M. (2016). A framework for fast and efficient cyber security network intrusion detection using apache spark. *Procedia Computer Science*, *93*, 824–831. doi:10.1016/j.procs.2016.07.238

Hasan, M., Islam, M. M., Zarif, M. I. I., & Hashem, M. M. A. (2019). Attack and anomaly detection in IoT sensors in IoT sites using machine learning approaches. *Internet of Things*, *7*, 100059. doi:10.1016/j.iot.2019.100059

Javaid, U., Siang, A. K., Aman, M. N., & Sikdar, B. (2018, June). Mitigating IoT device based DDoS attacks using blockchain. In *Proceedings of the 1st Workshop on Cryptocurrencies and Blockchains for Distributed Systems* (pp. 71-76). 10.1145/3211933.3211946

Kim, H., Kang, E., Broman, D., & Lee, E. A. (2020). Resilient Authentication and Authorization for the Internet of Things (IoT) Using Edge Computing. *ACM Transactions on Internet of Things*, *1*(1), 1–27. doi:10.1145/3375837

Kim, H., & Lee, E. A. (2017). Authentication and Authorization for the Internet of Things. *IT Professional*, *19*(5), 27–33. doi:10.1109/MITP.2017.3680960

Koroniotis, N., Moustafa, N., & Sitnikova, E. (2020). A new network forensic framework based on deep learning for Internet of Things networks: A particle deep framework. *Future Generation Computer Systems*, *110*, 91–106. doi:10.1016/j.future.2020.03.042

Kurakin, A., Goodfellow, I., & Bengio, S. (2016). Adversarial machine learning at scale. arXiv preprint arXiv:1611.01236.

Latif, S., Idrees, Z., Zou, Z., & Ahmad, J. (2020, August). DRaNN: A Deep Random Neural Network Model for Intrusion Detection in Industrial IoT. In *2020 International Conference on UK-China Emerging Technologies (UCET)* (pp. 1-4). IEEE. 10.1109/UCET51115.2020.9205361

Latif, S., Zou, Z., Idrees, Z., & Ahmad, J. (2020). A Novel Attack Detection Scheme for the Industrial Internet of Things Using a Lightweight Random Neural Network. *IEEE Access: Practical Innovations, Open Solutions*, *8*, 89337–89350. doi:10.1109/ACCESS.2020.2994079

Liang, C., Shanmugam, B., Azam, S., Jonkman, M., De Boer, F., & Narayansamy, G. (2019b, March). Intrusion Detection System for Internet of Things based on a Machine Learning approach. In *2019 International Conference on Vision Towards Emerging Trends in Communication and Networking (ViTECoN)* (pp. 1-6). IEEE. 10.1109/ViTECoN.2019.8899448

Liang, F., Hatcher, W. G., Liao, W., Gao, W., & Yu, W. (2019a). Machine Learning for Security and the Internet of Things: The Good, the Bad, and the Ugly. *IEEE Access: Practical Innovations, Open Solutions*, *7*, 158126–158147. doi:10.1109/ACCESS.2019.2948912

Luo, Z., Zhao, S., Lu, Z., Sagduyu, Y. E., & Xu, J. (2020, July). Adversarial machine learning based partial-model attack in IoT. *Proceedings of the 2nd ACM Workshop on Wireless Security and Machine Learning*.

Manuel, J., Joven, R., & Durando, D. (2018, February). OMG: Mirai-based Bot Turns IoT Devices into Proxy Servers. *Fortinet*. doi:10.1145/3395352.3402619

McCorduck, P., Minsky, M., Selfridge, O. G., & Simon, H. A. (1977, August). History of Artificial Intelligence. In IJCAI (pp. 951-954). Academic Press.

Misra, S., Krishna, P. V., Agarwal, H., Saxena, A., & Obaidat, M. S. (2011, October). A learning automata based solution for preventing distributed denial of service in internet of things. In *2011 international conference on internet of things and 4th international conference on cyber, physical and social computing* (pp. 114-122). IEEE. 10.1109/iThings/CPSCom.2011.84

Mnih, V., Kavukcuoglu, K., Silver, D., Graves, A., Antonoglou, I., Wierstra, D., & Riedmiller, M. (2013). *Playing atari with deep reinforcement learning*. arXiv preprint arXiv:1312.5602.

Mnih, V., Kavukcuoglu, K., Silver, D., Rusu, A. A., Veness, J., Bellemare, M. G., & Petersen, S. (2015). Human-level control through deep reinforcement learning. *Nature*, *518*(7540), 529–533. doi:10.1038/nature14236 PMID:25719670

Raza, S., Wallgren, L., & Voigt, T. (2013). SVELTE: Real-time intrusion detection in the Internet of Things. *Ad Hoc Networks*, *11*(8), 2661–2674. doi:10.1016/j.adhoc.2013.04.014

Regan, C. M. (2020). *A federated deep autoencoder for detecting IoT cyber attacks* (Master's Thesis). Faculty of the Department of Computer Science, Kennesaw State University.

Restuccia, F., D'Oro, S., & Melodia, T. (2018). Securing the internet of things in the age of machine learning and software-defined networking. *IEEE Internet of Things Journal*, *5*(6), 4829–4842. doi:10.1109/JIOT.2018.2846040

Russell, S., & Norvig, P. (2002). *Artificial intelligence: A modern approach*. Academic Press.

Sagduyu, Y. E., Shi, Y., & Erpek, T. (2019, June). IoT network security from the perspective of adversarial deep learning. *2019 16th Annual IEEE International Conference on Sensing, Communication, and Networking (SECON)*, 1-9. 10.1109/SAHCN.2019.8824956

Sagirlar, G., Carminati, B., & Ferrari, E. (2018, October). AutoBotCatcher: blockchain-based P2P botnet detection for the internet of things. In *2018 IEEE 4th International Conference on Collaboration and Internet Computing (CIC)* (pp. 1-8). IEEE.

Sanzhez-Iborra, R., & Skarmeta, A. F. (2020). TinyML-Enabled Frugal Smart Objects: Challenges and Opportunuties. *IEEE Circuits and Systems Magazine*, *20*(3), 4–18. doi:10.1109/MCAS.2020.3005467

Sanzhez-Iborra, R., & Skarmeta, A. F. (2020). TinyML-Enabled Frugal Smart Objects: Challenges and Opportunuties. *IEEE Circuits and Systems Magazine*, *20*(3), 4–18. doi:10.1109/MCAS.2020.3005467

Sari, A. (2019). Turkish national cyber-firewall to mitigate countrywide cyber-attacks. *Computers & Electrical Engineering*, *73*, 128–144. doi:10.1016/j.compeleceng.2018.11.008

Shafiq, M., Tian, Z., Sun, Y., Du, X., & Guizani, M. (2020). Selection of effective machine learning algorithm and Bot-IoT attacks traffic identification for internet of things in smart city. *Future Generation Computer Systems*, *107*, 433–442. doi:10.1016/j.future.2020.02.017

Shakeel, P. M., Baskar, S., Fouad, H., Manogaran, G., Saravanan, V., & Montenegro-Marin, C. E. (2020). Internet of things forensic data analysis using machine learning to identify roots of data scavenging. *Future Generation Computer Systems*.

Soro, S. (2020, September). *TinyML for Ubiqutious Edge AI*. MITRE Technical Report.

Tahsien, S. M., Karimipour, H., & Spachos, P. (2020). Machine learning based solutions for security of Internet of Things (IoT): A survey. *Journal of Network and Computer Applications*, *161*, 102630. doi:10.1016/j.jnca.2020.102630

Turing, A. M. (1950). Can a machine think. *Mind*, *59*(236), 433–460. doi:10.1093/mind/LIX.236.433

Uprety, A., & Rawat, D. B. (2020). *Reinforcement Learning for IoT Security: A Comprehensive Survey*. IEEE Internet of Things Journal.

Usman, M., Ahmed, I., Aslam, M. I., Khan, S., & Shah, U. A. (2017). SIT: A lightweight encryption algorithm for secure internet of things. *International Journal of Advanced Computer Science and Applications*, *8*(1).

Velliangiri, S., & Kasaraneni, K. K. (2020). Machine Learning and Deep Learning in Cyber Security for IoT. In *ICDSMLA 2019*. Springer.

Vu, L., Nguyen, Q. U., Nguyen, D. N., Hoang, D. T., & Dutkiewicz, E. (2020). Deep Transfer Learning for IoT Attack Detection. *IEEE Access : Practical Innovations, Open Solutions*, *8*, 107335–107344.

Waheed, N., He, X., & Usman, M. (2020). *Security & Privacy in IoT Using Machine Learning & Blockchain: Threats & Countermeasures*. arXiv preprint arXiv:2002.03488.

Wang, H., Barriga, L., Vahidi, A., & Raza, S. (2019, November). Machine Learning for Security at the IoT Edge-A Feasibility Study. In *2019 IEEE 16th International Conference on Mobile Ad Hoc and Sensor Systems Workshops (MASSW)* (pp. 7-12). IEEE.

Wang, P., Yao, C., Zheng, Z., Sun, G., & Song, L. (2018). Joint task assignment, transmission, and computing resource allocation in multilayer mobile edge computing systems. *IEEE Internet of Things Journal*, *6*(2), 2872–2884.

Xiao, L., Wan, X., & Han, Z. (2017). PHY-layer authentication with multiple landmarks with reduced overhead. *IEEE Transactions on Wireless Communications*, *17*(3), 1676–1687. doi:10.1109/TWC.2017.2784431

Xiao, L., Wan, X., Lu, X., Zhang, Y., & Wu, D. (2018). IoT security techniques based on machine learning: How do IoT devices use AI to enhance security? *IEEE Signal Processing Magazine*, *35*(5), 41–49. doi:10.1109/MSP.2018.2825478

Xu, G., Yu, W., Chen, Z., Zhang, H., Moulema, P., Fu, X., & Lu, C. (2015). A cloud computing based system for cyber security management. International Journal of Parallel. *Emergent and Distributed Systems*, *30*(1), 29–45. doi:10.1080/17445760.2014.925110

Yavuz, F. Y. (2018). *Deep learning in cyber security for Internet of Things* (Master's Thesis). Graduate School of Natural and Applied Sciences, Istanbul Sehir University.

Yuan, J., & Li, X. (2018). A reliable and lightweight trust computing mechanism for IoT edge devices based on multi-source feedback information fusion. *IEEE Access : Practical Innovations, Open Solutions*, *6*, 23626–23638.

Zeadally, S., Adi, E., Baig, Z., & Khan, I. A. (2020). Harnessing Artificial Intelligence Capabilities to Improve Cybersecurity. *IEEE Access : Practical Innovations, Open Solutions*, *8*, 23817–23837.

Zeadally, S., & Tsikerdekis, M. (2020). Securing Internet of Things (IoT) with machine learning. *International Journal of Communication Systems*, *33*(1), e4169.

Zhang, Q., Yang, L. T., Chen, Z., & Li, P. (2018). A survey on deep learning for big data. *Information Fusion*, *42*, 146–157.

ADDITIONAL READING

Alam, M., Shakil, K. A., & Khan, S. (Eds.). (2020). *Internet of Things (IoT) Concepts and Applications.* Springer. doi:10.1007/978-3-030-37468-6

Gupta, B. B., & Sheng, Q. Z. (2019). *Machine Learning for Computer and Cyber Security Principle, Algorithms, and Practices.* CRC Press. doi:10.1201/9780429504044

Li, J. H. (2018). Cyber security meets artificial intelligence: A survey. *Frontiers of Information Technology & Electronic Engineering, 19*(12), 1462–1474. doi:10.1631/FITEE.1800573

Li, S. S. & Xu, L. D. (2017). Securing the Internet of Thing. Elsevier Inc.

Milan, M. (2020). *Internet of Things: Concepts and System Design.* Springer.

Parisi, A. (2019). *Hands-On Artificial Intelligence for Cybersecurity: Implement smart AI systems for preventing cyberattacks and detecting threats and network anomalies.* Packt Publishing Ltd.

Sikos, L. F. (Ed.). (2019). AI in Cybersecurity (Intelligent Systems Reference Library (151)). Springer.

Tsukerman, A. (2019). *Machine Learning for Cybersecurity Cookbook: Over 80 recipes on how to implement machine learning algorithms for building security systems using Python.* Packt Publishing Ltd.

Wilkins, N. (2019). *Internet of Things: What You Need to Know About IoT, Big Data, Predictive Analytics, Artificial Intelligence, Machine Learning, Cybersecurity, Business Intelligence, Augmented Reality and Our Future.* Independently Published.

Xin, Y., Kong, L., Liu, Z., Chen, Y., Li, Y., Zhu, H., Gao, M., Hou, H., & Wang, C. (2018). Machine learning and deep learning methods for cybersecurity. *IEEE Access: Practical Innovations, Open Solutions, 6*, 35365–35381. doi:10.1109/ACCESS.2018.2836950

KEY TERMS AND DEFINITIONS

Artificial Intelligence: AI is a field of computer science addressing to automate computing problems that require human intelligence.

Artificial Neural Networks: Artificial neural networks, usually simply called neural networks, are computing systems vaguely inspired by the biological neural networks that constitute animal brains.

Blockchain: It is a growing list of blocks that are linked using cryptography. Each block contains a cryptographic hash of the previous block, a timestamp, and transaction data. A blockchain is resistant to modification of its data. It is primarily used in cryptocurrencies, most notably bitcoin.

Convolutional Neural Network: Convolutional neural network is a class of deep neural networks that mostly applied to analyzing visual imagery. They are generally used in image recognition, classification, face recognition, etc.

Cybercrime: It is a crime that involves a computer and a network. The computer may have been used in the commission of a crime, or it may be the target. Cybercrime may threaten a person, company or a nation's security and financial health.

Cybersecurity: Cybersecurity is the protection of computer systems and networks from the cyberattacks so that their hardware, software, or data are not disrupted or misdirected of the services that they provide.

Deep Neural Networks: A deep neural network is an artificial neural network with multiple layers between the input and output layers.

Edge Computing: It is a distributed computing paradigm that brings computation and data storage closer to the location where it is needed, to improve response times and save bandwidth.

Fog Computing: Fog computing or fog networking, also known as fogging (edge computing), is an architecture that uses edge devices (e.g., IoT devices, etc.) to carry out a substantial amount of computation, storage, and communication locally and routed over the internet backbone.

Information Gain: Information gain is the reduction in entropy or surprise by transforming a dataset and is calculated by comparing the entropy of the dataset before and after a transformation.

Internet of Things: Internet of things (IoT) is the interconnection of heterogeneous smart devices through the Internet with diverse application areas such as smart home, car, cities, healthcare, wearables, retail, grid, agriculture, and industry.

k-Nearest Neighbor: k-Nearest neighbor is a type of instance-based learning where the input consists of the k closest training examples in the feature space. The output depends on whether k-NN is used for classification or regression.

Chapter 8
Business Management and Strategy in Cybersecurity for Digital Transformation

Fahri Özsungur

(iD) https://orcid.org/0000-0001-6567-766X

Department of Labor Economics and Industrial Relations, Mersin University, Mersin, Turkey

ABSTRACT

Cyber security threatens vital elements of enterprises such as network, information, application, operational, sustainability, education, and trade secret. Digital transformation and widespread use of IoT caused by the pandemic reveal the importance of cybersecurity vulnerabilities. This study is prepared by a systematic review method for cybersecurity. The inspiration of this chapter is the cyberattacks that threaten the global economy and enterprises and the effects of cybercrime on management and strategy. The cybersecurity problem, which continues to increase with the pandemic in the manufacturing and service sector, is current and becoming a serious threat. This study reveals strategy development against cybersecurity threats; sustainability elements in management; measures to be taken against cybercrime, cyberattack, and cyberterrorism; and organizational and business culture management in digital transformation.

INTRODUCTION

Cybercrime and cyber attacks are among the most critical and important problems of today's digital World (Akhgar, Staniforth, & Bosco, 2014). The extraordinary situation that emerged with COVID-19 and the pandemic has made the global economy come to the fore in the operational processes of businesses. Digital elements, which are increasingly important, continue to be reflected in business life with digital transformation. The increasing effects of digital innovations on the managerial and strategic practices of the business have led to an increase in cyber attacks. Malicious attacks, cyber thieves are harming the global economy by seizing confidential and important information of businesses (Ismail, Shaaban, Naidu, & Serpedin, 2020).

DOI: 10.4018/978-1-7998-6975-7.ch008

Problems arising from cyber-attacks and systemic vulnerabilities of businesses require development, harmonization, and improvement in management and strategy (Hellström, 2007). Taking cybersecurity measures in the context of human resources, operations, sales, after-sales services, promotion, providing competitive advantage has become an important managerial and strategic need of today's businesses. It is a current issue to strengthen the strategies of businesses in the context of cybersecurity vulnerabilities, cyber-attacks, digital threats, cyber risks, and weaknesses due to these factors (Sallos, Garcia-Perez, Bedford, & Orlando, 2019). In the management and strategy literature, the management and strategy development of businesses and organizations is evaluated within a general framework (Phan, 2001; Chrisman, Hofer, & Boulton, 1988; Kotey & Meredith, 1997; Matricano, 2021). The theoretical framework and empirical research developed do not focus on strengthening strategy and managerial elements. This chapter brings to the literature that the requirements of today's digital world such as strengthening management and strategy, developing strategies based on digital and cyber protection, eliminating weaknesses in digital transformation. Eliminating the cyberattacks that threaten today's global economy and businesses and the weaknesses caused by digital transformation is a current issue and the chapter focuses on this issue. Therefore, in the chapter, digital transformation, effects of cybersecurity on businesses, data and information security, application and software security, network, and communication security, operational security, cyber-strategy development, sustainable training and adaptation, cybersecurity threats, cybercrime, cyberterrorism, cyber-management, and strategy issues are covered.

RESEARCH METHODOLOGY

This study was prepared by a systematic review method. The systematic review method consists of preparation for research → data collection → analysis of data → evaluation of data → implications → reporting (Beelmann, 2006; Petticrew & Roberts, 2008). The inspiration of this chapter is the cyberattacks that threaten the global economy and organizations, and the effects of cybercrime on management and strategy. The cybersecurity problem, which continues to increase with the pandemic in the manufacturing and service sector, is current and becoming a serious threat. In this context, the questions of the study were determined as follows:

- R1. What are the effects of cybersecurity on businesses?
- R2. What are the elements of cyber-strategy development in businesses?
- R3. How can cyber-management and strategy be strengthened in businesses?

After the study questions were determined, the keywords for literature review in academic databases (Google scholar, Web of Science, Emerald Insight, Taylor and Francis) were determined as follows: management, strategy, management and strategy, cyber, cyber attack, cybercrime, cybersecurity, digital transformation, digital management, digital strategy. 214 articles directly related to the topic were accessed in the search for keywords. The research, analysis, and reporting took approximately 1.5 weeks.

After the literature review was performed, the steps of summarizing, classifying, extracting data, discussing, categorizing, and presenting the information obtained from academic databases were followed in the study (Denyer & Tranfield, 2009; Martins et al., 2015). After these steps, the titles and content related to the researched subject were determined and reported.

CYBER-MANAGEMENT AND STRATEGY

The fact that cyber attacks and threats are increasingly affecting today's businesses and organizations in a negative way makes it necessary to take measures in this direction. The cyber approach to management and strategy provides important security measures in meeting digital transformation and innovation needs (Boeke, 2018). Cyber management and strategy approach provide added value in many areas such as human resources management, digital customer accounting, virtual marketing, virtual promotion, online training and communication, online purchasing and payment, digital operational transactions, digital procurement and logistics management, digital after-sales services.

In management and strategy, the cyber approach provides significant momentum in human resources and operational management. The efficient functioning of devices and systems brought into the business with digital transformation is important in terms of performance in human resources policy. Protection of personal data of employees and candidates depends on cybersecurity (Gordon & Loeb, 2006). On the other hand, protection of critical information such as business climate, culture, organizational structure, research and development, projects is necessary for the competitive advantage and sustainability of the business. It is necessary to integrate cybersecurity into the management and strategy of the enterprise in the execution of primary (inbound and outbound logistics, operations, marketing & sales, service) and support (firm infrastructure, human resources management, technology, procurement) activities (Hines, 1993; Porter, 2001; Nagy et al., 2018). Strategy development of the business in the face of evolving and changing digital innovations and threats strengthens the value chain.

Cybersecurity Threats

Cybersecurity is applications that aim to protect against the harmful effects of malicious software through smart and digital devices, computers and servers, electronic systems, and networks. These applications may cause financial and structural damages by threatening information security through the internet and electronic network. Operational, network, application, information, sustainability, and strategic security of businesses depend on cybersecurity.

Malicious attacks that threaten cybersecurity, such as social engineering, ransomware, denial-of-service attacks, cloud computing vulnerabilities attacks, cause financial losses to businesses (Rees et al., 2011). These attacks occurring in a global context cause significant limitations/weaknesses in today's business world, where dependence on digital devices is increasing. In the context of management strategy, cybersecurity threats often constitute the weaknesses of businesses (Razzaq et al., 2013).

Social engineering aims to seize the management of digital connection points that form social media accounts, e-blogs, e-mails, which form the communication link with their customers, with techniques such as pishing and scareware (Krombhol et al., 2015). These attacks, which manipulate human psychology, negatively affect the management and operational activities of businesses. Ransomware is a data-encrypting software (Brewer, 2016). Hackers require payment demand for the release of infected data. Hospitals, public institutions, and organizations, holdings are among the targets of these hackers. A denial-of-service attack is accomplished by temporarily or permanently interrupting the host's network service by sending superfluous requests to computers (Carl et al., 2006). These types of attacks target payment gateways, banks, credit card payment applications, web servers hosting payment applications (Yi et al., 2016). Commonly encountered cloud computing vulnerabilities attacks are as follows: Contractual breaches regarding the business network, cloud service providers lock-in, control problems related to end-user actions, misconfigured cloud storage, reliability and availability of service, lack of access restrictions, virtual machine escape, insecure application user interfaces, and cryptography, inadequate authentication, insufficient authorization, session riding, poor access management, theft of intellectual property, data alteration or deletion, internet dependency, loss of Access (Grobauer et al., 2010; Chou, 2013; Zhou et al., 2013). These threats and vulnerabilities expose the business' internet, digital and virtual networks to attack.

In major companies, cybersecurity threats arise due to supply chain stakeholders, halt and catch fire, illegal takeovers, weak passwords, worms and viruses, ransom attacks, employee errors, sabotage, ransomware, weak cyber security policies, industrial software errors. Small and medium-sized companies are most affected by malicious attacks (Warren & Hutchinson, 2000). Because the funding source these companies allocate for cybersecurity is very limited. On the other hand, large companies, especially holdings, are among the primary targets in the attack. Banks, financial institutions, intelligence, and telecommunication companies are among the priority sectors in the attack (Bendovschi, 2015; Watkins, 2014).

Cybercrime

Attacks such as unauthorized access to information systems through computer and internet networks such as espionage, financial theft, capturing data, theft of financial data and passwords, blocking the use of the system and log in, blocking or delaying communication, unauthorized recording of communication are the cybercrime activities (Yar & Steinmetz, 2019; Anderson et al., 2013). Such attacks involve attacks on personal and financial rights by violating the privacy of private and commercial life in the context of international and local law (McQuade, 2006). On the other hand, the employees of the business can also commit these crimes. Spoofing information regarding unfair competition is among cybercrime. Trade secrets of the business, information about the project, offers to be submitted forward in tenders are shared with third parties through these attacks.

Cybercrime typologies that emerge in businesses are phishing, hate speech, hacking, and digital pornography. These are carried out to damage the reputation of businesses, to capture confidential information, to reveal the financial data of the company. In Cybercrime typologies, confidential information is tried to be accessed illegally through the company's corporate website and computer networks.

Cyberterrorism

Cyber terrorism is the cyberattacks carried out through the computer network and the internet, which have serious damage to the values of society, the state, and humanity (Gordon & Ford, 2002). The purpose of these attacks is to damage the targets determined by activating the action plans of terrorist organizations (Weimann, 2005). Cyber terrorism in general does not target individuals. However, country or community leaders can be targeted for the purposes of terrorist organizations (Collin, 1997). Cyberattacks on a company's or holding's production capacity could be aimed at harming the country's oil or chemical industry. This purpose is evident especially in cyberattacks against some companies that play an important role in the export capacity of the country.

Cyber terrorism can cause consequences such as chaos, conflict, economic and political crisis, rebellion, loss of life (Chen et al., 2014). It is important for enterprises that cooperate with public institutions or offer public services through tenders to take the necessary measures in this regard (Denning, 2001).

Cyberterrorism can use the information networks of businesses as a tool by targeting the public. In this case, the confidential information of the state or the public can be seized by cyber terrorists.

Digital Transformation

Digital transformation is the creation of solutions by using digital elements in meeting social, organizational, sectoral, workplace, and business needs (Matt et al., 2015). Digital elements in organizational structuring, operational processes, information network, communication, organizational culture, business culture, organizational climate, education, adaptation, and many other issues are harmonized with these factors. It is important in terms of functionality to harmonize the digital elements with the organization and the components of the business. Digital transformation makes significant contributions to the structure of the organization and the businesses' relations with the external environment and internal functioning (Vial, 2019).

Employee training in human resources management, management of the recruitment process, determination of qualified employee criteria, online exams, database management related to curriculum vitae, work engagement and needs survey applications, social media usage have been affected by digital transformation (Vardarlier, 2020). This effect is important in terms of the adaptation of the employees to the job and the workplace and taking advantage of career opportunities. Digital transformation enables employees to work remotely in pandemic and extraordinary situations, to exchange information in employee-leader communication and interaction. The adaptation of the developing technology to the technical infrastructure of the business or organization enables information and feedback to be transmitted and obtained in a fast and efficient manner. Therefore, the transformation of digital elements into human resources management elements positively affects business efficiency.

Manufacturing, raw material supply, logistics benefit from digital resources in today's world. Manufacturing technologies are among some known Industrial internet of things (IIoT) applications such as smart robotics, industrial smart glasses, augmented reality, microgrid innovation, wearable technology, smart oil field innovator, Wi-Fi mesh network (Gibson et al., 2014). These applications provide benefits such as productivity and performance in manufacturing, quality in the communication network, innovation, time-saving, prevention of waste of labor, reduction of dependency on manpower, occupational health, and safety.

IIoT industry 4.0 is also called the digital factory, smart manufacturing (Jayaram, 2016; Zezulka et al., 2018). Real-time analytics can be performed with solutions designed for the operational application of data. By combining workloads, complex functions can be reduced to a simpler form. These innovations provide important outputs in the context of management and strategy. Thus, costs are reduced and the time to market products is shortened. IIoT and digital transformation provide improvement in the production system in terms of safety, efficiency, and performance.

Robot devices and automation provide important information to the production and planning team in the context of defects in production, error predictions, cause-effect inferences (Schneier, Schneier, & Bostelman, 2015). The quality of the product, error-free production in measurement and molds, assembly, and sustainable production are realized with this technological and digital transformation.

The complexity of information and the evaluation of many factors together create significant difficulties in terms of management. Thanks to this complexity IIoT, a large number of assets involved in production can be professionally and strategically managed. Turnover, efficiency, and constraint management can be improved through IIoT (Boyes et al., 2018).

Digital transformation is crucial in terms of shipment of products, logistics, delivery, customer satisfaction, after-sales services. Customer orientation is necessary for the sustainability of the business. Digital innovations play an important role in the rapid and efficient flow of information in customer feedback. On the other hand, follow-up of customers' complaints about products and services, performance in the return process is ensured by the contribution of digital transformation. Thus, three basic digital transformation outputs are obtained: business and performance improvement, interpretation and systematization of complex data, success, and sustainability in the digital economy.

Digital transformation assists to reduce energy costs (Llopis-Albert, Rubio, & Valero, 2021). In cases where physical interaction is mandatory, digital elements provide important convenience. Thanks to robotic applications and automation, labor costs are reduced and productivity is increased (Fernando,Mathath, & Murshid, 2016). On the other hand, the speed of reporting increases the contribution of planning to the strategy. However, besides these benefits of digital elements, there are also important risk factors. The most important threats to IIot, IoT, and digital networks are cyber attacks and vulnerabilities. These vulnerabilities can be eliminated through cybersecurity (Falco, Caldera, & Shrobe, 2018).

Cybersecurity's Effects on Business

Cybersecurity is the protection of data, servers, mobile devices, electronic systems, computers, and networks from malicious attacks (Kemmerer, 2003). This protection is provided through applications and software. These applications and software ensure the protection of information technology and the elimination of security threats arising from the transformation of technology. It also provides detailed information about possible threats, the severity, and extent of the attack, the software and encryption strength of the attack (Wu et al., 2018). Thus, strategic measures can be taken against malicious attacks that plan to infiltrate the business' network. The security of software providing remote control with mobile computing is provided by cybersecurity (Ten, Manimaran, & Liu, 2010).

Cybersecurity focuses on six basic functions:: 1) data and information security, 2) application and software security, 3) network and communication security, 4) operational security, 5) cyber-strategy development, 6) sustainable training, and adaptation (See Figure 1).

Data and Information Security

Information and data ensure the sustainability of the business and its internal functioning, flow in the implementation of the strategy, communication between units, continuity of relations with the external environment, performance in production and planning, communication in procurement and logistics, quality in total efficiency, and performance, corporate synergy, and the development of proactive behaviors (Xu et al., 2014; Jerman-Blažič, 2008). Data integrity is an important factor that needs to be protected in the context of the operational functions of the business. The data that is effective in making real-time and future-oriented decisions such as performance, efficiency, production, marketing, sales, customer volume, future customers are protected by cybersecurity.

Information is the facts learned from the external or internal environment of the business. The information to be obtained in learning organizations is important (Senge, 1995). Decisions on long and short-term implementation such as strategy formulation, plan, and tactics are taken through information. This is why information security is important in making decisions in the business. Data, which is effective in the operational management of the enterprise, is closely related to the information that is effective in making strategic decisions. Therefore, threats, risks, and security vulnerabilities arising in the data and information security of an enterprise can cause critical damages in financial, strategic, and managerial contexts.

Figure 1. Functions of cybersecurity

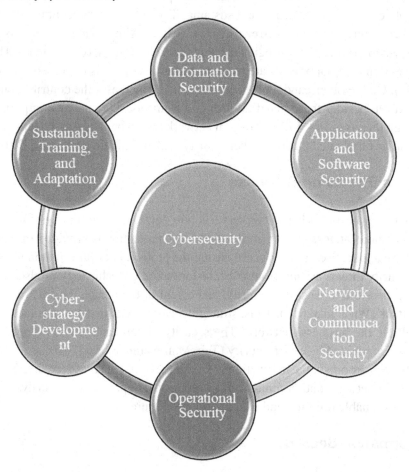

Application and Software Security

Compromised applications and software threaten the functionality of digital elements. This threat can lead to the disclosure of business secrets, to be seized the information of employees and leaders, and damage to production and service functions through IoT and IIot. Necessary precautions should be taken against cyber threats in the design, update, and control of software and applications. It is important for the security of the business that updates and checks are carried out in the context of new-age computer viruses and cyber-attacks (Dixit et al., 2012; Cass, 2001).

Applications and software are key factors in the production, planning, and logistics functions of businesses. Protecting these factors against cyber threats is necessary and important in delivering products to customers on time, ensuring efficiency and performance. These technological applications and software are applied in robots that have industrial use today.

In robotic automation, cobots (collaborative robots) designed for human-robot interaction are used. These new technology products used in industrial areas have the features of collaboration, suitable for risk analysis, light and compact structure, small footprint, flexible, low energy consumption, integrated force, torque sensor, easy integration into autonomous vehicles (Automated Guided Vehicles). Collaborative robots (CoBots) do not require periodic maintenance and have 360-degree rotation capability in all axes (UR3 and UR3e- sixth axis). These robots have conveyor tracking, force control, palletizing, bolting, g-code programming interfaces, and online training features (Simões, Soares, & Barros, 2020). Despite these features, 17 advanced adjustable embedded security functions are not fully sufficient for cybersecurity threats (Cherubini et al., 2016). For this reason, robots need to be constantly updated and software with special security shields due to their positive outputs, especially in the manufacturing sector, and cybersecurity vulnerabilities (Bi et al., 2020).

Possible cyber attacks on software and information systems of cobot and industrial robots may cause disruptions in production by compromising the security of employees. This situation can be encountered especially in remote control and management via the internet network. Vulnerabilities in software updates of robots create serious threats. For this reason, it is important to check the connections of the functions of cobots beforehand, detect security vulnerabilities, and take necessary cyber measures.

Vulnerabilities in IIoT and cobot software negatively affect the operations of many sectors such as food, agriculture, metal, automotive, electricity, electronics, technology, plastic, polymer, furniture, medicine, chemistry, laboratory, catering, logistics. This situation affects multifaceted functions such as supply, logistics, service, and production. In this case, customer satisfaction decreases, and the demand for products and services decreases. On the other hand, these applications and networks that keep employees away from doing dangerous work increase the risk of job security. Possible robotic automation and IIoT security threats can cause occupational accidents. These applications, which provide employees with a safe workplace, can reduce employee satisfaction due to possible cyber threats (Bayram, Üngan, & Ardıç, 2017).

Network and Communication Security

A computer network uses a set of common communication protocols. This tool that connects computers to each other provides information flow through digital interconnections and network nodes (Nguyen, Laurent, & Oualha, 2015). Thus, communication between the headquarters and branches can be maintained. Wired and wireless network technologies provide an important innovation for this communication (Flammini et al., 2009). While communication between devices is provided through these networks, it is also faced with important cyber threats.

Internet protocol (IP) has an important function in transporting packets to target IP addresses (Stallings, 1996). Vulnerabilities of these functions can occur during routing datagrams and encapsulating data into datagrams. The transition of IP header and IP data, in which Iot takes an active role, to the transport stage depends on taking security measures against cyber threats and the implementation of protocols. These risks may arise in communication protocols in the regulation of network traffic.

Operational Security

Internet protocol (IP) has an important function in transporting packets to target IP addresses. Vulnerabilities of these functions can occur during routing datagrams and encapsulating data into datagrams (Kumar et al., 2021). The transition of IP header and IP data, in which IoT takes an active role, to the transport stage depends on taking security measures against cyber threats and the implementation of protocols. These risks may arise in communication protocols in the regulation of network traffic.

Harmonized devices using advanced network technologies such as printers, faxes, cameras, and smart devices face the security risks of the computer network. Storage servers of the devices must be protected due to the security breaches that these risks and threats may pose. Protection of devices with a communication connection via network against cyber threats is important in the context of information security, trade secret, and operational sustainability.

Digital communication technologies, cloud computing, artificial intelligence are important technologies that use human-machine interaction and IIot in the production processes of smart production systems. However, these technologies are under malware and ransomware attacks. For this reason, it is necessary to realize innovation and develop strategies in the context of security in eliminating possible risks and threats that may arise due to security gaps.

Cyber-Strategy Development

The development of production technology has revealed innovations related to production capacity, efficient use of enterprise resources, and cloud manufacturing / Manufacturing-as-a-Service (MaaS) that saves time and effort (Chaudhuri et al., 2021). The traditional production resources related to the production, development, and design of the product are transformed into modern production design thanks to this technology. Planning, controlling, reporting, and managing production capacity and orders are carried out through cloud manufacturing. However, these innovations also include significant risks in the face of cyber threats.

Dissemination and mapping of information in production and service, software and update problems in digital transformation, enterprise software integration face significant cyber and information technology security threats. The theft of design models by virtual thieves can cause critical damage to the business. On the other hand, information about the factors that play an important role in the sustainability of the business such as customer portfolio, business secrets, profitability, efficiency, financial data, suppliers, distribution channels can be disclosed through cyber attacks. This situation makes it difficult for the company to be held in the market and causes it to lose its competitive advantage. In this case, the business should develop some proactive defense strategies against cyber attacks. These proactive defense strategies constitute the cyber strategies of the business. These are as follows: 1) Smell and feel (perception),2) track and investigate (focus),4) develop counter-moves, 5) take precautions against future attacks, update the system (Figure 2).

Smell and Feel (Perception)

Cyber-strategy can be improved by obtaining detailed information about cyber attacks and malware. The existing digital devices of the company, network, IoT and IIoT connections, data, information management centers, information distribution channels should be considered strategically. When cybersecurity risks and threats occur, the source of the problem should be identified. The source of the problem can often be detected by functional errors that occur in digital elements, IIoT, or network-originated errors in operational functions. Employees can report violations of data privacy or traces of malware can be detected in the company's databases. These situations can be detected in computer use, as well as they can be revealed by unusual traffic in the company's e-mail and social media accounts.

Figure 2. Businesses' cyber-strategy factors

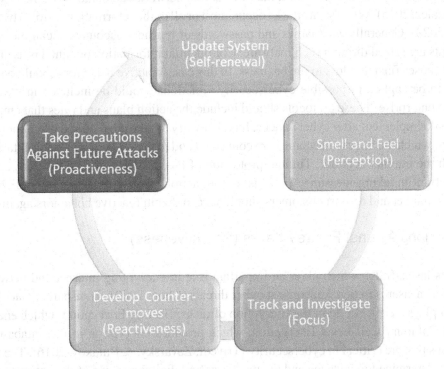

Social media accounts showcase the company's relationships with its customers, employees, external and internal environment, suppliers, and the public. For this reason, virtual applications must be protected against cyber-attack threats in order to protect the business image and to ensure reliability against customers. Spam posts, links shared in comments may contain malware. Virus scanner software must be integrated into the system in order to control these contents.

Track and Investigate (Focus)

The emerging cyberattacks and malware threats should be carefully examined by the business's IT department. The source of the attack, security vulnerabilities, software and databases, servers, and the size/risk level of the danger should be determined and reported to senior managers. Pishing issues caused by vulnerabilities and cyber-attacks may require red-level measures. Therefore, possible pishing problems are the first risk factor to be investigated. Spam is a yellow-level critical and dangerous factor. The risk factors in the orange category are suspicious e-mails and digital messages.

Administrative documents, trade secret documents, data related to manufacturing and planning, customer and stakeholder information should be stored, backed up, and protected in case of cyberattacks. Storage and backup should be performed on servers with reliable software. Servers that are not protected by software against cyber attacks pose a significant risk in deciphering information.

Develop Counter-Moves (Reactiveness)

Cyber attack aims to obtain information in the information network and database of the business (Ben-Asher & Gonzalez, 2015). When such attacks occur, most or all of the information is stolen by the attacker (Chen et al., 2020). Generally, usernames and passwords of business accounts, social media accounts, e-mail accounts are seized through such malware. Confidential information obtained is used against the company and causes financial loss to the business. In this case, reactive behaviors should be developed.

Protocols to be applied in possible cybersecurity violations should be included in the managerial strategy of the enterprise. These protocols should include the action plans and rules that employees and managers should implement after cyber attacks. It is necessary to take the required precautions to protect the accounts to which the attacked accounts are connected and to prevent other possible attacks that may occur through the internet network. Timing, protection of business interests and secrets, and personal data are important in taking measures. For this reason, actions that will damage the reliability of the business in the market and against customers should be avoided in reactive behaviors against attacks.

Take Precautions Against Future Attacks (Proactiveness)

Secure sockets layer (SSL), which plays an important role in encrypting internet and network traffic, is necessary for measures to be taken against cyber threats (Chou, 2002). Transparent Data Encryption (TDE), which plays a critical role in the encryption of disks, Backup Encryption, which encrypts SQL backups, and Column / Cell-Level Encryption, which provides encryption in the database, are SQL server functions that are critical in cybersecurity (Trivedi, Zavarsky, & Butakov, 2016). The future dangers should be determined in advance and the databases and digital systems of the enterprise should be protected with software and the software should be kept up to date.

Future attacks will have more complex encryption contexts than past attacks. For this reason, it is necessary to check the algorithm and update the security software. On the other hand, protection should be provided not to slow down the performance of system functions of antivirus software against cyber attacks in the context of the central processing unit. The measures to be taken for backing up the stored data, the security of the internet network, and closing security gaps should not adversely affect the system performance. The technological and digital infrastructure of the enterprise must have strong encryption and operating system against current and next-generation attacks.

The protection of the business against future attacks depends on the training of employees in the IT department or all related departments on these issues. Employees should be trained on security protocols, current problems, system infrastructure, IIoT and network systems of the enterprise, elimination of security gaps, new generation cyber attack types, and malicious software. It is necessary to prevent the disclosure of confidential information of the enterprise in training.

Update System (Self-renewal)

Updating the system ensures that to be prepared against possible cyber threats. It can be performed with software updates that have been strengthened and have new encryption techniques to protect software against cyber attacks and malware. Updating the system is crucial for compatibility in digital transformation. An update is required for efficiency in the operational functions of devices connected to the system. The update ensures that the system is protected against the new generation encryption features in cyber attacks and prevents the disclosure of confidential information and documents of the enterprise.

Updating may cause some problems in the functionality of the information stored in the database. If the digital infrastructures of the data are not compatible with the new technology or update version, there may be problems in reading and operational activities on the data. For this reason, the compatibility process of the technology and software of the data infrastructure should be followed closely in the update. Damaging software to older versions may result in data loss. The function and system compatibility level should be taken into consideration in the recovery of memory for software using the automatic garbage collector, such as Java.

Sustainable Training, and Adaptation

In the context of management and strategy, training is the transfer of strategic information to employees, leaders, stakeholders, customers, consumers, suppliers, sector representatives on specific issues. This transfer is carried out in subjects such as corporate cause-effect relationships, innovation, environmental analysis, opportunity-benefit-risk-threats analysis, entrepreneurship, technology, digital transformation in the relationships of individuals with the business. In today's digital world, training about cyber threats is important and necessary in the context of strategic management of the business.

Managerial strategies should take into account the protocols and principles related to developing technology and digital transformation. Although the strategies are a set of long-term plans, adaptation to the developing world conditions is required. The adaptation process required by digital transformation requires software and innovation. Especially the digital needs that emerged in the pandemic period clearly reveal this requirement. Virtual applications and online training come to the fore in extraordinary periods such as pandemics. The sustainability of the business, its ability to maintain its competitive advantage, promotion strategies, sustainability in strategic management, strategic human resources management, development of customer-business relations, ensuring employee-leader interaction depend on education on compliance in digital transformation and cyber threats.

In the context of information security, it is important to train employees about cyber threats and risks in the use of digital devices. Employees should be given continuous training on cybercrime, cyberattack, cyberterrorism, cybersecurity measures, emergency action plan. Protection of user name, and password information when logging in to the system, not clicking on links containing suspicious and malicious software in e-mails, ensuring information security in the use of networks and computers should be included in the training content. The ways to be followed and the measures to be taken in protecting computers and personal accounts belonging to the company against espionage and financial theft should be continuously conveyed to the employees. Some of this training should be carried out practically. On the other hand, employees working in the IT department should be subjected to a different training than other employees. In this training, there should be transferred the ways to protect sensitive and critical information of the enterprise such as a server, software, trade secrets, data, customer and employee information, supplier information. Sustainable training controls the sustainability of the business against possible cyber attacks by protecting the databases and secrets of the business.

SOLUTIONS AND RECOMMENDATIONS

Cyber attacks and cybercrime threaten today's businesses and the global economy. Although these threats constitute the weaknesses of businesses, they are critical risk factors in an operational and managerial context. Therefore, it is necessary and important to strengthen the business infrastructure in the context of cybersecurity. In the administrative context, cybersecurity requires coordination and cooperation in the relationship between the departments of the enterprise due to the security gaps that occur with digital transformation. Computer and network security should be protected in joint project development, in-house correspondence, and communication. On the other hand, software updates and new software should be considered in the context of business infrastructure in order to strengthen the system infrastructure.

Gircontrol plus-packaging, new CA-9S, RS 485, HUB Box, Modbus (RTU, TCP), automatic packaging systems, Industry 4.0. should be protected by software against cyber threats (Fovino, Carcano, Masera, & Trombetta, 2009; Huitsing, Chandia, Papa, & Shenoi, 2008). Protection of devices with a communication connection via network against cyber threats is important in the context of information security, trade secret, and operational sustainability. Since the transition of the IP header and IP data, in which IoT takes an active role, to the transport phase depends on taking security measures against cyber threats and the implementation of protocols, the necessary precautions should be taken strategically. Since spam posts, links shared in comments may contain malware, continuous training should be given to employees about the damages they may pose, security protocols, current problems, system infrastructure, IIoT and network systems of the enterprise, elimination of security vulnerabilities, new generation cyber attack types and malicious software. Administrative documents, trade secret documents, data related to production and planning, customer and stakeholder information should be stored, backed up, and protected in case of cyberattacks. Storage and backup should be performed on servers with reliable software.

Transparent data encryption (TDE), which plays a critical role in the encryption of disks, backup encryption, which encrypts SQL backups, Column / Cell-Level Encryption, which provides encryption in the database, are critical SQL Server functions in cybersecurity, and they must be protected by cybersecurity software (Coles & Landrum, 2009; Wiese, Waage, & Brenner, 2020). The protection of computers and personal accounts belonging to the company against espionage, financial theft, and the awareness level of employees on these issues should be increased. On the other hand, professional training to be received by employees of the IT department should be different from other employees and the confidentiality of sensitive data such as encryption related to the cybersecurity of the business should be ensured.

Human resources management and other strategic units of businesses should create emergency action plans regarding cyberattacks. It is recommended that departments such as production planning, marketing, procurement, and logistics create these action plans. In emergency action plans, factors such as possible cyber threats, technological deficiencies, protecting and backing up databases where confidential information of customers are kept should be taken into account.

FUTURE RESEARCH DIRECTIONS

Management and strategy development in cybersecurity and digital transformation should be explored empirically. For future research, it is recommended to investigate the effects of cybersecurity on human resource management, service, and manufacturing sectors. Besides, the measures taken by public institutions and organizations regarding cybersecurity and the strategies they have developed can be revealed with qualitative research.

CONCLUSION

This chapter was created with the aim of contributing to the management and strategy development of cybersecurity vulnerabilities and to be an inspiration for the strategies that businesses will develop against new generation cyberattacks and cybercrime. Although it is not empirical research, the findings revealed in the chapter provide important strategic and managerial foresight and principles to eliminate the threats, risks, and weaknesses that occur with the digital transformation of businesses that constitute the dynamics of the global economy and free market.

With this study, it was determined that cybersecurity focuses on six basic functions. These functions are data and information security, application, and software security, network and communication security, operational security, cyber-strategy development, sustainable training, and adaptation. Besides, cyber-strategy factors determined by the study were smell and feel (perception), track and investigate (focus), develop counter-moves, take precautions against future attacks, update system.

REFERENCES

Akhgar, B., Staniforth, A., & Bosco, F. (2014). *Cyber crime and cyber terrorism investigator's handbook*. Syngress.

Anderson, R., Barton, C., Böhme, R., Clayton, R., Van Eeten, M. J., Levi, M., & Savage, S. (2013). Measuring the cost of cybercrime. In *The economics of information security and privacy* (pp. 265–300). Springer. doi:10.1007/978-3-642-39498-0_12

Bayram, M., Üngan, M. C., & Ardıç, K. (2017). The relationships between OHS prevention costs, safety performance, employee satisfaction and accident costs. *International Journal of Occupational Safety and Ergonomics*, 23(2), 285–296. doi:10.1080/10803548.2016.1226607 PMID:27667202

Beelmann, A. (2006). Review of Systematic reviews in the social sciences. A practical guide [Review of the book Systematic reviews in the social sciences. A practical guide, by M. Petticrew & H. Roberts]. *European Psychologist*, 11(3), 244–245. doi:10.1027/1016-9040.11.3.244

Ben-Asher, N., & Gonzalez, C. (2015). Effects of cyber security knowledge on attack detection. *Computers in Human Behavior*, 48, 51–61. doi:10.1016/j.chb.2015.01.039

Bendovschi, A. (2015). Cyber-attacks–trends, patterns and security countermeasures. *Procedia Economics and Finance*, 28, 24–31. doi:10.1016/S2212-5671(15)01077-1

Bi, Z. M., Luo, M., Miao, Z., Zhang, B., Zhang, W. J., & Wang, L. (2020). Safety assurance mechanisms of collaborative robotic systems in manufacturing. *Robotics and Computer-integrated Manufacturing, 67*, 102022. doi:10.1016/j.rcim.2020.102022

Boeke, S. (2018). National cyber crisis management: Different European approaches. *Governance: An International Journal of Policy, Administration and Institutions, 31*(3), 449–464. doi:10.1111/gove.12309

Boyes, H., Hallaq, B., Cunningham, J., & Watson, T. (2018). The industrial internet of things (IIoT): An analysis framework. *Computers in Industry, 101*, 1–12. doi:10.1016/j.compind.2018.04.015

Brewer, R. (2016). Ransomware attacks: Detection, prevention and cure. *Network Security, 2016*(9), 5–9. doi:10.1016/S1353-4858(16)30086-1

Carl, G., Kesidis, G., Brooks, R. R., & Rai, S. (2006). Denial-of-service attack-detection techniques. *IEEE Internet Computing, 10*(1), 82–89. doi:10.1109/MIC.2006.5

Cass, S. (2001). Anatomy of malice [computer viruses]. *IEEE Spectrum, 38*(11), 56–60. doi:10.1109/6.963235

Chaudhuri, A., Datta, P. P., Fernandes, K. J., & Xiong, Y. (2021). Optimal pricing strategies for Manufacturing-as-a Service platforms to ensure business sustainability. *International Journal of Production Economics, 234*, 108065. doi:10.1016/j.ijpe.2021.108065

Chen, L., Yue, D., Dou, C., Chen, J., & Cheng, Z. (2020). Study on attack paths of cyber attack in cyber-physical power systems. *IET Generation, Transmission & Distribution, 14*(12), 2352–2360. doi:10.1049/iet-gtd.2019.1330

Chen, T., Jarvis, L., & Macdonald, S. (2014). *Cyberterrorism*. Springer. doi:10.21236/ADA603165

Cherubini, A., Passama, R., Crosnier, A., Lasnier, A., & Fraisse, P. (2016). Collaborative manufacturing with physical human–robot interaction. *Robotics and Computer-integrated Manufacturing, 40*, 1–13. doi:10.1016/j.rcim.2015.12.007

Chou, T. S. (2013). Security threats on cloud computing vulnerabilities. *International Journal of Computer Science and Information Technologies, 5*(3), 79–88. doi:10.5121/ijcsit.2013.5306

Chou, W. (2002). Inside SSL: The secure sockets layer protocol. *IT Professional, 4*(4), 47–52. doi:10.1109/MITP.2002.1046644

Chrisman, J. J., Hofer, C. W., & Boulton, W. B. (1988). Toward a system for classifying business strategies. *Academy of Management Review, 13*(3), 413–428. doi:10.5465/amr.1988.4306963

Coles, M., & Landrum, R. (2009). Transparent Data Encryption. In *Expert SQL Server 2008 Encryption* (pp. 127–150). Apress. doi:10.1007/978-1-4302-3365-7_6

Collin, B. C. (1997). The future of cyberterrorism: Where the physical and virtual worlds converge. *Crime and Justice International, 13*(2), 15–18.

Denning, D. E. (2001). Activism, hacktivism, and cyberterrorism: The Internet as a tool for influencing foreign policy. *Networks and netwars: The future of terror, crime, and militancy, 239*, 288.

Denyer, D., & Tranfield, D. (2009). Producing a systematic review. In D. A. Buchanan & A. Bryman (Eds.), *The Sage handbook of organizational research methods* (pp. 671–689). Sage Publications Ltd.

Dixit, N. K., Mishra, L., Charan, M. S., & Dey, B. K. (2012). The new age of computer virus and their detection. *International Journal of Network Security & Its Applications*, *4*(3), 79–96. doi:10.5121/ijnsa.2012.4305

Falco, G., Caldera, C., & Shrobe, H. (2018). IIoT cybersecurity risk modeling for SCADA systems. *IEEE Internet of Things Journal*, *5*(6), 4486–4495. doi:10.1109/JIOT.2018.2822842

Fernando, Y., Mathath, A., & Murshid, M. A. (2016). Improving productivity: A review of robotic applications in food industry. *International Journal of Robotics Applications and Technologies*, *4*(1), 43–62. doi:10.4018/IJRAT.2016010103

Flammini, A., Ferrari, P., Marioli, D., Sisinni, E., & Taroni, A. (2009). Wired and wireless sensor networks for industrial applications. *Microelectronics Journal*, *40*(9), 1322–1336. doi:10.1016/j.mejo.2008.08.012

Fovino, I. N., Carcano, A., Masera, M., & Trombetta, A. (2009). Design and implementation of a secure modbus protocol. In *International conference on critical infrastructure protection* (pp. 83-96). Springer. 10.1007/978-3-642-04798-5_6

Gibson, I., Rosen, D., Stucker, B., & Khorasani, M. (2014). *Additive manufacturing technologies* (Vol. 17). Springer.

Gordon, L. A., & Loeb, M. P. (2006). *Managing cybersecurity resources: a cost-benefit analysis* (Vol. 1). McGraw-Hill.

Gordon, S., & Ford, R. (2002). Cyberterrorism? *Computers & Security*, *21*(7), 636–647. doi:10.1016/S0167-4048(02)01116-1

Grobauer, B., Walloschek, T., & Stocker, E. (2010). Understanding cloud computing vulnerabilities. *IEEE Security and Privacy*, *9*(2), 50–57. doi:10.1109/MSP.2010.115

Hellström, T. (2007). Critical infrastructure and systemic vulnerability: Towards a planning framework. *Safety Science*, *45*(3), 415–430. doi:10.1016/j.ssci.2006.07.007

Hines, P. (1993). Integrated materials management: The value chain redefined. *International Journal of Logistics Management*, *4*(1), 13–22. doi:10.1108/09574099310804920

Huitsing, P., Chandia, R., Papa, M., & Shenoi, S. (2008). Attack taxonomies for the Modbus protocols. *International Journal of Critical Infrastructure Protection*, *1*, 37–44. doi:10.1016/j.ijcip.2008.08.003

Ismail, M., Shaaban, M. F., Naidu, M., & Serpedin, E. (2020). Deep learning detection of electricity theft cyber-attacks in renewable distributed generation. *IEEE Transactions on Smart Grid*, *11*(4), 3428–3437. doi:10.1109/TSG.2020.2973681

Jayaram, A. (2016). Lean six sigma approach for global supply chain management using industry 4.0 and IIoT. In *2016 2nd international conference on contemporary computing and informatics (IC3I)* (pp. 89-94). IEEE.

Jerman-Blažič, B. (2008). An economic modelling approach to information security risk management. *International Journal of Information Management, 28*(5), 413–422. doi:10.1016/j.ijinfomgt.2008.02.002

Kemmerer, R. A. (2003). Cybersecurity. In *25th International Conference on Software Engineering, 2003. Proceedings.* (pp. 705-715). IEEE. 10.1109/ICSE.2003.1201257

Kotey, B., & Meredith, G. G. (1997). Relationships among owner/manager personal values, business strategies, and enterprise performance. *Journal of Small Business Management, 35*, 37–64.

Krombholz, K., Hobel, H., Huber, M., & Weippl, E. (2015). Advanced social engineering attacks. *Journal of Information Security and Applications, 22*, 113-122.

Kumar, J., Kumar, M., Pandey, D. K., & Raj, R. (2021). Encryption and Authentication of Data Using the IPSEC Protocol. In *Proceedings of the Fourth International Conference on Microelectronics, Computing and Communication Systems* (pp. 855-862). Springer.

Llopis-Albert, C., Rubio, F., & Valero, F. (2021). Impact of digital transformation on the automotive industry. *Technological Forecasting and Social Change, 162*, 120343. doi:10.1016/j.techfore.2020.120343 PMID:33052150

Martins, A. I., Queirós, A., Silva, A. G., & Rocha, N. P. (2015). Usability evaluation methods: a systematic review. *Human Factors in Software Development and Design*, 250-273.

Matricano, D. (2021). Digital Business Transformations: An Investigation About Business-Driven and Technology-Enabled Strategies. In Handbook of Research on Management and Strategies for Digital Enterprise Transformation (pp. 173-195). IGI Global.

Matt, C., Hess, T., & Benlian, A. (2015). Digital transformation strategies. *Business & Information Systems Engineering, 57*(5), 339–343. doi:10.100712599-015-0401-5

McQuade, S. C. (2006). *Understanding and managing cybercrime*. Pearson/Allyn and Bacon.

Nagy, J., Oláh, J., Erdei, E., Máté, D., & Popp, J. (2018). The role and impact of Industry 4.0 and the internet of things on the business strategy of the value chain—The case of Hungary. *Sustainability, 10*(10), 3491. doi:10.3390u10103491

Nguyen, K. T., Laurent, M., & Oualha, N. (2015). Survey on secure communication protocols for the Internet of Things. *Ad Hoc Networks, 32*, 17–31. doi:10.1016/j.adhoc.2015.01.006

Petticrew, M., & Roberts, H. (2008). *Systematic reviews in the social sciences: A practical guide*. John Wiley & Sons.

Phan, D. D. (2001). E-business management strategies: A business-to-business case study. *Information Systems Management, 18*(4), 61–69. doi:10.1201/1078/43198.18.4.20010901/31466.7

Porter, M. E. (2001). The value chain and competitive advantage. *Understanding Business Processes, 2*, 50-66.

Razzaq, A., Hur, A., Ahmad, H. F., & Masood, M. (2013). Cyber security: Threats, reasons, challenges, methodologies and state of the art solutions for industrial applications. In *2013 IEEE Eleventh International Symposium on Autonomous Decentralized Systems (ISADS)* (pp. 1-6). IEEE. 10.1109/ISADS.2013.6513420

Rees, L. P., Deane, J. K., Rakes, T. R., & Baker, W. H. (2011). Decision support for cybersecurity risk planning. *Decision Support Systems, 51*(3), 493–505. doi:10.1016/j.dss.2011.02.013

Sallos, M. P., Garcia-Perez, A., Bedford, D., & Orlando, B. (2019). Strategy and organisational cybersecurity: A knowledge-problem perspective. *Journal of Intellectual Capital, 20*(4), 581–597. doi:10.1108/JIC-03-2019-0041

Schneier, M., Schneier, M., & Bostelman, R. (2015). *Literature review of mobile robots for manufacturing.* US Department of Commerce, National Institute of Standards and Technology. doi:10.6028/NIST.IR.8022

Senge, P. M. (1995). *Learning organizations.* Gilmour Drummond Publishing.

Simões, A. C., Soares, A. L., & Barros, A. C. (2020). Factors influencing the intention of managers to adopt collaborative robots (cobots) in manufacturing organizations. *Journal of Engineering and Technology Management, 57*, 101574. doi:10.1016/j.jengtecman.2020.101574

Stallings, W. (1996). IPv6: The new Internet protocol. *IEEE Communications Magazine, 34*(7), 96–108. doi:10.1109/35.526895

Ten, C. W., Manimaran, G., & Liu, C. C. (2010). Cybersecurity for critical infrastructures: Attack and defense modeling. *IEEE Transactions on Systems, Man, and Cybernetics. Part A, Systems and Humans, 40*(4), 853–865. doi:10.1109/TSMCA.2010.2048028

Trivedi, D., Zavarsky, P., & Butakov, S. (2016). Enhancing relational database security by metadata segregation. *Procedia Computer Science, 94*, 453–458. doi:10.1016/j.procs.2016.08.070

Vardarlier, P. (2020). Digital transformation of human resource management: digital applications and strategic tools in HRM. In *Digital Business Strategies in Blockchain Ecosystems* (pp. 239–264). Springer. doi:10.1007/978-3-030-29739-8_11

Vial, G. (2019). Understanding digital transformation: A review and a research agenda. *The Journal of Strategic Information Systems, 28*(2), 118–144. doi:10.1016/j.jsis.2019.01.003

Warren, M., & Hutchinson, W. (2000). Cyber attacks against supply chain management systems: A short note. *International Journal of Physical Distribution & Logistics Management, 30*(7/8), 710–716. doi:10.1108/09600030010346521

Watkins, B. (2014). The impact of cyber attacks on the private sector. Briefing Paper. *Association for International Affair, 12*, 1–11.

Weimann, G. (2005). Cyberterrorism: The sum of all fears? *Studies in Conflict and Terrorism, 28*(2), 129–149. doi:10.1080/10576100590905110

Wiese, L., Waage, T., & Brenner, M. (2020). CloudDBGuard: A framework for encrypted data storage in NoSQL wide column stores. *Data & Knowledge Engineering, 126*, 101732. doi:10.1016/j.datak.2019.101732

Wu, D., Ren, A., Zhang, W., Fan, F., Liu, P., Fu, X., & Terpenny, J. (2018). Cybersecurity for digital manufacturing. *Journal of Manufacturing Systems, 48*, 3–12. doi:10.1016/j.jmsy.2018.03.006

Xu, L., Jiang, C., Wang, J., Yuan, J., & Ren, Y. (2014). Information security in big data: Privacy and data mining. *IEEE Access: Practical Innovations, Open Solutions, 2*, 1149–1176. doi:10.1109/AC-CESS.2014.2362522

Yar, M., & Steinmetz, K. F. (2019). Cybercrime and society. *Sage (Atlanta, Ga.).*

Yi, P., Zhu, T., Zhang, Q., Wu, Y., & Pan, L. (2016). Puppet attack: A denial of service attack in advanced metering infrastructure network. *Journal of Network and Computer Applications, 59*, 325–332. doi:10.1016/j.jnca.2015.04.015

Zezulka, F., Marcon, P., Bradac, Z., Arm, J., Benesl, T., & Vesely, I. (2018). Communication systems for industry 4.0 and the iiot. *IFAC-PapersOnLine, 51*(6), 150–155. doi:10.1016/j.ifacol.2018.07.145

Zhou, F., Goel, M., Desnoyers, P., & Sundaram, R. (2013). Scheduler vulnerabilities and coordinated attacks in cloud computing. *Journal of Computer Security, 21*(4), 533–559. doi:10.3233/JCS-130474

KEY TERMS AND DEFINITIONS

Cyber Terrorism: The cyberattacks carried out through the computer network and the internet, which have serious damage to the values of society, the state, and humanity.

Cybercrime: Activities of attacks such as unauthorized access to information systems through computer and internet networks such as espionage, financial theft, capturing data, theft of financial data and passwords, blocking the use of the system and log in, blocking or delaying communication.

Cybersecurity: The protection of data, servers, mobile devices, electronic systems, computers, and networks from malicious attacks.

Digital Transformation: The creation of solutions by using digital elements in meeting social, organizational, sectoral, workplace, and business needs.

Internet Protocol (IP): An important function in transporting packets to target IP addresses.

Secure Sockets Layer (SSL): An important function in encrypting internet and network traffic, is necessary for measures to be taken against cyber threats.

Chapter 9
Cybersecurity for E–Banking and E–Commerce in Pakistan:
Emerging Digital Challenges and Opportunities

Tansif ur Rehman
 https://orcid.org/0000-0002-5454-2150
University of Karachi, Pakistan

ABSTRACT

Digital banking allows banks to make their new products more readily available, as they can package them with their essential software that has implications for cybersecurity. Internet presence also allows banks to extend their geographical reach without overbearing costs. In Pakistan, most internet offerings currently used by banks are more based on information than transactions; therefore, the issues for cybersecurity have gained high interest. The offerings on the websites by banks generally seem like electronic brochures. As they mainly offer company events, product information, along with a list of services rendered. Pakistan has various barriers to e-commerce, such as relatively few internet users, inadequate infrastructure (i.e., frequent power failures, fewer phone lines), and lack of cybersecurity for online transactions being hacked. The Government of Pakistan is rigorously working on these areas to overcome respective problems and progress in this sphere. This research focuses on the challenges for e-banking and e-commerce in Pakistan and issues relating to cybersecurity.

INTRODUCTION

Cybersecurity breaches have opened new digital challenges and threats for banks and their customers. Increases in cyberattacks is creating an unsafe digital environment. Electronic payment systems enable banks' customers to transact via internet-supported websites and banks of banks, known as electronic banking or net banking. It provides online access to banks if they have the means for it. Moreover, it offers different services, such as money transfer, bill payment, account verification, e-shopping, and

DOI: 10.4018/978-1-7998-6975-7.ch009

recharges. Online banking has notched its position since it operates in terms of ease and expediency, offers quick connectivity, cost-effectiveness, and could be performed anywhere. Internet also has offered hackers with easy access to exploit cyberspace for illegal activities. Shad (2019) suggests that cyber power depends on cybersecurity readiness —preparedness level against cyber threats —otherwise it transforms into cyber vulnerability. The author further argues that Pakistan faces wide-ranging cyber threats while it increasingly makes use of internet technologies but it seriously lacks in cyber readiness.

There exist many kinds of banks, viz., commercial, investment, private, and public. However, all have the same purpose of providing services relating to customers, enterprises, businesses, and government money as a vital prerequisite. Banks vary from lending and funding real estate and automobiles to major trade-relating deals in the contemporary era. Internet banking involves customers realizing the most varied banking practices that are not carried out within physical banking outlets. Such businesses range from conventional banking to mobile gadgets and are usually performed through the internet in which cyber-attacks are on the rise. Khan & Anwar (2020) in a study focuses on the cybersecurity framework present in Pakistan while reporting the key policy options for the state of Pakistan to deal with serious cybersecurity issues is the actual matter of concern?

Internet banking technology in the Asian region, especially in Pakistan, is comparatively less developed than in the Western world because of specific reasons. Full consideration of future e-banking in Pakistan would undoubtedly demand an investigation in various pertinent areas. The Electronic Transactions Ordinance was promulgated in 2002 to facilitate e-commerce in Pakistan, and it provided legal coverage to electronic transactions (e-Transactions). It also gave importance regarding Public-Key Infrastructure (PKI), which is software encryption technologies and services combination. It enables various enterprises to protect their communications and business transactions to a maximum extent on the internet.

In early 2000, the Government started an information-technology (I.T.) and e-commerce initiative. The banks were expected then to lead the way into e-commerce, respectively. However, the banking sector has been one of the leading spenders on information communications technology (ICT). Most progress in the e-commerce sector has been in e-government. Though some business-to-business (B2B) portals are available, they are designed more for information than facilitating transactions. There has been remarkable progress in the growth of e-commerce in Pakistan. In Pakistan, Internet users are growing fast, and internet access expanded from 29 cities in August 2000 to more than 6500 cities and towns by November 2018. Previously, optical fiber networks were only available in major cities, but now the respective networking is expanding exponentially.

Almost all renowned banks have equipped themselves with the latest technology significantly pertinent to enhance their services and have provided e-banking facilities to their customers. Now, customers can access their accounts without being physically present at their banks. Banks are offering more and more facilities to facilitate their customers with ease and convenience regarding e-banking. However, in Pakistan, this is not the case. As people still refrain from using e-banking in Pakistan because of various issues. The e-banking sector has exponentially grown in the last decade, and it has more chances of growth as organizations like banks still encourage clients to carry out e-transactions, like utility bill payments, access to account information, and money transfer.

Most of the prior studies have frequently focused only on the positive aspects of e-banking, e.g., advantages, trustworthiness, and innovations. This research will help banks formulate appropriate strategies to ensure customers' rapid migration to online banking, thus booming this self-service technology more efficiently and conveniently.

The establishment of National Centre for Cyber Security (NCCS) has been commenced by Government of Pakistan in June 2018 (NCCS 2018). The NCCS project is a joint initiative of Higher Education Commission (HEC) and Planning Commission. The Centre constitutes Research and Development (R&D) Labs in reputed universities of Pakistan which were shortlisted after the open call for proposals made by HEC in early 2018.

FOCUS OF THE RESEARCH

The comfort and expediency brought with electronic banking use caused a breakthrough that radically changed the business environment and an ever evolving digital space. Online banking worldwide is prevalent nowadays, and it is impossible to believe that this phenomenon did not exist long ago. Online banking commenced in the early 1980s when the largest banks in New York offered home-based facilities to their clients. The clients could view their bank statements and pay their bills and access their bank accounts anytime. Nevertheless, the revolution in e-banking started during the mid-1990s as the internet was recognized as a delivery means having potential prospective.

Though accessibility approach to banks and simplicity of managing individuals' accounts were beneficial and held immense promise, people quickly realized that this convenience has a price. Banks continually seek to develop protection and use different methodologies to maintain the system secure from cyber attacks, such as encoded business networks, two-tiered authentication, and several technologies to ensure that no one abuses the system. Researchers apply data analysis tools to review banks' business documents to understand how efficiently internal controls work and to highlight transactions that imply the possibility of forgery.

In general, this research focuses on the historical evolution of banking, advantages, disadvantages of e-banking, an overview of Pakistan's economy, internet usage, cybersecurity, growth of e-commerce in Pakistan, and e-banking global usage in Pakistan. In specific, it focuses on the prospects and barriers of e-banking and e-commerce in Pakistan.

RESEARCH METHODOLOGY

This research was formed by a systematic review method (Komba & Lwoga, 2020). In this method, the research objectives are determined, and an extensive literature review is done on the subject. The research findings are classified according to the subject's content (Petticrew & Roberts, 2006). Classified information is included in the study by organizing it as headings (Pawson et al., 2005). The flow of the study is formed by evaluating classified information and titles (Rahi, 2017). Thus, integrity is ensured by evaluating the researched subject with its contents (Victor, 2008).

As a result, this method was adopted, and these procedures were followed respectively. The information and data obtained from the literature review related to the research objectives were coded. The coded information was combined under the related topics. After classification and combining, the topics were sorted according to their level of relationship.

HISTORICAL EVOLUTION OF BANKING

Earliest Banks

Historical evidence shows that the first banks were probably the religious temples in the ancient world. They were most probably established around the 3rd millennium B.C. Scholars have also argued upon the very fact that these banks anticipated the invention of money as a result (Gilbart, 1919; Millet, 2002).

Deposits consisted of grain, and later on, other goods such as cattle and agricultural machinery were deposited. Eventually, precious metals like gold in compressed plates (i.e., easy to carry) and precious stones were deposited (Liverani, 2013). Temples and palaces were the safest places to store gold and other valuables securely, as they were frequently attended to and well built as sacred places (Schmandt-Besserat, 1992).

There are also records of loans from the 18th century B.C. in Babylon, made by temple priests to merchants. With the advent of Hammurabi's Code, circa 1754 BC (Prince, 1904), banking was developed well enough to justify laws governing banking operations and procedures.

Banking in the Western World

In 1565, the London Royal Exchange was established (Walvin, 2011). At that time, money changers were already called 'bankers.' Though the term bank' usually referred to their offices. It does not carry the meaning it does nowadays because of its usage and implications (Cameron, 2015; Davies & Bank, 2002).

Amsterdam, London, and Hamburg's ports served as the largest commercial centers in the late 17th century. Banking offices then were usually located near the centers of trade. Individuals, too, could participate in a lucrative business. East India traded via purchasing bills of credit from these banks (Davisson & Harper, 1972).

The price thus received for the commodities depending on the ships returning (which were usually delayed) and the type of cargo they carried (which often was not according to the plan formulated). It caused the commodities market to be very much volatile. Wars and conflicts also led to cargo seizures and ships' loss on several occasions (Parker, 1984).

E-BANKING

Internet banking allows customers to carry out financial transactions on a secure website operated by their retail or virtual bank. The onset of the internet and personal computers' popularity presented both an opportunity and a challenge for the banking industry. For many years, financial institutions have used robust computer networks to automate millions of daily transactions (Baker, 1999). Today, often, the only paper record is the customer's receipt at the point of sale, and now customers are connected to the internet via personal computers (Hamel, 2000) as banks envision similar economic advantages by adapting those same internal electronic processes to home usage.

AN OVERVIEW OF RETAIL AND CORPORATE BANKING

The branch of a bank that deals directly with retail customers are known as retail banking, while corporate banking is the part of the banking sector that deals with corporate customers. Retail banking is the public's first introduction to banking, with bank branches aplenty in most big cities. On the other hand, corporate banking deals with firms directly to offer deposits, credit, deposit plans, and checking accounts tailored to the needs of businesses rather than individuals (Majaski, 2019).

Retail Banking

Retail banking is a form of a financial institution that is available to the general public. Market banking, also known as personal banking, helps customers handle their money by providing basic banking facilities, loans, and financial advice. The term "retail banking" refers to a broad range of goods and services, including:

1. Automobile financing
2. Credit cards
3. Mortgages
4. Checking and savings accounts
5. Foreign currency and remittance services
6. Certificates of deposit (C.D.s)
7. Lines of credit such as home equity lines of credit (HELOCs) and other personal credit products

Clients of retail banking can also be given the following services, which are usually provided by another branch or subsidiary of the bank:

1. Private banking
2. Stock brokerage (discount and full-service)
3. Wealth management
4. Insurance

A client's level of tailored retail banking services is determined by their income level and length of association with the bank.

A teller or customer service agent would typically support a person with modest means, while an account manager or private banker would address the financial needs of a high-net-worth entity (HNWI) with a long history with the bank. While physical branches are still vital to express the sense of solidity and continuity that is so important in banking, thanks to the proliferation of automated teller machines (ATMs) and the prevalence of online and mobile banking, retail banking is now the field of banking that has been most impacted by technology (Majaski, 2019).

Corporate Banking

Corporate banking, also known as corporate banking, caters to a wide range of clients, from minor to mid-sized local companies with a few million dollars in revenue to multinational conglomerates with billions in profits and offices worldwide. Since the Glass-Steagall Act of 1933 divided the two practices, the concept was first used in the United States to differentiate it from investment banking. Although that legislation was abolished in the 1990s, most banks in the United States and elsewhere have been offering corporate and investment banking services under the same banner for many years (Majaski, 2019). Corporate banking is a significant source of benefit for most banks. However, as the largest provider of customer loans, it is also the cause of daily write-downs on defaulted loans. Corporations and other financial institutions may take advantage of the following goods and services provided by commercial banks:

1. Treasury and cash management services
2. Loans and other credit products
3. Commercial real estate
4. Equipment lending
5. Employer services
6. Trade finance

Commercial banks provide related services to their corporate customers through their investment banking branches, such as wealth management and bond underwriting.

Special Considerations

The banking sector is a vital component of the economy, both at home and abroad. First and foremost, consumers—both personal and business—deposit money into savings accounts, which banks can lend to others. Banks also assist in creating finance, the facilitation of commerce, and the formation of wealth. One of the most critical aspects of any economy is the finance market, which comprises retail and commercial banking.

When banks have issues, it has disastrous consequences for the economy. Take, for example, the financial crisis. The recession stemmed from the U.S. property bubble, and banks and financial institutions worldwide are undue exposure to derivatives and shares dependent on U.S. house values. Banks became more unable to lend money to each other or businesses. It caused a near-total freeze in the global banking and credit system, resulting in the worst global recession since the Great Depression (Majaski, 2019). Because of the global economy's near-death experience, regulators have revived their attention on the biggest banks, which are considered "too big to fail" due to their relevance to the global financial system.

GLOBAL CONTEXT OF E-BANKING

Modern, highly industrialized, technology-driven economies are now threatened with higher risks than ever before. Individuals need to protect themselves against the private risk that has been much increased. From the banks' viewpoint, internet banking is expected to lead to cost reductions and improved competitiveness. The industrial sector is undoubtedly one of the most significant service sectors for the national economy (The Financial Brand, 2018). This service delivery channel is being seen as a powerful tool. It can retain current web-based customers who continue using banking services from any location of their choice. Internet banking also provides opportunities for banks to develop their market by attracting a new customer base from existing internet users.

In the last five years, financial analysts have assessed financial services websites as laggards behind other industries in overall innovation. Internet banking sites currently score low in design and technology use compared to other retail websites, thus available. The current financial analysis indicates that the bank customers are the most satisfying ones if they are allowed to state when, where, and how they carry out their banking (Pedro, Ramalho, & Silva, 2018). Banks need to spend more time and increase investments in improving the connections with customers and differentiating customer experience. This aspect is now grabbing many banks' attention globally.

The financial analysts also suggest that the banks can learn few things from many non-bank industries, as they are exhibiting innovation to deal with the self-service options for their customers altogether (Pedro, Ramalho, & Silva, 2018). Internet technology possesses the potential to enable banks to enhance their internet offerings with potential features that will improve customer service interactions. It will allow them to increase the control of their e-banking experience altogether.

Due to the vital fact that financial transactions involve the transmission of sensitive and personal data, a significant factor influencing the consumer use of internet banking websites is the trust factor. The continuing instances of internet banking security violations and reports dwindle customers' trust in banks, especially online banking. Thus, issues pertinent to the adoption of internet banking must be factored in any plans to add to the customer's satisfaction and enhance the relevant security control features.

ADVANTAGES AND DISADVANTAGES OF E-BANKING

According to Nazaritehrani and Mashali (2020), Chao et al. (2019); Mahmood (2019); Rabiu et al. (2019); and YuSheng & Ibrahim (2020), the advantages as well as disadvantages of e-banking are enlisted.

Advantages

1. **Convenience:** Unlike a physical bank, online banking websites are never closed. They are available 24 hours a day, seven days a week, and they are only a mouse click away from the customer.
2. **Effectiveness:** Many online banking websites now offer sophisticated tools, including account aggregation, portfolio managing programs, rate alerts, as well as stock quotes, to facilitate customers to manage their assets more effectively than ever before.
3. **Efficiency:** Accessing and managing all bank accounts, including C.D.s, IRAs, and even securities, are now reachable from one secure website.
4. **Pervasiveness:** Even if a customer is abroad, he can easily log on instantly to his online bank and take care of his business whenever he needs it.
5. **Transaction speed:** Now, the online banks' websites execute and confirm the carried out transactions at or even swifter pace compared to ATM processing speed.

Disadvantages

1. **Banks' website modifications:** Even the most prominent banks periodically upgrade their online programs to add new features in unfamiliar places. In some cases, the customer has to re-enter account information, and it is a bit inconvenient for the customer to do so.

2. **Learning curve:** Banking websites can be challenging to navigate for the first time as customers become familiar with them over time.
3. **Start-up time consumption:** To register for the bank's online program, the customer has to provide her/his I.D. and sign a form at a bank branch they have an account.
4. **Trust factor:** The biggest hurdle to online banking is learning to trust it for many people. The question that usually bothers customers is; Is the transaction carried out?

According to Agarwal (2020) and Nollytech (2019), the advantages and disadvantages of e-banking are:

Advantages of E-Banking

1. **Easy to use:** With electronic banking, one can conveniently pay bills, pass money, check an account statement, and so on.
2. **Easy to open:** Creating and managing an online account is a breeze.
3. **It saves time:** Instead of waiting in a long line, which can be tedious and time-consuming, one can pay bills from their convenience.
4. **It saves details about transactions:** Since all transactions are done electronically, one does not need to keep receipts. As a result, one can obtain them at the touch of a button by requesting a digital statement of account from one's bank.
5. **Very easy and efficient:** Banks move funds quickly, and one can use it to handle several accounts conveniently.
6. **No time limit:** Yes, one can access account and conduct transactions anytime and on any day because it is open 24 hours a day, seven days a week. Even as long as there is an internet link, there is no barrier.
7. **Integrated banking services:** Integrated banking services allow the bank to invest in new markets and increase its customer base. Market share and profitability both increase as a result of this development.
8. **It makes for simple account monitoring:** One can keep track of all account transfers and balance at all times. One can now easily monitor and avoid any suspicious activity or danger to an account.
9. **Better funding makes it easier:** E-banking offers various customer service options, including call, text, and email. It makes it simple for customers to contact the bank if they have a problem.
10. **Security is assured:** The security and safety of customers' details are ensured by cutting-edge cryptography and security technology.

Disadvantages of E-Banking

1. **Limited access:** One can only access an online banking site while connected to the internet. As a result, it would not be essential if one does not have access to the internet.
2. **Hard for beginners:** If one is new to internet banking, one can encounter some difficulties that make it difficult to use the banking services.
3. **Banking information is not private:** If one does not adequately protect an account, one will find that the account information has spread through many devices. E.g., if one saves account numbers, ATM card pin code, and other personal information on the phone and loses it, they risk losing even more money if it falls into the wrong hands.

4. **An account may be hacked:** Do one realize that a third party can obtain online account records? If hackers have access to one's account's transaction password, for example, they can easily convert all of the money in an account to their own and withdraw it immediately.

5. **Server down:** When a bank server or a service provider's server is offline, one will not be able to make an internet transaction until the server is up and running again. Moreover, if it were very urgent, one would have to wait.

6. **Transaction Failure:** The transaction may fail. As a result, one must visit a bank to correct the situation. The failure of this transaction may be due to a lack of network connectivity, the bank's computer being down, or other factors. It is excruciatingly frustrating because it usually occurs when an individual is pressed for time to complete a deal with the other side.

7. **Notifications that bother:** Some service providers can send the same message 3 to 5 times to receive SMS warning fees. It can be aggravating at times.

8. **A third party may access an account:** If anyone mistakenly obtains a password, they will use an account for their gain. It is but one example of how dangerous online banking can be.

9. **Irreversible transactions:** One will not be able to reverse the transaction because the electronic banking system is incredibly swift. When one is on it, be cautious. One will not be able to reverse the transaction one has authorized. If one gives money to the wrong account, it will take God's grace to reclaim the funds.

10. **Constant updates and emails:** Did one know that not everybody enjoys receiving notifications or updates? The majority of debit reminder emails are vexing.

Table 1. Prominent Features of E-Banking in Pakistan

Prominent Features	Telephone Banking	Self Service Terminals	ATMs	Internet Banking
Balance enquires	√	√	√	√
Change ATM card PiN	√	√	√	√
Cheque book orders	√			√
Deposits			√	
Interim Statement	√	√		√
Rates	√	√		√
Stop orders	√			√
Stop payment of a cheque.	√	√		√
Transfer funds	√	√	√	√
Withdrawals			√	

OVERVIEW OF PAKISTAN'S ECONOMY

Pakistan has an overwhelming population of around 212 million. According to IMF (2017), it has the 25th largest economy in terms of purchasing power parity, 41st most extensive in terms of nominal gross domestic product. Unfortunately, Pakistan's GDP per capita is comparatively lower than the South Asian region's economy, i.e., only US$1541, and it ranks 148th on the list. Pakistan has a semi-industrialized economy encompassing agriculture, textiles, chemicals, food processing, and other relevant industries.

According to the Economic Survey of Pakistan 2017-18, the central bank of Pakistan, i.e., the State Bank, noted that the food inflation had pushed up overall inflation. Government borrowings from the State Bank reached alarming levels adding and resulting in inflationary pressures. As an underdeveloped country, Pakistan has undoubtedly suffered from decades of internal disputes, i.e., social and political nature, low foreign investments, and a costly ongoing confrontation with its neighboring countries. IMF-approved government policies, generous foreign assistance, and renewed access to the global markets for a few years have generated substantial macroeconomic recovery in Pakistan.

A few of the many challenges that Pakistan is facing are rising energy costs, inflation on the rise, depleting water resources, infrastructure deficits, and lack and drawbacks in social services, like education and health. From all the above-cited problems, economic and political instabilities, trade competitiveness, and human resource development are undoubtedly essential. Although the World Bank has its terms and conditions, it is ready to help Pakistan cope with its poverty reduction strategy to achieve Sustainable Development Goals.

The World Bank has also been working with Pakistan on different programs. This support is also continuing in investment loans, technical assistance, and programmatic operations in Pakistan and South Asia as a whole, where increasing global prices of petroleum products and food items are adversely affecting the lives of many.

INTERNET USAGE IN PAKISTAN

The Islamic Republic of Pakistan is a sovereign state located in South Asia. According to the Bureau of Statistics - 6th Population and Housing Census, Pakistan's population is 212,742,631. It is the fifth most populous country and the second-most populous Muslim country in the world after Indonesia. According to Internet World Stats (IWS), in Pakistan, the total number of internet users in October 2018 was 44,608,065, 22.2% of the total population.

GROWTH OF E-COMMERCE IN PAKISTAN

According to Pakistan Telecommunication Authority (2018), the percentage of broadband internet users in Pakistan as of October 2018 is around 30%. It reveals the development in this sphere during the last decade. Many banks and exchange companies now offer online funds transfers from overseas, like workers remittances. A few banks offer mobile phone banking, where customers can pay utility bills using their mobile phones.

The State Bank of Pakistan permitted the internet merchant accounts to process Internet vendors' financial transactions in February 2001. Transactions that occurred at that time used international credit cards, which were processed outside Pakistan. The users of the internet merchant accounts undertaking transactions outside Pakistan needed to submit electronic forms for their transactions valued at US$500 and more to their concerned banks. The banks then submit the same in a consolidated form monthly to the central bank, i.e., SBP.

The Central Board of Revenue (CBR), the tax authority in Pakistan, started allowing electronic filing of sales tax and federal excise returns by registered private and public companies in December 2005. It was said that it expected about 1,600 large taxpayers out of 22,000 to use the respective facility. The Government's efforts to promote the I.T. sector included establishing the Information Technology and Telecommunications Division in July 2000. Various other incentives were drafted for the commitment of resources for education and infrastructure building, and the Ministry of Science and Technology in August 2000 launched the National Information Technology Policy. It was developed by a team that included working groups encompassing cyber laws, e-commerce, human resource development, incentives for I.T. investment, internet development, I.T. fiscal issues, I.T. in Government and databases, I.T. market development and support, I.T. research and development, legislation and intellectual property rights, software export, telecom convergence, and deregulation.

E-BANKING'S GLOBAL USAGE AND PAKISTAN

Internet banking refers to using the internet as a remote delivery channel for banking services (Furst et al., 2004). Internet banking is becoming an increasingly important channel for Pakistani banks to facilitate banking services to individual customers and businesses. The banks offer internet banking in two ways; first, an existing bank with its physical offices can establish a website and offer internet banking to its customers and its traditional existing delivery channels. The second alternative is to establish a virtual internet-only bank. The computer server lies at the heart of an internet-only bank may be housed in either an office that serves as the legal address or at some other different location.

The internet-only banks may offer their customers the ability to make deposits and withdraw funds via ATMs or other remote delivery channels owned by other institutions, respectively. The internet banking service is presently being offered to two sets of clients, personal clients and business clients. Internet banking channels offer less waiting time with higher spatial convenience and a lower cost structure than traditional distribution channels. The success of e-banking can be gauged by identifying the number of currents and anticipated registered users worldwide (Hamilton, 1997).

DIGITAL ENTERPRISE TRANSFORMATION

"Ongoing digital transition through sectors became a given in 2019," Stephanie Overby (2020) said. Digital transition exhaustion became possible at the same time." Though Steve Hall (2020), President of ISG (a significant technology consulting and research organization), believes that "internet projects will continue to scale rapidly across industries in 2020." Chief information officers and companies have prepared their businesses for transition in many ways, but they have not gone all the way to changing their cultures to accept the change truly."

The integration of computerized technologies into the corporate realm is known as digital enterprise transformation, changing how a company handles and delivers service to its customers in general. Furthermore, continuing sociocultural shifts force businesses to test current criteria, experiment repeatedly, and become more familiar with malfunctioning and even loss (The Enterprisers Project, 2020).

DIGITAL ENTERPRISE TRANSFORMATION AND ICTS

Transactions created by information and communication technologies, such as telemedicine, e-commerce, and social media, give customers more options for connecting, chat, and shopping (Rouse, 2019). Progress in information and communication technologies has undoubtedly created many benefits, conveniences, and cost savings for businesses (Allen, 2019).

Digital learning management systems are now being used in higher education to use internet technology, and they have become a critical and invaluable platform for educational learning practices (Al-Amoush & Sandhu, 2019). Scholars such as Ayman Hassan Bazhair and Kamaljeet Sandhu have written extensively about enterprise resource planning (ERP) programs and their relationship to financial success (2015). However, perceived ease of use and perceived utility to consumer motivation are also essential factors in user adoption of Web-based eServices (Sandhu, 2008). The evaluation of customer contextual variables is needed for web-based electronic services, end-user acceptance, and deployment (Sandhu, 2009). These advantages include cost savings in fully automated business processes and a data transformation in companies that transform data produced by ICT into insights that drive new services and goods.

DIGITAL ENTERPRISE TRANSFORMATION IN CONTEMPORARY ERA

Banks that use Digital Enterprise Transformation will be able to gain significant comparative advantages:

1. It enables large-scale and rapid growth.
2. Organizational agility meets changing consumer demands.
3. The customer's future requirements are met.

Financial services companies benefit from Digital Enterprise Transformation because it makes them more stable, compliant, and digital (Allen, 2019). Employees, associates, clients, and stakeholders all have different experiences (Schenkel, 2019).

SOLUTIONS AND RECOMMENDATIONS

The E-banking system has been strengthened for years, with the advancement of the internet and aid of modernization and technology employed for data safety in cybersecurity. An increasing number of developments are shifting to the digital world daily, indicating a shift in mindset, industry prototypes, and cyber-security steps. Businesses experienced with that change hope their banks' services facilitate them constructively. It is possible to turn this anticipation into four features: creativity, simplicity, ease, and multichannel. It may also allow businesses to ask for new banking services by evading extensive and complicated procedures that depend on clients' physical existence in banks. It could be interactive apps for portable gadgets, smartwatches, tablets, and cellular phones. It could be a seamlessly flowing multichannel practice that keeps customers involved and has more regular contact with the institutions.

Discussions regarding the future of commercial organizations help the users to mull over various procedures, wherein they are changing. Although contemporary technologies like internet banking, mobile banking, and BitCoin facilitating the banks are popular, the evolutionary leap in the digital signature, encryption, Blockchain, data security, and numerous security-linked aspects could also be correlated with them. The advancements in technologies have led to an all-time digital world and, as it has become more comfortable and straightforward, business dealings are being integrated into our daily lives. This fact could be seen regarding payments made using cell phones. Regarding investment in information technology and business transactions linked to goods and services, the business field has continuously matured. The growth of Bank 3.0 (notion proposed by Brett King in 2012, it states that banking requires no physical space, as it is just an activity) arises from innovations, namely, cyber-security and cloud computing.

Banks should educate their customers about all benefits of mobile and e-banking and cybersecurity. Service charges of foreign banks should be reduced to be enabled to utilize their services and remain intact with these banks. More customized and featured mobile banking services should be introduced. These services are not sufficient, as mobile usage is on the rise, so this area needs a focus. During power cuts and frequent electricity breakdowns, accessing the internet becomes difficult; thus, mobile banking can help in this phase.

FUTURE RESEARCH DIRECTIONS

It is significant to note that individuals perceive e-banking differently, depending on whether they carry out transactions for themselves or their employers. A comparative analysis between one's thoughts pertinent to private e-banking and e-banking for work purposes as a corporate user can reveal some interesting facts. Therefore, a more in-depth analysis of the demographics and the user's background would help discover how these aspects influence corporate customers' decision-making and e-banking usage in Pakistan. Significant areas for conducting future research encompassing prospects of e-banking and e-commerce in Pakistan via engaging qualitative, qualitative, or eclectic approach can be gender adaptability of technology, incident response planning in Pakistan, the issues encompassing economic growth and stability in Pakistan, issues in the e-commerce sector of Pakistan, perceived and actual risk in e-commerce.

CONCLUSION

Internet banking is becoming an increasingly important channel for Pakistani banks to facilitate banking services to individual customers and businesses. The banks and post office departments in Pakistan are working on multiple delivery channels to facilitate citizens' delivery of payments in a minimum time frame with security and reliability. Banks and post offices across the country also facilitate workers' remittance from overseas Pakistanis within 24 hours and without charges.

As an underdeveloped country, Pakistan has undoubtedly suffered from decades of internal disputes, i.e., social and political nature, low foreign investments, and a costly ongoing confrontation with its neighboring countries. For a few years, IMF-approved government policies, generous foreign assistance, and renewed access to the global markets have generated reliable macroeconomic recovery in Pakistan.

Consequently, developments in detection technologies and safeguards also should be ensured. Big data technology is used by the most sophisticated anti-fraud programs by businesses to implement revolutionary predictive models online, allowing banks the prospect to identify and prevent apprehensive behavior as it happens. Banks, therefore, should employ an e-banking system whose protection is separated from customers. Security steps at all stages should be compulsory to keep this problem of scams under control. Improved technology and advanced machine-learning methods would provide banks with prospective access to advanced systems that are more reliable and competitive, hence reducing fraudulent activities.

Furthermore, the delivery of financial services via the internet should also be treated as a part of the overall customer service and distribution strategy. Thus, the relationship developed could then indeed be used as a gateway for product information delivery. These measures could also help in the rapid movement of customers to the e-banking environment. Finally, resulting in considerable savings in the operating costs for the respective banks across Pakistan.

The World Bank has also been working with Pakistan on different programs. This support is also continuing in investment loans, technical assistance, and programmatic operations in Pakistan and South Asia as a whole, where increasing global prices of petroleum products and food items are adversely affecting the lives of many. By engaging all stakeholders, these barriers can be reduced to a minimum extent, which ultimately will lead to the prospects of e-banking and e-commerce in Pakistan.

REFERENCES

Agarwal, A. (2020, May 8). *Advantages and disadvantages of internet banking.* ToughNickel. https://toughnickel.com/personal-finance/Advantages-and-Disadvantages-of-Internet-Banking

Al-Amoush, A. B., & Sandhu, K. (2019). A new model for acceptance of analytics in learning management systems at Jordanian universities. In Modern Technologies for Teaching and Learning in Socio-Humanitarian Disciplines (pp. 138-161). IGI Global.

Al-Furiah & Al-Braheem. (2009). Comprehensive study on methods of fraud prevention in credit card e-payment system. In *Proceedings of the 11th international conference on information integration and web-based applications & services. ACM.*

Allen, J. P. (2019). *Digital entrepreneurship.* Routledge. doi:10.4324/9780429506567

Anderson, R. J. (Ed.). (2008). *Security engineering: A guide to building dependable distributed systems.* Wiley.

Baker, C. R. (1999). An analysis of fraud on the internet. *Internet Research*, *9*(5), 348–360. doi:10.1108/10662249910297750

Bazhair, A. H., & Sandhu, K. (2015). Factors for the acceptance of enterprise resource planning (ERP) systems and financial performance. *System*, *14*(7), 16.

Cameron, R. E. (2015). *A concise economic history of the world: From Paleolithic times to the present* (5th ed.). Oxford University Press.

Carminati, M., Polino, M., Continella, A., Lanzi, A., Maggi, F., & Zanero, S. (2018). Security evaluation of a banking fraud analysis system. *ACM Transactions on Privacy and Security*, *21*(3), 1–31. Advance online publication. doi:10.1145/3178370

Chao, X., Kou, G., Peng, Y., & Alsaadi, F. E. (2019). Behavior monitoring methods for trade-based money laundering integrating macro and micro-prudential regulation: A case from China. *Technological and Economic Development of Economy, 25*(6), 1–16. doi:10.3846/tede.2019.9383

Davies, G., & Bank, J. H. (2002). *A history of money: From ancient times to the present day.* University of Wales Press.

Davisson, W. I., & Harper, J. E. (1972). *European economic history.* Appleton-Century-Crofts.

Furst, S. A., Reeves, M., Rosen, B., & Blackburn, R. S. (2004). Managing the life cycle of virtual teams. *The Academy of Management Executive, 18*(2), 6–20. doi:10.5465/ame.2004.13837468

Gilbart, J. W. (1919). *The history, principles, and practice of banking.* George Bell And Sons.

Government of Pakistan, Bureau of Statistics. (2017). *Provisional Summary Results of 6th Population and Housing Census - 2017.* https://bytesforall.pk/

Government of Pakistan, Ministry of Finance. (2018). *Economic Survey of Pakistan 2017-18.* http://www.finance.gov.pk/survey/chapters_18/overview_2017-18.pdf

Government of Pakistan. Electronic Transactions Ordinance, 2002. (2020). http://www.pakistanlaw.com/eto.pdf

Government of Pakistan. Pakistan Telecommunication Authority. (2018). *Telecom Indicators.* https://www.pta.gov.pk/en/telecom-indicators

Hall, S. (2020). *What is digital transformation?* https://enterprisersproject.com/what-is-digital-transformation

Hamel, G. (2000). *Leading the revolution.* Harvard Business School Press.

Hamilton, S. (1997). E-commerce for the 21st century. *Computer, 30*(5), 44–47. doi:10.1109/2.589909

Holtz, M., David, B., Deus, F. E., de Sousa, R. T. Jr, & Laerte, P. (2011). *A formal classification of internet banking attacks and vulnerabilities.* Academic Press.

Hutchins, E. M., Clopp, M. J., & Amin, P. R. (2011). *Intelligence-driven computer network defense informed by analysis of adversary campaigns and intrusion kill chains.* Lockheed Martin Corporation.

International Monetary Fund. (2017). *World Economic Outlook Database.* https://www.imf.org/external/pubs/ft/weo/2017/01/weodata/index.aspx

Internet World Stats. (2018). *World Internet Users and 2018 Population Stats.* https://www.internetworldstats.com/stats.htm

Khan, P., & Anwar, M. (2020). *Cybersecurity In Pakistan: Regulations, Gaps And A Way Forward.* Massey University. https://mro.massey.ac.nz/bitstream/handle/10179/16061/114-Article%20Text-223-1-10-20210122.pdf?sequence=1&isAllowed=y

Khrais, L. T. (2015). Highlighting the vulnerabilities of the online banking system. *Journal of Internet Banking and Commerce, 20*(3). Advance online publication. doi:10.4172/1204-5357.1000120

King, B. (2012). *Bank 3.0: Why banking is no longer somewhere you go but something you do*. Wiley. doi:10.1002/9781119198918

Kiyavash, N., Koushanfar, F., Coleman, T. P., & Rodrigues, M. (2013). A timing channel spyware for the CSMA/CA protocol. *IEEE Transactions on Information Forensics and Security, 8*(3), 477–487. doi:10.1109/TIFS.2013.2238930

Komba, M. M., & Lwoga, E. T. (2020). *Systematic review as a research method in library and information science.*. doi:10.4018/978-1-7998-1471-9.ch005

Liverani, M. (2013). *The ancient Near East: History, society, and economy*. Routledge. doi:10.4324/9781315879895

Mahmood, Y. N. (2019). The impact of quality service factors on banking service sector case study in Erbil banks. *Tikrit Journal of Administration and Economics Sciences, 2*(42).

Majaski, C. (2019, April 9). *Retail banking vs. corporate banking: What's the difference?* Investopedia. https://www.investopedia.com/articles/general/071213/retail-banking-vs-commercial-banking.asp

Millett, P. (2002). *Lending and borrowing in ancient Athens*. University Press.

Nazaritehrani, A., & Mashali, B. (2020). Development of e-banking channels and market share in developing countries. *Financial Innovation, 6*(12), 12. Advance online publication. 10.118640854-020-0171-z

NCCS. (2018). *National Centre for Cyber Security*. https://www.nccs.pk

Nollytech. (2019). *10 Advantages And Disadvantages of Electronic Banking*. https://nollytech.com/advantages-and-disadvantages-of-electronic-banking/

Overby, S. (2020). *What is digital transformation?* https://enterprisersproject.com/what-is-digitaltransformation

Parker, W. N. (1984). *Europe, America, and the wider world: Essays on the economic history of western capitalism*. Cambridge University Press.

Pawson, R., Greenhalgh, T., Harvey, G., & Walshe, K. (2005). Realist review - A new method of systematic review designed for complex policy interventions. *Journal of Health Services Research & Policy, 10*(1), 21–34. doi:10.1258/1355819054308530 PMID:16053581

Pedro, C. P., Ramalho, J. J. S., & Silva, J. V. (2018). The main determinants of banking crises in OECD countries. *Review of World Economics, 154*(1), 203–227. doi:10.100710290-017-0294-0

Petticrew, M., & Roberts, H. (2006). *Systematic reviews in the social sciences: A practical guide*. doi:10.1002/9780470754887

Prince, J. D. (1904). Review: The code of Hammurabi. *The American Journal of Theology, 8*(3), 601–609. doi:10.1086/478479

Rabiu, I. D., Ladan, S., Usman, H. A., & Garba, M. (2019). Impact of e-banking on the operational efficiency of banks in Nigeria. *International Journal of Academic Research in Business & Social Sciences, 9*(2). Advance online publication. doi:10.6007/IJARBSS/v9-i2/5527

Rahi, S. (2017). Research design and methods: A systematic review of research paradigms, sampling issues, and instruments development. *International Journal of Economics & Management Sciences, 06*(6). Advance online publication. doi:10.4172/2162-6359.1000403

Rouse, M. (2019). *ICT (Information and Communications technologies).* https://searchcio.techtarget.com/definition/ICT-information-and-communications-technology-or-technologies

Saeed, I. A., Campus, J. B., Selamat, M. A., Ali, M., & Abuagoub, M. A. (2013). A survey on malware and malware detection systems. *International Journal of Computers and Applications, 67*(16), 25–31. doi:10.5120/11480-7108

Sandhu, K. (2008). E-services acceptance model (E-SAM). In Advances in Computer and Information Sciences and Engineering (pp. 224–229). Springer. doi:10.1007/978-1-4020-8741-7_40

Sandhu, K. (2009). Measuring the performance of the electronic service acceptance model (E-SAM). *International Journal of Business Information Systems, 4*(5), 527–541. doi:10.1504/IJBIS.2009.025205

Schenkel, M. T., Farmer, S., & Maslyn, J. M. (2019). Process improvement in SMEs: The impact of harmonious passion for entrepreneurship, employee creative self-efficacy, and time spent innovating. *Journal of Small Business Strategy, 29*(1), 64–77.

Schmandt-Besserat, D. (1992). *Counting to cuneiform.* University of Texas Press.

Shad, M. (2019). Cyber Threat Landscape and Readiness Challenge of Pakistan. *Strategic Studies, 39*(1), 1-19. https://www.jstor.org/stable/10.2307/48544285

Singh, S., Cabraal, A., & Hermansson, G. (2006). What is your husband's name?: Sociological dimensions of internet banking authentication. In *Proceedings of the 18th Australia conference on Computer-Human Interaction: Design: Activities, Artefacts, and Environments.* ACM. 10.1145/1228175.1228217

The Enterprisers Project. (2020). *What is digital transformation?* https://enterprisersproject.com/whatis-digital-transformation

The Financial Brand. (2018). *The four pillars of digital transformation in banking.* https://thefinancial-brand.com/71733/four-pillars-of-digital-transformation-banking-strategy/

Victor, L. (2008). Systematic reviewing in the social sciences: Outcomes and explanation. *Enquire, 1*(1), 32–46.

Vila, J. A. (2015). *Identifying and combating cyber-threats in the field of online banking.* Academic Press. https://www.sslshopper.com/what-is-ssl.html

Walvin, J. (2011, February 17). Slavery and the building of Britain. *British Broadcasting Corporation.* http://www.bbc.co.uk/history/british/abolition/building_britain_gallery_02.shtml

YuSheng, K., & Ibrahim, M. (2019). Service innovation, service delivery, and customer satisfaction and loyalty in the banking sector of Ghana. *International Journal of Bank Marketing, 37*(5), 1215–1233. doi:10.1108/IJBM-06-2018-0142

ADDITIONAL READING

Ahanger, R. G. (2011). An investigation into the determinants of customers' preferences and satisfaction of internet banking (Empirical study of the Iranian banking industry). *Journal of Applied Sciences, 11*(3), 426–437. doi:10.3923/jas.2011.426.437

Casalo, L., Flavian, C., & Guinaliu, M. (2008). The role of usability and satisfaction in the consumer's commitment to a financial services website. *International Journal of Electronic Finance, 2*(1), 2008–2031. doi:10.1504/IJEF.2008.016883

Chavan, J. (2013). Internet banking - Benefits and challenges in an emerging economy. *International Journal of Research in Business Management, 1*(1), 19–26.

Laukkanen, T., Sinkkonen, S., & Laukkanen, P. (2009). Communication strategies to overcome functional and psychological resistance to Internet banking. *International Journal of Information Management, 29*(2), 111–118. doi:10.1016/j.ijinfomgt.2008.05.008

Munusamy, S., & Chelliah, W. M. (2010). Service quality delivery and its impact on customer satisfaction in the banking sector in Malaysia. *International Journal of Innovation, Management and Technology, 1*(4), 398–404.

Nupur, J. M. (2010). E-banking and customers' satisfaction in Bangladesh: An analysis. *International Review of Business Research Paper, 6*(4), 145–156.

Rahmath, S., & Hema, D. (2010). Customer perspectives on e-business value: A case study on internet banking. *Journal of Internet Banking and Commerce, 15*(1), 2–11.

Suh, H., & Han, I. (2002). Effect of trust on customer acceptance of internet banking. *Electronic Commerce Research and Applications, 1*(4), 7–63. doi:10.1016/S1567-4223(02)00017-0

Walker, R. H., Craig-Lees, M., Hecker, R., & Francis, H. (2002). Technology-enabled service delivery: An investigation of reasons affecting customer adoption and rejection. *International Journal of Service Industry Management, 13*(7), 91–106. doi:10.1108/09564230210421173

Westland, C. (2002). Transaction risk in e-commerce. *Decision Support Systems, 33*(1), 87–103. doi:10.1016/S0167-9236(02)00010-6

KEY TERMS AND DEFINITIONS

Banking: The services offered by a bank.

Barriers: Obstacles that cause hindrance.

E-Banking: Online banking, i.e., via the internet.

E-Commerce: Transactions conducted on the internet.

Remittance: A transfer of funds by an expatriate to his country of origin.

Telecommunications: It is the exchange of information over significant distances by electronic means.

Chapter 10
Demystifying Global Cybersecurity Threats in Financial Services

Deepika Dhingra
(iD) https://orcid.org/0000-0001-5967-8834
Bennett University, India

Shruti Ashok
Bennett University, India

Utkarsh Kumar
Bennett University, India

ABSTRACT

The financial sector across the globe ensures sustainable growth in the economy by mobilizing investments, funds, and savings. This chapter attempts to comprehend the current state of cybersecurity within the financial services industry worldwide. The chapter explores the different aspects of global cyber-attacks in financial sectors to elucidate the salient problems, issues, threats, safeguards, and solutions. As technology is progressing, highly technology-savvy criminals are becoming a new threat in the cybercrime space. The entire industry needs an intense transformation to create innovative, state-of-the-art information, and an up-to-date architecture of cybersecurity that is capable of confronting the continuous tides of cyber-attacks and data breaches on an everyday basis. The use of security tools like proxy servers, firewalls, multi-layered email strategy, virus security software, and effective governance strategies are necessary to protect financial sectors from cyber threats and attacks.

DOI: 10.4018/978-1-7998-6975-7.ch010

INTRODUCTION

The finance sector is complexly intertwined into the daily lives of individuals and across the globe and is the core of the world economy. These entities empower people and organizations to manage their trade, finances, and operate in various manners globally. To empower financial inclusion and enhance people's lives, financial companies are shifting their operations to digital platforms which exhibits huge potential for both sides. Since transactions in financial sector are sizable in both value and volume, it is a potential target for cyber threats from criminals, as gains from any such cyber-attack is apparently infinite. With such huge financial benefits and paybacks involved, coupled with low risk and detectability, the new age highly proficient cyber-devils are endeavoring to knock down the protective shields of ill-protected Banking, Financial Services, and Insurance (BFSI) sector. Thus, cybercrimes are emerging as a key concern in the global financial market, snowballing into a major threat. This fact is taken cognizance by the entire financial sector worldwide and many establishments have already accepted the fact that finance industry is the most attacked sector in Europe, Middle East and African regions.

In recent years, financial markets across the world have been affected by a quick rise in the number of cyber-attacks and incidents where data has been compromised (data breach) – and typically affected markets are characterized with higher volumes of digital financial transactions. Chebyshev (2019) in his study found mobile malware more prevalent in the developing world. Study by McAfee (2018) concluded that while Russia and most countries in Central Asia have the maximum reported cases of mobile malware, Asia has held the record for the maximum usage of mobile banking and digital payment applications and the continent is also witnessing increasing number of cyber-attacks on financial establishments. Just to name a few countries, Japan, Indonesia, Bangladesh, Philippines, Vietnam, and Taiwan have faced a series of cyber-attacks. This threat applies not only to banks, but also to asset management companies, exchanges, insurance companies, technology providers, clearing and settlement houses, and to supply chains institutions as well.

Figure 1. AIG Systemic Cyber Risk Study: Industries Most Likely to Face a Systemic Attack 2017 (Graphic: Business Wire)

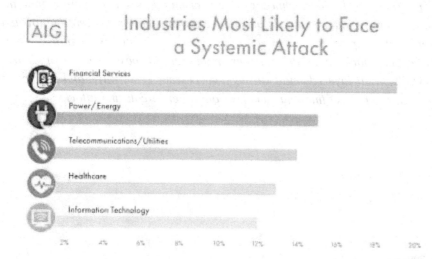

The financial sector across the world is troubled with the continuous waves of cyber assaults where exceptional instigators quietly conduct hi-tech data breaches, invasions, heists, and data thefts, etc. Consequently, there is huge financial loss every year. Cybersecurity Ventures has projected that due to cyber-crimes the world will face a loss of $6 trillion annually by 2021. Topics such as increasing cost, frequency, and magnitude of data breach are dominating the discussions on risk management as data compromise has shaken, hindered, and even paralyzed markets (temporarily). According to experts, confidential records and sensitive data worth billions of dollars have been compromised. As developed countries have made their defense stronger against cyber-crimes, the cyber attackers seem to have to shift their focus to new and evolving digital financial markets. Using insecure devices or ill-protected transmission lines may be the reason for digital transactions becoming more vulnerable in this part of the world.

Cyberthreat has become more alluring since the Covid-19 pandemic started. As new rules and regulations were imposed by the governments, employees and workers are being encouraged to work from home. This has brought new challenges as the system now is highly dependent on technology infrastructure, inviting many cyber threats to the new operating model. The dangers in the form of phishing or privacy invasion have become a significant hurdle for the companies resulting in exploitation of personal and company's information deterioration. Salaam et.al (2019) explored the cybersecurity risks to things, sensors, and monitoring systems and identified the implications to be distinct from the conventional networking systems in many aspects.

Not only financial institutions but security establishments are also developing new techniques to confront cyber threat. With rapid strides in technology and growing innovation, cyber attackers are quickly resorting to committing robberies of another nature and stature, continuing to escape security arrangements and attribution. The complexities of the finance sector only exacerbate complications and confusion, as banking and other financial services are now confronting completely different kinds of cyber threats. Amidst these threats, it becomes imperative that companies comprehend and understand cyber risk applicable to them as this knowledge can considerably improve the effectiveness of security & would result in better risk assessment and management in implementation and execution of new technologies and processes. Organizations must be proactively preparing strategies to confront cyber-attacks and secure themselves. This chapter will elaborate on the current state of cybersecurity within the financial services industry worldwide.

UNDERSTANDING CYBERSECURITY

In this new digital age, robberies are not done with weapons with masks being a thing of the past. Due to enhanced security, it is difficult for criminals to rob the banks and other financial establishments conventionally. As technology is progressing, sharp-minded and highly technology-savvy criminals are becoming a new threat in the cybercrime space. With an expanded threat landscape and new digital susceptibilities, the number of security breaches have increased in the last few years.

Defining Cyber Attacks and Security Threats/Breaches

According to a study conducted by Accenture in 2019, "Cyber-attacks are malevolent activities carried out against the institutions through the IT infrastructure via the Internet or the internal or external networks. These activities also comprise attacks against industrial control systems (ICS). Infiltration in the core networks or enterprise systems of the company is a consequence of breach of security. That is excluding the attacks stopped by the organization's firewall defenses."

However, for terms such as "cyberattack," "cybercrime," and "cyber incident," there are no globally adopted definitions. Some recent researches have made considerable endeavors to comprehend the impact of cybersecurity risk on the global financial industry and the need for suitable risk fortification and management. (Bouveret, 2019a; Bouveret, 2019b; Mohammed et al., 2020; Mugarura & Ssali, 2020; Humayun et al., 2020).

In general, a cyber-attack refers to an illegal and unapproved attempt to access sensitive and confidential data executed or committed using computers, network, or hardware devices. Cyber-activities that trouble the experts of financial market risk management are neither cybercrimes nor cyber-incidents and it is over-and under-inclusive to define the cyber threats that plague the financial services industry. Scrutinizing details of cyberattacks gives more useful points for determining the activities that instigate cybercrime, though; it is difficult and prominently more controversial. Alliances of activists and government use the term cyber-attack to define undesirable cyber invasions. The Joint Chiefs of Staff, US military explains a cyber-attack as:

A hostile act using computer or related networks or systems and intended to disrupt and/or destroy an adversary's critical cyber systems, assets, or functions. The intended effects of cyberattack are not necessarily limited to the targeted computer systems or data themselves—for instance, attacks on computer systems which are intended to degrade or destroy infrastructure or C2 capability. A cyberattack may use intermediate delivery vehicles including peripheral devices, electronic transmitters, embedded code, or human operators. The activation or effect of a cyberattack may be widely separated temporally and geographically from the delivery.

Various Depictions of Cyber-Attacks Clarifying the Methods and Rationale for These Incursions

1. **Lone Wolf Attacks**: These types of cyber-attacks are often carried out by prodigy teenagers who want to compromise international networks for the rush of quick fun and fame. These kinds of cyberattacks are some of the most difficult to detect and confront.
2. **Hacktivists Attacks**: These attacks are instigated by people who are driven to execute such attacks for moral or political reasons.
3. **Fraudulent and Criminal Activity**: These types of cyber-attacks are generally conducted by people who aim to get accessibility to customer data and other confidential information for their immoral advantages. These cybercriminals normally target retailers and banks as they possess a huge amount of customer data.
4. **Industrial Espionage:** This generally involves a lone wolf, targeting financial assets. These attacks are extremely complex.
5. **Cyberwarfare**: This is described as cyberattack against a country and furthering a political or a military campaign. These are the least common but can be the most hazardous even for developed countries.

Impact of Data Breach

Threat of data breaches continue to increase and affect the financial sector organizations such as banks and credit card companies. Because of the accessibility and the tremendous value of information, the financial sector organizations have always been the main target of cyber-attacks worldwide. Ameen et.al (2020) explored the rising number of data breaches on mobile devices and studied its effect on the security of customers' data and employee's compliance to cybersecurity. The International Data Corporation (IDC) had predicted that by 2020, one-fourth of the population in the world will be affected by data breach. The impact of breach of data in each company is distinct and depends on the event's duration, timing, and the industry. For instance, a data breach may cause more prominent and dire consequences for the financial sector in comparison to any other industry. Studies on cybersecurity hazards have found its direct correlation with escalating operational risks that ends in operational costs rise adversely affecting the economic results of banks and financial institutions (Kopp et al., 2017; Fitch, 2017; Aldasoro et al., 2020a; Aldasoro et al., 2020b).

To get deeper insights, we synthesize literature on four themes. Such as (i) ho According to a report by Boston Consulting Group, the probability of a cyberattack in financial services firms is 300 times more. Handling those attacks and their outcome carry a greater cost for banks and wealth managers than for any other sector. In this new world, which is extensively connected, these breaches are a looming threat for financial institutions and their customers.

Data breach stories grab attention worldwide and it is difficult to ignore stories about data breaches. Data is becoming more and more valuable to businesses and adversaries, particularly when it is related to customers and their financial transactions. To use data fraudulently, criminals target data that financial companies depend on to cater to their customers better. Any business that accepts payments from debit and credit cards is on the target which may be a further cause of breaches in financial institutions and their customers. A study in 2018 on cost of a data breach by The Ponemon Institute found that the global average cost of a data breach was $3.86 million and had increased by 6.4% from 2017. Even the smallest data breach can make big damage. Every stakeholder needs to understand the outcome of a data breach to assess the risk properly. It is believed that small businesses are too small to be targeted and do not prepare, which makes them even more susceptible to cyber-attacks. The next section elaborates on the consequences of a data breach.

Consequences of a Data Breach

Direct financial loss: As deliberated, several cyber-criminal groups target banks and other financial institutions to steal money. Profuse increase of ransomware, along with appropriate ransomware insurance policies, has established the cycle of crime and payment and has made it a cost for businesses in the modern world. With an increase in remote workers owing to COVID-19, companies need to re-evaluate basic network security guidelines and end-user training to substantially reduce the risk caused by ransomware. The cost of cybercrimes to financial institutions is far higher than any other business or industry. For a big financial company, a cyber breach may cost millions. Over-sightedness or a casual approach to cyber threats or data breaches can cripple businesses.

Data and credential theft: Cyber fraud leads to financial losses, but data theft can be far more damaging and worth for cybercriminals, particularly when it is sold on the Dark Web.

Network downtime and lost productivity: Service disruption for a week in 2018, costed UK-based TSB Bank nearly £200m. Though it was not a cyber-attack, an attack with the intent of destruction may sustain similar costs.

Reputation and competitiveness: The costs may be even higher when cybersecurity incidents influence brand loyalty and the trust of investors and customers, which can lead to customer churning. As financial organizations are experiencing the highest customer churning rate in any industry, this could be a worrying situation for financial institutions. The situation can lead to loss of revenue as well as damage to reputation, which can be cataclysmic.

Regulations and fines: Authorities throughout the world are becoming intolerant of data breaches and introducing stricter regulations, investigations, and penalties. One of the most stringent regulations recommended by the European Parliament for a breach of privacy, applicable from 25 May 2018, calls for a fine of 20 million euros, or 4% of annual revenues globally, whichever was the higher–the amount that would threaten several emerging companies.

Loss of Intellectual Property: Theft of intellectual property can create damage of very high magnitude, as a company can lose years of efforts on R&D investment, trade secrets or copyrighted material and even their competitive lead. Though, criminals also target strategies, designs, and blueprints, the loss can affect the competitiveness of financial institutions as some competitors would not hesitate to take advantage of stolen information.

Other Costs

Many intangible costs can disrupt a business for long even after the incident took place. Normally, the effects of operational interruption are miserably undervalued.

Costs commonly linked to a cyber breach may also comprise:

- Containment of breach and its remediation
- Damage control or recovery

Figure 2. Demonstrating possible consequential impacts of a cyberattack on financial institutions

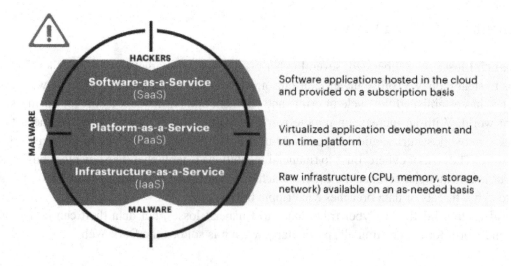

- Spending on new security software, hardware, and other services
- Expenses made on recovery of data.
- Incremental hiring

CYBERSECURITY IN THE FINANCIAL SECTOR

BFSI sector is the backbone of the economy of any nation and any intimidation to this industry may directly put the independent state into danger, hence cybersecurity in the financial sector has a great significance. The need to shield the customer's assets from cyber threats is of paramount importance in the BFSI sector. With transactions going cashless and online, the foundation of financial services industry and particularly banking lies in cultivating trustworthiness and integrity. As the BFSI sector is witnessing a digital overhaul in business operations and procedures comprehensively, this has made banks, insurance companies, payment firms, asset management companies, and other sectors of the financial industry a prime choice of target for the innumerable groups of highly skilled cybercriminals who use advanced technologies.

Cyber breach not only affects customers but also harms the institutions and the industry immensely. Institutions might need to pay a huge amount of money as ransom to release breached data and information. Consequently, they end up losing the confidence of investors and other stakeholders. In the financial sector, cybersecurity has great significance, and when the very foundation of financial services and particularly banking lies in cultivating trustworthiness and integrity, it becomes even more indispensable. Therefore, it is critical to build a threat-counter mechanism which is responsive, extremely robust, and resistant for all financial establishments in the country.

Significance of Cybersecurity in Financial Services Industry and its Importance to Investors and Customers

- Governments are promoting digital transactions and endorsing a cashless economy. People are increasingly using digital money, e-debit cards, and credit cards. Hence, it becomes essential that all measures of cybersecurity should be in place to safeguard customer's data and privacy.
- The events of data compromise and data breach can create challenges for financial institutions to retain the trust of their customers and investors creating an extremely serious problem for banks. Loss of trust in the institutions due to fragile cybersecurity system and data breaches can prompt the customers to take their money to safer institutions.
- The initial impact of cyber threat is felt by the customer as he is the first one to risk losing money, time, and efforts. It involves the cancellation of cards, checking portfolios and statements, and other complications associated with the event. The road to recovery from such events can be stressful and time-consuming.
- Financial companies need to be on their guard much more than companies in other industries. Companies in financial industry must bear costs for holding valued private information and confidential data as personal and confidential data in wrong hands can inflict immense damage. Even if corrective measures are immediately resorted to, sensitive data has already disclosed enough information to cause great damage.

ISSUES, THREATS, AND GENERIC TRENDS

Financial Institutions and Cyber Threats

Hackers exposing flaws in practices of cyber-security risk management, foreign involvement in corporates or conventional intelligence, terrorists creating havoc by piercing firewalls pose significant threat to financial institutions. Study by Senarak (2021) examined the relationships between cybersecurity hygiene and cyberthreats namely hacktivism, cyber criminality, cyber terrorism through questionnaire survey. Traditionally, policies on cybersecurity are designed to protect the firm's and investor's information from getting compromised. Though safeguarding data continues to be significant in the cyber risk space, cyberattacks threaten the networks that connect financial companies, clearinghouse, exchange, and payment systems including the new cybersecurity frontier. Financial institutions like investment banks, securities, commodities exchange, and broker-dealers tactically make efforts to foresee and defend against cyberattacks. According to regulators, cyber threats may "create a serious disaster in the financial lives of customers." Hence, financial institutions are concerned about cyber threats from both internal and external spheres, and infiltration testing is required to find out how secure a company is against these potential attacks.

This section categorizes cyber threats into three major types based on the attacker's motivations. This will help the finance industry to understand the relevant threats in a better manner:

1. **Data Theft:** Financial establishments particularly possess customer's sensitive and valued data in comparison to any other industry that fascinates both criminal and state-sponsored hackers. The personal information is secretly collected by hackers, to build a database that can be used in the future for different campaigns such as offering bribes, opportunities for blackmailing, craft phishing attacks. The stolen personal data may contain details that would enable criminals to steal funds from customer's accounts. On the other hand, criminals can also sell data on the dark web. Lastly, a very common phenomenon in the finance sector is when they receive ransom demand for not publishing stolen data from financial establishments.
2. **Data Integrity and Sabotage:** Sabotage refers to the interruption or ruining of systems and is one of the most common methods of extortion by cyber criminals. Ransomware is frequently used for such purposes, although distributed "denial-of-service" (DDoS) attacks are also rampant in this space. The risk of state-sponsored cyber-attack disrupting financial systems is more complexed, as it depends on the geopolitical relations between the two countries.
3. **Direct financial theft:** Cyber attackers often target different industries to steal funds by influencing or compromising finance branches. Though, banks are their exclusive targets from where they can steal millions of dollars in a single successful attempt.

COVID-19 PANDEMIC AND CYBERSECURITY

Various bodies in U.S, comprising of NASDAQ, Securities Exchange Commission, and FINRA10 have cautioned of spikes in market manipulation during the COVID-19 pandemic. As the pandemic spreads worldwide, financial companies are also rapidly modifying their operations. Muthuppalaniappan et. al (2021) studied the impact of cyberattack on the healthcare industry amidst COVID 1-19. Credential and identity thefts are poised to rise, particularly at the time when government authorities and financial establishments are implementing financial relief to individuals and businesses are being affected by the pandemic.

Why is COVID-19 Making Cyber Security Even Harder for the Financial Sector?

The financial sector throughout the world has accomplished an extraordinary task in 2020—they managed to shift most of the employees to a remote working environment in a short time. But at the same time, this accomplishment has produced new cybersecurity apprehensions. Pranggono & Arabo (2020) established a clear correlation between the pandemic and the rise in cyber-attacks targeting vulnerable sectors. Amidst pandemic, establishments had to be cautious regarding several issues comprising new fraudulent campaigns. Institutions have considerably beefed up their option for remote access for employees who were working out of physical locations. Financial entities quickly responded to the challenge but at the same time, fraudsters are also finding ways to make use of weaknesses of remotely working employees.

The following are some cybersecurity concerns that Financial Institutions need to keep in mind in FY 2020-2021 and 2021.

1. **A one-two punch:** Financial industry faced two front challenges concerning cybersecurity.
    a. The first was to quickly shift majority of employees to work from home set up. Subsequently, this brought in new challenges, required upgrading virtual private networking to provide accommodations for more users, secure data transfer, and support external access to internal resources.
    b. Secondly, credential and identity theft have grown multifold. Impostors are increasing their attempts and sophistication to acquire sensitive, private information. Consequently, cybercriminals get valid credentials and then use automated bots to log in. To confront these situations, financial institutions have conducted cybersecurity awareness and training programs.
2. **First-time user error:** Traditionally BFSI companies do not have much workforce working from home. It was a challenge for beginners to learn to work remotely this year. Traditionally, very few remote workforces can present new risks and security cavities when working for the first time — especially using unauthenticated personal devices and unsecured home Wi-Fi networks. Thus, employees who are unfamiliar with a remote working environment become susceptible to security threats.
3. **Talent Matters**: The pandemic compelled numerous firms to leverage a cloud environment but it generated a new set of problems. Though financial institutions are cognizant about the real cyber threat post pandemic, but currently the challenge is to hire the right talent. The security industry is doing good work in reaching out to talent, but the gap between demand and availability continues to widen as other industries are realizing the need for skilled staff. Largely, COVID-19 has highlighted that adversaries will take advantage of any disruption to breach the security of an institution. This comprises phishing attacks or ransomware.
4. **Beware of Sender**: As COVID-19 is spreading, adversaries have devised newer ways of dodging the customers. Financial institutions need to rethink about maintaining security in a hybrid environment where a part of the workforce can continue to work remotely, even after the invention of the vaccine. Virtual working adds complexities to cybersecurity procedures such as ensuring that best practices are followed, training recruits on risk, and repairing software remotely. Using work

devices from an unsecured network can introduce malware. Hence, usage policies must be brushed up and restructured for the 'new normal'.

5. **Attack Vectors on The Rise:** Cyber concerns and threats have increased during this pandemic. In the first quarter of 2020, attack on vectors of financial institutions had gone up immensely. The cloud vendor is a concerning factor, as these vendors think that they are invulnerable, and this perception leads to terrible consequences. Lallie at.al (2021) concluded that cyber-attacks in COVID times have risen considerably with an average of three to four attacks being reported daily.

6. **Only Going to Get Worse:** According to cyber experts, security threats will increase in 2021. Eventually, cybercriminals will understand that business email compromise is easier and more beneficial than other scams like ransomware. Besides, that remote working model is tough for workers to validate transaction requests from their workmates.

TRENDS AND FUTURE OF CYBER THREATS

Businesses are restructuring their operations for enhanced digital experiences yet are also increasingly becoming susceptible to threat. Keeping in view the potential impact of a cyber-attack, this section discusses the future of cyber threats and relevant trends that are being observed.

1. **Distractive Attacks:** There are times when security teams are confronting relatively mild disruptive attacks such as ransomware; attackers are stealthily conducting major activity somewhere else in the victim's network only.

2. **Targeted Ransomware:** Although, ransomware has been quite familiar, targeted ransomware attacks are on the rise. The footmarks of targeted attacks are considerably smaller in comparison to an outburst or spam operation. Attackers hit specific critical systems in targeted attacks and therefore can excerpt more money from a single prey.

3. **Supply chain attack:** Supply chain attacks seek to breach targets by compromising associated third parties and using them as an attack vector. Many highly targeted industries continue to invest in and enhance their security postures, compromising those industries through their supply chain is a real way to evade many security controls. Amid the diverse technologies available today, cloud computing has appeared as a real game-changer for businesses to innovative Supply Chain Management (SCM), swiftly and proficiently. In a very short span, the COVID-19 pandemic has amplified the role, aspects of cloud computing play in supply chain threats to crucial infrastructure, comprising the financial services industry. Threat actors in cyberspace are reaping benefits as industries shift focus of information security from enterprise arrangement to virtual and cloud environment that facilitates employees working remotely. Subsequently, cybercriminals exploit every core service of cloud across categories —SaaS (Software-as-a-Service), PaaS (Platform-as-a-Service), and IaaS (Infrastructure-as-a-Service) (Figure 2).

4. **Crypto jacking:** Crypto jacking is the illegal use of a computer to mine cryptocurrency, which can lead to leverage local and cloud processing power, and thus computer performance can be compromised. Due to the deterioration of system performance and the consequent drop in productivity, such attacks may sustain substantial opportunity costs.

Figure 3. Core service categories of cloud

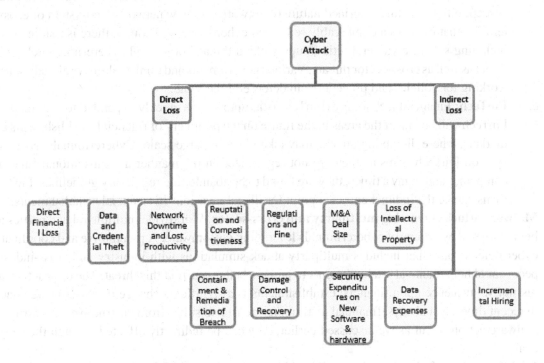

5. **Trickle-Down-Effect:** In today's scenario, criminals are not only developing their malware, but many of these actors are providing their customized services-for-hire on dark web markets, thus offering of "cybercrime-as-a-service" has witnessed a large increase. This has instigated a "trickle-down" effect, where advanced hacking capabilities have been made available to naïve cyber-criminals, partially resulting in the adoption of cutting-edge technology by criminals.

6. **Credential and identity theft:** Continued use of compromised credentials and identity is the foundation of targeted attacks and fraudulent activities. In times of COVID-19, financial organizations across the globe are rapidly modifying their operations, adversaries are also swiftly moving to reap benefits of the expanded attack surface. Mobile malware like EventBot5 and Cerberus which have the capability of stealing customer credentials of more than 200 financial organizations have surged in numbers. Establishments should continue to be cautious in their education awareness programs regarding security and anti-phishing to minimize the cyber-crime success rate around customer data, capturing credentials, and sensitive, private information.

7. **Advance Cyber threats from Emerging technologies**: Advanced threats emerging due to the development of new technologies and improvement in existing technologies such as:

    a. **Deep fakes:** As technology rapidly advances; cyber defenders and criminals are also exploring and using cutting-edge tools. Specifically, in recent days, the increased use of deep fake by mischievous players to enhance the effectiveness of their operations such as voice and face spoofing aims at exploiting human vulnerabilities. Financial establishments continue to confront compromised business e-mail and account takeover attacks.

    b.   **5G:** Fifth-generation networks build a considerably expanded, multidimensional cyberattack susceptibility. It is this redefined nature of networks—a new network "ecosystem of ecosystems"—that involves a comparably redefined cyber strategy. Though, there is risk involved, including software vulnerabilities, supply chain threats, organized cybercrime, intelligence threat as well as cross-sector threats. Various governments and think tanks have already started working for policies and procedures in defense of the same.

    c.   **FinTech:** Financial technology (FinTech) disruptors have quickly expanded to new markets. FinTech will be one of the areas in the future on the periphery of financial establishments and markets, where disrupting attacks may take place on large scale. Cybercriminals have their eyes on FinTech firms as they are not regularized in the manner as conventional financial companies and many a times, they are found to be abandoning regulatory guidelines. FinTech firms can be the indirect entrance point for illegal invasions in financial establishments.

8. **Malware attacks targeting multiparty and cross-sector**: Worldwide multiple related parties are being targeted by groups of cybercriminals leveraging ransomware. A preemptive and coordinated cyber defense plan that includes multiparty attack simulations with industry and cross-industry peers could help financial establishments to prepare better confront this threat. The destructive and disruptive influence upon financial establishments is a significant change in ransomware attacks in recent times. Not always, financial institutions are first to suffer from destructive and disruptive malware actions—but as we discussed earlier, they can be indirectly affected through the supply chain.

9. **Misinformation shakes trust in retail and banks**: It is not only COVID-19, misinformation and disinformation has also created issues for the financial industry. It has affected the financial market numerous times. As financial markets are vulnerable to manipulation, this creates chance for hackers to manipulate the system and cause both direct and indirect losses for the financial institutions that ultimately effects earnings. (Juma'h & Alnsour, 2020; Kamiya et al., 2020).

10. **Internal Threats:** Considering the trend of cybercrimes in Financial domain, most financial institutions are well prepared and protected and continuously upgrade themselves to confront external threats, but professionals from the industry believe that inside threat do pose a greater risk. From careless workers to software susceptibilities to obsolete hardware, these threats can manifest in several ways. Institutions are acting and launching programs to educate and train workers on protocols of cybersecurity.

Strategies to Combat Cyber Threat

Email is the most common entryway through which hackers enter. Thus, to strategize and implement a multi-layered email is a must.

- In an organization checks and balances are very much required. Every financial transaction must go through various checks and verifications, whether it is approved by the top management or a newly recruited employee.
- Basics on cybersecurity are not sufficient to confront criminals who are experts in hacking. For successful training, a tailor-made program is required to provide information in different ways to cater to all types of employees having different learning styles.

Even after the implementation of all strategies mentioned above, an employee with ill-intentions can be a source of extensive damage. Insider attacks with malevolent intentions are now becoming the most-costly attacks to be resolved. Institutions must closely with the network security team to identify and confront uncommon activities. Stringent policies should be adopted in granting access to employees.

Cybersecurity Constraints in Developing Countries

The challenges of cybersecurity are all about staying ahead by adopting precautionary measures before any threats exploit the system. In the era of digitalization, when cybercriminals are getting smarter, cybersecurity plays a significant role in shielding our private data.

Financial Services Providers and their customers, as well as supervisors and regulators of the financial sector, are facing challenges to adjust their behaviors, policies, and processes to confront mounting cyber threats and technological failures in an appropriate manner. A survey done by CGAP in 2018 showed that policymakers are cognizant of the concern. Policymakers are working to develop frameworks to regulate and build their capacity so that they are not only able to supervise but are also able to guide effectively for safeguarding their data and systems. Financial service providers are most prone to cyber threat. Smaller Financial service providers do not prioritize cyber challenges over other threats as the probability of an attack is considered small in their case. In general, mobile money operators are more prepared and better equipped to handle cyber risks, specifically international mobile network operators (MNOs), who abide by the international security standards set by the telecommunications sector.

Developing interest on topic among providers and policymakers is mitigating the sector's exposure to cyber risks. Though many a times, it is observed that these groups lack access to specialized and cybersecurity support services at a reasonable price, and they struggle to gather cyber threat information and good practices. On one hand in local labor markets there is a lack of cybersecurity resources, and on the other hand, specialized and experienced IT and data security professionals are in high demand and are expensive to hire. In this area, the global talent gap in developing countries is even more prominent. Professionals representing both public and private sectors would appreciate dialogue and collaborate initiatives to take on cybersecurity threats efficiently and comprehensively such as joint efforts on consumer education.

The Industry is Ill-Prepared

Whether in developed or developing and emerging economies, the BFSI industry has recognized the increasing threat of cybercrime. To help financial service providers safeguard their networks and customers, the industry has established standards and guidelines. Multi-factor authentication and the introduction of chip cards have decreased the theft of consumer credentials considerably, and on the other hand, artificial intelligence and machine learning are improving the industry's processes for fraud detection and resolution. Now FSPs (Financial Services providers) are increasingly investing in cyber defenses and resilience.

Whereas cyber defenses and best online practices have been embraced by developed countries and huge multinational FSPs, the industry in developing countries is still underprepared. Financial institutions in emerging markets particularly small and medium-sized can become an easy entrance door for cybercriminals to reach global financial systems. Several cases have been observed where adversaries have exploited the networking between financial establishments by intruding small banks to raid large financial institutions as smaller institutions are not well prepared, equipped, and protected. Throughout the (digital) financial services ecosystem, very little knowledge is available for evaluating susceptibilities, threats, and risks. When resources and capacity are limited, such analysis could help policymakers to support the weak aspects that pose a challenge to the strength and stability of the overall ecosystem of financial services.

Due to inadequate awareness and high imprudence, the users of mobile money frequently fall prey to social engineering attacks. Another study has highlighted the rising attacks on mobile banking systems. The susceptibilities are present on both the provider's and the user's side. Many mobile money applications lack basic control on security like data encryption that makes it easy for adversaries to intercept or eavesdrop transactions.

Policymakers' Capacity Constraints Inhibit Understanding and Effective Regulation and Supervision of Cybersecurity

Consumers and providers are on the target of cyber adversaries as supervisors and regulators possess and handle sensitive and confidential information that may be sufficient for criminals to hold them hostage. Moreover, supervisors and regulators are becoming more conscious of developing regulatory frameworks, supervisory processes, and industry guidance to make sure that the sector is implementing the required procedures and systems to protect, detect and efficiently handle cyber-attacks.

As customers and financial institutions are facing cyber challenges, the regulators have been asked to develop suitable and appropriate regulatory infrastructure to respond and stronger cyber resilience. In developing countries, law enforcement agencies are facing challenges to keep up with transformation in technology. This is enabling the cyber-crime-based economy to flourish. Encryption makes it more difficult for agencies to detect malevolent web traffic and track the criminal's communication. Criminals have also upskilled to escape investigators. Security agencies are struggling with a lack of resources (i.e., skills, funding, equipment, and training) to confront cybercrime, but furthermore, it is even more difficult to track down cross-border criminals.

There are some issues in many developing countries to address cybercrime such as inappropriate legislation, insufficient punishments, and not enough legal expertise required to prosecute cybercrimes. There is a significant presence of procedural hurdles, comprising jurisdiction issues, challenges in maintaining standards of evidence, and difficulties in explaining complex digital crimes to juries. There are several other reasons why criminals are often left to operate with impunity; for instance, lack of adequate evidence and extradition treaties with other countries and shortage of capability to investigate, locate or identify criminals, or take them into custody.

SOLUTION AND RECOMMENDATION

In developing markets, governments have started implementing cybersecurity strategies to set risk management standards and provide transparency in liabilities. Though, monitoring and management of cybersecurity need new resources and expertise, in developing countries, which are often not available. The research observes that regulators and providers in the financial sector are finding it tough to keep up with cyber adversaries, and they have limited resources and expertise.

According to a survey of 400 security professionals, the BFSI sector was found to be more "effective in detecting (56%) and containing (53%) than in preventing cyberattacks (31%)." Several strategies are mentioned below to help companies in the BFSI sector to be more preventative to cyber threats.

1. **Visibility:** If one can see, one can detect. BFSI industry has cross-segment traffic and to see the traffic, visibility is the most important thing that a solution should have. It is necessary for a company in the BFSI sector to have a solution that offers a centralized view of the routes and traffic between clients and servers. Hawk eye's view is the necessity for the present environment in the BFSI industry. Since the companies are using multiple clouds to operate, visibility is required to eliminate the requirement of multiple monitoring tools in silos. Visibility not only provides the Hawk eye view but also reduces the detection and response time and allows security teams to apply much-needed policies that reduce unauthorized movements and theft.

2. **Segmentation:** Segmentation is an important solution to prevent successful cyber-attacks. If the core financial data and workloads are micro-segmented and stored in a separate secure environment, then it will not be easy for attackers to take that data since the access will be provided based on the intent.

Organizations working in the BFSI sector would also be benefited from the adoption of the zero-trust security model. The Zero-trust model requires strict identity verification for all users. Every user would be strictly verified if it tries to access resources and secure places. It makes no difference whether the workloads are accessed from within or outside of the network perimeter. Multi-factor authentication (MFA) is required to enforce Zero-trust. It ensures that security is not compromised, and the user is verified on every level.

3. **Secured Endpoints:** Fully customizable solutions can help organizations working in the BFSI sector in securing endpoints, including ATM kiosks and transactional servers. Enabling process-level visibility and critical assets' control is the key to do it. It would ensure that only those processes which are whitelisted can run. With these solutions, ATM kiosks can be protected without costly patch management or system upgrades.

4. **Compliance Simplification:** There are tools to simplify compliance reporting and auditing and they can help the organizations working in the BFSI sector to meet their compliance requirements. The scope of compliance and IT audits like PCI-DSS, Gramm-Leach-Bliley Act (GLBA) can be reduced with the help of micro-segmentation. With the reduction in scope, risky guesswork can be eliminated, and consistent security and compliance can be ensured across all data centers of financial organizations. This will also help in saving manual effort, operational headache, and costs related to various IT and compliance audits.

5. **Strategic Governance And Implementation Of Correct Tools:** Security can get enhanced with improved value by adopting a preventive approach to tackle cybercrime related risks. A top-level governance strategy is required to incorporate risk related to cyberattacks into the enterprise risk strategy. The objective is to identify the gaps in the current cyber-attacks risk management strategy. A strategy cannot work for itself and it needs strong tools and technologies to prevent cyberattacks and safeguard institutions and sensitive data.

The use of security tools like proxy servers, firewalls, Security Incident and Event Management (SIEM), two-factor authentication, Privilege Identity Management (PIM), Web Application Filtering (WAF), Advanced Persistent Threats (APT), and File Integrity Management (FIM) are necessary for financial services companies to protect themselves from the threat of hackers and data breach.

6. **Multi-Layered Email Strategy:** Protection of sensitive data is the most important requirement for any financial institution. A multi-layered email strategy can work well to secure the data of customers. Since emails are the most common gateways that are used by black minds to access sensitive data. Multi-layer protection includes Domain Keys Identified Email (DKIM), Sender Policy Framework (SPF), and Domain-based Message Reporting and Conformance (DMARC).

7. **Up-To-Date Virus Security Software:** Weak virus protection software can increase the chances of a breach. In modern times, hackers are smart and fast and are equipped with new tools and technologies and ideas to enter illegally into a system. Since companies in the BFSI sector have sensitive data of customers, they should have their virus security software up to date to handle all those new tricks and tactics of modern-day hackers.

Solutions for Cybersecurity

Various solutions can be used to protect sensitive data, hard-earned money, and the trust of consumers by financial institutions, some of them are mentioned below:

1. **Cloud Computing:** Cloud computing is helping various organizations to take advantage of emerging technologies like machine learning. Cloud can help in reducing the risk. Data centers for big cloud providers have stringent physical security such as the use of biometrics for access which reduces vulnerabilities. Cloud service providers (CSPs), like Microsoft Azure, can help companies take benefits of evolving technologies, like machine learning, without investing a lot of money to make a team and in-house infrastructure. CSPs have frameworks and analytics to orchestrate information over the services and endpoints to quickly reveal threats and block them before they can damage privacy.

2. **Blockchain Technology – An emerging method of global payments:** Blockchain Technology is the need of the present to secure the future. Blockchain works as a digital ledger of economic transactions and it cannot be corrupted. It records all economic transactions and has transparency among its members and is not controlled by any nation or entity.

3. **Intrusion Detection System (IDS):** An IDS is a software application that monitors a system for malevolent activities. Any intrusion activity is reported to an administrator or collected centrally with the use of a security information system.

4. **Intrusion Prevention System (IPS):** An IPS works as a hawk eye on a network for any malevolent activities that attempt to exploit a known susceptibility. The main function of an IPS is to look for and identify any suspicious activity. It either detects and allows (IDS) or prevent (IPS) the possible threat such as brute force attacks, Denial of Service (DoS) attacks. The suspicious attempt is logged and blocked and then reported to the managers of the network or security operations center.

5. **Security Training:** Since employees are not competent enough to tackle the load of cyberattacks, professional security training is necessary to make them aware of various ways by which the sys-

tem can get breached and hackers and attackers can harm it deep. Reeves et.al (2021) discussed cybersecurity fatigue as a form of work disengagement specific to cybersecurity. This fatigue can be overcome by effective and continuous training related to various areas of information security. Some of the trainings that can be imparted by companies working in the BFSI sector are:

a. Security Awareness Training
b. Malware Reversing
c. Practical Web Application Penetration Testing
d. Practical Mobile Application Penetration Testing
e. Fraud methods training for financial institutions.

6. **Cyberattack Drill:** Penetration testing is an excellent way to examine some specific parts of the system. To get optimal protection, an organization needs to make sure that it has taken all the required precautions. Existing hardware and software solutions are examined to check their efficiency and planned attack simulations are performed by professionals to confirm whether the organization has the right security levels.

7. **Code Audit:** Reverse engineering is one of the unique areas of cybersecurity. Advanced Reverse Engineering methods are used by professionals to analyze black box software that enables to analyze potential threats. Since software development processes are long, they often result in multiple lines of code developed by team of developers, highly prone to mistake originated from humans. A secure code development cycle is an important measure to ensure the security of the final software. Detailed findings of vulnerabilities in the software are shared after the code audit and relevant training is given by professionals to raise awareness so that similar mistakes are not made in the future.

REGULATING CYBERSPACE

Finding appropriate solutions is the only way to address cyberthreats. Scrutinizing these solutions discloses critical prospects to alleviate endogenous cyber threats. This reveals that reliance on conventional solutions is a passive defense to cyberattacks. It also demonstrates the necessity of dynamic strategies and collaboration among businesses and government. Cyberspace is controlled by a collaborated work of state, national, and international guidelines. The uneven regulatory framework leaves substantial cracks in the oversight of cyberspace. Currently, there is no uniformity in international laws to control cyberspace and to precisely regulate cyberattacks, however, various organizations in different countries have made some efforts to regulate cyberattacks.

Ways to Address the Cybersecurity Resource Gap

Collaborated initiatives by both public and private sector, emerging efforts worldwide seek to consider and acknowledge the urgent need for information, training, technical advice, and incident response. Both developed, and developing markets exemplify various good practices where public sector agencies and/or providers come together to share information and help the financial services industry. Some of these efforts are led by the public sector, but most are private sector-led or comprise public-private partnerships.

1.   Some Governments Invest in Building Public Cybersecurity Support Structures for the Financial
     Sector

Cybersecurity efforts in developing markets, initiated by public agencies or governments often do not target the private sector as customers. Due to lack of resources and limited capacity, government initiatives on cybersecurity are likely to concentrate on public agencies and critical infrastructure - the significant assets for market firmness and reliability. Yet resources and capacity are often inadequate for effective training and education to staff, recruitment of technical experts, and provide the required support to supervisors and regulators.

Though agencies often face inadequate capacity and struggle to keep up with the speedy transformation in the cyber threat landscape, which impacts the support and advice they can offer to the industry. Very few countries have agencies that specialize in confronting threats to the financial services sector. Usually, these teams provide a very limited range of services; services are not available round the clock and rarely include an emergency response line.

2.   Financial Sector Providers and Associations are Leading Collaborative Efforts to Enhance their
     Cyber Resilience

Nowadays, in most developed countries, and many emerging and developing countries, players from the private sector are forming teams to share threat information and cooperate to fight against cybercrime and financial fraud. Several times banking associations have taken the initiative to formalize the interchange of cyber threats information. At times, only a few players will reach an agreement to work together at the initial stage and find a partnership with other players in due course of time. These partnerships are formed and are not necessarily limited to actors in the financial sector; they also include IT firms, intelligence, and telecommunications sectors. In recent times, a sharp increase has been observed in the number of cybersecurity and financial security firms ('FinSec' firms), often of a small size firm, that cater to the niche market and provide cybersecurity products and services to Financial Service Providers and fintech firms. Another interesting development is the increase in products about cyber insurance, particularly among the large multinational insurance organizations.

3.   Promising Cybersecurity Initiatives are Building on Public-Private Partnerships (PPP)

Public-private partnerships and cross-sectoral collaborations are inevitable in confronting cybercrime and mitigating risks effectively. Discussion on public-private partnership has already started in most of the countries in some way or another, predominantly in telecommunications and financial sectors.

Good practice examples include the following:

a.   **National Fintech-Cyber Innovation Lab in Israel** is led by the Ministry of Finance of the country.
     With the common objective, Cyber Directorate and Financial CERT are stimulating innovation in
     cyber industries and fintech and encouraging foreign investment. The Innovation Lab facilitates
     Israeli startups to develop, test, and exhibit new technology in cybersecurity for the financial
     industry.

b.   **Luxembourg's Cyber Competence Center** is a centralized center that supports individuals as
     well as public and private sectors to manage cybersecurity effectively. The center was founded in

2015, in a public-private partnership model two-thirds of its funds comes from the government and the rest from its commercial operations.

c.   **Nigeria's Electronic Fraud Forum** is an information exchange and knowledge sharing platform through public-private dialogue among key stakeholders on the issue of frauds including bank representatives, payment systems operators, mobile payment operators, security agencies, and the Central Bank of Nigeria. The Forum meets at regular intervals to collaborate on mitigating and handling frauds and reinstating public confidence in electronic payments and card usage.

4.   The Multi-Country Approach can Help Overcome the Resource Gap through Economies of Scale and Scope

In developing countries, two major challenges emerge while making cybersecurity support services available. First, developing countries have a limited number of experts in the cybersecurity domain, specifically experts that understand cyber threats in the context of Digital financial Sector (DFS). Second, the economies of a few developing countries may not create adequate in-house facility that can support an affordable cybersecurity resource center. Hence, regional cybersecurity resource centers can be an efficient solution to the gap in cybersecurity resources as it can utilize the availability of experts in the region and serve the countries in the region. Due to the participation of multiple countries, they can exchange cross-border information, share threats and trends in the region, work on early warning systems and share the experience of good practices with other regional and global platforms and they can be specialized in financial services and their associated sectors. All-encompassing efforts from multi-country are urgently required to support the growing DFS sector in developing countries that provide financially feasible and specialized services for the digitalized financial sector.

5.   Development Partners can Support the Sector to Become More Cyber Resilient

Development partners can play a significant role to support developing and emerging markets considering the resource gap in cybersecurity. Following are approaches to support the sector:

a.   Educating clients and partners and bringing data security and protection into program design.
b.   Developing curriculum and training to support public and private partners to implement good cybersecurity hygiene.
c.   Strengthening supervisors and regulators to build their capacity to impose and counsel the industry and customers on cybersecurity hygiene and fitting reactions to cyber instances. Additionally, it is also required to develop strategies for corporate cybersecurity.
d.   Supporting the public and private sectors on providing customer awareness on digitalized financial services, specifically for lower-income groups, as they may not be aware of the risks associated with using digital devices and services and do not have accessibility to support services.

FUTURE RESEARCH DIRECTIONS

Cybersecurity is a continual process that is creating countless opportunities and immense development for the future. Though there is a shortage of employees in the Cyber industry, which is a big pitfall for the advancing technology, the potential for AI and machine learning can be predominant at reducing cyberthreats and increasing digital platform productivity. As observed during the pandemic, most businesses have adopted the work from home culture thereby making cybersecurity for the digital world more critical for the future. The industry would need to push the Artificial Intelligence system to detect patterns emerging from repeated cyber-attacks. The future of cybersecurity is highly interconnected with the future information technology. The interconnection will make the network vulnerable hence advancing technology will need to be more adaptive and easily updatable. Studies over adaptive networks and automation will benefactor the online world. Consistent improvement and research on cyber mitigations would be a prudent way to embrace the digital transformation.

CONCLUSION

Cyberattacks are a central, persistent, and endemic threat, which will increase out of proportion in years to come12. Once former US President Obama said that cyberattacks can sabotage financial institutions, power grid, and air traffic control.13 These information structures are the backbone of the economy of any country.

Financial services are going digital at a faster rate than ever. The fast transformation and availability of technology to people is providing hackers access to a larger target. Financial services firms need to build their defense and capability reaction and recovery from potential attack if the sector is to continue to retain customer's confidence and trust. A wholesome approach towards the system can be a prominent way. Though never-ending threats can be a constant hurdle for cybersecurity, only advancing technology can be a proven primary solution to the problem. But practically, cybersecurity will never find a permanent solution to the problem.

Cybersecurity is not an IT problem – it is a business vital and calls for a system-wide approach. Implementation and execution of an inclusive strategy can help against hackers. International organizations and development partners should encourage public-private partnership to mitigate the problems pertaining to resources and expertise. Government authorities and providers must work together with their respective jurisdictions and global peers to share intelligence alerts and help each other to confront cyber adversaries at a rapidly growing risk landscape.

Besides, the topic of cybersecurity and data protection in the financial sector, discussions, and debates must be done on the use of personal data with responsibility. Unless the information systems and the data are protected against unauthorized accessibility and exploitation, data protection policies and regulations cannot be effective. The financial services industry needs to implement adequate and global standards of data security to confirm the trustworthy provider of the sector's offering of products and services.

The study discusses the existing solutions for risk management. The conventional solutions of risk management have depended on independently developed, applied, and imposed practices of risk management. The study terminates the traditional approach to risk management in the global financial industry. This chapter accentuates the development of a broad understanding of cyber risks and their management. Because of strict regulations, harsh competition, and changing behavior and expectations of customers, financial companies are embracing innovative and modern strategies. Financial companies are making use of cloud, mobile, social, and other technology trends to flare up growth and create customer trust. By shaping strong risk management programs, IT Security enables financial companies to innovate and compete with assurance.

REFERENCES

Aldasoro, I., Gambacorta, L., Giudici, P., & Leach, T. (2020a). *Operational and cyber risks in the financial sector.* BIS Working Paper No. 840. Basel, Switzerland: Bank for International Settlements.

Aldasoro, I., Gambacorta, L., Giudici, P., & Leach, T. (2020b). *The drivers of cyber risk.* BIS Working Paper No. 865. Basel, Switzerland: Bank for International Settlements.

Ameen, N., Tarhini, A., Shah, M. A., Madichie, N., Paul, J., & Choudrie, J. (2021). Keeping customers' data secure: A cross-cultural study of cybersecurity compliance among the Gen-Mobile workforce. *Computers in Human Behavior, 114.* doi:10.1016/j.chb.2020.106531

Bouveret, A. (2019a). Cyber Risk for the Financial Services Sector. *Journal of Financial Transformation, 49,* 29.

Bouveret, A. (2019b). Estimation of Losses Due to Cyber Risk for Financial Institutions. Journal of Operational Risk. Advance online publication. doi:10.21314/JOP.2019.224

Carter, W. A. (2017). *Forces shaping the cyber threat landscape for Financial Institutions.* SWIFT Institute, Working Paper No. 2016-004.

Chebyshev, V. (2019). *Mobile malware evolution.* Kaspersky Labs.

Defending the Digital Frontier. (2014). Retrieved from https://www.economist.com/sites/default/files/20140712_cyber-security.pdf

Fighting COVID-19-Related Financial Fraud. (2020). Retrieved from https://www.sec.gov/fighting-covid-19-related-financialfraud

Fitch. (2017, April). *Cybersecurity an Increasing Focus for Financial Institutions.* Retrieved from https://www.fitchratings.com/site/pr/1022468

Fraud and Coronavirus (COVID-19). (2020). Retrieved from https://www.finra.org/investors/insights/fraud-andcoronavirus-covid-19

Future Cyber Threats. (2020). Retrieved from https://acn-marketing-blog.accenture.com/wp-content/uploads/2020/09/2020Future of CyberThreats_Final.pdf

Humayun, M., Mahmood Niazi, N. J., Alshayeb, M., & Mahmood, S. (2020). Cyber Security Threats and Vulnerabilities: A Systematic Mapping Study. *Arabian Journal for Science and Engineering, 45*(4), 1–19. doi:10.100713369-019-04319-2

Juma'h, A. H., & Alnsour, Y. (2020). The effect of data breaches on company performance. *International Journal of Accounting & Information Management, 28*(2), 275–301. doi:10.1108/IJAIM-01-2019-0006

Kamiya, S., Kang, J-K., Jungmin, K., Milidonis, A., & Stulz, R. M. (2020). Risk management, firm reputation, and the impact of successful cyberattacks on target firms. *Journal of Financial Economics.*

Kopp, E., Kaffenberger, L., & Wilson, C. (2017). *Cyber Risk, Market Failures, and Financial Stability, Working Paper.* International Monetary Fund (WP/17/185).

Lallie, H. S., Shepherd, L. A., Nurse, J. R. C., Erola, A., Epiphaniou, G., Maple, C., & Bellekens, X. (2021). Cyber security in the age of COVID-19: A timeline and analysis of cyber-crime and cyber-attacks during the pandemic. *Computers & Security, 105*. doi:10.1016/j.cose.2021.102248

McKee, K., Kaffenberger, M., & Zimmerman, J. (2015). *Doing digital finance right: The case for stronger mitigation of customer risks.* Focus Note 103, CGAP. Retrieved from https://www.cgap.org/sites/default/files/Focus-Note-Doing-Digital-FinanceRight

Mind the Gap. Addressing Challenges to FinTech Adoption. (2018). Retrieved from https://www.accenture.com/_acnmedia/pdf-74/accenture-fintech-challenges-adoption.pdf

Mohammed, A. M., Idris, B., Saridakis, G., & Benson, V. (2020). *Information and communication technologies: a curse or blessing for SMEs?* (V. Benson & J. McAlaney, Eds.). Academic Press.

Morgan, S. (2020). *Cybercrime to Cost the World $10.5 Trillion Annually By 2025.* Retrieved from https://cybersecurityventures.com/hackerpocalypse-cybercrime-report-2016

Mugarura, N., & Ssali, E. (2020). Intricacies of anti-money laundering and cyber-crimes regulation. *RT Journal.*

Muthuppalaniappan, M., & Stevenson, K. (2021). Healthcare cyber-attacks and the COVID-19 pandemic: An urgent threat to global health. *International Journal for Quality in Health Care, 33*, 1353–4505.

Nasdaq warns of market manipulation amid Coronavirus outbreak. (2020). Retrieved from https://www.nasdaq.com/articles/nasdaq-warns-of-market-manipulation-amid-coronavirus-outbreak-2020-03-23

Pranggono, B., & Arabo, A. (2021). COVID-19 pandemic cybersecurity issues. *Internet Technology Letters*, *4*(2), e247. doi:10.1002/itl2.247

Reeves, A., Delfabbro, P., & Calic, D. (2021, January). Encouraging Employee Engagement with Cybersecurity: How to Tackle Cyber Fatigue. *SAGE Open*, *11*(1). Advance online publication. doi:10.1177/21582440211000049

Salam, A. (2020). Internet of Things for Sustainability: Perspectives in Privacy, Cybersecurity, and Future Trends. In *Internet of Things for Sustainable Community Development. Internet of Things (Technology, Communications and Computing).* Springer. doi:10.1007/978-3-030-35291-2_10

Senarak, C. (2021). Port cybersecurity and threat: A structural model for prevention and policy development. *The Asian Journal of Shipping and Logistics, 37*(1), 20-36. doi:10.1016/j.ajsl.2020.05.001

Chapter 11
Digital Transformation and Cybersecurity Challenges:
A Study of Malware Detection Using Machine Learning Techniques

Fatimah Al Obaidan
Imam Abdulrahman Bin Faisal University, Saudi Arabia

Saqib Saeed
https://orcid.org/0000-0001-7136-3480
Imam Abdulrahman Bin Faisal University, Saudi Arabia

ABSTRACT

Digital transformation has revolutionized human life but also brought many cybersecurity challenges for users and enterprises. The major threats that affect computers and communication systems by damaging devices and stealing sensitive information are malicious attacks. Traditional anti-virus software fails to detect advanced kind of malware. Current research focuses on developing machine learning techniques for malware detection to respond in a timely manner. Many systems have been evolved and improved to distinguish the malware based on analysis behavior. The analysis behavior is considered a robust technique to detect, analyze, and classify malware, categorized into two models: a static and dynamic analysis. Both types of previous analysis have advantages and limitations. Therefore, the hybrid method combines the strength of static and dynamic analyses. This chapter conducted a systematic literature review (SLR) to summarize and analyze the quality of published studies in malware detection using machine learning techniques and hybrid analysis that range from 2016 to 2021.

DOI: 10.4018/978-1-7998-6975-7.ch011

INTRODUCTION

Digital technologies have been widely used in the operations of business (Saeed, 2019), government (Saeed & Reddick, 2013) and nonprofit sector (Saeed & Rohde, 2013, Saeed & Shabbir, 2014). Such appropriated technology adoption has resulted in better productivity, cost effectiveness and enhanced customer satisfaction (Saeed et al., 2017). However, it has increased the probability of cybersecurity attacks on the technological infrastructures of the organizations. Such malicious attacks are carried out by software applications invented by hackers with a harmful purpose to obstruct the device's operations. The term malware was coined to name any computer program that has a malicious intention (Santos et al., 2009). Cohen *et.al* (1988) defined malware as a malicious code by attackers that harms our application programs and systems as well. The strength of these malicious programs is to evade any kinds of security restrictions (Harshalatha & Mohanasundaram, 2020).

Based on the research, it is becoming more challenging to identify malware because most malware programs tend to have several polymorphic layers to evade detections (Kumar & Ramamoorthy, 2017). Moreover, according to the studies, 80% of damaged systems were due to malware, whereas the remaining 20% system failures were from other factors. Generally, the malwares result in stealing and modifying the user information, malicious program collecting user sensitive information to be used illegally by attackers, and other severe implications (Pan et al., 2020). There are various forms of malware that contain worms, computer bugs, viruses, and other programs massively growing on the internet daily. Malwares are rising and growing explosively every day with various types and power, and pose an enormous threat to the security of sensitive information. Research studies showed that the manual examining and inspecting malware is considered inefficient and ineffective against malware's high spreading rate(Umamaheswaran et al., 2019).

The standard anti-virus software fails to detect the new malware programs and classify them into the same groups. Traditionally, anti-virus systems relied on two techniques for malware detection, which are signature-based and heuristic-based. The signature-based algorithm identifies the malware based on its unique hash. Simultaneously, the heuristic method comprises commands defined by specialists that monitor and analyze the malware behaviors. Despite the success of these methods, they fail to detect the unknown malware variants. Therefore, the security analysts have proposed behavior-based malwares. The primary purpose of this malware analysis is to provide any information regarding the malware's properties, strength, and behaviors in the given software. The malware behavior is categorized into two types which are static and dynamic analysis. The static analysis extracts the malware's feature from the source code or binary code and examines it without running the source code. Contrary, the dynamic analysis examines malware's executable by running it and observing its behavior. The categories of these analysis have advantages and limitations.

Static analysis, even though it is faster but malware can evade detection by using malware code obfuscations. In dynamic analysis, it's hard for malware to avoid detection since it's behavior monitored and observed during the runtime of the program (Gibert et al., 2020). The previous test requires operating on a simulated environment to track the malicious programs (Kumar & Ramamoorthy, 2017). Researchers have proposed various techniques that include analyzing the malware behaviors in static and dynamic analysis. Static analysis can detect malware based on binary code extracted as a feature for diagnosing and detecting other malware. Dynamic analysis can detect the behavior during the running time, which requires a virtual safety environment to observe and detect malware's behaviors. Compared with static and dynamic analysis, the hybrid analysis combines both analysis techniques to provide the best and precise malware detection using machine learning (ML) methods. Machine learning has evolved from the research of pattern recognition and computational learning field in the AI domain. ML focuses on the development of the algorithms that can learn and make a prediction on data. Traditional machine learning techniques depend on two primary types of analysis, which are static and dynamic analysis. A third group combines both of these analysis aspects to provide a robust system for malware detection, defined as hybrid analysis.

Therefore, the hybrid method integrates the static and dynamic analysis strengths used in ML models to detect and classify malware (Gibert et al., 2020). Moreover, machine learning models are considered the best methodology used to classify and detect new malware. The main purpose of this chapter is to provide a comprehensive review and a quick reference. Therefore, this chapter presents a systematic literature review that will investigate, analyze, and synthesize the literature focusing on malware detection applied with ML and hybrid methods to assist future research in detecting malware accurately.

This chapter is structured as follows: Section 2 provides the research questions and section 3 represents the associated literature. Section 4 provides the focus of this chapter. Section 5 describes the proposed methodology of SLR and section 6 represents the result and discussion of the research questions. Section 7 provides the future research direction. Section 8 represent the conclusion.

RESEARCH QUESTIONS

This section presents the research questions of our study which are following:

RQ1: What are the common features of static and dynamic analysis used in malware detection?
RQ2: What are the ML models used in the detection and classification of malware based on hybrid analysis?
RQ3: What are the performance measures applied in the articles of malware detection with ML techniques and hybrid analysis?

BACKGROUND

In 2016, Symantec recorded a significant increase in malware attacks that is equivalent to 286% percent and raised by 600% from 2016 to 2017 (Symantec, 2016). According to SonicWall's 2021 Cyber Report, the malware attacks began to slip downward in 2019, while decreased dramatically by 43% in 2020 (Sonicwall, 2020). Researchers at AV-Test have counted around 19.2 million new malwares in the first half of 2021 ("Malware Statistics & Trends Report | AV-TEST," n.d.).

Machine learning models have been investigated for malicious detection in recent years due to the used techniques that do not depend on strict rules, and as a result are considered a more robust solution. Different machine learning models have been provided, from basic fingerprint checking app, to static code inspection, to advanced dynamic behavior analysis (Gong et al., 2021).

MAIN FOCUS OF THE CHAPTER

Many recent studies have focused on malware detection, but few studies have considered machine learning based malware analysis. The presented literature review is divided into two categories of analysis, firstly we discuss static analysis, which is followed by dynamic analysis. These analysis methods are used with ML techniques for malware detection and classification.

Literature Reviews Based on Static Analysis

In this type of analysis, the features can be extracted without exectuing the software. An example of a static feature is the Windows Portable Executable file, where the features can be extracted in two ways, either from binary content of the file or the source file after appliyng decompile process to the assembly language. We present below most of the common features and information over static analysis. Ahmadi et al. (2016) have developed a platform that extracts malware feature to precisely detect malware based on static analysis. Firstly, the features are extracted statically from PE files and combined into a one feature vector through forward selection techniques. Then, instead of adding the feature to the model one by one, they consider the features as a subset that belongs to one category. The classification is implemented using the Gradient Boosting classifiers and XGBoots. The Microsoft Malware Classification Challenges dataset was used to evaluate, and they achieved comparable accuracy to the winner of the Kaggle's competition (Ahmadi et al, 2016).

Fuyong and Tiezhu (2017) have developed a technique that calculates each n-grams's bytes in the training sets by selecting the highest information gain of K n-grams as feature. The highest K n-grams are chosen to create a feature vector. Afterwards, they measured the average of each attribute of the feature vectors from the malware and benign datasets independently. Finally, a new portion of the program is classified into one of these types based on the vector's similar features. They used three different test samples to analyze the efficiency of the developed technique. The samples were collected from different sources in 2014 and 2015, using the Windows XP file system and the Open Malware Benchmark. Each dataset was classified using different classifiers. The highest accuracy was achieved by a method, which they named as Attribute Similarity (AS) when K is in the set {99, 199, 299, 399, 499, 599, 699, 799, 899, 999}, with 93.48% accuracy and the highest True Positive is 97.5% (Fuyong & Tiezhu, 2017). Furthermore, Sangal et al. (2020) have developed a classification-based technique for malware detection on the android platform based on a static feature. The extraction process of the static features done through android permission files and intents. The malware classification was applied using different models such as Decision Tree (J48) Naïve Bayes (NB), Random Forest, and K Nearest Neighbor (KNN). Random Forest obtained high performance at 96.05% (Sangal & Verma, 2020).

Literature Reviews Based on Dynamic Analysis

The dynamic technique comprises extracting features from the malware's execution at run time and observe its behavior in the running environment. In this section, we will describe the most common feature extracted through dynamic analysis. Mohaisen et al. (2015) have presented AMAL, which is mechanical behavior based on malware analysis. AMAL consists of two sub-models, AutoMal and MalLabel. AutoMal implements a tool to extract the features that describe the malware based on the memory, files of the system, and network. These features are extracted from malware samples in a virtualized environment.

On the other hand, MalLabel uses those features to build and train the classifiers to classify malware into families similar in behavior. In other words, the resulting feature vector is used to perform classification using ML classification such as SVM, DT, Logistic Regression, and K- Nearest Neighbor. The result shows AMAL's system's efficiency by detecting more than 99% and 98% precision in classification and clustering, respectively (Mohaisen et al., 2015). Okane et al. (2016) have evaluated the malware runtime tracks to observe two main points: First, the best set of opcode needed to develop a strong platform with no malicious attacks in the program. Second, the best time of the executing the programs to classify the malware and benign program accurately. The developed system applied the SVM classifier in the opcode density histograms that have been extracted at runtime of the program's execution to detect and analyze the malware (O'kane et al., 2016). Furthermore, Usman et al. (2021) proposed a novel hybrid approach using cyber threat, machine learning models, data forensics based on dynamic analysis. The approach was based on three steps: the preprocessing step where the IP reputation predicted by using DT model. The second step analyzed the malware behavior through dynamic analysis. Finally, they classified the identified malwares using the machine learning model such as SVM, DT and NB. The highest accuracy was achieved by Support Vector Machine with 98% (Usman et al., 2021). So far, we have represented the techniques that depend on a single model of a feature used for malware detection and classification. Nevertheless, the features extracted from the two types can be integrated to produce a strong classifier known as hybrid analysis.

Issues, Controversies, Problems

Despite the success achieved by static analysis, this type suffers from code obfuscation due to the malware properties to evade using different modern methods. While in dynamic analysis, there is some limitation on the observing processes, which is considered time-consuming. Moreover, the platform's environment needs to be closed and disconnected from other devices to prevent malware spread over the platform and the harm that it will cause. Thus, combining the strengths of both analysis will build a robust analysis behavior known as hybrid analysis.

Literature Reviews Based on Hybrid Analysis

The third technique combines the strengths of both static and dynamic analysis and then uses it as an input in machine learning models for malware classification. The hybrid analysis is the main focus of this chapter. Liu et al. (2016) have conducted a hybrid malware detection scheme on the android platform, which can detect the malware behaviors based on static and dynamic analysis. First, they decompile the application using apktool. If the application is successfully decompiled, then static analysis can be performed to extract the features from manifest.xml files such as API keywords and permissions. The feature is combined into one vector and passed to ML classifiers to classify the files as malware or benign. When the application decompiled incorrectly, the dynamic analysis is performed on the application. The application installs and executes an emulator device to trace the system calls using the Strace tool to capture the malware's dynamic behavior. They evaluated the performance using ML classifiers such as SVM, NB, and KNN. The experimental result provided accuracy with 99.28% (Liu et al., 2016).

Furthermore, Yang et al. (2017) conducted an experiment on the android platform to detect malware using hybrid analysis and ML technique. Firstly, static analysis is applied to extract the software's package features, components, and permission features. Secondly, the software's dynamic behavior character was obtained using a dynamic tool to format the static and dynamic features. Finally, to deal with feature eigenvector in the two stages, they used a machine learning technique to classify malicious software. The experiment result showed that the proposed method of using a hybrid approach with machine learning in the test stage of the dataset gave a more accurate result in malware detection than the typical detection engine, while its ability to classify the malicious malware into their families become stronger. The ML classifiers used were SVM, DT, Random Forest, where the optimal performance was achieved by Random forest with an accuracy of 95.9% (Yang et al., 2017). Similarly, Sun et al.(2017) have developed a Monet detection system, which can detect several types of malwares. Monet used hybrid analysis as behavior-based techniques for malware classification combined with ML techniques. The static feature extracted from the Manifest.xml file and disassembled the code file while the dynamic behavior was captured during the application's execution. The dataset size was 3723 malware and 500 legitimate applications were used for evaluation of Monet performance. The experimental result showed good performance for malware detection with 99% accuracy (Sun et al., 2017).

Furthermore, Arshad et .al (2018) have proposed SAMADroid, that combined three levels of hybrid malware detection techniques for android OS. The three-level of analysis are static and dynamic, local remote hosts, and machine learning techniques. Drebin is a static malware detection framework used to extract static features while it fails to extract the dynamic feature. In dynamic analysis, the features are extracted as system calls at runtime. The level 2 contained a hybrid of the local host and remote host. On the localhost, dynamic analysis was applied to take realistic inputs using a programming tool. For user input and system calls that were generated previously, were passed to the remote server. The machine learning techniques used to evaluate the proposed method using SVM, Random Forest, Decision Tree, and Naïve Bayes, the optimal performance was achieved by static features using Random Forest with 99.07% accuracy (Arshad et al., 2018).

Moreover, He et al. (2018) have proposed the hybrid analysis technique to detect malware in JavaScript code. The data sample used in the static features was 1500, which was collected from different web pages, and categorized based on four features. For dynamic analysis, the Jalangi framework was used to monitor malicious code characteristics during the run time. Additionally, the malicious code of JavaScript was detected and classified using Random Forest classifier with 94.76% accuracy (He et al., 2018). Kumar et al.(2019) have developed a technique by combining both static and dynamic techniques to detect malware into four initial groups using a Random Forest classifier. They applied a new process known as early-stage detection, which stopped early before the analysis is fully executed. The static analysis was used to extract the Portable Executable (PE) header features such as file header, optional header, and section header. Also, they extracted the information from the section table, such as the number of sections, their size, section virtual address, etc. The extracted features depend on significant resources such as network and system calls from the dynamic analysis. Afterwards, they applied feature reduction by the Information Gain method. The results were evaluated based on different classifiers such as DT, Random Forest, Neural Network, and K-NN. Kumar et al., (2019) have developed a framework based on API call sequences' static and dynamic features. They identified the relations and the differences between the static and dynamic API call sequences based on observing multiple types of malware behaviors. Their study depends on multimodal approaches that collect numerous features on unimodal or one classifier to develop a hybrid feature vector. The hybrid feature used to evaluate the effectiveness of their approach used as an input to train four classifiers, including K-Nearest Neighbor, Random Forest, and Decision Tree for detecting and classifying malwares (Han et al., 2019).

Catak et al. (2019) have built a benchmark for Windows OS API calls consisting of various kinds of malwares. The experiment relied on examining the portable executable file (PE) to extract the malware feature, the static feature extracted was MD5 signatures hash algorithm using VirusTotal tool. The result of this process is to classify each malware with a label. Secondly, the dynamic features were extracted from running the malware in the Cuckoo sandbox to record the malware behavior representing API call sequences report. The collected data was saved into MongoDB in JSON format. Then each API call sequence assigned a specific label based on the malware features. Finally, they used Long Short Term Memory (LSTM) as a classification machine learning method. The LSTM method was compared with traditional ML and achieved high accuracy than KNN, DT, and SVM (Catak et al., 2020) . Similarly, Yen et al. (2019) have proposed a malware detection process using hybrid process behavior to extract static and dynamic features. The analysis features were combined with a deep neural network for Windows OS malware classification. Firstly, they analyzed the malware to collect the API call and then generated a call graph represented by the adjacency matrix. The transformation step from the call graph to embedding representation is done by training an embedded graph model. Finally, the adjacency matrix contains the signal information of the call graph. The behavior observed in sandbox VM and API call sequence was recorded with their associated parameters for dynamic analysis. Deep learning used the three types of fusion neural network to build malware classifier. The best result was achieved with accuracy at 83.17% on classifying 80 malware into their families with a dataset consist of 4519 malware samples (Yen et al., 2019).

Vinayakumar et al. (2019) have evaluated several kinds of traditional MLA, and the deep learning architectures for malware detection, classification using using multiple samples. They removed all dataset biases in their experimental analysis by splitting the public and private datasets to train and test models using various timescales. In order to arrive at effective zero-day malware detection, they proposed a novel image processing technique with optimal parameters for ML algorithms and deep learning architectures. They combined the visualization process with deep learning architectures for static, dynamic, and image-based hybrid approaches applied in big data to build a robust intelligent malware detection model. The static analysis was applied using the Windows-static-brain-droid (WSBD) approach that extracts multiple types of features such as PE file, format-agnostic feature (raw byte), and strings. All static features were passed into the SVM classifier for classification. The dynamic analysis was applied based on PE file using Windows-dynamic-brain-droid (WDBD) approach. Finally, they evaluated the performance of traditional ML with deep learning architecture, and in most cases, the deep learning outperformed the traditional ML algorithms (Vinayakumar et al., 2019).

Rhode et al. (2019) have proposed a simulated lab experiment that collects two types of features, machine metrics as a static feature and API calls as a dynamic feature. The Psutil library was used to extract the static feature as machine metrics that included user and system CPU usage, memory and swap usage, the received and transmitted bytes, and the received and transmitted packets. The dynamic analysis extracted the API calls from the Cuckoo sandbox VM. The two types of features were applied on multimodal which collected the features into a single vector, then used as an input in the machine learning classifiers Neural Network, SVM, DT and Random Forest for malware detection (Rhode et al., 2019). Furthermore, Mantoo and Khurana (2019) have conducted their research on malware detection in android OS mobile phones. Their study's analysis approach was based on a hybrid of static, dynamic, and intrinsic features. They used the K Nearest Neighbor (KNN) and Logistic regression as machine learning models to detect malwares based on the extracted features. The features were extracted from several files of an android platform such as Mainfest.xml file, .apk files using apktool, and permissions packages by using any available emulator in the static analysis. For dynamic analysis, the features were extracted from system calls through installing the application into an android emulator called Genymotion with logs of its system calls. Moreover, they used linear discriminant analysis as an evaluation technique to evaluate the impact on the detection rate. The conducted study was applied to the public dataset of Androtrack. Both classifiers Logistic regression and KNN achieved optimal performance on detecting malware with 97.5% accuracy (Mantoo & Khurana, 2020).

Kuo et al.(2019) have conducted their study based on malware detection in the android platform using hybrid extracted features. The android file's permission characteristics were extracted as a static feature while the API call sequences as a dynamic feature. Machine learning classifiers were applied to evaluate the performance of the proposed method in malware detection rate. The experiment results of SVM and Random Forest classifiers were compared with Arshad et al. and showed a better accuracy performance of 88% and 89%, respectively. (Kuo et al., 2019). Moreover, other researchers analyzed the android platform to detect malware based on the hybrid analysis. Singh et al.(2019) have proposed an android detection technique based on dynamic and static analysis. They extracted the static features from the android Mainfest.xml file, which was divided into two types standard and non-standard permission. They used different tools such as AXMLPrinter2 and apktool to decompile the application to extract the features. In order to measure the effectiveness of the proposed method, they used Linear SVM (LSVM) as a machine learning classifier that achieved an accuracy of 99.6% (Singh et al., 2019).

Souza et al. (2020) have constructed their detection technique based on a hybrid approach and artificial neural network with a fuzzy system to build an expert system in the cybernetic invasion. The system relied on the fuzzy rules, where a hybrid model generated the rules to enable the extracted feature to construct the expert system to be able to work autonomously in cyberattack identification. The neural network model was trained based on the hidden layer to avoid the overfitting problem. The features were extracted from network architecture using three different layers used to prepare the fuzzy neural network model. Based on the experiment result, the fuzzy neural network achieved high accuracy than other classifiers such as DT (J48), Random Forest, and Naïve Bayes with 99.89% (Souza et al., 2020). Moreover, Darabian et al. (2020) have presented the strength analysis for detecting malicious code using static and dynamic approaches. The static feature extracted from the PE file's opcode sequence while the dynamic feature captured API calls of 1500 PE malware samples during the runtime in the Cuckoo sandbox environment. They evaluated the performance using the neural classifiers, which are Conventional Neural Network (CNN), Long Short Term Memory (LSTM), and Attention Based LSTM (ATT-LSTM). The high accuracy achieved by ATT-LSTM classifier with a 99% detection rate (Darabian et al., 2020).

As to conclude, the static analysis aims to find the malicious characteristics of an executable application or program without actually running it. In contrast, the dynamic analysis only monitors and analyzes the program's behavior during the execution time in the controlled environment. The integration of both analysis provides a new approach known as the hybrid approach. Table 1 summarizes all research studies that used different types of behavior analysis: static, dynamic, and hybrid. The table also shows the machine learning techniques used within previous studies and the accuracy result of malware detection. In this chapter, we have presented a SLR to collect the recent malware detection studies that used the hybrid approach based on the methodological criteria given in the next section.

Table 1. Comparison of three different analysis based on classification techniques and accuracy

Ref.	Static analysis	Dynamic analysis	Hybrid analysis	Accuracy	Dataset size	Training	Testing	Classification Technique
(Ahmadi et al., 2016)	√			-	21741	10868	10873	XGBoots
(Fuyong & Tiezhu, 2017)	√			93.48%	194 KB	70 KB	-	NB, SVM, DT, AS
(Sangal & Verma, 2020)	√			96.05%	1522	K-fold cross validation		DT, NB, RF, and KNN
(Mohaisen et al., 2015)		√		99%	more than 115,000	10-fold cross validation		SVM, DT, KNN and Logistic Regression
(O'kane et al., 2016)		√		-	350	-	-	SVM
Usman et al. (2021)		√		98%	7.3K malware applications	70%	30%	SVM, DT and NB
(Liu et al., 2016)			√	99.28	500	-	-	SVM, NB, KNN
(Yang et al., 2017)			√	95.9%	3378	70%	30%	SVM, DT and **Random Forest**
(Arshad et al., 2018)			√	99.07%	5560	66%	34%	SVM, RF, DT, NB
(He et al., 2018)			√	94.76%	-	-	-	Random Forest
(N. Kumar et al., 2019)			√	98.65%	1500	70%	30%	DT, RF, NN, and K-NN
(Han et al., 2019)			√	97.89%	-	-	-	KNN, RF and DT
(Catak, Yazi, Elezaj, & Ahmed, 2020)			√	-	7107	80%	20%	LSTM
(Yen et al., 2019)			√	83.17%	4519	3661	451	deep learning neural network
(Vinayakumar et al., 2019)			√	90.4% 96.6%	69,860	60%	40%	CNN, DNN (deep learning)
(Rhode et al., 2019)			√	92%	376	-	-	NN, SVM, Random Forest
(Mantoo & Khurana, 2020)			√	97.5%	600	-	-	Logistic regression and KNN
(Kuo et al., 2019)			√	89%	5500	1000	4500	SVM, RF
(A. K. Singh et al., 2019)			√	99.6%	10500	3000	-	LSVM
(Souza et al., 2020)			√	99.89%	2.598	70%	30%	fuzzy neural network DT (J48), RF, NB
(Darabian et al., 2020)			√	99%	1500	70%	15%	(CNN), (LSTM), Attention Based LSTM (ATT-LSTM).

RESEARCH METHODOLOGY

In this section, we explain the applied methodology. Figure 1 shows the steps of SLR, which are divided into three stages.

1. Planning review
   The first step describes the objective and the purpose of the systematic literature review

2. Conducting review
   The second step comprised the major content of the SLR that include
   a. Search strategy: describe the search source and terms for collected studies
   b. Selection Criteria: identify the included and excluded studies in SLR
   c. Quality Criteria: assess the quality of selected literature and the purpose of SLR
   d. Data Extraction: determine the procedure of feature extraction
   e. Data Synthesis: summarize the result of collected studies

3. Reporting review
   This process will be represented in solution and recommendation section, which will report the result of the selected studies.

a. Search Strategy

This step describes the method we used to collect all studies related to malware detection using machine learning based on the hybrid analysis. We applied a search term of binary expression combined with "OR" or "AND". The search term was (malware OR malicious behavior) AND (detect OR detection OR classification) AND (machine learning OR ML OR data mining techniques OR deep learning) AND (hybrid analysis OR static and dynamic OR API calls OR neural network). The search term was used to search in six digital libraries, listed as following:

i.   IEEE Library
ii. Google Scholar
iii. SpringerLink
iv. ScienceDirect
v.   IAU Digital library
vi. ResearchGate

The search process carried on these e-databases, in main journals and conferences, listed in Table 2. All studies related to the search term have been considered, in the range between 2016 to 2020.

Figure 1. Overview of SLR process (Pan et al., 2020)

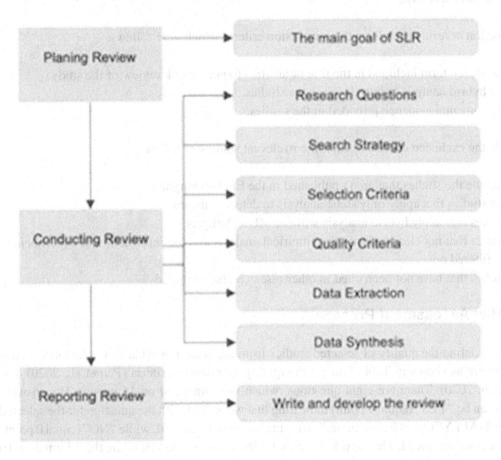

Table 2. Journals and Conferences

Category	Acronym	Name
Journals	-	Computer Virology and Hacking Techniques
	-	Grid Computing
	DTRP	ACM of Digital Threats: Research and Practice
	-	IEEE Access
		Computers & Security
Conference	(ICCE)	International Conference on Consumer Electronics
	(ICCCS)	IEEE International Conference on Computer and Communication Systems
	(EAIS)	IEEE Conference on Evolving and Adaptive Intelligent Systems
	ICAIS	International Conference on Artificial Intelligence and Security
	(CSE)	IEEE International Conference on Computational Science and Engineering
	(AsiaJCIS)	Asia Joint Conference on Information Security
	(APSEC)	Asia-Pacific Conference on Software Engineering
	(DSN)	International Conference on Dependable Systems and Networks
	(ICRIC)	International Conference on Recent Innovations in Computing

b. Selection Criteria

The selection criteria depends on three inclusion criteria which is as follows:

i.   The search term included in the title or abstract to get a quick review of the study
ii. The hybrid analysis is introduced in the studies.
iii. Experimental evidence provided in the studies.

While the exclusion criteria to filter the irrelevant studies as follow

i.   Exclude the studies that aren't published in the English language
ii. The studies that apply only static analysis to detect malware
iii. Studies that apply hybrid analysis without ML techniques
iv. Studies that not clearly clarify the empirical analysis and the information of experimental results are filtered out
v.   Studies that have not been cited in other research also excluded

c. Quality Assessment Process

In order to define the quality of selected studies from the selection criteria, we performed an analysis questionnaire as shown in Table 3 to get the quality assessment criteria (Pan et al., 2020), (Sohan & Basalamah, 2020). There are eight questions, which were imposed on 15 papers. The answers to the question can be "YES" (equal 1 point) indicating that we agreed with the question for the selected study, for "PARTIALLY" (equal 0.5 point) indicates that we partially agreed, while "NO" (equal 0 point) which implies that we disagreed. The maximum score for the study is 8 points, while the minimum is 0 points.

Table 3. Quality assessment

ID	Quality criteria	Yes	Partially	NO
1	Is the purpose of the study clear?			
2	Does hybrid analysis technique stated clearly?			
3	Are the extracted features clearly defined?			
4	Is the machine learning technique clearly defined?			
5	Does the study provide a source code or any tool?			
6	Are the result clearly stated?			
7	Does the study provide the measurement performance?			
8	Does the study add value or contribution to this paper?			

d. Data Extraction

This step is considered an essential part for accurately extracting meaningful information from each selected study and based on the extracted information; we can answer the research questions. Figure 2 provides an overview of the data extraction method.

i.   The publication year and publication source for journals and conferences
ii. Hybrid analysis methods that depend on the static and dynamic features
iii. An empirical experiment that includes a support tool for static and dynamic analysis, performance measures and ML techniques

Figure 2. Data Extraction Process

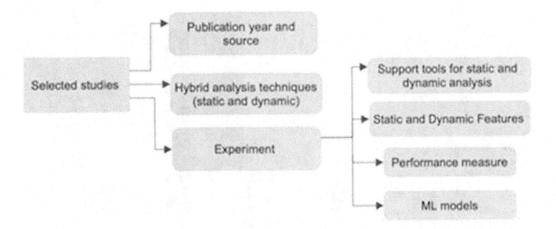

e. Data Synthesis

This step will summarize the result of data extraction to provide conclusive answers to the research questions. The result will be collected and saved in an excel file to be presented as a pie chart and histogram to provide a clear view of the selected studies' information.

SOLUTIONS AND RECOMMENDATIONS

This section will present the results of selected studies to answer the research questions. Firstly, we will provide the publication time and publication source. Then, we will analyze the quality of the selected studies based on quality questionaries. Finally, we present the answer for each research question with appropriate discussion.

The Annual Number of Studies and the Publication Source

Figure 3 provides an overview of the number of selected studies that start in 2016 and end in 2020. The figure displays the number of studies published over the years. In 2016 and 2017, we encountered only one published study in each year, while in 2018, two studies were published. Furthermore, the number of studies was raised in 2019 as nine articles were published. According to this figure, the highest proportion of studies published in 2019. The main source of the selected articles and the number of articles related to the publication source are shown in Table 4.

Figure 3. The annual publication of studies

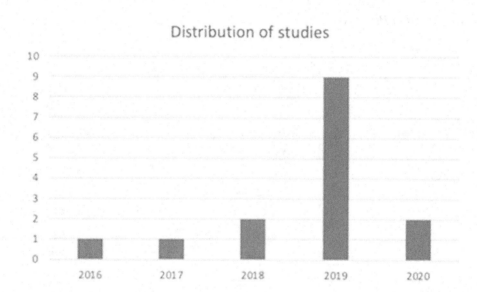

Quality Assessment Result

We have presented the quality questions in the previous section to analyze the quality of the selected articles. Table 5 shows the answers for the quality assessments, where we can see that most of the questions were answered positively, where Q2 and Q3 mostly positive. The answer of Q5 shows that some studies provide a tool or source code, where the rest either mention the tool's name or not described very well. The result of Q7 shows that the performance measurement was expressed very well by measuring different parameters in some studies, while the remaining studies only provide one measured parameter.

In Table 6, we categorized the scores of the quality assessment into three groups: very high (7.5 and above), high (7), and average (6.5 and below), and assign the percentage for each category.

As illustrated in Table 7, most of the selected studies have a high-quality score above 7.5, while the least score of studies was 6.5, which is considered the average of scores.

Table 4. Publication source of selected studies

Type	Name	Ref.
Journal	IEEE Access	(Arshad et al., 2018) (Vinayakumar et al., 2019)
	Computers & Security	(Han et al., 2019)
	Computer Virology and Hacking Techniques	(A. K. Singh et al., 2019)
	Grid Computing	(Darabian et al., 2020)
Conference	International Conference on Consumer Electronics	(Liu et al., 2016)
	International Conference on Artificial Intelligence and Security	(Yang et al., 2017)
	Asia-Pacific Conference on Software Engineering	(He et al., 2018)
	Asia Joint Conference on Information Security	(N. Kumar et al., 2019)
	International Conference on Dependable Systems and Networks Industry Track	(Rhode et al., 2019)
	International Conference on Recent Innovations in Computing ICRIC	(Mantoo & Khurana, 2020)
	IEEE 4th International Conference on Computer and Communication Systems	(Kuo et al., 2019)
	2020 IEEE Conference on Evolving and Adaptive Intelligent Systems	(Souza et al., 2020)

Table 5. Result of quality questionnaire

ID	Quality criteria	Yes	Partially	NO
1	Is the purpose of the study clear?	15(100%)	0	0
2	Does hybrid analysis technique stated clearly?	14 (93.3%)	1 (6.7%)	0
3	Are the used feature clearly defined?	13(86.7%)	2 (13.3%)	0
4	Is the machine learning technique clearly stated?	15 (100%)	0	0
5	Does the study provide a source code or any tool?	10 (66.7%)	3 (20%)	2(13.3%)
6	Are the result clearly stated?	15 (100%)	0	0
7	Does the study clearly state the measurement performance?	12 (80%)	3 (20%)	0
8	Does the study add value or contribution to this SLR?	15 (100%)	0	0

Table 6. Scores of quality questions

Score category	No. of studies	Percentages
very high (7.5 and above)	10	66.7%
high (7)	2	13.3%
average (6.5 and below)	2	13.3%

Table 7. Quality scores of selected studies

Paper	Score	Paper	Score
Liu et al.(2016)	8	Darabian et al.(2020)	8
He *et al.* (2018)	8	Yang et al. (2017)	7.5
Kumar et al.(2019)	8	Vinayakumar et al. (2019)	7.5
Hen et al.(2019)	8	Arshad et .al (2018)	7
Catak **et al. (2019)**	8	Rhode et al. (2019)	7
Mantoo and Khurana (2019)	8	Yen et al.(2019)	6.5
Kuo et al.(2019)	8	Souza et al. (2020)	6.5
Singh et al. (2019)	8		

RESULT AND DISCUSSION OF RESEARCH QUESTION

In this section, we have answered the research questions with more details and discussions.

a.   *RQ1.*what are the common features of static and dynamic analysis used in malware detection?

The features extracted from static and dynamic analysis can be integrated to produce a robust technique known as hybrid analysis. Due to this advantage, recent studies tend to use a hybrid analysis for malware detection and classification with ML techniques to provide accurate results. Based on the selected studies, we have divided the features into six categories, as shown in Table 8.

Table 8. Common features used in hybrid techniques

Category	Ref.	No. of papers
Android characteristics features	[13] [14] [16] [24] [25] [26]	6
PE headers and API calls	[18] [20] [22]	3
Machine metrics and API calls	[23]	1
JavaScript code	[17]	1
Call graph and API calls	[19] [21]	2
Opcode and API calls	[27] [28]	2

The table illustrates the category of hybrid analysis that integrates the static and dynamic analysis features. The prevalent features used by most of the studies were android characteristics features, followed by PE header and API calls. The number of studies that used call graphs and opcode with API calls as hybrid features were only two studies for each category. The smallest number of studies were carried out by JavaScript and machine metrics features.

b.   *RQ2*.what are the ML models used for malware detection and classification based on hybrid analysis?

Machine learning models used a protocol to detect malware by producing sets of features. The developed features can be used in the training set to train the ML classifiers such as SVM, DT, Naïve Bayas, etc. The test sets' features are used to test the accurate number of detection and classification of malware to validate the classifiers. The last step to evaluate the detection model's performance using different measurement metrics such as Accuracy, Precision, F-score, and Recall. Figure 4 shows the popular machine learning models used in the selected studies. The highest percentage of tasks by Random forest classifier is 22%, followed by SVM and DT with 14% for each classifier. The smallest portion was carried out by Fuzzy neural network, LSVM, and Logistic regression with 3%.

Figure 4. ML models used in the studies

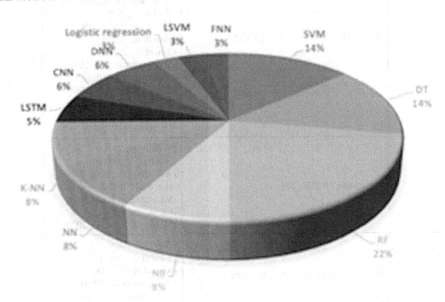

c.   *RQ3*.What are the performance measures applied in the articles on malware detection with ML techniques and hybrid analysis?

The performance measures are used to examine the ability of classifiers to detect and classify malware. Table 9 provides the performance measures used in the selected articles. True positive (TP), True Negative (TN), False positive (FP), and False Negative (FN) are considered the basic measure parameters. TP is the benign number that accurately predicted, where TN the number of benign that falsely predicted. FN the number of malware correctly predicted, while FP the number of malware incorrectly predicted.

The main measures used in the studies for empirical evidence evaluation are:

i.   Accuracy: the ratio of precisely detected malware samples upon the total size. Most of the selected studies applied accuracy measures.

ii.   Precision: the ratio of correctly detected malware and it was used in seven studies.

iii. False Positive Rate: FPR identifies the ratio of benign that is incorrectly detected as malware. This measure was only used by six of the studies.

iv. True Positive Rate: Recall, TPR provides the ratio of correctly detected malware across the total number of samples and is considered the second commonly used in the studies.

v. F-score: measured by the TPR and Precision, which was used in six studies.

Table 9. Performance measured by selected studies

Performance measure	Definition	Ref.	No. of studies
Accuracy	Acc= (TP +TN) /(TP +FN+FP+TN)	(Liu et al., 2016) (Yang et al., 2017) (Arshad et al., 2018) (He et al., 2018) (A. K. Singh et al., 2019) (Kuo et al., 2019) (N. Kumar et al., 2019) (Han et al., 2019) (Yen et al., 2019) (Vinayakumar et al., 2019) (Rhode et al., 2019) (Catak, Yazi, et al., 2020) (Mantoo & Khurana, 2020) (Souza et al., 2020) (Darabian et al., 2020)	14
Preision	Precision= TP /(FP+TP)	(Yang et al., 2017) (He et al., 2018) (A. K. Singh et al., 2019) (Han et al., 2019) (Vinayakumar et al., 2019) (Catak, Yazi, et al., 2020) (Mantoo & Khurana, 2020)	7
FPR	False Positive Rate = FP /(TN + FP)	(Liu et al., 2016) (Yang et al., 2017) (Arshad et al., 2018) (N. Kumar et al., 2019) (A. K. Singh et al., 2019) (Darabian et al., 2020)	6
Recll	True Positive Rate = TP /(FN + TP)	(Liu et al., 2016) (Yang et al., 2017) (Arshad et al., 2018) (He et al., 2018) (A. K. Singh et al., 2019) (Han et al., 2019) (Kuo et al., 2019) (N. Kumar et al., 2019) (Vinayakumar et al., 2019) (Catak, Yazi, et al., 2020) (Mantoo & Khurana, 2020)	11
F-Masure	F-Measure= Recall*Precision*2/(Recall + Precision)	(He et al., 2018) (Han et al., 2019) (Rhode et al., 2019) (Vinayakumar et al., 2019) (Catak, Yazi, et al., 2020) (Darabian et al., 2020)	6
AUC	Area Under the Curve = ½ *(sensitivity + specificity)	(Yang et al., 2017) (Souza et al., 2020)	2

In summary, we compared and analyzed the selected studies based on the extracted features of static and dynamic analysis, the measurement accuracy, and the machine learning models, as shown in Table 10.

Table 10. Comparison of hybrid analysis extracted features and the accuracy percentage of machine learning techniques

Ref.	Static analysis	Dynamic analysis	Precision	Accuracy	Classification Technique
(Liu et al., 2016)	Permission	API call system	-	99.28	SVM, NB, KNN
(Yang et al., 2017)	permission features	DroidBox tool	95.9%	95.9%	SVM, DT and **Random Forest**
(Arshad et al., 2018)	Suspicious API calls	APIs call	-	99.07%	SVM, RF, DT, NB
(He et al., 2018)	JavaScript code from web pages	*Jalangi* framework	94.80%	94.76%	Random Forest
(N. Kumar et al., 2019)	(PE) header	system calls, network data	-	99.74%	DT, RF, NN, and K-NN
(Han et al., 2019)	API call function	API call sequences	97.45%	97.89%	KNN, RF and DT
(Catak, Yazi, et al., 2020)	MD5 (hash)	API calls	40%	-	LSTM
(Yen et al., 2019)	API call	API call sequence captured of sandbox		83.17%	deep learning neural network
(Vinayakumar et al., 2019)	PE and row byte using **(WSBD)**	PE using **(WDBD)**	86.1% 94.0%	90.4% 96.6%	CNN, DNN (deep learning)
(Rhode et al., 2019)	Machine metrics from Psutil python library	API calls **captured of sandbox**	-	92%	NN, SVM, Random Forest
(Mantoo & Khurana, 2020)	.apk files and Mainfest. xml files	API calls system	97.0%	97.5%	Logistic regression and KNN
(Kuo et al., 2019)	Permission files (Android packages)	API call sequences	-	89%	SVM, RF
(A. K. Singh et al., 2019)	Mainfest.xml file	API calls sequences	99.5%	99.6%	LSVM
(Souza et al., 2020)	Binary static analysis to extract from VirusDataset file	Analyzing the features in Expert system at running time	-	99.89%	fuzzy neural network DT (J48), RF, NB
(Darabian et al., 2020)	Opcode sequence	API call sequence	-	99%	(CNN), (LSTM), Attention Based LSTM (ATT-LSTM).

FUTURE RESEARCH DIRECTIONS

For future work, we provide some recommendations for future researchers interested in this domain: the malware datasets are preferred to be available and public so that it can be easily accessed and used by other researchers. Moreover, many security analysts tend to use automation and predictable tools for detecting malwares. Based on our investigation, we noticed that a few studies were conducted using tools or platform, therefore we recommend that that more future studies should use these automation and prediction tools for malware detection.

CONCLUSION

Digital transformation has introduced different cybersecurity threats in many domains. Current research focuses on developing machine learning methods for malware detection due to their advantages to keep up with malware's evolving speed. The security analysts have proposed malware behavior-based approach, which provides information about the malware's nature, strength, and behavior in the given software. The malware behavior can be categorized into static and dynamic analysis. Both classes of analysis have advantages and limitations. The hybrid method combines the strength of both static and dynamic approaches. This study represents a systematic literature review of malware detection using a machine learning technique based on the hybrid analysis. Particularly, this SLR performed over several studies ranging from 2016 to 2020. It represents the malware detection based on different analysis behaviors that are static, dynamic, and focused on the hybrid analysis and performance model for each machine learning technique used to detect and classify the malicious code. We have collected fifteen studies from different digital libraries based on searching and selection criteria. Then we have evaluated the quality of the selected studies by applying quality questionnaires for each study. The quality analysis edthat most of the studies have high scores. After that, we present the result of this paper by answering the investigated research questions presented in the previous section to fulfill the findings. Overall, we conclude that most studies have high-quality work and success in detecting malware using machine learning models based on the hybrid analysis.

REFERENCES

Ahmadi, M., Ulyanov, D., Semenov, S., Trofimov, M., & Giacinto, G. (2016). Novel Feature Extraction, Selection and Fusion for Effective Malware Family Classification. In *Proceedings of the Sixth ACM Conference on Data and Application Security and Privacy* (pp. 183–194). New York, NY: Association for Computing Machinery. 10.1145/2857705.2857713

Arshad, S., Shah, M. A., Wahid, A., Mehmood, A., Song, H., & Yu, H. (2018). SAMADroid: A Novel 3-Level Hybrid Malware Detection Model for Android Operating System. *IEEE Access: Practical Innovations, Open Solutions*, 6, 4321–4339. doi:10.1109/ACCESS.2018.2792941

Catak, F. O., Yazi, A. F., Elezaj, O., & Ahmed, J. (2020). Deep learning based Sequential model for malware analysis using Windows exe API Calls. *PeerJ. Computer Science*, 6(July), 1–23. doi:10.7717/peerj-cs.285 PMID:33816936

Catak, F. O., Yazı, A. F., Elezaj, O., & Ahmed, J. (2020). Deep learning based Sequential model for malware analysis using Windows exe API Calls. *PeerJ. Computer Science*, 6, e285. doi:10.7717/peerj-cs.285 PMID:33816936

Darabian, H., Homayounoot, S., Dehghantanha, A., Hashemi, S., Karimipour, H., Parizi, R. M., & Choo, K.-K. R. (2020). Detecting Cryptomining Malware: A Deep Learning Approach for Static and Dynamic Analysis. *Journal of Grid Computing, 18*(2), 293–303. doi:10.100710723-020-09510-6

Fuyong, Z., & Tiezhu, Z. (2017). Malware Detection and Classification Based on N-Grams Attribute Similarity. In *2017 IEEE International Conference on Computational Science and Engineering (CSE) and IEEE International Conference on Embedded and Ubiquitous Computing (EUC)*. IEEE. 10.1109/CSE-EUC.2017.157

Gibert, D., Mateu, C., & Planes, J. (2020). The rise of machine learning for detection and classification of malware: Research developments, trends and challenges. *Journal of Network and Computer Applications, 153*(July), 102526. doi:10.1016/j.jnca.2019.102526

Gong, L., Lin, H., Li, Z., Qian, F., Li, Y., Ma, X., & Liu, Y. (2021). Systematically Landing Machine Learning onto Market-Scale Mobile Malware Detection. *IEEE Transactions on Parallel and Distributed Systems, 32*(7), 1615–1628. doi:10.1109/TPDS.2020.3046092

Han, W., Xue, J., Wang, Y., Huang, L., Kong, Z., & Mao, L. (2019). MalDAE: Detecting and explaining malware based on correlation and fusion of static and dynamic characteristics. *Computers & Security, 83*, 208–233. doi:10.1016/j.cose.2019.02.007

Harshalatha, P., & Mohanasundaram, R. (2020). Classification of malware detection using machine learning algorithms: A survey. *International Journal of Scientific and Technology Research, 9*(2), 1796–1802.

He, X., Xu, L., & Cha, C. (2018). Malicious JavaScript Code Detection Based on Hybrid Analysis. In *2018 25th Asia-Pacific Software Engineering Conference (APSEC)* (pp. 365–374). 10.1109/APSEC.2018.00051

Kumar, N., Mukhopadhyay, S., Gupta, M., Handa, A., & Shukla, S. K. (2019). Malware Classification using Early Stage Behavioral Analysis. In *2019 14th Asia Joint Conference on Information Security (AsiaJCIS)*. IEEE. 10.1109/AsiaJCIS.2019.00-10

Kumar, V. V., & Ramamoorthy, S. (2017). A Novel method of gateway selection to improve throughput performance in MANET. *Journal of Advanced Research in Dynamical and Control Systems, 9*, 420–432. doi:10.1109/AsiaJCIS.2019.00-10

Kuo, W., Liu, T., & Wang, C. (2019). Study on Android Hybrid Malware Detection Based on Machine Learning. In *2019 IEEE 4th International Conference on Computer and Communication Systems (ICCCS)* (pp. 31–35). 10.1109/CCOMS.2019.8821665

Liu, Y., Zhang, Y., Li, H., & Chen, X. (2016). A hybrid malware detecting scheme for mobile Android applications. In *2016 IEEE International Conference on Consumer Electronics (ICCE)* (pp. 155–156). 10.1109/ICCE.2016.7430561

Malware Statistics & Trends Report | AV-TEST. (n.d.). Retrieved April 19, 2021, from https://www.av-test.org/en/statistics/malware/

Mantoo, B. A., & Khurana, S. S. (2020). Static, Dynamic and Intrinsic Features Based Android Malware Detection Using Machine Learning. In P. K. Singh, A. K. Kar, Y. Singh, M. H. Kolekar, & S. Tanwar (Eds.), *Proceedings of ICRIC 2019* (pp. 31–45). Cham: Springer International Publishing. 10.1007/978-3-030-29407-6_4

Mohaisen, A., Alrawi, O., & Mohaisen, M. (2015). AMAL: High-fidelity, behavior-based automated malware analysis and classification. *Computers & Security, 52*, 251–266. doi:10.1016/j.cose.2015.04.001

O'kane, P., Sezer, S., & McLaughlin, K. (2016). Detecting obfuscated malware using reduced opcode set and optimised runtime trace. *Security Informatics, 5*(1), 2. Advance online publication. doi:10.118613388-016-0027-2

Pan, Y., Ge, X., Fang, C., & Fan, Y. (2020). A Systematic Literature Review of Android Malware Detection Using Static Analysis. *IEEE Access: Practical Innovations, Open Solutions, 8*, 116363–116379. doi:10.1109/ACCESS.2020.3002842

Rhode, M., Tuson, L., Burnap, P., & Jones, K. (2019). LAB to SOC: Robust Features for Dynamic Malware Detection. In *2019 49th Annual IEEE/IFIP International Conference on Dependable Systems and Networks – Industry Track* (pp. 13–16). 10.1109/DSN-Industry.2019.00010

Saint Yen, Y., Chen, Z. W., Guo, Y. R., & Chen, M. C. (2019). *Integration of Static and Dynamic Analysis for Malware Family Classification with Composite Neural Network.* Retrieved from https://arxiv.org/abs/1912.11249

Sangal, A., & Verma, H. K. (2020). A Static Feature Selection-based Android Malware Detection Using Machine Learning Techniques. In *2020 International Conference on Smart Electronics and Communication (ICOSEC)* (pp. 48–51). 10.1109/ICOSEC49089.2020.9215355

Santos, I., Penya, Y. K., Devesa, J., & Bringas, P. G. (2009). N-grams-based File Signatures for Malware Detection. *ICEIS, 9*(2), 317–320.

Singh, A. K., Jaidhar, C. D., & Kumara, M. A. A. (2019). Experimental analysis of Android malware detection based on combinations of permissions and API-calls. *Journal of Computer Virology and Hacking Techniques, 15*(3), 209–218. doi:10.100711416-019-00332-z

Sohan, M. F., & Basalamah, A. (2020). A Systematic Literature Review and Quality Analysis of Javascript Malware Detection. *IEEE Access: Practical Innovations, Open Solutions, 8*, 190539–190552. doi:10.1109/ACCESS.2020.3031690

Sonicwall. (2020). 2021 SonicWall Cyber Threat Report. *2020 SonicWall*, 1–38. Retrieved from https://www.sonicwall.com/resources/2020-cyber-threat-report-pdf/

Souza, P. V. de C., Guimarães, A. J., Rezende, T. S., Araujo, V. S., do Nascimento, L. A. F., & Batista, L. O. (2020). An Intelligent Hybrid Model for the Construction of Expert Systems in Malware Detection. In *2020 IEEE Conference on Evolving and Adaptive Intelligent Systems (EAIS)* (pp. 1–8). 10.1109/EAIS48028.2020.9122770

Sun, M., Li, X., Lui, J. C. S., Ma, R. T. B., & Liang, Z. (2017). Monet: A User-Oriented Behavior-Based Malware Variants Detection System for Android. *IEEE Transactions on Information Forensics and Security*, *12*(5), 1103–1112. doi:10.1109/TIFS.2016.2646641

Symantec. (2016). Internet security threat report. *Network Security, 21*(2), 1–3. Retrieved from https://linkinghub.elsevier.com/retrieve/pii/S1353485805001947

Umamaheswaran, S., Lakshmanan, R., Vinothkumar, V., Arvind, K. S., & Nagarajan, S. (2019). New and robust composite micro structure descriptor (CMSD) for CBIR. *International Journal of Speech Technology*, 1–7. doi:10.100710772-019-09663-0

Usman, N., Usman, S., Khan, F., Jan, M. A., Sajid, A., Alazab, M., & Watters, P. (2021). Intelligent Dynamic Malware Detection using Machine Learning in IP Reputation for Forensics Data Analytics. *Future Generation Computer Systems*, *118*, 124–141. doi:10.1016/j.future.2021.01.004

Vinayakumar, R., Alazab, M., Soman, K. P., Poornachandran, P., & Venkatraman, S. (2019). Robust Intelligent Malware Detection Using Deep Learning. *IEEE Access: Practical Innovations, Open Solutions*, *7*, 46717–46738. doi:10.1109/ACCESS.2019.2906934

Yang, F., Zhuang, Y., & Wang, J. (2017). Android Malware Detection Using Hybrid Analysis and Machine Learning Technique. In X. Sun, H.-C. Chao, X. You, & E. Bertino (Eds.), *Cloud Computing and Security* (pp. 565–575). Springer International Publishing. doi:10.1007/978-3-319-68542-7_48

ADDITIONAL READING

Fatima, A., Maurya, R., Dutta, M. K., Burget, R., & Masek, J. (2019). Android Malware Detection Using Genetic Algorithm based Optimized Feature Selection and Machine Learning. In 2019 42nd International Conference on Telecommunications and Signal Processing (TSP) (pp. 220–223). 10.1109/TSP.2019.8769039

HR., S. (2019). Static Analysis of Android Malware Detection using Deep Learning. In *2019 International Conference on Intelligent Computing and Control Systems (ICCS)* (pp. 841–845). 10.1109/ICCS45141.2019.9065765

Ijaz, M., Durad, M. H., & Ismail, M. (2019). Static and Dynamic Malware Analysis Using Machine Learning. In 2019 16th International Bhurban Conference on Applied Sciences and Technology (IBCAST) (pp. 687–691). 10.1109/IBCAST.2019.8667136

Ki, Y., Kim, E., & Kim, H. K. (2015). A Novel Approach to Detect Malware Based on API Call Sequence Analysis. *International Journal of Distributed Sensor Networks*, *11*(6), 659101. doi:10.1155/2015/659101

Kriti, V., Virmani, J., & Agarwal, R. (2020). Deep feature extraction and classification of breast ultrasound images. *Multimedia Tools and Applications*, *79*(37–38), 27257–27292. doi:10.100711042-020-09337-z

Somasundaram, S., Kasthurirathna, D., & Rupasinghe, L. (2019). Mobile-based Malware Detection and Classification using Ensemble Artificial Intelligence. The Institute of Electrical and Electronics Engineers, Inc. (IEEE) Conference Proceedings. Sri Lanka Institute of Information Technology,Faculty of Computing,Malabe,Sri Lanka: The Institute of Electrical and Electronics Engineers, Inc. (IEEE).

Tajoddin, A., & Abadi, M. (2019). RAMD: Registry-based anomaly malware detection using one-class ensemble classifiers. *Applied Intelligence*, *49*(7), 2641–2658. doi:10.100710489-018-01405-0

Wyrwinski, P., Dutkiewicz, J., & Jedrzejek, C. (2020). Ensemble malware classification using neural networks. Communications in Computer and Information Science, 1284 CCIS, 125–138. doi:10.1007/978-3-030-59000-0_10

Chapter 12
Digital Transformation of Cyber Crime for Chip-Enabled Hacking

Romil Rawat

Shri Vaishnav Vidyapeeth Vishwavidyalaya, India

Vinod Mahor

IPS College of Technology and Management, Gwalior, India

Anjali Rawat

Independent Researcher, India

Bhagwati Garg

Union Bank of India, Gwalior, India

Shrikant Telang

ⓘ https://orcid.org/0000-0001-5477-865X

Shri Vaishnav Vidyapeeth Vishwavidyalaya, India

ABSTRACT

The heterogeneous digital arena emerged as the open depiction for malicious activities, and cyber criminals and terrorists are targeting the cyber depiction for controlling its operation. In the dark web (DW), diverse illegal hacking communities are using the sensing-chip webnet to transfer their bots for tracking the user activity so that criminal activities could be accomplished like money laundering, pornography, child trafficking, drug trafficking, arms and ammunition trafficking, where professionals could also be hired and contracted for generating flood infringement and ransomware infringement.

DOI: 10.4018/978-1-7998-6975-7.ch012

INTRODUCTION

Malevolent-Process-Design (MPD) refers to a broad cybernated-invasion and digital transformation genre that is loaded into the system. Typically, the gadget is compromised to the enemy's benefit without the knowledge of the legitimate owner. Some excellent genres of MPD include malicious code designs to access the gadget covertly and modify surveillance processes (Jang-Jaccard, 2014). In a variety of ways, it infects digital processes, e.g. spreads from foolish users into opening stained directories, and allows users to enter MPD sharing websites or infected gadgets. It can spread from gadget and containing attached logic and processes (Zamojski, 2019). For convenience, labor problems and safety, vehicle autonomy (Valluripally, 2019) is now widely used in urban culture. The Hyperspace of web enabled chips is an inherent depiction network that can connect any chip-enabled-net centers in order to help track and handle chip-enabled vehicles. Unfortunately, the main complications of this neoteric technology fueled by connectivity protocols of the 5th century are surveillance, cybernated violation and connection failures (Kakkar,2020). It creates unparalleled opportunities to bind both human and machine-to-machine beings. In such a model, dossier surveillance is a very salient task (Zhou, 2020). There's no protected spectrum sharing mechanism. Available research rely on a incorporated forum to validate any arrangement on spectrum sharing that is impuissant with numerous cybernated infringement, including single point of compromise, Web flooding invasion and violation, etc. In contrast, they concentrate solely on the usage of energy, while neglecting protection and surveillance issues that are salient for spectrum sharing. Secondly, self-interested and rational H2H clients share their scaled resources without sufficient financial incentives because of co-channel interference and other costs. In fact, private awareness is the cost of spectrum sharing for the H2H user, which adds to the statistics asymmetry between the authenticated centers and the H2H user. Available methods typically assume for fully aware of the particulars on the H2H side, which may be unworkable for real-world use (Kadoguchi, 2020). Semantic relationships between cybernated infringement infrastructure junctions from the perspective of a heterogeneous statistics webnet (HIN). However, most of these works rely mainly on analogous knowledge webnet or bipartite graphs, which are unable to detect higher-level semantic interactions between various types of junction. Knowledge webnet, HIN includes various types of junction or associations that have distinct semantic meanings (Malhotra, 2021).

The economic loss due to the cybernated –terrorism increasing rapidly due to which it is necessary for inquisitor to work on the processes which will prove to be beneficial for the community. By ability to improve road traffic, fuel comfort and piloting through the use of wireless dossier relay, car platooning has associated the inquisitors.

The vehicles participating in the platoon are basically capable of exchanging inter-vehicle dossier with each other, which actually results in an upgraded achievement of the operation goals, benefiting by parameters collected from embedded designed vehicular systems. Dossier exchange between platoons is done mainly by Vehicular Adhoc Webnet (VANET) Dedicated Short Range Relay (DSRR) (Lalar, 2020) that has been used for surveillance guarantees and secure dossier sharing. They are currently part of a broad genre of neoteric developed systems, called the Cybernated Physical Modeling Phase (Kaur, 2020), having been seen from a specific point of view on vehicle platoons. Thus, we believe that there is a lot of cyber espionage in cyber space, including this illicit stuff. These days, it is expected to detect violation in advance and establish active protection by using the cybernated-invasion cyber espionage (Roddy, 2020). The below diagram 1 shows about the available types of infringement linked to Wireless Sensor Webnet for creating malfunctioning and irregularities into the structure. The objective is to present the Brain-Intelligent Chip Junction (BICJ) mechanization is used as assistive mechanization for patients similarly as sound subjects to control gadgets only by brain development. Anyway, the peril analogous with the maltherapy of this mechanization remains to a great extent neglected. Late revelations have shown that BICJ are possibly powerless against cybernated guiltiness. This opens the possibility of neuro-malfeasance, growing the scope of computer-malfeasance to neurological gadgets. The work investigates such a neuro-malfeasance likewise called as brain hijacking (BH) as it centers on the unlawful permission to and control of neurological statistics and computation. As neurological figuring underlies insight, conduct and our self-assurance as people, a cautious investigation of the arising peril of kindhearted BH is central, and good defends against this peril should be viewed as from the get-go in arrangement and guideline. This commitment is highlighted bringing issues to light of the arising peril of kindhearted BH and adventures out developing a good and authentic reflection on that peril.

Figure 1. Diverse types of infringement linked to Wireless Sensor Webnet

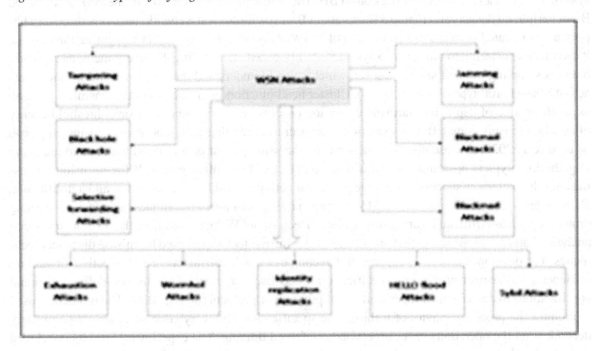

Background

In the last few epochs, DN has been one of the most contested issues in cybernated surveillance circles. For others, anonymous webnet on the Hyperspace is a way of gaining freedom. Most neoteric's media sources find out the DN and its Tor browser are commonly used for illegal activities (Jang-Jaccard, 2014). Similarly, spam or spear phishing e-mails may be delivered to other victims. Credentials may also be used as commodities sold or exchanged in subway outlets (Safaldin, 2020). Company Insider reported over one billion Android users globally during 2014. Government agencies are also pursuing chip-enabled-net applications for Android. Google's technology architecture is now pervasive and will continue to grow. The strength of an application-based architecture is the simplicity, interoperability and versatility it offers to consumers. However, the same versatility also enables and attracts the production of MPD. It discusses the methods used in static analysis of Android MPD. It discusses the key research efforts used to analyze applications for leakage of consent and seclusion issues (Birajdar, 2013).

The terminology BH enlightens towards the chance of co-opting Brain-Intelligent Chip Junction (BICJ) (Kakkar,2020) and other neurological engineering gadgets to get to or manipulating neurological statistics from the brain offers an overview of the potential sorts of BH to which BICJ are or may get subject in the near future and provides an inventory of the particular moral ramifications of BH. The moral concerns we examine in relation to BH might be found in relation to other technologies too, we propose that their particular blend with respect to BICJ warrants a separate conversation, particularly given the current and not out of the ordinary progress in BICJ research and utility and the point is to provide a systematic therapy BH (Kakkar,2020) in relation to the divergent integrants of BICJ. This contribution is pointed toward promoting a public discussion over the likely infringements to neuro surveillance analogous to the conceivably ubiquitous availability of BICJ among the general public, and ventures out building up a systematic moral and legitimate reflection on BH. The below figure 2 –shows the framework of IoT based Brain Peripheral designs and Figure 3 shows about Brain Neurological Network. Intrusion discovery has been a complicated problem in examination of WSW. According to a variety of categorization criteria, it can be categorized into numerous ways. incongruity based encroaching discovery methods regularly requires sampling training set and test set, which helps to understand the standard patterns and create activity-based prototype (Agrawal, 2014). Cluster head junction monitored the other member junction as an alternative of deploying intrusion detect ion process on every junction to save threshold energy of attached sensing chips . But this solution is subject to check that only motionless sensing chips can be used (Cao,2020). Misuse discovery depends on the principles of pattern coordination and matching in gathering atypical operations which is used to detect webnet infringement. If the intrusion process matches the pattern as successful then the particular activity considered as intrusion and a notification alarm is generated (De Bruijn, 2017). Most common misuse discovery techniques include deep learning prototype such as Artificial Neurological Webnet, Deep Belief Webnet. Additionally, the state transition analysis, feature analysis and expert process are major misuse techniques used for misuse discovery techniques. The developed process is capable of detecting black hole infringement and selective forwarding infringement. The main principle of specification-based discovery method is to use pre-defined rules and specifications to describe the proper working of program or protocol (Senol, 2020). The protocol is used to monitor the process behavior of webnet. The specification discoverybased methods are completely dependent on the operations of the object and reinforced training. The experimental results concluded that a higher discovery rate is capable of detecting intrusions if proper set of operation were assigned to the discovery process (Mirea, 2019). Their states have already been supervised by the intrusion discovery process during the operation of systems (Villalva,2018). A warning was activated as the actions of the gadget deviated from the predefined state. The findings showed a higher discovery rate compared to other equivalent two anomaly-based discovery systems.

The literature have perceived express surveillance ambush impacting BICJ uprightness, seclusion, accessibility, and prosperity, thorough investigation and miss pertinent concerns (Safaldin, 2020). All the more unequivocally, the use of neuro-arousement BICJ in clinical circle presents serious weaknesses that can fundamentally influence the client's ailment (Ali, 2020). BICJ previously existing on the retail outlet would benefit by the utilization of hearty surveillance courses of action, decreasing their impact, especially in clinical circle. Besides, the expansion of BICJ to neoteric retail stores, e.g., computer games or diversion, creates extensive peril as far as dossier mystery. In this exceptional condition, clients' very own insights, for instance, thoughts, emotions, sexual direction, or strict feelings, are under encroachments if surveillance measures are not embraced. In addition, contemporary BICJ approaches, for instance, the usage of silicon-based Junction, present neoteric surveillance confusion in view of the expansion in the volume of obtained dossier and the use of possibly impuissant development (Zhou, 2020). The automation insurgency of neoteric ages, gotten together with improvement, for instance, the Hyperspace of Things (HoT), acquires speeding up the production of neoteric gadgets lacking surveillance principles and courses of action subject to the thoughts of surveillance - by-plan and seclusion-by-plan (Zhou, 2020). This transformation also brings to reality forthcoming and troublesome situations, where we highlight as models the immediate hand-off between brains, known as Brain-by-Brain (BbB) or Brain-network, and brains related with the Hyperspace (Brain-to-Hyperspace (BtH)), which will require basic endeavors from the surveillance crystal. The current forms simply consider the sign getting measure, missing the impelling of neurons. These plans present divergent requests of the BICJ progression, as some don't think about the age of brain signals as a phase, or bunch assorted phases in only one, without giving measurements about their jobs (Valluripally,2019). Divergent plans, as recommended in (Ali, 2020), are puzzling a direct result of the portray as neoteric phases, changes, and dossier exchanged between disparate phases. Regarding utilizes, a couple of creators portray a nonexclusive phase of employments (Lalar, 2020) while others deal with orders sent off outer gadgets (Senol, 2020). Also, a few works describe the info sent by utility to clients (Zhou,2020). To homogenize the BICJ progression and address the already missing or perplexing centers, we present another variant of the BICJ progression with five phases (with plainly portrayed tasks, insights sources, and yields) that think about both obtainment and induction limits.

Figure 2. IoT based Brain Peripheral design

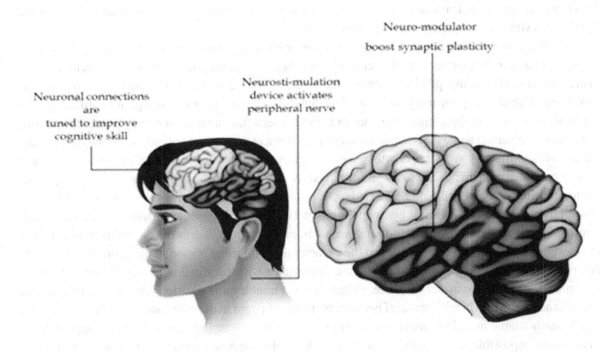

Figure 3. Brain Neurological Network

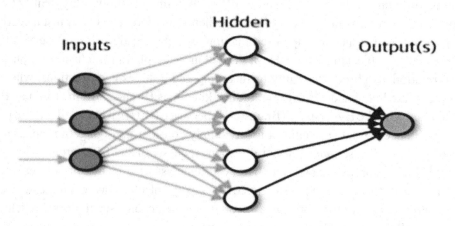

RESEARCH METHODOLOGY

The most well-known kind of brain embeds is the deep brain incitement (DBI) system. It comprises of embedded electrodes positioned deep inside the brain (Zhou, 2020) associated with wires running under the skin, which carry signals from an embedded stimulator. The stimulator comprises of a battery, a little processor, and a wireless relay radio wire that allows doctors to program functions a lot of like a cardiac pacemaker, with the principle qualification being that it directly Junction with the brain. DBI is a phenomenal instrument for treating a wide range of dysfunction. It is most widely used to treat Parkinson's sickness, frequently with dramatic results.

Targeting divergent brain regions with divergent incitement parameters (Zhou, 2020) gives neurosurgeons increasingly precise control over the human brain (Kakkar, 2020), allowing them to mitigate distressing side effects. this precise control of the brain, combined with the wireless control of stimulators, likewise opens an opportunity for benevolent ambush to go past the more straightforward harms that could accompany controlling insulin siphons or cardiac inserts, into a realm of deeply troubling ambush. Examples of potential ambush incorporate altering incitement settings so patients with chronic torment are caused significantly greater agony than they would experience without incitement. Or a Parkinson's patient could have their capacity to move restrained. A refined ambush might actually even initiate behavioral changes, for example, hyper-sexuality or obsessive betting, or even exert a restricted form of control over the patient's behavior by invigorating parts of the brain associated with reward learning to reinforce certain activities. Albeit these hacks would be hard to accomplish as they would require a significant level of mechanization capability and the capacity to monitor the person in question, an adequately determined ambush could manage it. There are suggested answers for making inserts more resistant to cybernated -ambush, yet makers of these gadgets are in a troublesome position when trying to actualize surveillance features. There's a tradeoff between planning a system with perfect surveillance and a system that is really usable in reality. Inserts are intensely constrained by actual size and battery limit, making many plans impossible. These gadgets should be effectively available to medical staff in an emergency, implying that some form of "secondary passage" control is just about a need. Neoteric and energizing features, for example, having the option to control inserts utilizing a Smartphone (Souri, 2018) or over the hyperspace, must be adjusted against the increased peril that such features can provide. Brain inserts are getting more typical. As they get approved for treating more illnesses, become cheaper, and get more features, increasing numbers of patients will be embedded with them. This is something to be thankful for overall at the same time, similarly as a more intricate and interconnected hyperspace resulted in greater cybernated - surveillance peril, more advanced and ubiquitous brain inserts will present enticing targets to criminals. Consider how a terrorist could manage admittance to a government official's brain or how coercive shakedown would be on the off chance that someone could alter how you act and think. These are scenarios that are probably not going to remain purely in the realm of sci-fi for any longer.

Neuro -Cyber Threat Issues

The problems of innovation abuse and surveillance of natural statistics are particularly critical with regards to neuro-technology as this kind of innovation applies (either directly or indirectly) to very salient body communicative organs. The brain not just contributes fundamentally to life-looking after processes, (for example, nutrition and respiration) yet additionally to resources, and our self-ID as conscious creatures or persons. Therefore, misusing neurological gadgets for cybernated criminal purposes may not just infringement the actual surveillance of the users yet in addition impact their behavior and alter their self-recognizable proof as persons. Cybernated criminal exercises enabled by the abuse of neurological gadgets neuro-malfeasance. It is worth noticing that neuro-malfeasance doesn't necessarily include direct admittance to the brain and to brain statistics. Rather, neuro-offender exercises are destined to occur, at present, in a manner that influences the brain just indirectly, for instance by restricting, adjusting or disrupting function in the gadgets that Junction brain calculation. This sort of peril is already critical at the current degree (Lalar, 2020) of sending of neurological designs. Neurological supervised robotic appendages used to make up for the mechanism deficiencies of excised patients are possibly impuissant to being precisely destroyed by benevolent actors, which would deprive the users of their reacquired mechanism capacities. The below figure 4 outlines about the IoT-Brain tiered Architecture.

Dark Web Illicit Intruders

There are three essential tier of the Hyperspace -Surface web, Deep web, and DW. First, there is the "Surface Web", which refers to anything that typical search engines like Facebook, Google and Yahoo can find. Secondly, Deep Web is that tier which generally provides access to academic, proprietary details, web-forums requiring registrations. Basically, these are the web pages that cannot be accessed directly through the typical search engines. This can be ingressed only through specialized coherence such as the Tor webnet. A webnet like Tor can be downloaded by anyone and it lets its users browse the web anonymously. This webnet was developed to protect online relay among military and governmental agencies in the US and to facilitate open-source cyber espionage gathering. Hidden webnet such as Tor let users exchange messages while maintaining their anonymity through a process known as "onion routing". Analogous to the tier of an onion, DW hides identities by wrapping tier around people's relay, making them untraceable. With the advent of the case of Silk Road (Nazah, 2020), DW became a major perpetrator of cybernated crimes, thus negatively impacting cybernated surveillance (Martin, 2020). It is an illegal pharmacy sold in trade for crypto currency for unauthorized and dangerous products. The largest dark emporium in DW, launched by a Canadian, was shut down by the United States Authorities. For illicit medicines and unlicensed pharmaceuticals, the Silk Road was a popular emporium. Black depth is a place in the DW of trafficking in human beings. Many websites, such as TOR, which encourage seclusion, are valuable tools for whistleblowers, advocates and surveillance agencies. Dark Webnet is also a forum for intruder to leak genre statistics. Since 2011, crypto emporiums, anonymous hyperspace exchanges where illegal drugs are traded, have been working, but there is a shortage of awareness to track illicit sites to trade drugs analysis including appraisal category. We examine the various explanations for crypto emporium purchases by oriented analyses of this difficult-to-approach category and parameters analysis framed from the point of view of crime seduction, economic estimation, and drift and neutralization strategies (Ali, 2020). The creation of the Darknet (DN) as a parallel webnet in the 21st century allowed the illicit trade in small arms as established by the United Nations. The investigators used investigative techniques to observe six gun sales locations in the DN over a six-month span to locate firearm vendors, the nature and scale of guns for sale, the manufacturer, the price in Bitcoin, and the key national origins of the firearms. This is the first research of its kind to investigate the illicit selling of weapons on the DN. This evidence can be used by enforcement agencies to capture and close down those pages and provide insight into the essence of the illicit weapons trade in the DW (Lalar, 2020).

Figure 4. IoT-Brain tiered Architecture

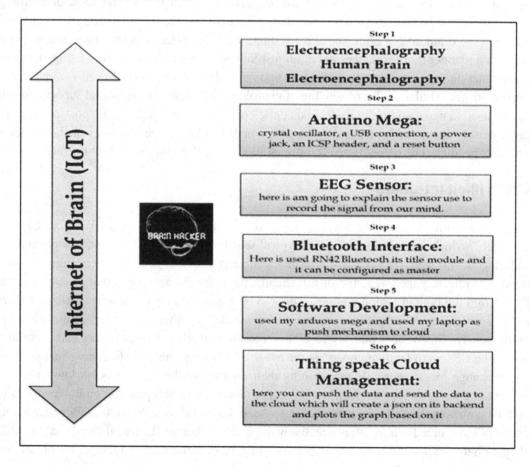

Techniques and Algorithm Used b+y Infringement Wireless Sensor

Sensing chips in WSW are resource-restricted resources, whereas existing dossier processing strategies have complex protection measures that influence webnet existence with large processing and response times (Safaldin, 2020). WSW consist a spatially dispersed reduced small-scale sensor process with a wireless-Signal-transceiver to detect diverse physical events and to capture dossier under all types of conditions. As opposed to other wired and WSW should be tailored to the extreme sphere. The Deep advanced Learning-based Surveillance approaches adversary design on a cluster-based analogous webnet analyzed. Acting together in the WSW, the clump of comparable small sensor junction with an equal energy level gathers statistics from divergent sensing areas. To forward the dossier received, each sensor junction has a wireless coherence. The sensor junction changes its characteristics to be dynamic and self-governing, such as the duty succession and cluster head WSW are highly impuissant to flooding infringements during the implementation of WSW in the hostile sphere where the sensing chip junction are physically collected and exploited (Roundy, 2010),The hybrid algorithm uses sophisticated encryption methods and hash functions for cryptographic requirements. The message is broken into three parts in this algorithm and Dual encryptions are applied in parallel with the sub-message. Based on criteria such as execution time, encryption, and decryption this suggested algorithm is analyzed. The result reveals that the suggested encryption binaries perform well in terms of encryption and decryption time (Souri, 2018). Diverse functions, accuracy, processing time, false signaled alarming values and detection analyzed rate, the suggested methods are tested. The results showed that the other comparative algorithms suggested by the seven wolves of the suggested GWOSVM-IDS dominate (Wagner, 2017).

THEORETICAL FRAMEWORK

Dossier produced by your hyperspace program, by your geological region, by balancing on the web structures or by creating on your console can uncover private insights, for instance, your sexual direction or your political conviction framework. Imagine what insights may be assembled with permission to your thoughts. The progression of Brain-Intelligent Chip Junction constrains us to think about this issue, as these gadgets are prepared for partner computers straightforwardly to the brain. Science and neurotechnology haven't beaten sufficiently a lot to engage mind-perusing, yet as of now there are customer grade gadgets which can enroll delicate neurological signs. Electro-encephalography (EEG) (Zhou, 2020) headsets, for instance, are used in emporium discourses to separate emotions and careless responses to specific items or events. This mental dossier can be prepared to uncover basic insights about an individual.

Neurotechnology surveillance issues aren't neoteric: there could be cases of provocation, coordinated malfeasance or individual dossier traffic, much equivalent to those previously happening in other computerized areas. In any case, what's going on is the idea of neurological dossier. As these are created straightforwardly in the brain, they can encode sensitive clinical measurements and clues concerning our character and the private instruments controlling our own choices. To exhibit the real factors inquisitor have attempted to hack monetarily accessible neurotech. They will probably extricate measurements which may be useful to cybernated crooks (Zamojski, 2019), thusly highlighting potential surveillance imperfections. Clusters of inquisitor and technologists have exhibited that it's possible to plant spyware in a Brain-Intelligent Chip Junction — unequivocally, one proposed to control computer games with the mind—that engages them to take insights from the client. By embeddings subliminal pictures in the videogame, saltines were prepared to test the player's careless mental response to unequivocal lifts, for instance, postal locations, bank nuances or human faces. They were prepared to accumulate measurements including a Visa's PIN number and a place of home. Master has attempted several gadgets himself and hacked a brand-name EEG headset and figured out how to block the neurological dossier sent by the gadget to combined inserted models. If you can handle these signs, you can get insights with respect to disease, scholarly limits or even a client's inclinations and inclinations, In the most dire outcome imaginable, a bidirectional Junction — that is, one that peruses brain signals just as exudes them, for example as nerve beats (to a prosthetic arm, to a wheelchair or to the sensory system itself)— may be hacked to genuinely hurt the client or someone else, To forestall a potential homicide attempt by hijacking of the gadget .

Attacks on Various Network Tier

Limited memory and less computational limit of remote sensing chips webnet make them powerless of refusal of administration illicit espionage. Remote sensing chips hubs are conveyed and dispersed at divergent spots for divergent applications and there are inherent outcomes of actual harm or annihilation of hubs by assailants. Hub catching may result into modification of equipment and programming of WSW hub (Schmeelk,2015). Assailants or gatecrashers can abuse the restricted webnet assets and make them inaccessible for genuine clients. It changes the routing dossier of webnet and influences the correspondence antagonistically. A can be utilized to distinguish confusion illicit espionage. Specific sending is a webnet tier illicit espionage. In this sort of illicit espionage, a fake hub acts like a real hub and redirect the bundles to an off-base way yet specifically drops a portion of the bundles so it gets troublesome to distinguish the interruption. Affirmation based routing, multi statistics stream and location dependent on neighboring dossier can be utilized to distinguish this sort of interruption. Sink opening illicit espionage is statistics connect tier illicit espionage. In this illicit espionage (Nazah, 2020), an interloper accompanies a concurrence with a sensing chips hub or presents a phony hub in the sensing chips webnet. At the point when a produced hub draws in the webnet traffic, an illicit espionage is produced. When the illicit espionage is effective, the produced hub can perform divergent glitches like dropping all bundles, dropping particular parcels and adjustment of statistics. In Sybil illicit espionage, a malignant sensing chips hub takes divergent personalities to play out an illicit espionage. In remote sensing chips webnet, all the sensing chips hubs work obligingly yet this sort of illicit espionage focuses on this collaboration and upset the routing and correspondence measure. Wormhole illicit espionage is an statistics interface tier interruption. In this kind of illicit espionage, a malevolent or phony hub enlists the entire dossier and redirects it to wrong way. This illicit espionage can be framed without the statistics on cryptography of real remote sensing chips hub. In remote sensing chips webnet, routing conventions use Hello parcels for location of neighbors. In this kind of illicit espionage, counterfeit (Birajdar, 2013) bundles are utilized to cover hi parcels and to pull in the sensing chips hubs. Assailants with adequate radio assets and preparing capacities can produce this sort of illicit espionage.

Design Flaws Techniques of Cybernated Criminals for MPD Designing

Infringement of Malevolent-Process-Design (MPD) requires thorough forensic investigative practices are the techniques of evaluation-resistance used by designers of MPD. Dossier unpacking, code overwriting (Botta, 2016), and power shift obfuscation are the most common of these techniques. The aim of our study is to simplify the MPD analysis by returning to the traditional prototype of analysis-then-execute, which has the benefit of having the illegitimate code under the inquisitor's control before it is implemented. Through associating dynamic and the static approaches to establishes and maintains for control the dossier -flow processing that shape the coherence from which the observer recognizes and applies the code, we approach these goals. The ability to upgrade these evaluate to include dynamically operate and revised code before it runs is a key value of our methodology. (Camara, 2015) Neoteric, the most widely used filtering programming strategy that emphasizes the same relation is impression-based recognition. Identification of MPD focused mainly on performing static investigations to review the code-structure mark of malevolent codes rather than the behavioral approaches of the feature. Using a predefined set of known infringements, the impression-based approach finds interruptions. Although in a modular program, this structure has the ability to recognize MPD, a steady revision of the predefined impression database is needed. In addition, due to the continually changing presence of portable MPD, it is less efficient in identifying malicious activity using a impression-based approach. In order to arrange a risky letter, impression-based strategies rely on exceptional rudimentary byte examples or standard articulations, known as signs. For starters, a record's static highlights are used to decide if it is an MPD. The main usefulness of impression-based methods is their thoroughness, since they follow all possible protocols for executing the document (Chakladar, 2019). Through static or dynamic analysis, malicious behavior in software is described. In the one hand, the binary index is dissected by function while a possible malicious MPD fragment is statically evaluated. In the other hand, dynamic analysis directly observes the study's behavior: the so-called MPD sample is carried out within an independent, frequently virtualized laboratory setup and is used by selected statistics providers to create a system report (i.e. trace) and the sample sequentially invokes the API calls. The method of extracting behavior patterns is generally split into diverse phases and can be based on multiple service providers. The API call traces using Malheur, the cluster structure traces each cluster, and searches for patterns with the Sequitur compression algorithm, resulting in a grammar that is context-free. The trends found by collaborating domain experts are called 'rules' since the rules are part of a context-free grammar (Jang-Jaccard, 2014). The MPD sample used is an executable file format that is not human-readable when doing MPD study. As a consequence, the file is decrypted using many methods such that knowledge can be retrieved from MPD. Analysis has two primary methods, namely static analysis and dynamic analysis; both techniques are therefore basic or advanced in nature (Jang-Jaccard, 2014). Some neoteric experiments have examined methods to significantly speed up the recognition approach of MPD. Visual analytics falls into Big Dossier sphere where complex facts involve the analysis of details that combines automation with human experts' analytical reasoning. Affinity mining is a machine learning technique in visual analytics that relies on an understanding of the correlations in distance measurements that have neoteric been used to define MPD. In this study, we give the view of the matrix of affinity between divergent programs of MPD that are commonly used for infringement. In addition, to demonstrate a large variance in behavior patterns, we use the imagine approach to compare MPD dossier sets (Valluripally,2019). The Figure 5 below show about the Cryptographic algorithms designed for entrusting the web-models and to create shield for surveillance purposes.

Figure 5. Cryptographic algorithms used for surveillance purposes

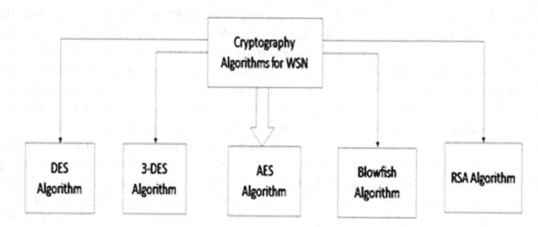

Loop Holes of Diversified Webnet

Consumers of digital gadget and chip-enabled-net phones are building a secured network classified society and demand a secure, quantified mobile broadband user experience everywhere and at any time. In the next generation of mobile web networks, meeting these criteria is a critical obstacle we must face (Valluripally,2019) (. The aim of statistics fusion is to reduce or exclude redundant, converge and other processes so that the statistics collected from multiple sensing chip junctions is concise and reliable (Zamojski,2019). In WSW, the most salient subject is the durability of the webnet, which is defined by the webnet explicitly or implicitly. In this post, for WSW, diversified webnet prototype is suggested to extend the web net's life and their corresponding cluster heads by applying a weighted positioned probability and calculated threshold function to the decision (Zamojski, 2019).

There are diverse paradoxes currently confronting decision makers in the world of cybernated defense. Choosing one direction may be at the cost of another direction, though there are reasons for heading both directions. Cybernated surveillance strategies and decision-making take place within dynamic sphere in which audiences from a diverse community, the policy sector (Schmeelk, 2015) and the government must engage. Responsibilities are scattered through many governmental authorities at the national and local level, with varied complication and complication, making it impossible to undertake concerted action. Society is made up of diverse actors who may want surveillance but have varying perceptions about the role of government in maintaining surveillance and surveillance in cybernated space. Governments may play minor or main roles in cybernated surveillance Politics must adapt to social demands establish policy and distribute money, whereas public agencies must fulfill the priorities set. This can sound like a straightforward partnership, but the reality is far more complicated and nuanced, as the functions of stakeholders are frequently (Lalar, 2020) contradictory and paradoxical. One such contradiction is that policymakers want to protect cybernated surveillance, but at the same time they want access to dossier from people and organizations for monitoring purposes. The entire debate of 'backdoor' access to dossier shows the paradox that policymakers have faced. Governments, on the one hand, want businesses and people to defend them, but on the other hand, they do not want to use encryption and other cybernated surveillance methods, which might allow intruder and criminals to conceal their traces (Birajdar, 2013). Governments are attempting to do an immense amount of work in the fields of cybernated (defense, web-warfare and cyber-deterrence), to determine the situation within the context of technical advances, to take steps by recognizing risks and complication, to set goals in accordance with their needs by making inherent forecasts, to establish plans and policies, and to enforce them effectively. With the rise in the usage of Digital processes and the universal use of the Hyperspace, which is an increasing webnet and statistics relay (Valluripally,2019) webnet all over the world, substantial change has been made relative to the past in the work done to avoid and eradicate the dangers, complication, hazards, etc that are taking place in tandem with changes in the world. In this sense, in addition to increasing productivity by removing shortcomings and inadequacies relevant to cybernated defense techniques and policies against cybernetic infringement and accidents, It is felt that it will be fitting to discuss the problem of cybernetic deterrence, which is a neoteric hot topic of discussion and research, with a systemic approach coupled with cybernetic surveillance techniques and policies (Safaldin, 2020). Snort, widely distributed worldwide, is one of the most popular IDS/IPS applications (Mirea, 2019). Since it is an open-source project, its users can freely customize it and feed rules to the Snort engine from various sources (e.g. not only form Snort homepage). Experts usually provide a cybernetic community with the impressions (in the form of receptive rules) of an attack on applications such as Snort. It is generally fairly easy to determine patterns for deterministic infringement that can reliably discern individual infringement. It also happens when malicious software (e.g. worm) is supplied to communicate with the command and control center or other instance of such software via the trough webnet using the same method and algorithm (Valluripally,2019).The below diagram 6 outlines the variant of cybernated-frauds and web enabled crime use by hidden tiered internet invaders.

SOLUTIONS AND RECOMMENDATIONS

A programmer could plant spyware in a Brain-Intelligent Chip Junction that engages them to take insights from the client to suggest automation measures, for instance, block chain and unified learning, to dodge the preparing of neurological signs in brought together data sets. Thusly, a disparate cluster of inquisitors from the University of Washington has recommended that neuro-motorization gadgets play out an in-situ division of brain wave integrants prior to sending them. Accordingly, a Brain-Intelligent Chip Junction (Zhou,2020) can limit the insights handed-off to its control gadget and simply send measurements that is pertinent to the work waiting be finished. For instance, an EEG detecting gadget planned to control a wheelchair would simply send the integrant of brain waves which encodes measurements relating to enhancement reason, holding other integrants similar to, state, energetic sensations. By confining the capacity and transmission of crude neurological dossier, openings for hoodlums to seize supportive insights are limited as well.

Divergent research are investigating to relate the human brain (Zhou,2020) to a computer Junction, has applied to begin testing its gadget on people. The framework has been taken a stab at a monkey that had the alternative to control a computer with its brain and focused in on patients with extreme neurological conditions with envisions an eventual fate of superhuman discernment.

The gadget the firm has made involves a little test containing more than 3,000 electrodes (Ali, 2020) affixed to versatile strings - more slender than a human hair - which would then have the option to screen the activity of 1,000 neurons. The upside of this framework, as indicated by the firm, is that it is prepared to target exceptionally express territories of the brain, which would make it carefully more secure. It would in like manner have the alternative to explore chronicles using AI, which would then work out what kind of prompting to give a patient.

The brain to a Junction would make another level of stunning scholarly (Lalar, 2020) in the human brain as people as of now have through their telephones. The advancing researches are also coordinated and have been taken a stab at monkeys, with the animal prepared to control a computer with its brain. The plans will require numerous ages of work to oversee particular and good challenges, yet the development could be a major development in attempting to moderate certain genuine ailments like epilepsy and Parkinson's."

Figure 6. Types of frauds analogous to cybernated crime

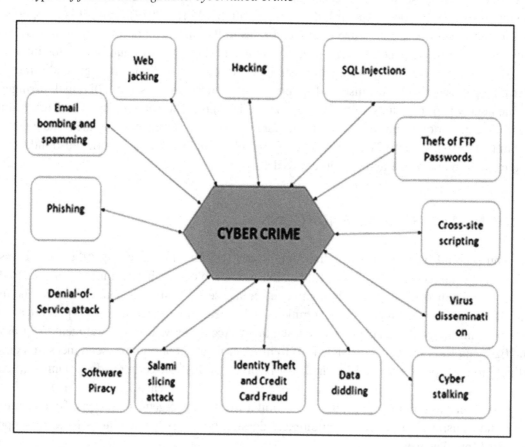

FUTURE RESEARCH DIRECTIONS

In this Chapter we address the effect of MPD on the webnet of wireless sensing gadget. The approaches for discovery is compared and evaluated by diverse main criteria, such as genre methods, dossier analytics methods, number of the uses, precision element, and case analysis. In discovery techniques, the benefit and drawback of each process is discussed. In dossier processing, the bulk of the selected objects are behavioral strategies Any selection criteria such as core definition, usefulness and drawbacks, type of algorithm and type of dossier mining methodology evaluate discovery approaches. The selected findings are reviewed and addressed according to current approaches. In the DW, cybernetic criminals are constantly aware of the approaches used to track them. This carries with it higher complication. International boundaries remain one of the most daunting complications for Surveillance enforcement and cyber espionage forces. The scale of the hidden web demands more productive methods to mitigate the risks faced by the DW. In order to identify offenders with sophisticated methods, the black emporium place and purchases there must be traced. The Dark Webnet framework, unhindered, fractured and multitiered, makes the identification of criminals more demanding.

CONCLUSION

This chapter performs a worldwide and comprehensive analysis of the literature of BICJ in terms of surveillance and wellbeing. Chiefly, we have assessed the ambush, effects and countermeasures that BICJ arrangements suffer from the software's Architectonic plan and execution perspectives. At first, we suggested a brought together version of the BICJ succession to incorporate neurological dossier procurement and incitement processes. Once having a homogeneous BICJ succession plan. The work ventured out addressing the issue of BH and raising awareness on the moral and surveillance suggestions analogous with the benevolent utilization of BICJ innovation. An overview of the conceivable vulnerability sources of BICJ and their analogous sorts of BH was offered. Additionally, an inventory of the major moral ramifications of BH through BICJ was provided. Further interdisciplinary examination is required to broadly dissect those ramifications and to build up a normative and regulatory framework that allows amplifying the advantages of BICJ innovation while limiting its possible peril. BICJ utility have the capability of fundamentally improving life grade in patients (particularly in patients suffering severe neuromuscular dysfunction) and empowering upgraded and more personalized user experience in relay, gaming and entertainment for general users. The possible advantages of this innovation might be tempered if surveillance issues and moral lawful considerations remain unaddressed. The Discussion ought to include the collaboration of ethicists, neuroscientists, engineers, computer inquisitor, CS experts, and lawyers. At long last, we provide our vision regarding BICJ trends and portray that the current amelioration of BICJ towards interconnected gadgets is generating tremendous surveillance concerns and difficulties, which will increase in the near future.

REFERENCES

Agrawal, M., Singh, H., Gour, N., & Kumar, M. A. (2014). Evaluation on malware analysis. *International Journal of Computer Science and Information Technologies*, 5(3), 3381–3383.

Ali, S., Humaria, A., Ramzan, M. S., Khan, I., Saqlain, S. M., Ghani, A., & Alzahrani, B. A. (2020). An efficient cryptographic technique using modified Diffie–Hellman in wireless sensor networks. *International Journal of Distributed Sensor Networks*, 16(6), 1550147720925772. doi:10.1177/1550147720925772

Birajdar, G. K., & Mankar, V. H. (2013). Digital image forgery detection using passive techniques: A survey. *Digital Investigation*, 10(3), 226–245. doi:10.1016/j.diin.2013.04.007

Botta, A., De Donato, W., Persico, V., & Pescapé, A. (2016). Integration of cloud computing and internet of things: A survey. *Future Generation Computer Systems*, *56*, 684–700. doi:10.1016/j.future.2015.09.021

Camara, C., Peris-Lopez, P., & Tapiador, J. E. (2015). Security and privacy issues in implantable medical devices: A comprehensive survey. *Journal of Biomedical Informatics*, *55*, 272–289. doi:10.1016/j.jbi.2015.04.007 PMID:25917056

Cao, L., Cai, Y., & Yue, Y. (2020). Data Fusion Algorithm for Heterogeneous Wireless Sensor Networks Based on Extreme Learning Machine Optimized by Particle Swarm Optimization. *Journal of Sensors*, *2020*, 2020. doi:10.1155/2020/2549324

Chakladar, D. D., & Chakraborty, S. (2019). Feature extraction and classification in brain-computer interfacing: Future research issues and challenges. In *Natural Computing for Unsupervised Learning* (pp. 101–131). Springer. doi:10.1007/978-3-319-98566-4_5

De Bruijn, H., & Janssen, M. (2017). Building cybersecurity awareness: The need for evidence-based framing strategies. *Government Information Quarterly*, *34*(1), 1–7. doi:10.1016/j.giq.2017.02.007

Jang-Jaccard, J., & Nepal, S. (2014). A survey of emerging threats in cybersecurity. *Journal of Computer and System Sciences*, *80*(5), 973–993. doi:10.1016/j.jcss.2014.02.005

Kadoguchi, M., Kobayashi, H., Hayashi, S., Otsuka, A., & Hashimoto, M. (2020, November). Deep Self-Supervised Clustering of the Dark Web for Cyber Threat Intelligence. In *2020 IEEE International Conference on Intelligence and Security Informatics (ISI)* (pp. 1-6). IEEE.

Kakkar, A. (2020). A survey on secure communication techniques for 5G wireless heterogeneous networks. *Information Fusion*, *62*, 89–109. doi:10.1016/j.inffus.2020.04.009

Kaur, S., & Randhawa, S. (2020). Dark Web: A Web of Crimes. *Wireless Personal Communications*, *112*(4), 2131–2158. doi:10.100711277-020-07143-2

LalarS.BhushanS.SurenderM. (2020). Hybrid Encryption Algorithm to Detect Clone Node Attack in Wireless Sensor Network. *Available at* SSRN 3565864. doi:10.2139srn.3565864

Malhotra, P., Singh, Y., Anand, P., Bangotra, D. K., Singh, P. K., & Hong, W. C. (2021). Internet of Things: Evolution, Concerns and Security Challenges. *Sensors (Basel)*, *21*(5), 1809. doi:10.339021051809 PMID:33807724

Martin, J., Munksgaard, R., Coomber, R., Demant, J., & Barratt, M. J. (2020). Selling drugs on dark-web cryptomarkets: Differentiated pathways, risks and rewards. *British Journal of Criminology*, *60*(3), 559–578. doi:10.1093/bjc/azz075

Mirea, M., Wang, V., & Jung, J. (2019). The not so dark side of the darknet: A qualitative study. *Security Journal*, *32*(2), 102–118. doi:10.105741284-018-0150-5

Nazah, S., Huda, S., Abawajy, J., & Hassan, M. M. (2020). Evolution of Dark Web Threat Analysis and Detection: A Systematic Approach. *IEEE Access: Practical Innovations, Open Solutions*, *8*, 171796–171819. doi:10.1109/ACCESS.2020.3024198

Roddy, A. L., & Holt, T. J. (2020). An Assessment of Hitmen and Contracted Violence Providers Operating Online. *Deviant Behavior*, 1–13. doi:10.1080/01639625.2020.1787763

Roundy, K. A., & Miller, B. P. (2010, September). Hybrid analysis and control of malware. In *International Workshop on Recent Advances in Intrusion Detection* (pp. 317-338). Springer. 10.1007/978-3-642-15512-3_17

Safaldin, M., Otair, M., & Abualigah, L. (2020). Improved binary gray wolf optimizer and SVM for intrusion detection system in wireless sensor networks. *Journal of Ambient Intelligence and Humanized Computing*, 1–18. doi:10.100712652-020-02228-z

Schmeelk, S., Yang, J., & Aho, A. (2015, April). Android malware static analysis techniques. In *Proceedings of the 10th annual cyber and information security research conference* (pp. 1-8). Academic Press.

Senol, M., & Karacuha, E. (2020). Creating and Implementing an Effective and Deterrent National Cyber Security Strategy. *Journal of Engineering (Stevenage, England)*.

Souri, A., & Hosseini, R. (2018). A state-of-the-art survey of malware detection approaches using data mining techniques. *Human-centric Computing and Information Sciences*, 8(1), 1–22. doi:10.118613673-018-0125-x

Valluripally, S., Sukheja, D., Ohri, K., & Singh, S. K. (2019, May). IoT Based Smart Luggage Monitor Alarm System. In *International Conference on Internet of Things and Connected Technologies* (pp. 294-302). Springer.

Villalva, D. A. B., Onaolapo, J., Stringhini, G., & Musolesi, M. (2018). Under and over the surface: A comparison of the use of leaked account credentials in the Dark and Surface Web. *Crime Science*, 7(1), 1–11. PMID:31984202

Wagner, M., Rind, A., Thür, N., & Aigner, W. (2017). A knowledge-assisted visual malware analysis system: Design, validation, and reflection of KAMAS. *Computers & Security*, 67, 1–15. doi:10.1016/j.cose.2017.02.003

W. Zamojski, J. Mazurkiewicz, J. Sugier, T. Walkowiak, & J. Kacprzyk (Eds.). (2019). Engineering in Dependability of Computer Systems and Networks: *Proceedings of the Fourteenth International Conference on Dependability of Computer Systems DepCoS-RELCOMEX*, July 1–5, 2019, Brunów, Poland (Vol. 987). Springer.

Zhou, Z., Chen, X., Zhang, Y., & Mumtaz, S. (2020). Blockchain-empowered secure spectrum sharing for 5G heterogeneous networks. *IEEE Network*, 34(1), 24–31. doi:10.1109/MNET.001.1900188

Chapter 13
Evolution of Malware in the Digital Transformation Age

Shahid Alam
ⓘ https://orcid.org/0000-0002-4080-8042
Adana Alparsalan Turkes Science and Technology University, Turkey

ABSTRACT

As corporations are stepping into the new digital transformation age and adopting leading-edge technologies such as cloud, mobile, and big data, it becomes crucial for them to contemplate the risks and rewards of this adoption. At the same time, the new wave of malware attacks is posing a severe impediment in implementing these technologies. This chapter discusses some of the complications, challenges, and issues plaguing current malware analysis and detection techniques. Some of the key challenges discussed are automation, native code, obfuscations, morphing, and anti-reverse engineering. Solutions and recommendations are provided to solve some of these challenges. To stimulate further research in this thriving area, the authors highlight some promising future research directions. The authors believe that this chapter provides an auspicious basis for future researchers who intend to know more about the evolution of malware and will act as a motivation for enhancing the current and developing the new techniques for malware analysis and detection.

INTRODUCTION

As we are advancing into the new digital transformation age, most of the enterprises have been adapting to this new pace of technology by adopting leading-edge technologies like cloud, mobile, big data, and the Internet of things. At the same time, organizations are facing a new wave of security attacks, which are posing a severe impediment in implementing these technologies. WannaCry ransomware attack in 2017 affected many leading organizations around the globe. The ransomware was a CryptoWorm (used cryptography to design the malicious software) (Zouave et al., 2020) and targeted Microsoft Windows operating system by encrypting the data and demanding ransom payments in the CryptoCurrency (Narayanan et al., 2016). Within a day the ransomware infected more than 230,000 computers in over 150 countries. Stuxnet, malware (malicious software), was used to cause substantial damage to supervisory

DOI: 10.4018/978-1-7998-6975-7.ch013

control and data acquisition systems. Targeting industrial control systems, the malware infected over 200,000 computers. Shamoon, another similar malware, was used for cyber warfare against some of the national oil companies in the middle east. Recently, Twitter got hacked where hackers were able to steal US high profile accounts, and Magellan Health, a Fortune 500 company, faced a sophisticated ransomware attack that affected thousands of patients. Cyberattacks are on the rise and pose a serious threat to a company's financial and other resources. A chronological timeline of such and other high-profile cybersecurity attacks on different companies is shown in Figure 1. As we can see from Figure 1 the number of breaches (break into an account to steal information, including passwords, banking, etc.) of user accounts of a company range from 134 million accounts in the year 2008 – 538 million accounts in the year 2020. The average cost of a malware attack on a company is 2.4 million USD. These attacks highlight the vulnerabilities of the current cyberinfrastructure. They also emphasize the importance of the integration of cybersecurity as part of the new scenario for digital transformation.

Figure 1. A chronological timeline of high-profile cybersecurity attacks from 2008 to 2020 with affected accounts in millions

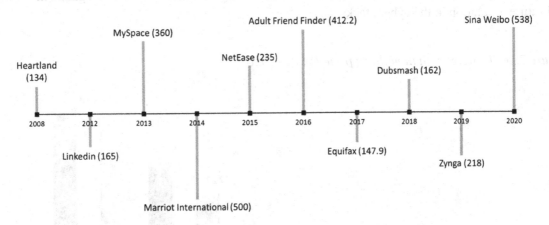

Most of the cyberattacks are executed by installing malware that carries out different malicious activities. According to a recent report by AV-TEST, an independent IT security institute, the total number of new malicious programs are on the rise. The malware growth reported by AV-TEST is shown in Figure 2. As we can see from Figure 2, the number of malware programs grew from 65.26 million in the year 2011 – 1101.88 million in the year 2020. This shows a significant growth (almost 16 times) in the number of malware programs in these ten years. The numbers can be explained by the fact, that initially, malware writers were hobbyists but now the professionals have become part of this group because of the incentives attached to it, such as financial gains, intelligence gathering, and cyber warfare, etc. Moreover, the malware writers are adopting reusable software development methodologies, and also using obfuscation (Linn & Debray, 2003) to create new malware that is a copy (variant) of the original malware. Malware has also grown in sophistication, from a simple file infection virus to programs that can propagate through networks, can change their shape and structure (polymorphic and metamorphic malware) with a variety of complex modules to execute malicious activities. Malware writers have also adapted to new platforms, such as smartphones and IoTs, etc. The research in the defense and analysis techniques by academia and industry goes side by side with this growth of malware attacks. Several techniques and methods have been developed to mitigate the effects of these attacks. The main goal is to know the structure and behavior of malware, by using static, dynamic, or hybrid analysis techniques. If it is found that the program is a variant of previous malware, or its behavior is suspicious then appropriate actions are taken to take care of the malware program. These actions can be quarantining, repairing, or deleting the malware program, and isolating the effected computers and networks, etc. This has become a race between malware and antimalware techniques and approaches. The techniques and approaches in both these areas are evolving at their own pace.

In this chapter, after a basic introduction to malware, we discuss the evolution of malware in the new digital transformation age, and the developments of some of the antimalware techniques to neutralize or mitigate their effects. We also discuss how and what techniques malware writers are using to hide (obfuscate) their malicious code. Some new types, such as polymorphic and metamorphic malware, and some of the key and advanced techniques for detecting such and other malware are discussed. The main goal of the chapter is to give the reader a basic and some advanced perspective about the evolution of malware and antimalware techniques in the new digital transformation age. This will give the reader an understanding and equip him/her with motivation, knowledge, and tools to defend against the current and future escalation in the cyberattacks.

Figure 2. Malware growth in millions from 2011 to 2020

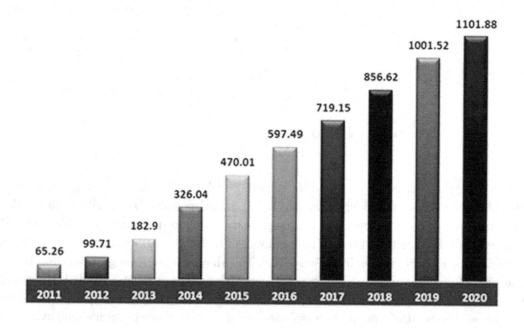

BACKGROUND

Malware

One of the earliest definitions of malware, also called malicious code, is given by Gary McGraw and Greg Morrisett (McGraw & Morrisett, 2000): *Malicious code, is any code added, changed, or removed from a software system to intentionally cause harm or subvert the intended function of the system.* A malware carries out activities, such as stealing passwords, setting up a back door, etc. Antimalware software detects, neutralizes, and mitigates the effects of malware. There are two basic detection approaches, anomaly-based and signature-based. The first approach uses the knowledge of a normal program to decide if the program under inspection is malicious or not. The second approach uses the characteristics of a malicious program to decide if the program under inspection is malicious or not. To prevent analysis and detection, malware writers are using different techniques to hide the malware, such as compression, encryption, obfuscation, and detection of reverse engineering, etc. Reverse engineering is an amalgamation of different techniques used during malware analysis. For example, to evade detection, if a malware detects reverse engineering will not perform any malicious activity.

Malware Classification

During the digital transformation, malware has also evolved into a complex and reusable piece of software. The following are some of the traditional classifications of malware.

- **Virus**: A computer program that replicates itself by modifying and inserting its own code to other computer programs. After this replication, the areas affected are then infected with a virus.
- **Worm**: A computer program that replicates itself to spread to other computers through networks. The major difference between a virus and a worm is that when a virus starts spreading to other computers, it becomes a worm.
- **Trojan**: It is a virus that misleads the users of its true intent. The name is derived from the ancient Greek story of the deceptive Trojan horse.
- **Spyware**: A malicious software that collects private information about a person or organization and delivers it to another entity for harmful purposes.
- **Ransomware**: A malicious software that threatens to publish or block access to the victim's data unless a ransom is paid.
- **Rootkit**: A computer program that enables access to a computer or its software that is otherwise not accessible and hides or hides the other software. Some advanced malware programs use a rootkit to hide.

Malware Analysis and Detection

There are three main approaches for malware analysis, static analysis, dynamic analysis, and hybrid, i.e., combining both, static and dynamic, in one. **Static analysis** is performed without executing the program, whereas **dynamic analysis** is performed when the program is executing. Both have their advantages and disadvantages. To maximize the benefits both these approaches are combined into one and are called the hybrid approach. Malware forensic is also another static analysis technique that is performed when the program completes executing. The main purpose of forensic is to get details about the damage done by the malware program and to get more insight into the behavior of the program for its future detections.

As mentioned before there are two main approaches for malware detection, signature-based and anomaly-based. Both these detection approaches can employ one of the three different analysis approaches static, dynamic, or hybrid. The difference between these two detection approaches is the way they gather information to detect malware. **Signature-based** detection is performed using pattern matching techniques, looking for a particular signature (pattern) of the malware. Usually, the signatures are stored in a database and then used for comparison in the detection process. These signatures or patterns are usually preconfigured and predetermined by domain experts and need an update whenever new malware or their variants arrive. Another drawback is that such a detection mechanism will not be able to detect new (zero-day – malware whose signatures are not yet in the database) or previously unknown malware. To its advantage, this mechanism uses fewer resources and is faster than other techniques. Most of the antimalware programs use signature-based techniques to detect malware. **Anomaly-based** detection is performed by differentiating between the normal and abnormal behavior of a system/program. A model of normal system/program behavior is built, called profiles, that are then used to detect new behavior that significantly deviates from these profiles. The advantage is that this mechanism may detect zero-day malware attacks. This mechanism needs more resources and can be very time-consuming. One of the limiting factors of this approach is its high percentage of false positives. Like signature-based new behaviors/profiles could be added to enhance detection.

Malware Reverse Engineering

Malware reverse engineering is the process of gaining insight into a malware program to determine its functionality, origin, and potential impact on the system. By knowing these details, security engineers are then able to find and create solutions that can neutralize and mitigate the program's malicious effects. A reverse engineer uses a set of tools to investigate these details. The popular WannaCry malware was reverse engineered to discover the mechanisms (a kill switch in this case) to stop its spread. Some of the basic tools (there are many types but here we only include the main tools) used for reverse engineering a malware program are as follows.

Disassemblers (e.g. IDA Pro) – A disassembler takes apart an executable program and produces its assembly code. Sometimes a decompiler is also used to produce the source code. Through this process, binary instructions are converted into higher-level constructs that are easier to understand by a human. **Debuggers** (e.g. OllyDbg, WinDbg, GDB) – To get more insight into a program reverse engineers to use debuggers to manipulate the execution of a program. Debuggers let the engineer control part of the program while it is running. For example, a portion of the current program's memory can be inspected for finding possible exploits present in the malware. Debuggers also help when dealing with obfuscated code. **Network Analyzers** (e.g. Wireshark, Network Miner) – Network Analyzers help engineers to find how the malware is interacting with other machines on the network, such as what connections are being made and what data is being sent. **Sandboxing** (e.g. Cuckoo Sandbox) – To limit the infection and protect the environment malware programs are run inside a sandbox. Sandbox tools help the reverse engineer to observe the program's behavior and output activity in a proactive layer of security. It also allows dumping the process memory to have a better picture of what is happening in memory. **Patching** (e.g. *x*64Dbg) – Complex and modern-day malware contain defense mechanisms to detect if they are being reverse engineered. In such cases, it becomes impossible to reverse engineer such a malware program. To eliminate these defense mechanisms a reverse engineer uses patching, i.e., modifying the malicious code. The engineer will identify the defense mechanisms in a malware program, remove them, and save the updated malware program as a new executable to be analyzed without the impact of the defense mechanisms.

EVOLUTION OF MALWARE

The *Creeper*, generally considered as the world's first virus, was written in 1971. It was a harmless program that was able to spread (creep) to other computers using local connections. The program would display I'M THE CREEPER: CATCH ME IF YOU CAN. It was written for mainframe computers running the TENEX operating system. The first PC virus was written for MS-DOS in 1986 called *Brain*. This virus did no harm and came complete with the names, addresses, and phone numbers of the authors. The main purpose of this virus was to replace the boot sector of a floppy disk to protect the software from illegal copying. The first ransomware was written in 1989 called *AIDS Trojan*. Before this, the viruses were mostly harmless. This virus would render all the files inaccessible on the computer and demand money to be sent to a specific address to undo the damage. The first social engineering attack was carried out by the virus called *Melissa* in 1999. This attack led to one of the biggest malware attacks of the time carried out by the virus *ILOVEYOU* in the year 2000. It was sent through an email disguised as a love letter. This virus would overwrite files, steal usernames, passwords, IP addresses, and more, and then send itself to everyone on the victim's email contact list. After this, it would lock the victim out of her/his email address. It compromised 45 million computers (10% of all connected computers at the time) and caused over 8 billion US dollars in damages. In the year 2010 malware evolution took a major leap. Till now malware was a threat to businesses, personal finances, etc. *Stuxnet*, a self-replicating malware discovered in 2010 was responsible for attacking the nuclear facilities of different countries. To prevent detection, it used a rootkit to hide on the infected machine. Various variants of this malware were latterly used for similar purposes. Symantec, a leading antimalware company, reported that Stuxnet was a complex piece of code. Different news agencies (BBC, The Guardian, and The New York Times) at that time reported that the complexity of the code indicates only a nation-state would have the ability to produce it. Stuxnet and the reports that followed indicated a start of a cyberwar, i.e., now it is possible to launch a cyberattack rather than a military strike on the nuclear facilities or other sensitive facilities of a country. Recently, with the introduction of cryptocurrency, malware attacks are focused more on mining and stealing the cryptocurrency. Cryptojacking, Clop Ransomware, and Mount Locker are some of the emerging forms of malware. *Cryptojacking* steals the computer resources for stealing and mining cryptocurrency. *Clop Ransomware* encrypts all files in an enterprise and demands payments to decrypt the files. *Mount Locker* is also ransomware attacking enterprises demanding multi-million US dollars in ransoms. A chronological timeline of these and other notable malware programs is shown in Figure 3.

Hidden Malware

One of the emerging major challenges plaguing malware detection is obfuscation. To prevent software applications from reverse engineering attacks, even legitimate developers are encouraged to obfuscate their code. Similar techniques are used by malware writers to prevent analysis and detection. Obfuscation can be used to create variants of the same malware in-order to evade detection. Initial obfuscators were simple and were detected by simple signature-based detectors. With the new digital transformation, the malware programs also start using complex codes, and to counter the simple signature-based detection techniques the obfuscation methods have evolved in sophistication and diversity. Such techniques obscure code to make it difficult to understand, analyze, and detect malware embedded in the code. There is basic three types of techniques to obfuscate the code and are discussed below.

Figure 3. A chronological timeline of notable malware programs from 1970 to 2020

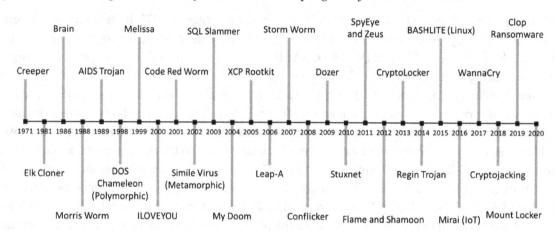

Packing is a technique where malware is packed (compressed) to avoid detection. An antimalware program needs to unpack the malware before it can analyze it. Entropy analysis is generally used to detect packing, but to unpack, the packing algorithm used to pack the program must be known. Legitimate software also uses packing for its distribution and deployment. Therefore, to differentiate between a legitimate software program and a malicious program, it must be unpacked.

Polymorphism is an encryption technique that mutates the code of a static binary to avoid detection. A new version of mutation is performed during each run of the infected program. With each run, the malware is decrypted and written to memory for execution. Therefore, with each new run, the malware signature changes. The functionality of the malware does not change with the run of the program, i.e., the opcode is semantically the same for each instance. It is possible for the current signature-based technique to use semantic analysis to detect such malware during runtime.

Metamorphism is a technique that mutates the dynamic binary code to avoid detection. It does not use any encryption or decryption and changes the opcode with each run of the infected program. It never keeps the opcode in memory. This phenomenon is also called dynamic code obfuscation. There are two types of metamorphic malware based on the channel of communication. *Closed-world malware* – where there is no external communication and the malware generates the newly mutated code using a binary transformer or a metalanguage. *Open-world malware* – where there is communication with other sites on the Internet and the malware updates themselves with new features through this communication.

Obfuscations

The main objective of obfuscations is to change the structure of a program without changing the behavior of the program. Here we discuss some of the obfuscations/mutations used in polymorphic and metamorphic malware.

Instruction Reordering: This technique changes the order of instructions with a commutative or associative operator. This changes the structure of a program but keeps the behavior the same. Here is a simple example of instruction reordering shown in Figure 4:

Figure 4. An example of instruction reordering with the corresponding original and modified C and assembly codes

```
              Original – C code
a = 10;  b = 20;
x = a * b;
              Assembly code
movl [rbp-0xc], 0xa ; a = 10
movl [rbp-0x8], 0x14 ; b = 20
mov eax, [rbp-0xc] ;
imul eax, [rbp-0x8] ; a * b
mov [rbp-0x4], eax ; x = a * b
```

```
              Modified – C code
a = 10;  b = 20;
x = b * a;
              Modified assembly code
movl [rbp-0xc], 0xa ; a = 10
movl [rbp-0x8], 0x14 ; b = 20
mov eax, [rbp-0x8] ; (reordered)
imul eax, [rbp-0xc] ; b * a (reordered)
mov [rbp-0x4], eax ; x = b * a
```

After reordering the two instructions the original and modified codes have different byte sequences (signatures). Other instructions can also be reordered if there is no dependency exists between the instructions.

Register Renaming: In this technique, registers are reassigned in a fragment of a binary code. This changes the byte sequences of the code. A signature-based detector will not be able to match the signature if it is searching for a specific register. In the following example shown in Figure 5, register eax is renamed to edx:

Figure 5. An example of register renaming with the corresponding original and modified assembly code

```
         Original assembly code
lea eax, [RIP+0x203768]
add eax, 0x10
jmp eax
```

```
         Modified assembly code
lea edx, [RIP+0x203768]
add edx, 0x10
jmp edx
```

Branch Functions: To obscure the flow of control in a program a branch function is used. The target of all unconditional branches in the program is changed by the address of a branch function. To keep the behavior of the program intact, the branch function makes sure the branch is correctly transferred to the right target for each branch.

Jump Tables: Compilers use jump tables to implement switch-case statements in a language. Operating system used jump tables to implement function and system calls. To modify the flow of control of a program a malware writer uses either one or a combination of the following strategies. An artificial jump table is created, artificial jumps are added to the existing jump table or the target of a jump in the table is changed to point to malicious code.

Self-Modifying Code: Self-modifying code changes its structure at runtime for benign or malicious purposes. An optimizing program may change its instructions to improve performance. A malware program may change its instructions at runtime to hide code to prevent reverse engineering or to evade detection from antimalware programs. Self-modifying code is mostly used by polymorphic or metamorphic malware. The following example shown in Figure 6 depicts a snippet of a self-modifying original and obfuscated (order of instructions and flow of control changed) code:

Figure 6. An example of a self-modifying code with the corresponding original and modified assembly code

```
             Original assembly code
             mov  ebx,  0x402364
             add  ebx,  0x100
             push edx
      loop:  mov  edx,  [ebx]
             mov  [ecx], edx
             dec  ebx
             inc  ecx
             cmp  ebx,  (0x402364+0x100)
             jne  loop
             pop  edx
```

```
             Modified assembly code
             mov  ebx,  0x402364
             jmp  j2
      loop:  mov  edx,  [ebx]
             mov  [ecx], edx
             jmp  j3
      j1:    jmp  j4
      j2:    add  ebx,  0x100
             push edx
             jmp  loop
      j3:    dec  ebx
             inc  ecx
             jmp  j1
      j4:    cmp  ebx,  (0x402364+0x100)
             jne  loop
             pop  edx
```

In the above example, the code modifies its instructions by copying data (that contains code) from the data section to the code section of the program.

Here we have just discussed a few of the possible obfuscations that can be used to alter the signature of a program. The first two are simple (trivial) obfuscations, whereas the last two are complex (non-trivial) obfuscations that change the control flow of a program and are difficult to detect. For a detailed discussion of various obfuscation techniques, the reader is referred to (Nagra & Collberg, 2009). As we mentioned before these and various other obfuscations are used by malware writers to create variants (copies) of the original malware to evade detection. Some of the previous studies while evaluating the resilience of commercial antimalware programs against variants of known malware found that most of the antimalware programs are not able to successfully detect the variants. Here we present the results of one of the recent such studies (Alam et al., 2017). A small experimental study was carried out to evaluate the resilience of commercial antimalware tools against variants of known malware. For this experimental study, 192 malware variants were generated from 30 different families (class/type) of Android malware. 16 commercial antimalware tools were tested with these variants. To generate these variants, following

7 obfuscations were applied: NOP = no-operation insertion; CND = call indirection; FND = function indirection; RDI = removing debug information; RVD = reversing order; RNF = renaming fields; RNM = renaming methods. The results of this experimental study are shown in Table 1. The majority, i.e., 11 out of 16 of these tools performed very poorly, with overall detection rates ranging from 8.33% – 72.91%. Only 5 of the tools performed significantly better than others with a detection rate of more than 80%. Overall, the commercial antimalware tools perform better in this recent experimental study than in the previous studies/reports, which indicates that their malware analysis and detection techniques are continuously being improved. These results reveal that just by applying some basic obfuscations to a malware program it is possible to deceive an antimalware program.

Table 1. Detection results of the 16 commercial anti-malware programs tested with 192 variants of 30 malware families

Antimalware	Detection Rate (%)							
	NOP	CND	FND	RDI	RVD	RNF	RNM	Overall
Kaspersky	92.85	92.58	92.00	92.59	96.43	93.10	92.59	93.22
Sophos	92.85	92.58	92.00	85.18	96.43	93.10	92.59	92.18
AVG	78.57	85.71	92.00	92.59	78.57	93.10	92.59	87.50
BitDefender	85.71	92.58	92.00	85.18	85.71	86.20	85.18	86.45
DrWeb	85.71	53.57	84.00	85.18	89.28	79.31	85.18	80.31
ESET	89.28	53.57	84.00	88.88	17.85	89.65	85.18	72.91
Microsoft	39.28	75.00	88.00	33.33	32.14	34.48	33.33	40.10
VIPRE	17.85	57.14	32.00	14.81	14.28	13.79	14.81	21.35
Symantec	14.28	53.57	8.00	3.70	7.14	10.34	7.40	15.10
Qihoo-360	10.71	53.57	8.00	7.40	7.14	6.89	7.40	14.58
Fortinet	10.71	53.57	8.00	7.40	7.14	6.89	7.40	14.58
TrendMicro	3.57	53.57	4.00	7.40	3.57	3.57	3.70	11.45
McAfee	7.14	53.57	4.00	3.70	3.57	3.57	3.70	11.45
TotalDefense	7.14	53.57	0.00	0.00	0.00	0.00	0.00	8.85
Malwarebytes	3.57	53.57	0.00	0.00	0.00	0.00	0.00	8.33
Panda	3.57	53.57	0.00	0.00	0.00	0.00	0.00	8.33

Detection

There are two basic techniques for malware analysis and detection. We have already defined these two, here we discuss the advantages and disadvantages of static analysis versus dynamic analysis.

Static Analysis: This analysis is performed on a program without executing the program and is mostly used by antimalware software for automatic malware analysis and detection. Simple static analysis is usually based on string or instruction sequence scanning and matching (Szor, 2005). More sophisticated methods rely on control flow analysis (Aho et al., 2007), value set analysis (Balakrishnan & Reps, 2010), opcode-based analysis (Bilar, 2007) or more complex methods such as model checking (Clarke et al., 1999), etc. (1) Static analysis captures all the paths taken by an executable program and is easier to automate. (2) There is no need to run the program to detect the malware, so there is no possibility of infecting the endpoint system. (3) Depending on the method used, static analysis has the potential of being used in real-time malware detection. (4) These advantages make static analysis suitable to be used in an industrial antimalware software product. Besides these *advantages*, static analysis has some *disadvantages*. (1) When conducted manually, static analysis can be time-consuming. (2) It is difficult for a static analysis tool to support different platforms. (3) When a program cannot be unpacked, then the instructions on the disk will be different than the instruction at runtime. (4) This makes it non-trivial for a static analysis tool to detect malware that introduces changes during runtime, such as metamorphic malware.

Dynamic Analysis: This analysis is performed on a program when the program is executing and is mostly used by antimalware software for manual malware analysis to either, get a specific signature of a malware to be used later, or find an anomaly for malware detection. (1) This analysis is very useful when a program cannot be unpacked during static analysis. (2) The program automatically unpacks itself when it runs. This makes it trivial for a dynamic analysis tool to detect malware that introduces changes during runtime, such as metamorphic malware. (3) With appropriate tools, dynamic analysis is easier to perform on any platform. (4) The dynamic analysis may produce a high detection rate but is not suitable for real-time detection. Besides these *advantages*, dynamic analysis has some *disadvantages*. (1) Dynamic analysis is unable to capture all the paths of a program for malware detection. One possible solution to this problem is to force a conditional branch to take multiple paths, which is a non-trivial problem to solve. This solution is time-consuming and may render the analysis impractical. (2) With dynamic analysis, there is a possibility of infecting the endpoint system. (3) Anti-reverse engineering techniques make dynamic analysis unreliable for malware detection. (4) Running a program in a controlled environment for automatic analysis may take more time than performing an automatic static analysis on the same program. These disadvantages make dynamic analysis unsuitable to be used in an industrial antimalware software product.

Issues and Challenges

Automation: This is one of the main challenges posed by the current malware programs. The number of new malware programs including their variants is increasing significantly (as shown in Figure 1) and we need to automate the process of malware analysis and detection. Manual detection is time-consuming and prone to errors, and moreover it does not scale well to the exponential rise in the rate of new unique malware generated. We have moved into the new digital age, but malware analysis is still a manual task. We need to apply the new technologies, such as artificial intelligence, cloud computing, and deep learning, and integrate them with other classic techniques, such as program analysis, programming languages, information flow analysis to successfully automate the process of malware analysis and detection.

Native Code: Another major challenge is the successful analysis of the native code present in a malware program to improve the detection. Native code is any machine code that is directly executed by a processor. Most of the malware programs on Windows are native-code programs. 86% of the most popular Android applications contain native code, making native code a plausible threat for Android. Successful reverse engineering of native code is non-trivial. Almost all the static analysis-based malware detection systems for Android operating on a bytecode level, this means malware present as native code will not be detected on Android. Another issue plaguing in analyzing native code is designing and developing a cross-architecture malware analyzer. Native code for each processor/architecture (Intel, ARM, etc.) is different, and handling these differences while analyzing the native code is non-trivial, i.e., a separate binary (native code) analyzer is to be developed for each processor.

Obfuscation: Another issue facing malware detection is obfuscation. As we mentioned before, obfuscations are used by malware writers to make their code more difficult to analyze or to create variants of the same malware to evade detection. To protect their software, even legitimate developers are encouraged to obfuscate their code. This makes it difficult to differentiate between a legitimate and malicious program. As shown in Table 1, the majority of the commercial antimalware programs were not able to successfully detect the variants. The morphing of a malware program during runtime using different obfuscation techniques makes it difficult to detect the malware.

Morphing: Transforming shape (structure) of a malware program during runtime using different morphing techniques, such as polymorphism and metamorphism, makes it difficult to detect the malware. Some of these malware programs do not contain any malicious code, and when they feel safe (i.e., when they are not being analyzed) they download the malicious code from the Internet. Dynamic analysis is generally used to detect such complex malware, but it has its drawbacks. Moreover, these malware programs use anti-reverse engineering techniques to avoid such detection.

Anti-Reverse Engineering: Modern malware programs use anti-reverse engineering techniques to avoid detection. Some of these techniques are sandbox detection, debugger detection, and binary instrumentation detection, etc. Such malware programs become non-trivial and sometimes impossible to detect even after using a hybrid analysis. These types of malware may require a deep manual analysis by an expert malware analyst. However, by the time this analysis is complete, the malware may have inflicted the damage.

SOLUTIONS AND RECOMMENDATIONS

So far, we have discussed some of the issues and challenges plaguing malware analysis and detection. Now we are to going to present and discuss some of the practical solutions to these issues and challenges. We present two systems that attempt to solve the above challenges and issues. The first system called MAIL (malware analysis intermediate language) utilizes static analysis and semantic signature-based techniques, and the second system utilizes dynamic analysis and anomaly-based techniques.

MAIL (Malware Analysis Intermediate Language)

MAIL, an intermediate language, is a step towards automating and optimizing malware analysis and detection. Intermediate languages are used in compilers to translate the source code into a form that is easy to optimize and provide portability. Here we discuss some of the reasons why we need to transform a malware program into an intermediate language.

1. Most of the malware programs are analyzed as binaries (in executable form). The first step during static malware analysis is to disassemble the program into its assembly code. There are typically hundreds of instructions in an assembly language. For example, the number of instructions in popular ISAs (Instruction Set Architectures), Intel, ARM, and IBM PowerPC, range from 200+ to 500+.

For a successful analysis, this number of instructions needs to reduce considerably. To reduce this number, functionally equivalent assembly instructions can be grouped in one intermediate language.

2. Moreover, these instructions contain much complexity that makes their analysis much difficult. An intermediate language abstracts the instructions and makes the language more transparent to static analysis. By using simpler instructions, the intermediate language makes the static analysis much simpler.

3. Another advantage of using an intermediate language is that it can be used with different platforms, such as Intel and ARM the two most popular architectures in current computers (Windows and smartphones). This way we do not have to perform separate static analysis for each platform.

4. An intermediate language can be easily translated into a string, a tree, or a graph and hence can be optimized for various analyses that are required for malware analysis and detection, such as pattern matching and data mining.

MAIL provides an abstract representation of an assembly program and hence the ability for a tool to automate malware analysis and detection. By translating binaries compiled for different platforms to MAIL, a tool can achieve platform independence. Each MAIL statement is annotated with patterns that can be used by a tool to optimize malware analysis and detection. There are other intermediate languages for malware analysis being used in research and industry. The reason for choosing and discussing MAIL here is its well-defined formal model and detailed explanation of its application and use in automating and optimizing malware analysis and detection. The interested reader is referred to (Alam et al., 2017, 2013) for more information about MAIL and its use. Here we give a short introduction to MAIL and how it can be used for automating and optimizing malware analysis and detection.

Design of MAIL

MAIL is designed as a small, simple, and extensible language. There are 8 basic statements in MAIL. Some of them are *assignment*, *control*, *conditional*, *libcall*, and *jump* statements. For example, the control statement represents the following control instructions:

```
control::= ('if' condition (jump | assignment))
            ('else' (jump | assignment))? ;
```

Instructions in an assembly language can be mapped to one of the 8 statements of MAIL. Here is an example of the translation from binary (hex dump) to MAIL of a small piece of code from a real malware program:

```
Hex dump      x86 assembly                   MAIL Statement
 83c0ff       ADD EAX, -0x1    -->     EAX = EAX + -0x1;          (assign)
 83f800       CMP EAX,  0x0    -->     compare(EAX, 0x0);         (libcall)
   743a       JZ   0x401267    -->     if (ZF == 1) jmp 0x401267; (control)
```

In the above example, the hex dump is first converted to Intel x86 assembly and then translated to MAIL statements. Here we see 3 MAIL statements, *assignment*, *libcall*, and *control*. The first statement decrements the register EAX, the second statement compares the value in EAX to 0, and the third statement jumps to an address (a location in the program) if the zero-flag (ZF) is 1. Compare is one of the libs of MAIL and sets the zero-flag based on the results of the comparison. We can see from the above example that it is much simpler to understand the MAIL statements, and hence the meaning (semantics) of the program, than the assembly code or the hex dump.

MAIL Patterns for Annotation

MAIL program can also be annotated using different patterns available in the language. These annotations assign patterns to MAIL statements that can be used latter for pattern matching during malware analysis and detection. There are total of 21 patterns in MAIL and are explained as follows in Table 2:

Here is an example of a MAIL annotated program shown in Table 3:

This program consists of five ASSIGN, one CALL, two JUMP_CONSTANT (jump to a known/constant address), one STACK, one LIBCALL, and one CONTROL_CONSTANT (jump to a known/constant address) statements. These annotations/patterns can be used/applied to extract and select important features and characteristics of a program for malware analysis and detection.

Table 2. MAIL Patterns

ASSIGN	An assignment statement. e.g: EAX = EAX + ECX;
ASSIGN CONSTANT	An assignment statement including a constant. e.g: EAX = EAX + 0x01;
CONTROL	A control statement where the target of the jump is unknown. e.g: if (ZF == 1) JMP [EAX+ECX+0x10];
CONTROL CONSTANT	A control statement where the target of the jump is known. e.g: if (ZF == 1) JMP 0x400567;
CALL	A call statement where the target of the call is unknown. e.g: CALL EBX;
CALL CONSTANT	A call statement where the target of the call is known. e.g: CALL 0x603248;
FLAG	A statement including a flag. e.g: CF = 1;
FLAG STACK	A statement including ag register with stack. e.g: EFLAGS = [SP=SP-0x1];
HALT	A halt statement. e.g: HALT;
JUMP	A jump statement where the target of the jump is unknown. e.g: JMP [EAX+ECX+0x10];
JUMP CONSTANT	A jump statement where the target of the jump is known. e.g: JMP 0x680376
JUMP STACK	A return jump. e.g: JMP [SP=SP-0x8]
LIBCALL	A library call. e.g: compare(EAX, ECX);
LIBCALL CONSTANT	A library call including a constant. e.g: compare(EAX, 0x10);
LOCK	A lock statement. e.g: lock;
STACK	A stack statement. e.g: EAX = [SP=SP-0x1];
STACK CONSTANT	A stack statement including a constant. e.g: [SP=SP+0x1] = 0x432516;
TEST	A test statement. e.g: EAX and ECX;
TEST CONSTANT	A test statement including a constant. e.g: EAX and 0x10;
UNKNOWN	Any unknown assembly instruction that cannot be translated.
NOTDEFINED	The default pattern. e.g: All the new statements when created are assigned this default value.

Table 3. MAIL annotated program

Offset	MAIL Statement	Pattern
000129	RAX = RAX + 0xf;	(ASSIGN)
00012d	[sp=sp+1] = 0x132; call (0x4b8);	(CALL_C)
000132	jmp (0xed6);	(JMP_C)
000138	jmp (0x068);	(JMP_C)
00013e	EDI = EDI;	(ASSIGN)
000140	[sp=sp+0x1] = EBP;	(STACK)
000141	EBP = ESP;	(ASSIGN)
000143	EAX = [EBP+0x8];	(ASSIGN)
000146	EAX = [EAX];	(ASSIGN)
000148	compare([EAX], 0xe06d7363);	(LIBCALL)
00014e	if (ZF == 0) jmp 0x17a;	(CONTROL_C)

Application of MAIL

To show how to utilize MAIL, here we discuss 2 of the previous research applying MAIL to analyze and detect malware.

DroidClone (Alam et al., 2021) uses MAIL to find code clones in Android applications. DroidClone serializes a MAIL program to a string for efficient matching. Features are extracted by serializing each function in a MAIL program. These are also assigned weights based on their frequencies. Features are selected using TF-IDF (term frequency and inverse document frequency) and a signature is built. A SimScore is computed for each sample in the dataset. The samples with their SimScore values are used for training a classifier for malware detection. A new sample is tagged as malware if SimScore of the sample is greater than or equal to a certain threshold. During the evaluation, DroidClone achieved a detection rate of 94.2% and a false positive rate of 5.6%. DroidClone was able to successfully provide resistance against all the trivial and some non-trivial obfuscations.

DroidNative (Alam et al., 2017) is a tool that uses specific control flow patterns to reduce the effect of obfuscations, provides automation and platform independence, and is the first system that operates at the Android native code level. DroidNative builds an annotated control flow graph (ACFG) (Alam et al., 2015) of an Android application. ACFG analyzes a control flow graph derived from an application and annotates it using MAIL patterns in-order to capture the control flow semantics of the program. Annotating the CFG of a MAIL program allows much smaller CFGs to be reliably analyzed for malware detection than are traditionally used in CFG based techniques. For example, an application being analyzed is broken into smaller ACFGs which become that application's signature. At detection time, the ACFGs within that signature are compared to the ACFGs of known malware, and if a high percentage of ACFGs in the application match that of known malware, then the application can be tagged as malware. This matching is also very fast because the individual ACFGs being compared against are small. DroidNative also uses another technique called the sliding window of difference (SWOD) (Alam et al., 2015) for signature building. SWOD is an opcode-based technique for malware detection. One of the main advantages of using opcodes for detecting malware is that detection can be performed in real-time. However, it also has some challenges: (1) The patterns of opcodes can be changed by using a different compiler, the same compiler with a different level of optimizations, or if the code is compiled for a different platform. (2) Obfuscations introduced by malware variants can change the opcode distributions. (3) The execution time depends on the number of features selected for mining in a program. Selecting too many features results in a high detection rate but also increases the execution time. Selecting too few features has the opposite effect. SWOD is a window that represents differences in MAIL patterns distributions and hence makes the analysis independent of different compilers, compiler optimizations, instruction set architecture, and operating systems. It uses a statistical analysis of MAIL patterns' distributions to develop a set of heuristics that help in selecting the appropriate number of features and reduces the runtime cost. When tested with traditional malware variants, DroidNative achieved a detection rate of 99.48%, compared to the detection rates of commercial tools that range from 8.33% to 93.22% as shown in Table 1.

Dynamic Malware Analysis

So far, we have discussed techniques utilizing static analysis. Here we are going to describe the basic steps of how to perform dynamic malware analysis. The first step during dynamic malware analysis is to unpack the program. Once the program is unpacked, it is executed in a controlled environment, such as a sandbox, etc. These controls include the ability to stop execution at any point for inspection of the program. Generally, debugging, and binary instrumentation is used to control malware execution. The duration of execution depends on various factors, such as the available time and extent of the analysis. The dynamic analysis will include a mechanism to explore the full behavior of the malware, such as forward symbolic execution to explore multiple execution paths in the malware program. After the execution and analysis is complete a report is generated. For example, if the malware stole the password, the analysis report should identify which functions were responsible, and how it was stolen e.g., from the memory or through a phishing attack, etc. As discussed before, one of the main advantages of dynamic analysis is that it makes it possible to fully analyze packed, polymorphic, and metamorphic malware. Anti-reverse engineering is used by modern malware to avoid detection by dynamic analysis. There are some techniques, such as patching, that can be used in a dynamic analysis to defeat anti-reverse engineering methods. During patching, the anti-malware engineer will identify the defense mechanisms in a malware program, remove them, and save the updated malware program as a new executable to be analyzed without the impact of the defense mechanisms. This is a non-trivial process and may require an expert anti-malware engineer to successfully perform such a process.

Most of the dynamic analysis platforms execute the malware for a limited time before terminating the analysis. Therefore, one of the techniques to evade dynamic analysis employed by the malware is to use delay mechanisms, such as sleep commands. CIASandbox (Lin et al., 2016) utilizes a virtual machine (VM) to execute the malware and collects information about the system calls through the traces left in the VM's memory and stack. VTCSandbox (Lin et al., 2018) extends CIASandbox to utilize the VM time controller to manipulate time inside the VM and accelerate analysis of the malware. The tick counter inside the VM is manipulated to speed up the execution inside the VM. This helps skip the sleep time or other delays employed by malware to suspend their operations.

MEGDroid (Hasan et al., 2021) is a model-driven approach recently proposed for dynamic Android malware analysis. MEGDroid enhances the model-driven event generation process by generating appropriate events for malware analysis using model-to-model and model-to-code transformations. Another advantage that MEGDroid provides is the inclusion of human in the loop to take his/her experience and knowledge into account to further improve malware analysis.

DeepAMD (Imtiaz et al., 2021), a recent proposed technique utilizes deep artificial neural networks (ANN) to analyze and detect Android malware. DeepAMD performs both static and dynamic analysis. The static layer utilizes a binary classifier and classify the samples either as malware or benign. The dynamic layer is then used to further classify the malware (which is detected by the static layer as malware) into 4 different categories. The static layer achieves an accuracy of 93.4% for malware classification, whereas the dynamic layer achieves an accuracy of 80.3% for malware category classification. This shows that deep ANN are promising for analyzing and detecting malware but still there is a lot of room for improvement.

Memory Forensic Analysis

Sometimes it is not possible to perform dynamic analysis of a malware program in a controlled environment. For example, when the program is not able to finish its execution and crashes, or some advance attacks or malicious behaviors leave no track on the hard drive. In such cases, analysis is performed on memory dumps called memory forensic analysis. The first step is to acquire memory. Next, the memory dump is analyzed to extract data relating to malware and associated information that can provide additional context. Various tools, such as Volatility Suite, are available for such purpose.

FUTURE RESEARCH DIRECTIONS

Malware analysis and detection techniques are trying to keep pace with the new emerging threats and attacks because of the digital transformation. To stimulate further research in this thriving area, this section discusses some of the future research directions including the problems and challenges faced.

Automation

To completely automate successful malware analysis and detection is non-trivial. There are a lot of works, some of them discussed in this chapter, that have tried to completely automate this process, achieving only partial success. Currently, a suspicious malware program goes through static analysis. If the static analysis fails to detect the program as malware, it goes through dynamic analysis. If the dynamic analysis fails to detect the program as the malware it goes through a manual analysis by a malware analysis expert. There are some caveats during this whole process. (1) What if the static or dynamic analysis falsely detects the program as malware. With more false positives during the analysis more of the benign programs will be rejected. This may not be a problem where the security of the system has a higher priority, otherwise, this may significantly affect the business. (2) What if during the analysis process more of the programs are detected as benign. This will require a greater number of manual analysis. If the program is positively detected as benign, then this will waste the time and money spent on the manual process. These caveats highlight the limitations to completely automate the process of malware analysis and detection. Successful partial automation will reduce the number of false positives and increase the number of true positives.

Web and Mobile Malware

With the proliferation of mobile and web applications, such as social networking, Financial services, and software as a service, etc., current mobile and web malware have also started using sophisticated obfuscations to make it difficult to analyze and detect them. JavaScript is widely used for developing web applications and can change the code at runtime, which also makes JavaScript more inclined to obfuscations such as metamorphism. The lightweight dynamic analysis combined with static analysis may be suitable to analyze applications that run inside a web browser for malware detection, such as a combination of JavaScript, HTML, and CSS (cascading style sheets) that relies on a common web browser to render the application. Such a hybrid system can use an already processed structure (e.g. an abstract syntax tree of the JavaScript) by the web browser for malware analysis and detection.

Embedded Systems Malware

With the digital transformation comes the new wave of intelligent embedded systems (including Internet of Things – IoTs), such as routers, switches, modern SCADA (supervisory control and data acquisition), PLC (programmable logic controllers), EPOS (electronic point of sale) and automotive systems, home devices (scanners, printers, toasters, and refrigerators, etc.), and medical devices, etc. These intelligent devices, with more CPU power and memory (from the previous such devices), are prone to more sophisticated malware attacks. Because of their limited energy resources, running a complete malware detector on these devices is quite challenging. To combat this challenge, malware detection can be provided as an in-cloud service. In the next few paragraphs, we describe the challenges and issues of in-cloud malware analysis and provide some future directions to mitigate these issues.

In-cloud Malware Analysis

Cloud computing is an environment where a program or an application runs on several connected computers. These computers can be physical or virtual. A physical server may be running multiple virtual servers. These virtual servers are disassociated from the physical server, and hence can move around and scale up and down on the fly without affecting the client. The word in-cloud refers to the services provided by a cloud to its users. Malware analysis and detection can be one of the services that can be provided as an in-cloud service. The current state of the art in-cloud malware analysis and detection has some advantages and disadvantages, which are listed below:

1. Advantages
    a. It improves the detection rate by combining multiple antimalware engines.
    b. It is extensible. Other antimalware engines can be easily added.
    c. It provides deep malware analysis, such as dynamic analysis, for resource-constrained devices.
    d. It provides correlation of information between antimalware engines, such as sharing the behavior of a malware program that can enhance the malware detection.
2. Disadvantages
    a. It increases the false positive rate. More antimalware engines can produce more false positives.
    b. Running a file on the client and then replicating on the cloud can expose the client to possible malware.
    c. It highly depends on the trust and privacy provided by the cloud.
    d. A full replication of the client is required to detect the new generation of malware, such as polymorphic and metamorphic malware.

For a complete malware analysis and detection system, a combination of static and dynamic analysis is used. Such a system is more suitable for in-cloud based malware analysis and detection. Here we present a hybrid in-cloud layered malware analysis and detection system. Figure 7 gives an overview of such a system.

Figure 7. An overview of the hybrid in-cloud layered malware analysis and detection system

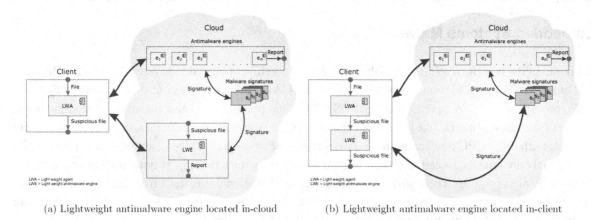

(a) Lightweight antimalware engine located in-cloud   (b) Lightweight antimalware engine located in-client

As shown in Figure 7, the client can run either an LWA (lightweight agent) or an LWE (lightweight antimalware engine) depending on the resources available, that can scan/detect files and send only a suspicious file to the cloud for further analysis and detection. The cloud can run multiple malware detection engines to analyze the file, shown as $e_1, e_2, e_3 \ldots \ldots e_m$, where m is the number of antimalware engines currently available in the cloud. After a new malware is found its signature is stored in the database of malware signatures, shown as $s_1, s_2, s_3 \ldots \ldots s_k$, where k is the current number of malware signatures in the database. More details about this system are given in (Alam et al., 2014). To shield the client from the malware, the in-cloud malware analysis and detection system described above has three layers, LWA, LWE, and antimalware engines. These layers separate the execution of the file (dynamic analysis) under detection. This also reduces the bandwidth required for transferring the files from the client to the cloud.

Adversarial Machine Learning and Malware Analysis

Artificial intelligence powered technologies such as machine learning, deep learning, reinforcement learning, game theory, and others can provide solutions to some of the main challenges faced by malware analysis and detection in the new digital transformation age. A recent proposed artificial intelligence technology Adversarial Machine Learning (Huang et al., 2011) is a technique that generates a class of attacks that deteriorate the performance of classifiers on specific tasks. This helps develop approaches to counter these attacks and strengthen malware detection system by improving the classifiers. A recent study (Hu and Tan, 2017) proposed a Generative Adversarial Networks (GoodFellow et al., 2014) based approach, that takes original samples and produce adversarial examples to defeat machine learning malware detectors. Another recent research (Martins et al., 2020) presents a systematic review of the application of adversarial machine learning to intrusion and malware detection. 20 recent research works were studied, and the authors concluded that adversarial attacks could retrograde the performance of the intrusion and malware classifiers. All the classifiers studied show similar results on normal data, but most of them got effected except neural networks and random forests on the manipulated data.

The best defense against any cybersecurity system is to know the current and future risks to the system. These and other such research, that are still in their infancy, inspire studies about adversarial systems and potential risks to malware analysis and detection systems and provide guidance and direction to reduce these risks. There is a need to do further research to develop new techniques and methods to apply adversarial machine learning to improve malware analysis and detection systems.

CONCLUSION

In this chapter, after a basic introduction and a brief history of malware, we discussed the evolution of malware in the new digital transformation age, and the developments of some of the antimalware techniques to neutralize or mitigate their effects. This chapter discusses and answers some of the following questions. How malware affects our lives and what are some of the complications and challenges it creates in the new digital transformation age? What are some of the emerging techniques in this area, such as in-cloud malware analysis, and adversarial machine learning, etc., that have evolved because of the digital transformation? How malware writers create such complex malware using different techniques, such as obfuscation, etc.? How these malware programs avoid detection by some of the techniques used by the current security architectures? How malware writers create variants (copies) of the original malware so that it is not detected by an anti-malware program?

Recently malware has plummeted in smartphones, especially Android phones. These devices provide third party applications from a variety of markets. It poses strong security and privacy issues through malicious software that gets installed and collects sensory data and personal information from these devices. Initially, simple techniques (using simple signatures) were used to detect malware. Now, these have evolved to detect some of the complex malware, polymorphic, and metamorphic malware.

We have also discussed some of the key challenges and issues, such as automation, native code, obfuscations, morphing, and anti-reverse engineering, plaguing malware analysis and detection. Solutions and recommendations were provided to solve some of these challenges and issues. To stimulate further research in this area, we have highlighted some future research directions. We believe this chapter, provides a promising basis for future researchers interested to know more about the evolution of malware and will act as a motivation for improving the current and developing new techniques for malware analysis and detection.

REFERENCES

Aho, A. V., Lam, M. S., Sethi, R., & Ullman, J. D. (2007). Compilers: Principles, techniques, and tools (2nd ed.). Academic Press.

Alam, S., Horspool, R. N., & Traore, I. (2013, November). MAIL: Malware Analysis Intermediate Language: a step towards automating and optimizing malware detection. In *Proceedings of the 6th International Conference on Security of Information and Networks* (pp. 233-240). 10.1145/2523514.2527006

Alam, S., Qu, Z., Riley, R., Chen, Y., & Rastogi, V. (2017). DroidNative: Automating and optimizing detection of Android native code malware variants. *Computers & Security, 65*, 230-246.

Alam, S., & Sogukpinar, I. (2021). DroidClone: Attack of the android malware clones - A step towards stopping them. *Computer Science and Information Systems, 18*(1), 67–91. doi:10.2298/CSIS200330035A

Alam, S., Sogukpinar, I., Traore, I., & Coady, Y. (2014, September). In-cloud malware analysis and detection: State of the art. In *Proceedings of the 7th International Conference on Security of Information and Networks* (pp. 473-478). 10.1145/2659651.2659730

Alam, S., Sogukpinar, I., Traore, I., & Horspool, R. N. (2015). Sliding window and control flow weight for metamorphic malware detection. *Journal of Computer Virology and Hacking Techniques, 11*(2), 75–88. doi:10.100711416-014-0222-y

Alam, S., Traore, I., & Sogukpinar, I. (2015). Annotated control flow graph for metamorphic malware detection. *The Computer Journal, 58*(10), 2608–2621. doi:10.1093/comjnl/bxu148

Balakrishnan, G., & Reps, T. (2010). WYSINWYX: What you see is not what you eXecute. *ACM Transactions on Programming Languages and Systems, 32*(6), 1–84. doi:10.1145/1749608.1749612

Bilar, D. (2007). Opcodes as predictor for malware. *International Journal of Electronic Security and Digital Forensics, 1*(2), 156-168.

Clarke, E. M., Grumberg, O., & Peled, D. A. (1999). *Model checking. The MIT Press.*

Goodfellow, I. J., Pouget-Abadie, J., Mirza, M., Xu, B., Warde-Farley, D., Ozair, S., Courville, A., & Bengio, Y. (2014). *Generative Adversarial Networks.* arXiv:1406.2661.

Hasan, H., Ladani, B. T., & Zamani, B. (2021). MEGDroid: A Model-Driven Event Generation Framework for Dynamic Android Malware Analysis. *Information and Software Technology, 135*, 106569. doi:10.1016/j.infsof.2021.106569

Hu, W., & Tan, Y. (2017). *Generating adversarial malware examples for black-box attacks based on gan.* arXiv:1702.05983.

Huang, L., Joseph, A. D., Nelson, B., Rubinstein, B. I., & Tygar, J. D. (2011). Adversarial machine learning. *Proceedings of the 4th ACM workshop on Security and artificial intelligence*, 43–58. 10.1145/2046684.2046692

Imtiaz, S. I., Rehman, S., Javed, A. R., Jalil, Z., Liu, X., & Alnumay, W. S. (2021). DeepAMD: Detection and identification of Android malware using high-efficient Deep Artificial Neural Network. *Future Generation Computer Systems, 115*, 844–856. doi:10.1016/j.future.2020.10.008

Lin, C. H., Pao, H. K., & Liao, J. W. (2018). Efficient dynamic malware analysis using virtual time control mechanics. *Computers & Security, 73*, 359–373. doi:10.1016/j.cose.2017.11.010

Lin, C. H., Tien, C. W., Chen, C. W., Tien, C. W., & Pao, H. K. (2015, September). Efficient spear-phishing threat detection using hypervisor monitor. In *2015 International Carnahan Conference on Security Technology (ICCST)* (pp. 299-303). IEEE. 10.1109/CCST.2015.7389700

Linn, C., & Debray, S. (2003, October). Obfuscation of executable code to improve resistance to static disassembly. In *Proceedings of the 10th ACM conference on Computer and communications security* (pp. 290-299). 10.1145/948109.948149

Martins, N., Cruz, J. M., Cruz, T., & Abreu, P. H. (2020). Adversarial machine learning applied to intrusion and malware scenarios: A systematic review. *IEEE Access: Practical Innovations, Open Solutions*, *8*, 35403–35419. doi:10.1109/ACCESS.2020.2974752

McGraw, G., & Morrisett, G. (2000). Attacking malicious code: A report to the infosec research council. *IEEE Software*, *17*(5), 33–41. doi:10.1109/52.877857

Nagra, J., & Collberg, C. (2009). *Surreptitious Software: Obfuscation, Watermarking, and Tamperproofing for Software Protection: Obfuscation, Watermarking, and Tamperproofing for Software Protection*. Pearson Education.

Narayanan, A., Bonneau, J., Felten, E., Miller, A., & Goldfeder, S. (2016). *Bitcoin and cryptocurrency technologies: a comprehensive introduction*. Princeton University Press.

Szor, P. (2005). *The Art of Computer Virus Research and Defense*. Addison Wesley Professional.

Zouave, E., Bruce, M., Colde, K., Jaitner, M., Rodhe, I., & Gustafsson, T. (2020). *Artificially intelligent cyberattacks*. Academic Press.

KEY TERMS AND DEFINITIONS

Abstract Syntax Tree: In computer science, an abstract syntax tree (AST), or just syntax tree, is a tree representation of the abstract syntactic structure of source code written in a programming language.

Binary Instrumentation: It is a technique that modifies a binary program, either pre-execution or during execution to get more insights (behaviors) into the program.

Bytecode: Bytecode is a program code that has been compiled from source code into low-level code designed for a software interpreter.

Cloud Computing: Cloud computing is the on-demand availability of computer system resources, especially data storage and computing power, without direct active management by the user.

Computer Forensics: Computer forensics is a branch of digital forensic science pertaining to evidence found in computers and digital storage media.

Control Flow: In computer science, control flow is the order in which individual statements, instructions, or function calls of an imperative program are executed or evaluated.

Cryptocurrency: Any form of currency that only exists digitally, that usually has no central issuing or regulating authority but instead uses a decentralized system to record transactions and manage the issuance of new units, and that relies on cryptography to prevent counterfeiting and fraudulent transactions.

Cyberattack: An attempt to gain illegal access to a computer or computer system for the purpose of causing damage or harm.

Debugging: In computer programming and software development, debugging is the process of finding and resolving bugs within computer programs, software, or systems.

Decompiler: A decompiler is a computer program that takes an executable file as input and attempts to create a high-level source file that can be recompiled successfully.

Embedded Systems: An embedded system is a combination of computer hardware and software designed for a specific function or functions within a larger system.

Endpoint System: An endpoint system is a remote computing device that communicates back and forth with a network to which it is connected. Some examples of endpoints include Desktops, laptops, smartphones, servers, workstations, and internet-of-things devices.

Instruction Set Architecture: In computer science, an instruction set architecture (ISA) is an abstract model of a computer.

Metalanguage: A form of language or set of terms used for the description or analysis of another language.

Obfuscation: To obfuscate something means to make it so that it is not clear or transparent, much like dirty water makes it hard to see to the bottom of a pond.

Opcode: In computing, an opcode (operation code) is the portion of a machine language instruction that specifies the operation to be performed.

Symbolic Execution: In computer science, symbolic execution (also symbolic evaluation) is a means of analyzing a program to determine what inputs cause each part of a program to execute.

Virtual: Not physically existing as such but made by software to appear to do so.

Vulnerability: Vulnerability refers to the inability (of a system or a unit) to withstand the effects of a hostile environment.

Chapter 14
A Study of Advancing E–Banking and Cybersecurity for Digital Enterprise Transformation in Pakistan

Tansif ur Rehman
iD https://orcid.org/0000-0002-5454-2150
University of Karachi, Pakistan

ABSTRACT

In this technological era, almost all renowned banks have equipped themselves with the latest technology significantly pertinent to enhance their services and have provided e-banking facilities to their customers. Nevertheless, cybersecurity has been the focus of many organizations. Banks are offering more facilities to facilitate their customers with ease and convenience regarding e-banking. However, in Pakistan this is not the case. As people still refrain from using e-banking in Pakistan because of various issues, the e-banking sector has exponentially grown in the last decade. It has more chances of growth as enterprises such as banks still encourage clients to carry out e-transactions, like utility bill payments, access to account information, and money transfer. During this process, cybercriminals attempt to steal customer data and hack their online sessions. With regards to e-banking fraud, digitization has caused a revolution. Cybercriminals have employed various tools to steal crucial information through identity theft, trojans, viruses, and phishing.

INTRODUCTION

Financial, savings, private, and public banks are among the various types of enterprises which are vulnerable to cybersecurity threats. All, however, share the same goal of delivering services to consumers, companies, and government funds as a necessary prerequisite on cyberspace. In today's world, banks are undergoing digital enterprise transformation and conduct financial activities from lending and purchasing real estate and vehicles to large trade-related transactions (Holzhauer, 2021). These digital transac-

DOI: 10.4018/978-1-7998-6975-7.ch014

tions are increasingly targeted by cyberhackers which leads to cybersecurity breaches. Consequently, bank cybersecurity should be monitored regularly in these organizations since the cyberworld is a risky abode, and without any safety regulations, there is a potential to endeavor to steal money, amongst other circumstances of risks and hazards (Frazier, 2021; Phaneuf, 2021a). Customers that use internet banking have access to a wide range of banking services that are not available in physical banking locations. These enterprises vary from traditional banking to mobile devices and are usually conducted over the internet (Marous, 2021; Overby, 2020). However, many of these services have a higher risk of data theft, data intrusion, data hack, as cybersecurity is not clearly understood by the customers and many of the cybersecurity software installed are unregistered, or out of date, non-compliant, having no upgrades, and having the minimum protection from cyber-attacks.

As business dealings could be performed simply by a single click, it has altered individuals' behavior concerning the way they spend. The simplicity and expediency attract customers in the way that commercial institutions protect their money. Commercial institutions protect their monecious to clients (Amoros, 2019; Phaneuf, 2021b; Singh et al., 2006). The harm caused by cyber-attack to any financial organization is hard to calculate as the effect is not only in economic terms. However, other components make it challenging to assess, for example, harms to organizations' prestige and credibility, lack of organizations' faith in institutions and clients. Thus, the price of institutions' cyber-attack will be significantly more extensive than the amount taken out by cyber-attackers.

While the e-banking system has been introduced for several years, cybercrime cases started to be recorded drastically during the last decade, especially in the last few years with the emergence of social media, which often reveals people's information vulnerabilities. Consequently, the employment of e-banking has decreased, while the risks have risen exponentially (Amoros, 2019; Zaidi, 2021). Nevertheless, because of other aspects, for example, new cryptographic systems, it has added potency lately. If the customers decide to be robbed, none of this is beneficial since it mainly executes it. Cybercriminals exploit customers' naivety and inexperience in data safety. Risks to such methods are produced to a similar degree as protection methods are promoted (Carminati et al., 2018; Overby, 2020). The harms caused by scams are worth millions of dollars globally each year. These scams contribute to consumer humiliation and an extensive adaptation period for concerned banks and high expenditures (Al-Furiah & Al-Braheem, 2009).

Electronic payment systems, also known as electronic banking or net banking, allow bank customers to transact through internet-based websites and banks. It gives banks internet access if they have the resources. It also provides various services, including money transfers, bill payments, account verification, e-shopping, and recharges (Li et al., 2021). Online banking has risen to prominence because it is convenient and straightforward to use, provides fast access, is cost-effective, and can be done anywhere. With these benefits, online forgery, wherein an individual's account is utilized to transfer funds for commercial gains, is becoming a spotlight for cyber fraud. To deceive account holders, methods such as phishing, voice phishing, downloading of Trojans, and other malicious software could motivate cybercriminals to make easy cash.

At present, fraud through online banking is at the top of cybercrime lists in nations worldwide. Therefore, it is a crucial era for banks' security and for authentication strategies to be competitive. There are, however, advanced tools and technologies built by cybercriminals to invade banking networks. E-banking networks must have reliable security protocols capable of accurately identifying users and then authorizing connections, hence reducing fraud. Two critical identification schemes, i.e., distinctive secret data previously held by customers and bank passwords, and unique device features needed to access device fingerprinting services. However, if any of these were breached, the entire cybersecurity system would be harmed (Khrais, 2015).

Thus, e-banking in Pakistan is less developed than in first-world countries (Akhlaq, 2011). A thorough examination of future e-banking in Pakistan will undoubtedly necessitate research in several fields. This research aims to identify the issues that prevent respective customers from adopting e-banking services in Pakistan. In Pakistan, the Electronic Transactions Ordinance (ETO) was passed in 2002 to promote e-commerce activities further, and it gave legal protection to e-transactions. It also placed a premium on Public-Key Infrastructure, a set of digital encryption technology and facilities. It allows multiple businesses to encrypt their online correspondence and business activities to the most significant degree possible.

Much previous research has tended to concentrate only on the beneficial implications of e-banking, such as benefits (Suganthi, Balachandher, & Balachandran, 2001); trustworthiness (Suh & Han, 2002); innovations (Gerrard & Cunningham, 2003). This research was carried out in Karachi because it is the largest city of Pakistan, with a population of 149 million, and has a multi-ethnic blend of people from Pakistan. It will assist banks in developing suitable plans to ensure that consumers migrate to online banking as quickly as possible, allowing this self-service technology to grow more effectively and conveniently.

BACKGROUND

Online banking is still widely used worldwide, and it is difficult to imagine that it did not exist not long ago. In the early 1980s, the central banks in New York began offering home-based banking services to their customers. Clients may access their bank accounts, display their bank statements, pay their bills, and view their bank statements at any time. Nonetheless, the e-banking movement began in the mid-1990s, when the internet was recognized as a distribution medium with promise. The comfort and expediency brought with electronic banking use caused a breakthrough that radically changed the business environment.

While the openness with which banks were approached and the ease with which individuals' accounts were managed were advantageous and held great promise, people soon discovered that this convenience came at a cost. Through the intrusion of networks, cyber offenders began to see the potential in e-banking to achieve malicious motivation for monetary benefits. E-banking scams quickly substituted traditional banking fraud strategies. Nevertheless, as a result, technical advances embraced by the banking field seeking growth have opened the vista of advanced levels of cyber threats. It perhaps caused the system with new susceptibilities and complications.

In the present era, hackers are looking for these vulnerabilities and finding and employing new tactics regarding vulnerabilities in modern banking systems. Different studies have been carried out regarding crucial subject matter under review, i.e., online banking scams. Studies on this aspect encompass preemptive protection steps, improving the framework, and identification of forgeries. Banks constantly improve security and use various methods to keep the infrastructure secure, including encrypted business networks, two-tiered authentication, and various techniques to ensure that no one exploits the system. Researchers use data analysis software to examine bank business records to determine how adequate internal controls are and identify transactions forged.

When safety and security measures taken by banks tighten, so makes progress by hackers in technology, as they maintain to keep themselves a step ahead of others. Therefore, it takes a few hours to understand security steps in that direction, i.e., technology equivalent to the technologies applied by these cybercriminals. Hence, this sector requires highly skilled professionals in cybersecurity, having avid minds and those who can diligently work encompassing security of e-banking systems and have the capability to realize countermeasures for all potential internet banking forgeries.

FOCUS OF THE RESEARCH

In the present era, hackers are looking for these vulnerabilities and finding and employing new tactics regarding vulnerabilities in modern banking systems. Different studies have been carried out regarding crucial subject matter under review, i.e., online banking scams. Studies on this aspect encompass preemptive protection steps, improving the framework, and identification of forgeries. Banks constantly improve security and use various methods to keep the infrastructure secure, including encrypted business networks, two-tiered authentication, and various techniques to ensure that no one exploits the system. Researchers use data analysis software to examine bank business records to determine how adequate internal controls are and identify transactions forged.

When safety and security measures taken by banks tighten, so makes progress by hackers in technology, as they maintain to keep themselves a step ahead of others. Therefore, it takes a few hours to understand security steps in that direction, i.e., technology equivalent to the technologies applied by these cybercriminals. Hence, this sector requires highly skilled professionals in cybersecurity, having avid minds and those who can diligently work encompassing security of e-banking systems and have the capability to realize countermeasures for all potential internet banking forgeries. In general, this research is conducted to analyze the issues that prevent customers from adopting e-banking services. Specifically, this study focuses on ascertaining the problems associated with adopting e-banking services in Pakistan from the customer's perspective rather than the bank's perspective.

OBJECTIVES OF THE RESEARCH

The objectives of the research are to discuss the nature and techniques of attacks by cybercriminals, to highlight security techniques in the contemporary era, to understand the perceived risks of customers regarding e-banking services in Pakistan, to highlight the registration process of e-banking services in Pakistan, to explore the aspects encompassing the security of the system in Pakistan, and to critically analyze the reliability of transactions over the internet in Pakistan.

E-BANKING IN GLOBAL CONTEXT

The industrial sector is undoubtedly one of the most significant service sectors for the national economy (Chavan, 2013; Li et al., 2021; The Financial Brand, 2018). Risks to modern, highly advanced, technology-driven societies are now more significant than ever before (Hettiarachchi, 2013; Lee, 2009). Individuals must safeguard themselves against the vastly increased private harm (Suki, 2010). From the banks' perspective, internet banking is supposed to result in cost savings and increased competition (Polasik & Wisniewski, 2009).

This method of service distribution is regarded as an essential weapon (Elleithy, 2008; Li et al., 2021). It will keep new web-based consumers who want to use banking facilities anywhere they want (Bai, Law, & Wen, 2008). Digital banking also allows banks to expand their customer base by drawing new customers from existing internet users (Dannenberg & Keller, 1998; Suganthi, Balachandher, & Balachandran, 2001).

Financial experts have rated financial services websites as lagging behind other sectors in terms of overall innovation over the last five years (Li et al., 2021). Unlike other shopping websites, internet banking pages rank poorly in terms of architecture and technological use. According to recent financial research, bank customers are the most satisfied when choosing when, where, and how they conduct their banking (Pedro et al., 2018). Banks must devote more time and resources to strengthening customer relationships and differentiating customer experiences (Gao & Owolabi, 2008). It is a subject attracting many banks around the world (Eckenrode, 2006; Kephart, 2005).

According to financial experts, banks should learn a few lessons from many non-bank sectors, demonstrating ingenuity in dealing with self-service solutions for their clients (Li et al., 2021; Pedro et al., 2018). Internet technology can allow banks to expand their internet services with potential features that will increase customer service experiences (Li et al., 2021; Yiu, Grant, & Yiu, 2021; Yiu, Grant, & Degar, 2007). It will give them more leverage over their e-banking experience as a whole (Sayar & Wolfe, 2007; Yu & Lo, 2007).

Since financial transactions include the sharing of sensitive as well as personal data (Laukkanen, Sinkkonen, & Laukkanen, P., 2009), the confidence factor is a significant factor affecting customer usage of internet banking websites (Ortega, Martinez, & Hoyos, 2007; Suh & Han, 2002). Customers' confidence in banks, especially online banking, is eroding due to the continued occurrences of internet banking security breaches and studies (Fox, 2005). As a result, all efforts to improve customer loyalty and expand applicable security monitoring functionality must consider concerns related to the introduction of internet banking (Li et al., 2021; Kuisma, Laukkanen, & Hiltunen, 2007; Lallmahamood, 2007).

NATURE AND PURPOSE OF CYBER-ATTACKS

The contemporary banking sector necessitates having thorough technological awareness of cyber-attacks and the weaknesses they are focused on increasing rapidly. Therefore, it requires adequate safety and security initiatives to counter the increasing problems of e-banking scams. Moreover, cyber-attacks are growing at a large scale that cyber developers should be equipped with advanced technical knowledge and skills. Each cyber-attack is designed to bypass the authentication structures applied by banks to facilitate their clients. Cyber-attacks are usually based on the software developed by cybercriminals, either on the victims' computers (i.e., malware) or through different forms of social engineering to attract victims to a phony website (phishing) or through installing rogue applications on their mobile gadgets (Vila, 2015).

The critical trajectories on which cyber-attacking strategies can be built are explained by Holtz et al. (2011). Credential theft is a form of cybercrime in which a victim's proof of identity is stolen. After a good password breach, the perpetrator would have the same account rights as the victim. The first step of a credential-based assault is credential theft. A common and prevailing cyber-attack in which cybercriminals use malware or phishing, attempt to gain consumer credentials through login as valid users, and perform monetary transactions. Rather than stealing passwords of users through the authentication method, it is pretty complicated if cyber-attackers take complete control of their devices, and after that, the users' devices are utilized to access e-banking execute forgeries. Content manipulation happens between the user and browser in the application layers. The intruder may alter and control data without the users' knowledge. The attacker modifies the database by inserting a few more profiles and configuring the passwords for them; this allows unauthorized parties to access confidential business information while remaining undetected.

TECHNIQUES OF ATTACKS

Cyber-attacks are primarily carried out using web tools and are now readily accessible on the internet. These web tools can secure classified data, replace a forged page with an authentic website, and users are tricked into the input on these fake websites. The following are some kinds of common cyber-attacks that could intrude on the security systems of banks:

1. **Malware:** E-commerce and e-government are employed widely in the contemporary era by public and private organizations. Cybercriminals have frequently targeted such systems and services. Amongst monetarily focused cybercriminals, malware viz. banking Trojans are popular. Malware cyber-attacks could be generally defined in network-linked and non-network-linked features (Kiyavash et al., 2013; Saeed et al., 2013) as spyware, adware, backdoors, worms, trojans, and rootkits. Spyware is a malicious malware that gathers information about an individual or organization and sends it to another party that affects the user, such as by breaching their privacy or jeopardizing the protection of their computer. Adware is software that creates money for its creator by displaying internet ads in its user interface or on a screen shown to the user during the installation process. A backdoor is any mechanism that allows permitted and unauthorized users to bypass standard security measures and obtain high-level user access (also known as root access) to an operating device, network, or software program. A machine worm is a malicious software program with the primary goal of infecting other machines while operating on compromised devices. A machine worm is a self-replicating malware that spreads to uninfected machines by duplicating itself. Trojans belong to the significant class of malware that is employed widely in e-banking frauds. A rootkit is a malicious software that grants unauthorized users privileged access to a device and restricted software zones. Keyloggers, banking login stealers, password stealers, antivirus disablers, and bots for DDoS attacks are examples of malicious techniques found in a rootkit.

Trojans have several methods of operating, which can help regarding the performance of skills, such as sniffing, spamming, and backdoors. Sniffing is the method of continuously tracking and recording all data packets that travel across a network. Network/system administrators use sniffers to track and troubleshoot network traffic. Attackers use sniffers to intercept data packets containing personal data such as passwords and account records. Spamming is the practice of sending multiple unsolicited messages (spam) to large groups of people for commercial advertising, non-commercial proselytizing, any illegal purpose (especially the fraudulent purpose of phishing) or simply sending the same message to the same user over and over again.

Trojans are known to be one of the most tenacious malware that, in a considerable time, could dodge traditional firewall and antivirus competencies that help hackers to gain classified data (Hutchins et al., 2011). Trojans lead to one of the most severe security risks to e-banking since they are designed to carry out forgery in the banking sector. Trojan banking malware codes are set up on the users' computer via a typical computer virus and worm to collect information (i.e., authentication, activities of the users' information, and classified data like credit card particulars) when the victims use e-banking. However, the most critical is the "key loggers" that collect, register, interpret the users' keystrokes, and even capture images on the display when e-banking sessions are in progress. Leading loggers also record the actions of users on typical websites (Vila, 2015).

2. **Man-in-the-Middle Attack:** Typically, by concealing their identification (for instance, by DNS poisoning), the hackers who can control Wi-Fi access points, switches, DNS, as well as network routers are capable of attracting users, and it seems as though the information is originated from a reliable source. Hence, users do not know that they have visited the forger's website rather than the official. Throughout the period, victims' data are dispatched to perpetrators, who could then employ the data to do business scams. These cyber-attacks could be performed through false credentials that make the users assume that the websites they have logged into are safe and authentic without understanding that the perpetrators' website's SSL certificate is forged.

3. **Brute Force Attacks:** In this method, with software aid, the cyber-attacker attempts to breach the protection and get accessibility to texts, users' I.D.s, and passwords. Automated software is employed in brute force cyber-attacks to produce several predictions to obtain the required data. It is a tactic to predict victims' crucial information like a password.

4. **Phishing:** It is a deceptive tactic involving social engineering (referring to individuals being psychologically coerced to carry out certain acts or expose sensitive data) and technological deception (Anderson, 2008). Since an authentic-looking website and email can be a hoax, confidential data viz., passwords, usernames, debit and credit card data are reclaimed. Some outlets that claim to be legitimate, namely, auction websites, social websites, online payment platforms, banks, are usually used by cybercriminals for this forgery.

5. **Fraudulent certificates:** Through issuing forged security documents, impostors build pages that resemble genuine websites to trick consumers into revealing their data. Moreover, by exploiting the one-security step (i.e., the green padlock on internet browsers) all internet users have been taught to trust, cybercriminals could then steal their money. These padlocks are thought to depict that a secure digital record is engaged. Nevertheless, they can now be obtained for free by cybercriminals. In reality, fake documents' placement does not imply that licensed operators or certifying agents have been engaged in unlawful activities.

SECURITY TECHNIQUES IN CONTEMPORARY ERA

Security techniques adopted by banks usually comprise digital certificates, two-factor authentication (2FA), and captcha. The emerging security techniques encompassing banks are deep learning, analysis tools, big data, certificate transparency, and HTTP security response headers.

Figure 1. Taxonomy of E-Banking Attacks, Divided by Attack Target

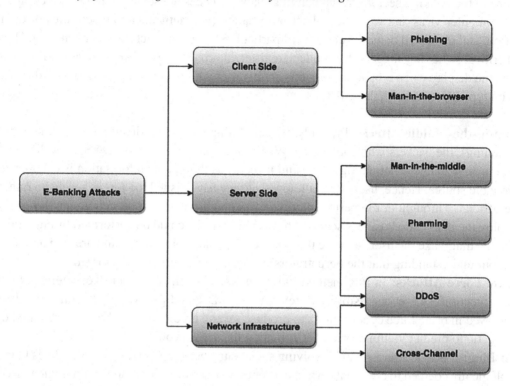

RESEARCH METHODOLOGY

Primary as well as secondary sources are used in this research. For primary sources, the formulated questionnaire was used for e-banking customers in Karachi (Pakistan). Secondary data sources include past research, the internet, policy manuals, and newspapers. For fulfilling the objectives of this research study, a survey was conducted. Questionnaires were distributed, and this study's total response rate remains 92%, which is very high for this kind of investigation, thus creating a foundation for acquiring reliable answers.

The questionnaire consisted of three sections. The first section gathered customer information, such as the introduction. The second section was about the banking services the customer is currently using. In contrast, the third section inquired about the respondents' perspective on e-banking services and their satisfaction level regarding the traditional banking system in Pakistan. In both ways, i.e., analytically and technically, data were treated, and results are presented in a tabular form and the analysis of graphical images. The sample size was 100, and data was collected from local banks located in six districts of Karachi, i.e., District Central, District East, District Korangi, District Malir, District South, and District West.

ICTS AND DIGITAL ENTERPRISE TRANSFORMATION

Progress in information and communication technologies has undoubtedly created many benefits, conveniences, and cost savings for businesses (Allen 2019). These advantages include cost savings in highly automated business processes, data revolution in firms that are turning data generated by Information and Communication Technologies into insights that drive new services and products, and ICT-enabled transactions such as telemedicine, e-shopping, and social media that allow consumers to have more choices (Rouse, 2019).

ICTS AND E-BANKING RELATED ISSUES

The typical person is gaining experience and trust online and is gradually using the internet to perform critical activities in their everyday lives, according to general internet usage (Akhlaq, 2011; Kawai, 2019; Vondracek et al., 2019). It involves making financial transfers and obtaining financial records (Allen, 2019; Chavan, 2013; Dannenberg & Kellner, 1998). Allen (2019) believes that organizations that use Digital Enterprise Transformation will gain significant competitive advantages because it unleashes creativity on a large scale. Customers' future demands are addressed rapidly, and changing marketplace requirements are met through organizational agility. Saadullah Khan (2009) addressed the main roadblocks to ICT acceptance as well as e-banking. He has defined the following elements: the registration process's complexity, the transaction's usability, potential harm, and the system's security.

Figure 2. Taxonomy of Bank Security Mechanisms, Divided into Physical and Virtual

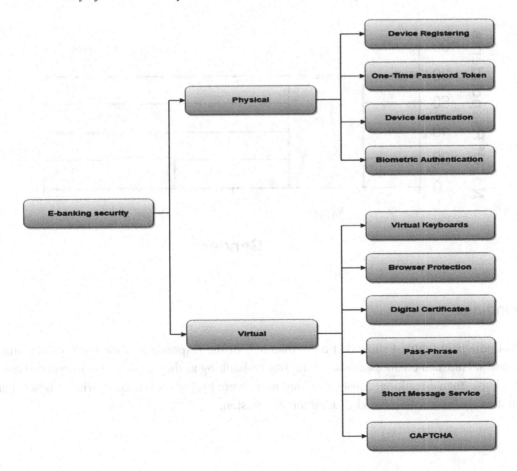

CORE ISSUES OF E-BANKING IN PAKISTAN

Four issues were identified and selected for investigation regarding the adoption of e-banking in Pakistan in this study, perceived (anticipated) risk, registration process complexity, security of the system, and transaction's reliability.

DATA

Findings

Pakistan has a patriarchal system, i.e., it has a male-dominated society and a male-dominated government. In Pakistan, the female labor force penetration is less than 30%, i.e., half of the global average (Ahmed, 2021). The data findings in figure 3 show that more than 80% of the e-banking users were males, as Pakistani females are mostly restricted to domestic chores. The majority of women work in the informal sector, where they are employed as domestic workers, home-based workers, and piece-rate workers for manufacturing companies without any legal security (Ahmad, 2018).

Figure 3. Gender participation and roles

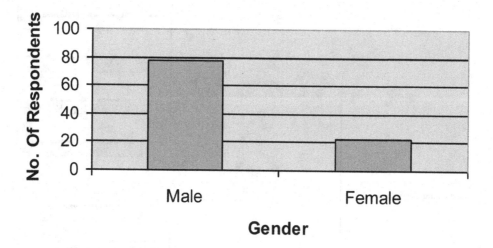

Data Findings

The data findings in figure 4 show that more than half of the respondents were bankers, accountants, and engineers. Pakistani businesspeople refrain from e-banking as they think that conventional banking is more reliable than e-banking. Most e-banking users were highly professional, which shows that occupation directly links with e-banking adoption in Pakistan.

Figure 4. Occupation roles and professional categories

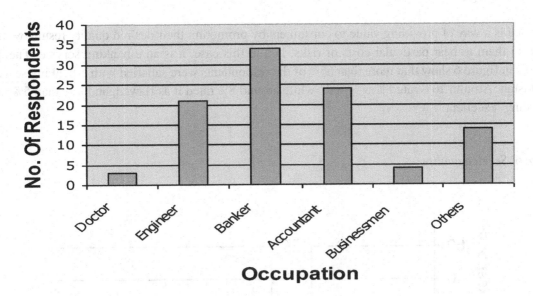

Data Findings

Income is the money received by a person or a company in exchange for labor, the production of a good or service, or the investment of resources. Wages and salaries are the most common sources of income for most people. Businesses make money by selling products or services for more than they cost to produce, i.e., in this case, it is the income level of e-banking users in Pakistan. The data findings in figure 5 show that more than half of the respondents' salary was between 20000 and 40000, which is higher than the average salary, i.e., 18754 PKR (Pakistan Bureau of Statistics, 2018) and minimum-salary in Pakistan, i.e., 17500 PKR (Sadiq, 2020). Income level has a direct relation to e-banking usage in Pakistan.

Figure 5. Income level distribution

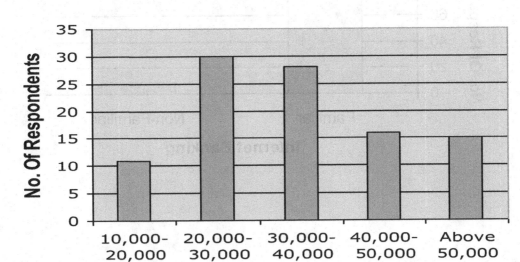

Data Findings

A service is a way of providing value to consumers by promoting their desired quality results without requiring them to bear particular costs or risks, i.e., in this case, it is an e-banking service. The data findings in figure 6 show that more than 65% of the respondents were satisfied with e-banking services in Pakistan. Around 20% rated it as 'good,' while around 8% rated it as flawed, and less than 5% rated it as being 'excellent.

Figure 6. Service quality

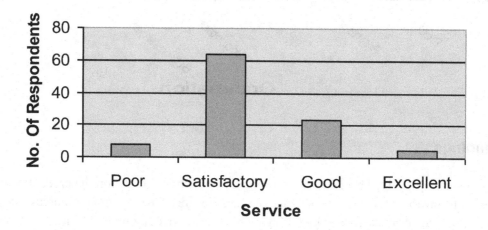

Figure 7. Internet Banking Familiarity

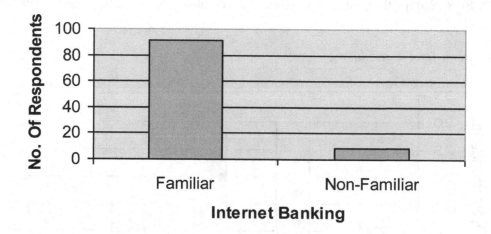

DATA

Findings

Familiarity is the quality or state of being familiar with a phenomenon, i.e., in this case, it is electronic banking. If an individual is not aware of a product or service, then there is a chance that the adoption rate will be much lower. The data findings in figure 7 show that more than 90% of the respondents had familiarity with internet banking in Pakistan, which is a good sign of its acceptance in the future.

DISCUSSION

Almost 89% of banks in Pakistan are online. They have launched their websites and rendering e-services to their customers which has significantly increased the cybersecurity attacks. Unfortunately, in Pakistan, e-banking services are not yet fully catering to the customers' expectations as most of the banks' websites are static and have very minute information according to the customer's point of view. There is also no live support for their customers, and there is a big communication gap between the banks' management and customers. After analysis of the data, there were three main findings of this research. First, banks should enhance the security level of the virtual environment. Second, the banks have to implement such policies, which create a more secure environment for carrying out reliable transactions. Third, the banks should minimize the level of perceived (anticipated) risks in the e-transaction environment to gain their customers' trust. Few banks offer email contact facilities to their customers. If the banks want to understand and cater to their customers' requirements and expectations, they have to improve their services, i.e., more secure and fast operations. In simple words, the banks should keep in mind what kind of services they offer in the market and how secured and controlled they are. Engaging people in banking over the internet and attracting customers' needs should be considered along with all pertinent aspects of e-banking's secure environment in the Pakistani context.

MAIN FINDINGS OF THE STUDY

In Pakistan, the development and the use of internet banking are still at a very early stage. Like any other technology, e-banking comes with a lot of perceived risks to the customers. The bank's management should take initiatives to manage and control all its pertinent risks. They should also implement new and revised security policies, improve internal communication, evaluate and upgrade their services as per customer's expectations. They must also develop innovative contingency plans to minimize these perceived (anticipated) risks further. The banks can undoubtedly enhance their ability to control and manage various cyber risks inherent from e-transaction's activities. They should also implement more security to minimize the respective risks and increase customer authentication, like personal identification numbers and audit trials.

The respondent's data also reveals that the registration process of e-banking in Pakistan is not very complicated and still needs some improvement. More convenience needs to be added to the customer's side, and in return, the customers will associate themselves more with the internet banking system vehemently.

The respective research findings reveal that security is the most critical issue for customers while adopting e-banking services. The banks must ensure a more secure online environment for their customers, and initiatives should also be taken to illustrate authenticity, confidentiality, and online transactions' integrity. So, the customers feel safe to transact via the internet as insecurity issues make it difficult for them to develop their trust in Pakistan's e-banking system.

The respondents' data also reveal that banks' websites should also provide proper functioning to their customers and should be operative all time. It is also significant for the customers that their bank's homepage never freezes, especially after filling in all of the respective information, because it could create irritation and confusion. It should also be noted that accurate and problem-free links and page download times are of great concern to e-banking customers in Pakistan. Transactions should be secured as well as paid more attention to e-banking service providers. E-banking websites must have accurate and updated information. These websites should also provide information about investments, stocks, and foreign exchange to gain prospective customers' attention.

SOLUTIONS AND RECOMMENDATIONS

To research with the corporate customers and trade finance to investigate more of the external and internal issues of e-banking system and customer's adoption intention towards it. Banks should install hardened operating systems, i.e., the system's software and firewalls should be configured to the highest security settings in consonance with the level of protection as per the customer's requirement. Banks should conduct regular system as well as data integrity checks. They must also implement a multi-tier application architecture that differentiates session controls, business logic, presentation logic, server-side input validation, database access, deploying stringent user authentication in wireless local area networks, and protecting sensitive data the help of strong encryption and integrity controls. Banks should also increase their ability to control as well as manage various risks inherent from e-transaction activities. Banks also need to implement more security to minimize the associated risks to increase their customer authentication, such as personal identification numbers and audit trails. Secure connections should be ensured. Official banking apps should be used. When a session is completed, a user should always log out. Antivirus, firewalls, and updated software should be used. Account details should not be given on cellular phone and email. Secure Wi-Fi networks to be used for e-banking. A strong password should be used. Passwords and login details should not be saved on computers and e-devices. The bank account's activity should be regularly checked. One should never open or click ambiguous links and emails.

The substantial change from traditional to digital banking using technology and cybersecurity is focused on effectiveness and trust. The most automated, innovative, and safe supply of goods and amenities could promote the digital banking experience, the crux of the Bank 3.0 idea. However, it would be necessary to associate this modern paradigm with bank information security. Besides recognizing new corporate models, procedures, and innovations that would help customers to adapt to the definition of Bank 3.0, chief executive officers who plan to provide this distinctive feature must strengthen the notion that this would not be conceivable without investments in cyber-security.

Finally, from a technical, organizational, and cultural standpoint, Bank 3.0 should be flexible enough to permit itself to adjust to the fast-evolving market and technology environs constantly. Hence, procedures, resources, and infrastructure are linked to the fundamentals that a company should progressively cover. It comprises implementation, from operational, organizational, technical, or technological, to legal and governing problems. With all this in mind, would a company have the comprehensive ability to assure its security, despite many business worlds?

FUTURE RESEARCH DIRECTIONS

E-banking is undoubtedly a developing technology in Pakistan and across the globe. Various issues influence the customer's intentions to adopt e-banking. In this research, the researcher has tried to investigate some pertinent issues, and there still is room for further investigations regarding the adoption of e-banking in the Pakistani context. Individuals' perceptions of e-banking vary based on whether they conduct transactions for themselves or for their employers, which is fascinating. Comparing one's views on private e-banking vs. e-banking for business purposes as a corporate customer can show some fascinating details. As a result, a more detailed examination of the demographics and user's context will aid in determining how these factors affect corporate customers' decision-making and e-banking consumption in Pakistan. Customers' preferred method of performing future research encompassing acceptance problems of e-banking in Pakistan is to use a contextual, qualitative, or eclectic approach can be customer's preferences, cybersecurity, gender's adaptability of modern technology, and perceived and actual risks.

In the future, banking institutions would probably experience more safety and modernization challenges. Every day, a growing number of technologies are moving to the digital realm, signaling a transformation in attitude, business prototypes, and cyber-security measures. Businesses who have been affected by the move expect that their banks' programs will positively help them. This anticipation can be expressed in four ways: imagination, versatility, convenience, and multichannel. It can also allow companies to request new banking facilities without going through lengthy and complex processes that rely on clients' physical presence in banks. It could be interactive apps for smartphones, smartwatches, tablets, and other mobile devices. It may be a streamlined multichannel practice that keeps consumers engaged and in touch with institutions on a more frequent basis.

The concept of the e-banking system has been strengthened for many years, not only with the advancement of the internet but also with the aid of modernization and technology employed for data safety. Information security also has some weaknesses that cybercriminals could at certain stages apply to intrude networks, steal, or capture classified information. Users should think of different protocols evolving as a result of discussions about the future of business organizations. While modern banking technology such as online banking, mobile banking, and Bitcoin is widely used, the evolution in digital signatures, cryptography, Blockchain, computer protection, and other security-related issues may also be connected to them.

Technology advances have resulted in an all-digital world, and corporate transactions are increasingly being blended into our everyday lives as they have become more convenient and transparent. It can be seen in the case of purchases made with mobile phones. The business area has evolved in terms of information technology investment and business activities involving products and services. The emergence of Bank 3.0 (a concept suggested by Brett King in 2012 that argues that banking does not need physical space because merely it is an activity) is fueled by technological advancements such as cyber-security and cloud computing.

However, it is notable that this development resulted from the transformation of models and that the advent of digital banking was one of the monetary market's most significant experiments, promoting major alterations with regards to its customers' conduct. Soon, we could see a significant conceptual shift in fiscal organizations; they stop to be banks and transform into monetary aides in the age of Bank 3.0, all occurring online and with minor intervention from institutions and people.

CONCLUSION

Cyber frauds have become illegal globally, consisting of professional and educated criminals having excellent technical skills and accessibility to very specialized resources and understanding how the business system functions. However, with a growing number of people, the degree of sophistication of frauds is increasing progressively. As a result, advancements in identification technology and precautions must be assured. The most advanced anti-fraud systems use big data analytics to apply disruptive statistical algorithms digitally, giving banks the ability to detect and deter suspicious activity as it occurs.

In the high-tech anti-fraud systems, machine learning has also changed into a critical enabler, and significant development in its role could be seen in the future. New generations of risk modeling are beginning to substitute the mathematical, probability-based method that has been applied so far through machine-learning systems built for detecting forged banking records transactions in large quantities. A myriad of cyber frauds people face in the modern world often occur at the user's end, wherein hackers deceive users into presenting their private data and classified details that are then applied to cyber-attackers ' advantages to performing fraudulent activities. As a result, banks can use an e-banking system that is protected from customers. Moreover, to keep the scammers under control, security measures should be required at all times.

Computer professionals are trying to build anti-fraudulent programs that are more responsive to multifaceted collusion trends and frauds that are often a prominent feature of skillfully conducted cyber-fraud. The anti-fraud sensitive systems would also help banks establish a better position between detecting frauds and facilitating clients to perform their businesses without hindrance. Improved technologies and innovative machine-learning approaches will give banks access to more advanced solutions that are more reliable and competitive, reducing fraudulent activities.

This study's findings identified a lack of system security concerns as the prime reason for the slow adoption of e-banking as derived from the respondents' data. The bank management should build strong system security to attract their customers and to develop their trust. Low reliability of transactions is one of the most critical issues that include worries about the system's security. The registration process of e-banking also needs improvement. The findings also reveal that the respondents have a greater security concern level as customers do not have much confidence to engage in significant financial transactions via the internet.

Furthermore, providing banking services over the internet should be considered part of a more significant consumer support and distribution approach. As a result, the partnership established may be used as a portal for product information distribution. These initiatives may also aid in the migration of consumers to the electronic banking world. Finally, this has resulted in significant cost cuts for the respective banks across Pakistan.

REFERENCES

Ahmad, I. (2018, March 10). No country for working women. *The Express Tribune*. https://tribune.com.pk/story/1655699/6-no-country-working-women#:~:text=women%20workforce%20engagement.-,Though%20women%20constitute%2049%25%20of%20Pakistan's%20population%2C%20they%20constitute%20only,higher%20than%20women%20(24.8%25)

Ahmed, A. (2020, February 19). Female labour force share on the rise in Pakistan, unlike India. *Dawn*. https://www.dawn.com/news/1535374

Akhlaq, M. A. (2011). Internet banking in Pakistan: Finding complexities. *Journal of Internet Banking and Commerce, 16*(1), 1–14.

Al-Furiah & Al-Braheem. (2009). Comprehensive study on methods of fraud prevention in credit card e-payment system. In *Proceedings of the 11th international conference on information integration and web-based applications & services. ACM.*

Allen, J. P. (2019). *Digital entrepreneurship*. Routledge. doi:10.4324/9780429506567

Amoros, J. E., Ciravegna, L., Mandakovic, V., & Stenholm, P. (2019). Necessity or opportunity? The effects of State fragility and economic development on entrepreneurial efforts. *Entrepreneurship Theory and Practice, 43*(4), 725–750. doi:10.1177/1042258717736857

Anderson, R. J. (Ed.). (2008). *Security engineering: A guide to building dependable distributed systems*. Wiley.

Bai, B., Law, R., & Wen, I. (2008). The impact of website quality on customer satisfaction and purchase intentions: Evidence from Chinese online visitors. *International Journal of Hospitality Management, 27*(3), 391–402. doi:10.1016/j.ijhm.2007.10.008

Carminati, M., Polino, M., Continella, A., Lanzi, A., Maggi, F., & Zanero, S. (2018). Security evaluation of a banking fraud analysis system. *ACM Transactions on Privacy and Security, 21*(3), 1–31. Advance online publication. doi:10.1145/3178370

Chavan, J. (2013). Internet banking - Benefits and challenges in an emerging economy. *International Journal of Research in Business Management, 1*(1), 19–26.

Dannenberg, M., & Kellner, D. (1998). The bank of tomorrow with today's technology. *International Journal of Bank Marketing, 16*(2), 90–97. doi:10.1108/02652329810206743

Eckenrode. (2006). *Building a more responsive banking industry: The bell is ringing but are banks salivating?* The Tower Group.

Elleithy, K. (2008). *Innovations and advanced techniques in systems, computing sciences and software engineering*. Springer. doi:10.1007/978-1-4020-8735-6

Fox, S. (2005). *The state of online banking*. Pew Internet & American Life Project. http://www.pewInternet.org/pdfs/PIP_Online_Banking_2005.pdf#search='The%20State%20of%20Online%20Banking%20Pew

Frazier, L. (2021, March 22). Digital banking trends evolve in 2021, but customer needs stay the same. *Forbes*. https://www.forbes.com/sites/lizfrazierpeck/2021/03/22/digital-banking-trends-evolve-in-2021-but-customer-needs-stay-the-same/?sh=6de017101cd3

Gao, P., & Owolabi, O. (2008). Consumer adoption of internet banking in Nigeria. *International Journal of Electronic Finance, 2*(3), 284–299. doi:10.1504/IJEF.2008.020598

Gerrard, P., & Cunningham, B. (2003). The diffusion of internet banking among Singapore consumers. *International Journal of Bank Marketing, 21*(1), 16–28. doi:10.1108/02652320310457776

Government of Pakistan. (2002). *Electronic Transactions Ordinance*. http://www.pakistanlaw.com/eto.pdf

Government of Pakistan, Pakistan Bureau of Statistics. (2018). *Pakistan average monthly wages*. https://www.ceicdata.com/en/pakistan/average-monthly-wages-by-industry/average-monthly-wages

Hettiarachchi, H. A. H. (2013). Factors affecting customer adoption of internet banking. *Kelaniya Journal of Management, 2*(2), 68–87. doi:10.4038/kjm.v2i2.6551

Holtz, M., David, B., Deus, F. E., de Sousa, R. T. Jr, & Laerte, P. (2011). *A formal classification of internet banking attacks and vulnerabilities*. Academic Press.

Holzhauer, B. (2021, January 11). Digital banking is the new normal in 2021: What to expect from banks. *Forbes*. https://www.forbes.com/advisor/banking/digital-banking-as-new-normal-2021-what-to-expect/

Hutchins, E. M., Clopp, M. J., & Amin, P. R. (2011). *Intelligence-driven computer network defense informed by analysis of adversary campaigns and intrusion kill chains*. Lockheed Martin Corporation.

Kawai, N. (2019). Historical transition of psychological theories of fear: The view of fear in behaviorism. In *The Fear of Snakes* (pp. 1–18). Springer. doi:10.1007/978-981-13-7530-9_1

Kephart, J. O. (2005). *Research challenges of autonomic computing*. IBM Research. https://domino.research.ibm.com/library/cyberdig.nsf/papers/5E932DBBECF5EBCF85257067004EE94C/$File/rc23692.pdf

Khan, S. (2009). *Adoption issues of internet banking in Pakistani' firms* (Unpublished Master Thesis). Lulea University of Technology, Lulea, Sweden.

Khrais, L. T. (2015). Highlighting the vulnerabilities of online banking system. *Journal of Internet Banking and Commerce, 20*(3). Advance online publication. doi:10.4172/1204-5357.1000120

King, B. (2012). *Bank 3.0: Why banking is no longer somewhere you go but something you do*. Wiley. doi:10.1002/9781119198918

Kiyavash, N., Koushanfar, F., Coleman, T. P., & Rodrigues, M. (2013). A timing channel spyware for the CSMA/CA protocol. *IEEE Transactions on Information Forensics and Security, 8*(3), 477–487. doi:10.1109/TIFS.2013.2238930

Kuisma, T., Laukkanen, T., & Hiltunen, M. (2007). Mapping the reasons for resistance to internet banking: A means-end approach. *International Journal of Information Management, 27*(2), 75–85. doi:10.1016/j.ijinfomgt.2006.08.006

Lallmahamood, M. (2007). An examination of an individual's perceived security and privacy of the internet in Malaysia and the influence of this on their intention to use e-commerce: Using an extension of the technology acceptance model. *Journal of Internet Banking and Commerce, 12*(3), 1–26.

Laukkanen, T., Sinkkonen, S., & Laukkanen, P. (2009). Communication strategies to overcome functional and psychological resistance to Internet banking. *International Journal of Information Management, 29*(2), 111–118. doi:10.1016/j.ijinfomgt.2008.05.008

Lee, M. C. (2009). Factors influencing the adoption of internet banking: An integration of TAM and TPB with perceived risk and perceived benefit. *Electronic Commerce Research and Applications, 8*(3), 130–141. doi:10.1016/j.elerap.2008.11.006

Li, F., Lu, H., Hou, M., Cui, K., & Darbandi, M. (2021). Customer satisfaction with bank services: The role of cloud services, security, e-learning and service quality. *Technology in Society, 64*, 101487. doi:10.1016/j.techsoc.2020.101487

Marous, J. (2021, March 29). The evolution of banking: 2021 and beyond. *The Financial Brand.* https://thefinancialbrand.com/111080/evolution-future-digital-banking-baas-transformation/

Ortega, B., Martinez, J., & Hoyos, M. J. M. (2007). An analysis of web navigability in Spanish internet banking. *Journal of Internet Banking and Commerce, 12*(3), 1–8.

Overby, S. (2020). *What is digital transformation?* https://enterprisersproject.com/what-is-digitaltransformation

Pedro, C. P., Ramalho, J. J. S., & Silva, J. V. (2018). The main determinants of banking crises in OECD countries. *Review of World Economics, 154*(1), 203–227. doi:10.100710290-017-0294-0

Phaneuf, A. (2021a, January 15). The disruptive trends & companies transforming digital banking services in 2021. *Business Insider.* https://www.businessinsider.com/digital-banking

Phaneuf, A. (2021b, January 15). The future of retail, mobile, online, and digital-only banking technology in 2021. *Business Insider.* https://www.businessinsider.com/future-of-banking-technology

Polasik, M., & Wisniewski, T. P. (2009). Empirical analysis of internet banking adoption in Poland. *International Journal of Bank Marketing, 27*(1), 32–52. doi:10.1108/02652320910928227

Rouse, M. (2019). *ICT (Information and Communications technologies).* https://searchcio.techtarget.com/definition/ICT-information-and-communications-technology-or-technologies

Sadiq, N. (2020, October 26). Minimum wage. *The News International.* thenews.com.pk/print/734687-minimum-wage#:~:text=Like%20all%20other%20countries%2C%20Pakistan,social%20security%20and%20overtime%20pay

Saeed, I. A., Campus, J. B., Selamat, M. A., Ali, M., & Abuagoub, M. A. (2013). A survey on malware and malware detection systems. *International Journal of Computers and Applications, 67*(16), 25–31. doi:10.5120/11480-7108

Sayar, C., & Wolfe, S. (2007). Internet banking market performance: Turkey versus the U.K. *International Journal of Bank Marketing, 25*(3), 122–141. doi:10.1108/02652320710739841

Singh, S., Cabraal, A., & Hermansson, G. (2006). What is your husband's name?: Sociological dimensions of internet banking authentication. In *Proceedings of the 18th Australia conference on Computer-Human Interaction: Design: Activities, Artefacts and Environments*. ACM. 10.1145/1228175.1228217

Suganthi, R., Balachandher, K. G., & Balachandran, S. (2001). Internet banking patronage: An empirical investigation of Malaysia. *Journal of Internet Banking and Commerce, 6*(1).

Suh, B., & Han, I. (2002). Effect of trust on customer acceptance of internet banking. *Electronic Commerce Research and Applications, 1*(3-4), 247–263. doi:10.1016/S1567-4223(02)00017-0

Suki, N. M. (2010). An empirical study of factors affecting internet banking adoption among Malaysian consumers. *Journal of Internet Banking and Commerce, 15*(2), 2–11.

The Financial Brand. (2018). *The four pillars of digital transformation in banking.* https://thefinancial-brand.com/71733/four-pillars-of-digital-transformation-banking-strategy/

Vila, J. A. (2015). *Identifying and combating cyber-threats in the field of online banking.* Academic Press. https://www.sslshopper.com/what-is-ssl.html

Vondracek, F. W., Lerner, R. M., & Schulenberg, J. E. (2019). *Career development: A life-span developmental approach.* Routledge., doi:10.4324/9781315792705

Yiu, C. S., Grant, K., & Degar, D. (2007). Factors affecting the adoption of internet banking in Hong Kong, implications for the banking sector. *International Journal of Information Management, 27*(5), 330–351. doi:10.1016/j.ijinfomgt.2007.03.002

Yu, C. S., & Lo, Y. F. (2007). Factors encouraging people to adopt online banking and discouraging adopters to use online banking services. In *Proceeding of Business and Information, Tokyo, Japan: International Conference on Business and Information.*

Zaidi, E. (2021, March 3). Future of e-banking tied to digital inclusion of masses. *The News International.* https://www.thenews.com.pk/print/798127-future-of-e-banking-tied-to-digital-inclusion-of-masses

ADDITIONAL READING

Ahanger, R. G. (2011). An investigation into the determinants of customers' preferences and satisfaction of internet banking (Empirical study of Iranian banking industry). *Journal of Applied Sciences, 11*(3), 426–437. doi:10.3923/jas.2011.426.437

Casalo, L., Flavian, C., & Guinaliu, M. (2008). The role of usability and satisfaction in the consumer's commitment to a financial services website. *International Journal of Electronic Finance, 2*(1), 2008–2031. doi:10.1504/IJEF.2008.016883

Hamel, G. (2000). *Leading the revolution.* Harvard Business School Press.

Munusamy, S., & Chelliah, W. M. (2010). Service quality delivery and its impact on customer satisfaction in the banking sector in Malaysia. *International Journal of Innovation, Management and Technology, 1*(4), 398–404.

Nupur, J. M. (2010). E-banking and customers' satisfaction in Bangladesh: An analysis. *International Review of Business Research Paper, 6*(4), 145–156.

Rahmath, S., & Hema, D. (2010). Customer perspectives on e-business value: A case study on internet banking. *Journal of Internet Banking and Commerce, 15*(1), 2–11.

Suh, H., & Han, I. (2002). Effect of trust on customer acceptance of internet banking. *Electronic Commerce Research and Applications, 1*(4), 7–63. doi:10.1016/S1567-4223(02)00017-0

Walker, R. H., Craig-Lees, M., Hecker, R., & Francis, H. (2002). Technology-enabled service delivery: An investigation of reasons affecting customer adoption and rejection. *International Journal of Service Industry Management, 13*(7), 91–106. doi:10.1108/09564230210421173

Westland, C. (2002). Transaction risk in e-commerce. *Decision Support Systems, 33*(1), 87–103. doi:10.1016/S0167-9236(02)00010-6

KEY TERMS AND DEFINITIONS

Adoption Issues: The act of embracing ideas or technology.
Banking: The services offered by a bank.
E-Banking: Online banking, i.e., via the internet.
Perceived Risks: Uncertainty a consumer has while using electronic services.
Reliability: The quality of being trustworthy.

Chapter 15
Advancing Cybersecurity for Business Transformation and Enterprise Architecture Projects:
Deep Learning Integration for Projects (DLI4P)

Antoine Trad
ⓘ https://orcid.org/0000-0002-4199-6970
IBISTM, France

ABSTRACT

In this chapter, the author bases his research project on his authentic mixed multidisciplinary applied mathematical model for transformation projects. His mathematical model, named the applied holistic mathematical model for projects (AHMM4P), is supported by a tree-based heuristics structure. The AHMM4P is similar to the human empirical decision-making process and is applicable to any type of project; it is aimed to support the evolution of organisational, national, or enterprise transformation initiatives. The AHMM4P can be used for the development of the cybersecurity subsystems, enterprise information systems, and their decision-making systems, based on artificial intelligence, data sciences, enterprise architecture, big data, deep learning, and machine learning. The author attempts to prove that an AHMM4P-based action research approach can unify the currently frequently-used siloed MLI4P and DLI4P trends.

INTRODUCTION

In this chapter, the author presents a Project based generic concept for decision making that is based on DLI4P; where the AHMM4P manages various types of algorithms. A transformation depends on the capacities of the decision-making system and the profile of the Business Transformation Manager (or simply the *Manager*) and his team; who are supported by a holistic framework (Trad & Kalpić, 2020a).

DOI: 10.4018/978-1-7998-6975-7.ch015

The role of Deep Learning Integration for Projects (DLI4P) and the AHMM4P is essential for managing various type of algorithms in a transformation project. All the author's research publications deal with Business Transformation Projects' (or simply a *Project*) complexity as well as the use of underlying Decision-Making System for Projects (DMS4P) and Enterprise Architecture Integration for Projects (EAI4P). The author's framework promotes *Project* technics to ensure success, by: 1) modelling artefacts; 2) implementing Machine Learning Integration for Projects (MLI4P) and DLI4P components; 3) EAI4P support; 4) the use of a Generic Project Pattern (GPP) as an interface; and 5) using complex algorithmics.

Figure 1. EAI4P cycles synchronize with Project resources

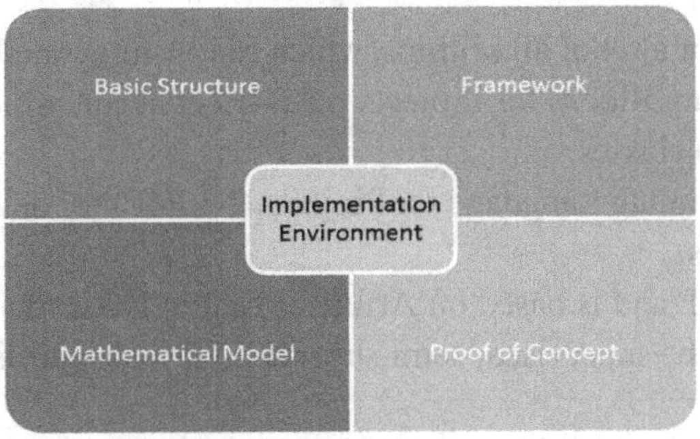

As shown in Figure 1, the implementation of such *Project*s requires significant knowledge of EAI4P. GPP handles DLI4P calls and offers: 1) a generic data architecture; 2) an interfaces; and 3) data and modules modelling. GPP is a part of the Selection management, Architecture-modelling, Control-monitoring, Decision-making, Training management and Project management Framework (SmAmCmDmTmPmF, for simplification in further text the term Transformation, Research, Architecture, Development framework or *TRADf* will be used). As shown in Figure 1, *Project* resources interact with all the enterprise's (or simply an *Entity*) architecture phases, using the data Building Blocks for Projects (dBB4P) or the holistic brick (Trad & Kalpić, 2020a). GPP is MLI4P's main interface and the trends of using DLI4P for 2021, is tremendous, as shown in Figure 2 (Kapoor, 2021).

Figure 2. The growing role of MLI4P and DLI4P on Hyperautomation (Kapoor, 2021)

AHMM's Application and Instantiation for a Specific Domain

Domain	= Geopolitical Analysis (GA)	(14)
AHMM(*Domain*)	= $\bigcup$ ADMs + MMs(*Domain*)	(15)

keywords are: Deep Learning, Cybersecurity, Mathematical models, Strategic Vision, Financial Technology, Risk Management, Atomic Building Blocks, Requirements Engineering, Business Transformation Projects, Enterprise Architecture, Critical Success Factors/Areas, Performance Indicators.

This chapter like all other works related to framework has a specific structure and uses sections with bullet points.

BACKGROUND

DLI4P uses the GPP as an interface to interact with the EAI4P and has the following characteristics:

- Is a composite model, or a set of algorithms, which can be integrated in various types of *Projects*.
- Uses the atomic Building Blocks for Projects (aBB4P) concept; which corresponds to an autonomous set of objects and classes.
- Uses a Natural Programming Language for Projects (NLP4P) for development of various types of scenarios and interfaces.
- DLI4P is part of MLI4P and is based on Artificial Neural Networks (ANN) using representation learning. Learning can be supervised, semi-supervised or unsupervised.

The author's global research topic and final Research Question (RQ) (hypothesis #1-1) is: "Which business transformation manager's characteristics and which type of support should be assured for the implementation phase of a business transformation project?" The targeted business domain is any business environment that uses: 1) complex technologies; and 2) frequent transformation iterations. For this phase of research, the sub-question (or hypothesis #2-3) is: "What is the impact of the DLI4P on *Projects and risk management like* cybersecurity?"

MAIN FOCUS OF THE CHAPTER

In this chapter the focus is on DLI4P's usages, that are a part of the Decision making (Dm) module, and it tries to prove that such a concept can be built on a loosely coupled EAI4P. It uses the Data Management Concepts for Projects (DMC4P) to interface various types of data sources. The DLI4PAI uses the AHMM4P, which manages algorithms that are used to analyse data and offer conclusions. *Projects* are increasingly complex and data is global; these huge amounts of data are full of valuable operational information.

Intelligence Basics

Intelligence is a concept that is older than Information and Communication Systems (ICS) and inspects if it is possible to create machines that contain *human like* cognitive abilities. This concept has influenced academicians, researchers and other scientific fields. It emerged as a practical domain in the middle of the 20th century. In 1950, Alan Turing (an English computer scientist, cryptanalyst, mathematician and theoretical biologist) developed a fundamental test for machine intelligence, which is known as the *Turing Test* (Schmelzer, 2021).

Data Sciences Basics

Data Sciences Integration for Projects (DSI4P) represents the entire process of finding meaning in data and MLI4P algorithms are often used to assist in this search because they are capable of learning from data; whereas DLI4P is a sub-field of MLI4P with enhanced capabilities. DSI4P's basics are (Guru99, 2021):

- It involves extracting insights in the context of vast amounts of data, by using scientific methods, algorithms and processes. It helps in finding hidden patterns from raw data. DSI4P is the result of evolution of statistics, data analysis and Big Data for Projects (BGD4P).
- It is cross functional and tries to extract knowledge from structured or unstructured databases.
- It translates business problems into a RDP4P and then translates them into solutions.
- It includes, statistics, visualization, DLI4P, MLI4P and DL4P concepts.
- Its process includes: discovery, data preparation, model planning, model building, operationalize and the communication of results.
- It predicts business solutions as it looks backward, where DSI4P looks forward.
- Possible applications are 1) Internet search; 2) Recommendation systems; 3) Image and Speech recognition; 4) Gaming world; 5) Online price comparison; and 6) many other…
- Its biggest challenges are: various information, data formats and sources.

DLI4P Basics

DLI4P basics are (Grossfeld, 2020):

- Intelligence has two major concepts: MLI4P and DLI4P and it's important to know the differences and to know their insides.
- DLI4P is an evolution of MLI4P, where it uses ANN that enables machines to make accurate decisions without human support.
- MLI4P is basically:
  - *Algorithms that parse data, learn from that data, and then apply what they've learned to make informed decisions… An easy example of a MLI4P is an on-demand music streaming service, where a decision on which new songs to recommend to a listener. MLI4P associates listener's preferences with other listeners who have a similar musical taste. This technique, which is often simply touted as Artificial Intelligence (AI), is used in many services that offer automated recommendations.*
  - Supports different types of automated tasks from multiple industries.
  - Involves a complex algorithm that serve a goal function.
- The main difference between DLI4P and MLI4P are:
  - DLI4P is a subset of MLI4P; and technically is they function in a similar way, however, their capabilities are different. DLI4P is what powers human-like AI.
  - Basic MLI4P models to improve need guidance, like, if an algorithm returns an inaccurate prediction, then a specialist makes adjustments. A DLI4P model's algorithm is autonomous if a prediction is accurate using ANN.
  - A DLI4P model is able to learn as like it has its own brain.

- A DLI4P model is designed to continually analyze data with a logic structure similar to the human by using ANN. The ANN is inspired by the biological human brain, leading to a process of learning that's far more capable than that of standard MLI4P models.
- DLI4P models can be risky and can draw incorrect conclusions, but when it functions, then it is considered as a scientific marvel that many consider being the backbone of true intelligence based *Projects*.
- An example of DLI4P is Google's AlphaGo hat learned to play the game called Go, which is known for requiring sharp intellect and intuition.
- To main differences are:
  - MLI4P uses algorithms to parse data, learn from that data, and make informed decisions based on what it has learned
  - DLI4P structures algorithms in layers to create an ANN that can learn and make decisions autonomously.
- The role of data:
  - Massive data (or *Big Data Era*), is this phase's major issue.
  - There is need for a powerful DLI4P for massive data, where DLI4P models' fuel is massive data that can use these algorithms.
- MLI4P and DLI4P in customer services, applications for customer services utilize MLI4P algorithms where the priorities are: self-service, increase agent productivity and workflows robustness.
- Data used by algorithms comes from customer queries, which includes relevant contexts. Aggregation of contexts leads to accurate predictions, this makes DLI4P crucial for businesses.

A Composite AI Model

AI, DSI4P, MLI4P and DLI4P, composite model's basics are (Schmelzer, 2021):

- The used terms are rough classifications that are in constant evolution and *TRADf* is in fact a mixed method that is an advanced version of DLI4P.
- DLI4P is powerful and when combining it with DSI4P and other AI domains gives the capability for managing massive data and delivering recommendations.
- It leads to solving the challenge of complex *Project* problems; like:
  - Predictive analytics forecasts of customer behavior, business trends and events based on analysis of constantly changing criterias.
  - Intelligent conversational systems which support interactive communications with various parties.
  - Anomaly detection systems that can respond to continually evolving threats and enforce cybersecurity and fraud detection.
  - Hyperpersonalization systems enable targeted advertising, product recommendations, financial guidance and medical care and other services.
  - Major financial crimes.
- Even if they are separate concepts which individually offer capabilities, combing them is transforming the business ecosystems.
- The author's framework goes even further to combine them with EAI4P and other fields.

RESEARCH DEVELOPMENT PROCESS FOR PROJECTS

As shown in Figure 3, the Research and Development Process for Projects (RDP4P) focuses on the impacts of the mechanistic EAI4P integration and uses a mixed hyper-heuristics based methodology (Vella, Corne, & Murphy, 2009). The RDP4P is based on an extensive cross-functional Literature Research Process for Projects (LRP4P), an adapted Qualitative Analysis for Artificial Analysis (QLA4P) methodology and on a Proof of Concept (PoC) for the proposed hypotheses.

Figure 3. The mixed method flow diagram (Trad & Kalpić, 2020a)

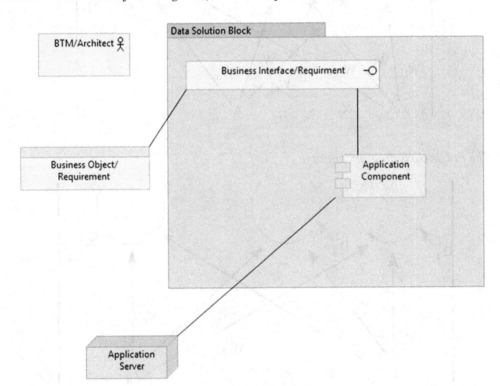

Projects and business engineering fields use a PoC or prototyping to establish GPP's and DLI4P's (Camarinha-Matos, 2012): 1) feasibility; 2) viability; 2) major technical issues; and 3) offer recommendations. Where GPP is an interface to all AI modules with EAI4P; and as shown in Figure 4; uses the Knowledge Management System for Projects (KMS4P) to store solutions.

The PoC is used to prove the feasibility of GPP's interaction with MLI4P and DLI4P. The PoC is based on a defined case that uses data class diagram for a data transaction, as shown in Figure 5; where an MLI4P module is called.

Figure 4. The PoC's overall diagram of components

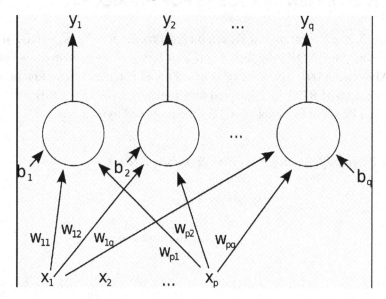

Figure 5. The PoC's class diagram package

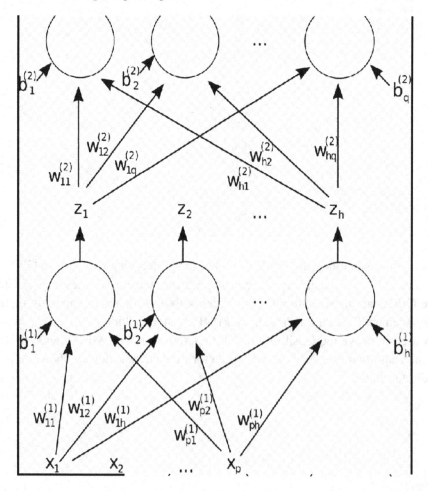

Critical Success Areas, Factors, GPP and DLI4P

Critical Success Area (CSA) is a selected set of Critical Success Factors (CSF), where the CSF is a set of Key Performance Indicators (KPI), where each KPI corresponds/maps to a single *Project* requirement and/or problem type. For a given requirement (or problem), an *Entity* architect can identify the initial set of CSAs and their CSFs to be managed by the GPP to support the DMS4P, by calling DLI4P modules. Hence the CSFs are important for the mapping between the problem types, knowledge constructs, organisational items. Therefore, CSFs reflect possible problem types that must meet strategic *Project* goals and predefined constraints. Measurements are used to evaluate performance in each of the CSA sets, where CSFs (and KPIs) can be internal or external to the environment.

THE TARGETED APPLICATION DOMAIN AND INTERACTION

Main Stages

This chapter's targeted application domain characteristics are (OMNI-SCI, 2021):

- This exploration step: is the principal difference between DSI4P and Data Analytics Integration for Projects (DAI4P); where the DSI4P has a macro view, aiming to propose precise questions about data to extract and to have more insights.
- Modelling: fits the data into the model using MLI4P algorithms and the model selection depends on the type of data and the business requirement.
- Definition: DSI4P includes the mining of large datasets of raw data, both structured and unstructured, in order to identify patterns and extract actionable insight from them. It includes, statistics, inference, computer science, predictive analytics, DLI4P, MLI4P and BGD4P.
- Lifecycle, the 1st stage in an MLI4P process involves: acquiring data, extracting data and entering data into the system. The 2nd stage: is maintenance, which includes Data Warehouses Integration for Projects (DWI4P), data cleansing, data processing, data staging and EAI4P (data architecture).
- Processing follows and is a combination of DLI4P and DSI4P's fundamental activities; and the next is the analysis stage and predictive analysis, QLA4P and text mining activities.
- During the final stage, a specialist communicates insights; and this involves data visualization, data reporting, the use of various Business Intelligence Integration for Projects (BII4P) tools.

Combining Fields and a Holistic View

DAI4P has more to do with placing historical data in context and less to do with predictive modelling and DLI4P. DAI4P needs precise questions and unlike DSI4P does not create statistical models or use DLI4P tools. DLI4P is predictive and the relationship between the DAI4P and data is retrospective (OMNI-SCI, 2021). The AHMM4P based GPP gives the possibility to combine all these disciplines in a holistic manner.

RDP4P's CSF's

Based on the business case's (and its CSA) LRP4P process managed and weighted the most important CSFs that were used.

Table 1. The RDP4P's CSFs that have an average of 9.0

	Critical Success Factors	KPIs	Weightings Ranges	Values
1	RDP4AJ	Feasible	From 1 to 10	9
2	AHMM4AJ	PossibleClassification	From 1 to 10	9
3	DMC4AJ	AutomatedRules	From 1 to 10	9.1
4	PLATFORM	IntegrationPossible	From 1 to 10	9
5	EA4AJ	AdvancedStage	From 1 to 10	9
6	ENVIRONMENT	Advanced	From 1 to 10	9.4
7	GAP	IntegrationPossible	From 1 to 10	8.5
8	ASSEMBLING	IntegrationPossible	From 1 to 10	8.4

EvaPA

RESULT: 8.925

As shown in Table 1, the result's aim is to prove or justify the RDP4P's feasibility; and the result permits to move to the next CSA that is the AHMM4P.

AHMM4P'S SUPPORT FOR DLI4P

The *TRADf* is based on AHMM4P based GPP, which in turn supports the DLI4P, DSI4P, QNA4P and QLA4P based scenario(s), to interface the DMS4P, as shown in Figure 6.

Figure 6. The overview

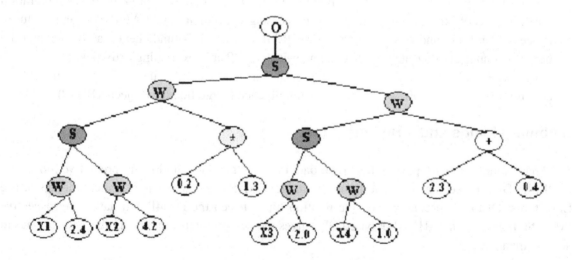

A Generic Holistic Approach

The *TRADf* proposes a holistic approach to analyse events and eventually manage possible risks to help Application and Problem Domains (APD) managers to avoid major *Project* pitfalls. Traditionally, complex risk concepts, were associated with a single origin or CSF; mainly personified to concretise a complex situation, like cybersecurity. Pitfalls may be defined as a violation of an internal risk's related CSF that can be due to various types of problems or constraints; where in DLI4P's concept it can be applied for example, for: 1) estimating *Project* risks; 2) APD risk initiatives; 3) special domains, like geopolitical events or telecommunication implementations; 4) tracking financial crimes and cybersecurity; and 3) other CSFs...

The Microartefacts' Distributed Architecture Model for the GPP

The AHMM4P has a dynamic defined nomenclature to facilitate GPP's integration with EAI4P model, and its Architecture Development Method for Projects (ADM4P). The AHMM4P is the *Entity's* holistic structural model that supports a set of multiple coordinated DLI4P processing to deliver solutions that correspond to various just in time processing schemes which use the same *Project's* central pool of CSAs and CSFs. The basic AHMM4P nomenclature, is presented in Figure 7, to the reader in a simplified form, to be easily understood on the cost of a holistic formulation of the AHMM4P's basics for GPP, DLI4P, MLI4P, QNA4P and QLA4P. The DMS4P uses an AHMM4P's instance to solve a *Project* problem.

Figure 7. The applied AHMM4P's basics nomenclature (Trad & Kalpić, 2020a)

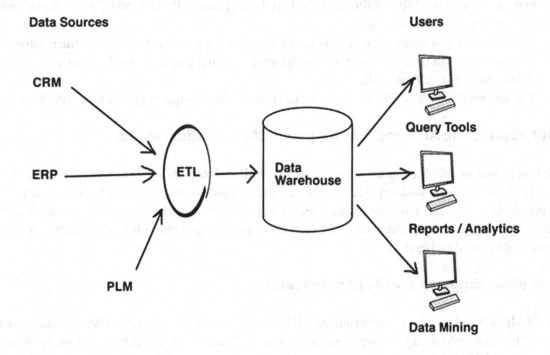

AHMM4P's instances supports the GPP; using CSFs weightings and ratings (in phase 1), and based on multicriteria evaluation (selected and defined constraints). The symbol $\sum$ indicates summation of all the relevant named set members, while the indices and the set cardinality have been omitted. AHMM4P's role should be understood in a broader sense, more like set unions. As shown in Figure 7:

- The abbreviation "mc" can be used, and stands for micro, which depends on the granularity.
- The symbol $\sum$ indicates summation of weightings/ratings, denoting the relative importance of the set members selected as relevant. Weightings as integers range in ascending importance from 1 to 10 (or another range defined by GPP based analysists).
- The symbol $\underline{U}$ indicates sets union.
- The proposed AHMM4P supports GPP as an interface model; using CSFs weightings and ratings evaluation.
- The selected corresponding weightings to: CSF ϵ { 1 ... 10 }; are integer values, that are presented in tables. The rules were presented in the RDP4P section.
- The selected corresponding ratings to: CSF ϵ { 0.00% ... 100.00% } are floating point percentage values.

The AHMM4P's Structure for GPP and DLI4P Based Solutions

The AHMM4P's has a composite structure that can be viewed as follows:

- The static view has a similar static structure like the relational model's structure that includes sets of CSAs/CSFs that map to tables and the ability to create them and apply actions on these tables; in the case of AHMM4P for GPP and DLI4P, is done by using QNA4P and QNA4P microartefacts and not tables (Lockwood, 1999).
- In the behavioural view, these actions are designed using a set of AHMM4P nomenclature, the implementation of the AHMM4P is in the internal scripting language, used also to tune the CSFs (Lazar, Motogna, & Parv, 2010).
- The skeleton of the *TRADf* uses microartefacts' scenarios to support just-in-time GPP requests.

Entity/Enterprise Architect as an Applied Mathematical Model

The EAI4P and its ADM4P are the kernel of this RDP4P and they are the basics of its *TRADf;* where the AHMM4P is GPP's skeleton. The LRP4P has shown that existing LRP4P's resources on DLI4P, are practically inexistent. This pioneering research work is cross-functional and links all the DLI4P or QLA4I/QNA4P based microartefacts to an *Entity*; where the main reasoning component is a DLI4P engine that is based on heuristics.

Heuristics, Empirics and Action Research

The DLI4P is based on a set of synchronized AHMM4P instances, where each AHMM4P can launch a QLA4P beam-search based heuristic processing (Kim, & Kim, 1999). Weightings and ratings concept support the AHMM4P to process a GPP request for an optimal analysis or solution for a given *Entity's Project* problem. Actions Research Integration for Projects (ARI4P) (Berger, & Rose, 2015) can be considered as a set of continuous beam-search heuristics processing phases and is similar to design, analysis and architecture processes, like the ADM4P (Järvinen, 2007). Fast changing *Entity's* change requests may provoke an important set of events and problems that can be hard to predict and solve; that makes the GPP various types of actions useless and complex to implement. The AHMM4P is responsible for the DLI4P that uses QLA4P heuristic process for *Entity's* problem solving and synchronizes a set of AHMM4P instances which have also separate heuristics processes and are supported by a dynamic tree algorithm, as shown in Figure 8 (Nijboer, Morin, Carmien, Koene, Leon, & Hoffman, 2009) that manages tree nodes and their correlation with memorized patterns that are combinations of data states and heuristic goal functions. The AHMM4P capacities are measured by analysing the *TRADf's* AHMM4P tree.

Figure 8. The applied heuristics tree algorithm (Nijboer, Morin, Carmien, Koene, Leon & Hoffman, 2009)

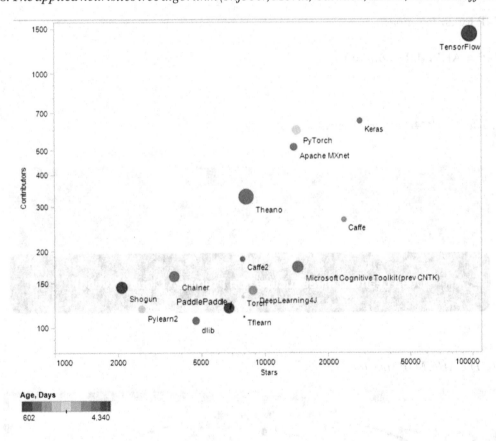

Holistic ARI4P based heuristics enables reflective practice that is the basis of a holistic approach to develop EAI4P based GPP solutions, where its kernel and skeleton are a dynamic DMS4P (Leitch, & Day, 2006). GPP bridges the EAI4P with MLI4P, DLI4P, QLA4P and QNA4P methods (Loginovskiy, Dranko, & Hollay, 2018). Where the author estimates that MLI4P, DLI4P, QLA4P and QNA4P methods are subsets (that can be combined) of the ARI4P which is *TRADf's* main stub.

The Applied GPP Transformation Mathematical Model

GPP is a part of the *TRADf* that uses microartefacts to support just-in-time DMS4P actions. The GPP based component and interface, are based on a light version of the ADM4P, having a systemic approach. A *Project* using GPP is the combination of GPP based, EAI4P methodology (like the TOGAF's ADM4P) and the proposed AHMM4P, that is presented in Figures 9 and 10.

The generic AHMM can applied to any specific domain; in this chapter and RDP4P's phase, the *Domain,* is GPP based and the AHMM4P = AHMM(APD), as shown in Figure 10; where AHMM can applied to any domain and any concept.

The proposed combination can be modelled after the following formula for the GPP Transformation Mathematical Model (GAIPTMM) that abstracts the *Project* for a given *Entity*:

(AHMM4P for an *Iteration*):

iAHMM4P = AHMM4P(*Iteration*);

Figure 9. The AHMM4P generic structure

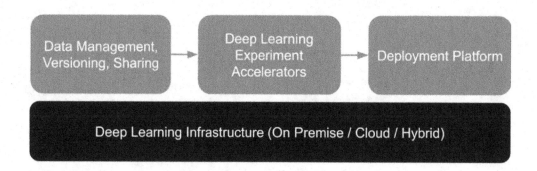

Figure 10. The AHMM4P structure

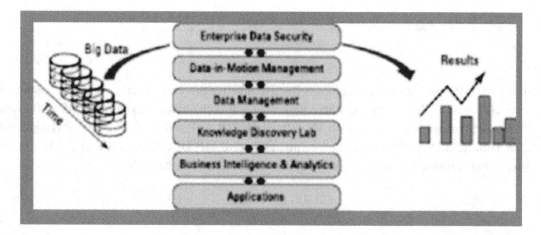

iAHMM4P=Weigthing$_1$*iAHMM4P_Qualitative+Weigthing$_2$* iAHMM4P _Quantitative (16).

The *Project's* AHMM4P (PAHMM4P) = $\sum$ iAHMM4P for an ADM4P's instance (17).

(GAIPTMM):

GAIPTMM = $\sum$ PAHMM4P instances (18).

The Main Objective Function for GPP based (MOFGAIP) of the GAIPTMM's formula can be optimized by using constraints and with extra variables that need to be tuned using the AHMM4P. The variable for maximization or minimization can be, for example, the *Project* success, costs or other (Dantzig, 1949). For this chapter's PoC the success will be the main and only constraint and success is quantified as a binary 0 or 1. Where the MOF4P definition will be:

Minimize risk GAIPTMM Function (GAIPTMMf) (19).

The AHMM4P is based on a concurrent and synchronized *TRADf*, which uses concurrent threads that can make various AHMM4P instances run in parallel and manage information through the use of the AHMM4P's NLP4P. The GAIPTMM is the combination of the GPP, *Project* and EAI4P methodologies and a holistic AHMM4P that integrates the *Entity* or organisational concept, ICS that have to be formalized using a functional development environment like *TRADf's* NLP4P.

The AHMM4P's CSFs

Based on the LRP4P, the most important AHMM4P's CSFs that are used are evaluated to the following:

Table 2. The AHMM4P CSFS have an average of 9.0

Critical Success Factors	KPIs		Weightings
CSF_DLI4AI_AHMMAI_TRADf_Integration	Complex	▼	From 1 to 10. **08 Selected**
CSF_DLI4AI_AHMMAI_InitialPhase	Proven	▼	From 1 to 10. **10 Selected**
CSF_DLI4AI_AHMMAI_PoC	Complex	▼	From 1 to 10. **08 Selected**
CSF_DLI4AI_AHMMAI_Qualitative&Quantitative	Feasible	▼	From 1 to 10. **09 Selected**
CSF_DLI4AI_AHMMAI_Final_Instance	Proven	▼	From 1 to 10. **10 Selected**
CSF_DLI4AI_AHMMAI_ADM4AI_Integration	Proven	▼	From 1 to 10. **10 Selected**
CSF_DLI4AI_AHMMAI_APD_Interfacing	Complex	▼	From 1 to 10. **08 Selected**

valuation

As shown in Table 2, the result's aim is to prove or justify that it is complex but possible to implement atheAHMM4P in the *Entity's* ICS. The next CSA to be analysed is DMC4P as an interface.

DATA AND ALGORITMIC SUPPORT

The Model's Unit of Work

A holistic alignment, identification and classification of all the RDP4P's resources must be done, so that the research process can start. A holistic alignment needs also, to define the Unit of Work (UoW) or the "1:1" mapping concept.

Data Solution Blocks

Upon a concrete *Project* requirement, the *Manager* issues a a contract to resolve this requirement by using EAI4P. EAI4P ensures that new requirements are managed accordingly to the *Project's* records and objectives. The requirement is linked to an instance of a newly created data Building Block for Projects (dBB4P) and its instance (a data Solution Block for Projects, dSB4P). The dBB4P is a part of GPP; and as shown in Figure 11, the *TRADf* uses the GPP and DLI4P that includes the pattern on how to integrate data solution blocks which are instances of the dBB4Ps.

Figure 11. The PoC's dSB4P diagram

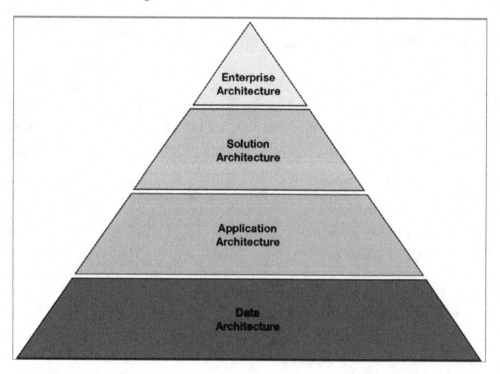

ARTIFICIAL NEURAL NETWORKS

Basics

ANNs are computing systems inspired by the biological neural networks that constitute the brain and it is based on a collection of connected nodes called *artificial neurons* (AN), which simulates the neurons in a biological brain. A connection, or the synapses in a biological brain, transmits a signal to other neurons. ANs receive a signal, processes it and signals neurons that are connected to it. The signal at a connection is represented with a real number and the output of each neuron is evaluated by a non-linear function of the sum of its inputs. The connections are known as edges; neurons and edges have a weighting (CSF) that adjusts as learning proceeds. The weighting increases or decreases the strength of the signal at a given connection. Neurons are aggregated into layers that perform different transformations on their inputs. Signals travel from the input layer to the output layer (Wikipedia, 2021a).

Figure 12. One layered ANN (Wikipedia, 2021a)

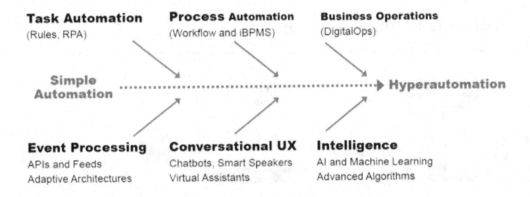

Training

ANNs are trained by processing samples, each of which contains a known input and result, forming probability-weighted associations between the two, then are stored in and internal storage. ANN's training is usually conducted by evaluating the difference between the output (result) and a reference output. If needed, ANN adjusts its weighted associations according to a learning rule and using the gap value. Iterative adjustments will tune ANN's output to converge to the target output. After a defined number of adjustments, the training can be terminated based on a defined conditions (supervised learning) (Wikipedia, 2021a).

Models

ANNs started with architecting the human brain to execute tasks that algorithms failed to do then diverted to optimize empirical results, by abandoning attempts to remain coherent with the brain. Neurons are interconnected in different patterns, to connect outputs of some neurons to the input of others. The ANN forms a weighted graph. An ANN has a collection of simulated neurons, where each neuron is a node which is connected to other nodes using relations that correspond to the biological axon-synapse-dendrite connections. Each relation has a weighting, which determines the node's influence (Wikipedia, 2021a).

Anns Components

Neurons

ANNs contain ANs which are conceptually derived from biological neurons. ANs have inputs and produce a single output which is sent to a set of neurons. Inputs can be a sample of data or can be the outputs of other Ans, as shown in Figure 13. The final output neurons of the ANN terminate the processing. Output's valuation is the weighted sum of all the inputs. The weighted sum is sometimes called the activation and is then passed through an activation function to deliver the output.

Figure 13. Multi-layered ANN (Wikipedia, 2021a)

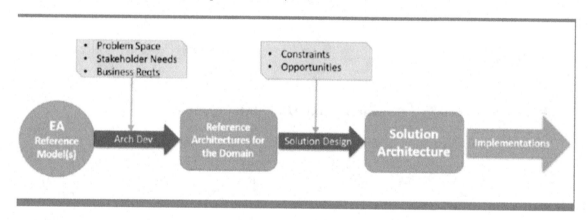

Connections and Weights

ANNs contain connections and each connection provide the output of one ANN as an input to another neuron. Each connection is assigned a weighting that represents its relative importance.

Propagation Function

It computes AN's input from other ANs outputs and their connections as a weighted sum. A bias term can be added to the result of the propagation.

Organization

In DLI4P, ANs are organized in multiple layers. ANs of one layer can connect to ANs of the preceding layers. The layer that receives external data is the input layer and the layer that delivers the result is the output layer and in between there are hidden layers.

Learning

Learning is the adaptation of the ANN to improve a task by considering sample observations. Learning involves adjusting the weighting of the ANN to improve the accuracy of the result. Learning is complete when examining additional observations does not usefully reduce the error rate. Even after learning, the error rate typically does not reach 0. If after learning, the error rate is too high, the network typically must be redesigned. This is done by defining a cost function that is evaluated periodically during learning. As long as its output continues to decline, learning continues (Wikipedia, 2021a).

Learning Rate

The learning rate defines the size of the corrective steps that the model takes to adjust for errors in each observation. A high learning rate shortens the training time, but with lower ultimate accuracy, while a lower learning rate takes longer, but with the potential for greater accuracy.

LEARNING PARADIGMS

Supervised Learning

Supervised learning uses a set of paired inputs and desired outputs. The learning task is to produce the desired output for each input. In this case the cost function is related to eliminating incorrect deductions.

Unsupervised learning

In unsupervised learning, input data is given along with the cost function that depends on the task (the model domain) and any a priori assumptions (the implicit properties of the model, its parameters and the observed variables).

Reinforcement Learning

In applications such as playing video games, an actor takes a string of actions, receiving a generally unpredictable response from the environment after each one. The goal is to win the game, i.e., generate the most positive (lowest cost) responses. In reinforcement learning, the aim is to weight the ANN (devise a policy) to perform actions that minimize long-term (expected cumulative) cost.

Self-learning

Self-learning is a system with only one input and only one output, by using an action. It has neither external advice input nor external reinforcement input from the environment.

Neural Trees

As already mentioned, ARI4P can simulate the DLI4P by adapting an ANN to a heuristic tree. A goal functions and rules are modelled according to the tested problem and delivering a solution, as shown in Figure 14.

Figure 14. The tree structure of an ANN (Pavlopoulos, Vrettaros, & Drigas, 2008)

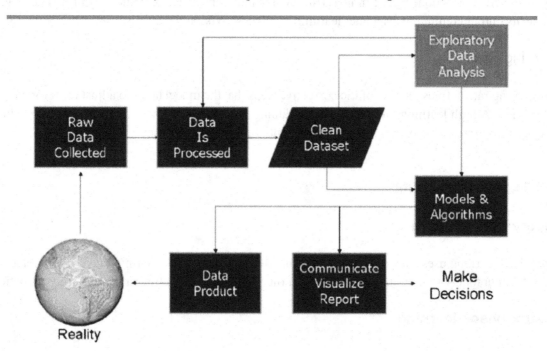

DMC4P's CSF's

Based on the business case's (and its CSA) LRP4P process managed and weighted the most important CSFs that were used.

As shown in Table 3, the result's aim is to prove or justify the RDP4P's feasibility; and the result permits to move to the next CSA that is the data access, architecture and agility.

Table 3. The DMC4P's CSFs that have an average of 9.10

Critical Success Factors	KPIs		Weightings
CSF_DMC4AI_Interface_Data	Feasible	▼	From 1 to 10. **09 Selected**
CSF_DMC4AI_Interface_Transformation	Proven	▼	From 1 to 10. **10 Selected**
CSF_DMC4AI_Interface_Mapping	Proven	▼	From 1 to 10. **10 Selected**
CSF_DMC4AI_Interface_EA4AI	Proven	▼	From 1 to 10. **10 Selected**
CSF_DMC4AI_Interface_CSF_CSA	Feasible	▼	From 1 to 10. **09 Selected**
CSF_DMC4AI_Interface_ANN	Complex	▼	From 1 to 10. **08 Selected**
CSF_DMC4AI_Interface_Learning	Feasible	▼	From 1 to 10. **09 Selected**
CSF_DMC4AI_Interface_Tree	Complex	▼	From 1 to 10. **08 Selected**

valuation

THE DLI4P PLATFORM

Basic Roadmap

The major notions to implement a DLI4P oriented platform are (Veneberg, 2014);

- EAI4P supports the traceability and monitoring subsystem using standard patterns, but is not wise to out-source for GPP applications, because of the strategic goals. Combining DMS4P and DLI4P consolidates the *Entity's* support for business specialists, without the need to trace use data.
- For massive digital data structures, Data Base Management System (DBMS) implemented to access, read and write datasets and d DBMS is a collection of inter-related data.
- DMS4Ps lack data traceability and monitoring in respect for DLI4P processes, where *Project* teams need instructions on how to trace datasets and events.

Enterprise Service Bus and Enterprise Application Integration

An Enterprise Service Bus (ESB) implements an enterprise-wide communication subsystem between mutually interacting applications in a SOA paradigm. An ESB promotes modularity, agility and flexibility in relation to the ICS and *Project*. It is used in Enterprise Application Integration (EAI) approach for heterogeneous and complex services-based *Projects*. *Project*s must use ESB to glue the various data sources of the business environment, through the use of the technology stack and data connectors, which permit a holistic data services' management.

Extraction, Transform and Load

ETL processes are defined as accessing data stored in various locations and transforming them in order to enable their unification, quality or normalization. The DLI4P, proposes the separation of data processing activities; that enables data services to access data without bothering about various data sources' complexities. As shown in Figure 15, the ETL processes are responsible for the access of data from heterogeneous data sources.

Figure 15. Various data sources (Tamr, 2014)

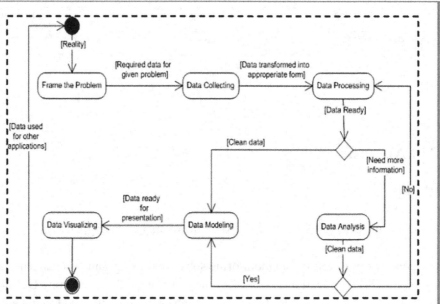

BGD4P for DLI4P

BGD4P for Projects (BGD4P) has the following characteristics (SAS, 2021):

- BGD4P refers to data that is massive, fast or complex that is very complex to process using existing ICS' resources.
- Managing massive data for DLI4P can managed by BGD4P that is based on the now-mainstream definition of big data as the three V's: 1) Volume; 2) Velocity; and 3) Variety.
- Volume: *Entities* collect data from a variety of sources, including business transactions, smart (IoT) devices, industrial equipment, videos, social media and more. In the past, storing it would have been a major volume problem.
- Velocity: The evolution of ICS' and data streams with extreme speed, requests just-in-time processing. It is mainly a problem of performance and scalability.

- Variety: *Entity's* data have various types of formats, from structured, numeric data in traditional databases to unstructured text documents, emails, videos... That needs a unique transformation platform.

Libraries, Components and Platforms

Libraries, Components and Platforms for DLI4P are (Clark, 2018; Hershey, 2020):

- DLI4P is exponentially growing and is based on data representations, Figure 16 shows the major Libraries.
- DLI4P presents huge opportunities, like new revenue potential, product ideas, cost reductions, etc. An *Entity* starts a *Project* with a small team which should PoC a use case to prove its feasibility.
- Building a DLI4P platform is a complex and it is costly to build such platforms, and off-the-shelf tools to put together their platform is an option, as shown in Figure 17. This includes storing massive datasets, needing GPUs for computation, and provisioning hardware for deployment, managing the infrastructure needed for DLI4P.
- The experiment-driven nature of DSI4P is fundamentally different from software engineering, so the related tools and methods are not sufficient for collaborating on model building.
- Building models is complex and need dozens of trainings runs to find effective hyperparameters.
- Deployment platform to support the gap between development and deployment.

Figure 16. The major DLI4P libraries (Clark, 2018)

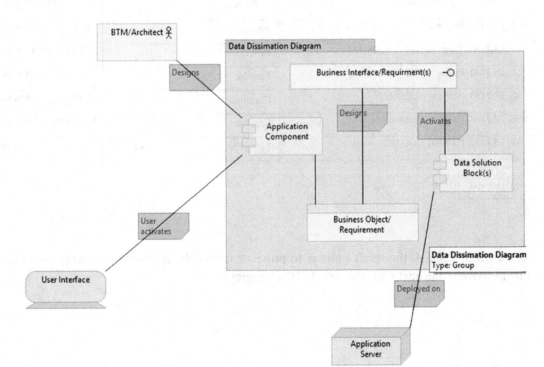

Figure 17. The DLI4P platform (Hershey, 2020)

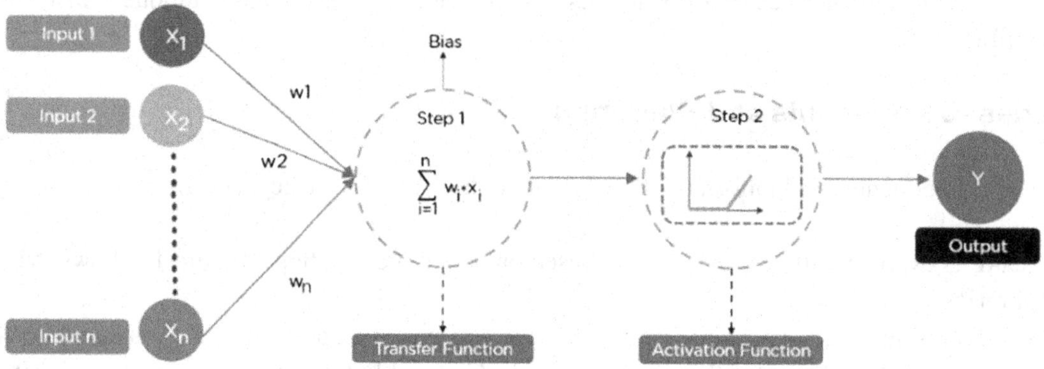

Platform's CSF's

Based on the business case's (and its CSA) LRP4P process managed and weighted the most important CSFs that were used.

Table 4. The Platform's CSFs that have an average of 9.0

Critical Success Factors	KPIs		Weightings
CSF_DLI4AI_Platform_Roadmap	Complex	▼	From 1 to 10. **08 Selected**
CSF_DLI4AI_Platform_ESB_EAI	Feasible	▼	From 1 to 10. **09 Selected**
CSF_DLI4AI_Platform_Legacy_Mainframes	Proven	▼	From 1 to 10. **10 Selected**
CSF_DLI4AI_Platform_EA4AI_ADM4AI	Proven	▼	From 1 to 10. **10 Selected**
CSF_DLI4AI_Platform_CSF_CSA	Feasible	▼	From 1 to 10. **09 Selected**
CSF_DLI4AI_Platform_Scalability	Complex	▼	From 1 to 10. **08 Selected**
CSF_DLI4AI_Platform_Performance	Feasible	▼	From 1 to 10. **09 Selected**
CSF_DLI4AI_Platform_BGD4AI	Complex	▼	From 1 to 10. **09 Selected**

valuation

As shown in Table 4, the result's aim is to prove or justify the RDP4P's feasibility; and the result permits to move to the next CSA that is EAI4P's integration.

EAI4P'S INTEGRATION

EAI4P Principles and Basics

The main EAI4P's principles and basics are:

- MLI4P may be complex in large *Entities* dealing with types of cybersecurity risks and situations.
- DMS4P and DMC4P are implemented using existing BI solutions, combined with DWI4P for storing operational data.
- EAI4P is often used for strategy purposes and provides an overview of complex *Entity* architectures, showing business entities and relations.
- EAI4P accommodates DMC4P to enable data-driven EAI4P. Actually, there is no concept that enables BGD4P integrate in data-driven EAI4P.
- ADM4P supports a data-driven *Entity*; through a specific adaption of the ADM4P permits that DMC4P and BGD4P has on each phase within the ADM4P to support DLI4P.

Figure 18. The layers of data-driven EAI4P

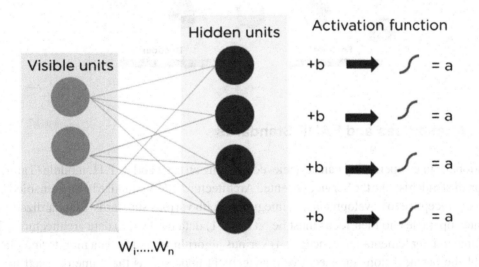

EAI4P Layers

EAI4P's main layers characteristics depend on (Sarkar, 2018):

- Lack of reproducibility and reusable artifacts: DLI4P analyses and modules are to be reproducible.
- Lack of collaboration: siloed should be removed, even though specialists work in an isolated manner.
- Technical debt: there is a lack of standards and EAI4P concepts for DLI4P.

- Build reusable assets: it is important not just to focus on DLI4P but also on Non-Functional Requirements for Projects (NFR4P).
- DLI4P needs to implement EAI4P based *Projects*, to define solutions, application and data models. For this goal there is a need to define layered EAI4P as shown in Figure 19.
- EAI4P based GPP is capable of: 1) envisioning end-to-end solutions: 2) to improve and transform the *Entity*.
- Structured evolution is essential to DLI4P that is an innovative field, that needs GPP as an interface.

Figure 19. Layered EAI4P Hierarchy (Sarkar, 2018)

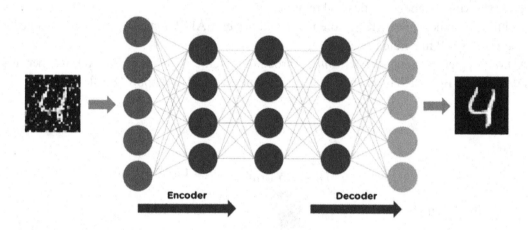

The Role of Resources and EAI4P Standards

Standardization for inter-operability can be achieved by using an ESB and its ETL module (Tamr, 2014). The evolution of standards, like the Service Oriented Architecture (SOA) standards, have enabled DLI4Ps to become more receptive to development and integration with various standards. Standardized *Projects* have to be inter-operable and their focus must be on their: 1) data models; 2) data architectures; 3) software modelling and implementation concepts; 4) various algorithms; and 5) data monitoring platforms. Regardless of the business domain, executive management understands the immense need for agility and the integration of DLI4P using GPP as an interface.

Application Reference Model

Application Reference Model (ARM), as shown in Figure 20, categorizes the system, applications' standards and ICS that support the delivery of service capabilities, allowing various *Entities* to share common solutions. EAI4P's data architect and a *Project's* data analyst, can use the standard ARM, which is not on for analytics, but is also used for EAI4P. ARM is a used, for mapping business APD to *Entity's* applications.

Figure 20. An ARM implementation

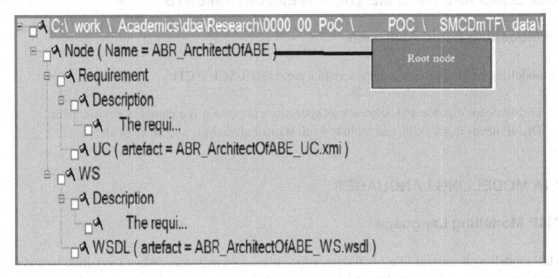

EAI4P's CSF's

Based on the business case's (and its CSA) LRP4P process managed and weighted the most important CSFs that were used.

Table 5. The EAI4P's CSFs that have an average of 9.0

Critical Success Factors	KPIs		Weightings
CSF_EA4AI_Integration_Principles	Feasible	▼	From 1 to 10. **09 Selected**
CSF_EA4AI_Integration_DLI4AI_Strategy	Feasible	▼	From 1 to 10. **09 Selected**
CSF_EA4AI_Integration_Standards	Feasible	▼	From 1 to 10. **09 Selected**
CSF_EA4AI_Integration_EA4AI	Proven	▼	From 1 to 10. **10 Selected**
CSF_EA4AI_Integration_CSF_CSA	Feasible	▼	From 1 to 10. **09 Selected**
CSF_EA4AI_Integration_Layers	Complex	▼	From 1 to 10. **08 Selected**
CSF_EA4AI_Integration_Modelling_Languages	Proven	▼	From 1 to 10. **10 Selected**
CSF_EA4AI_Integration_ARM	Complex	▼	From 1 to 10. **08 Selected**

valuation

As shown in Table 5, the result's aim is to prove or justify the RDP4P's feasibility; and the result permits to move to the next CSA that is modelling and implementation environments.

MODELLING AND IMPLEMENTATION ENVURONMENTS

The Modelling Basic Approach

The modelling basic approach's characteristics are (OMNI-SCI, 2021):

- DLI4P needs capable and autonomous specialists because it is a complex environment.
- DLI4P needs many skills that include from statistical analysis and other fields.

DATA MODELLING LANGUAGES

EAI4P Modelling Language

EAI4P modelling languages like ArchiMate, which is an open and independent modelling language for *Entity* functional, enterprise and data architectures. ArchiMate is supported by many vendors and consulting companies; and it provides instruments to enable *Entity* architects to describe, analyse and visualize the relationships among business (including data) domains in an clear manner (The Open Group, 2013b).

Unified Modelling Language

Unified Modelling Language (UML) can be used with DLI4P in the following contexts (Sikander, & Khiyal, 2018):

- To model data concepts and implementations; like the Data Flow Diagram (DFD) is an artefact that represents a flow of data through a process or a system (usually an ICS).
- The DFD also provides information on the outputs and inputs of each object (like a table) and the process itself. The DFD has no control flow, there are no Dynamic Rules for Projects (DR4P) and no loops. Specific operations based on the data can be represented by a flowchart.
- A UML Diagram, is essential to illustrate a conceptual model to a precise *Project* problem with the component or class diagrams.
- In the context of the process of data analysis, integrates three models as shown in Figure 21, it is the process of inspecting, cleaning, converting and modelling of data, in order to obtain particular results. Raw data is collected from various sources and transformed into usable information streams for DMS4P and DLI4P processing. The UML state diagram for DLI4P process is shown in Figure 22.

Figure 21. The MLI4P process flowchart (Sikander, & Khiyal, 2018)

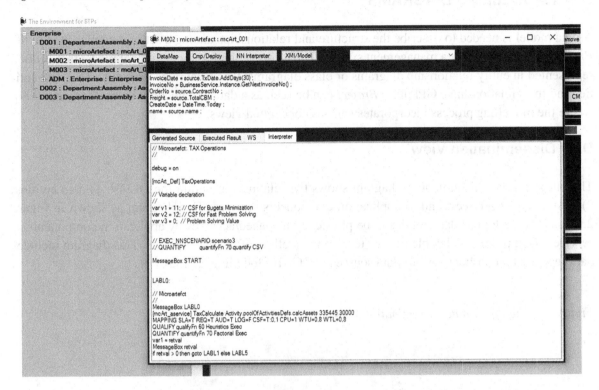

Figure 22. An MLI4P process flowchart, using the UML state diagram (Sikander, & Khiyal, 2018)

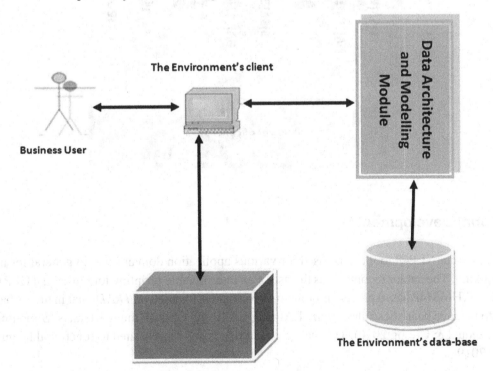

DATA MODELLING DIAGRAMS

A data model is needed to describe the structure and relationships among a set of data managed in the *Project* and stored in a data management system. The most common is the relational model that is often represented in entity-relationship diagrams or class diagrams; these diagrams basically show data entities and their relationships. GPP for a *Project* can be seen as a data architectural view (Merson, 2009); where the modelling process incorporates various conceptual views.

Data Dissemination View

The purposed data dissemination diagram shows the relationship within the DLI4P: 1) data entities; 2) business data services; and 3) application components/services. This diagram as shown in Figure 23, presents the logical data entities to be physically managed/accesses by application components or services. That permits a flexible architecture and modelling of the data sources. This diagram includes data services that abstract various data sources (TOGAF Modelling, 2015a).

Figure 23. The PoC's data dissemination view

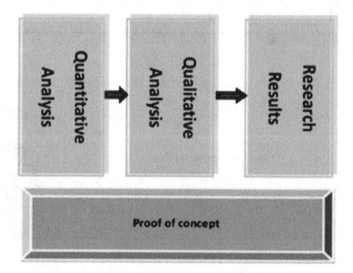

Functional Development

TRADf's internal NLP4P tool can be used for various application domains and in general for hard systems' thinking. The author recommends the use of an interpretable scripting for building a GPP (Moore, 2014). The AHMM4P based process is domain-driven and is founded on *TRADf* that in turn is based on a NLP4P to manage heuristics/rules, *Entity*/EAI4P, QLA4P and QNA4P microartefacts (Simonin, Bertin, Traon, Jezequel & Crespi, 2010). The main characteristics and facts related to functional languages are (Clancy, 2019):

- Functional programming reaches for stardom in finance.
- Financial institutions are adopting functional programming or NLP4P as an alternative to the dominant imperative approach.
- NLP4P results with less bugs as it is stricter, and easier to check and to test.
- It has in-built concurrency constructs, and are optimal for distributed ledgers. Distributed ledgers may find a wide application in the derivatives industry.
- It lacks skilled developers, as well as its memory and speed drawbacks.
- They will become more relevant with the adoption of the Distributed Ledger Technology (DLT) in finance.
- NLP4P make testing easier because of immutability.
- It will continue to spread, as *Entities* become aware of its advantages, but as other, complementary technologies advance.

Environments CSFs

Based on the business case's (and its CSA) LRP4P process managed and weighted the most important CSFs that were used.

Table 6. The environment's CSFs that have an average of 9.40

Critical Success Factors	KPIs	Weightings
CSF_Modelling_Implementation_DLI4AI_Interface	Proven ▾	From 1 to 10. **10 Selected**
CSF_Modelling_Implementation_Modelling_Languages	Proven ▾	From 1 to 10. **10 Selected**
CSF_Modelling_Implementation_Diagrams	Feasible ▾	From 1 to 10. **09 Selected**
CSF_Modelling_Implementation_Functional_Dev	Feasible ▾	From 1 to 10. **09 Selected**
CSF_Modelling_Implementation_CSF_CSA	Proven ▾	From 1 to 10. **10 Selected**
CSF_Modelling_Implementation_ADM4AI_Integration	Proven ▾	From 1 to 10. **10 Selected**
CSF_Modelling_Implementation_APD_Interfacing	Complex ▾	From 1 to 10. **08 Selected**

valuation

As shown in Table 6, the result's aim is to prove or justify the RDP4P's feasibility; and the result permits to move to the next CSA that is the GPP's components integration

GPP'S MAIN COMPONENTS INTEGRATION

GPP's Construct

The GPP's construct has the following characteristics (OMNI-SCI, 2021):

- It should simulate the human brain's functioning using ICS; that includes learning, logical reasoning and auto-correction.
- It supports the *Entity's* system to learn, auto-correct and reasoning and to draw inferences in an independent manner.
- It is generic and has a holistic approach because it can handle a many types of activities, like the humans, all of which demand reasoning, judgment, and thought.
- It uses specialized methods to handle specific tasks.
- It uses neural networks and it needs also to teach its DMS4P to think like a human brain and that needs an extraordinary amount of data. This is the intersection of DSI4P (=the field), GPP (=the goal) and DLI4P (=the process).

USE OF STATISTICS

Statistics Methods' Integration

The Integration of statistics methods have the following characteristics (OMNI-SCI, 2021):

- DLI4P is a broad, cross functional domain that is used in applied business management, ICS, economics, mathematics and software engineering along with statistics.
- DLI4P main challenges require the collection, processing, management, analysis and visualization of large quantities of data.
- There is a close relation between DLI4P and BGD4P. BGD4P exists for unstructured formats and includes some non-numeric data.
- Statistics is also a broad field demanding APD expertise and it focuses on the study of numerical and categorical data; where statistics is an APD that sees use in numerous other verticals.
- DLI4P employs statistical protocols to design the RDP4P and to ensure that its results are valid.

Integration Using GPP

DLI4P's integration has the following characteristics (OMNI-SCI, 2021):

- It is a function of GPP processes data and generates patterns to be used by the DMS4P.
- It is a type of DLI4P, that is focused on ANN that can master unstructured or unlabelled data, without any type of human assistance.
- It uses hierarchical ANNs to be used in DLI4P and are like the human brain.
- DLI4P uses a hierarchy of functions that enables a nonlinear approach to problems' solving.
- BGD4P is mainly unstructured, so the DLI4P is important subset of MLI4P.

Business Intelligence Integration Using GPP

The BII4P has the following characteristics (OMNI-SCI, 2021):

- BII4P is a subset of data analysis, and it analyses existing data for insights into business trends.
- BII4P gathers data from internal and external sources, prepares and processes it for a specific use, and then creates dashboards with the data to resolve business problems.
- MLI4P is a more exploratory, future-facing approach and it analyses all relevant data, current or past, structured or unstructured. Having the goal of smarter, more informed DMS4P processing.

GPP's CSF's

Based on the business case's (and its CSA) LRP4P process managed and weighted the most important CSFs that were used.

Table 7. GPP's CSFs that have an average of 8.50

Critical Success Factors	KPIs		Weightings
CSF_DLI4AI_GAIP_Construct	Feasible	▼	From 1 to 10. **09 Selected**
CSF_DLI4AI_GAIP_DSI4AI	Complex	▼	From 1 to 10. **08 Selected**
CSF_DLI4AI_GAIP_Statistics	Feasible	▼	From 1 to 10. **09 Selected**
CSF_DLI4AI_GAIP_BGD4AI	Complex	▼	From 1 to 10. **08 Selected**
CSF_DLI4AI_GAIP_DLI4AI	Feasible	▼	From 1 to 10. **09 Selected**
CSF_DLI4AI_GAIP_BII4AI	Complex	▼	From 1 to 10. **08 Selected**
CSF_DLI4AI_GAIP_Finance	Feasible	▼	From 1 to 10. **09 Selected**
CSF_DLI4AI_GAIP_Transformation	Complex	▼	From 1 to 10. **08 Selected**

| valuation |

As shown in Table 7, the result's aim is to prove or justify GPP's feasibility; and the result permits to move to the next CSA that is the assembling the DLI4P component.

ASSEMBLING DLI4P COMPONENTS

The Analysis Processes

The Process

DLI4P's Application Programming Interface (API) can be used to avoid common pitfalls, because of expensive, complex and monolithic nature, the barrier to integrate DLI4P using GPP, has been simplified with the introduction of simpler entry-level and distributed platform becomes a viable *start small and grow* approach (Gartner, 2020).

People

To motivate stakeholders, it is imperative that there is a strong relationship between the DLI4P and the *Entity's* business results. This is complex because of ICS' silo structure; when integrating data silos, reducing duplicates, improving data quality and creating a semantically consistent view of master data; are all very important (Gartner, 2020).

Technology

To assess impacts related to *Projects*, firstly is to assess DLI4P's solutions to a given problem and whether the *Entity* is ready to be applied. It is recommended to start with a PoC and assess an end solution. Secondly, as it is imperative not to start with ICS/technology integration, and where EAI4P needs to inspect the existing *Entity's* processes significantly (Gartner, 2020).

DLI4P Algorithms

Ans are known as nodes, and as shown in Figure 24, are stacked next to each other in three layers: 1) The input layer; 2) The hidden layer(s); and 3) The output layer.

Nodes receive with inputs and these inputs are calculated with weightings and adds a bias. Finally, a nonlinear function (activation function) is applied to select the neuron to be fired. DLI4P algorithms promote self-learning representations, based on ANNs to simulate brain-like processing. Processing use input to extract features, group objects and discover patterns; like training machines for self-learning, this occurs at multiple levels, using the algorithms to implement models which use algorithms (Biswal, 2021).

Restricted Boltzmann Machines

RBM is a stochastic ANN that learns from a probability distribution over a set of inputs. It is used for dimensionality reduction, classification, regression, collaborative filtering, feature learning and topic modelling. RBMs constitute the building blocks of DBNs and its layers: 1) Visible units; and 2) Hidden units. A visible unit is connected to all hidden units. RBMs have a bias unit that is connected to all the visible units and the hidden units and they have no output nodes, as shown in Figure 25.

Figure 24. ANN schema

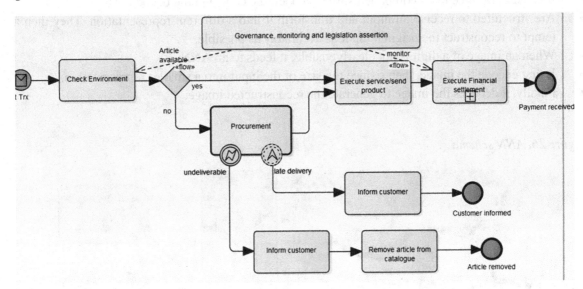

Figure 25. RBM schema

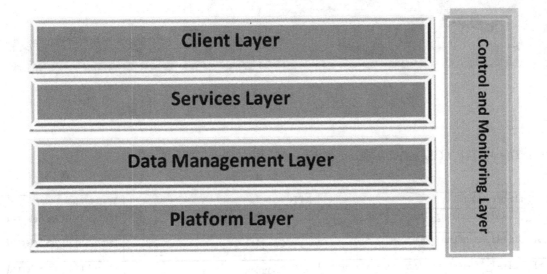

Autoencoders

Autoencoders are a specific type of feedforward ANN in which the input and output are identical, and is specialized to solve unsupervised learning problems. They are trained ANNs that replicate the data from the input layer to the output layer. Autoencoders are used for purposes such as pharmaceutical discovery, popularity prediction and image processing. As shown in Figure 26 it functions as follows:

- It consists of three main components: the encoder, the code and the decoder.
- Are structured to receive an input and transform it into a different representation. They then attempt to reconstruct the original input as accurately as possible.
- When an image of a digit is not clearly visible, it feeds to an ANN.
- It first encode the image, then reduce the size of the input into a smaller representation.
- Finally, it decodes the image to generate the reconstructed image.

Figure 26. ANN schema

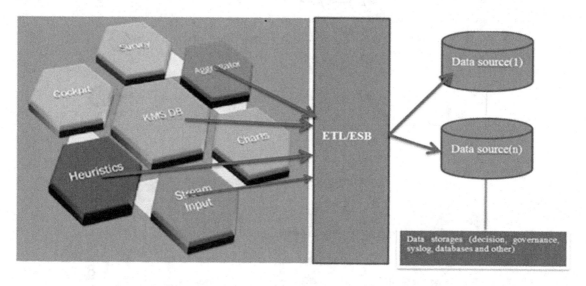

Table 8. The MLI4P's CSFs that have an average of 8.40

Critical Success Factors	KPIs		Weightings
CSF_DLI4AI_Assembling_Analysis_Processes	Complex	▼	From 1 to 10. 08 Selected
CSF_DLI4AI_Assembling_DDProject	Complex	▼	From 1 to 10. 08 Selected
CSF_DLI4AI_Assembling_Integration_Components	Complex	▼	From 1 to 10. 08 Selected
CSF_DLI4AI_Assembling_EA4AI_ADM4AI	Proven	▼	From 1 to 10. 10 Selected
CSF_DLI4AI_Assembling_CSF_CSA	Feasible	▼	From 1 to 10. 09 Selected
CSF_DLI4AI_Assembling_Set_of_Algorithms	Complex	▼	From 1 to 10. 08 Selected
CSF_DLI4AI_Assembling_RBM	Complex	▼	From 1 to 10. 08 Selected
CSF_DLI4AI_Assembling_Autoencoders	Complex	▼	From 1 to 10. 08 Selected

valuation

DLI4P's CSF's

Based on the business case's (and its CSA) LRP4P process managed and weighted the most important CSFs that were used.

As shown in Table 8, the result's aim is to prove or justify the RDP4P's feasibility.

THE PROOF OF CONCEPT

Author's RDP4P, is based on AHMM4P and ARI4P that can adapt to any type of MLI4P problem and used algorithm.

Basics

This RDP4P's hypothesis by using a PoC, which has been developed using the Microsoft Visual Studio 2019. The PoC contains *TRADf*'s major components for the DLI4P's processing, and primarily will be tested using the ARI4P's mixed reasoning engine, which is based on the heuristics model. This PoC serves to confirm the research's RQ. The used goal function calculates the best solution for the encountered problems. The PoC's results are presented in the form of a set of recommendations.

CSFs, Rules and Constraints Setup

The ARI4P's process execution starts with the use of the imputed data collection in the *TRADf's* data storage and then these data are filtered using the selected set of CSFs. The execution of the QLA4P part follows. The inputted data collection is considered to be the root or initial node that helps in the establishment of the basic state that is enhanced with the adopted solution(s). The ARI4P's tree reasoning goal is to select the optimal solution(s).

The Tree and Resources

The DMS4P's decision tree's collection of nodes contains the following resources, as shown in Figure 27, which are based on the unbundling of the system: 1) the executed actions; 2) the constraints; 3) the *Project* problem; and 4) the solutions. Each tree node is a CSF suggestion and it is linked to a concrete data state, which in turn contains an aggregate of a resource linked with a 1:1 mapping link.

Possible Solutions

The selected CSFs were fed in the DMS4P's heuristics engine in order to reveal DLI4P prerequisites for a selected *Project* problem or request. The CSFs were configured and weighted; afterwards they were processes in order to deliver a set of possible solutions. The DMS4P starts with the initial set of selected CSFs that correspond to a specific problem or request; then the grounded hyper-heuristics processing is launched to find a set of possible solution(s) in the form of possible improvements or suggestions of needed actions (Jaszkiewicz, & Sowiñski, 1999). The author's aim is to convert their relevant research outcomes into a set of managerial recommendations for DLI4P's usage; and the *TRADf* a hyper-heuristics

Figure 27. A view on the DMS4P's decision tree's solution nodes

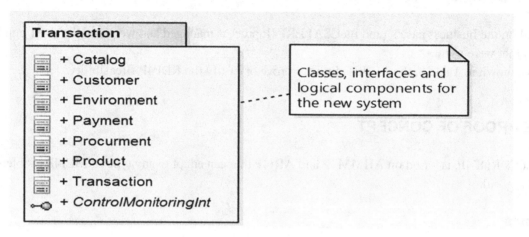

tree processing model template that is suitable for a wide class of problem instances (Vella, Corne, & Murphy, 2009).

The PoC Processing

The PoC uses an internal set of CSFs' that are presented in Tables 1 to 8. These CSFs have bindings to specific RDP4P resources, where the AHMM4P formalism was designed using an NLP4P microartefacts. In this chapter's tables and the result of the processing of the DMS4P, as illustrated in Table 9, shows clearly that the DLI4P is feasible.

The AHMM4P's main constraint is that CSAs for simple research components, having an average result below 8.5 will be ignored. In the case of the MLI4P's implementation an average result below 6.5 will be ignored. As shown in Table 9 the average is 9.0. DLI4P's processing model represents the relationships between this research's requirements, NLP4P generic and microartefacts, unique identifiers and the CSAs. The PoC was achieved using *TRADf* client's interface. From the *TRADf* client's interface, the NLP4P development setup and editing interface can be launched. Once the development setup interface is activated the NLP4P interface can be launched to implement the needed microartefact scripts to process the defined three CSAs. These scripts make up the kernel knowledge system and the DMS4P set of actions that are processed in the background. The DLI4P uses GPP that automatically

Table 9. The MLI4P based RDP4P's outcome

	Critical Success Factors	KPIs	Weightings Ranges	Values		
1	RDP5AI	HighlyFeasible	From 1 to 10.	9,25		
2	AHMM4AI	PossibleClassification	From 1 to 10.	10	EvaPA	
3	DMC4AI	AutomatedExists	From 1 to 10.	9,4		
4	PLATFORM	IntegrationPossible	From 1 to 10.	9		
5	EA4AI	AdvancedStage	From 1 to 10.	9		
6	ENVIRONMENT	Advanced	From 1 to 10.	9,4		
7	GAIP	IntegrationPossible	From 1 to 10.	8,5		
8	ASSEMBLING	IntegrationPossible	From 1 to 10.	8,4	RESULT:	9,11875

Figure 28. The edited NLP4P script and flow

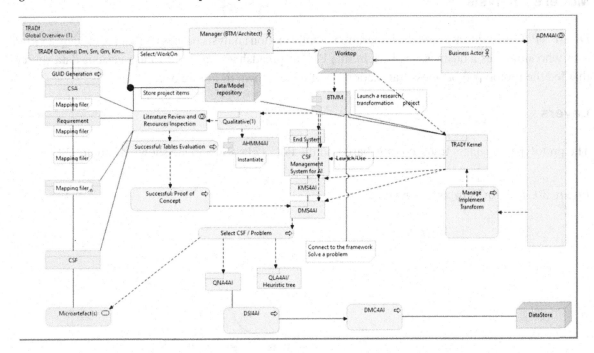

generates actions which make calls to QLA4P and QNA4P modules, that manages the edited NLP4P script and flow, as shown in Figure 28.

DLI4P structures, serve various APDs and in this PoC the functional domain are information analysis and decision making of a business transaction's log; where the data that results from business transactions are logged and used in the data analysis process, as shown in Figure 29.

Figure 29. The PoC's data interface view

Basic MM's Nomenclature

Iteration	= An integer variable that denotes a *Project/ADM iteration*

microRequirement	= KPI	(1)
CSF	= Σ KPI	(2)
CSA	= Σ CSF	(3)
Requirement	= $\bigcup$ microRequirement	(4)
microKnowledgeArtefact	= $\bigcup$ knowledgeItem(s)	(4)
neuron	= action $\circ$ data + microKnowledgeArtefact	(5)
microArtefact	= $\bigcup$ (e)neurons	(6)
microEntity or Enterprise	= $\bigcup$ microArtefact	(7)
Entity or Enterprise	= $\bigcup$ microEntity	(8)
microArtefactScenario	= $\bigcup$ microArtefactDecisionMaking	(9)
Decision Making/Intelligence	= $\bigcup$ microArtefactScenario	(10)
EnityIntelligence	= $\bigcup$ Decision Making/InteligenceComponent	(11)
MM(*Iteration*) as an instance	= EnityIntelligence(*Iteration*)	(12)

Model's Analysis

DLI4P's PoC took into account the integration of information analysis processes that are used by a virtual user who simulates a business analyst. In this PoC a spreadsheet was built to use various data sources that fed the prototyped business transactions system, as shown in Figure 30.

Layers

The prototyped business transaction is based on the PoC's class model, as shown in Figure 30.

Figure 30. The PoC's transaction view

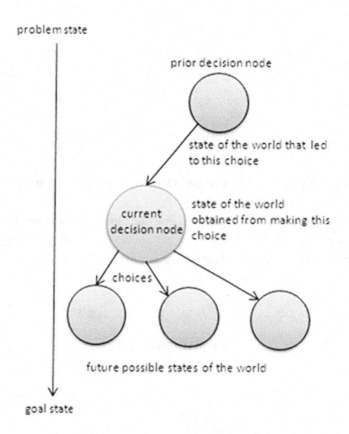

As shown in Figure 31, the data architecture and modelling PoC's layers are:

- Data architecture using TOGAF and GPP to link DLI4P to various artefacts.
- The client layer that contains the following packages based on: DBMS, Microsoft Excel, Flat Files Interfaces and a Client web interface.
- The data services layer that contains a data services hub.
- The data management layer that contains the following packages: an entity relational model, an extensible mark-up language transformer and a database interface.

Figure 31. The PoC's layers view

The Generic AHMM's Formulation

$$AHMM \qquad = \bigcup ADMs + MMs \qquad (13)$$

SOLUTIONS AND RECOMMENDATIONS

This chapter's and its PoC's list of the most important technical and managerial recommendations:

- The *Managers* should be supported with DLI4Ps tools that can integrate with the EAI4P principles (IBM, 2015a).
- The role of data standards is important; today there are many standards concerning the DLI4P. The *Manager* must propose a solution on how to integrate these various data standards in the *Project*.
- GPP services enable DLI4P's usage, that glues the various models to the business environment.
- Unbundling through the use of business data services uses the DMS4P well integrated in the context of a system that applies a holistic approach.
- The data services and dBB4Ps must unify the implementation and usage of data models.
- To define DLI4P's default CSFs and CSAs.
- Data transformation models need a meta-model to show the relationships between various types of data models and data sources.
- Define a data normalization and inter-operability paradigm that must be based on various standards.
- Define a business process and a data architecture and modelling integration paradigm to enhance the KMS4P.
- Develop an agile MVC4P pattern that is dynamically created for each business transaction. This MVC4P uses a dBB4P and its instance
- Define the ADM4P's integration with the proposed concept where the data building and solution blocks are the basic artefacts that circulate through the ADM4P.
- Define business architecture integration paradigm that is needed to manage the implementation of the dBB4Ps.
- Define conceptual views that can be built to simplify the application of the DLI4P. Such views can also be the used to simplify the *Entity*'s data-model that links various data sources.
- Create basic class diagrams for the DLI4P(s) to be the central artefact that is defined in the initial phase and then calibrated in all other phases.
- An in-house ARI4P can replace commercial DLI4P tools.

CONCLUSION

The RDP4P is based on DLI4P and is mainly motivated by high failure rates in *Projects*. The DLI4P feasibility is presented in the PoC and is to present the needed GPP and DLI4P concepts for a *Project*. There are several trends shaping the future of DLI4P; first, DLI4P tasks in the life-cycle are automated that increases the *Entity's* ROI. Another important element is that DLI4P resources become accessible to more people. A third important trend is the tension between the right to privacy, the need to regulate and the state of transparency. DLI4P has the ability to make DLI4P algorithms transparent, that makes regulatory oversight possible.

FUTURE RESEARCH DIRECTIONS

The future research on cybersecurity should study holistically enterprise information systems and their digital decision-making systems, based on Artificial Intelligence, Data Sciences, Enterprise Architecture, Big Data, Deep Learning and Machine Learning which can lead to a better understanding of intertwining these different domains and finding newer research outcomes and solutions that can measure and solve the critical problems facing the cybersecurity. The business transformation manager's characteristics for emphasising which type of support should be assured for the implementation phase of a business transformation project?" which needs to be unravelled. The targeted business domain should be further deeply explored which is any business environment that uses: 1) complex technologies, what are the scope and functions; and 2) frequent transformation iterations which can lead to further understanding of the systems engineered for cybersecurity.

REFERENCES

Biswal, A. (2021). *Top 10 Deep Learning Algorithms You Should Know in 2021*. Simplilearn. Simplilearn.com/tutorials/deep-learning-tutorial/deep-learning-algorithm

Camarinha-Matos, L. M. (2012). *Scientific research methodologies and techniques- Unit 2: Scientific method. Unit 2: Scientific methodology. PhD program in electrical and computer engineering*. Uninova.

Clancy, L. (2019). *Functional programming reaches for stardom in finance*. CME Group. https://www.risk.net/risk-management/6395366/functional-programming-reaches-for-stardom-in-finance

Clark, D. (2018). *Top 16 Open Source Deep Learning Libraries and Platforms*. KDnuggets. https://www.kdnuggets.com/2018/04/top-16-open-source-deep-learning-libraries.html

Dantzig, G. (1949). *Programming of Interdependent Activities: II Mathematical Model*. Academic Press.

E-Business Definition. (2014). *E-Business*. Accessed and reviewed in April 2019, http://dictionary.reference.com/browse/e-business.Dictionary.com

Gartner. (2020). *Three Essentials for Starting and Supporting Master Data Management*. ID G00730039. Gartner Inc. https://www.gartner.com/doc/reprints?id=1-24MIGFGU&ct=201119&st=sb

Grossfeld, B. (2020). *Deep learning vs MLI4P: a simple way to understand the difference.* Zendesk. https://www.zendesk.com/blog/machine-learning-and-deep-learning/

Guru99. (2021). *Data Science Tutorial for Beginners: What is, Basics & Process.* https://www.guru99. com/data-science-tutorial.html

Hershey, D. (2020). *Building an Enterprise Deep Learning Platform.* Determined AI. https://determined-ai.medium.com/building-a-deep-learning-platform-21a4a9dd90fe

IBM. (2015a). *Modelling the Entity data architecture.* IBM.

Järvinen, P. (2007). Action Research is Similar to Design Science. *Quality & Quantity, 41*(1), 37–54. Retrieved August 10, 2018, from https://link.springer.com/article/10.1007/s11135-005-5427-1

Jaszkiewicz, J., & Sowiński, R. (1999). The 'Light Beam Search' approach - an overview of methodology and applications. *European Journal of Operational Research, 113*(2), 300–314. doi:10.1016/S0377-2217(98)00218-5

Kapoor, A. (2021). *Artificial Intelligence and Machine Learning: 5 Trends to Watch Out for in 2021. AI Zone.* DZone. https://dzone.com/articles/artificial-intelligence-amp-machine-learning-5-dev

Kim, K., & Kim, K. (1999). Routing straddle carriers for the loading operation of containers using a beam search algorithm. Elsevier. *Computers & Industrial Engineering, 36*(1), 109–136. doi:10.1016/S0360-8352(99)00005-4

Lazar, I., Motogna, S., & Parv, B. (2010). Behaviour-Driven Development of Foundational UML Components. Department of Computer Science. Babes-Bolyai University. Cluj-Napoca, Romania. doi:10.1016/j.entcs.2010.07.007

Leitch, R., & Day, Ch. (2000). *Action research and reflective practice: towards a holistic view.* Taylor & Francis. Retrieved February 10, 2018, from https://www.tandfonline.com/doi/ref/10.1080/0965079 0000200108?scroll=top

Lockwood, R. (2018). *Introduction The Relational Data Model.* Retrieved January 29, 2019, from http://www.jakobsens.dk/Nekrologer.htm

Loginovskiy, O. V., Dranko, O. I., & Hollay, A. V. (2018). *Mathematical Models for Decision-Making on Strategic Management of Industrial Enterprise in Conditions of Instability.* Conference: Internationalization of Education in Applied Mathematics and Informatics for HighTech Applications (EMIT 2018). Leipzig, Germany.

Merson, P. (2009). *Data Model as an Architectural View. Technical Note. CMU/SEI-2009-TN-024.* Research, Technology, and System Solutions.

Moore, J. (2014). *Java programming with lambda expressions-A mathematical example demonstrates the power of lambdas in Java 8.* Retrieved March 10, 2018, from, https://www.javaworld.com/article/2092260/java-se/java-programming-with-lambda-expressions.html

Nijboer, F., Morin, F., Carmien, S., Koene, R., Leon, E., & Hoffman, U. (2009). Affective brain-computer interfaces: Psychophysiological markers of emotion in healthy persons and in persons with amyotrophic lateral sclerosis. In *3rd International Conference on Affective Computing and Intelligent Interaction and Workshops*. IEEE. 10.1109/ACII.2009.5349479

OMNI-SCI. (2021). *Data Science - A Complete Introduction*. OMNI-SCI. https://www.omnisci.com/learn/data-science

Pavlopoulos, J., Vrettaros, J., & Drigas, A. (2008). The Development of a Self-assessment System for the Learners Answers with the Use of GPNN. *Emerging Technologies and Information Systems for the Knowledge Society, First World Summit on the Knowledge Society, WSKS 2008, Athens, Greece, September 24-26, 2008. Proceedings*. 10.1007/978-3-540-87781-3_37

Sarkar, D. (2018). *Get Smarter with Data Science — Tackling Real Enterprise Challenges. Take your Data Science Projects from Zero to Production*. Towards Data Science. https://towardsdatascience.com/get-smarter-with-data-science-tackling-real-enterprise-challenges-67ee001f6097

SAS. (2021). *History of Big Data*. SAS. https://www.sas.com/en_us/insights/big-data/what-is-big-data.html

Schmelzer, R. (2021). *Data science vs. MLI4P vs. AI: How they work together*. TechTarget. https://searchbusinessanalytics.techtarget.com/feature/Data-science-vs-machine-learning-vs-AI-How-they-work-together?track=NL-1816&ad=937375&asrc=EM_NLN_144787081&utm_medium=EM&utm_source=NLN&utm_campaign=20210114_An%20open%20source%20database%20comparison

Sikander, M., & Khiyal, H. (2018). *Computational Models for Upgrading Traditional Agriculture*. Preston University. https://www.researchgate.net/publication/326080886

Simonin, J., Bertin, E., Traon, Y., Jezequel, J.-M., & Crespi, N. (2010). Business and Information System Alignment: A Formal Solution for Telecom Services. In *2010 Fifth International Conference on Software Engineering Advances*. IEEE. 10.1109/ICSEA.2010.49

Tamr. (2014). *The Evolution of ETL*. Tamr. http://www.tamr.com/evolution-etl/

The Open Group. (2011). *Open Group Standard-TOGAF® Guide, Version 9.1*. The Open Group.

The Open Group. (2013b). *ArchiMate®*. Retrieved May 03, 2014, from https://www.opengroup.org/subjectareas/Entity/archimate

TOGAF Modelling. (2015a). *Data dissemination view*. TOGAF Modelling. http://www.TOGAF-modelling.org/models/data-architecture-menu/data-dissemination-diagrams-menu.html

Trad, A., & Kalpić, D. (2020a). *Using Applied Mathematical Models for Business Transformation. Author Book*. IGI-Global. doi:10.4018/978-1-7998-1009-4

Vella, A., Corne, D., & Murphy, C. (2009). *Hyper-heuristic decision tree induction*. Sch. of MACS, Heriot-Watt Univ.

Veneberg, R. (2014). *Combining enterprise architecture and operational data-to better support decision-making. University of Twente*. School of Management and Governance.

Wikipedia. (2021a). Artificial neural network. *Wikipedia, the free encyclopedia.* https://en.wikipedia.org/wiki/Artificial_neural_network

KEY TERMS AND DEFINITIONS

TRADf: Is the research's framework.

Chapter 16
Cybersecurity and Electronic Services Oriented to E–Government in Europe

Teresa Magal-Royo
ⓘ https://orcid.org/0000-0002-7640-6264
Universitat Politécnica de Valencia, Spain

José Macário de Siqueira Rocha
Leading Management Technology, Spain

Cristina Santandreu Mascarell
Universitat Politécnica de Valencia, Spain

Rebeca Diez Somavilla
Universitat Politécnica de Valencia, Spain

Jose Luis Giménez López
Universitat Politécnica de Valencia, Spain

ABSTRACT

Cybersecurity in Europe as the rest of the world has been legislated for only 20 years. Numerous governmental institutions such as councils offer electronic services through their recently created electronic offices. In all of them, the volume of citizens who register temporarily or permanently to request online services related to the processing of documents and services with the government has increased significantly since the pandemic. Confinement has forced users to request numerous online services where authentication is one of the most relevant aspects to access safely and securely. European Union through the Connecting Europe Mechanism, CEF projects of the European Health Executive Agency, and Digital HaDEA has allowed numerous institutions to connect through the eIDAS created to establish trust in electronic transactions between individuals, organizations, and government entities across European member states.

DOI: 10.4018/978-1-7998-6975-7.ch016

INTRODUCTION

This chapter shows the importance of digital services for public services around the world and in particular to Europe. The European Union has been working on the regulation and control of secure digital transactions in Europe for more than 20 years and it will mention the existing regulations including the concepts Electronic identification (eID) and Electronic IDentification, Authentication and trust Services (eIDAS) used by both companies as public institutions.

Due to confinement, the increase in electronic services in public electronic offices worldwide has increased enormously and therefore it is necessary to pose new challenges in the control and management of sensitive data of citizens who access and share their data with administrations public.

On the other hand, the problems related to cyberattacks are very similar to those that we can find in private companies, therefore, the most important challenge for Europe will be, on the one hand, the detection of the types of massive attacks that can affect the use of data of citizens of the electronic headquarters and on the other the containment plans that are needed to control it at European level

Finally, we will mention examples of CEF projects that promote the implementation and use of the mechanisms offered by the European Union in the eiDAS regulation in electronic public services throughout Europe.

As cybersecurity remains a challenge for government websites: Only 20% of all URLs assessed meet half of the 14 basic security criteria evaluated. This underlines the importance of significantly enhancing website security levels to ensure that users can trust public sector websites and services. (EC, 2020)

In fact, e-Government refers to the use by national or local governmental authorities of ICTs that can reshape the relations with citizens and businesses. It contributes to the evolution of smart cities when ICTs are integrated in strategies for citizen participation to public services and policy, (Webster & Leleux, 2018).

The report e-Government Benchmark 2020 created by European Commission, shows remarkable improvements across the board. More than three out of four public services can be fully completed online (78%). Users can find the services they are looking for via portal websites 95% of the time, and information about these services online nearly 98% of the time. European countries should improve the implementation of digital enablers in eGovernment service delivery. Users use their own national eID for only half (57%) of the services that require online identification. Moreover, only half (54%) of online forms contain pre-filled data to ease completion. Users who want to obtain a service from another European country can do so in 62% of the services for citizens and 76% of the services for businesses. Citizens can use their own national eID solution for only 9% of the services from other countries. For businesses this number jumps to 36%. The cross-border use of digital public services are problems with access to procedures requiring authentication. Foreign national eIDs are accepted for only 9% of the services that citizens can access with a domestic eID. This indicates that the cross-border acceptance of eIDs still requires more research and implementation in national or local governmental institutions.

e- Government as a Challenge in Europe

Governments are institutions that contribute to governance a country or a region. Representative governments seek and receive citizen support, but they also need the active cooperation of their public servants (Carter & Belanger, 2005). E-governance, meaning electronic governance, has evolved as an information-age model of governance that seeks to realise processes and structures for harnessing the potentialities of information and communication technologies (ICTs) at various levels of government and the public sector. E-governance is the commitment to utilize appropriate technologies to enhance governmental relationships, both internal and external, in order to advance democratic expression, human dignity and autonomy, support economic development and encourage the fair and efficient delivery of services. As a concept, e-governance can be perceived to be contextually inclusive as an electronic democracy and electronic government (Caffrey & Okot-Uma, 1999), (Okot-Uma, 2001).

Electronic government (e-government) and the use of electronic services in public sector organizations, called public e-services, are currently significant issues. The term e-service is a service delivered electronically (Scupola, Henten, & Nicolajsen, 2009). The term public can also be interpreted as systems that are available for public use (Sundgren, 2005), including privately supplied e-services.

According with Saxena (2005) there are the following dimensions that reflect the functions of government itself:

- e-services. Electronic delivery of government information, programmes, and services
- e-commerce. Electronic exchange of money for goods and services, such as citizens paying taxes.
- e-management. Use of ICTs to improve the management of government improving the flow of information within government offices.

Public e-service is related to e-services delivered by governmental organizations and Public e-services-Usually constitute the mediation of that service and should be available to citizens, (Riley, 2000). Public e-services thus become a matter of citizen rights to access of public information including the governance control of a institution (Karlsson et. al., 2012), (Lindgren &Jansson, 2013).

Nowadays, increasing adoption of new technologies has been change expectations about how governments are delivering public services and are creating public value in the society. National and regional government plays an important and increasing role in coordinating the smart cities development. Smart cities technologies have many potential applications that will arise as technologies will gain widespread application. Municipal government service delivery is one of these applications having an increasing impact. Local government can understand and act in line with challenges and opportunities specific to their region as to become more effective, efficient and responsive. (Lytras & Şerban, 2020). The new digital environment helps governments to be more open, transparent, coherent and relations more participative and requires policies for digital technologies al all level of public sector, (Yildiz, 2007).

However, future challenges related to the supervision of the information data provided by citizens have made it necessary to improve strategies related to data protection, electronic identity, levels of cybersecurity control in transactions carried out by European citizens (European Commission, 2017), (Nixon et al. 2009),

The European Union Agency for Cybersecurity, ENISA has defined almost the most important threats in European. In 2020, the top threat was Malware. In fact, the years 2019 and 2020 brought significant changes in the cyber threat landscape. ENISA define two significantly aspects to contributed to these changes: The coronavirus disease (COVID-19) pandemic and the continuous threats increase in the global cyberspace, (ENISA2020a).

The COVID-19 pandemic forced to international and national coordination in healthcare services, teleworking, distance learning at schools and Universities, increasing of interpersonal communication systems, control of lockdown measures, teleconferencing and many others. (ENISA, 2020c).

The European Commission is promoting its plan called Blockchain Strategy aimed at The European Commission is promoting its plan called Blockchain Strategy aimed at establishing programs to improve these certain aspects related to the use of databases and secure transactions. The EC strategy is to create a legal and regulatory framework related to Blockchain technology that must be compatible with European data protection and privacy regulations. Among the most important aspects foreseen are 1) Environmental sustainability 2) Data protection, 3) Electronic Identity, 3) Cybersecurity, 4) Interoperability Blockchain technology must respect and be compatible with the evolving electronic identity framework of Europe, but also improve its usefulness. This includes being compatible with electronic signature regulations, such as eIDAS, as well as supporting an identity framework common to all European countries in the future. (European Commission, 2021).

Figure 1. Threat Landscape mapping in Europe
Source: (ENISA, 2020b)

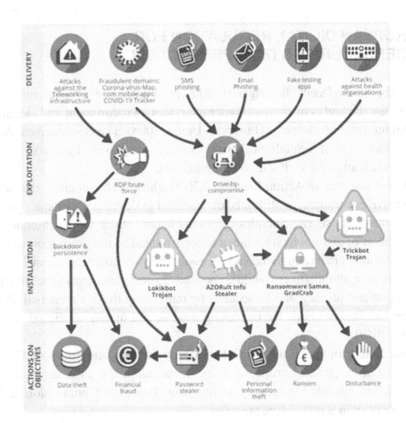

The Connecting Europe Facility, CEF Building Blocks promoted by European Union are advanced connected technologies. Big Data Test Infrastructure, Context Broker, eArchiving, eDelivery, eID, eInvoicing, eSignature and eTranslation support the security, interoperability, support and compliance with the complex legislation of smart city projects. The Building Blocks support secure environments, where data is safely handled and stored. They are based on open European standards and technical specifications, ensuring systems can communicate with each other all across Europe. The Building Blocks offer free supporting services (such as conformance testing and training) and grants, allowing cities to save time and money in the implementation of complex digital projects. (European Commission, 2021)

Distributed ledger technology (DLT) is a new technology that allows users from different locations to validate and update transactions in a synchronized way across the network.

The most used DTL is blockchain. The use of this technology by governments reduces the bureaucracy and will increase both the efficiency of the process (reducing economic costs, time and complexity of information exchanges; boost productivity) and promote trusting services in governmental public record-keeping (reduce errors, increase speed, transparency, accountability and security). In fact, blockchain´s model data are public resources that own citizens can change but only with their consent. The main innovation of this technology is that the transactions are automatically be verified and recorded through cryptographic algorithms, making unnecessary the human intervention, the central authority or the points of control of third parties, (Guendueza, et al. 2020).

EUROPEAN DIGITAL REGULATION FOR CYBERSECURITY & DATA PROTECTION

Since the Malmö Declaration signed in 2009, progress has been made to modernise public administrations across Europe and deliver cross border eServices, eProcurement and electronic identification (eID) for digital information exchange (European Union, 2009). The eGovernment Action Plan 2011-2015 led to the development of technological enablers that are key to facilitate access to and use of public services and identification for verification of digital data.

The eGovernment Action Plan 2016-2020 which both recognize that service-oriented, reliable and innovative government at all levels are essential to develop a dynamic, productive and European society. In that Plan, seven principles were established, which were subsequently endorsed by the Tallinn Declaration of 2017, which included aspects related to the promotion of electronic services in public administrations in a centralized and accessible way on different channels. (European Union, 2017).

Moreover, all initiatives should go beyond the compliance with the legal framework on personal data protection and privacy, and IT security by integrating those elements in the design phase. These were important pre-conditions for increasing trust in and uptake of digital services in Europa, (European Union, 2019)

Since the adoption of the EU Cybersecurity Strategy, the European Commission has stepped up its efforts to better protect Europeans online. It has adopted a set of legislative proposals, in particular on network and information security. In that time, European Commission. articulates the EU's vision of cybersecurity in terms of five priorities:

- Promote cyber resilience.
- Control and reduce cybercrime.
- Develope cyber defence policy and legal capabilities related to the Common Security and Defence Policy (CSDP).
- Develope industrial and technological resources for cyber-security.
- Establish a coherent international cyberspace policy for the European Union and promote core EU values.

The EU made regulatory progress to better protect citizens from online crime, including the establishment of a European Cybercrime Center and the proposed legislation on attacks against information systems (IP / 10/1239), including the launch of a Global Alliance to Fight Child Sexual Abuse Online (IP / 12/1308). The strategy included the objective of developing and financing a network of national centers of excellence in cybercrime to facilitate training and capacity building in each European country coordinated with a global center.

In 2013 the Commission proposed the Directive on security of network and information systems (NIS Directive) aiming at ensuring a high common level of cybersecurity in the EU in the future.

The Digital Single Market Strategy was presented in 2015 to fight against cybercrime included as one of the three pillars of the European Agenda on Security. In 2016, European Commission presented an additional measure to boost the cybersecurity industry and to control cyber-threats through a Directive on security of network and information systems by the European Parliament.

The NIS Directive was adopted by the European Parliament in 2016 and member states had 21 months to get pass the Directive into their national laws and a further 6 months to identify essential service operators.

Sum up, several EU legislative actions contribute to the fight against cybercrime:

- 2001-Framework Decision on combating fraud and counterfeiting of non-cash means of payment, which defines the fraudulent behaviours that EU States need to consider as punishable criminal offences. The Commission is assessing the need to revise this Framework Decision to cover new forms of money transmissions like virtual currencies and other aspects, with a plan to come forward with any new initiative for the first quarter of 2017.
- 2011-Directive on combating the sexual exploitation of children online and child pornography which better addresses new developments in the online environment, such as grooming (offenders posing as children to lure minors for the purpose of sexual abuse). This legislation had to be transposed by 2013 and the Commission is currently verifying implementation. Two reports on implementation were issued at the end of 2016.
- 2013- Directive on attacks against information systems, which aims to tackle large-scale cyber-attacks by requiring Member States to strengthen national cybercrime laws and introduce tougher criminal sanctions. This Directive had to be implemented by Member States by September 2015 and the Commission is currently checking implementation. Five infringement procedures for partial or noncommunication have been launched in December 2015. An implementation report will be published in 2017.
- 2018- Proposals for Regulation and Directive facilitating cross-border access to electronic evidence for criminal investigations.
- 2019- Directive on non-cash payment fraud. The directive updates the legal framework, removing obstacles to operational cooperation and enhancing prevention and victims' assistance, to make law enforcement action against fraud and counterfeiting of non-cash means of payment more effective.
- 2020- Proposal for Interim Regulation on the processing of personal and other data for the purpose of combatting child sexual abuse.

Table 1. European Security normative

Normative	Description
ISO/IEC27001	ISO/IEC 27001:2013: "Information technology -- Security techniques -- Information security management systems -- Requirements".
ISO/IEC27005	ISO/IEC 27005:2018: "Information technology — Security techniques — Information security risk management"
EN 419 241-2	CEN EN 419 241-2: "Trustworthy Systems Supporting Server Signing - Part 2: Protection profile for QSCD for Server Signing"
EN 319 401	ETSI EN 319 401 (v2.2.1): "Electronic Signatures and Infrastructures (ESI); General Policy Requirements for Trust Service Providers".
EN 319 411-1	ETSI EN 319 411-1 (v1.2.2): "Electronic Signatures and Infrastructures (ESI); Policy and security requirements for Trust Service Providers issuing certificates; Part 1: General requirements".
EN 319 411-2	ETSI EN 319 411-2 (v1.1.1): "Electronic Signatures and Infrastructures (ESI); Policy and security requirements for Trust Service Providers issuing certificates; Part 2: Requirements for trust service providers issuing EU qualified certificates".
EN 319 421	ETSI EN 319 421 (v1.1.1): "Electronic Signatures and Infrastructures (ESI); Policy and Security Requirements for Trust Service Providers issuing Time-Stamps".
TS 119 431-1	ETSI TS 119 431-1 (v1.1.1): "Electronic Signatures and Infrastructures (ESI); Policy and security requirements for trust service providers; Part 1: TSP service components operating a remote QSCD / SCDev".
TS 119 441	ETSI TS 119 441 (v1.1.1): "Electronic Signatures and Infrastructures (ESI); Policy requirements for TSP providing signature validation services".
TS 119 511	ETSI TS 119 511: "Electronic Signatures and Infrastructures (ESI); Policy and security requirements for trust service providers providing long-term preservation of digital signatures or general data using digital signature techniques".
EN 319 521	ETSI EN 319 521 (v1.1.1): "Electronic Signatures and Infrastructures (ESI); Policy and security requirements for Electronic Registered Delivery Service Providers".
EN 319 531	ETSI EN 319 531 (v1.1.1): "Electronic Signatures and Infrastructures (ESI); Policy and security requirements for Registered Electronic Mail Service Providers".

Source: (ENISA, 2021)

EUROPEAN INSTITUTIONS RELATED TO CYBERSECURITY

The European Union has several coordinated institutions to control actions related to cyberattacks threats since the beginning of 2010. The three main institutions are; The European Union Agency for Network and Information Security, (ENISA), The EU Computer Emergency Response Team (CERT-EU) and The Europol's Cybercrime Centre (EC3) among many specific associations and agencies. (Markopoulou, Papakonstantinou, & Hert, 2019).

All of them analyse, verify and promote implementation of measures against cyberattacks at European level that affect European citizens, companies or institutions. Year after year, the three institutions´ reports shows the verifications carried out from different points of view and issues.

ENISA was set up in 2004 to contribute to the overall goal of ensuring a high level of network and information security achieving a high common level of cybersecurity across Europe. The European Commission and the High Representative of the Union for Foreign Affairs and Security Policy presented a new EU Cybersecurity Strategy at the end of 2020.The document promotes to build resilience to cyber threats and ensure citizens and businesses benefit from trustworthy digital technologies. These three instruments are regulatory, investment and policy initiatives. They address three areas of EU action,

1) Resilience, technological sovereignty and leadership; 2) Operational capacity to prevent, deter and respond, 3) Cooperation to advance a global and open cyberspace.

ENISA helps the European Commission, the Member States and the business community to address, respond and specially to prevent NIS problems. The main activities run by ENISA include:

- Collect and analize data on security incidents in Europe and emerging risks.
- Promote risk assessment and risk management methods to enhance capability to deal with information security threats.
- Run of pan-European cyber exercises.
- Support Computer Emergency Response Teams (CERTs) cooperation in the Member States
- Aware-raising and cooperation between different actors in the information security field.

The CERT-EU was set up in 2012 with the aim to provide effective and efficient response to information security incidents and cyber threats for the EU institutions, agencies and bodies. is composed of IT security experts from the main EU Institutions. After a pilot phase of one year and a successful assessment by its constituency and its peers, the EU Institutions have decided to set up a permanent Computer Emergency Response Team (CERT-EU) for the EU institutions, agencies and bodies. The team was made up of IT security experts from the main EU Institutions (European Commission, General Secretariat of the Council, European Parliament, Committee of the Regions, Economic and Social Committee). The CERT-EU cooperates with other CERTs in the Members States and with specialised IT security companies in order to respond to information security incidents and cyber threats.

CERT-EU's mission is to contribute to the security of the ICT infrastructure of all Union institutions, bodies and agencies ('the constituents') by helping to prevent, detect, mitigate and respond to cyber-attacks and by acting as the cyber-security information exchange and incident response coordination hub for the constituents. The scope of CERT-EU's activities covers prevention, detection, response and recovery CERT-EU will operate according to the following key values:

- Highest standards of ethical integrity;
- High degree of service orientation and operational readiness.
- Effective responsiveness in case of incidents an emergencies and maximum commitment to resolve the issues.
- Building on, and complementing the existing capabilities in the constituents.
- Facilitating the exchange of good practices between constituents and peers.
- Fostering a culture of openness within a protected environment, operating on a need-to-know basis.

The EC3 was set up in 2013 as part of The European Union Agency for Law Enforcement Cooperation, (EUROPOL) wich promote combatting and preventing cross-border cybercrime by:

- serve as the central hub for criminal information and intelligence;
- support Member States' operations and investigations by means of operational analysis, coordination and expertise;
- provide strategic analysis products;

- reach out to cybercrime related law enforcement services, private sector, academia and other non-law enforcement partners.

Each year, EC3 publishes the Internet Organised Crime Threat Assessment (IOCTA), its flagship strategic report on key findings and emerging threats and developments in cybercrime. The IOCTA demonstrates how wide and varied cybercrime is and how EC3 is a key part of Europol's, and the EU's, response. EC3 takes a three-pronged approach to the fight against cybercrime: detection, strategy and operations.

AUTHENTIFICATION SYSTEMS in EUROPE

European citizens who move freely through Member States face the problem that their eID documents from their home state do not allow access to electronic services of another Member State in which they are currently present. This may be an undue restriction on EU citizens' use of these services. Administrations, at the other hand, cannot provide services to European citizens from other Member States with the same ease and efficiency as their own citizens. So there is a need to extend these digital services beyond national borders and beyond the user group of national citizens. At the same time, European and national data protection laws and regulations must be respected and may not be undermined by cross-border distribution of personal data.

Improving the interoperability of electronic identification and authentication systems is thus a European task and a task for all Member States. In 2010, ENISA promote a report related to the eID in this moment (Górniak et al.,2010). This report visualizes the security risks of electronic authentication in cross-border solutions, in two different projects.

- The European Health Insurance Card (EHIC) facilitates access to health care services for insured European citizens during temporary stays abroad. NETC@RDS for eEHIC ID is a pan-European project supported by the EU eTEN programme. It facilitates medical treatment of European citizens by using an electronically readable European health insurance card.
- STORK (Secure idenTity acrOss boRders linKed) is a large-scale pilot project in the ICT Policy Support programme to simplify administrative formalities by providing secure online access to public services across EU borders.

The report addressed some major issues which were related to critical factor such as:

- establishing the legal and contractual framework
- identifying the citizen through credentials
- authenticating system participants across borders
- making online connections secure
- bridging technological differences
- establishing and agreeing on a common security policy

In 2014, ENISA propose an ID authority as a source of the electronic identity based on the person's personal data. An ID authority can be a health insurance register or a civil register which establishes the root of all personal data for the application. The IT systems of the cross-border adapter are obviously the focus in any security evaluation of an electronic cross-border authentication process. As this component bridges not only two separate IT systems but also two separate sets of governing laws, a careful analysis of the security issues involved is strongly recommended for any specific application. By covering these factors in electronic cross-border authentication, the national goals of eID solutions can be extended successfully to a pan-European solution.

ELECTRONIC ACCESS IN EUROPE. THE EIDAS NODE

Electronic identification and trust services for electronic transactions in the internal market also known as eIDAS Regulation, (EU-N° 910/2014) provides a regulatory environment for electronic identification of natural and legal persons for electronic services based on electronic signatures, registered delivery services and certificates for institutional website authentication.

This Regulation remove existing barriers to the cross-border through use of electronic identification means used in each Member States to access to public services. This Regulation does not aim to intervene with regard to electronic identity management systems and related institutional infrastructures established in Member States. The aim of this Regulation is to ensure that for access to cross-border online services offered by Member States, secure electronic identification and authentication is possible.

One objective of this Regulation is to enhance the trust of enterprises and consumers in the European market and to promote the use of trust services and products. eIDAS Regulation introduces the notions of qualified trust service (QTS) and qualified trust service provider (QTSP) with a view to implement their compliance with the eIDAS high-level security requirements and obligations. The eIDAS Regulation introduced the notions of qualified trust service (QTS) and qualified trust service provider (QTSP) with a view to indicating requirements and obligations that ensure high-level security and a higher presumption of their legal effect.

Qualified Electronic Signature (QES) has the equivalent legal effect to handwritten signature. The consequences of a security incident can have a higher impact on a QTSP. In fact, previous issued QES lose their qualified status and issued certificates cannot be used for QES anymore. A security incident may cause the withdrawal of its qualified status and so the loss of its business line and customers (e.g. customers which need qualified certificates to access to a administrative or legal public e-services).

A QTSP is a TSP that has been granted a qualified status and is supervised by its national supervisory body (SB). The eIDAS Regulation defines nine types of QTS:

1. Provision of qualified certificates for electronic signature
2. Provision of qualified certificates for electronic seals
3. Provision of qualified certificates for website authentication (institutional/private)
4. Qualified validation service for qualified electronic signatures (QESig)
5. Qualified validation service for qualified electronic seal (QESeal)
6. Qualified preservation service for qualified electronic signature (QESig)
7. Qualified preservation service for qualified electronic seal (QESeal)
8. Qualified temporal stamping service
9. Qualified electronic registered delivery service

In general, each European state member designates its own set of parties responsible for this. These are public administrations that provide online services to European citizens.

The eIDAS-Node implementer can be a separate organisation to the eIDAS-Node operator, or both roles can be played by the same organisation. During the eIDAS eID deployment process, eIDAS-Node implementers and operators will need to execute the solution nationally to connect to the eIDAS Network and to (optionally) integrate national Identity Providers and Attribute Providers.

Those public administrations providing online services (at national level) which require eID assurance, will be obliged under the eIDAS Regulation to also provide access to users from other European countries (who are using a national eID which has been notified).

To enable cross-border access to their online services, Service Providers will be supported by the European states members to connect to the eIDAS-Node in their country. In the future a wide range of Service Providers, both in the public and private sectors, will likely be connected at the national level.

Figure 2. eIDAS Network
Source: CEF Digital, Connecting Europe, 2021

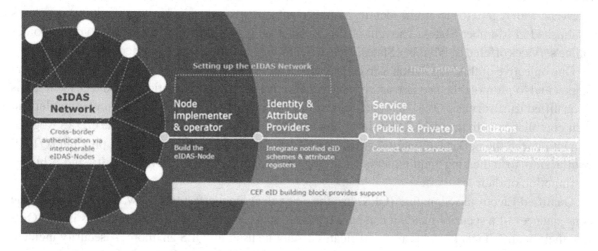

SOLUTIONS AND RECOMMENDATIONS

In Spain the authentication gateway is Cl @ ve 2.0 is a system aimed at unifying and simplifying electronic access by citizens to public services. Its main purpose is to allow citizens to identify themselves before to access to a public e-services in the Administration by means of fixed keys (username and password), to avoid the need to remember different keys for different services.

The design of Cl@ve is based on a federated electronic identities system, which comprises different elements as 1) Electronic administration service providers (SP): Entities providing electronic services to citizens and using the platform for identification and authentication of same, 2) Identification and authentication service providers (IdP): Entities providing identification and authentication mechanisms of citizens to be used as common means by other entities, 3) Identification Gateway / Manager: Intermediation system which enables service providers to access different identification mechanisms and selection of same by the users.

Cl@ve complements current access systems using electronic ID and digital certificate, offering at the same time the possibility to carry out cloud-based signature operations with personal certificates protected on remote servers.

Cl@ve is a common platform for the identification, authentication and electronic signature, an interoperable, horizontal system which helps the Spanish Government to avoid implementation and management of its own identification and signature systems. Citizens will be able to use different identification methods to deal with Public Administrations electronically. The Cl@ve system was approved by Resolution adopted by the Council of Ministers, on the meeting held on 19 September 2014. Its terms and conditions of use are established by the Directorate for Information and Communication Technologies of the Spanish Government. Cl@ve includes the use of identification systems based on fixed keys (username and password systems) as well as digital certificates (including electronic ID). Regarding the fixed codes, Cl@ve accepts three possible uses:

- DNIe/Electronic certificate
- Temporary Cl@ve (PIN Cl@ve): Password system valid for a short period of time, oriented for users who use the services sporadically; it corresponds to the PIN24H systems of the State Tax Administration Agency, AEAT.
- Permanent Cl@ve: Password system valid for a long, limited period of time, intended for regular users. It is designed for the access system by means of username and password, reinforced by one-time keys sent by SMS, to the Social Security services. This system will also enable citizens' access to cloud-based signature.

Figure 3. Cl@ve identification access
Source: Spanish Government, 2021

Some examples have been developed through CEF projects as program Connecting Europe Facility (CEF) Telecom. Nowadays is developed in the project named Connecting Public Administrations to the Spanish eIDAS Node, eID4Spain-19. The main objective of this project is to connect the public electronic services provided by two Spanish public administrations (Provincial Council of Valladolid and the Andalusian Health Service) to the Spanish eIDAS node via Cl @ ve 2.0 to allow cross-border authentication of European citizens online following eIDAS regulation.

Provincial Council of Valladolid

The Provincial Council has an electronic website which seeks the effective implementation of public e-services are being made available to all european Public Administrations . The Provincial Council of Valladolid is currently connected to a previous version of the CL @ VE spanish platform, but it is not linked to the european eIDAS node. The scope of this action is to adapt regional public e-services so that they are connected to Cl @ ve 2.0. To persist the information of the users who access the electronic services of the Provincial Council of Valladolid after the authentication process.

The proposal will facilitate the insertion and management of data for all interested parties, whether they are nationals or European citizens through the use of data for the authentication and processing of electronic services.

The platform is currently designed to work with the data of Spanish citizens in a third-party database named TangramBPM stores the contact information (e.g. name or company name, postal address, email address for electronic notifications, etc...) but it will necessary to adapt the data model to be able to implement the access of european citzens.

TangramBPM provides a solution for the processing of files and management of the electronic office. It allows citizens and companies access to information, procedures and services available to the public institution, such as access to the bulletin board, official agency bulletins and public e-services. The platform is based on open source software like Activity, Alfresco, Postgres, Liferay, etc.... and uses enabling elements offered by the electronic Administration of the Government of Spain (eg Notific @, Cl@ve, @firma, etc ...). The services and procedures created by the Valladolid Provincial Council have been adapted to receive the response from the Spanish eIDAS node and the new user authentication system that provides access to European citizens from each country connected to your eIDAS node.

Andalusian Health Service

The Andalusian Health Service (SAS) provides its service to more than 8 million users and not including citizens of European countries who travel to Andalusia. The solution proposed by SAS is intended to offer digital health services to users who travel from European countries such as Germany, France and Italy. DIRAYA is the system used in the Andalusian Health Service to support electronic medical records. It integrates user´s healthcare information of each citizen cared for in the Andalusian healthcare centres.

The digital platform response both to the mobility of patients and to a comprehensive healthcare provision model, provided by multidisciplinary professional teams from different healthcare settings. DIRAYA is one of the most advanced comprehensive systems for Healthcare Management in Europe and the patient database (BDU) that allows obtaining the Andalusian Single Health History Number (NHUSA). DIRAYA pursues the total elimination of analog documents for the use and management of digital documents.

Figure 4. Institutional website Provincial Council of Valladolid
Source: (Provincial Council of Valladolid, 2021)

The SAS uses the ClicSalud + platform, it presents a security based on digital certificates, connected with Cl @ ve, through the regional gateway ProxyCl @ ve, and allows both the authentication and the electronic identification of Spanish citizens through the DNI or NIE. The document number sent in the affirmative authentication response by Cl @ ve is used to search the patient's database (BDU) and obtain the Andalusian Health History Number (NHUSA). Normally, the patient from the European Union identifies himself with a national identification document of his country or by passport. Once the NHUSA has been obtained, the user will be able to access the public e-services of the ClicSalud + platform. It will allow European citizens access through the eIDAS node and thus access reports and diagnostic tests carried out in the SAS in its healthcare services.

Figure 5. Institutional website Andalusian Health Service
Source: (The Andalusian Health Service, 2021)

FUTURE RESEARCH DIRECTIONS

COVID-19 Pandemic has activated massive accesses to online public services in the present years and It is need of a rapid review of data control protocols because of the increase and traffic of information that affects the databases used.

Taking into account the increase in the use of electronic public services throughout Europe, new unknowns arise related to the information that users should know about the data provided when connecting and authenticating within a public electronic service. In fact, effective cyberattacks communications is often hidden from the public and does not help the real transparency on the use and control of electronic services. One of the important challenges will be the way to communicate to the user that a cyberattack is taking place and what are the measures adopted by each service at the government level and how it will affect access to their data.

Since 2017 and through the publication of the document called Resilience, deterrence and defence: building a solid cybersecurity for the EU, the European Commission announced the intention to support the creation of a network of competence centres in cybersecurity, with a European Centre of competence in cybersecurity to stimulate the development and deployment of cybersecurity technology. However, the increase has been so significant in the last two years that European legislation must be prepared to coordinate not only its member states but also take into account international legislation with other more or less advanced countries so that attacks made from outside the European Union can be prosecuted and controlled from their origin.

CONCLUSION

The advancement of new technologies in e-government environments in Europe have necessitated the creation of legal and technological mechanisms so that secure communication throughout Europe is effective. In the coming years and due to the impact of COVID-19 due to confinement and the increase in data traffic in digital environments, it increased considerably or only at a private level but also with communication with public services.

The public services offered by any public institution in Europe face the challenge not only to create digital environments with services to citizens, but they must be controlled and secure. This security must include containment plans on cyberattacks at any level reported at national and European level since more and more the exchange of data at European level will be a fact. The monitoring and reporting of security problems in e-government environments from the European institutions will help to improve at a pan-European level the perception and confidence in the use of public services in Europe.

ACKNOWLEDGMENT

This research was supported by European Health and Digital Executive Agency – HaDEA within the framework program Connecting Europe Facility (CEF) Telecom and developed in the project named Connecting Public Administrations to the Spanish eIDAS Node, eID4Spain-19. [Action N°: 2019-ES-IA-0040].

REFERENCES

Caffrey, L., & Okot-Uma, R. W. O. (1999). Government secure intranets. Information Technology & Globalisation Series. Commonwealth Secretariat.

Carter, L., & Belanger, F. (2005). The utilization of e-government services: Citizen trust, innovation and acceptance factors. *Journal of Information Systems*, *15*(1), 5–25. doi:10.1111/j.1365-2575.2005.00183.x

Commission of the European Communities. (2006). *A strategy for a Secure Information Society – "Dialogue, partnership and empowerment"*. Retrieved from https://ec.europa.eu/information_society/doc/com2006251.pdf

ENISA. (2020a). *The year in review*. ENISA Threat Landscape. Retrieved from: https://www.enisa.europa.eu/publications/year-in-review

ENISA. (2020b). *Threat Landscape 2020 - List of top 15 threats*. The European Union Agency for Cybersecurity, ENISA. Retrieved from: https://www.enisa.europa.eu/topics/threat-risk-management/threats-and-trends/threat-landscape-mapping-infographic-2020/view

ENISA. (2020c). *Telecom Security During A Pandemic. Telecom security good practices and lessons learned from the COVID-19 outbreak*. doi:10.2824/239478

ENISA. (2021). *Security Framework for Qualified Trust Service Providers*. The European Union Agency for Cybersecurity, ENISA retrieved from: https://www.enisa.europa.eu/publications/security-framework-for-qualified-trust-providers

European Commission. (2013). *Cybersecurity Strategy of the European Union: An Open, Safe and Secure Cyberspace*. Retrieved from https://eeas.europa.eu/archives/docs/policies/eu-cyber-security/cybsec_comm_en.pdf

European Commission. (2017). *EU-Wide Digital Once-Only Principle for Citizens and Businesses. Policy Options and Their Impacts: Final Report*. EU Official Publications. doi:10.2759/393169

European Commission. (2017). *Ministerial Declaration on eGovernment - the Tallinn Declaration*. Retrieved from https://ec.europa.eu/digital-single-market/en/news/ministerial-declaration-egovernment-tallinn-declaration

European Commission. (2019). *European eGovernment Action Plan 2016-2020*. Retrieved from: https://ec.europa.eu/digital-single-market/en/european-egovernment-action-plan-2016-2020

European Commission. (2020). *EGovernment Benchmark 2020 eGovernment that works for the people*. Insight Report. doi:10.2759/24753

European Commission. (2021). *Blockchain Strategy. Shaping Europe's digital future*. Retrieved from https://digital-strategy.ec.europa.eu/en/policies/blockchain-strategy

European Commission. (2021). *About Connecting Europe Facility (CEF). Joinup platform*. Retrieved from: https://joinup.ec.europa.eu/collection/connecting-europe-facility-cef/about

European Parliament. (2015). *eGovernment. Using technology to improve public services and democratic participation*. EPRS | European Parliamentary Research Service. doi:10.2861/150280

European Union. (2009). *Ministerial Declaration on eGovernment*. 5th Ministerial eGovernment Conference, Malmö, Sweden. Retrieved from: https://ec.europa.eu/digital-single-market/sites/digital-agenda/files/ministerial-declaration-on-egovernment-malmo.pdf

European Union (2014) Regulation (EU) No 910/2014 of the European Parliament and of the Council of 23 July 2014 on electronic identification and trust services for electronic transactions in the internal market and repealing Directive 1999/93/EC. OJ L 257, 28.8.2014, p. 73–114. https://eur-lex.europa.eu/legal-content/EN/TXT/?uri=uriserv%3AOJ.L.2014.257.01.0073.01.ENG

Górniak, S., Naumann, I., Hartmann, D., & Körting, S. (2010). *Security Issues in Cross-border Electronic Authentication.* Retrieved from: https://www.enisa.europa.eu/publications/xborderauth

Guendueza, A. A., Mettlerb, T., & Schedlera, K. (2020). Technological frames in public administration: What do public managers think of big data? *Government Information Quarterly, 37*(1), 101406. Advance online publication. doi:10.1016/j.giq.2019.101406

Karlsson, F., Holgersson, J., Söderström, E., & Hedström, K. (2012). Exploring user participation approaches in public e-service development. *Government Information Quarterly, 29*(2), 158–168. doi:10.1016/j.giq.2011.07.009

Lindgren, I., & Gabriella Jansson, G. (2013). Electronic services in the public sector: A conceptual framework. *Government Information Quarterly, 30*(2), 163–172. doi:10.1016/j.giq.2012.10.005

Lytras, M. D., & Şerban, A. C. (2020). E-Government Insights to Smart Cities Research: European Union (EU) Study and the Role of Regulations. *IEEE Access: Practical Innovations, Open Solutions, 8*, 65313–65326. doi:10.1109/ACCESS.2020.2982737

Markopoulou, D., Papakonstantinou, V., & Hert, P. (2019). The new EU cybersecurity framework: The NIS Directive, ENISA's role and the General Data Protection Regulation. *Computer Law & Security Review, 35*(6), 105336. Advance online publication. doi:10.1016/j.clsr.2019.06.007

Nixon, P. G., Koutrakou, V. N., & Rawal, R. (2009). *Understanding E-Government in Europe. Issues and Challenges.* Routledge Taylor & Group.

Okot-Uma, R. (2000). Electronic Governance: Reinventing Good Governance. *Proceedings of African Computing and Telecommunications Summit.*

Riley, T. B. (2000). Electronic Governance and Electronic Democracy: Living and Working in the Wired World. Academic Press.

Saxena, K. (2005). Towards excellence in e-governance. *International Journal of Public Sector Management, 18*(6), 498–513. doi:10.1108/09513550510616733

Scupola, A., Anders Henten, A., & Hanne Westh Nicolajsen, H. (2009). E-Services: Characteristics, Scope and Conceptual Strengths. *International Journal of E-Services and Mobile Applications, 1*(3), 1–16. Advance online publication. doi:10.4018/jesma.2009070101

Sundgren, B. (2005). What is a public information system? *International Journal of Public Information Systems, 1*(1), 81–99.

Webster, C. W. R., & Leleux, C. (2018). Smart governance: Opportunities for technologically-mediated citizen co-production. *Information Polity, 23*(1), 95–110. doi:10.3233/IP-170065

Yildiz, M. (2007). E-government research: Reviewing the literature, limitations, and ways forward. *Government Information Quarterly*, 24(3), 646–665. doi:10.1016/j.giq.2007.01.002

ADDITIONAL READING

Council of the European Union. (2018). European Union Cyber Defence Policy Framework, update Retrieved from https://data.consilium.europa.eu/doc/document/ST-14413-2018-INIT/en/pdf

European Commission. (2021). eIDAS-Node version 2.5. Retrieved from https://ec.europa.eu/cefdigital/wiki/display/CEFDIGITAL/eIDAS-Node+version+2.5

European Union Agency for Cybersecurity. ENISA (2020). ENISA programming document 2020–2022 Retrieved from https://www.enisa.europa.eu/publications/corporate-documents/enisa-programming-document-202020132022

Nai-Fovino, I., & Neisse, R.;'Lazari, A.; Ruzzante, G. (2018). European Cybersecurity Centre of Expertise - Cybersecurity Competence Survey. EUR 29330 EN. *Publications Office of the European Union, Luxembourg, JRC111211*. Advance online publication. doi:10.2760/42369

Nai-Fovino, I., Neisse, R., Lazari, A., Ruzzante, G., Polemi, N., & Figwer, M. (2018). *European Cybersecurity Centres of Expertise Map - Definitions and Taxonomy. EUR 29332 EN*. Publications Office of the European Union., doi:10.2760/622400

KEY TERMS AND DEFINITIONS

Blockchain: Is a digital record of transactions. The name comes from its structure, in which individual records, called blocks, are linked together in single list, called a chain. Blockchains are used for recording transactions made with cryptocurrencies. Each transaction added to a blockchain is validated by multiple computers on the Internet.

Cryptography: The application of mathematical processes on data-at-rest and data-in-transit to provide the security benefits of confidentiality, authentication, integrity and non-repudiation. Cryptography includes three primary components: symmetric encryption, asymmetric encryption and hashing. Symmetric encryption is used to provide confidentiality. Asymmetric encryption is used to provide secure symmetric key generation, secure symmetric key exchange (via digital envelopes created through the use of the recipient's public key) verification of source, verification/control of recipient, digital signature (a combination of hashing and use of the sender's private key) and digital certificates (which provides third-party authentication services). Hashing is the cryptographic operation that produces a representational value from an input data set. A before and after hash can be compared in order to detect protection of or violation of integrity.

Cyberattack: Any attempt to violate the security perimeter of a logical environment. An attack can focus on gathering information, damaging business processes, exploiting flaws, monitoring targets, interrupting business tasks, extracting value, causing damage to logical or physical assets or using system resources to support attacks against other targets.

Distributed Ledger Technology (DLT): Is a digital system for recording the transaction of assets in which the transactions and their details are recorded in multiple places at the same time. Unlike traditional databases, distributed ledgers have no central data store or administration functionality. In a distributed ledger, each node processes and verifies every item, thereby generating a record of each item and creating a consensus on each item's veracity. A distributed ledger can be used to record static data, such as a registry, and dynamic data, i.e., transactions.

Electronic Authentication: The electronic process of establishing confidence in user identities presented to an information system. The process of proving an individual is a claimed identity. Authentication is the first element of the AAA services concept, which includes Authentication, Authorization, and Accounting. Authentication occurs after the initial step of identification (i.e. claiming an identity). Authentication is accomplished by providing one or more authentication factors—Type 1: something you know (e.g., password, PIN, or a combination of them), Type 2: something you have (e.g. smart card, RSA SecureID FOB, or USB drive), and Type 3: something you are (e.g. biometrics—fingerprint, iris scan, retina scan, hand geometry, signature verification, voice recognition, and keystroke dynamics).

Electronic Authorization: The security mechanism determining and enforcing what authenticated users are authorized to do within a computer system. The dominant forms of authorization are DAC, MAC and RBAC. DAC (Discretionary Access Control) manages access using ACL (Access Control Lists) on each resource object where users are listed along with the permissions or privileges granted or denied them. MAC (Mandatory Access Control) manages access using labels of classification or clearance on both subjects and objects, and only those subjects with equal or superior clearance are allowed to access resources. RBAC (Role Based Access Control) manages access using labels of a job role that has been granted the permissions and privileges needed to accomplish a specific job or role.

Electronic Identification (eID): Is a digital solution for proof of identity of citizens or organizations. They can be used to view to access benefits or services provided by government authorities, banks or other companies, for mobile payments, etc.

Electronic Identification, Authentication, and trust Services (eIDAS).: Is an EU regulation on electronic identification and trust services for electronic transactions in the European Single Market. It was established in EU Regulation 910/2014. Ensures that people and businesses can use their own national electronic identification schemes (eIDs) to access public services available online in other EU countries.

Fifth Anti-Money Laundering Directive (AML5): Is the standard for the prevention of money laundering and terrorist financing. AML5, entered into force on July 9, 2018 at community level, with effective application at national level on January 10, 2020.

Identity Verification: Is a process that ensures a person's identity matches the one that is supposed to be. Identity verification ensures that there is a real person behind a process and proves that the one is who he or she claims to be, preventing both a person from carrying out a process on our behalf without authorization, and creating false identities or commit fraud.

Information Security Incident: Single or a series of unwanted or unexpected information security events that have a significant probability of compromising business operations and threatening information security.

Malware: Malicious software designed specifically to damage or disrupt a system, attacking confidentiality, integrity and/or availability.

Network Resilience: The ability of a network to: (1) provide continuous operation (i.e., highly resistant to disruption and able to operate in a degraded mode if damaged); (2) recover effectively if failure does occur; and (3) scale to meet rapid or unpredictable demands.

Network Security: Is concerned with hardware, software, basic communication protocols, network frame structure, and communication mechanisms factors of the network. Information Security in the network context deals with data integrity, confidentiality, availability, and non-repudiation while is sent across the network.

Risk Assessment: The product or process which collects information and assigns values to risks for the purpose of informing priorities, developing, or comparing courses of action, and informing decision making. The appraisal of the risks facing an entity, asset, system, or network, organizational operations, individuals, geographic area, other organizations, or society, and includes determining the extent to which adverse circumstances or events could result in harmful consequences.

Risk Management Process: Systematic application of management policies, procedures and practices to the activities of communicating, consulting, establishing the context and identifying, analysing, evaluating, treating, monitoring, and reviewing risk.

Vulnerability: A characteristic or specific weakness that renders an organization or asset (such as information or an information system) open to exploitation by a given threat or susceptible to a given hazard. Characteristic of location or security posture or of design, security procedures, internal controls, or the implementation of any of these that permit a threat or hazard to occur. Vulnerability (expressing degree of vulnerability): qualitative or quantitative expression of the level of susceptibility to harm when a threat or hazard is realized.

Chapter 17
Advanced Cyber Security and Internet of Things for Digital Transformations of the Indian Healthcare Sector

Jonika Lamba

The NorthCap University, Gurugram, India

Esha Jain

 https://orcid.org/0000-0002-0152-8566

The NorthCap University, Gurugram, India

ABSTRACT

Cybersecurity is not just about fortification of data. It has wide implications such as maintaining safety, privacy, integrity, and trust of the patients in the healthcare sector. This study methodically reviews the need for cybersecurity amid digital transformation with the help of emerging technologies and focuses on the application and incorporation of blockchain and the internet of things (IoT) to ensure cybersecurity in the well-being of the business. It was found in the study that worldwide, advanced technology has been used in managing the flow of data and information, India should focus on maintaining the same IT-enabled infrastructure to reduce causalities in the nation and on the other hand improve administration, privacy, and security in the hospital sector. Depending on the network system, resource allocation, and mobile devices, there is a need to prioritize the resources and efforts in the era of digitalization.

INTRODUCTION

As per available reports spending of the Indian government on healthcare is estimated to be 1.5% of the total GDP which is low as far as the population of the nation is considered. The spending of the government in the healthcare sector is too low in comparison to other nations. The healthcare sector theaters a pivotal part in the accomplishment and prosperity of a nation, so the government should devote

DOI: 10.4018/978-1-7998-6975-7.ch017

considerable resources to the upliftment of the living conditions of people. The government has taken various steps to improve the present condition of the healthcare sector by framing policies such as the National Health Policy 2017 focused on plummeting infant mortality rate and providing access to good quality healthcare services to the people of the nation. The current situation in the country is alarming and the COVID-19 pandemic had forced nations to rethink the present health care infrastructure as the government alone will not be able to cope up with the present situation (Jain & Lamba, 2020). It need support from the big industrialists to fasten the process of developing the infrastructure for the COVID-19 patients. The time has come where a nation can sustain only based on investment in the well-being care sector due to drastic changes in the environment, pollution level, and modern living habits. The well-being care sector is one of the most important pillars of the Indian economy as it supports the rest of the sectors in smooth functioning.

A healthy nation will be able to face any pandemic and will emerge out of being a winner in the period of disguise. The health care sector is one of the most important pillars of the Indian economy as it supports the rest of the sectors in smooth functioning. A healthy nation will be able to face any pandemic and will emerge out of being a winner in the period of disguise. With the advancement in information and technology, every sector has get influenced to some extent. The need for data management and organization has paved the way for evolving know-hows such as Blockchain and the Internet of Things (IoT) (Miraz et al., 2020; Aich et al., 2019). Blockchain is the technology that integrates healthcare and data. The distinguishing features of blockchain such as transparency, data attribution, accurate and reliable reporting and data analytics help in resolving rigorous data management issues in clinical trials (Omar et al., 2020; Rathee, 2020; Fekih & Lahami, 2020; Fekih et al., 2020). The healthcare sector shown tremendous improvement such as patient retention, data integrity, privacy and regulatory compliances due to adoption of blockchain advanced application. The peculiarities of advanced technology such as Blockchain and how it improved the operations in the healthcare domain with the assistance of its key features and innovative applications. The major risks and opportunities related to technology adoption have also been discussed in the study.

The impact of COVID 19 on the economy of different countries has been studied and it was analyzed that COVID 19 had seriously impacted the healthcare sector (Attia et al. 2019; McGhin et al., 2019; Epiphaniou et al. 2019; Hasselgren et al., 2020). The use of advanced tools and applications such as Artificial Intelligence (AI), Internet of Things (IoT), Unmanned Aerial Vehicles (UAVs) and Blockchain etc., helps in reducing the influence of contagion on the environment (Chamola et al., 2020).

The Healthcare sector is the most important domain of a nation's prosperity. Data and health integration can solve many difficult problems in the healthcare sector. It facilitates exchange and dealings in the database that can be shared across authorized operators. It is peer-to-peer disseminated ledger know-how. It consists of majorly three components which are namely distributed network, shared record, and digital transaction. Blockchain technology ensures that no one can change any information or record and that can be done with the permission of all authorized operators in the system. Blockchain is the most used technology to assemble scattered data and at the critical time, it serves its purpose at best (Abdellatif et al., 2020; Ray et al., 2020). This technology has brought many changes in the well-being sector and in the way, data is managed in the hospital industry. The availability of crucial data at the right point in time has saved many lives (Alladi et al., 2019). Looking at the outdated healthcare infrastructure, emerging technologies have raised the expectations from blockchain and the Internet of Things (Hussein et al., 2019). Emerging technologies such as the Internet of Things (IoT), blockchain, artificial intelligence, machine learning, and big data all together have brought a drastic change in data compilation and management (Abdullah & Jones, 2019). These technologies help in maintaining the confidentiality of patients and provide access to a secure platform for the exchange of information. Step by step implementation of these evolving technologies will brighten the future of the healthcare sector in the long run. Maintaining the privacy of patients and the exchange of transactions between hospitals lead to the proper treatment of patients with less time frame. This helps in the organization of patients' records such as their chronicles related to laboratory tests, patient history of ailment, surgery records, medicine ledger, disease registries, and lab results, etc. With the help of master keys patients, records can be grasped in a quick manner that will facilitate the management of data on the other hand. Block-chain technology has the budding to renovate the hospital sector and bring revolutionary changes which will be beneficial for both patients and hospitals. Though it is quite costly to integrate with the existing infrastructure it is expected that its benefits will outweigh outlays in the extended run. It will also have a promising future in supply change management and claim settlement. Evolving technologies such as big data, the internet of things (IoT), blockchain, and machine learning will together have the potential to bring digital transformation in every sphere of the healthcare industry. Blockchain technology can renovate medical trials, SCM, remedy supply administration, and avert frauds in the healthcare business (Kumar & Mallick, 2018; Akram et al., 2020).

REVIEW OF LITERATURE

Martin et al. (2017) stated that digital transformation in the healthcare sector has huge potential for improving the level of services for the patients. The cyber security threats such as ransomware highlighted the significance of the cyber security to ensure safety of patient records. Due to the inherent limitations of healthcare sector, this sector encounters the largest cyber risk in its security position. The healthcare sector is the soft and easy target for the attackers due to loopholes in its security mechanism and it offers plenty of valuable data.

Pilkington (2017) examined the requirement of distributed ledger technology in the hospital and medicine segment after encountering the problems with private and public enterprises for retrieving data related to patients. The distributed ledger technology has acknowledged the remarkable role for the organization and compilation of electronic health records (Bell et al., 2018). The study aroused the fast-mounting demand for medical equipment by the consumers and figure out the role of public-private relationships for designing blockchain technologies for the health care sector.

Rose (2017) stated that online medicine ordering i.e., telemedicine is not a new concept in the nation but the outburst of COVID 19 has made this mobile health concept very much popular. The concept of mhealth has led to wider integration of hospitals and patients and resulted in wider reach and participation (Celesti et al., 2020). The chapter focused on the alarming usage of electronic media and health apps in the period of novel coronavirus which will help to overcome the fear of infection due to physical interaction between people (Kalla et al., 2020; Ahmad et al., 2021). The study explored the upsurge in the concept of mhealth and what are its developments, and what kind of opportunities are being offered by this emerging concept in the medical industry. The challenges and threats posed by this concept were also covered by the study.

Teoh & Mahmood (2017) stated that the digital economy is possible with the help of cyber security. The cyber space is becoming very challenging and there are new advancements with each passing day. This calls for the enactment of National cybersecurity strategy (NCSS) to protect the digital economy in the phase of drastic online transformation (Brunetti et al., 2020). The adoption of NCSS is not mandatory but it will help in continuous growth and prosperity in the online world.

Rabah (2018) said that data is the new blood in the economy. Data management is required in every field whether it is healthcare, manufacturing, retail, food, transport, service, operational and agriculture, etc. and demand for professionals in big data is also increasing day by day. It played a crucial role in identifying the needs of consumers and supplying requisite goods at the best price to remain ahead of their competitors. Developing knowledges such as the, blockchain, artificial intelligence, Internet of Things (IoT), machine learning, and big data all together have brought a drastic change in data compilation and management. This will lead to a promising industrial revolution. The study focused on the implementation of evolving technology in healthcare and any other domains it answered many questions related to the application of technology in the fast-changing era of digitalization. Data is the basis of evolving artificial intelligence and helps in the growth of every sector of the economy.

Attia et al. (2019) focused on security architecture in the field of IoT and blockchain for reviewing the healthcare applications. Various appropriate examples have been used to validate this framework at design level. In advanced technology framework, devices are connected and information needs to be placed in a highly secure environment.

Abraham et al. (2019) examined that Healthcare sector is most vulnerable to cyber security. The cyber risk due to malware, ransomware, hacking and phishing, etc,. pose serious threats in the operation of healthcare sector. The United States (US) healthcare domain found that due to excessive legality and discordant systems, application of cyber security has become difficult. The governance, securities laws, compliance regulations futher complicate the challenge of cyber security into the system.

Dai et al. (2019) dicussed about the opportunities and challenges of IoT in the technology driven environment. There are number of loopholes noticed in the IoT applications such as privacy, security, decentralization and deprived interoperability. The study also discussed how blockchain adoption helped in overcoming the challenges caused by IoT.

Epiphaniou et al. (2019) explored the peculiarities of advanced technology such as Blockchain and how it improved the operations in the healthcare domain with the assistance of its key features and innovative applications. The major risks and opportunities related to technology adoption have also been discussed in the study.

Meske et al. (2019) examined the possibilities of online shoving in medical clinics and reasoned that computerized poking in medical clinics can decidedly impact the utilization of innovation, new worth creation, the difference in structures, and subsequently monetary elements of advanced change, supporting guardians as well as overseers.

Ricciardi et al. (2019) found that the influence of the digitalization process has been thoughtful, and it is projected to be more thoughtful in nearby future (Jain & Lamba, 2021). The study evaluated whether health care services contributed in a significant manner to the goals of health care processes and systems. Optimally decision should be taken at which level digital services should be introduced based on the evidence from the medical industry.

Alam (2020) emphasized how blockchain can be fruitful in the mobile health (mhealth) of patients. Patients nowadays are more knowledgeable and need to know all information related to their health on a real-time basis and this would empower them. The blockchain phenomena will boost mobile health and its applications and usage. The combination of the Internet of Things (IoT) and blockchain will provide a unique identification number to the connected device in the framework including mobile and medical devices. This will be helpful for the patients to monitor their health and reduce the cost of physically visiting the hospitals. In a nutshell, the adoption of emerging advancements in the field of technology will provide relief and comfort to effectively monitor patient's health problems and it will also benefit the doctors and hospital staff to perform their duties while maintaining integrity in the system.

Chamola et al. (2020) inspected the impression of COVID 19 on the budget of diverse countries and it also analyzed that COVID 19 had seriously impacted the healthcare sector. The use of advanced tools and applications such as, Internet of Things (IoT), Unmanned Aerial Vehicles (UAVs), Artificial Intelligence (AI) and Distributed expertise etc., helps in reducing the influence of pandemic on the economy.

El-Gazzar & Stendal (2020) studied the advantages and challenges faced by the health care sector with the application of blockchain technology and how the innovation in the information and technology sector enhanced the exchange of patient-sensitive data and empowered the patients and found that adoption of this distributed ledger technology may raise the problems of the health care sector instead of solving them. It was found that there is a requirement of using more cases to understand the sharing of information with the health care domain (Khezr et al., 2019).

Fekih & Lahami (2020) examined that blockchain technology applications in the medicine and well-being domain. The research in this sector is emerging rapidly. The advanced technology is used for patient monitoring, reviewing drug supply chain and sharing the electronic medicinal histories. The study also focused on the limitations of blockchain also.

Mathy et al. (2020) studied the influence of digitalization on the supply chain of the hospital industry. The digitalization of the supply chain had raised concerns for decision-makers in the healthcare sector. These are usually valued with techniques such as return on investments, Health technology assessments (HTA), etc. The introduction of ADS (automated dispensing system) in French hospital central pharmacy with a posteriori evaluation from the opinion of hospitals. It has led to hidden cost assuagement which does not generate any cash flow i.e., financial flow and it has not been valued. When they are given weightage, the results changed dramatically, as the profitability changes from negative to positive. Importance should be given to these hidden costs and gains as they had a drastic impact on the evaluation of the organization's impact.

Moro Visconti & Morea (2020) explored the influence of making digital the smart hospital project financing (PF) promoted by pay-for-performance (P4P) inducements. Electronic stages facilitate the exchange of information between different agents. Submission to healthcare public-private firms (PPPs) has importantly led to the steadiness of electronic stages with the well-being problems and the intricacy of the shareholder's interface. Digital savings can be very useful for all the stakeholders and it has proved beneficial in the digitalization of supply chains and is significantly contributing towards a patient-centric approach. Digitalization of the medicine sector will be beneficial for surveillance of infectious disease, supplement massive healthcare intervention, provide timely and accurate data, and helps in the decongestion of hospitals during the COVID 19 period.

Omar et al. (2020) explored the prospects in the well-being domain wide the applications of Blockchain technology. The distinguishing features of blockchain such as transparency, data attribution, accurate and reliable reporting and data analytics help in resolving rigorous data management issues in clinical trials. The healthcare sector shown tremendous improvement such as patient retention, data integrity, privacy and regulatory compliances due to adoption of blockchain advanced application.

Ratthe (2020) discussed about the wide applications of IoT such as healthcare, agriculture, public safety, smart phones and smart homes. The IoT is now considered as IoE "Internet of Everything". It has undertaken a drastic revolution in the field of advanced technology. It has a promising future ahead.

Singh & Singh (2020) studied the integration of blockchain and the Internet of Things (IoT) in the agriculture and healthcare sector predominantly. With emerging advancements and innovations these technologies will transform the food and healthcare industry (Kumar et al., 2018). It was discovered that 20% of papers are accessible in agriculture and 14% obtainable in the hospital sector that integrated blockchain with AI and IoT. It will help in managing healthcare and nutrition stock chain administration (Farouk et al., 2020).

Srivastava et al. (2020) The technology of the Internet of Things (IoT) has increased the usage of blockchain applications in the well-being sector. The aim is to reap maximum benefits from the request of blockchain in the well-being domain. The sphere of blockchain has reached many sectors besides the financial sector, the chapter focused on IoT applications specifically in the well-being sector by making use of distributed ledger expertise (Clauson et al., 2018). This is a challenging area of research as per today's scenario and the chapter dealt with positive attributes of this technology and what will be its future implications has been discussed in detail in the study. The author emphasized exploring this new horizon and IoT integration with the blockchain.

Tripathi et al. (2020) found that blockchain helped to overcome the failure of privacy and security-related issues. The study explored the technical and communal hurdles while adopting Smart Healthcare Systems (SRS) by exploring the views of experts and operators and observed the role of blockchain as the remarkable to facilitate the security and veracity of the system (Mistry et al., 2020).

Caldarelli et al. (2021) intended to inspect and overwhelmed the barricades to the extensive acceptance of blockchain technology and reinforced the impression that the blockchain explanation could be an appreciated add-on in maintainable supply chains. However, a high thoughtful knowledge of technology and widespread statement with patrons is obligatory for fruitful incorporation.

Foster et al (2021) stated the remarkable advancement in the field of technology and how it is going to decide the survival and growth in the wake of digitalization in the future. The technologies have been become agile such as blockchain, Machine learning, IoT, Virtual Reality have fostered the digital transactions in the country. These tools are going to decide the which sector will flourish in the 2021. Innovations and research in education industry are shaping the future of the nation.

Kamble et al. (2021) acknowledged intrant heaviness, companion willingness, apparent practicality, and seeming comfort of use as the most persuading aspects for blockchain acceptance.

Mathivathanan et al. (2021) recognized the espousal barricades and showed that the absence of commercial consciousness and acquaintance with distributed expertise on what it can deliver for upcoming supply chains, are the greatest powerful barricades that obstruct blockchain espousal. These barricades delay and influence trades choice to create a blockchain-enabled supply chain and that other barricades act as subordinate and related variable star in the implementation procedure.

Sharma & Joshi (2021) recognized barricades in the direction of the implementation of distributed technology in Indian hospital and well-being industry and recommended that low-slung consciousness linked to permissible subjects and little provision from upper level of organization have supreme pouring control.

OBJECTIVE OF THE STUDY

The aim of the study is as follows:

Primary Objectives

- To study the need for cyber-security amid digital transformation with the aid of emerging technologies.
- To study the application and combination of blockchain and the Internet of Things (IoT) for ensuring cyber-security in the healthcare industry.

Secondary Objectives

- To study the various innovations in the healthcare sector concerning technology adoption.
- To study the worldwide applications and developments of blockchain in the well-being domain.
- To study measures to mitigate cyber risk in wake of digitalization.

RESEARCH METHODOLOGY

This article methodically reviews the present literature published in peer-reviewed journals related to the application of blockchain and the Internet of Things (IoT) in the healthcare industry to overcome cyber risk in the period of digitalization. The information gathered in this study has been taken from authentic sources of secondary data collection including past studies. The study is a descriptive analysis of need for cyber-security amid digital transformation with the support of emerging technologies and the integration of blockchain and the Internet of Things (IoT) in the hospital sector and also throw some light on the worldwide applications of blockchain in the healthcare domain to ensure security and integrity in the phase of digital transformation.

USE OF DIGITAL TECHNOLOGY IN HEALTHCARE SECTOR

Technology has become the most important need of every sector. The technologies in the healthcare domain have wide applications from hospital administration applications to surgery and cancer research to eradicate the flaws in the system and make the patient experience with the hospital as pleasant as possible and improve overall efficacy in the well-being business (Jain, 2020).

Administrative

The use of IoT and blockchain has organized the administrative work in hospitals. The AI applications help in calculating the waiting time for a patient and also ask preliminary questions which makes it easier for the doctors and professionals to pact with patients in an operative manner. This has led to the more efficient and effective functioning of hospitals in the country.

Surgical Treatment

The use of machine learning, and robotics has been widely used in surgical procedures. During the COVID-19 period (Chamola et al., 2020) robotics has helped a lot in discharging services to patients and eradicate the chances of catching an infection. Robots are assisting doctors from minor surgeries to open-heart operations. Healthtech had a bright future ahead and the pandemic situation made the need for further advancement in the field of robotics. Augmented Reality (AR) is also helping doctors in explaining concepts to patients more clearly.

Medicine Development

Medicine and drug development is an important area of research and this has become all the way more vital due to the emergence of a pandemic. Healthcare and pharmaceutical companies are using artificial intelligence and paving new methods of drug development. It has simplified the process of drug development and reduce the period as well leading to the optimal drug. The patients and drug suitability can be checked via artificial intelligence.

Fitness

A healthy body is a must for keeping other things workable. There has been advancement in the number of applications that guide people on how to keep themselves healthy including wearables to keep a record of several steps in a day, sleep schedule measurement, weight reducing tips, etc.

Fault Reduction and Diagnostics

Early detection of disease can save millions of lives so the integration of Healthtech in the field of diagnosis is of paramount importance. Integration of technology in the field of genetics, pathology, diagnosis fields helped in the early detection of deadly diseases such as cancers and provided solutions with accuracy to treat can patients.

Psychological Well-Being

In today's era keeping your mind healthy is of paramount importance in one's life. Due to the continuously changing environment and increasing competition, it has become vital to pay attention to mental health. Disease such as depression, PTSD, Alzheimer's, etc. are arousing so there is a need to tackle these problems by inventing telemedicine apps where patients can access counselors online and exposure therapies can also be helpful to revive patients from depression.

APPLICATIONS OF DIGITAL TECNOLOGY IN THE HEALTHCARE SECTOR

- **Eradicating Centralization:** With the emergence of blockchain in technological advancement things changed drastically, earlier only authorized representatives had access to the repository of patient information but the introduction of blockchain led to decentralization where every user can access the information available on digital or cloud platform without any authorization and hurdles.
- **Enhanced data security and confidentiality:** The usage of blockchain leads to the removal of concerns related to data security and privacy concerns as they transform the exchange process,

now information is accessible in an encrypted format only which is difficult to decode. Moreover, the use of master and primary keys leads to the chronological arrangement of data and enhanced the security of patient records and details.

- **Control over patient records and ownership:** The patient's consent should be taken before using their treatment records. Using blockchain technology patients can monitor where data has been used and what are replications of that. The patients possess the ultimate control over their records and should not part on their privacy at any cost.

- **The atmosphere of Trust:** The step-by-step adoption of blockchain in the health care sector ensures the integrity of the system while sharing information. The uncluttered and see-through features of blockchain boost the trust and help various stakeholders of the health care sector in the implementation of numerous applications of data compilation, arrangement, retrieval, and management.

- **Claim Verification:** The use of blockchain in the healthcare domain has simplified the process of claim adjudication as it will make the process of verifying documents of patients much easier and reliable.

- **Data Accessibility:** The data stored on multiple nodes in the blockchain is easily available on the available to all the entitled users and their chances of data theft or loss are also minimal due to the security framework developed by blockchain and IoT technology and there will no corruption on part of data accessibility.

NEED FOR CYBERSECURITY IN PHASE OF DIGITAL TRANSFORMATION

The pace of digitalization in the market today calls for security issues as well, the emerging cyber-crimes such as hacking of websites, bank frauds, ATM card fraud, Call center fraud and Napster case etc., arose the fear of cyber threat in the business (Srivastava et al., 2020). The benefits offered by digitalization are numerous but challenges also need to be addressed on an immediate basis. In data driven society security of information needs to be maintained, to secure trust of public in technology. Recently the data of Dominos company related to credit card information of customers have been leaked which possess the threat to personal information of the customers. The advanced research in cyber security is providing tools and mechanism to control the menace of digital frauds. There have been several laws enacted at national and international level to control the menace of frauds by technocrats. The advancement in the IT sector is commendable but it offers certain challenges and threats also. These applications include Augmented Reality (AR), Big Data, Blockchain, Robotics and Virtual Reality and many more. There is a need for controlling cyber risk by strict application of security measures in the system and appointment of Chief Information Security Officer to maintain the safety of dealings in the business. The malicious activities need to be curbed to better use the leading advancement in the information technology sector. It need to be focused that no digital transformation should be taken without understanding its security implications. The Healthcare sector is a data enrich sector which is more lucrative to cyber attackers to impede the security of the system.

CYBER SECURITY ROADMAP

- **Consider Cyber Security Risk:** Recognize core and assignment perilous roles and formulate an reservoir of susceptible assets and allot a risk influence score to each susceptible asset.
- **Escalating cybersecurity risk and measures:** Evaluate the adverse consequences linked with diverse outbreak set-ups. Then estimate the outlay of suggested risk reduction measures such as prevention, recognition and retrieval and use of erudite analytics to guess the likelihood of adverse consequences and allied outlay.
- **Collaborating cybersecurity activities and results:** Upsurge transparency about cybersecurity strategy and measures. Adapt communications and attain a certain level of shared understanding and accord on inferences of cybersecurity events.

EMERGING MEDICAL DEVICES IN THE ERA OF DIGITALIZATION

The upsurge of digitization has taken over the world. All the evolving technologies like Cloud-based solutions, the Internet of Things (IoT) and Artificial Intelligence (AI), and many others are serving individuals animate a healthier and relaxed lifespan. The service division has been promoted a lot from digitization especially in the health care industry.

Patient-Generated Health Data (PGHD): It is a healthcare mobile application that provides information related to symptoms, lifestyle, the healing process, disease, treatment history, habits, and many more. It provides a critical analysis of the patient's disease history and helps in reducing the number of visits to a clinic.

Wearable Devices: Digital wearable devices always provide continuous nursing of health. It provides facilities such as quality of sleep, heart rate, steps walked, and more. They are widely used in the North American region.

Communication Channels: The recent developments in communication technology helps in keeping updated on all details related to their treatment such as instant messaging, emergency calls (SOS Signals), real-time video calls, and many more. By incorporating all these facilities in a mobile application companies are planning to offer real-time sustenance to patients in the time of need.

Geolocation: It is one of the distinguishing features of every mobile health application. It allows patients to locate nearby hospitals' addresses, clinics, and medical stores. It also has a provision in case of emergency when the patient is unable to locate his current location then he can make emergency calls. During the COVID 19 phase, it helps to locate COVID hot spots during the pandemic phase. It helps in fighting against the deadly virus. For instance, the government of the nation has developed an app named "Aarogya Setu" that uses geolocation and Bluetooth data to aware the users in the case of COVID 19 patients adjacent.

Contact Tracing: To combat the spread of this deadly virus infection and the practice of returning to a new world of normal requires the use of contact tracing. It helps in silent tracking of the COVID 19 patients and alerts the people promptly regarding any of their contacts who tested positive of this deadly disease.

Internet of Things (IoT): It has provided significant assistance in the era of digitalization; it helps in the collection of data from the connected devices and transmits it to the health care service provider. It can be vigilant for the doctors as they will be informed if anything wrong happens to a patient or any values crosses the threshold limits. The problem of depression has been well monitored by the usage of these technologies.

Cloud-based Solutions: EMR (Electronic Medical Records) have been integrated with EHR (Electronic Health Records) with cloud-based solutions that allow easy access to the patient treatment history, their recovery process, medical bills, insurance plans, and many more. With the emergence of cloud-based solutions and infrastructure, hospitals and healthcare companies promise to render better services at a relative lessor cost.

ELEMENTS OF ADVANCED BLOCKCHAIN TECHNOLOGY

- **Distributed Ledger Technology:** Blockchain is a record of all transactions in a peer-to-peer system. It is a dispersed ledger technology that ensures that everyone in the network has access to the information without any delay.
- **Encryption of Information:** The use of blockchain ensures that information is encrypted and leads to secure transfer of information. In short, it maintains the integrity and security of the data.
- **No need for Third Party:** All the authorized users in the system can directly share information amongst themselves that reduces the need for any third-party organization to authenticate the dealings.
- **Smart Contracts:** It permitted the agreement on additional business logic and automatic enforcement of the expected behavior of dealings or assets embodied in blockchain technology.

CYBER THREATS IN THE DIGITAL TRANSFORMATION OF HEALTHCARE SECTOR

- **Ransomware:** With the help of this malware the wrongdoers are trying to stop users from accessing their systems or data and even to delete their files unless a fees is paid to attackers.
- **Information theft for Impact:** Now a days there is common practice of stealing the data and information just for the sake of publicity stunts such as in case of high profile people, politicians and celebrities their health data is used for publicity purpose.
- **Stealing data for financial gains:** The attackers steal the information such personal information including names, address, credit card details, etc to use them for unethical monetary gains.
- **Denial of Service attacks:** It often used by attacker to cause disruption in the network by blocking the network with artificial requests, blackmail and activism.
- **Phishing:** It is a common fraud technique where a link is send over email and the victim by clicking on the link gives the way to intruder to access his/her system. Due to this victim faces huge financial loss.
- **Malevolent attacks:** These types of attacks can lead to complete or partial loss od data related to customers, accounts and financial dealings leading to serious regulatory desecrations.

WORLDWIDE ADVANCED TECHONLOGY APPLICATIONS IN HEALTHCARE SECTOR

Factom

It is widely used in information technology and enterprise system in Austin, Texas. It develops products that assist the healthcare sector to store data related to patients on the organization's blockchain that is available to hospital staff and operators only. Only authorized people can access the information stored in the Factom security chip. It laboring blockchain distributed technology for data handling and store information in a secured manner digitally.

Medicalchain

It is widely used in maintaining health records electronically and blockchain assists that only in London, England. It ensures the privacy of patients as outsiders cannot access the patient's confidential information and doctors, professionals and laboratories can access information from a record origin as well. With the help of blockchain, they can maintain the information from the origin and protect the confidentiality of patients.

Guardtime

It is used in cybersecurity in Irvine, California. It is being applied in the healthcare sector for cybersecurity applications. It is very much helpful for government and healthcare companies to integrate blockchain with cybersecurity applications.

Simplyvital Health

This company is using decentralized technology in the healthcare domain in Watertown, Massachusetts. It provides an open database where pertinent information is stored and made available to health care professionals for further research in the healthcare industry. Patients' information can be accessed in a time-effective manner and information can be shared for obtaining coordination.

Coral Health Research and Discovery

It employs blockchain to speed up the process of administration, care process and automate other health operations queries and improve the resulting information. It led to smart contracts between patients and professionals in the medical industry.

Robomed

This company does the task of gathering information related to patients with the help of AI and share the information gathered with healthcare benefactors. It is put up in Moscow, Russia, and used blockchain technology to securely access and share information with professionals and healthcare operators only.

Patientory

It focused on maintaining the confidentiality of patient's data in Atlanta. Georgia. It provided end-to-end encryption of data and information. All patient's information has been placed under one roof from where all doctors, professionals, surgeons can retrieve the information as per their requirement by employing blockchain technology.

RECENT DEVELOPMENTS IN BLOCKCHAIN TECHNOLOGY

- **Blockchain As a Service (BaaS):** This trend has been made famous more in 2020 as blockchain has been integrated with start-up ventures. The users can make their online products with the assistance of blockchain. These products can take the form of decentralized applications and smart contracts, all the more it offers services that don't require blockchain infrastructure. Companies such as Microsoft and Amazon making blockchain applications need of the hour to remain competitive.
- **Coalesced Blockchain Transfers to the Center Phase:** It is one of the latest and demanding trends in blockchain technology. The case used has been increased with the help of federated blockchain. It led to decentralization where diverse authorities can control nodes of blockchain. It has sped up the processing speed and will provide a more customized outlook.
- **High Demand of Stablecoins:** To stabilize the volatility in the cryptocurrencies blockchain stable coins will be in high demand in the year 2021.
- **Blockchain Networks:** These networks have fastened the process of exchange of data and sharing of information from one network to another integrated via blockchain.
- **Lucrative to Government Organizations:** Government agencies are required to monitor a huge volume of data, blockchain applications will reduce the burden of storage by providing a separate database for a specific activity. The adoption of distributed ledger technology will improve the functioning of government departments.
- **Blockchain integration with Artificial Intelligence:** The combination of blockchain and artificial intelligence can boost the machine learning concept and blockchain can make AI more understandable and comprehensive. It can trace why conclusions are reached in machine learning and enhance the application domain of emergent technology.

MEASURES TO MITIGATE CYBER RISK IN WAKE OF DIGITALIZATION

Depending on the nature of business, complexity of dealings and usage of network, the measures should the adopted to prevent cyber risk in light of digitalization in the economy.

- Identification of the risk at the initial phase helps in prevention of a big problem from originating. Depending on the network system, allocation of resources and mobile devices, there is a need to prioritize the resources and effort in wake of digitalization.

- The practice of restricting the permission to access the system is one of the common ways to mitigate cyber risk. Use of passwords and proper administration will help in achievement of cyber security in the system.
- Encryption devices makes sure that data that is private and confidential is not available to people outside the organization domain.
- Use of proper software and firewall applications serve the purpose of cyber security in digital transactions.
- Periodic monitoring of the system also helps in maintaining security of the system in the network and often ensure smooth functioning of the system as well. The information security manager should be alert all the time to ensure the integrity and trust in the system.
- A proper response strategy also helps in overcoming the severity of cyber-attacks. The strategy helps in fetching legal remedies and reduces the monetary impact of unwanted dealings in the system.
- There is need for timely backup and customized training for ensuring reliability and integrity at all stages of organization.
- The vetting needs to be done for cloud service providers to ensure compliance with auditing standards such as SAS 70 and FIPS 200.
- Deploying AI automated structures that proactively notice and prevent outbreaks on web and devices.
- A risk management regimes needs to be set up and embedded into cybersecurity of the business dealings

MAJOR FINDINGS OF THE STUDY

- The introduction of advanced tehnology in digital world led to decentralization where every user can access the information available on digital or cloud platforms without any authorization and hurdles.
- The digital transformation led to smart contracts between patients and professionals in the medical industry.
- Cybersecurity ensures the privacy of patients as outsiders cannot access the patient's confidential information and doctors, professionals and laboratories can access information from a record origin as well.
- Digital wearable devices always provide continuous nursing of health. It provides facilities such as quality of sleep, heart rate, steps walked, and more.
- The step-by-step adoption of blockchain in the well-being sector ensures the integrity of the system while sharing information. The uncluttered and see-through features of blockchain boost the trust and help various stakeholders of the health care sector in the implementation of numerous applications of data compilation, arrangement, retrieval, and management.
- Emerging technologies such as the Internet of Things (IoT), blockchain, artificial intelligence, machine learning, and big data all together have brought a drastic change in data compilation and management. These technologies help in maintaining the confidentiality of patients and provide access to a secure platform for the exchange of information.

- Internet of Things (IoT) has provided significant assistance in the era of digitalization; it helps in the collection of data from the connected devices and transmits it to the health care service provider.
- Government agencies are required to monitor a huge volume of data, blockchain applications will reduce the burden of storage by providing a separate database for a specific activity.
- It is very much helpful for government and healthcare companies to integrate blockchain with cybersecurity applications.
- It is highly recommended to maintain adequate documentation on the technical standards followed and aspired to be followed by the businesses and that need to be driven by adequate policy and top managerial employees. It further suggested that top and senior management should be guided by a competent and professional Chief Inforamtion Security Officer.
- Identification of the risk at the initial phase helps in prevention of a big problem from originating. Depending on the network system, allocation of resources and mobile devices, there is a need to prioritize the resources and effort in wake of digitalization.
- The use of blockchain in the healthcare domain has simplified the process of claim adjudication as it will make the process of verifying documents of patients much easier and reliable.
- The use of master and primary keys leads to the chronological arrangement of data and enhanced the security of patient records and details.

SOLUTIONS AND RECOMMENDATIONS

The healthcare sector is very soft target of the malicous attackers so security needs to be fostered at every level of business transactions. It is highly recommended to maintain adequate documentation on the technical standards followed and aspired to be followed by the businesses and that need to be driven by adequate policy and top managerial employees. It further suggested that top and senior management should be guided by a competent and professional Chief Inforamtion Security Officer. The information security manager should be alert all the time to ensure the integrity and trust in the system.he following security measures should be pracrices such as use of proper software and firewall applications that serve the purpose of cyber security in digital transactions and continous monitoring of the system also helps in maintaining security of the system in the network and often ensure smooth functioning of the system as well. A proper response strategy also helps in overcoming the severity of cyber-attacks. The strategy helps in fetching legal remedies and reduces the monetary impact of unwanted dealings in the system. There is need for timely backup and customized training for ensuring reliability and integrity at all stages of organization.

FUTURE RESEARCH DIRECTIONS

The cybercrime is a universal challenge, the present study mainly discussed about the cyber security threats, measures and digital advancement in the healthcare sector. There is scope for other sectors to analyse the cyber security impications in the era of digitalization. The effective cybersecurity must become an vital part of healthcare domain and further guidelines and compliance actions should be subject of imminent research tactics.

CONCLUSION

Cybersecurity is not just about protection of data it has wide implications such as maintaining safety, privacy, integrity, trust of the patients in the healthcare sector. The need for data management and organization has paved ways for advanced technologies such as Blockchain and the Internet of Things (IoT). The Healthcare sector is the most important domain of a nation's prosperity. Data and health integration can solve many difficult problems in the healthcare sector. It facilitates exchange and dealings in the database that can be shared across authorized operators. Advanced technology such as Blockchain is peer-to-peer disseminated ledger know-how. It consists of majorly three components which are namely distributed network, shared record, and digital transaction. The healthcare industry has undergone various reforms since the evolution of blockchain and Internet of Things (IoT) technology came into the picture. The emergence of these techniques has led to a drastic improvement in the field of Hospital administration, Medicine development, Surgery, Mental Health, and cybersecurity, etc. During the COVID 19 phase, the most affected sector was healthcare where technological advancement was much needed. Robotics helped the nations to face this pandemic with strength.

The technologies in the healthcare domain have wide applications from hospital administration to surgery and cancer research to eradicate the flaws in the system and make the patient experience with the hospital as pleasant as possible and improve overall efficiency in the healthcare industry. Emerging technologies such as the Internet of Things (IoT), blockchain, artificial intelligence, machine learning, and big data all together have brought a drastic change in data compilation and management. This will lead to a promising industrial revolution. The study focused on the implementation of evolving technology in the healthcare sector. Worldwide, blockchain technology has been used in managing the flow of data and information and ensuring security in the system, India should focus on maintaining the same blockchain-enabled infrastructure to reduce causalities in the nation. The adoption of these techniques has led to the secure transfer of information and helped in maintaining the confidentiality of patient's health records.

"Healthcare is an important sector of Indian Economy. Both government and technocrats should work together in the best possible manner by exploiting emerging technologies so that it leads to improvement of healthcare services and the well-being of the nation."

ACKNOWLEDGMENT

This study received no explicit grant from any funding agency in the public, commercial, or not-for-profit divisions.

REFERENCES

Abdellatif, A. A., Al-Marridi, A. Z., Mohamed, A., Erbad, A., Chiasserini, C. F., & Refaey, A. (2020). Health: Toward secure, blockchain-enabled healthcare systems. *IEEE Network*, *34*(4), 312–319. doi:10.1109/MNET.011.1900553

Abdullah, T., & Jones, A. (2019, January). eHealth: challenges far integrating blockchain within healthcare. In *2019 IEEE 12th International Conference on Global Security, Safety and Sustainability (ICGS3)* (pp. 1-9). IEEE.

Abraham, C., Chatterjee, D., & Sims, R. R. (2019). Muddling through cybersecurity: Insights from the US healthcare industry. *Business Horizons*, *62*(4), 539–548. doi:10.1016/j.bushor.2019.03.010

Ahmad, R. W., Salah, K., Jayaraman, R., Yaqoob, I., Ellahham, S., & Omar, M. (2021). The role of blockchain technology in telehealth and telemedicine. *International Journal of Medical Informatics*, *148*, 104399. doi:10.1016/j.ijmedinf.2021.104399 PMID:33540131

Aich, S., Chakraborty, S., Sain, M., Lee, H. I., & Kim, H. C. (2019, February). A review on benefits of IoT integrated blockchain-based supply chain management implementations across different sectors with case study. In *2019 21st international conference on advanced communication technology (ICACT)* (pp. 138-141). IEEE. 10.23919/ICACT.2019.8701910

Akram, S. V., Malik, P. K., Singh, R., Anita, G., & Tanwar, S. (2020). Adoption of blockchain technology in various realms: Opportunities and challenges. *Security and Privacy*, *3*(5), e109. doi:10.1002py2.109

Alam, T. (2020). mHealth Communication Framework using blockchain and IoT Technologies. *International Journal of Scientific & Technology Research*, *9*(6).

Alladi, T., Chamola, V., Parizi, R. M., & Choo, K. K. R. (2019). Blockchain applications for industry 4.0 and industrial IoT: A review. *IEEE Access: Practical Innovations, Open Solutions*, *7*, 176935–176951. doi:10.1109/ACCESS.2019.2956748

Attia, O., Khoufi, I., Laouiti, A., & Adjih, C. (2019, June). An IoT-blockchain architecture based on hyperledger framework for health care monitoring application. In *NTMS 2019-10th IFIP International Conference on New Technologies, Mobility and Security* (pp. 1-5). IEEE Computer Society.

Bell, L., Buchanan, W. J., Cameron, J., & Lo, O. (2018). Applications of blockchain within healthcare. *Blockchain in Healthcare Today, 1*(8).

Brunetti, F., Matt, D. T., Bonfanti, A., De Longhi, A., Pedrini, G., & Orzes, G. (2020). Digital transformation challenges: Strategies emerging from a multi-stakeholder approach. *The TQM Journal*, *32*(4), 697–724. doi:10.1108/TQM-12-2019-0309

Caldarelli, G., Zardini, A., & Rossignoli, C. (2021). Blockchain adoption in the fashion sustainable supply chain: Pragmatically addressing barriers. *Journal of Organizational Change Management*, *34*(2), 507–524. doi:10.1108/JOCM-09-2020-0299

Celesti, A., Ruggeri, A., Fazio, M., Galletta, A., Villari, M., & Romano, A. (2020). Blockchain-based healthcare workflow for tele-medical laboratory in federated hospital IoT clouds. *Sensors (Basel)*, *20*(9), 2590. doi:10.339020092590 PMID:32370129

Chamola, V., Hassija, V., Gupta, V., & Guizani, M. (2020). A comprehensive review of the COVID-19 pandemic and the role of IoT, drones, AI, blockchain, and 5G in managing its impact. *IEEE Access: Practical Innovations, Open Solutions*, *8*, 90225–90265. doi:10.1109/ACCESS.2020.2992341

Clauson, K. A., Breeden, E. A., Davidson, C., & Mackey, T. K. (2018). Leveraging blockchain technology to enhance supply chain management in healthcare: an exploration of challenges and opportunities in the health supply chain. *Blockchain in Healthcare Today, 1*(3), 1-12.

Dai, H. N., Zheng, Z., & Zhang, Y. (2019). Blockchain for Internet of Things: A survey. *IEEE Internet of Things Journal, 6*(5), 8076–8094. doi:10.1109/JIOT.2019.2920987

El-Gazzar, R., & Stendal, K. (2020). Blockchain in health care: Hope or hype? *Journal of Medical Internet Research, 22*(7), e17199. doi:10.2196/17199 PMID:32673219

Epiphaniou, G., Daly, H., & Al-Khateeb, H. (2019). Blockchain and healthcare. In *Blockchain and Clinical Trial* (pp. 1–29). Springer. doi:10.1007/978-3-030-11289-9_1

Farouk, A., Alahmadi, A., Ghose, S., & Mashatan, A. (2020). Blockchain platform for industrial healthcare: Vision and future opportunities. *Computer Communications, 154*, 223–235. doi:10.1016/j. comcom.2020.02.058

Fekih, R. B., & Lahami, M. (2020, June). Application of blockchain technology in healthcare: a comprehensive study. In *International Conference on Smart Homes and Health Telematics* (pp. 268-276). Springer.

Foster, I., Lopresti, D., Gropp, B., Hill, M., & Schuman, K. (2021). *A National Discovery Cloud: Preparing the US for Global Competitiveness in the New Era of 21st Century Digital Transformation.* arXiv preprint arXiv:2104.06953.

Hasselgren, A., Kralevska, K., Gligoroski, D., Pedersen, S. A., & Faxvaag, A. (2020). Blockchain in healthcare and health sciences—A scoping review. *International Journal of Medical Informatics, 134*, 104040. doi:10.1016/j.ijmedinf.2019.104040 PMID:31865055

Hussein, A. H. (2019). Internet of things (IOT): Research challenges and future applications. *International Journal of Advanced Computer Science and Applications, 10*(6), 77–82. doi:10.14569/ IJACSA.2019.0100611

Jain, E. (2020). Digital Employability Skills and Training Needs for the Indian Healthcare Industry. In *Opportunities and Challenges in Digital Healthcare Innovation* (pp. 113–130). IGI Global. doi:10.4018/978-1-7998-3274-4.ch007

Jain, E., & Lamba, J. (2020). Covid-19: Economic Hardship and Financial Distress in Indian Economy. *International Journal of Disaster Recovery and Business Continuity, 11*(3), 3081–3092.

Jain, E., & Lamba, J. (2021). Management and Digitalization Strategy for Transforming Education Sector: An Emerging Gateway Persuaded by COVID-19. In Emerging Challenges, Solutions, and Best Practices for Digital Enterprise Transformation (pp. 69-83). IGI Global.

Kalla, A., Hewa, T., Mishra, R. A., Ylianttila, M., & Liyanage, M. (2020). The role of blockchain to fight against COVID-19. *IEEE Engineering Management Review, 48*(3), 85–96. doi:10.1109/ EMR.2020.3014052

Kamble, S. S., Gunasekaran, A., Kumar, V., Belhadi, A., & Foropon, C. (2021). A machine learning based approach for predicting blockchain adoption in supply Chain. *Technological Forecasting and Social Change, 163*, 120465. doi:10.1016/j.techfore.2020.120465

Khezr, S., Moniruzzaman, M., Yassine, A., & Benlamri, R. (2019). Blockchain technology in healthcare: A comprehensive review and directions for future research. *Applied Sciences (Basel, Switzerland), 9*(9), 1736. doi:10.3390/app9091736

Kumar, N. M., & Mallick, P. K. (2018). Blockchain technology for security issues and challenges in IoT. *Procedia Computer Science, 132*, 1815–1823. doi:10.1016/j.procs.2018.05.140

Kumar, T., Ramani, V., Ahmad, I., Braeken, A., Harjula, E., & Ylianttila, M. (2018, September). Blockchain utilization in healthcare: Key requirements and challenges. In *2018 IEEE 20th International Conference on e-Health Networking, Applications and Services (Healthcom)* (pp. 1-7). IEEE.

Martin, G., Martin, P., Hankin, C., Darzi, A., & Kinross, J. (2017). Cybersecurity and healthcare: How safe are we? *BMJ (Clinical Research Ed.), 358*. doi:10.1136/bmj.j3179 PMID:28684400

Mathivathanan, D., Mathiyazhagan, K., Rana, N. P., Khorana, S., & Dwivedi, Y. K. (2021). Barriers to the adoption of blockchain technology in business supply chains: A total interpretive structural modelling (TISM) approach. *International Journal of Production Research*, 1–22.

Mathy, C., Pascal, C., Fizesan, M., Boin, C., Délèze, N., & Aujoulat, O. (2020, July). Automated hospital pharmacy supply chain and the evaluation of organisational impacts and costs. In Supply chain forum: An international journal (Vol. 21, No. 3, pp. 206-218). Taylor & Francis.

McGhin, T., Choo, K. K. R., Liu, C. Z., & He, D. (2019). Blockchain in healthcare applications: Research challenges and opportunities. *Journal of Network and Computer Applications, 135*, 62–75. doi:10.1016/j.jnca.2019.02.027

Meske, C., Amojo, I., Poncette, A. S., & Balzer, F. (2019, July). The Potential Role of Digital Nudging in the Digital Transformation of the Healthcare Industry. In *International Conference on Human-Computer Interaction* (pp. 323-336). Springer. 10.1007/978-3-030-23538-3_25

Miraz, M. H. (2020). Blockchain of things (BCoT): The fusion of blockchain and IoT technologies. In *Advanced Applications of Blockchain Technology* (pp. 141–159). Springer. doi:10.1007/978-981-13-8775-3_7

Mistry, I., Tanwar, S., Tyagi, S., & Kumar, N. (2020). Blockchain for 5G-enabled IoT for industrial automation: A systematic review, solutions, and challenges. *Mechanical Systems and Signal Processing, 135*, 106382. doi:10.1016/j.ymssp.2019.106382

Moro Visconti, R., & Morea, D. (2020). Healthcare digitalization and pay-for-performance incentives in smart hospital project financing. *International Journal of Environmental Research and Public Health, 17*(7), 2318. doi:10.3390/ijerph17072318 PMID:32235517

Omar, I. A., Jayaraman, R., Salah, K., Yaqoob, I., & Ellahham, S. (2020). Applications of blockchain technology in clinical trials: Review and open challenges. *Arabian Journal for Science and Engineering*, 1–15.

Pilkington, M. (2017). Can blockchain improve healthcare management? Consumer medical electronics and the IoMT. *Consumer Medical Electronics and the IoMT.*

Rabah, K. (2018). Convergence of AI, IoT, big data and blockchain: a review. *The Lake Institute Journal, 1*(1), 1-18.

Rathee, G., Sharma, A., Saini, H., Kumar, R., & Iqbal, R. (2019). A hybrid framework for multimedia data processing in IoT-healthcare using blockchain technology. *Multimedia Tools and Applications,* 1–23. doi:10.100711042-019-07835-3

Rathee, P. (2020). Introduction to Blockchain and IoT. In *Advanced Applications of Blockchain Technology* (pp. 1–14). Springer. doi:10.1007/978-981-13-8775-3_1

Ray, P. P., Dash, D., Salah, K., & Kumar, N. (2020). Blockchain for IoT-based healthcare: Background, consensus, platforms, and use cases. *IEEE Systems Journal.* Advance online publication. doi:10.1109/JSYST.2020.2963840

Ricciardi, W., Pita Barros, P., Bourek, A., Brouwer, W., Kelsey, T., Lehtonen, L., Anastasy, C., Barros, P., Barry, M., Bourek, A., Brouwer, W., De Maeseneer, J., Kringos, D., Lehtonen, L., McKee, M., Murauskiene, L., Nuti, S., Ricciardi, W., Siciliani, L., & Wild, C. (2019). How to govern the digital transformation of health services. *European Journal of Public Health, 29*(Supplement_3), 7–12. doi:10.1093/eurpub/ckz165 PMID:31738442

Rose, K. J. (2017). Mobile Health: Telemedicine's Latest Wave but This Time It's for Real. In L. Menvielle, A. F. Audrain-Pontevia, & W. Menvielle (Eds.), *The Digitization of Healthcare.* Palgrave Macmillan. doi:10.1057/978-1-349-95173-4_9

Sharma, M., & Joshi, S. (2021). Barriers to blockchain adoption in health-care industry: an Indian perspective. *Journal of Global Operations and Strategic Sourcing.*

Singh, P., & Singh, N. (2020). Blockchain With IoT and AI: A Review of Agriculture and Healthcare. *International Journal of Applied Evolutionary Computation, 11*(4), 13–27. doi:10.4018/IJAEC.2020100102

Srivastava, A., Jain, P., Hazela, B., Asthana, P., & Rizvi, S. W. A. (2021). Application of Fog Computing, Internet of Things, and Blockchain Technology in Healthcare Industry. In *Fog Computing for Healthcare 4.0 Environments* (pp. 563–591). Springer. doi:10.1007/978-3-030-46197-3_22

Srivastava, G., Parizi, R. M., & Dehghantanha, A. (2020). The future of blockchain technology in healthcare internet of things security. *Blockchain Cybersecurity, Trust and Privacy,* 161-184.

Teoh, C. S., & Mahmood, A. K. (2017, July). National cyber security strategies for digital economy. In *2017 International Conference on Research and Innovation in Information Systems (ICRIIS)* (pp. 1-6). IEEE. 10.1109/ICRIIS.2017.8002519

Tripathi, G., Ahad, M. A., & Paiva, S. (2020, March). S2HS-A blockchain based approach for smart healthcare system. In Healthcare (Vol. 8, No. 1, p. 100391). Elsevier.

Chapter 18
Digital Transformation of E–Commerce Services and Cybersecurity for Modernizing the Banking Sector of Pakistan:
A Study of Customer Preferences and Perceived Risks

Tansif ur Rehman
https://orcid.org/0000-0002-5454-2150
University of Karachi, Pakistan

ABSTRACT

The practice of protecting computers, websites, mobile devices, electronic services, networks, and digital data from malicious attacks is known as cybersecurity. Since political, military, private, financial, and medical institutions collect, process, and maintain massive volumes of data on computers and other devices, cybersecurity is critical. Sensitive data, such as intellectual property, financial data, personal records, or other forms of data, can make up a large amount of the data. Improper access or disclosure to that data can have profound implications. Technology has undoubtedly made a significant change in every aspect of life in Pakistan, whether it is a financial or non-financial sphere. Technology's usage is thoroughly utilized by banks worldwide. They have started adopting it frequently because of the immense need to achieve goals and satisfy customer needs more efficiently. Almost all leading banks have now provided e-commerce facilities. Over time, more and more services and facilities are offered to bank customers conveniently via e-commerce products.

DOI: 10.4018/978-1-7998-6975-7.ch018

INTRODUCTION

E-commerce has been promoted worldwide as a primary enabler for youth entrepreneurship and a job-creating catalyst (Ahmed, 2019; Kshetri, 2007). Despite favorable internet and smartphone demographics and rising e-commerce adoption, Pakistan's e-commerce market is still tiny compared to comparable countries such as Indonesia and India and poses serious cybersecurity challenges. Due to various technological, sociopolitical, and cognitive hurdles, Pakistan's true E-Commerce potential has yet to be realized and along with that a robust cybersecurity for safeguarding the trust of the digital users. With over 36 million internet digital subscribers, over 40 million smartphone digital users, over 30 million broadband internet users, expanding 4G LTE penetration, and massive social media adoption, the future looks bright and can provide enormous benefits to the country's economy and the people. Pakistan has all of the required indicators and is fast advancing to kick-start an e-commerce boom that will stimulate the economy and also create jobs for the people and newer tech industries around which the country can modernise. The Alibaba group's recent acquisition of www.Daraz.pk, Pakistan's largest online marketplace, may significantly affect the country's e-commerce growth (Ahmed, 2019).

Increased internet connectivity, higher capacity, better logistics penetration, and distribution systems, and the availability of alternative payment mechanisms such as COD and mobile payments have contributed to an increasing trend in B2C and C2C e-commerce in recent years. Overall the progress has been astonishing. The increased traffic on B2C and C2C websites, hundreds of which are now among Pakistan's top 500 websites by traffic, is evidence of much more modernization to follow (Ahmed, 2019). The expansion of structured retail into e-commerce and the growing number of e-commerce portals with multimillion-dollar investments, such as Yayvo.com, 24hrs.pk, and Daraz.pk, is further evidence of the important role that the digital technology has to offer. Furthermore, the buyer's and almost every established consumer brand's rapid embrace of social media adds to the belief that e-commerce is gaining traction in Pakistan.

In 1987, ATMs were introduced in Pakistan (Abbasi, 2013), and they have gained much popularity. Now, internet and mobile banking services are offered on a large scale to facilitate Pakistan's respective customers. Remittances from foreign countries also play a crucial role in the financial sector's stability, and thus banks are bringing customers even closer to their banks. This study's primary focus is on e-commerce facilities offered by banks, i.e., local and foreign, with relevance to customers' individual and collective perceptions of these services. This study will highlight the areas where e-commerce services have lapses.

While the internet provides some anonymity, more and more ways that personal information can be compromised on cyberspace and there is an enormous risk to privacy of the people. One can reduce the cyber risk of an Internet mishap by using awareness as a safety net. Being vigilant when using the internet helps secure data, devices, and money. Young people are particularly vulnerable because they put a high value on creating an online identity, and many websites request personal information and privacy can be compromised on cyberspace. While many people are aware of setting up strict privacy controls on their accounts and preventing email scams, it is essential to educate them about the dangers of providing personal information online and cybersecurity (ReachOut Australia, 2021).

Since they are heterogeneous, with various minor transactions executed by individuals across several networks, cross-border remittances are difficult to monitor due to vast networks. Understanding of the available digital transaction networks and the capacity to collect or approximate digital data that covers all heavily used channels are prerequisites for enhancing data on remittances which also has risks associated with cybersecurity. The financial structure, the overall administrative climate of the sending and receiving countries, the ease and costs associated with using these channels, and the demographic characteristics of the senders and receivers may all influence the transaction channels used and may also lead to higher cybersecurity risks (IMF, 2008).

Service satisfaction is described as a metric that defines how well a company's services satisfy the needs of its customers. One of the most critical metrics of customer buying intentions and loyalty is service satisfaction. The customer experience of the highest caliber will capture customers' hearts and make a company visible in the target market. Nowadays, with social media playing such a significant role in decision-making, it is essential to keep an eye on its support. Expect consumers would be unconcerned with an organization's offerings if it does not care about their happiness (Survicate, 2021).

E-commerce, which can easily be conducted on digital devices such as laptops, tablets, and smartphones, can be thought of as a digital equivalent of catalog shopping. As a result, it is regarded as a highly revolutionary technology, but nevertheless carries a high risk for cybersecurity (Bloomenthal, 2020).

The ease of keeping financial facilities right at hand is one of the critical advantages of e-banking and m-banking. There is no need to go to a bank or ATM to wait for it to open to check account balance, move money, pay bills, or read a statement. One can do all such activities on a phone or screen and on a digital platform. While money transfer transactions can stop when banks close, one may review the account balance or get an account statement at any time. If one uses e-banking and m-banking services, bank account and personal information are accessible, but may also lurking behind is a cyber risk from a hacker. The bank will give an individual a collection of passwords that one will use to log in to an account and make transactions. This link information is easily forwarded to, and the account is still safe. Most banks need to set up two-step authentication, which requires entering a one-time password (OTP) sent to your registered mobile phone number before you can make a bank transaction (Goodreturns, 2020).

Internet banking fraud is a form of theft or fraud that involves unlawfully withdrawing money from a bank account and transferring money to a separate bank account using online technologies. Internet banking fraud is a form of identity theft that is typically carried out using phishing techniques. To check account records, make payments, pay bills, pass money, print statements, and so on, internet banking is now commonly used. The user identity is usually the customer identification number, with a password given to secure purchases. However, an individual can potentially slip into the pit of cybercriminals due to stupidity or stupid errors (WorldJute.Com, 2002).

Every year, many security breaches in electronic banking (e-Banking) systems are identified, highlighting the need to protect and warn consumers about the risk of being exposed to malicious cyber-actions. Financial firms and investors are aware that cyber-attacks and financial frauds are getting more sophisticated and are being carried out by a new breed of criminals. This class is becoming more advanced, and they are incorporating technologies into their technique (Vrincianu & Popa, 2010).

Cybersecurity refers to safeguarding internet-connected devices, including hardware, software, and data, against cyber threats. Individuals and businesses use the technique to prevent unwanted entry to data centers and other computerized networks. A solid cybersecurity policy will have a decent protection stance against malicious threats aimed at gaining access to, altering, deleting, destroying, or extorting confidential data from an organization's or user's networks. Cybersecurity is often crucial in avoiding attacks that attempt to disable or interrupt the functionality of a machine or computer. The value of cybersecurity continues to intensify as the number of people, computers, and systems in the digital enterprise grow, along with the increasing deluge of data, much of which is sensitive or confidential.

The problem is exacerbated by the increasing number and complexity of cyber attackers and assault techniques (Shea, 2021).

Maintaining cybersecurity in an ever-changing threat environment is a difficult task for any business. Traditional reactive methods, which focused resources on defending structures against the most well-known threats while leaving lesser-known threats undefended, are no longer adequate. A more constructive and flexible strategy is needed to keep up with changing security threats. Several important cybersecurity consulting companies will help. To protect against known and unknown risks, the National Institute of Standards and Technology (NIST) advises using continuous surveillance and real-time analyses as part of a risk management process (Shea, 2021).

According to Sharon Shea (2021), automation has been a critical component in ensuring that businesses are safe from the amount and complexity of cyber threats. In areas of high-volume data sources, artificial intelligence (AI) and machine learning can help improve cybersecurity in three ways:

1. **Detection of threats:** AI platforms can process data to detect and forecast known and unknown threats.
2. **Augmentation by humans:** Warnings and routine activities often overburden security professionals. AI will assist in reducing warning exhaustion by quickly triaging low-risk warnings and automating big data processing and other routine activities, allowing humans to focus on more complex tasks.
3. **Answer to a threat:** Security protections are also generated and implemented automatically by AI systems.

Assault detection, malware discovery, traffic identification, enforcement analysis, and more are advantages of cybersecurity automation.

FOCUS OF THE RESEARCH

Until recently, Pakistani internet users were addicted to free content and services; however, due to the reduction in e-commerce barriers to a certain degree, as discussed above, there is a growing movement toward the transactional existence of e-commerce. Despite favorable demographics and lower e-commerce barriers, there has been no investigation into why e-commerce is still in its infancy in Pakistan (Ahmed, 2019). While increased e-commerce adoption is a positive sign for Pakistan's economic development, there are still significant gaps in many areas where serious efforts are needed to jumpstart e-commerce growth. This research's main objective is to make a comparative analysis of e-commerce banking of local and foreign banks in Pakistan based on customer preferences and perceived risks that customers associate with it. The e-commerce perspective in the banking sector is identified and explored and represented in an operational definition of e-commerce.

E-COMMERCE BARRIERS IN DEVELOPED COUNTRIES

In the literature, a variety of obstacles have been identified as hurdles to e-commerce in developed countries. Economic and technical, cognitive, sociocultural, and legal and political obstacles have all been identified. If external barriers such as physical, technical, legal, and political barriers exist, cognitive barriers exist within organizations or individuals. According to Molla and Licker (2005), in the early stages of e-commerce adoption, cognitive factors in a country are more significant than environmental factors, but as e-commerce adoption grows, environmental factors become more critical. Nonetheless, e-commerce adoption is influenced by a mixture of cognitive and environmental influences (Ahmed, 2019).

Internet infrastructure and diffusion rate, logistics infrastructure, scale problems, credit card penetration, and availability of online payment methods are some of the economic and technical barriers listed in the literature. Unreliability and a shortage of telecommunication networks are the key reasons for poor internet diffusion rates in developed countries (Mercer, 2006). Low internet diffusion rates have also been linked to power shortages and poor quality energy networks, as seen in Tanzania (Ahmed, 2019; Mercer, 2006). The number of people who engage in e-commerce is directly proportional to the rate of internet diffusion and scale issues and a poor return on investment. As a result, many small developed nations, such as the Caribbean (Fraser & Wresch, 2005), have poor internet penetration. As most e-commerce sites heavily rely on high-quality photographs to display their goods, slow internet speed and reduced bandwidth availability to internet users have also been identified as an obstacle to telecom infrastructure and products and services. Low internet speeds result in slow image downloads on a website, inconvenient for the user (Ahmed, 2019).

However, in recent years, the massive growth of mobile providers in developed countries has accelerated internet adoption rates exponentially. According to PTA, Pakistan's overall teledensity increased to 78 percent in March 2014, up from 4.31 percent in 2003, and the number of broadband internet subscribers (both fixed and wireless) increased to 3.34 million from 26 thousand in 2006. Similarly, the number of smartphone subscribers has increased from 0.5 million in 2004 to 136 million today. As a result, Pakistani customers are increasingly adopting e-commerce (Ahmed, 2019).

The lack of credit cards for a significant proportion of the population of most developed countries has slowed e-commerce acceptance. Low credit card penetration rates were a significant stumbling block in e-commerce operations in India and South America (Hawk, 2004; Hilbert, 2001). As a result, cash-on-delivery is a common payment mechanism in most developed countries (Biederman, 2000). Furthermore, banks in developed countries cannot support online credit card payments; thus, online retailers must rely on an international payment portal, resulting in additional operating costs (Kenny, 2003).

In the online sale of goods, road and logistics networks and distribution systems play a critical role. In most developed countries, poor logistics has historically been a significant barrier to e-commerce development (Ahmed, 2019; Kenny, 2003). Local courier services in developed countries lack size and penetration, whereas extensive multinational courier services such as FedEx and DHL are too expensive for internet retailers to use. TCS, Pakistan's largest courier firm, is the only one with logistics coverage throughout the country (excluding most parts of Balochistan). TCS, too, has to rely on small delivery firms to supply in certain far-flung villages and cities. The rest of the firms, such as OCS, Leopard, Speedex, and many others, are either regionally oriented or represent Pakistan's major cities.

Furthermore, weak delivery service in terms of late deliveries, cash collection inaccuracies, and loss and harm to products has been identified as a barrier to e-commerce adoption (Ahmed, 2019; Hawk, 2004). As a result, many internet retailers in developed countries are forced to either build their distribution network in larger cities or switch to franchising. Shophive.com, for example, delivers to consumers in Lahore and Islamabad with its riders. In India, Babyoye.com has established its distribution network in larger cities such as Mumbai and Delhi, but it relies on its franchisees to stock products and sell merchandise to many smaller cities.

The term "sociocultural boundaries" refers to social conventions and traditions. Technological and political challenges are more challenging to address than sociocultural and emotional barriers (Ahmed, 2019; Tigre & Dedrick, 2004). Personal relationships and face-to-face encounters are significant in Asian societies, for example. People find it challenging to engage in a transactional relationship with a company or individual because of the impersonal aspect of e-commerce. It leads to a lack of confidence in e-commerce and a reluctance to shop online. Similarly, sociocultural obstacles have been identified to include a lack of confidence in courier and distribution services (Fraser & Wresch, 2005). The confidence factor is linked to a lack of the rule of law and an inadequate regulatory system for e-commerce.

Individuals' perceptual maps and patterns are referred to as cognitive boundaries (Kshetri, 2007). Lack of understanding, experience, and expertise in using the internet and e-commerce and linguistic barriers are examples of cognitive barriers. Since the majority of web content and software is written in English, and the majority of the population in developed countries cannot read or write English, the majority of the population will be unable to participate in e-commerce until the web content and software are written in their language (Ahmed, 2019; Kenny, 2003). Most Chinese websites communicate with their consumers in official language accounts for the relatively higher acceptance of e-commerce in China. Similarly, a lack of command of the English language leads to a lower computer and internet literacy level. As a result, a lack of English language proficiency or the lack of official language web content results in a lower e-commerce acceptance rate and a lower internet dissemination rate. In addition to these, organizational cognitive obstacles have been identified to include a lack of commitment to adapt and SMEs' restricted use of internet banking and web portals (Ahmed, 2019; Zaied, 2012). Furthermore, SMEs have identified difficulties in identifying and maintaining eligible people with e-commerce expertise and qualifications as a barrier to e-commerce (Kaynak et al., 2005).

Because of their links to traditional institutions, legal and political hurdles take longer and are more challenging to resolve than other environmental obstacles. The main legal and political hurdles in developed countries have been the absence of a legal and regulatory framework, ambiguous and complicated processes and rules, and a lack of e-commerce standards and legislation (Ahmed, 2019; MacGregor, 2010). After 2002, Pakistan has enacted a host of e-commerce-related laws, including the Electronic Transaction Ordinance, the Electronic Data Protection Act, and the Electronics Crimes Ordinance, followed by the Electronic Crimes Bill 2010, which is still awaiting approval in the national assembly. However, the legislation's implementation and usefulness remain primarily in doubt.

THE CURRENT STATE OF AFFAIRS AND THE BARRIERS TO E-COMMERCE GROWTH

Due to a variety of technological, sociocultural, legal, political, and cognitive obstacles, the true potential of E-Commerce could not be realized in emerging economies like Pakistan in the past (Ahmed, 2019). According to a range of reports, inferior ICT technology, inadequate transportation and logistics networks, low credit card penetration, confidence problems, a lack of training and capacity building, and a limited or absent legal and institutional infrastructure are the key obstacles to e-commerce development in developing countries like Pakistan (Bingi et al., 2000; Panagariya, 2000).

In recent years, there has been a rising trend in B2C and C2C e-commerce. It can be due to a host of positive developments over the last decade that have gone relatively unnoticed but have provided e-commerce and e-entrepreneurs in Pakistan a new lease on life. Among the enhancements are:

1. Due to intensified competition among courier firms, distribution services have improved, and logistics penetration has increased.
2. Improved internet speed and broadband/WiMax coverage in more than 180 Pakistani cities, allowing for faster connectivity to e-commerce pages.
3. Higher educational attainment is a result of HEC's investment in higher education and increased internet literacy.
4. The rapid adoption of online social networking sites such as Facebook provides sellers with an engaging and feedback-focused forum to reach buyers. As a result, it aids in the resolution of trust problems between seller and buyer.
5. Payment innovation, such as courier firms collecting cash on delivery (CoD), mobile payment systems like Telenor's Easypaisa (available in 18,000+ shops throughout Pakistan) and UBL's Omni (available in 600+ towns and cities), and internet funds transfer through many banks like UBL and Standard Chartered.

Pakistani internet users have primarily consumed free entertainment, news, sports, education, and employment-related content and services. Early promising B2C e-commerce startups (such as emarkaz.com and 786gifts.com) focused on delivering presents and greetings to Pakistanis living abroad. However, in recent years, Pakistan has seen an increase in B2C e-commerce adoption. The increased traffic on B2C and C2C websites is proof of this. In Pakistan, for example, there was not a single B2C website among the top 500 websites by internet traffic until two years ago (Ahmed, 2019).

Pakistani internet users have primarily consumed free entertainment, news, sports, education, and employment-related content and services. Early promising B2C e-commerce startups (such as emarkaz.com and 786gifts.com) focused on delivering presents and greetings to Pakistanis living abroad (Ahmed, 2019). However, in recent years, Pakistan has seen an increase in B2C e-commerce adoption. The increased traffic on B2C and C2C websites is proof of this. In Pakistan, for example, there was not a single B2C website among the top 500 websites by internet traffic until two years ago. Today, however, Shophive.com, which sells computers and electronics, is the 129th most visited website in Pakistan; Daraz.pk, which sells fashion and clothing, is ranked 198th; Symbios.pk is ranked 252, Techcity.pk is 440th, and Beliscity.com is 478th. The number of online startups founded by young university graduates in Pakistan, such as Hometownshoes.com, Hmgte.com, Babyplanet.pk, and Gadgets.pk, demonstrates the country's growing interest in e-commerce (Ahmed, 2019).

Furthermore, a host of well-known high-street fashion brands and designers, such as Bareeze, Uniworth, HSY, Gul Ahmed, BnB Accessories, and Al-Karam, have recognized the value of the online platform and have launched their online stores. The entrance of high-street brands into e-commerce is also bolstering online shopping trust and helping to shape consumer purchase habits (Ahmed, 2019). The unexpected entrance of TCS into e-commerce is one of the most compelling evidence of increased e-commerce adoption in Pakistan. TCS is the premium courier business that manages deliveries for almost any e-commerce website in Pakistan, owing to its extensive understanding of its e-commerce potential. TCS jumped into e-commerce as TCSConnect.com in May 2012, selling books, electronics, and cosmetics to Pakistani customers, using its vast logistic network and e-commerce distribution expertise.

The importance of social media, especially social networks, in e-commerce adoption, cannot be overstated. Most national and multinational consumer brands and retailers are increasingly interested in social media, especially Facebook, as evidence of their interest in e-commerce. About every well-known consumer brand and the high-street store has established a Facebook page in recent years to reach new and current consumers, create identities, have exclusive deals, and promote and sell their goods and services.

E-BANKING IN A GLOBAL CONTEXT

Credit researchers have rated financial services websites as lagging behind other sectors in overall innovation over the last five years. Online banking sites have a poor appearance and technological use as compared to other shopping portals. According to recent financial studies, bank customers are the happiest when it comes to where, when, and how they bank (Pedro et al., 2018). Banks must devote more time and resources to strengthening client relationships and delivering exceptional customer services. It is a subject that is attracting the interest of many banks around the world. Contemporary societies are today exposed to more significant dangers than they have ever been. Individuals must safeguard themselves against the vastly increased private harm. From the banks' perspective, internet banking is supposed to result in cost savings and increased competition. The manufacturing sector is, without a doubt, one of the country's most important service industries (The Financial Brand, 2018). This method of service distribution is regarded as an essential weapon. It will keep new web-based consumers who want to use banking facilities from anywhere they want. Digital banking also allows banks to expand their customer base by drawing new customers from existing internet users.

According to financial analysts, banks should take a few cues from various non-banking industries, showing creativity in coping with self-service options for their customers (Pedro et al., 2018). IT can help banks develop their online services by adding features that improve customer service experiences. It will allow them greater control over their whole e-banking experience. Customer trust is a significant factor impacting their usage of internet banking websites because financial transfers involve exchanging private and personal data. Due to repeated internet banking security breaches and reports, customers' trust in banks, especially online banking, is eroding. As a result, all attempts to increase customer satisfaction and extend relevant security monitoring capabilities must consider questions about the implementation of internet banking.

E-COMMERCE BANKING IN PAKISTAN

E-Banking Evolution in Pakistan

'SBP Mandate' emerged as a significant event in August 2002 as the State Bank of Pakistan directed all scheduled banks in Pakistan to join any of the two switches available, i.e., 1Link and MNET. It also directed that both switches should be connected. All scheduled banks of Pakistan thus became able to participate in the necessary online transaction exchange process. Banking customers became able to use an ATM card on any ATM within Pakistan, and through a synergy of three critical forces, i.e., Government, financial, and the private sector.

E-Banking Initiative in Pakistan

Banking has now surpassed four walls of a branch and extended beyond it. In advanced countries, customers enjoy much more facilities than in Pakistan. Though e-banking in Pakistan started a bit late, with time, it has been in the line for chasing up this aspect globally. With the advent and common usage of the internet, banks were forced globally to incorporate e-banking. Though Pakistani banks are still far behind other global counterparts, this phase is still growing. For instance, the lack of merchant accounts in Pakistan is also affecting the situation.

A key factor of e-banking's low penetration level is the lack of computers in Pakistan. Another factor is not allowing people with computers and internet facilities because of a lack of services offered by banks and security concerns, and ineffective legal framework. Electronic Transactions Ordinance 2002 proved to be a landmark step in this direction as it provided legal recognition to digital signatures and reduced documentation and such risks associated with the usage of the electronic medium of business.

The high cost is also one of the factors prohibiting the usage of the newly offered services. It is seen that because of apprehensions about security, clients take refuge behind the high cost. They also believe that these facilities' use is low in the sphere of services, thus rendered (Eisenmann & Trispas, 2002). Capital intensive nature of such operations is also a factor slowing down its process. Investments in the technology sphere by banks are adversely affecting pay-outs to shareholders and depositors. From a banking sector expert's perspective, they term it as only a brief phase.

Secure Mobile Payments (SMS Based)

In 2009, the chairman of Pakistan's Telecommunication Authority (PTA), Dr. Muhammad Yaseen, had the honor to inaugurate the first SMS-based secure mobile payments technology in Pakistan. According to the Pakistan Telecommunication Authority, this technology initiative was designed to enable more than 96 million mobile users in 2009 to interact with financial institutions and conduct transactions via mobile in a convenient and reliable aspect. It has undoubtedly provided an efficient and secure enough platform for M and e-banking services, i.e., to provide customers anytime, anywhere convenient. It will expand into new financial services dimensions for customers to interact with a patented and protected medium.

The Role of Remittances in Pakistan

Remittances undoubtedly constitute one of the largest and resilient sources of foreign exchange earnings for developing countries like Pakistan, so it is an important phenomenon. For instance, the flow of workers' remittances to developing countries has steadily grown during the past three decades. In Pakistan, workers' remittances raised a lot during the last decade as it has grown enormously. According to the State Bank of Pakistan, remittances in Pakistan increased by 21% to $2 billion in October 2018 (The Express Tribune, 2018). The USA, United Arab Emirates, Saudi Arabia accounted for more than 80% of the remittances total inflow. The State bank of Pakistan also claimed that Pakistan's remittances might reach $22bn in 2019 (Pakistan Today, 2018). It allows individuals to improve their living standards and consumption (Laudon & Traver, 2001). Foreign remittances have a crucial role in alleviating poverty (Hamel, 2000). Remittances also revive economic growth (Choi & Whinston, 1999). The removal of entry barriers and competition in the remittance market enhances its infrastructure (Hamilton, 1997).

Activities Permissible by the State Bank of Pakistan

Pakistan's central bank is the State Bank of Pakistan (SBP). The State Bank of Pakistan Order 1948 established its constitution, which remained essentially unchanged until January 1, 1974, when the bank was nationalized, and the extent of its functions was greatly expanded. The State Bank of Pakistan Act 1956, as amended, is the foundation of the bank's activities today. The company's offices are in Karachi, Pakistan's financial hub (State Bank of Pakistan, 2021).

The SBP Banking Services Corporation (SBP-BSC), a wholly-owned subsidiary of the central bank, is the operating arm of the bank, with branch offices in 16 cities across Pakistan, including the capital city of Islamabad and the four provincial capitals. Other wholly-owned branches of the State Bank of Pakistan include the National Institute of Banking and Finance (NIBAF), which provides instruction to commercial banks, the Deposit Protection Corporation (DPC), and control of Pakistan Security Printing Corporation (PSPC). The activities permissible by the State Bank of Pakistan include opening and maintaining (Business-to-business account), fund transfers (Account-to-account), fund transfers (Person-to-person), cash-in/out, payment of bills, payments of the merchant, and the loan repayment and disbursement (State Bank of Pakistan, 2021).

ESSENTIALS OF DIGITAL ENTERPRISE TRANSFORMATION

There are eight crucial Digital Enterprise Transformation developments that IT and business leaders should be aware of, according to The Enterprisers Project (2020):

1. Rapid introduction of digital operating models, which have cross-functional units that are interconnected.
2. A shakeout (due to rivals' investments in significant data regulation and analytic advancement).
3. Continued mergers and acquisitions in the information technology outsourcing market.
4. Metrics for measuring the performance of digital enterprise transformation.
5. Broadening the use of public clouds.
6. Consultancies should shape new digital alliances.
7. Improve the application of artificial intelligence and machine learning.
8. The long-term value of a digital project should be considered.

TRANSFORMATION OF THE BANKING SECTOR AND DIGITAL ENTERPRISE TRANSFORMATION

According to the Boston Consulting Group, credit unions and banks should rely on the following pillars when developing a digital transformation strategy:

1. Re-imagining the interactive experience of a customer.
2. Using data to the full potential.
3. Redefining the current business paradigm.
4. Creating a technologically focused organization.

(The Financial Brand, 2018).

Allen (2019) defines digital transformation as "more than just enabling smartphone and web functionality." Traditional banking providers must balance simplicity with a digital speed that allows for human contact (Pedro et al., 2018). At critical points in a customer's experience, it can be reflective and defensive. Although four out of five financial organizations believe that digital transformation can fundamentally alter the banking industry and entirely change the competitive environment, According to the Boston Consulting Group, 43% of executives agree that their company has yet to develop a digital strategy. Surprisingly, one out of every five financial executives considers their credit union and company to be "market-leading" when it comes to digital transformation (The Financial Brand, 2018).

DIFFERENT TYPES OF CYBERSECURITY SERVICES

According to Consolidated Technologies, Inc.(2018) and ReachOut Australia (2021), cybersecurity services are the overarching processes to ensure this security and protect against common cyber threats. Cybersecurity refers to a company's defense against unauthorized or fraudulent use of electronic data, and cybersecurity services are the coordinating processes put in place to achieve this security and protect against common cyber threats. Forcepoint (2021) is of the view that the following are examples of typical threats that cybersecurity providers target:

1. **Ransomware:** Ransomware is a form of malware that encrypts a system and then asks to pay a "ransom" to decrypt it and regain access.
2. **Malware:** It is also known as malicious malware, is a virus that is installed on a computer device with the intent of compromising the data's availability, credibility, or secrecy. Malware applications remain undetectable, but they have evolved into one of the most severe external challenges to enterprise networks today.
3. **DDoS** (Distributed Denial of Service) attacks: DDoS attacks delay website response time by overloading a network with traffic requests. It is sometimes used as a diversionary tactic by suspects while they commit other forms of crimes.
4. **Phishing:** Phishing is a technique used by cybercriminals to collect data by impersonating an actual company official. They will usually send an email with an alert about an account and a connection to a bogus website asking for passwords or other personal details.

VARIOUS CYBERSECURITY SOLUTIONS

According to IT Governance (2021), cybersecurity uses a wide range of network security mechanisms to secure the files, networks, and systems against these and other types of attacks. The below are only a few of the various cybersecurity options available:

1. **Data loss protection:** Data is critical in day-to-day operations, and data loss prevention techniques ensure that data is still available.

2. **Encryption:** Data encryption means that hackers will be unable to read the information even though it is compromised. If an individual often transfers data from one device to another, encryption is particularly critical because data can be compromised during the transfer.
3. **Solutions for anti-virus and anti-malware:** One of the most basic cybersecurity solutions in any computer network is anti-virus and anti-malware applications. It scans the computer for threats and prevents viruses from gaining access to files.
4. **Firewalls:** Firewalls regulate the movement of outgoing and incoming network traffic to protect against malware threats and untrusted networks.
5. **Risk and compliance management:** To comply with government laws or industry requirements, many businesses need cybersecurity services. Risk and security assessment is a dedicated solution that addresses these requirements.
6. **Web filtering:** Web filtering prevents workers from accessing inappropriate resources on the company's network by mistake, resulting in data loss.

OBSTACLES SOLVED BY CYBERSECURITY

In Juliana De Groot's (2020) work, every day, businesses of all sizes and types face various potential security threats. Cybersecurity tools can help with issues like these:

1. **External threats:** Hackers are getting more adept at circumventing conventional firewalls and stealing information. Cybersecurity providers guarantee that the firewalls, anti-virus applications, and other security solutions are up to date and ready to secure networks.
2. **Employee negligence:** It is by far the most common cause of data breaches. Web monitoring and other cybersecurity techniques reduce the possibility of human error by preventing workers from visiting potentially malicious websites or becoming victims of phishing scams.
3. **Unsecured cloud storage:** As cloud servers are standard now, so do security breaches in cloud storage. In 2017, IBM estimated that misconfigured cloud servers were responsible for almost 70% of all data breaches. Network monitoring providers ensure that the cloud networks are safe enough to prevent data breaches.
4. **Insider illegal activity:** Unfortunately, data theft from inside an enterprise is one of the most difficult truths for all small and large corporations. Security solutions protect the data from the inside out so that only people need to know to access it.
5. **Subpar IT processes:** Small companies do not always have the funding or expertise to keep up with evolving risks and security best practices. Many businesses put their infrastructure at risk because they lack the funds to employ a committed IT team. Outsourced or cloud-based cybersecurity tools, on the other hand, are a low-cost option for avoiding revenue loss in the event of a security violation.
6. **Protection of third-party apps:** Not all systems are designed with the wellbeing of the business in mind. Many third-party applications lack adequate or easily updatable protection features. Cybersecurity filters out this risky software and implements the security features that many apps lack.

RESEARCH METHODOLOGY

Three locals and three foreign banks were selected, and a sample size of 15 account holders from each bank was taken. This research was carried out in Karachi (Pakistan) because all of the head offices were located in Karachi's premises, and it is the financial hub of Pakistan. The primary data was collected through questionnaires filled by the pertinent customers, and secondary data sources include banking policy manual and the internet. The results are represented in the form of pie charts and analysis following it. This list includes only those banks based on which comparative analysis is conducted. The local banks of Pakistan selected for this research are Allied Bank Limited, MCB Bank Limited, and United Bank Limited. The foreign banks that operate in Pakistan are Deutsche Bank AG, Industrial and Commercial Bank of China Limited, and Standard Chartered Pakistan.

DATA ANALYSIS

Cleaning, transforming, and modeling data to discover valuable knowledge for business decision-making is known as data analysis. Data analysts' goal is to derive valuable knowledge from data and make decisions based on that information. The results are represented in the form of pie charts and analysis following it.

1. Are you aware of e-commerce banking products (M-banking, E-banking, and Foreign remittances) services offered by banks?
    a) Yes
    b) No

Figure 1. Awareness of E-Commerce Products

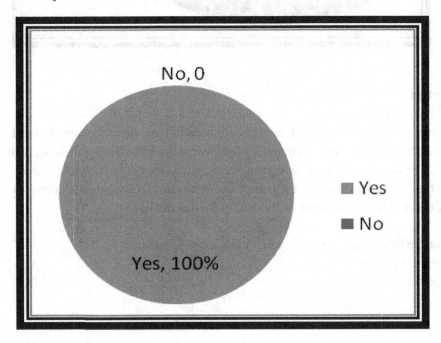

Data Findings

The data findings in figure 1 show that it is a good sign for banks, as all respondents were aware of e-commerce products and related services which is also an important indicator of technology penetration deeper into the society and community of Pakistan. Through e-commerce banks can reach vast markets that are geographically distributed and the only means of reach is through a digital network. Pakistan has been investing in building a modern digital infrastructure that will benefit the country, the people, and the busines community.

2. In which bank will you like to have an account in the future?
   a. Foreign bank
   b. Local bank

Figure 2. Bank Preference

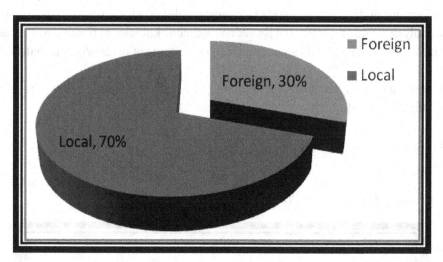

Data Findings

The data findings in figure 2 show that most people want to have their accounts in local banks instead of foreign banks, and it was also seen that very few people are maintaining their accounts in local and foreign banks. The data reveals some interesting information about the customers having diverse interests based on their needs and habits for banking. The banks need to investigate deeper the attitudes and preference of the people and what drives them to make that decision.

3. Which of the following e-commerce service is more reliable?
   a. Mobile Banking
   b. Internet Banking

Figure 3. Type of E-Commerce Product

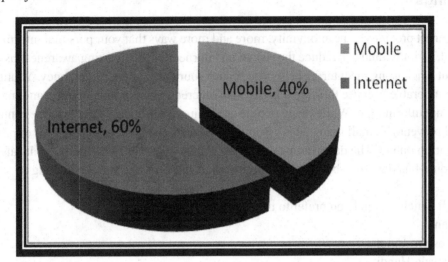

Data Findings

The data findings in figure 3 show that more people mostly rely on e-banking than mobile banking; this may be because of a delayed response on mobile service. Overall, the results are conclusive that the drive towards a digital product in each of the categories identified has a very valuable role to play and the balance in each category will be based on peoples preferences and desires. Such information also unravels the need for making more reliable and modern internet and mobile services and products that can fulfill the needs of the people.

4. Is it safe to disclose details on e-banking or m-banking?
    a. Yes
    b. No

Figure 4. Safety in Disclosing Details

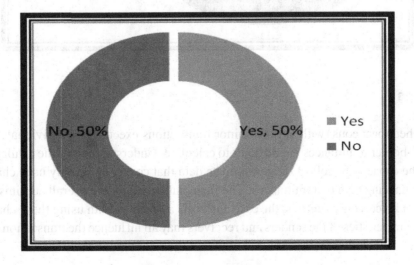

Data Findings

While the internet provides some anonymity, more and more ways that your personal information can be compromised, an individual can reduce the risk of an internet mishap by using awareness as a safety net. Being vigilant when using the internet helps you secure your data, device, and money. Young people are particularly vulnerable because they put a high value on creating an online identity, and many websites request personal information. While many people are aware of setting up strict privacy controls on their accounts and preventing email scams, it is essential to educate them about the dangers of providing personal information online. The data findings in figure 4 show that half of the people felt safe to disclose their details on e-banking or m-banking. In contrast, half felt insecure about revealing it.

5. Through which channel you prefer to transfer funds abroad?
    a. Banks
    b. Western Union
    c. Hawala/Hundi
    d. Others

Figure 5. Channel for Fund Transfer Abroad

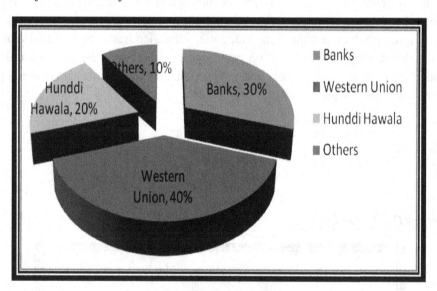

Data Findings

Since they are heterogeneous, with various minor transactions executed by individuals across several networks, cross-border remittances are difficult to calculate. Understanding of the available transaction networks and the capacity to collect or approximate data that covers all heavily used channels are prerequisites for enhancing data on remittances. The financial structure, the overall administrative climate of the sending and receiving countries, the ease and costs associated with using these channels, and the demographic characteristics of the senders and receivers may all influence the transaction channels used.

The data findings in figure 5 show that most people use the Western Union as they feel a bit reluctant because of the security questions asked by banks when they want to transfer their funds. While 30% of the respondents maintain their accounts with their banks, they cannot face securities-related questions.

6.   The services which your bank is rendering, are you satisfied with it?
    a.   Yes
    b.   No

Figure 6. Service Satisfaction

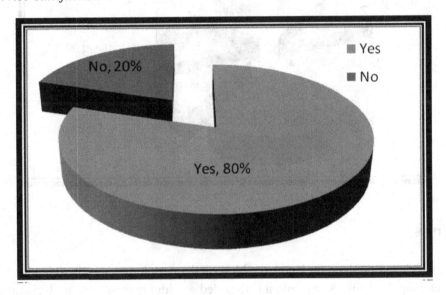

Data Findings

Service satisfaction is described as a metric that defines how well a company's services satisfy the needs of its customers. One of the most critical metrics of customer buying intentions and loyalty is service satisfaction. The customer experience of the highest caliber will capture customers' hearts and make a company visible in the target market. Nowadays, with social media playing such a significant role in decision-making, it is essential to keep an eye on its support. Expect consumers would be unconcerned with an organization's offerings if it does not care about their happiness. The data findings in figure 6 show that most of the respondents are satisfied with their bank's services. At the same time, some felt that their banks should improve their services.

7.   What are the foremost transactions you carry out via e-commerce?
    a.   Checking current balance
    b.   Money transfers
    c.   Create Fixed Deposits Online
    d.   Pay Bills
    e.   Order a Checkbook

f.   Request Stop Payment on a Cheque

g.   Request a Demand Draft

Figure 7. Main Transactions

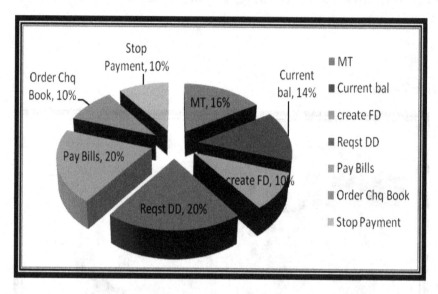

Data Findings

E-commerce, which can be done on laptops, tablets, and smartphones, can be thought of as a digital equivalent of catalog shopping. As a result, it is regarded as a highly revolutionary technology. The data findings in figure 7 show that respondents like to do all such transactions via e-banking as most of the respondents use internet banking for such types of transactions as compared with m-banking.

8.   Do you know about the available benefits of e-banking and m-banking?

a.   Yes

b.   No

Data Findings

The ease of keeping financial facilities right at hand is one of the critical advantages of e-banking and m-banking. There is no need to go to a bank or ATM to wait for it to open to check account balance, move money, pay bills, or read a statement. Individuals can do anything on the phone or screen. While money transfer transactions can stop when banks close, an individual may review an account balance or get an account statement at any time. If an individual uses e-banking and m-banking services, their bank account and personal information are accessible. The data findings in figure 8 show that most respondents are aware of the benefits of m-banking and e-banking.

Figure 8. Benefits of E & M Banking

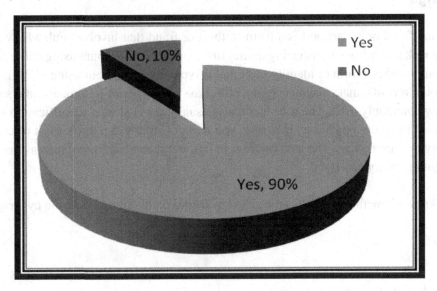

9. Do you know about methods that can be used for committing any cyberfraud?
    a. Yes
    b. No

Figure 9. Awareness of Methods of Frauds

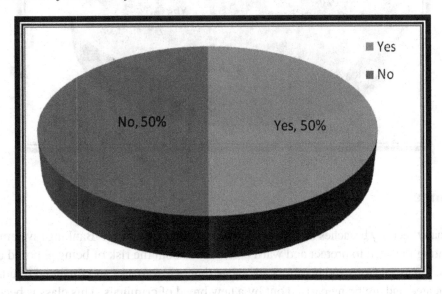

Data Findings

Internet banking fraud or cyberfraud is a form of theft or fraud that involves unlawfully withdrawing money from a bank account and transferring money to a separate bank account using online technologies. Internet banking fraud is a form of identity theft that is typically carried out using phishing techniques. To check account records, make payments, pay bills, pass money, print statements, and so on, internet banking is now commonly used. The user identity is usually the customer identification number, with a password given to secure purchases. However, you will potentially slip into the pit of cybercriminals due to stupidity or stupid errors. The data findings in figure 9 show that 50% of respondents were aware of the techniques used for any fraud.

10. Do you know all methods which can be used to secure online transactions on cyberspace?
     a. Yes
     b. No

Figure 10. Methods to Secure Transactions

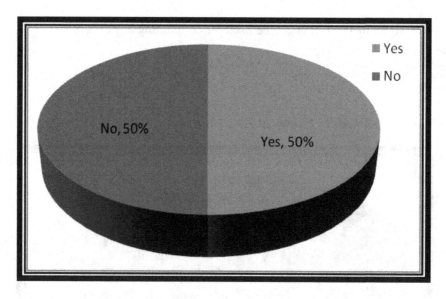

Data Findings

Every year, many security breaches on cyberspace in electronic banking (e-Banking) systems are identified, highlighting the need to protect and warn consumers about the risk of being exposed to malicious cyber-actions. Financial firms and investors are aware that cyber-attacks and financial frauds are getting more sophisticated and are being carried out by a new breed of criminals. This class is becoming more advanced, and they are incorporating technologies into their technique. The data findings in figure 10 show that 50% of the respondents are unaware of the bank's initiatives to secure customer's transactions via software and methods.

11. Are you being educated by the bank about e-commerce services on cyberspace?
    a. Yes
    b. No

Figure 11. Educating about E-Commerce

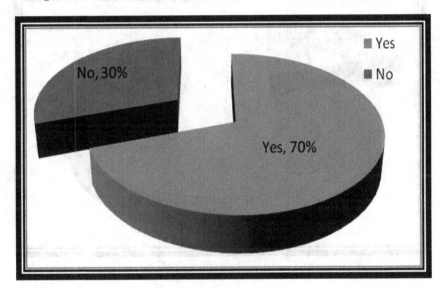

Data Findings

The data findings in figure 11 show that few respondents felt that they were not educated appropriately about e-commerce banking and its benefits on cyberspace. The reasons being that cyberspace may not offer direct educational tools that users are accustomed in offline mode. The banks and the financial institutions may not actively promote cybersecurity so that the customers are not panicked and will therefore refrain from using e-commerce. Higher levels of education for cybersecurity may bring transparency and awareness of important issues that the customers should be aware of and take action if suspicious activities are noticed.

12. Will you like to use M-banking or E-banking instead of visiting the bank in the upcoming time?
    a. Yes
    b. No

Data Findings

The data findings in figure 12 show that most respondents preferred using M-banking and E-banking as compared to conventional banking. Though M-Banking and E-Banking offers a wider choice and convenience to do banking at the privacy of one's home or office or in a private place, nevertheless it also has higher risks from hackers accessing the digital financial transaction online and stealing the money. If there are no cyber safeguards on the M-Banking and E-Banking websites its can also lead to unauthorized access to the customers' accounts which can result in financial losses.

Figure 12. Banking Preference

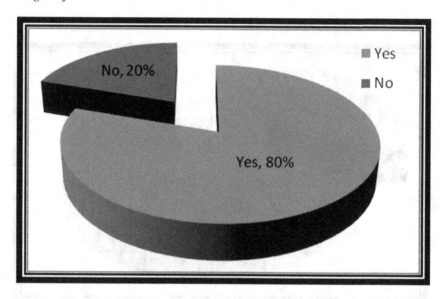

13. What are the benefits of E-banking or M-banking?
    a. Transparency
    b. Convenience
    c. Time
    d. Speed

Figure 13. Benefits Seen by Customers

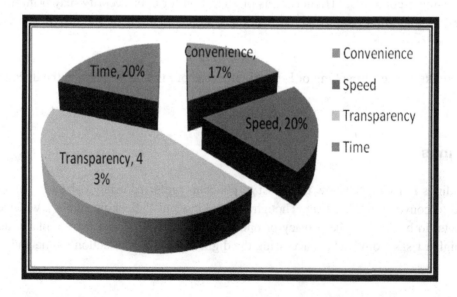

Data Findings

The data findings in figure 13 show that transparency by M and e-banking is one of the highest motivating factors for customers, and then after that they prefer speed and time, while convenience is also one of the many motivating factors of M and e-banking. This demonstrates that transparency can be an important factor for the customers, which may also be linked to speedier digital transactions as well as to convenience. But how that plays into the customers perceptions is an important area of study and that more research is needed that can provide valuable information about customers attitudes.

Table 1. Summary of important findings

Research Measurement Variables	Validation
The data findings in figure 1 show that it is a good sign for banks, as all respondents were aware of e-commerce products and related services.	Yes
The data findings in figure 2 show that most people want to have their accounts in local banks instead of foreign banks, and it was also seen that very few people are maintaining their accounts in local and foreign banks.	Yes
The data findings in figure 3 show that more people mostly rely on e-banking than mobile banking; this may be because of a delayed response on mobile service.	Yes
The data findings in figure 4 show that half of the people felt safe to disclose their details on e-banking or m-banking. In contrast, half felt insecure about revealing it.	Yes
The data findings in figure 5 show that most people use the Western Union as they feel a bit reluctant because of the security questions asked by banks when they want to transfer their funds. While 30% of the respondents maintain their accounts with their banks, they cannot face securities-related questions.	Moderate
The data findings in figure 6 show that most of the respondents are satisfied with their bank's services. At the same time, some felt that their banks should improve their services.	Moderate
The data findings in figure 7 show that respondents like to do all such transactions via e-banking as most of the respondents use internet banking for such types of transactions as compared with m-banking.	Yes
The data findings in figure 8 show that most respondents are aware of the benefits of m-banking and e-banking.	Yes
The data findings in figure 9 show that 50% of respondents were aware of the techniques used for any fraud.	Yes
The data findings in figure 10 show that 50% of the respondents are unaware of the bank's initiatives to secure customer's transactions via software and methods.	Yes
The data findings in figure 11 show that few respondents felt that they were not educated appropriately about e-commerce banking and its benefits.	Yes
The data findings in figure 12 show that most respondents preferred using M-banking and E-banking as compared to conventional banking.	Yes
The data findings in figure 13 show that transparency by M and e-banking is one of the highest motivating factors for customers, and then they prefer speed and time, while convenience is also one of the many motivating factors of M and e-banking.	Yes

SUMMARY OF FINDINGS

Many people choose M and e-banking as a new way to manage their money, as they seek it as a valuable option. More people are being attracted to technology for personal banking purposes, as it is a safe and convenient way to utilize financial services and maintain bank accounts and conduct business the whole day, i.e., 24 hours. It saves time by using online banking via mobile phones and personal computers.

Basic transactions can be completed quickly from PC and mobile phones from anywhere and anytime. It is also convenient and, above all, transparent. Complicated transactions and investment decisions have been much facilitated, as people find it comparatively convenient to access their financial information. Customers have various customized services with less or free cost and choose a bank of their own choice accordingly.

A wide range of financial products and services are being offered by banks, like free checking of accounts and bill paying services via the internet. Most of the banks offer free e-banking for a few of their services, but they charge their customers for others. In m-banking, banks also charge fees for a few of their services and transactions. Foreign banks that are operating in Pakistan are offering comparatively fewer e-commerce services. At the same time, local banks in Pakistan have more e-commerce services. Foreign banks are also charging more fees as compared to local banks. It is one of the reasons that people are more attracted to local banks. People use mobile phones for transactions, like balance checking, e-statements, and transaction alert. Most people use e-banking for credit card bill payments, transferring money, stop payments, checkbook requests. It was seen that local banks have a comparatively high customer base as compared to foreign banks. It is because of the customer's high balance requirements and charges related to performing their financial transactions. One of the lapses observed in products and services is service charges, because of which few customers utilize M and e-banking. No bank in Pakistan is altogether offering a full range of electronic services.

SOLUTIONS AND RECOMMENDATIONS

According to Identity Theft Resource Centre (2018), small and large companies should use one of three categories of cybersecurity technologies to incorporate IT protection at a size and budget that suits them best:

1. **IT security/cybersecurity as a solution:** More products and services, including cybersecurity, are now accessible through the cloud in the era of software as a service (SaaS). Cybersecurity is an important subject. SaaS (Software as a Service) is an outsourced model in which you pay for cybersecurity applications monthly. It enables you to stay on top of the new technologies at a low cost.
2. **Outsourced:** Outsourcing cybersecurity allows companies to spend less time on time-consuming compliance programs and more time on more profitable projects as a third-party team monitors security.
3. **In-house:** Many major companies with their security teams in order to provide cybersecurity services. This do-it-yourself strategy helps you take care of security and privacy when working with employees familiar with a company and its specific requirements.

Policymakers should be able to formulate practical strategies based on field data and statistics to estimate the scale of the e-commerce industry. Investors and developers should be able to spot e-commerce opportunities and make well-informed decisions based on-field results. Incorporating the perspectives of both e-business owners and customers would aid policymakers in gaining a deeper view of the e-commerce industry environment and trends to better balance policies with market conditions. Identifying and integrating the perspectives of core stakeholders will illustrate the most critical issues that an e-commerce strategy can solve. Furthermore, learning from our other countries, especially India, will aid in developing and implementing best practices in e-commerce policy. Banks should promote online banking services, and promotional activities should be implemented respectively. Customers who are not technologically sophisticated should be appealed to by banks as services should be simple enough to use. Banks should offer more services, and online applications for new account opening, complaints, and corporate banking via the internet should be specially focused on. Massive liquidity is in the market during Muslim festivals, like Eid and Ramzan. E-banking can solve many liquidity problems, as it is possible to take advantage of the banks.

FUTURE RESEARCH DIRECTIONS

The forecasts by cyber experts are that cybercriminals will target remote employees until 2021. Many organizations' legacy security infrastructure, such as VPNs, would be the weak point. CSOs and CISOs will pursue integration through defense technologies to deal with limited budgets. Breach of security in the healthcare industry may be fatal. Financial institutions should be aware that further threats are on the way. COVID-19 compelled businesses to speed up their digital transformation activities. Because of the introduction of emerging technology and the number of internet users, most of the world's population is at risk of data leakage. It is interesting to see how people's views of e-banking differ depending on whether they perform transactions independently or for their employers. As a corporate client, contrasting one's views on private e-banking vs. e-banking for commercial purposes will reveal some interesting information. As a result, a more in-depth look at the demographics and consumer background would help assess how these aspects influence corporate customers' decision-making and e-banking use in Pakistan. Significant areas for conducting future research encompassing e-commerce via engaging qualitative, qualitative, or eclectic approach can be computer-focused and computer-assisted crimes, cybersecurity issues in e-commerce, incident response planning, issues of gender, and technology adaptability.

CONCLUSION

Some of the advantages of introducing and managing cybersecurity practices are, cybersecurity provides data theft defense for businesses, data and network security are also protected. Unauthorized account control is avoided. In a hack, there is a faster recovery time, end-user and endpoint system security is enhanced. Regulatory adherence and continuity of operations are ensured. Developers, investors, clients, owners, and staff have more confidence in the company's credibility and trust.

Hackers, data theft, anonymity, risk control, and evolving cybersecurity policies are constant cybersecurity threats. The number of cyberattacks is unlikely to decline anytime soon. Furthermore, expanded intrusion access points, such as the internet of things (IoT), increase the need to protect networks and computers. The ever-changing essence of security threats is one of the most challenging aspects of cybersecurity. New assault avenues arise as new developments emerge and as technology is used in new or diverse forms. It can be challenging to keep up with the constant improvements and advancements in threats and update procedures to guard against them. Among the issues is ensuring that aspects of cybersecurity are kept up to date to safeguard against future weaknesses. Smaller businesses without employees or in-house facilities can find this particularly challenging.

Furthermore, organizations may collect a wealth of information about people who use one or more of their programs. The risk of a cybercriminal attempting to steal personally identifiable information (PII) increases as more data is gathered. A company that stores PII in the cloud, for example, may be the target of a ransomware attack. Organizations should do everything possible to avoid a cloud leak. Employees can carry viruses into the workplace on their laptops or mobile devices, so cybersecurity initiatives should include end-user education. Employees who receive regular security awareness training would be more able to keep their workplace safe from cyber threats. Another issue confronting cybersecurity is a scarcity of trained cybersecurity staff. If companies gather and use more data, the need for cybersecurity professionals to analyze, monitor, and respond to incidents expands. The workplace distance between required cybersecurity employment and security experts, according to (ISC)2, is estimated to be 3.1 million (Shea, 2021).

E-commerce has been hailed as one of the most critical enablers of young entrepreneurship and work worldwide. Despite favorable internet and smartphone demographics and rising e-commerce adoption, Pakistan's e-commerce industry is still tiny compared to other comparable countries. Along with the challenges of customer service, payments, and logistics, Pakistan's explosive e-commerce development is being hampered by the lack of institutions and trade bodies to fund and encourage it. According to the researcher, the formulation of a rational e-commerce policy focused on field data and ground realities and the successful execution of such policy is critical in providing the enabling environment. According to the researcher, the formulation of a rational e-commerce policy based on field data and ground realities and successful implementation of such policy is critical in creating an enabling environment for e-commerce growth.

The Pakistani e-commerce market has grown significantly since its humble beginnings in the early 2000s, with major players such as Daraz and Yayvo emerging in 2017. According to our preliminary report, payments and logistics continue to be the most significant obstacles for Pakistani businesses. Many of these problems could be alleviated if the Government had enough funding and rewards. Our exhaustive search revealed no government or autonomous agency in Pakistan whose primary goal is to establish and implement policies to promote e-commerce development. The importance of such an organization for e-commerce development cannot be overstated. There are no government or private body that can offer unbiased advice, training, or consultancy on technical (e.g., website construction, configuration, and maintenance) and commercial (e.g., business model, online business processes, and online marketing) facets of e-commerce to an SME or entrepreneur who needs to use the online platform for their business. E-commerce and information and communication technology (ICT) has been marketed worldwide as a primary enabler for youth entrepreneurship and a career creator (Kshetri, 2007). Young entrepreneurs under the age of 30 have established some of the most promising and high-growth e-commerce companies in most countries, including Pakistan.

Pakistan can become a major exporter of quality goods and services by establishing a robust e-commerce industry within the country and overseas, that will benefit the people including the young professionals to gain employment and provide income for their families, start new businesses, and new tech startups. Pakistan also has a strategic role to play as it can become a major exporter in the region and export large numbers of products/services to neighboring countries such as India which enjoys close cultural relationship amongst its people having similar customs and interests, traditions, languages, food & tastes, clothing & fashion, movies, tourism, and handicrafts etc., and India's economy growing at a faster rate and Pakistan's product and services being top quality and very popular and in high demand in India. Pakistan can easily connect to vast e-commerce opportunities provided by the Indian e-commerce industry and access to vast digital markets, which can benefit both countries in trade and commerce and establish closer business relationship.

Mobile and information technology in Pakistan have empowered businesses and customers by facilitating them in making better investment decisions. On the other side, technology has helped banks offer a wide range of new products, raise productivity, operate more efficiently, expand geographically, and compete globally. The banking industry in Pakistan is now providing more outstanding quality and value-oriented services. Internet banking has now become an appropriate survival strategy as the banking industry worldwide has transformed. Customer's banking services are now offered at a much lower cost and have surely empowered people with complete freedom while choosing their means regarding financial services.

While operational, reputational, security, cross-border, and strategic risks are related to mobile and internet banking. The banks should have a disaster recovery plan with efficacy as well as a comprehensive risk management tool. It should not be confined only to the bank but to the banking system as a whole. Undoubtedly, the internet has created many opportunities for the banking sector's players. New entrants have the benefits of having the latest technology, while a conventional bank's goodwill provides them with an exceptional opportunity to lead online. Existing services will not help banks alone to hold their customers but will also enable them to learn how to capitalize on customer's different relationships regarding online financial services.

REFERENCES

Abbasi, W. A. K. (2013, April 25). Pakistan's e-banking - past, present, and future. *Business Recorder.* https://fp.brecorder.com/2013/04/201304251178401/

Ahmed, R. (2019). *E-commerce in Pakistan: Challenges & opportunities.* Lahore School of Economics. https://aisel.aisnet.org/cgi/viewcontent.cgi?article=1012&context=whiceb2019

Al-Furiah & Al-Braheem. (2009). A comprehensive study on methods of fraud prevention in credit card e-payment system. In *Proceedings of the 11th international conference on information integration and web-based applications & services. ACM.*

Allen, J. P. (2019). *Digital entrepreneurship.* Routledge. doi:10.4324/9780429506567

Anderson, R. J. (Ed.). (2008). *Security engineering: A guide to building dependable distributed systems.* Wiley.

Biederman, D. (2003). E-commerce comes to Asia. *Traffic World, 26*(9), 23.

Bingi, P., Mir, A., & Khamalah, J. (2000). The challenges facing global e-commerce. *Information Systems Management, 17*(4), 26–35. doi:10.1201/1078/43193.17.4.20000901/31249.5

Bloomenthal, A. (2020, November 24). Electronic commerce (e-commerce). *Investopedia.* https://www.investopedia.com/terms/e/ecommerce.asp

Carminati, M., Polino, M., Continella, A., Lanzi, A., Maggi, F., & Zanero, S. (2018). Security evaluation of a banking fraud analysis system. *ACM Transactions on Privacy and Security, 21*(3), 1–31. Advance online publication. doi:10.1145/3178370

Choi, S. Y., & Whinston, A. B. (1999). The future of e-commerce: Integrate and customize. *Computer*, *32*(1), 133–138. doi:10.1109/2.738310

Consolidated Technologies, Inc. (2018, October 26). *What is a cybersecurity solution?* https://consoltech.com/blog/cybersecurity-saas/

De Groot, J. (2020, October 5). What is cyber security? Definition, best practices & more. *Digital Guardian*. https://digitalguardian.com/blog/what-cyber-security

Eisenmann, T., & Trispas, M. (Eds.). (2002). *Internet business models: Text and cases*. McGraw-Hill Irwin.

Forcepoint. (2021). *What is cybersecurity? Cybersecurity defined, explained, and explored*. https://www.forcepoint.com/cyber-edu/cybersecurity

Fraser, S., & Wresch, W. (2005). National competitive advantage in e-commerce efforts: A report from five Caribbean nations perspectives. *Global Development and Technology*, *4*(1), 27–44. doi:10.1163/1569150053888236

Goodreturns. (2020, February 27). *Mobile banking: What are the advantages and disadvantages?* https://www.goodreturns.in/2014/12/05/mobile-banking-what-are-the-advantages-disadvantages-325811.html

Government of Pakistan. Electronic Transactions Ordinance, 2002. (2021). http://www.pakistanlaw.com/eto.pdf

Government of Pakistan. State Bank of Pakistan. (2021). https://dnb.sbp.org.pk/bprd/2011/C11.htm

Government of Pakistan. State Bank of Pakistan Act, 1956. (2021). http://www.na.gov.pk/uploads/documents/1302514100_374.pdf

Hamel, G. (2000). *Leading the revolution*. Harvard Business School Press.

Hamilton, S. (1997). E-commerce for the 21st century. *Computer*, *30*(5), 44–47. doi:10.1109/2.589909

Hawk, S. (2004). Comparison of B2C e-commerce in developing countries. *Electronic Commerce Research*, *14*(3), 181–199. doi:10.1023/B:ELEC.0000027979.91972.36

Hilbert, M. (2001). *Latin America on its path into the digital age: Where are we?* CEPAL/ECLAC.

Holtz, M., David, B., Deus, F. E., de Sousa, R. T. Jr, & Laerte, P. (2011). *A formal classification of internet banking attacks and vulnerabilities*. Academic Press.

Hutchins, E. M., Clopp, M. J., & Amin, P. R. (2011). *Intelligence-driven computer network defense informed by analysis of adversary campaigns and intrusion kill chains*. Lockheed Martin Corporation.

Identity Theft Resource Centre. (2018). *Data breach reports*. https://www.idtheftcenter.org/wp-content/uploads/2018/09/2018-August-Data-Breach-Package.pdf

International Monetary Fund. (2008). *Chapter 2 - Understanding remittances: Demography, transaction channels, and regulatory aspects*. https://www.imf.org/external/np/sta/bop/2008/rcg/pdf/ch2.pdf

IT Governance. (2021). *What is cyber security? Definition and best practices*. https://www.itgovernance.co.uk/what-is-cybersecurity

Kaynak, E., Tatoglu, E., & Kula, V. (2005). An analysis of the factors affecting the adoption of electronic commerce by SMEs: Evidence from an emerging market. *International Marketing Review*, 22(6), 632–640. doi:10.1108/02651330510630258

Kenny, C. (2003a). Development's false divide. *Foreign Policy*, (134), 76–77. doi:10.2307/3183524

Kenny, C. (2003b). The internet and economic growth in less-developed countries: A case of managing expectations? *Oxford Development Studies*, 31(1), 99–113. doi:10.1080/1360081032000047212

Khrais, L. T. (2015). Highlighting the vulnerabilities of the online banking system. *Journal of Internet Banking and Commerce*, 20(3). Advance online publication. doi:10.4172/1204-5357.1000120

King, B. (2012). *Bank 3.0: Why banking is no longer somewhere you go but something you do*. Wiley. doi:10.1002/9781119198918

Kiyavash, N., Koushanfar, F., Coleman, T. P., & Rodrigues, M. (2013). A timing channel spyware for the CSMA/CA protocol. *IEEE Transactions on Information Forensics and Security*, 8(3), 477–487. doi:10.1109/TIFS.2013.2238930

Kshetri, N. (2007). Barriers to e-commerce and competitive business models in developing countries: A case study. *Electronic Commerce Research and Applications*, 6(4), 443–452. doi:10.1016/j.elerap.2007.02.004

Laudon, K. C., & Traver, C. G. (2001). *E-commerce: Business, technology, society*. Addison-Wesley.

MacGregor, R., & Kartiwi, M. (2010). Perception of barriers to e-commerce adoption in SMEs in a developed and developing country: A comparison between Australia and Indonesia. *Journal of Electronic Commerce in Organizations*, 8(1), 61–82. doi:10.4018/jeco.2010103004

Mercer, C. (2006). Telecentres and transformations: Modernizing Tanzania through the internet. *African Affairs*, 105(419), 243–264. doi:10.1093/afraf/adi087

Molla, A., & Licker, P. S. (2005). Perceived e-readiness factors in e-commerce adoption: An empirical investigation in a developing country. *International Journal of Electronic Commerce*, 10(1), 83–110. doi:10.1080/10864415.2005.11043963

Pakistan Today. (2018, November 2). *Pakistan's remittances may reach $22bn in FY19*. https://profit.pakistantoday.com.pk/2018/11/02/pakistans-remittances-may-reach- 22bn-in-fy19/

Panagariya, A. (2000). E-commerce, WTO, and developing countries. *World Economy*, 23(8), 959–979. doi:10.1111/1467-9701.00313

Pedro, C. P., Ramalho, J. J. S., & Silva, J. V. (2018). The main determinants of banking crises in OECD countries. *Review of World Economics*, 154(1), 203–227. doi:10.100710290-017-0294-0

ReachOut Australia. (2021). *Disclosing personal information*. https://schools.au.reachout.com/articles/disclosing-personal-information

Saeed, I. A., Campus, J. B., Selamat, M. A., Ali, M., & Abuagoub, M. A. (2013). A survey on malware and malware detection systems. *International Journal of Computers and Applications*, 67(16), 25–31. doi:10.5120/11480-7108

Shea, S. (2021). Cybersecurity. *SearchSecurity*. https://searchsecurity.techtarget.com/definition/cybersecurity#:~:text=Cybersecurity%20is%20the%20protection%20of,centers%20and%20other%20computerized%20systems

Singh, S., Cabraal, A., & Hermansson, G. (2006). What is your husband's name? Sociological dimensions of internet banking authentication. In *Proceedings of the 18th Australia conference on Computer-Human Interaction: Design: Activities, Artefacts, and Environments*. ACM. 10.1145/1228175.1228217

Survicate. (2021). *Customer satisfaction: Why it's still important in 2021*. https://survicate.com/customer-satisfaction/importance-customer-satisfaction/

The Enterprisers Project. (2020). *What is digital transformation?* https://enterprisersproject.com/whatis-digital-transformation

The Express Tribune. (2018, November 10). *Remittances increase by 21% to $2 billion*. https://tribune.com.pk/story/1844098/2-remittances-increase-21-2-billion/

The Financial Brand. (2018). *The four pillars of digital transformation in banking*. https://thefinancial-brand.com/71733/four-pillars-of-digital-transformation-banking-strategy/

Tigre, P. B., & Dedrick, J. (2004). E-commerce in Brazil: Local adaptation of global technology. *Electronic Markets*, *14*(1), 36–47. doi:10.1080/1019678042000175289

Vila, J. A. (2015). *Identifying and combating cyber-threats in the field of online banking*. Academic Press. https://www.sslshopper.com/what-is-ssl.html

Vrincianu, M., & Popa, L. A. (2010). Considerations regarding the security and protection of e-banking services consumers' interests. *Academy of Economic Studies, Bucharest, Romania, 12*, 28. https://core.ac.uk/download/pdf/6492899.pdf

WorldJute.Com. (2002). *Internet banking frauds*. http://www.worldjute.com/ebank1.html#:~:text=Internet%20Banking%20Fraud%20is%20a,through%20techniques%20such%20as%20phishing.

Zaied, A. N. (2012). Barriers to e-commerce adoption in Egyptian SMEs. *International Journal of Information Engineering and Electronic Business*, *4*(3), 9. doi:10.5815/ijieeb.2012.03.02

ADDITIONAL READING

Abdou, H. A., English, J., & Adewunmi, P. O. (2014). An investigation of risk management practices in electronic banking: The case of the UK banks. *Banks and Bank Systems, 9*(3).

Acohido, P., & Swartz, J. (2008). *Zero-day threat: The shocking truth of how banks and credit bureaus help cyber crooks steal your money and identity*. Union Square Press.

Afuah, A., & Tucci, C. L. (2001). *Internet business models and strategies*. McGraw-Hill Irwin.

Anghelache, G. V., Cozmanca, B. O., Handoreanu, C. A., Obreja, C., Olteanu, A. C., & Radu, A. N. (2011). Operational risk - An assessment at the international level. *International Journal of Mathematical Models and Methods in Applied Sciences*, *1*(5), 184–192.

Chen, S. (2001). *Strategic management of e-business*. Wiley and Sons.

Kirkpatrick, R. (2009). *1969: The year everything changed*. Skyhorse Publishing Inc.

Krishnamurthy, S. (2003). *E-commerce management: Text and cases*. Thompson Learning.

Kumar, M., Sareen, M., & Barquissau, E. (2012). Relationship between types of trust and level of adoption of internet banking. *Problems and Perspectives in Management*, *10*(1), 82–92.

Rayport, J. F., & Jaworski, B. (2001). *Electronic commerce*. McGraw-Hill.

KEY TERMS AND DEFINITIONS

Banking: The services offered by a bank.

Customer Preferences: Expectations that drive customer decisions.

E-Commerce: Transactions conducted on the internet.

Foreign Banks: Banks based in another country.

Local Banks: Locally owned and operated banks.

Perceived Risks: Uncertainty, a consumer has while using electronic services.

Compilation of References

Abbas Fadhil Al-Husainy, M., & Al-Shargabi, B. (2020). Secure and Lightweight Encryption Model for IoT Surveillance Camera. *International Journal of Advanced Trends in Computer Science and Engineering*, 9(2), 1840–1847. doi:10.30534/ijatcse/2020/143922020

Abbasi, W. A. K. (2013, April 25). Pakistan's e-banking - past, present, and future. *Business Recorder*. https://fp.brecorder.com/2013/04/201304251178401/

Abdellatif, A. A., Al-Marridi, A. Z., Mohamed, A., Erbad, A., Chiasserini, C. F., & Refaey, A. (2020). Health: Toward secure, blockchain-enabled healthcare systems. *IEEE Network*, 34(4), 312–319. doi:10.1109/MNET.011.1900553

Abdullah, T., & Jones, A. (2019, January). eHealth: challenges far integrating blockchain within healthcare. In *2019 IEEE 12th International Conference on Global Security, Safety and Sustainability (ICGS3)* (pp. 1-9). IEEE.

Abeshu, A., & Chilamkurti, N. (2018). Deep learning: The frontier for distributed attack detection in fog-to-things computing. *IEEE Communications Magazine*, 56(2), 169–175. doi:10.1109/MCOM.2018.1700332

Ablon, L. (2018). *Data Thieves: The Motivations of Cyber Threat Actors and Their Use and Monetization of Stolen Data*. The RAND Corporation. Retrieved from: https://www.rand.org/content/dam/rand/pubs/testimonies/CT400/CT490/RAND_CT490.pdf

Abraham, C., Chatterjee, D., & Sims, R. R. (2019). Muddling through cybersecurity: Insights from the US healthcare industry. *Business Horizons*, 62(4), 539–548. doi:10.1016/j.bushor.2019.03.010

Abu Al-Haija, Q., & Zein-Sabatto, S. (2020). An Efficient Deep-Learning-Based Detection and Classification System for Cyber-Attacks in IoT Communication Networks. *Electronics (Basel)*, 9(12), 2152. doi:10.3390/electronics9122152

Abusnaina, A., Khormali, A., Alasmary, H., Park, J., Anwar, A., & Mohaisen, A. (2019, July). Adversarial learning attacks on graph-based IoT malware detection systems. *2019 IEEE 39th International Conference on Distributed Computing Systems (ICDCS)*, 1296-1305. 10.1109/ICDCS.2019.00130

Aceto, G., Persico, V., & Pescapé, A. (2020). Industry 4.0 and health: Internet of Things, big data, and cloud computing for Healthcare 4.0. *Journal of Industrial Information Integration*, 18, 100129. doi:10.1016/j.jii.2020.100129

Ackerman, G. (2020). *Israel Power Plants Have Fended Off Cyber Attacks, Minister Says*. Bloomberg. Retrieved from https://www.bloomberg.com/news/articles/2020-01-29/israel-power-plants-have-fended-off-cyber-attacks-minister-says

ACSC. (2021). *Australian Cyber Security Centre. The cyber security principles*. Retrieved from: https://www.cyber.gov.au/acsc/view-all-content/guidance/cyber-security-principles

Adlam, R., & Haskins, B. (2019). A permissioned blockchain approach to the authorization process in electronic health records. In *2019 International Multidisciplinary Information Technology and Engineering Conference (IMITEC)*, (pp. 1-8). IEEE 10.1109/IMITEC45504.2019.9015927

Agarwal, A. (2020, May 8). *Advantages and disadvantages of internet banking*. ToughNickel. https://toughnickel.com/personal-finance/Advantages-and-Disadvantages-of-Internet-Banking

Agrawal, M., Singh, H., Gour, N., & Kumar, M. A. (2014). Evaluation on malware analysis. *International Journal of Computer Science and Information Technologies*, *5*(3), 3381–3383.

Ahmad, I. (2018, March 10). No country for working women. *The Express Tribune*. https://tribune.com.pk/story/1655699/6-no-country-working-women#:~:text=women%20workforce%20engagement.-,Though%20women%20constitute%2049%25%20of%20Pakistan's%20population%2C%20they%20constitute%20only,higher%20than%20women%20(24.8%25)

Ahmadi, M., Ulyanov, D., Semenov, S., Trofimov, M., & Giacinto, G. (2016). Novel Feature Extraction, Selection and Fusion for Effective Malware Family Classification. In *Proceedings of the Sixth ACM Conference on Data and Application Security and Privacy* (pp. 183–194). New York, NY: Association for Computing Machinery. 10.1145/2857705.2857713

Ahmad, R. W., Salah, K., Jayaraman, R., Yaqoob, I., Ellahham, S., & Omar, M. (2021). The role of blockchain technology in telehealth and telemedicine. *International Journal of Medical Informatics*, *148*, 104399. doi:10.1016/j.ijmedinf.2021.104399 PMID:33540131

Ahmed, A. (2020, February 19). Female labour force share on the rise in Pakistan, unlike India. *Dawn*. https://www.dawn.com/news/1535374

Ahmed, M. E., & Kim, H. (2017, April). DDoS attack mitigation in Internet of Things using software defined networking. In *2017 IEEE third international conference on big data computing service and applications (BigDataService)* (pp. 271-276). IEEE. 10.1109/BigDataService.2017.41

Ahmed, K. D., & Askar, S. (2021). Deep Learning Models for Cyber Security in IoT Networks: A Review. *International Journal of Science and Business*, *5*(3), 61–70.

Ahmed, R. (2019). *E-commerce in Pakistan: Challenges & opportunities*. Lahore School of Economics. https://aisel.aisnet.org/cgi/viewcontent.cgi?article=1012&context=whiceb2019

Aho, A. V., Lam, M. S., Sethi, R., & Ullman, J. D. (2007). Compilers: Principles, techniques, and tools (2nd ed.). Academic Press.

Aich, S., Chakraborty, S., Sain, M., Lee, H. I., & Kim, H. C. (2019, February). A review on benefits of IoT integrated blockchain-based supply chain management implementations across different sectors with case study. In *2019 21st international conference on advanced communication technology (ICACT)* (pp. 138-141). IEEE. 10.23919/ICACT.2019.8701910

AIRC. (2008). *Attack Intelligence Research Center Annual Threat Report: 2008 Overview and 2009 Predictions*. Attack Intelligence Research Center, Alladin Knowledge Systems. Available online at http://www.aladdin.com/pdf/airc/AIRC-Annual-Threat-Report2008.pdf

Aishath Murshida, A., Chaithra, B. K., Nishmitha, B., Raghavendra, S., & Mahesh Prasanna, K. (2019). Survey on Artificial Intelligence. *International Journal on Computer Science and Engineering*, *7*(5), 1778–1790.

Akhgar, B., Staniforth, A., & Bosco, F. (2014). *Cyber crime and cyber terrorism investigator's handbook*. Syngress.

Akhlaq, M. A. (2011). Internet banking in Pakistan: Finding complexities. *Journal of Internet Banking and Commerce*, *16*(1), 1–14.

Akhtar, A. (2021) *The Microsoft Exchange hack shows attackers are working 'smarter, not harder,' experts say.* Business Insider. Retrieved from https://www.businessinsider.com.au/microsoft-exchange-server-hack-why-cyberattack-matters-2021-3?r=US&IR=T

Akhtar, A. (2021). The Microsoft Exchange hack shows attackers are working 'smarter, not harder,' experts say. *Business Insider Australia.* Retrieved from: https://www.businessinsider.com.au/microsoft-exchange-server-hack-why-cyberattack-matters-2021-3?r=US&IR=T

Akram, S. V., Malik, P. K., Singh, R., Anita, G., & Tanwar, S. (2020). Adoption of blockchain technology in various realms: Opportunities and challenges. *Security and Privacy, 3*(5), e109. doi:10.1002py2.109

Alam, S., Qu, Z., Riley, R., Chen, Y., & Rastogi, V. (2017). DroidNative: Automating and optimizing detection of Android native code malware variants. *Computers & Security, 65*, 230-246.

Al-Amoush, A. B., & Sandhu, K. (2019). A new model for acceptance of analytics in learning management systems at Jordanian universities. In Modern Technologies for Teaching and Learning in Socio-Humanitarian Disciplines (pp. 138-161). IGI Global.

Alam, S., Horspool, R. N., & Traore, I. (2013, November). MAIL: Malware Analysis Intermediate Language: a step towards automating and optimizing malware detection. In *Proceedings of the 6th International Conference on Security of Information and Networks* (pp. 233-240). 10.1145/2523514.2527006

Alam, S., & Sogukpinar, I. (2021). DroidClone: Attack of the android malware clones - A step towards stopping them. *Computer Science and Information Systems, 18*(1), 67–91. doi:10.2298/CSIS200330035A

Alam, S., Sogukpinar, I., Traore, I., & Coady, Y. (2014, September). In-cloud malware analysis and detection: State of the art. In *Proceedings of the 7th International Conference on Security of Information and Networks* (pp. 473-478). 10.1145/2659651.2659730

Alam, S., Sogukpinar, I., Traore, I., & Horspool, R. N. (2015). Sliding window and control flow weight for metamorphic malware detection. *Journal of Computer Virology and Hacking Techniques, 11*(2), 75–88. doi:10.100711416-014-0222-y

Alam, S., Traore, I., & Sogukpinar, I. (2015). Annotated control flow graph for metamorphic malware detection. *The Computer Journal, 58*(10), 2608–2621. doi:10.1093/comjnl/bxu148

Alam, T. (2020). mHealth Communication Framework using blockchain and IoT Technologies. *International Journal of Scientific & Technology Research, 9*(6).

Albrechtsen, E., & Hovden, J. (2010). Improving information security awareness and behaviour through dialogue, participation and collective reflection. An intervention study. *Computers & Security, 29*(4), 432–445. doi:10.1016/j.cose.2009.12.005

Aldasoro, I., Gambacorta, L., Giudici, P., & Leach, T. (2020a). *Operational and cyber risks in the financial sector.* BIS Working Paper No. 840. Basel, Switzerland: Bank for International Settlements.

Aldasoro, I., Gambacorta, L., Giudici, P., & Leach, T. (2020b). *The drivers of cyber risk.* BIS Working Paper No. 865. Basel, Switzerland: Bank for International Settlements.

Alexander, K. (2020). *Israeli-Gulf cyber cooperation.* Modern Diplomacy. Retrieved from https://moderndiplomacy.eu/2020/12/23/israeli-gulf-cyber-cooperation/

Al-Furiah & Al-Braheem. (2009). A comprehensive study on methods of fraud prevention in credit card e-payment system. In *Proceedings of the 11th international conference on information integration and web-based applications & services. ACM.*

Al-Furiah & Al-Braheem. (2009). Comprehensive study on methods of fraud prevention in credit card e-payment system. In *Proceedings of the 11th international conference on information integration and web-based applications & services. ACM.*

Al-Garadi, M. A., Mohamed, A., Al-Ali, A., Du, X., Ali, I., & Guizani, M. (2020). A survey of machine and deep learning methods for internet of things (IoT) security. *IEEE Communications Surveys and Tutorials, 22*(3), 1646–1685. doi:10.1109/COMST.2020.2988293

Al-Hujran, O., Al-Debei, M. M., Chatfield, A., & Migdadi, M. (2015). The imperative of influencing citizen attitude toward e-government adoption and use. *Computers in Human Behavior, 53*, 189–203. doi:10.1016/j.chb.2015.06.025

Ali, S., Humaria, A., Ramzan, M. S., Khan, I., Saqlain, S. M., Ghani, A., & Alzahrani, B. A. (2020). An efficient cryptographic technique using modified Diffie–Hellman in wireless sensor networks. *International Journal of Distributed Sensor Networks, 16*(6), 1550147720925772. doi:10.1177/1550147720925772

Alladi, T., Chamola, V., Parizi, R. M., & Choo, K. K. R. (2019). Blockchain applications for industry 4.0 and industrial IoT: A review. *IEEE Access: Practical Innovations, Open Solutions, 7*, 176935–176951. doi:10.1109/ACCESS.2019.2956748

Allen, J. P. (2019). *Digital entrepreneurship.* Routledge. doi:10.4324/9780429506567

Al-Odat, Z. A., Srinivasan, S. K., Al-qtiemat, E., Dubasi, M. A. L., & Shuja, S. (2018). *Iot-based secure embedded scheme for insulin pump data acquisition and monitoring.* arXiv preprint arXiv:1812.02357.

Alotaibi, B., & Alotaibi, M. (2020). A Stacked Deep Learning Approach for IoT Cyberattack Detection. *Journal of Sensors, 2020*, 1–10. doi:10.1155/2020/8828591

Aloul, F. A. (2012). The Need for Effective Information Security Awareness. *Journal of Advances in Information Technology, 3*(3), 176–183. doi:10.4304/jait.3.3.176-183

Alrashdi, I., Alqazzaz, A., Aloufi, E., Alharthi, R., Zohdy, M., & Ming, H. (2019, January). Ad-iot: Anomaly detection of iot cyberattacks in smart city using machine learning. In *2019 IEEE 9th Annual Computing and Communication Workshop and Conference (CCWC)* (pp. 0305-0310). IEEE.

Ameen, N., Tarhini, A., Shah, M. A., Madichie, N., Paul, J., & Choudrie, J. (2021). Keeping customers' data secure: A cross-cultural study of cybersecurity compliance among the Gen-Mobile workforce. *Computers in Human Behavior, 114.* doi:10.1016/j.chb.2020.106531

Amoros, J. E., Ciravegna, L., Mandakovic, V., & Stenholm, P. (2019). Necessity or opportunity? The effects of State fragility and economic development on entrepreneurial efforts. *Entrepreneurship Theory and Practice, 43*(4), 725–750. doi:10.1177/1042258717736857

Anderson, H. S., Kharkar, A., Filar, B., Evans, D., & Roth, P. (2018). Learning to evade static PE machine learning malware models via reinforcement learning. arXiv preprint arXiv:1801.08917.

Anderson, R. J. (Ed.). (2008). *Security engineering: A guide to building dependable distributed systems.* Wiley.

Anderson, R., Barton, C., Böhme, R., Clayton, R., Van Eeten, M. J., Levi, M., & Savage, S. (2013). Measuring the cost of cybercrime. In *The economics of information security and privacy* (pp. 265–300). Springer. doi:10.1007/978-3-642-39498-0_12

Andrews, L., Gajanayake, R., & Sahama, T. (2014). The Australian general public's perceptions of having a personally controlled electronic health record. *International Journal of Medical Informatics, 83*(12), 889–900. doi:10.1016/j.ijmedinf.2014.08.002 PMID:25200198

Andročec, D., & Vrček, N. (2018, January). Machine learning for the Internet of things security: A systematic review. *The 13th International Conference on Software Technologies.* 10.5220/0006841205970604

Angraal, S., Krumholz, H. M., & Schulz, W. L. (2017). Blockchain technology: Applications in health care. *Circulation: Cardiovascular Quality and Outcomes, 10*(9), e003800. doi:10.1161/CIRCOUTCOMES.117.003800 PMID:28912202

Arkin, D. (2018). *The world needs multi-layered, multi-dimensional cybersecurity systems.* Israel Defense. Retrieved from https://www.israeldefense.co.il/en/node/32887

Arnold, M. (2014). Banks Face Rising Threat from Cybercrime. *Financial Times.* Retrieved from: http://www.ft.com/intl/cms/s/0/5fd20f60-4d67-11e4-8f75-00144feab7de.html#axzz3FOFcGxgh

Arshad, S., Shah, M. A., Wahid, A., Mehmood, A., Song, H., & Yu, H. (2018). SAMADroid: A Novel 3-Level Hybrid Malware Detection Model for Android Operating System. *IEEE Access: Practical Innovations, Open Solutions, 6,* 4321–4339. doi:10.1109/ACCESS.2018.2792941

Atienza, A. A., Zarcadoolas, C., Vaughon, W., Hughes, P., Patel, V., Chou, W.-Y., & Pritts, J. (2015). Consumer Attitudes and Perceptions on mHealth Privacy and Security: Findings from a Mixed-Methods Study. *Journal of Health Communication, 20*(6), 673–679. doi:10.1080/10810730.2015.1018560 PMID:25868685

Attia, O., Khoufi, I., Laouiti, A., & Adjih, C. (2019, June). An IoT-blockchain architecture based on hyperledger framework for health care monitoring application. In *NTMS 2019-10th IFIP International Conference on New Technologies, Mobility and Security* (pp. 1-5). IEEE Computer Society.

Atzori, L., Iera, A., & Morabito, G. (2010). The internet of things: A survey. *Computer Networks, 54*(15), 2787–2805. doi:10.1016/j.comnet.2010.05.010

Aunger, C. (2020). *It's Time to Re-engineer Healthcare Cybersecurity.* Forbes Technology Council. Available from www.forbes.com/sites/forbestechcouncil/2020/08/05/its-time-to-re-engineer-health-care-cybersecurity/?sh=e74c6f412784

Australian Digital Health Agency (ADHA). (2019). *My Health Record.* Available from https://www.myhealthrecord.gov.au/for-you-your-family/what-is-my-health-record

Australian Government. (2016). *MyHRCs Rule 2016.* Available from https://www.legislation.gov.au/Details/F2016C00607

Australian Government. (2019). *My Health Record Statistics.* Available from https://www.myhealthrecord.gov.au/sites/default/files/my_health_record_dashboard_-_28_july_2019.pdf?v=1565831963

Aytes, K., & Connolly, T. (2004). Computer Security and Risky Computing Practices: A Rational Choice Perspective. *Journal of Organizational and End User Computing, 16*(3), 22–40. doi:10.4018/joeuc.2004070102

Aziz, A., & Singh, K. (2019). Lightweight security scheme for Internet of Things. *Wireless Personal Communications, 104*(2), 577–593. doi:10.100711277-018-6035-4

Bagayogo, F. F., Lapointe, L., & Bassellier, G. (2014). Enhanced use of IT: A new perspective on post-adoption. *Journal of the Association for Information Systems, 15*(7), 3. doi:10.17705/1jais.00367

Bai, B., Law, R., & Wen, I. (2008). The impact of website quality on customer satisfaction and purchase intentions: Evidence from Chinese online visitors. *International Journal of Hospitality Management, 27*(3), 391–402. doi:10.1016/j.ijhm.2007.10.008

Bajak, F., Tucker, E., & O'Brien, M. (2021). *Chinese Hackers Blamed for Massive Microsoft Server Hack.* The Diplomat. Retrieved from https://thediplomat.com/2021/03/chinese-hackers-blamed-for-massive-microsoft-server-hack/

Bajak, F., Tucker, E., & O'Brien, M. (2021). Chinese Hackers Blamed for Massive Microsoft Server Hack. *The Diplomat.* Retrieved from: https://thediplomat.com/2021/03/chinese-hackers-blamed-for-massive-microsoft-server-hack/

Baker, C. R. (1999). An analysis of fraud on the internet. *Internet Research, 9*(5), 348–360. doi:10.1108/10662249910297750

Balakrishnan, G., & Reps, T. (2010). WYSINWYX: What you see is not what you eXecute. *ACM Transactions on Programming Languages and Systems, 32*(6), 1–84. doi:10.1145/1749608.1749612

Baldwin, J. L., Singh, H., Sittig, D. F., & Giardina, T. D. (2017). Patient portals and health apps: Pitfalls, promises, and what one might learn from the other. *Health Care, 5*(3), 81–85. PMID:27720139

Banfield, J. M. (2016). *A study of information security awareness program effectiveness in predicting end-user security behavior* (Master Thesis). Eastern Michigan University.

Bansler, J. P., Havn, E. C., Schmidt, K., Mønsted, T., Petersen, H. H., & Svendsen, J. H. (2016). Cooperative epistemic work in medical practice: An analysis of physicians' clinical notes. *Computer Supported Cooperative Work, 25*(6), 503–546. doi:10.100710606-016-9261-x

Barabási, A. L. (2018). A képlet [The Formula]. *Libri.*

Bayram, M., Üngan, M. C., & Ardıç, K. (2017). The relationships between OHS prevention costs, safety performance, employee satisfaction and accident costs. *International Journal of Occupational Safety and Ergonomics, 23*(2), 285–296. doi:10.1080/10803548.2016.1226607 PMID:27667202

Bazhair, A. H., & Sandhu, K. (2015). Factors for the acceptance of enterprise resource planning (ERP) systems and financial performance. *System, 14*(7), 16.

Beaudry, A., Vaghefi, I., Bagayogo, F., & Lapointe, L. (2020). Impact of IT user behavior: Observations through a new lens. *Communications of the Association for Information Systems, 46*(1), 15. doi:10.17705/1CAIS.04615

Beelmann, A. (2006). Review of Systematic reviews in the social sciences. A practical guide [Review of the book Systematic reviews in the social sciences. A practical guide, by M. Petticrew & H. Roberts]. *European Psychologist, 11*(3), 244–245. doi:10.1027/1016-9040.11.3.244

Bélanger, F., & Carter, L. (2008). Trust and risk in e-government adoption. *The Journal of Strategic Information Systems, 17*(2), 165–176. doi:10.1016/j.jsis.2007.12.002

Bell, L., Buchanan, W. J., Cameron, J., & Lo, O. (2018). Applications of blockchain within healthcare. *Blockchain in Healthcare Today, 1*(8).

Ben-Asher, N., & Gonzalez, C. (2015). Effects of cyber security knowledge on attack detection. *Computers in Human Behavior, 48*, 51–61. doi:10.1016/j.chb.2015.01.039

Bendovschi, A. (2015). Cyber-attacks–trends, patterns and security countermeasures. *Procedia Economics and Finance, 28*, 24–31. doi:10.1016/S2212-5671(15)01077-1

Bhuyan, S. S., Bailey-DeLeeuw, S., Wyant, D. K., & Chang, C. F. (2016). Too Much or Too Little? How Much Control Should Patients Have Over EHR Data? *Journal of Medical Systems, 40*(7), 174. doi:10.100710916-016-0533-2 PMID:27272134

Bhuyan, S. S., Kabir, U. Y., Escarino, J. M., Ector, K., Palakodeti, S., ... Dobalian, A. (2020). Transforming Healthcare Cybersecurity from Reactive to Proactive: Current Status and Future Recommendations. *Journal of Medical Systems, 44*(98), 98. Advance online publication. doi:10.100710916-019-1507-y PMID:32239357

Biederman, D. (2003). E-commerce comes to Asia. *Traffic World, 26*(9), 23.

Big News Network. (2021). *Israeli manufacturers launch cybersecurity HQ following rise in attacks*. Retrieved from https://www.bignewsnetwork.com/news/267448715/israeli-manufacturers-launch-cybersecurity-hq-following-rise-in-attacks

Bilar, D. (2007). Opcodes as predictor for malware. *International Journal of Electronic Security and Digital Forensics*, *1*(2), 156-168.

Bingi, P., Mir, A., & Khamalah, J. (2000). The challenges facing global e-commerce. *Information Systems Management*, *17*(4), 26–35. doi:10.1201/1078/43193.17.4.20000901/31249.5

Birajdar, G. K., & Mankar, V. H. (2013). Digital image forgery detection using passive techniques: A survey. *Digital Investigation*, *10*(3), 226–245. doi:10.1016/j.diin.2013.04.007

Biswal, A. (2021). *Top 10 Deep Learning Algorithms You Should Know in 2021*. Simplilearn. Simplilearn.com/tutorials/deep-learning-tutorial/deep-learning-algorithm

Bi, Z. M., Luo, M., Miao, Z., Zhang, B., Zhang, W. J., & Wang, L. (2020). Safety assurance mechanisms of collaborative robotic systems in manufacturing. *Robotics and Computer-integrated Manufacturing*, *67*, 102022. doi:10.1016/j.rcim.2020.102022

Blanco, R., Cilla, J. J., Briongos, S., Malagón, P., & Moya, J. M. (2018, November). Applying cost-sensitive classifiers with reinforcement learning to IDS. In *International Conference on Intelligent Data Engineering and Automated Learning* (pp. 531-538). Springer. 10.1007/978-3-030-03493-1_55

Bloomenthal, A. (2020, November 24). Electronic commerce (e-commerce). *Investopedia*. https://www.investopedia.com/terms/e/ecommerce.asp

Bob, Y. J. (2020). *Cyber authority to victims post-Shirbit hack: Get new identity cards*. The Jerusalem Post. Retrieved from https://www.jpost.com/breaking-news/shirbit-hackers-to-leak-more-documents-by-9-am-if-money-not-received-651276

Bob, Y. J. (2020). *NSA, Israeli, UK cyber chiefs confront new hacker threats in corona era*. The Jerusalem Post. Retrieved from https://www.jpost.com/jpost-tech/nsa-israeli-uk-cyber-chiefs-confront-new-hacker-threats-in-corona-era-639475

Bob, Y. J. (2020). *With no cyber law, can gov't stop Shirbit-style cyberattacks?* The Jerusalem Post. Retrieved from https://www.jpost.com/israel-news/cyber-lawyer-to-post-law-needs-amending-to-bolster-cybersecurity-650949

Boeke, S. (2018). National cyber crisis management: Different European approaches. *Governance: An International Journal of Policy, Administration and Institutions*, *31*(3), 449–464. doi:10.1111/gove.12309

Bogle, A. (2018). *Healthcare data a growing target for hackers, cybersecurity experts warn*. Available from https://www.abc.net.au/news/science/2018-04-18/healthcare-target-for-hackers-experts-warn/9663304

Boss, S. R. (2007). *Control, perceived risk and information security precautions: external and internal motivations for security behavior* (PhD Thesis). University of Pittsburgh.

Botta, A., De Donato, W., Persico, V., & Pescapé, A. (2016). Integration of cloud computing and internet of things: A survey. *Future Generation Computer Systems*, *56*, 684–700. doi:10.1016/j.future.2015.09.021

Boukerche, A., & Coutinho, R. W. (2020). Design Guidelines for Machine Learning-based Cybersecurity in Internet of Things. *IEEE Network*.

Bouveret, A. (2019b). Estimation of Losses Due to Cyber Risk for Financial Institutions. Journal of Operational Risk. Advance online publication. doi:10.21314/JOP.2019.224

Bouveret, A. (2019a). Cyber Risk for the Financial Services Sector. *Journal of Financial Transformation*, *49*, 29.

Boyes, H., Hallaq, B., Cunningham, J., & Watson, T. (2018). The industrial internet of things (IIoT): An analysis framework. *Computers in Industry, 101*, 1–12. doi:10.1016/j.compind.2018.04.015

Brewer, R. (2016). Ransomware attacks: Detection, prevention and cure. *Network Security, 2016*(9), 5–9. doi:10.1016/S1353-4858(16)30086-1

Broeders, D. (2021). Private active cyber defense and (international) cyber security—pushing the line? *Journal of Cybersecurity, 7*(1). doi:10.1093/cybsec/tyab010

Browne, R. (2021). Bitcoin falls after U.S. seizes most of Colonial ransom. *CNBC Tech*. Retrieved from: https://www.cnbc.com/amp/2021/06/08/bitcoin-btc-price-slides-as-us-seizes-most-of-colonial-ransom.html

Brunetti, F., Matt, D. T., Bonfanti, A., De Longhi, A., Pedrini, G., & Orzes, G. (2020). Digital transformation challenges: Strategies emerging from a multi-stakeholder approach. *The TQM Journal, 32*(4), 697–724. doi:10.1108/TQM-12-2019-0309

Buchanan, B. G. (2005). A (very) brief history of artificial intelligence. *AI Magazine, 26*(4), 53–53.

Bulgurcu, B., Cavusoglu, H., & Benbasat, I. (2010). Information security policy compliance: An empirical study of rationality-based beliefs and information security awareness. *Management Information Systems Quarterly, 34*(3), 523–548. doi:10.2307/25750690

Burton-Jones, A., & Grange, C. (2013). From use to effective use: A representation theory perspective. *Information Systems Research, 24*(3), 632–658. doi:10.1287/isre.1120.0444

Burton-Jones, A., & Volkoff, O. (2017). How can we develop contextualized theories of effective use? A demonstration in the context of community-care electronic health records. *Information Systems Research, 28*(3), 468–489. doi:10.1287/isre.2017.0702

Bygstad, B., & Øvrelid, E. (2021). Managing two-speed innovation for digital transformation. *Procedia Computer Science, 181*, 119–126. doi:10.1016/j.procs.2021.01.111

Caffrey, L., & Okot-Uma, R. W. O. (1999). Government secure intranets. Information Technology & Globalisation Series. Commonwealth Secretariat.

Cahane, A. (2018). *The New Israeli Cyber Draft Bill – A Preliminary Overview*. The Federmann Cyber Security Research Center. Retrieved from https://csrcl.huji.ac.il/news/new-israeli-cyber-law-draft-bill#_ftn1

Caldarelli, G., Zardini, A., & Rossignoli, C. (2021). Blockchain adoption in the fashion sustainable supply chain: Pragmatically addressing barriers. *Journal of Organizational Change Management, 34*(2), 507–524. doi:10.1108/JOCM-09-2020-0299

Callinan, R. (2021). UnitingCare cyber attack claimed by notorious ransom gang REvil/Sodin. *ABC News*. Retrieved from: https://mobile.abc.net.au/news/2021-05-06/qld-uniting-care-hack-revil-revealed/100118590

Camara, C., Peris-Lopez, P., & Tapiador, J. E. (2015). Security and privacy issues in implantable medical devices: A comprehensive survey. *Journal of Biomedical Informatics, 55*, 272–289. doi:10.1016/j.jbi.2015.04.007 PMID:25917056

Camarinha-Matos, L. M. (2012). *Scientific research methodologies and techniques- Unit 2: Scientific method. Unit 2: Scientific methodology. PhD program in electrical and computer engineering*. Uninova.

Cameron, R. E. (2015). *A concise economic history of the world: From Paleolithic times to the present* (5th ed.). Oxford University Press.

Canner, B. (2021). RockYou2021 is Largest Password Leak at 8.4 Billion Entries. *Solutions Review*. Retrieved from: https://solutionsreview.com/identity-management/rockyou2021-is-largest-password-leak-at-8-4-billion-entries/

Cao, L., Cai, Y., & Yue, Y. (2020). Data Fusion Algorithm for Heterogeneous Wireless Sensor Networks Based on Extreme Learning Machine Optimized by Particle Swarm Optimization. *Journal of Sensors, 2020*, 2020. doi:10.1155/2020/2549324

Carl, G., Kesidis, G., Brooks, R. R., & Rai, S. (2006). Denial-of-service attack-detection techniques. *IEEE Internet Computing, 10*(1), 82–89. doi:10.1109/MIC.2006.5

Carminati, M., Polino, M., Continella, A., Lanzi, A., Maggi, F., & Zanero, S. (2018). Security evaluation of a banking fraud analysis system. *ACM Transactions on Privacy and Security, 21*(3), 1–31. Advance online publication. doi:10.1145/3178370

Carter, W. A. (2017). *Forces shaping the cyber threat landscape for Financial Institutions*. SWIFT Institute, Working Paper No. 2016-004.

Carter, L., & Belanger, F. (2005). The utilization of e-government services: Citizen trust, innovation and acceptance factors. *Journal of Information Systems, 15*(1), 5–25. doi:10.1111/j.1365-2575.2005.00183.x

Cascio, W. F., & Montealegre, R. (2016). How technology is changing work and organizations. *Annual Review of Organizational Psychology and Organizational Behavior, 3*(1), 349–375. doi:10.1146/annurev-orgpsych-041015-062352

Cass, S. (2001). Anatomy of malice [computer viruses]. *IEEE Spectrum, 38*(11), 56–60. doi:10.1109/6.963235

Catak, F. O., Yazi, A. F., Elezaj, O., & Ahmed, J. (2020). Deep learning based Sequential model for malware analysis using Windows exe API Calls. *PeerJ. Computer Science, 6*(July), 1–23. doi:10.7717/peerj-cs.285 PMID:33816936

Catalini, C. (2017). How blockchain technology will impact the digital economy. *Blockchains Smart Contracts Internet Things, 4*, 2292-2303. https://ide.mit.edu/sites/default/files/publications/IDE%20Research%20Paper_v0517.pdf

Cathelat, B. (2019). *Smart Cities - Shaping the Society of 2030*. Global Sociology Study Report. NETEXPLO, Observatory. Paris, France. United Nations Educational, Scientific and Cultural Organization (UNESCO). Retrieved from: https://unesdoc.unesco.org/ark:/48223/pf0000367762.locale=es

Cattaruza, A. (2020). *A digitális adatok geopolitikája ("Geopolitics of Digital Data")*. Pallas Athéné Könyvkiadó.

Celesti, A., Ruggeri, A., Fazio, M., Galletta, A., Villari, M., & Romano, A. (2020). Blockchain-based healthcare workflow for tele-medical laboratory in federated hospital IoT clouds. *Sensors (Basel), 20*(9), 2590. doi:10.339020092590 PMID:32370129

Chakladar, D. D., & Chakraborty, S. (2019). Feature extraction and classification in brain-computer interfacing: Future research issues and challenges. In *Natural Computing for Unsupervised Learning* (pp. 101–131). Springer. doi:10.1007/978-3-319-98566-4_5

Chamola, V., Hassija, V., Gupta, V., & Guizani, M. (2020). A comprehensive review of the COVID-19 pandemic and the role of IoT, drones, AI, blockchain, and 5G in managing its impact. *IEEE Access: Practical Innovations, Open Solutions, 8*, 90225–90265. doi:10.1109/ACCESS.2020.2992341

Chandrakar, P. (2021). A Secure Remote User Authentication Protocol for Healthcare Monitoring Using Wireless Medical Sensor Networks. In *Research Anthology on Telemedicine Efficacy* (pp. 549–572). Adoption, and Impact on Healthcare Delivery. www.igi-global.com/chapter/a-secure-remote-user-authentication-protocol-for-healthcaremonitoring-using-wireless-medical-sensor-networks/

Chao, H. C., Wu, H. T., & Tseng, F. H. (2021). AIS Meets IoT: A Network Security Mechanism of Sustainable Marine Resource Based on Edge Computing. *Sustainability, 13*(6), 3048. doi:10.3390u13063048

Chao, X., Kou, G., Peng, Y., & Alsaadi, F. E. (2019). Behavior monitoring methods for trade-based money laundering integrating macro and micro-prudential regulation: A case from China. *Technological and Economic Development of Economy*, 25(6), 1–16. doi:10.3846/tede.2019.9383

Chaudhuri, A., Datta, P. P., Fernandes, K. J., & Xiong, Y. (2021). Optimal pricing strategies for Manufacturing-as-a Service platforms to ensure business sustainability. *International Journal of Production Economics*, 234, 108065. doi:10.1016/j.ijpe.2021.108065

Chavan, J. (2013). Internet banking - Benefits and challenges in an emerging economy. *International Journal of Research in Business Management*, 1(1), 19–26.

Chebyshev, V. (2019). *Mobile malware evolution.* Kaspersky Labs.

Chen, L., Xu, L., Gao, Z., Lu, Y., & Shi, W. (2018). Tyranny of the majority: On the (im)possibility of correctness of smart contracts. *IEEE Security and Privacy*, 16(4), 30–37. doi:10.1109/MSP.2018.3111240

Chen, L., Yue, D., Dou, C., Chen, J., & Cheng, Z. (2020). Study on attack paths of cyber attack in cyber-physical power systems. *IET Generation, Transmission & Distribution*, 14(12), 2352–2360. doi:10.1049/iet-gtd.2019.1330

Chen, L., Zhou, S., & Xu, J. (2018). Computation peer offloading for energy-constrained mobile edge computing in small-cell networks. *IEEE/ACM Transactions on Networking*, 26(4), 1619–1632. doi:10.1109/TNET.2018.2841758

Chen, T., Jarvis, L., & Macdonald, S. (2014). *Cyberterrorism.* Springer. doi:10.21236/ADA603165

Cherubini, A., Passama, R., Crosnier, A., Lasnier, A., & Fraisse, P. (2016). Collaborative manufacturing with physical human–robot interaction. *Robotics and Computer-integrated Manufacturing*, 40, 1–13. doi:10.1016/j.rcim.2015.12.007

Choi, S. Y., & Whinston, A. B. (1999). The future of e-commerce: Integrate and customize. *Computer*, 32(1), 133–138. doi:10.1109/2.738310

Chou, T. S. (2013). Security threats on cloud computing vulnerabilities. *International Journal of Computer Science and Information Technologies*, 5(3), 79–88. doi:10.5121/ijcsit.2013.5306

Chou, W. (2002). Inside SSL: The secure sockets layer protocol. *IT Professional*, 4(4), 47–52. doi:10.1109/MITP.2002.1046644

Chrisman, J. J., Hofer, C. W., & Boulton, W. B. (1988). Toward a system for classifying business strategies. *Academy of Management Review*, 13(3), 413–428. doi:10.5465/amr.1988.4306963

Cichocki, A., & Kuleshov, A. P. (2021). Future trends for human-ai collaboration: A comprehensive taxonomy of ai/agi using multiple intelligences and learning styles. *Computational Intelligence and Neuroscience.*

Cisco. (2020). *2020 Global Network Trends Report.* https://www.cisco.com/c/m/en_us/solutions/enterprise-networks/networking-report.html

Clancy, L. (2019). *Functional programming reaches for stardom in finance.* CME Group. https://www.risk.net/risk-management/6395366/functional-programming-reaches-for-stardom-in-finance

Clark, D. (2018). *Top 16 Open Source Deep Learning Libraries and Platforms.* KDnuggets. https://www.kdnuggets.com/2018/04/top-16-open-source-deep-learning-libraries.html

Clarke, E. M., Grumberg, O., & Peled, D. A. (1999). *Model checking. The MIT Press.*

Clarke, N., Stewart, G., & Lacey, D. (2012). Death by a thousand facts. *Information Management & Computer Security*, 20(1), 29–38. doi:10.1108/09685221211219182

Claughton, D., & Beilharz, N. (2021). JBS Foods pays $14.2 million ransom to end cyber attack on its global operations. *ABC Rural*. Retrieved from: https://www.abc.net.au/news/rural/2021-06-10/jbs-foods-pays-14million-ransom-cyber-attack/100204240

Clauson, K. A., Breeden, E. A., Davidson, C., & Mackey, T. K. (2018). Leveraging blockchain technology to enhance supply chain management in healthcare: an exploration of challenges and opportunities in the health supply chain. *Blockchain in Healthcare Today, 1*(3), 1-12.

ClearSky Cyber Security Ltd. (2020). *Pay2Kitten - Pay2Key Ransomware – A New Campaign by Fox Kitten.* Retrieved from https://www.clearskysec.com/wp-content/uploads/2020/12/Pay2Kitten.pdf

Coles, M., & Landrum, R. (2009). Transparent Data Encryption. In *Expert SQL Server 2008 Encryption* (pp. 127–150). Apress. doi:10.1007/978-1-4302-3365-7_6

Collin, B. C. (1997). The future of cyberterrorism: Where the physical and virtual worlds converge. *Crime and Justice International, 13*(2), 15–18.

Colonial Pipeline cyber attack. (2021, June 5). In *Wikipedia*. Retrieved from: https://en.wikipedia.org/wiki/Colonial_Pipeline_cyber_attack

Commission of the European Communities. (2006). *A strategy for a Secure Information Society – "Dialogue, partnership and empowerment"*. Retrieved from https://ec.europa.eu/information_society/doc/com2006251.pdf

Commission of the European Communities. (2006). *A strategy for a Secure Information Society – "Dialogue, partnership and empowerment"*. Retrieved from: https://ec.europa.eu/information_society/doc/com2006251.pdf

Commonwealth of Australia. (2012). *MyHRCs Act 2012 (Australia)*. Available from https://www.legislation.gov.au/Series/C2012A00063

Commonwealth of Australia. (2015). *MyHRCs Regulation 2012 (Australia)*. Available from https://www.legislation.gov.au/Details/F2016C00093

Conaty-Buck, S. (2017). Cyber security and healthcare records. Tips for ensuring patient safety and privacy. *American Nurse Today, 12*(9), 62–65.

Connell, A., Palko, T., & Yasar, H. (2013, November). Cerebro: A platform for collaborative incident response and investigation. In 2013 IEEE international conference on technologies for homeland security (HST) (pp. 241-245). IEEE. doi:10.1109/THS.2013.6699007

Consolidated Technologies, Inc. (2018, October 26). *What is a cybersecurity solution?* https://consoltech.com/blog/cybersecurity-saas/

Coventry, L., & Branley, D. (2018). Cybersecurity in healthcare: A narrative review of trends, threats and ways forward. *Maturitas, 113*, 48–52. doi:10.1016/j.maturitas.2018.04.008 PMID:29903648

Csizmadia N. (2016). *Geopillanat* [Geomoment]. L'Harmattan Kiadó.

Cybertech Group. (2021). *Cybertech Global UAE-Dubai Conference agenda*. Retrieved from https://www.cybertech-conference.com/program

Da Costa, K. A., Papa, J. P., Lisboa, C. O., Munoz, R., & de Albuquerque, V. H. C. (2019). Internet of Things: A survey on machine learning-based intrusion detection approaches. *Computer Networks, 151*, 147–157. doi:10.1016/j.comnet.2019.01.023

Dai, H. N., Zheng, Z., & Zhang, Y. (2019). Blockchain for Internet of Things: A survey. *IEEE Internet of Things Journal*, *6*(5), 8076–8094. doi:10.1109/JIOT.2019.2920987

Daim, T., Lai, K. K., Yalcin, H., Alsoubie, F., & Kumar, V. (2020). Forecasting technological positioning through technology knowledge redundancy: Patent citation analysis of IoT, cybersecurity, and Blockchain. *Technological Forecasting and Social Change*, *161*, 120329. doi:10.1016/j.techfore.2020.120329

Daniel, S., Christopher, W., & Luke, B. (2018). Digital Transformation of Business Models-Best Practice, Enabler, and Roadmap. *International Journal of Innovation Management*, *21*(8), 1–13.

Dannenberg, M., & Kellner, D. (1998). The bank of tomorrow with today's technology. *International Journal of Bank Marketing*, *16*(2), 90–97. doi:10.1108/02652329810206743

Dantzig, G. (1949). *Programming of Interdependent Activities: II Mathematical Model*. Academic Press.

Darabian, H., Homayounoot, S., Dehghantanha, A., Hashemi, S., Karimipour, H., Parizi, R. M., & Choo, K.-K. R. (2020). Detecting Cryptomining Malware: A Deep Learning Approach for Static and Dynamic Analysis. *Journal of Grid Computing*, *18*(2), 293–303. doi:10.100710723-020-09510-6

Darknet market. (2021, June 8). In *Wikipedia*. Retrieved from: https://en.wikipedia.org/wiki/Darknet_market

Darknet. (2021, June 8). In *Wikipedia*. Retrieved from: https://en.wikipedia.org/wiki/Darknet

Davidson, H. (2019). My Health Record failed to manage cybersecurity and privacy risk- audit finds. *The Guardian*. Available from https://www.theguardian.com/australia-news/2019/nov/25/my-health-record-failed-to-manage-cybersecurity-and-privacy-risks-audit-finds

Davidson, S., De Filippi, P., & Potts, J. (2018). Blockchains and the economic institutions of capitalism. *Journal of Institutional Economics*, *14*(4), 639–658. doi:10.1017/S1744137417000200

Davies, G., & Bank, J. H. (2002). *A history of money: From ancient times to the present day*. University of Wales Press.

Davisson, W. I., & Harper, J. E. (1972). *European economic history*. Appleton-Century-Crofts.

De Bruijn, H., & Janssen, M. (2017). Building cybersecurity awareness: The need for evidence-based framing strategies. *Government Information Quarterly*, *34*(1), 1–7. doi:10.1016/j.giq.2017.02.007

De Groot, J. (2020, October 5). What is cyber security? Definition, best practices & more. *Digital Guardian*. https://digitalguardian.com/blog/what-cyber-security

De Souza, C. A., Westphall, C. B., Machado, R. B., Sobral, J. B. M., & dos Santos Vieira, G. (2020). Hybrid approach to intrusion detection in fog-based IoT environments. *Computer Networks*, *180*, 107417. doi:10.1016/j.comnet.2020.107417

Defending the Digital Frontier. (2014). Retrieved from https://www.economist.com/sites/default/files/20140712_cybersecurity.pdf

Defense, I. (2021). *Cybertech Dubai: An exciting Holocaust Remembrance Day ceremony was held during the conference*. Retrieved from https://www.israeldefense.co.il/node/49233

Del Fiol, G., Kohlmann, W., Bradshaw, R. L., Weir, C. R., Flynn, M., Hess, R., Schiffman, J. D., Nanjo, C., & Kawamoto, K. (2020). Standards-based clinical decision support platform to manage patients who meet guideline-based criteria for genetic evaluation of familial cancer. *JCO Clinical Cancer Informatics*, *4*(4), 1–9. doi:10.1200/CCI.19.00120 PMID:31951474

Denning, D. E. (2001). Activism, hacktivism, and cyberterrorism: The Internet as a tool for influencing foreign policy. *Networks and netwars: The future of terror, crime, and militancy, 239*, 288.

Denyer, D., & Tranfield, D. (2009). Producing a systematic review. In D. A. Buchanan & A. Bryman (Eds.), *The Sage handbook of organizational research methods* (pp. 671–689). Sage Publications Ltd.

Department of Health. (2016, March). MyHRC *Stastics*. Canberra: Australian Government. Available from https://myhealthrecord.gov.au/internet/mhr/publishing.nsf/

Department of Home Affairs. (2020). *Australia's Cyber Security Strategy*. Available from https://www.homeaffairs.gov.au/about-us/our-portfolios/cyber-security/strategy

Desman, M. B. (2003). The Ten Commandments of Information Security Awareness Training. *Information Systems Security, 11*(6), 39–44. doi:10.1201/1086/43324.11.6.20030101/40430.7

Diesch, R., Pfaffa, M., & Krcmar, H. (2020). A Comprehensive Model of Information Security Factors for Decision-Makers. *Computers & Security, 92*, 1–21. doi:10.1016/j.cose.2020.101747

Dilek, S., Çakır, H., & Aydın, M. (2015). Applications of artificial intelligence techniques to combating cyber crimes: A review. *International Journal of Artificial Intelligence & Applications, 6*(1), 21–39. doi:10.5121/ijaia.2015.6102

Diro, A. A., & Chilamkurti, N. (2018). Distributed attack detection scheme using deep learning approach for Internet of Things. *Future Generation Computer Systems, 82*, 761–768. doi:10.1016/j.future.2017.08.043

Dixit, N. K., Mishra, L., Charan, M. S., & Dey, B. K. (2012). The new age of computer virus and their detection. *International Journal of Network Security & Its Applications, 4*(3), 79–96. doi:10.5121/ijnsa.2012.4305

Dombe, A. R. (2021). *Servers of Ben Gurion University breached*. Israel Defense. Retrieved from https://www.israeldefense.co.il/en/node/47630

Domínguez, C. M. F., Ramaswamy, M., Martinez, E. M., & Cleal, M. G. (2010). A Framework For Information Security Awareness Programs. *Issues in Information Systems, 6*(1), 402–409.

Dorn, A. W., & Webb, S. (2019). Cyberpeacekeeping: New Ways to Prevent and Manage Cyberattacks. *International Journal of Cyber Warfare & Terrorism, 9*(1), 19–30. doi:10.4018/IJCWT.2019010102

Easttom, C., & Butler, W. (2021). The Iran-Saudi Cyber Conflict. *International Journal of Cyber Warfare & Terrorism, 11*(2), 29–42. doi:10.4018/IJCWT.2021040103

E-Business Definition. (2014). *E-Business*. Accessed and reviewed in April 2019, http://dictionary.reference.com/browse/e-business.Dictionary.com

Eckenrode. (2006). *Building a more responsive banking industry: The bell is ringing but are banks salivating?* The Tower Group.

Ehrenfeld, J. M. (2017). WannaCry, Cybersecurity and Health Information Technology: A time to act. *Journal of Medical Systems, 41*(7), 104. doi:10.100710916-017-0752-1 PMID:28540616

Eisenmann, T., & Trispas, M. (Eds.). (2002). *Internet business models: Text and cases*. McGraw-Hill Irwin.

El-Gazzar, R., & Stendal, K. (2020). Blockchain in health care: Hope or hype? *Journal of Medical Internet Research, 22*(7), e17199. doi:10.2196/17199 PMID:32673219

Elleithy, K. (2008). *Innovations and advanced techniques in systems, computing sciences and software engineering*. Springer. doi:10.1007/978-1-4020-8735-6

ENISA. (2020a). *The year in review*. ENISA Threat Landscape. Retrieved from: https://www.enisa.europa.eu/publications/year-in-review

ENISA. (2020b). *Threat Landscape 2020 - List of top 15 threats*. The European Union Agency for Cybersecurity, ENISA. Retrieved from: https://www.enisa.europa.eu/topics/threat-risk-management/threats-and-trends/threat-landscape-mapping-infographic-2020/view

ENISA. (2020c). *Telecom Security During A Pandemic. Telecom security good practices and lessons learned from the COVID-19 outbreak*. doi:10.2824/239478

ENISA. (2021). *Security Framework for Qualified Trust Service Providers*. The European Union Agency for Cybersecurity, ENISA retrieved from: https://www.enisa.europa.eu/publications/security-framework-for-qualified-trust-providers

Epiphaniou, G., Daly, H., & Al-Khateeb, H. (2019). Blockchain and healthcare. In *Blockchain and Clinical Trial* (pp. 1–29). Springer. doi:10.1007/978-3-030-11289-9_1

Eremia, M., Toma, L., & Sanduleac, M. (2017). The Smart City Concept in the 21st Century. *Procedia Engineering*, *181*, 12–19. doi:10.1016/j.proeng.2017.02.357

Estrin, D. (2018). *In Israel, teaching kids cyber skills is a national mission*. The Times of Israel. Retrieved from https://www.timesofisrael.com/in-israel-teaching-kids-cyber-skills-is-a-national-mission/

European Commission. (2013). *Cybersecurity Strategy of the European Union: An Open, Safe and Secure Cyberspace*. Retrieved from https://eeas.europa.eu/archives/docs/policies/eu-cyber-security/cybsec_comm_en.pdf

European Commission. (2013). *Cybersecurity Strategy of the European Union: An Open, Safe and Secure Cyberspace*. Retrieved from: https://eeas.europa.eu/archives/docs/policies/eu-cyber-security/cybsec_comm_en.pdf

European Commission. (2017). *EU-Wide Digital Once-Only Principle for Citizens and Businesses. Policy Options and Their Impacts: Final Report*. EU Official Publications. doi:10.2759/393169

European Commission. (2017). *Ministerial Declaration on eGovernment - the Tallinn Declaration*. Retrieved from https://ec.europa.eu/digital-single-market/en/news/ministerial-declaration-egovernment-tallinn-declaration

European Commission. (2019). *European eGovernment Action Plan 2016-2020*. Retrieved from: https://ec.europa.eu/digital-single-market/en/european-egovernment-action-plan-2016-2020

European Commission. (2019a). *Connecting Europe Facility in Telecom*. Retrieved from: https://ec.europa.eu/digital-single-market/en/connecting-europe-facility

European Commission. (2019b). *eIDAS cooperation network portal*. Retrieved from: https://ec.europa.eu/cefdigital/wiki/display/EIDCOOPNET/eIDAS+Cooperation+Network

European Commission. (2019c). *What are the benefits of eID?* Retrieved from: https://ec.europa.eu/cefdigital/wiki/display/CEFDIGITAL/Benefits+of+eID

European Commission. (2020). *EGovernment Benchmark 2020 eGovernment that works for the people*. Insight Report. doi:10.2759/24753

European Commission. (2021). *About Connecting Europe Facility (CEF). Joinup platform*. Retrieved from: https://joinup.ec.europa.eu/collection/connecting-europe-facility-cef/about

European Commission. (2021). *Blockchain Strategy. Shaping Europe's digital future*. Retrieved from https://digital-strategy.ec.europa.eu/en/policies/blockchain-strategy

European Parliament Council. (2014). Regulation (EU) N° 910/2014 of the European Parliament and of the Council of 23 July 2014 on electronic identification and trust services for electronic transactions in the internal market and repealing Directive 1999/93/EC. *Official Journal of the European Union*. L 257/73. European Legislation Identifier (ELI) Retrieved from: https://eur-lex.europa.eu/legal-content/EN/TXT/PDF/?uri=CELEX:32014R0910&from=EN

European Parliament. (2015). *eGovernment. Using technology to improve public services and democratic participation*. EPRS | European Parliamentary Research Service. doi:10.2861/150280

European Union (2014) Regulation (EU) No 910/2014 of the European Parliament and of the Council of 23 July 2014 on electronic identification and trust services for electronic transactions in the internal market and repealing Directive 1999/93/EC. OJ L 257, 28.8.2014, p. 73–114. https://eur-lex.europa.eu/legal-content/EN/TXT/?uri=uriserv%3AOJ .L.2014.257.01.0073.01.ENG

European Union. (2009). *Ministerial Declaration on eGovernment*. 5th Ministerial eGovernment Conference, Malmö, Sweden. Retrieved from: https://ec.europa.eu/digital-single-market/sites/digital-agenda/files/ministerial-declaration-on-egovernment-malmo.pdf

Falco, G., Caldera, C., & Shrobe, H. (2018). IIoT cybersecurity risk modeling for SCADA systems. *IEEE Internet of Things Journal*, *5*(6), 4486–4495. doi:10.1109/JIOT.2018.2822842

Fang, H., Qi, A., & Wang, X. (2020). Fast Authentication and Progressive Authorization in Large-Scale IoT: How to Leverage AI for Security Enhancement. *IEEE Network*, *34*(3), 24–29. doi:10.1109/MNET.011.1900276

Farivar, F., Haghighi, M. S., Jolfaei, A., & Alazab, M. (2019). Artificial Intelligence for Detection, Estimation, and Compensation of Malicious Attacks in Nonlinear Cyber-Physical Systems and Industrial IoT. *IEEE Transactions on Industrial Informatics*, *16*(4), 2716–2725. doi:10.1109/TII.2019.2956474

Farouk, A., Alahmadi, A., Ghose, S., & Mashatan, A. (2020). Blockchain platform for industrial healthcare: Vision and future opportunities. *Computer Communications*, *154*, 223–235. doi:10.1016/j.comcom.2020.02.058

Fehér, K. (2016). *Kezdő hackerek kézikönyve [The Handbook of Novice Hackers]*. BBS-INFO Kiadó.

Fehér, K. (2018). *Hacker-technikák [Hacker Techniques]*. BBS-INFO Kiadó.

Fekih, R. B., & Lahami, M. (2020, June). Application of blockchain technology in healthcare: a comprehensive study. In *International Conference on Smart Homes and Health Telematics* (pp. 268-276). Springer.

Fernández-Alemán, J. L., Carrión Señor, I., Lozoya, P. L. O., & Toval, A. (2013). Security and privacy in electronic health records: A systematic literature review. *Journal of Biomedical Informatics*, *46*(3), 541–562. doi:10.1016/j.jbi.2012.12.003 PMID:23305810

Fernando, J., & Dawson, L. (2009). The health information system security threat lifecycle: An informatics theory. *International Journal of Medical Informatics*, *78*(12), 815–826. doi:10.1016/j.ijmedinf.2009.08.006 PMID:19783203

Fernando, Y., Mathath, A., & Murshid, M. A. (2016). Improving productivity: A review of robotic applications in food industry. *International Journal of Robotics Applications and Technologies*, *4*(1), 43–62. doi:10.4018/IJRAT.2016010103

Fighting COVID-19-Related Financial Fraud. (2020). Retrieved from https://www.sec.gov/fighting-covid-19-related-financialfraud

Fitch. (2017, April). *Cybersecurity an Increasing Focus for Financial Institutions*. Retrieved from https://www.fitchratings.com/site/pr/1022468

Flammini, A., Ferrari, P., Marioli, D., Sisinni, E., & Taroni, A. (2009). Wired and wireless sensor networks for industrial applications. *Microelectronics Journal, 40*(9), 1322–1336. doi:10.1016/j.mejo.2008.08.012

Florin, M. V., & Sachs, R. (2019). *Critical Infrastructure Resilience - Lessons from Insurance.* Retrieved from https://www.researchgate.net/publication/339271660_Critical_Infrastructure_Resilience_-_Lessons_from_Insurance

Forcepoint. (2021). *What is cybersecurity? Cybersecurity defined, explained, and explored.* https://www.forcepoint.com/cyber-edu/cybersecurity

Fortson, D. (2017, Apr. 2). 90% of all attempts logins are by cyber-hackers. The Sunday Times, p. 5.

Forum, I. S. (2003). *The standard of good practice for the information security.* Information Security Forum.

Foster, I., Lopresti, D., Gropp, B., Hill, M., & Schuman, K. (2021). *A National Discovery Cloud: Preparing the US for Global Competitiveness in the New Era of 21st Century Digital Transformation.* arXiv preprint arXiv:2104.06953.

Fovino, I. N., Carcano, A., Masera, M., & Trombetta, A. (2009). Design and implementation of a secure modbus protocol. In *International conference on critical infrastructure protection* (pp. 83-96). Springer. 10.1007/978-3-642-04798-5_6

Fox, S. (2005). *The state of online banking.* Pew Internet & American Life Project. http://www.pewInternet.org/pdfs/PIP_Online_Banking_2005.pdf#search='The%20State%20of%20Online%20Banking%20Pew

Fragidis, L. L., & Chatzoglou, P. D. (2018). Implementation of a nationwide electronic health record (EHR). *International Journal of Health Care Quality Assurance, 31*(2), 116–130. doi:10.1108/IJHCQA-09-2016-0136 PMID:29504871

Fraser, S., & Wresch, W. (2005). National competitive advantage in e-commerce efforts: A report from five Caribbean nations perspectives. *Global Development and Technology, 4*(1), 27–44. doi:10.1163/1569150053888236

Fraud and Coronavirus (COVID-19). (2020). Retrieved from https://www.finra.org/investors/insights/fraud-andcoronavirus-covid-19

Frazier, L. (2021, March 22). Digital banking trends evolve in 2021, but customer needs stay the same. *Forbes.* https://www.forbes.com/sites/lizfrazierpeck/2021/03/22/digital-banking-trends-evolve-in-2021-but-customer-needs-stay-the-same/?sh=6de017101cd3

Furst, S. A., Reeves, M., Rosen, B., & Blackburn, R. S. (2004). Managing the life cycle of virtual teams. *The Academy of Management Executive, 18*(2), 6–20. doi:10.5465/ame.2004.13837468

Future Cyber Threats. (2020). Retrieved from https://acn-marketing-blog.accenture.com/wp-content/uploads/2020/09/2020Future of CyberThreats_Final.pdf

Fuyong, Z., & Tiezhu, Z. (2017). Malware Detection and Classification Based on N-Grams Attribute Similarity. In *2017 IEEE International Conference on Computational Science and Engineering (CSE) and IEEE International Conference on Embedded and Ubiquitous Computing (EUC).* IEEE. 10.1109/CSE-EUC.2017.157

Gajek, S., Lees, M., & Jansen, C. (2020). IIoT and cyber-resilience: Could blockchain have thwarted the Stuxnet attack? *AI & Society.* Advance online publication. doi:10.100700146-020-01023-w

Gal-Ezer, J., Beeri, C., Harel, D., & Yehudai, A. (2018). *A High-School Program in Computer Science.* The Open University of Israel. Retrieved from https://www.openu.ac.il/personal_sites/download/galezer/high-school-program.pdf

Galindo-Martín, M., Castaño-Martínez, M., & Méndez-Picazo, M. (2019). Digital transformation, digital dividends and entrepreneurship: A quantitative analysis. *Journal of Business Research, 101*, 522–527. doi:10.1016/j.jbusres.2018.12.014

Gambrell, J., & Zion, I. B. (2021). *Iran calls Natanz atomic site blackout 'nuclear terrorism'*. AP News. Retrieved from https://apnews.com/article/middle-east-iran-358384f03b1ef6b65f4264bf9a59a458

Gao, P., & Owolabi, O. (2008). Consumer adoption of internet banking in Nigeria. *International Journal of Electronic Finance*, *2*(3), 284–299. doi:10.1504/IJEF.2008.020598

Gartner. (2020). *Three Essentials for Starting and Supporting Master Data Management*. ID G00730039. Gartner Inc. https://www.gartner.com/doc/reprints?id=1-24MIGFGU&ct=201119&st=sb

Gauhar, A., Ahmad, N., Cao, Y., Khan, S., Cruickshank, H., Qazi, E. A., & Ali, A. (2020). xDBAuth: Blockchain Based Cross Domain Authentication and Authorization Framework for Internet of Things. *IEEE Access: Practical Innovations, Open Solutions*, *8*, 58800–58816. doi:10.1109/ACCESS.2020.2982542

Gerrard, P., & Cunningham, B. (2003). The diffusion of internet banking among Singapore consumers. *International Journal of Bank Marketing*, *21*(1), 16–28. doi:10.1108/02652320310457776

Geusebroek, J. (2012). *Cyber Risk Governance-Towards a framework for managing cyber related risks from an integrated IT governance perspective* (Master's thesis). Institute of Information and Computing Sciencem, Utrecht University.

Gibert, D., Mateu, C., & Planes, J. (2020). The rise of machine learning for detection and classification of malware: Research developments, trends and challenges. *Journal of Network and Computer Applications, 153*(July), 102526. doi:10.1016/j.jnca.2019.102526

Gibson, I., Rosen, D., Stucker, B., & Khorasani, M. (2014). *Additive manufacturing technologies* (Vol. 17). Springer.

Gilbart, J. W. (1919). *The history, principles, and practice of banking*. George Bell And Sons.

Glaser, F. (2017). *Pervasive decentralisation of digital infrastructures: A framework for blockchain enabled system and use case analysis*. doi:10.24251/HICSS.2017.186

Gobierno de España. (2015). *BOE-A-2015-14215*. Resolución de 14 de diciembre de 2015, de la Dirección de Tecnologías de la Información y las Comunicaciones, por la que se establecen las prescripciones técnicas necesarias para el desarrollo y aplicación del sistema Cl@ve. Retrieved from: https://www.boe.es/eli/es/res/2015/12/14/(3)/con

Gobierno de España. (2019). *Portal Cl@ve*. Retrieved from: https://clave.gob.es

Gong, C., & Ribiere, V. (2020). Developing a unified definition of digital transformation. *Technovation*.

Gong, L., Lin, H., Li, Z., Qian, F., Li, Y., Ma, X., & Liu, Y. (2021). Systematically Landing Machine Learning onto Market-Scale Mobile Malware Detection. *IEEE Transactions on Parallel and Distributed Systems*, *32*(7), 1615–1628. doi:10.1109/TPDS.2020.3046092

Goodchild, M. (2007). Citizens as sensors: The world of volunteered geography. *GeoJournal*, *69*(4), 211–221. doi:10.100710708-007-9111-y

Goodfellow, I. J., Pouget-Abadie, J., Mirza, M., Xu, B., Warde-Farley, D., Ozair, S., Courville, A., & Bengio, Y. (2014). *Generative Adversarial Networks*. arXiv:1406.2661.

Goodhue, D. L., & Straub, D. W. (1991). Security concerns of system users: A study of perceptions of the adequacy of security. *Information & Management*, *20*(1), 13–27. doi:10.1016/0378-7206(91)90024-V

Goodreturns. (2020, February 27). *Mobile banking: What are the advantages and disadvantages?* https://www.goodreturns.in/2014/12/05/mobile-banking-what-are-the-advantages-disadvantages-325811.html

Goran, J., LaBerge, L., & Srinivasan, R. (2017). Culture for a digital age. *The McKinsey Quarterly*.

Gordon, L. A., & Loeb, M. P. (2006). *Managing cybersecurity resources: a cost-benefit analysis* (Vol. 1). McGraw-Hill.

Gordon, S., & Ford, R. (2002). Cyberterrorism? *Computers & Security, 21*(7), 636–647. doi:10.1016/S0167-4048(02)01116-1

Górniak, S., Naumann, I., Hartmann, D., & Körting, S. (2010). *Security Issues in Cross-border Electronic Authentication.* Retrieved from: https://www.enisa.europa.eu/publications/xborderauth

Government of Pakistan, Bureau of Statistics. (2017). *Provisional Summary Results of 6th Population and Housing Census - 2017.* https://bytesforall.pk/

Government of Pakistan, Ministry of Finance. (2018). *Economic Survey of Pakistan 2017-18.* http://www.finance.gov.pk/survey/chapters_18/overview_2017-18.pdf

Government of Pakistan, Pakistan Bureau of Statistics. (2018). *Pakistan average monthly wages.* https://www.ceicdata.com/en/pakistan/average-monthly-wages-by-industry/average-monthly-wages

Government of Pakistan. (2002). *Electronic Transactions Ordinance.* http://www.pakistanlaw.com/eto.pdf

Government of Pakistan. Electronic Transactions Ordinance, 2002. (2020). http://www.pakistanlaw.com/eto.pdf

Government of Pakistan. Electronic Transactions Ordinance, 2002. (2021). http://www.pakistanlaw.com/eto.pdf

Government of Pakistan. Pakistan Telecommunication Authority. (2018). *Telecom Indicators.* https://www.pta.gov.pk/en/telecom-indicators

Government of Pakistan. State Bank of Pakistan Act, 1956. (2021). http://www.na.gov.pk/uploads/documents/1302514100_374.pdf

Government of Pakistan. State Bank of Pakistan. (2021). https://dnb.sbp.org.pk/bprd/2011/C11.htm

Governo de Portugal. (2019). *Sistema Autenticação.gov.* Retrieved from: https://www.autenticacao.gov.pt

Gracia, D. B., & Ariño, L. C. (2015). Rebuilding public trust in government administrations through e-government actions. *Revista Española de Investigación de Market, 19*(1), 1–11. doi:10.1016/j.reimke.2014.07.001

Granjal, J., Monteiro, E., & Silva, J. S. (2015). Security for the internet of things: a survey of existing protocols and open research issues. *IEEE Communications Survey Tutor, 17*(3), 1294–1312. Retrieved from: https://ieeexplore.ieee.org/document/7005393

Grech, A., & Camilleri, A. F. (2017). *Blockchain in education.* Publications Office of the European Union. doi:10.2760/60649

Greenlalgh, T., Hinder, S., Stramere, K., Bratan, T., & Russell, J. (2010). Adoption, non-adoption, and abandonment of a personal electronic health record: Case study of HealthSpace. *Biomedical Journal, 341,* c5814. doi:10.1136/bmj.c581 PMID:21081595

Greenlee, M. (2021). *Cybersecurity for Healthcare: Addressing Medical Image Privacy.* Available from https://securityintelligence.com/articles/cybersecurity-for-healthcare-problems-and-solutions/

Griggs, K. N., Ossipova, O., Kohlios, C. P., Baccarini, A. N., Howson, E. A., & Hayajneh, T. (2018). Healthcare blockchain system using smart contracts for secure automated remote patient monitoring. *Journal of Medical Systems, 42*(7), 130. doi:10.100710916-018-0982-x PMID:29876661

Grobauer, B., Walloschek, T., & Stocker, E. (2010). Understanding cloud computing vulnerabilities. *IEEE Security and Privacy, 9*(2), 50–57. doi:10.1109/MSP.2010.115

Grossfeld, B. (2020). *Deep learning vs ML14P: a simple way to understand the difference.* Zendesk. https://www.zendesk.com/blog/machine-learning-and-deep-learning/

Guendueza, A. A., Mettlerb, T., & Schedlera, K. (2020). Technological frames in public administration: What do public managers think of big data? *Government Information Quarterly, 37*(1), 101406. Advance online publication. doi:10.1016/j.giq.2019.101406

Guo, H., Li, W., Nejad, M., & Shen, C. C. (2019, July). Access control for electronic health records with hybrid blockchain-edge architecture. In *2019 IEEE International Conference on Blockchain (Blockchain)* (pp. 44-51). IEEE. 10.1109/Blockchain.2019.00015

Gupta, G. P., & Kulariya, M. (2016). A framework for fast and efficient cyber security network intrusion detection using apache spark. *Procedia Computer Science, 93*, 824–831. doi:10.1016/j.procs.2016.07.238

Gupta, R., Tanwar, S., Tyagi, S., Kumar, N., Obaidat, M. S., & Sadoun, B. (2019). Habits: Blockchain-based telesurgery framework for Healthcare 4.0. *2019 International Conference on Computer, Information and Telecommunication Systems (CITS)*, 1–5. 10.1109/CITS.2019.8862127

Gurinaviciute, J. (2021). 5 biggest cybersecurity threats: How hackers utilize remote work and human error to steal corporate data. *Security.* Retrieved from: https://www.securitymagazine.com/articles/94506-5-biggest-cybersecurity-threats

Guru99. (2021). *Data Science Tutorial for Beginners: What is, Basics & Process.* https://www.guru99.com/data-science-tutorial.html

Haaretz. (2020a). *Iran Says One of Two 'Large Scale' Cyber Attacks Targets Country's Ports.* Retrieved from https://www.haaretz.com/israel-news/tech-news/iran-says-one-of-two-cyber-attacks-targets-country-s-ports-1.9239908

Haaretz. (2020b). *UAE Hit With Cyberattacks in Response to Ties With Israel, Official Says.* Retrieved from https://www.haaretz.com/israel-news/tech-news/uae-hit-with-cyberattacks-in-wake-of-israel-deal-official-says-1.9351738

Hall, S. (2020). *What is digital transformation?* https://enterprisersproject.com/what-is-digital-transformation

Hamel, G. (2000). *Leading the revolution.* Harvard Business School Press.

Hamilton, S. (1997). E-commerce for the 21st century. *Computer, 30*(5), 44–47. doi:10.1109/2.589909

Han, W., Xue, J., Wang, Y., Huang, L., Kong, Z., & Mao, L. (2019). MalDAE: Detecting and explaining malware based on correlation and fusion of static and dynamic characteristics. *Computers & Security, 83*, 208–233. doi:10.1016/j.cose.2019.02.007

Harman, L. B., Flite, C. A., & Bond, K. (2012). Electronic Health Records: Privacy, Confidentiality, and Security. *AMA Journal of Ethics, 14*(9), 712–719. doi:10.1001/virtualmentor.2012.14.9.stas1-1209 PMID:23351350

Harman, T., Mahadevan, P., Mukherjee, K., Chandrashekar, P., Venkiteswaran, S., & Mukherjea, S. (2019). Cyber resiliency automation using blockchain. *2019 IEEE International Conference on Cloud Computing in Emerging Markets (CCEM)*, 51–54. 10.1109/CCEM48484.2019.00011

Harshalatha, P., & Mohanasundaram, R. (2020). Classification of malware detection using machine learning algorithms: A survey. *International Journal of Scientific and Technology Research, 9*(2), 1796–1802.

Hasan, H., Ladani, B. T., & Zamani, B. (2021). MEGDroid: A Model-Driven Event Generation Framework for Dynamic Android Malware Analysis. *Information and Software Technology, 135*, 106569. doi:10.1016/j.infsof.2021.106569

Hasan, M., Islam, M. M., Zarif, M. I. I., & Hashem, M. M. A. (2019). Attack and anomaly detection in IoT sensors in IoT sites using machine learning approaches. *Internet of Things, 7*, 100059. doi:10.1016/j.iot.2019.100059

Hasselgren, A., Kralevska, K., Gligoroski, D., Pedersen, S. A., & Faxvaag, A. (2020). Blockchain in healthcare and health sciences—A scoping review. *International Journal of Medical Informatics, 134*, 104040. doi:10.1016/j.ijmedinf.2019.104040 PMID:31865055

Hawk, S. (2004). Comparison of B2C e-commerce in developing countries. *Electronic Commerce Research, 14*(3), 181–199. doi:10.1023/B:ELEC.0000027979.91972.36

He, X., Xu, L., & Cha, C. (2018). Malicious JavaScript Code Detection Based on Hybrid Analysis. In *2018 25th Asia-Pacific Software Engineering Conference (APSEC)* (pp. 365–374). 10.1109/APSEC.2018.00051

Hellström, T. (2007). Critical infrastructure and systemic vulnerability: Towards a planning framework. *Safety Science, 45*(3), 415–430. doi:10.1016/j.ssci.2006.07.007

Henriette, E., Feki, M., & Boughzala, I. (2016). *Digital transformation challenges.* Paper presented at the Mediterranean Conference on Information Systems (MCIS), Samos, Greece.

Henriette, E., Feki, M., & Boughzala, I. (2015). The shape of digital transformation: a systematic literature review. *Ninth Mediterranean Conference on Information Systems (MCIS)*, 1-13.

Henry, R., Herzberg, A., & Kate, A. (2018). Blockchain access privacy: Challenges and directions. *IEEE Security and Privacy, 16*(4), 38–45. doi:10.1109/MSP.2018.3111245

Hershey, D. (2020). *Building an Enterprise Deep Learning Platform.* Determined AI. https://determined-ai.medium.com/building-a-deep-learning-platform-21a4a9dd90fe

Hettiarachchi, H. A. H. (2013). Factors affecting customer adoption of internet banking. *Kelaniya Journal of Management, 2*(2), 68–87. doi:10.4038/kjm.v2i2.6551

Hilbert, M. (2001). *Latin America on its path into the digital age: Where are we?* CEPAL/ECLAC.

Hines, P. (1993). Integrated materials management: The value chain redefined. *International Journal of Logistics Management, 4*(1), 13–22. doi:10.1108/09574099310804920

Hintze, A. (2016). Understanding the Four Types of Artificial Intelligence. *Government Technology.* Retrieved from: https://www.govtech.com/computing/Understanding-the-Four-Types-of-Artificial-Intelligence.html

HIPPA Journal. (2019). *2019 Healthcare Data Breach Report.* Available from https://www.hipaajournal.com/2019-healthcare-data-breach-report/

Hobbs, P. (2003). The Use of Evidentiality in Physicians' Progress Notes. *Discourse Studies, 5*(4), 451-478.

Holtz, M., David, B., Deus, F. E., de Sousa, R. T. Jr, & Laerte, P. (2011). *A formal classification of internet banking attacks and vulnerabilities.* Academic Press.

Holzhauer, B. (2021, January 11). Digital banking is the new normal in 2021: What to expect from banks. *Forbes.* https://www.forbes.com/advisor/banking/digital-banking-as-new-normal-2021-what-to-expect/

Hu, W., & Tan, Y. (2017). *Generating adversarial malware examples for black-box attacks based on gan.* arXiv:1702.05983.

Huang, L., Joseph, A. D., Nelson, B., Rubinstein, B. I., & Tygar, J. D. (2011). Adversarial machine learning. *Proceedings of the 4th ACM workshop on Security and artificial intelligence*, 43–58. 10.1145/2046684.2046692

Huitsing, P., Chandia, R., Papa, M., & Shenoi, S. (2008). Attack taxonomies for the Modbus protocols. *International Journal of Critical Infrastructure Protection, 1*, 37–44. doi:10.1016/j.ijcip.2008.08.003

Humayun, M., Mahmood Niazi, N. J., Alshayeb, M., & Mahmood, S. (2020). Cyber Security Threats and Vulnerabilities: A Systematic Mapping Study. *Arabian Journal for Science and Engineering*, *45*(4), 1–19. doi:10.100713369-019-04319-2

Hussein, A. H. (2019). Internet of things (IOT): Research challenges and future applications. *International Journal of Advanced Computer Science and Applications*, *10*(6), 77–82. doi:10.14569/IJACSA.2019.0100611

Hutchins, E. M., Clopp, M. J., & Amin, P. R. (2011). *Intelligence-driven computer network defense informed by analysis of adversary campaigns and intrusion kill chains*. Lockheed Martin Corporation.

Hyperledger Fabric. (2020a). *Blockchain network, 2.2*. https://hyperledger-fabric.readthedocs.io/en/release-2.2/network/network.html

Hyperledger Fabric. (2020b). *Membership Service Provider, 2.2*. https://hyperledger-fabric.readthedocs.io/en/release-2.2/membership/membership.html

Hyperledger Fabric. (2020c). *Private Data, 2.2*. https://hyperledger-fabric.readthedocs.io/en/release-2.2/private-data/private-data.html#what-is-a-private-data-collection

Ibarra, D., Igartua, J. I., & Ganzarain, J. (2018). *Engineering Digital Transformation*. Springer.

IBM Security. (2020). *New Destructive Wiper "ZeroCleare" Targets Energy Sector in the Middle East*. Retrieved from https://www.ibm.com/downloads/cas/OAJ4VZNJ

IBM. (2015a). *Modelling the Entity data architecture*. IBM.

IBM. (2021). *Today's chief security challenges*. Retrieved from: https://www.ibm.com/it-infrastructure/us-en/resources/power/it-security-challenges/

IBM. (2021). *What is quantum computing?* Retrieved from: https://www.ibm.com/quantum-computing/what-is-quantum-computing/

Identity Theft Resource Centre. (2018). *Data breach reports*. https://www.idtheftcenter.org/wp-content/uploads/2018/09/2018-August-Data-Breach-Package.pdf

Im, G. P., & Baskerville, R. L. (2005). A longitudinal study of information system threat categories: The enduring problem of human error. *ACM SIGMIS Database: the DATABASE for Advances in Information Systems*, *36*(4), 68–79. doi:10.1145/1104004.1104010

Imtiaz, S. I., Rehman, S., Javed, A. R., Jalil, Z., Liu, X., & Alnumay, W. S. (2021). DeepAMD: Detection and identification of Android malware using high-efficient Deep Artificial Neural Network. *Future Generation Computer Systems*, *115*, 844–856. doi:10.1016/j.future.2020.10.008

Innovation and Networks Executive Agency. (2015). *Connecting public services to the Spanish eIDAS node*. Retrieved from: https://ec.europa.eu/inea/en/connecting-europe-facility/cef-telecom/2015-es-ia-0087

Innovation and Networks Executive Agency. (2016). *eIDAS2Business: Making private businesses benefit from eIDAS*. Retrieved from: https://ec.europa.eu/inea/en/connecting-europe-facility/cef-telecom/2016-eu-ia-0066

Innovation and Networks Executive Agency. (2018). *Authentication and eSignature in Portuguese services*. Retrieved from: https://ec.europa.eu/inea/en/connecting-europe-facility/cef-telecom/2018-pt-ia-0045

Innovation and Networks Executive Agency. (2019a). *CEF Telecom 2019 Report*. Retrieved from: https://ec.europa.eu/inea/sites/inea/files/cefpub/cef-telecom-brochure-2019-final_web.pdf

Innovation and Networks Executive Agency. (2019b). *Trust Services and Electronic identification.* Retrieved from: https://ec.europa.eu/digital-single-market/en/trust-services-and-eid

Innovation and Networks Executive Agency. (2019c). *eID Documentation*: Country overview Retrieved from: https://ec.europa.eu/cefdigital/wiki/display/CEFDIGITAL/Country+overview

Innovation and Networks Executive Agency. IEA (2017). *Development of an eIDAS – openNCP Connector for cross border eHealth.* Retrieved from: https://ec.europa.eu/inea/en/connecting-europe-facility/cef-telecom/2017-eu-ia-0044

Intel. (2019). *Intel in Israel.* Retrieved from https://www.intel.com/content/www/us/en/corporate-responsibility/intel-in-israel.html

International Monetary Fund. (2008). *Chapter 2 - Understanding remittances: Demography, transaction channels, and regulatory aspects.* https://www.imf.org/external/np/sta/bop/2008/rcg/pdf/ch2.pdf

International Monetary Fund. (2017). *World Economic Outlook Database.* https://www.imf.org/external/pubs/ft/weo/2017/01/weodata/index.aspx

International Organization for Standardization. (2014). *ISO 37120:2014: Sustainable development of communities-Indicators for city services and quality of life.* International Organization for Standardization. Retrieved from: https://www.iso.org/standard/62436.html

International Organization for Standardization. (2018). *ISO 37120:2018: Sustainable Cities and Communities-Indicators for City Services and Quality of Life.* Retrieved from: https://www.iso.org/standard/68498.html

International Organization for Standardization. (2019). *ISO 37122:2019: Sustainable Cities and Communities — Indicators for Smart Cities.* Retrieved from: https://www.iso.org/standard/69050.html

Internet World Stats. (2018). *World Internet Users and 2018 Population Stats.* https://www.internetworldstats.com/stats.htm

Ismail, M., Shaaban, M. F., Naidu, M., & Serpedin, E. (2020). Deep learning detection of electricity theft cyber-attacks in renewable distributed generation. *IEEE Transactions on Smart Grid, 11*(4), 3428–3437. doi:10.1109/TSG.2020.2973681

Israel Cyber Alliance. (2021). *Cyber security is Israel.* Retrieved from https://israelcyberalliance.com/cyber-security-in-israel-2/

Israel Innovation Authority - Startup Nation Central. (2019). *High Tech Human Capital Report 2019.* Retrieved from https://www.startupnationcentral.org/wp-content/uploads/2020/02/Start-Up-Nation-Centrals-High-Tech-Human-Capital-Report-2019-2.pdf

Israel National Cyber Directorate. (2019). *Best Practices Hardening Computer Systems.* Retrieved from https://www.gov.il/BlobFolder/generalpage/hardingcomputersystem/en/hardening.pdf

Israel National Cyber Directorate. (2020). *Draft public address on improvements and additions to defense theory.* Retrieved from https://www.gov.il/he/departments/publications/Call_for_bids/tohag_draft

Israel National Cyber Directorate. (2020). *The Israeli cyber industry continues to grow: record fundraising in 2020.* Retrieved from https://www.gov.il/en/departments/news/2020ind

Israel National Cyber Directorate. (2020). *The Israeli Police Cyber Unit arrested suspects of stealing hundreds of thousands of ILS from Israeli citizens.* Retrieved from https://www.gov.il/en/departments/news/accounttakeover

Israel National Cyber Directorate. (2021). *Cyber protection for the organization.* Retrieved from https://www.gov.il/he/departments/topics/organization_cyber_protection

IT Governance. (2021). *What is cyber security? Definition and best practices.* https://www.itgovernance.co.uk/what-is-cybersecurity

IUCC. (2021). *Inter-University Computation Center Cyber & Data Security Services.* Retrieved from https://www.iucc.ac.il/en/infrastructuretechnologies/cyber/

Jain, E., & Lamba, J. (2021). Management and Digitalization Strategy for Transforming Education Sector: An Emerging Gateway Persuaded by COVID-19. In Emerging Challenges, Solutions, and Best Practices for Digital Enterprise Transformation (pp. 69-83). IGI Global.

Jain, E. (2020). Digital Employability Skills and Training Needs for the Indian Healthcare Industry. In *Opportunities and Challenges in Digital Healthcare Innovation* (pp. 113–130). IGI Global. doi:10.4018/978-1-7998-3274-4.ch007

Jain, E., & Lamba, J. (2020). Covid-19: Economic Hardship and Financial Distress in Indian Economy. *International Journal of Disaster Recovery and Business Continuity*, *11*(3), 3081–3092.

Jalali, M. S., & Kaiser, J. P. (2018). Cybersecurity in Hospitals: A Systematic, Organizational Perspective. *Journal of Medical Internet Research*, *20*(5), e10059. doi:10.2196/10059 PMID:29807882

Jalali, M. S., Razak, S., Gordon, W., Perakslis, E., & Madnick, S. (2019). Health care and cybersecurity: Bibliometric analysis of the literature. *Journal of Medical Internet Research*, *21*(2), e12644. doi:10.2196/12644 PMID:30767908

Jang-Jaccard, J., & Nepal, S. (2014). A survey of emerging threats in cybersecurity. *Journal of Computer and System Sciences, 80*(5), 973-993. doi:10.1016/j.jcss.2014.02.005

Järvinen, P. (2007). Action Research is Similar to Design Science. *Quality & Quantity, 41*(1), 37–54. Retrieved August 10, 2018, from https://link.springer.com/article/10.1007/s11135-005-5427-1

Jaszkiewicz, J., & Sowiñski, R. (1999). The 'Light Beam Search' approach - an overview of methodology and applications. *European Journal of Operational Research*, *113*(2), 300–314. doi:10.1016/S0377-2217(98)00218-5

Javaid, U., Siang, A. K., Aman, M. N., & Sikdar, B. (2018, June). Mitigating IoT device based DDoS attacks using blockchain. In *Proceedings of the 1st Workshop on Cryptocurrencies and Blockchains for Distributed Systems* (pp. 71-76). 10.1145/3211933.3211946

Jayaram, A. (2016). Lean six sigma approach for global supply chain management using industry 4.0 and IIoT. In *2016 2nd international conference on contemporary computing and informatics (IC3I)* (pp. 89-94). IEEE.

Jerman-Blažič, B. (2008). An economic modelling approach to information security risk management. *International Journal of Information Management*, *28*(5), 413–422. doi:10.1016/j.ijinfomgt.2008.02.002

Joffre, T. (2020). *State comptroller to review preparedness for cyberattack on elections.* The Jerusalem Post. Retrieved from https://www.jpost.com/israel-news/state-comptroller-to-review-preparedness-for-cyberattack-on-elections-651380

Johnston, A. C., Warkentin, M., McBride, M., & Carter, L. (2017). Dispositional and situational factors: Influences on information security policy violations. *European Journal of Information Systems*, *25*(3), 231–251. doi:10.1057/ejis.2015.15

Jones, M. D., Hutcheson, S., & Camba, J. D. (2021). Past, present, and future barriers to digital transformation in manufacturing: A review. *Journal of Manufacturing Systems*. Advance online publication. doi:10.1016/j.jmsy.2021.03.006

Juma'h, A. H., & Alnsour, Y. (2020). The effect of data breaches on company performance. *International Journal of Accounting & Information Management*, *28*(2), 275–301. doi:10.1108/IJAIM-01-2019-0006

Kabir, O. (2020). *UAE views Israel as a strategic cybersecurity partner, says head of national cyber authority.* Calcalist. Retrieved from https://www.calcalistech.com/ctech/articles/0,7340,L-3874096,00.html

Kadoguchi, M., Kobayashi, H., Hayashi, S., Otsuka, A., & Hashimoto, M. (2020, November). Deep Self-Supervised Clustering of the Dark Web for Cyber Threat Intelligence. In *2020 IEEE International Conference on Intelligence and Security Informatics (ISI)* (pp. 1-6). IEEE.

Kahan, R. (2020). *Pay2Key hackers claim they breached IAI servers.* Calcalist. Retrieved from https://www.calcalistech.com/ctech/articles/0,7340,L-3883010,00.html

Kakkar, A. (2020). A survey on secure communication techniques for 5G wireless heterogeneous networks. *Information Fusion, 62,* 89–109. doi:10.1016/j.inffus.2020.04.009

Kalkan, K., & Rasmussen, K. (2020). TruSD: Trust framework for service discovery among IoT devices. *Computer Networks, 178*(4).

Kalla, A., Hewa, T., Mishra, R. A., Ylianttila, M., & Liyanage, M. (2020). The role of blockchain to fight against COVID-19. *IEEE Engineering Management Review, 48*(3), 85–96. doi:10.1109/EMR.2020.3014052

Kamble, S. S., Gunasekaran, A., Kumar, V., Belhadi, A., & Foropon, C. (2021). A machine learning based approach for predicting blockchain adoption in supply Chain. *Technological Forecasting and Social Change, 163,* 120465. doi:10.1016/j.techfore.2020.120465

Kamiya, S., Kang, J-K., Jungmin, K., Milidonis, A., & Stulz, R. M. (2020). Risk management, firm reputation, and the impact of successful cyberattacks on target firms. *Journal of Financial Economics.*

Kane, Palmer, Phillips, Kiron, & Buckley. (2015). Strategy, Not Technology, Drives Digital Transformation. MIT Sloan Management Review and Deloitte University Press.

Kapoor, A. (2021). *Artificial Intelligence and Machine Learning: 5 Trends to Watch Out for in 2021. AI Zone.* DZone. https://dzone.com/articles/artificial-intelligence-amp-machine-learning-5-dev

Karlsson, F., Holgersson, J., Söderström, E., & Hedström, K. (2012). Exploring user participation approaches in public e-service development. *Government Information Quarterly, 29*(2), 158–168. doi:10.1016/j.giq.2011.07.009

Katz, F. H. (2006). The effect of a university information security survey on instruction methods in information security. *Proceedings of the 2nd annual conference on Information security curriculum development,* 43-48.

Kaur, S., & Randhawa, S. (2020). Dark Web: A Web of Crimes. *Wireless Personal Communications, 112*(4), 2131–2158. doi:10.100711277-020-07143-2

Kawai, N. (2019). Historical transition of psychological theories of fear: The view of fear in behaviorism. In *The Fear of Snakes* (pp. 1–18). Springer. doi:10.1007/978-981-13-7530-9_1

Kaynak, E., Tatoglu, E., & Kula, V. (2005). An analysis of the factors affecting the adoption of electronic commerce by SMEs: Evidence from an emerging market. *International Marketing Review, 22*(6), 632–640. doi:10.1108/02651330510630258

Kelly, S., & Resnick-Ault, J. (2021). One password allowed hackers to disrupt Colonial Pipeline, CEO tells senators. "Not a Colonial123-type password. *IT News.* Retrieved from: https://www.itnews.com.au/news/one-password-allowed-hackers-to-disrupt-colonial-pipeline-ceo-tells-senators-565

Kelly, J. M. (2020). Australia would benefit from US-Style health Information Security regulation. *The Journal of Law and Technology, 1*(2), 1–24.

Kemmerer, R. A. (2003). Cybersecurity. In *25th International Conference on Software Engineering, 2003. Proceedings.* (pp. 705-715). IEEE. 10.1109/ICSE.2003.1201257

Kenny, C. (2003a). Development's false divide. *Foreign Policy,* (134), 76–77. doi:10.2307/3183524

Kenny, C. (2003b). The internet and economic growth in less-developed countries: A case of managing expectations? *Oxford Development Studies*, *31*(1), 99–113. doi:10.1080/1360081032000047212

Kephart, J. O. (2005). *Research challenges of autonomic computing*. IBM Research. https://domino.research.ibm.com/library/cyberdig.nsf/papers/5E932DBBECF5EBCF85257067004EE94C/$File/rc23692.pdf

Kerai, P., Wood, P., & Martin, M. (2014). A pilot study on the views of elderly regional Australians of personally controlled electronic health records. *International Journal of Medical Informatics*, *83*(3), 201–209. doi:10.1016/j.ijmedinf.2013.12.001 PMID:24382474

Khan, P., & Anwar, M. (2020). *Cybersecurity In Pakistan: Regulations, Gaps And A Way Forward*. Massey University. https://mro.massey.ac.nz/bitstream/handle/10179/16061/114-Article%20Text-223-1-10-20210122.pdf?sequence=1&isAllowed=y

Khan, S. (2009). *Adoption issues of internet banking in Pakistani' firms* (Unpublished Master Thesis). Lulea University of Technology, Lulea, Sweden.

Khezr, S., Moniruzzaman, M., Yassine, A., & Benlamri, R. (2019). Blockchain technology in healthcare: A comprehensive review and directions for future research. *Applied Sciences (Basel, Switzerland)*, *9*(9), 1736. doi:10.3390/app9091736

Khraisat, A., & Alazab, A. (2021). A critical review of intrusion detection systems in the internet of things: Techniques, deployment strategy, validation strategy, attacks, public datasets and challenges. *Cybersecurity*, *4*(1), 18. doi:10.118642400-021-00077-7

Khrais, L. T. (2015). Highlighting the vulnerabilities of the online banking system. *Journal of Internet Banking and Commerce*, *20*(3). Advance online publication. doi:10.4172/1204-5357.1000120

Kierkegaard, P. (2011). Electronic health record: Wiring Europe's healthcare. *Computer Law & Security Review*, *27*(5), 503–515. doi:10.1016/j.clsr.2011.07.013

Kim, H., Kang, E., Broman, D., & Lee, E. A. (2020). Resilient Authentication and Authorization for the Internet of Things (IoT) Using Edge Computing. *ACM Transactions on Internet of Things*, *1*(1), 1–27. doi:10.1145/3375837

Kim, H., & Lee, E. A. (2017). Authentication and Authorization for the Internet of Things. *IT Professional*, *19*(5), 27–33. doi:10.1109/MITP.2017.3680960

Kim, K., & Kim, K. (1999). Routing straddle carriers for the loading operation of containers using a beam search algorithm. Elsevier. *Computers & Industrial Engineering*, *36*(1), 109–136. doi:10.1016/S0360-8352(99)00005-4

Kim, M. I., & Johnston, K. B. (2002). Personal Health Records: Evaluation of Functionality and Utility. *Journal of the American Medical Informatics Association: JAMIA*, *9*(2), 171–180. doi:10.1197/jamia.M0978 PMID:11861632

King, B. (2012). *Bank 3.0: Why banking is no longer somewhere you go but something you do*. Wiley. doi:10.1002/9781119198918

Kiyavash, N., Koushanfar, F., Coleman, T. P., & Rodrigues, M. (2013). A timing channel spyware for the CSMA/CA protocol. *IEEE Transactions on Information Forensics and Security*, *8*(3), 477–487. doi:10.1109/TIFS.2013.2238930

Klonoff, D. (2017). Fog computing and edge computing architectures for processing data from diabetes devices connected to the medical Internet of Things. *Journal of Diabetes Science and Technology*, *11*(4), 647–652. doi:10.1177/1932296817717007 PMID:28745086

Knapp, K. J., Marshall, T. E., Morrow, D. W., & Rainer, R. K. (2006). The Top Information Security Issues Facing Organizations: What Can Government Do to Help? *Information System Security*, *15*(4), 51–58. doi:10.1201/1086.106 5898X/46353.15.4.20060901/95124.6

Kogosowski, M. (2021). *UAE cyber security head calls for joint exercise with Israel*. Israel Defense. Retrieved from https://www.israeldefense.co.il/en/node/49182

Koi, T. (2020). *Kiberfegyvereket loptak el a FireEye-től* [Cyberweapons stolen from FireEye]. HWSW. Retrieved from https://www.hwsw.hu/hirek/62656/fireeye-red-team-betores-hacker-kiberbiztonsag.html

Komba, M. M., & Lwoga, E. T. (2020). *Systematic review as a research method in library and information science..* doi:10.4018/978-1-7998-1471-9.ch005

Kopp, E., Kaffenberger, L., & Wilson, C. (2017). *Cyber Risk, Market Failures, and Financial Stability, Working Paper*. International Monetary Fund (WP/17/185).

Koroniotis, N., Moustafa, N., & Sitnikova, E. (2020). A new network forensic framework based on deep learning for Internet of Things networks: A particle deep framework. *Future Generation Computer Systems*, *110*, 91–106. doi:10.1016/j.future.2020.03.042

Kotey, B., & Meredith, G. G. (1997). Relationships among owner/manager personal values, business strategies, and enterprise performance. *Journal of Small Business Management*, *35*, 37–64.

Kranz, J., & Haeussinger, F. (2013). Information security awareness: its antecedents and mediating effects on security compliant behavior. *International Conference on Information Systems*, 1-16.

Krawiec, R., & White, M. (2016). *Blockchain: Opportunities for health care*. Available from: https://www2.deloitte.com/content/dam/Deloitte/us/Documents/public-sector/us-blockchainopportunities-for-health-care.pdf

Krombholz, K., Hobel, H., Huber, M., & Weippl, E. (2015). Advanced social engineering attacks. *Journal of Information Security and Applications, 22*, 113-122.

Krunger, H. A., & Kearney, W. D. (2006). A prototype of assessing information security awareness. *Computers & Security*, *25*(4), 289–296. doi:10.1016/j.cose.2006.02.008

Kshetri, N. (2007). Barriers to e-commerce and competitive business models in developing countries: A case study. *Electronic Commerce Research and Applications*, *6*(4), 443–452. doi:10.1016/j.elerap.2007.02.004

Kuisma, T., Laukkanen, T., & Hiltunen, M. (2007). Mapping the reasons for resistance to internet banking: A means-end approach. *International Journal of Information Management*, *27*(2), 75–85. doi:10.1016/j.ijinfomgt.2006.08.006

Kumar, D., & Sanicola, L. (2021). Pipeline outage causes U.S. gasoline supply crunch, panic buying. *Reuters*. Retrieved from: https://www.reuters.com/business/energy/us-fuel-supplies-tighten-energy-pipeline-outage-enters-fifth-day-2021-05-11/

Kumar, N., Mukhopadhyay, S., Gupta, M., Handa, A., & Shukla, S. K. (2019). Malware Classification using Early Stage Behavioral Analysis. In *2019 14th Asia Joint Conference on Information Security (AsiaJCIS)*. IEEE. 10.1109/AsiaJCIS.2019.00-10

Kumar, T., Ramani, V., Ahmad, I., Braeken, A., Harjula, E., & Ylianttila, M. (2018, September). Blockchain utilization in healthcare: Key requirements and challenges. In *2018 IEEE 20th International Conference on e-Health Networking, Applications and Services (Healthcom)* (pp. 1-7). IEEE.

Kumar, J., Kumar, M., Pandey, D. K., & Raj, R. (2021). Encryption and Authentication of Data Using the IPSEC Protocol. In *Proceedings of the Fourth International Conference on Microelectronics, Computing and Communication Systems* (pp. 855-862). Springer.

Kumar, N. M., & Mallick, P. K. (2018). Blockchain technology for security issues and challenges in IoT. *Procedia Computer Science, 132*, 1815–1823. doi:10.1016/j.procs.2018.05.140

Kuo, W., Liu, T., & Wang, C. (2019). Study on Android Hybrid Malware Detection Based on Machine Learning. In *2019 IEEE 4th International Conference on Computer and Communication Systems (ICCCS)* (pp. 31–35). 10.1109/CCOMS.2019.8821665

Kuo, T. T., Kim, H. E., & Ohno-Machado, L. (2017). Blockchain distributed ledger technologies for biomedical and health care applications. *Journal of the American Medical Informatics Association: JAMIA, 24*(6), 1211–1220. doi:10.1093/jamia/ocx068 PMID:29016974

Kurakin, A., Goodfellow, I., & Bengio, S. (2016). Adversarial machine learning at scale. arXiv preprint arXiv:1611.01236.

LalarS.BhushanS.SurenderM. (2020). Hybrid Encryption Algorithm to Detect Clone Node Attack in Wireless Sensor Network. *Available at* SSRN 3565864. doi:10.2139srn.3565864

Lallie, H. S., Shepherd, L. A., Nurse, J. R. C., Erola, A., Epiphaniou, G., Maple, C., & Bellekens, X. (2021). Cyber security in the age of COVID-19: A timeline and analysis of cyber-crime and cyber-attacks during the pandemic. *Computers & Security, 105*. doi:10.1016/j.cose.2021.102248

Lallmahamood, M. (2007). An examination of an individual's perceived security and privacy of the internet in Malaysia and the influence of this on their intention to use e-commerce: Using an extension of the technology acceptance model. *Journal of Internet Banking and Commerce, 12*(3), 1–26.

Langer, G. (2017). Cybersecurity Issues in Healthcare Information Technology. *Journal of Digital Imaging, 30*(1), 117–125. doi:10.100710278-016-9913-x PMID:27730416

Latif, S., Idrees, Z., Zou, Z., & Ahmad, J. (2020, August). DRaNN: A Deep Random Neural Network Model for Intrusion Detection in Industrial IoT. In *2020 International Conference on UK-China Emerging Technologies (UCET)* (pp. 1-4). IEEE. 10.1109/UCET51115.2020.9205361

Latif, S., Zou, Z., Idrees, Z., & Ahmad, J. (2020). A Novel Attack Detection Scheme for the Industrial Internet of Things Using a Lightweight Random Neural Network. *IEEE Access: Practical Innovations, Open Solutions, 8*, 89337–89350. doi:10.1109/ACCESS.2020.2994079

Laudon, K. C., & Traver, C. G. (2001). *E-commerce: Business, technology, society.* Addison-Wesley.

Laukkanen, T., Sinkkonen, S., & Laukkanen, P. (2009). Communication strategies to overcome functional and psychological resistance to Internet banking. *International Journal of Information Management, 29*(2), 111–118. doi:10.1016/j.ijinfomgt.2008.05.008

Lautman, O. (2015). *Israeli Business Culture.* Academic Press.

Lazar, I., Motogna, S., & Parv, B. (2010). Behaviour-Driven Development of Foundational UML Components. Department of Computer Science. Babes-Bolyai University. Cluj-Napoca, Romania. doi:10.1016/j.entcs.2010.07.007

Lee, M. C. (2009). Factors influencing the adoption of internet banking: An integration of TAM and TPB with perceived risk and perceived benefit. *Electronic Commerce Research and Applications, 8*(3), 130–141. doi:10.1016/j.elerap.2008.11.006

Lehnbom, E. C., McLachlan, A., & Brien, J. A. (2012). A qualitative study of Australians' opinions about personally controlled electronic health records. *Studies in Health Technology and Informatics*, *178*, 105–110. PMID:22797027

Leichman, A. K. (2018). *The Israeli high-school kids earning high-tech salaries*. Israel21C. Retrieved from https://www.israel21c.org/the-israeli-high-school-kids-earning-high-tech-salaries/

Leitch, R., & Day, Ch. (2000). *Action research and reflective practice: towards a holistic view*. Taylor & Francis. Retrieved February 10, 2018, from https://www.tandfonline.com/doi/ref/10.1080/09650790000200108?scroll=top

Leitold, H. (2011). Challenges of eID Interoperability: The STORK Project. In S. Fischer-Hübner, P. Duquenoy, M. Hansen, R. Leenes, & G. Zhang (Eds.), *Privacy and Identity Management for Life. Privacy and Identity 2010. IFIP Advances in Information and Communication Technology, 352*. Springer. doi:10.1007/978-3-642-20769-3_12

Levush, R. (2019). *Israel: Knesset Passes Amendment Law Recognizing Role of National Cyber Directorate in Protecting Cyberspace*. The Library of Congress. Retrieved from https://www.loc.gov/law/foreign-news/article/israel-knesset-passes-amendment-law-recognizing-role-of-national-cyber-directorate-in-protecting-cyberspace/

Liang, C., Shanmugam, B., Azam, S., Jonkman, M., De Boer, F., & Narayansamy, G. (2019b, March). Intrusion Detection System for Internet of Things based on a Machine Learning approach. In *2019 International Conference on Vision Towards Emerging Trends in Communication and Networking (ViTECoN)* (pp. 1-6). IEEE. 10.1109/ViTECoN.2019.8899448

Liang, F., Hatcher, W. G., Liao, W., Gao, W., & Yu, W. (2019a). Machine Learning for Security and the Internet of Things: The Good, the Bad, and the Ugly. *IEEE Access: Practical Innovations, Open Solutions*, *7*, 158126–158147. doi:10.1109/ACCESS.2019.2948912

Li, F., Lu, H., Hou, M., Cui, K., & Darbandi, M. (2021). Customer satisfaction with bank services: The role of cloud services, security, e-learning and service quality. *Technology in Society*, *64*, 101487. doi:10.1016/j.techsoc.2020.101487

Lin, C. H., Pao, H. K., & Liao, J. W. (2018). Efficient dynamic malware analysis using virtual time control mechanics. *Computers & Security*, *73*, 359–373. doi:10.1016/j.cose.2017.11.010

Lin, C. H., Tien, C. W., Chen, C. W., Tien, C. W., & Pao, H. K. (2015, September). Efficient spear-phishing threat detection using hypervisor monitor. In *2015 International Carnahan Conference on Security Technology (ICCST)* (pp. 299-303). IEEE. 10.1109/CCST.2015.7389700

Lindgren, I., & Gabriella Jansson, G. (2013). Electronic services in the public sector: A conceptual framework. *Government Information Quarterly*, *30*(2), 163–172. doi:10.1016/j.giq.2012.10.005

Linn, C., & Debray, S. (2003, October). Obfuscation of executable code to improve resistance to static disassembly. In *Proceedings of the 10th ACM conference on Computer and communications security* (pp. 290-299). 10.1145/948109.948149

Liu, Y., Zhang, Y., Li, H., & Chen, X. (2016). A hybrid malware detecting scheme for mobile Android applications. In *2016 IEEE International Conference on Consumer Electronics (ICCE)* (pp. 155–156). 10.1109/ICCE.2016.7430561

Liverani, M. (2013). *The ancient Near East: History, society, and economy*. Routledge. doi:10.4324/9781315879895

Llopis-Albert, C., Rubio, F., & Valero, F. (2021). Impact of digital transformation on the automotive industry. *Technological Forecasting and Social Change*, *162*, 120343. doi:10.1016/j.techfore.2020.120343 PMID:33052150

Lockwood, R. (2018). *Introduction The Relational Data Model*. Retrieved January 29, 2019, from http://www.jakobsens.dk/Nekrologer.htm

Loginovskiy, O. V., Dranko, O. I., & Hollay, A. V. (2018). *Mathematical Models for Decision-Making on Strategic Management of Industrial Enterprise in Conditions of Instability*. Conference: Internationalization of Education in Applied Mathematics and Informatics for HighTech Applications (EMIT 2018). Leipzig, Germany.

Luck, M. (2019). Entrapment behind the firewall: the ethics of internal cyber-sting. *Australasian Journal of Information Systems, 23*. Retrieved from: https://journal.acs.org.au/index.php/ajis/article/view/1886/843

Luo, Z., Zhao, S., Lu, Z., Sagduyu, Y. E., & Xu, J. (2020, July). Adversarial machine learning based partial-model attack in IoT. *Proceedings of the 2nd ACM Workshop on Wireless Security and Machine Learning.*

Lyngaas, S. (2020). *Israel, UAE say they're allies in cyberspace. They have plenty of tech power to draw upon.* Cyber-Scoop. Retrieved from https://www.cyberscoop.com/israel-uae-cybersecurity-deal-tech-firms/

Lytras, M. D., & Şerban, A. C. (2020). E-Government Insights to Smart Cities Research: European Union (EU) Study and the Role of Regulations. *IEEE Access: Practical Innovations, Open Solutions, 8*, 65313–65326. doi:10.1109/ACCESS.2020.2982737

MacGregor, R., & Kartiwi, M. (2010). Perception of barriers to e-commerce adoption in SMEs in a developed and developing country: A comparison between Australia and Indonesia. *Journal of Electronic Commerce in Organizations, 8*(1), 61–82. doi:10.4018/jeco.2010103004

Mahmood, Y. N. (2019). The impact of quality service factors on banking service sector case study in Erbil banks. *Tikrit Journal of Administration and Economics Sciences, 2*(42).

Majaski, C. (2019, April 9). *Retail banking vs. corporate banking: What's the difference?* Investopedia. https://www.investopedia.com/articles/general/071213/retail-banking-vs-commercial-banking.asp

Malhotra, P., Singh, Y., Anand, P., Bangotra, D. K., Singh, P. K., & Hong, W. C. (2021). Internet of Things: Evolution, Concerns and Security Challenges. *Sensors (Basel), 21*(5), 1809. doi:10.339021051809 PMID:33807724

Malware Statistics & Trends Report | AV-TEST. (n.d.). Retrieved April 19, 2021, from https://www.av-test.org/en/statistics/malware/

Mamonov, S., & Benbunan-Fich, R. (2018). The impact of information security threat awareness on privacy-protective behaviors. *Computers in Human Behavior, 83*, 32–44. doi:10.1016/j.chb.2018.01.028

Mantoo, B. A., & Khurana, S. S. (2020). Static, Dynamic and Intrinsic Features Based Android Malware Detection Using Machine Learning. In P. K. Singh, A. K. Kar, Y. Singh, M. H. Kolekar, & S. Tanwar (Eds.), *Proceedings of ICRIC 2019* (pp. 31–45). Cham: Springer International Publishing. 10.1007/978-3-030-29407-6_4

Manuel, J., Joven, R., & Durando, D. (2018, February). OMG: Mirai-based Bot Turns IoT Devices into Proxy Servers. *Fortinet.* doi:10.1145/3395352.3402619

Marcus, J. (2020). *Iran navy 'friendly fire' incident kills 19 sailors in Gulf of Oman.* BBC. Retrieved from https://www.bbc.com/news/world-middle-east-52612511

Margit, M. (2020). *Israel to launch 'Cyber Defense Shield' for health sector.* The Jerusalem Post. Retrieved from https://www.jpost.com/israel-news/israel-to-launch-cyber-defense-shield-for-health-sector-627304

Markopoulou, D., Papakonstantinou, V., & Hert, P. (2019). The new EU cybersecurity framework: The NIS Directive, ENISA's role and the General Data Protection Regulation. *Computer Law & Security Review, 35*(6), 105336. Advance online publication. doi:10.1016/j.clsr.2019.06.007

Marous, J. (2021, March 29). The evolution of banking: 2021 and beyond. *The Financial Brand.* https://thefinancialbrand.com/111080/evolution-future-digital-banking-baas-transformation/

Marshall, T. (2016). *A földrajz fogságában ("Prisoners of Geography").* Park Könyvkiadó.

Martin, N. (2021). *Israeli entrepreneurs have starting building larger companies.* Israel Hayom. Retrieved from https://www.israelhayom.com/2021/04/04/israeli-cyber-startups-ride-covid-wave-with-no-sign-of-stopping/

Martin, G., Martin, P., Hankin, C., Darzi, A., & Kinross, J. (2017). Cybersecurity and healthcare: How safe are we? *BMJ (Clinical Research Ed.), 358.* doi:10.1136/bmj.j3179 PMID:28684400

Martin, J., Munksgaard, R., Coomber, R., Demant, J., & Barratt, M. J. (2020). Selling drugs on darkweb cryptomarkets: Differentiated pathways, risks and rewards. *British Journal of Criminology, 60*(3), 559–578. doi:10.1093/bjc/azz075

Martins, A. I., Queirós, A., Silva, A. G., & Rocha, N. P. (2015). Usability evaluation methods: a systematic review. *Human Factors in Software Development and Design,* 250-273.

Martins, N., Cruz, J. M., Cruz, T., & Abreu, P. H. (2020). Adversarial machine learning applied to intrusion and malware scenarios: A systematic review. *IEEE Access: Practical Innovations, Open Solutions, 8,* 35403–35419. doi:10.1109/ACCESS.2020.2974752

Martins, R. P. (2018). Punching Above Their Digital Weight: Why Iran is Developing Cyberwarfare Capabilities Far Beyond Expectations. *International Journal of Cyber Warfare & Terrorism, 8*(2), 32–46. doi:10.4018/IJCWT.2018040103

Massachusetts Institute of Technology. (2020). Can We Escape the Technology Trap? Carl Frey interview by Paul Michelman. *MIT Sloan Management Review's Three Big Points podcast.* Massachusetts Institute of Technology. Retrieved from: https://sloanreview.mit.edu/audio/can-we-escape-the-technology-trap/

Matarazzo, M., Penco, L., Profumo, G., & Quaglia, R. (2021). Digital transformation and customer value creation in Made in Italy SMEs: A dynamic capabilities perspective. *Journal of Business Research, 123,* 642–656. doi:10.1016/j.jbusres.2020.10.033

Mathivathanan, D., Mathiyazhagan, K., Rana, N. P., Khorana, S., & Dwivedi, Y. K. (2021). Barriers to the adoption of blockchain technology in business supply chains: A total interpretive structural modelling (TISM) approach. *International Journal of Production Research,* 1–22.

Mathy, C., Pascal, C., Fizesan, M., Boin, C., Délèze, N., & Aujoulat, O. (2020, July). Automated hospital pharmacy supply chain and the evaluation of organisational impacts and costs. In Supply chain forum: An international journal (Vol. 21, No. 3, pp. 206-218). Taylor & Francis.

Matricano, D. (2021). Digital Business Transformations: An Investigation About Business-Driven and Technology-Enabled Strategies. In Handbook of Research on Management and Strategies for Digital Enterprise Transformation (pp. 173-195). IGI Global.

Matt, C., Hess, T., & Benlian, A. (2015). Digital transformation strategies. *Business & Information Systems Engineering, 57*(5), 339–343. doi:10.100712599-015-0401-5

Ma, Y., & Fang, Y. (2020). Current status, issues, and challenges of blockchain applications in education. *International Journal of Emerging Technologies in Learning, 15*(12), 20–31. doi:10.3991/ijet.v15i12.13797

McAfee, A., & Brynjolfsson, E. (2017). *Machine, Platform, Crowd: Harnessing Our Digital Future* (1st ed.). Kindle Edition.

McCorduck, P., Minsky, M., Selfridge, O. G., & Simon, H. A. (1977, August). History of Artificial Intelligence. In IJCAI (pp. 951-954). Academic Press.

McGhin, T., Choo, K. K. R., Liu, C. Z., & He, D. (2019). Blockchain in healthcare applications: Research challenges and opportunities. *Journal of Network and Computer Applications, 135*, 62–75. doi:10.1016/j.jnca.2019.02.027

McGraw, G., & Morrisett, G. (2000). Attacking malicious code: A report to the infosec research council. *IEEE Software, 17*(5), 33–41. doi:10.1109/52.877857

McKee, K., Kaffenberger, M., & Zimmerman, J. (2015). *Doing digital finance right: The case for stronger mitigation of customer risks.* Focus Note 103, CGAP. Retrieved from https://www.cgap.org/sites/default/files/Focus-Note-Doing-Digital-FinanceRight

McQuade, S. C. (2006). *Understanding and managing cybercrime.* Pearson/Allyn and Bacon.

Medhekar, A. (2021). Digital Health Innovation Enhancing Patient Experience in Medical Travel. In *Research Anthology on Telemedicine Efficacy, Adoption, and Impact on Healthcare Delivery. Edition1* (pp. 199–223). IGI Global. doi:10.4018/978-1-7998-8052-3.ch011

Medhekar, A., & Nguyen, J. (2020). My Digital Healthcare Record: Innovation, Challenge and Patient Empowerment. In K. Sandhu (Ed.), *Opportunities and Challenges in Digital Healthcare Innovation* (pp. 131–150). IGI Global., doi:10.4018/978-1-7998-3274-4.ch008

Medhekar, A., & Wong, H. (2020). Medical Travellers' Perspective on Factors Affecting Medical Tourism to India. *Asia Pacific Journal of Tourism Research, 25*(12), 1295–1310. doi:10.1080/10941665.2020.1837893

Mercer, C. (2006). Telecentres and transformations: Modernizing Tanzania through the internet. *African Affairs, 105*(419), 243–264. doi:10.1093/afraf/adi087

Merriam-Webster. (2021). *Cybersecurity.* Available from https://www.merriam-webster.com/dictionary/cybersecurity

Merson, P. (2009). *Data Model as an Architectural View. Technical Note. CMU/SEI-2009-TN-024.* Research, Technology, and System Solutions.

Meske, C., Amojo, I., Poncette, A. S., & Balzer, F. (2019, July). The Potential Role of Digital Nudging in the Digital Transformation of the Healthcare Industry. In *International Conference on Human-Computer Interaction* (pp. 323-336). Springer. 10.1007/978-3-030-23538-3_25

Millett, P. (2002). *Lending and borrowing in ancient Athens.* University Press.

Mind the Gap. Addressing Challenges to FinTech Adoption. (2018). Retrieved from https://www.accenture.com/_acnmedia/pdf-74/accenture-fintech-challenges-adoption.pdf

Miraz, M. H. (2020). Blockchain of things (BCoT): The fusion of blockchain and IoT technologies. In *Advanced Applications of Blockchain Technology* (pp. 141–159). Springer. doi:10.1007/978-981-13-8775-3_7

Mirea, M., Wang, V., & Jung, J. (2019). The not so dark side of the darknet: A qualitative study. *Security Journal, 32*(2), 102–118. doi:10.105741284-018-0150-5

Misra, S., Krishna, P. V., Agarwal, H., Saxena, A., & Obaidat, M. S. (2011, October). A learning automata based solution for preventing distributed denial of service in internet of things. In *2011 international conference on internet of things and 4th international conference on cyber, physical and social computing* (pp. 114-122). IEEE. 10.1109/iThings/CPSCom.2011.84

Mistry, I., Tanwar, S., Tyagi, S., & Kumar, N. (2020). Blockchain for 5G-enabled IoT for industrial automation: A systematic review, solutions, and challenges. *Mechanical Systems and Signal Processing, 135*, 106382. doi:10.1016/j.ymssp.2019.106382

Mitnick, K., & Simon, W. (2002). *The Art of Deception: Controlling the Human Element of Security.* Wiley Publishing, Inc.

Mnih, V., Kavukcuoglu, K., Silver, D., Graves, A., Antonoglou, I., Wierstra, D., & Riedmiller, M. (2013). *Playing atari with deep reinforcement learning.* arXiv preprint arXiv:1312.5602.

Mnih, V., Kavukcuoglu, K., Silver, D., Rusu, A. A., Veness, J., Bellemare, M. G., & Petersen, S. (2015). Human-level control through deep reinforcement learning. *Nature, 518*(7540), 529–533. doi:10.1038/nature14236 PMID:25719670

Modic, D., & Anderson, R. (2014). Reading this may harm your computer: The psychology of malware warnings. *Computers in Human Behavior, 41*, 71–79. doi:10.1016/j.chb.2014.09.014

Mohaisen, A., Alrawi, O., & Mohaisen, M. (2015). AMAL: High-fidelity, behavior-based automated malware analysis and classification. *Computers & Security, 52*, 251–266. doi:10.1016/j.cose.2015.04.001

Mohammed, A. M., Idris, B., Saridakis, G., & Benson, V. (2020). *Information and communication technologies: a curse or blessing for SMEs?* (V. Benson & J. McAlaney, Eds.). Academic Press.

Molla, A., & Licker, P. S. (2005). Perceived e-readiness factors in e-commerce adoption: An empirical investigation in a developing country. *International Journal of Electronic Commerce, 10*(1), 83–110. doi:10.1080/10864415.2005.11043963

Moore, J. (2014). *Java programming with lambda expressions-A mathematical example demonstrates the power of lambdas in Java 8*. Retrieved March 10, 2018, from, https://www.javaworld.com/article/2092260/java-se/java-programming-with-lambda-expressions.html

Morgan, S. (2020). *Cybercrime to Cost the World $10.5 Trillion Annually By 2025.* Retrieved from https://cybersecurityventures.com/hackerpocalypse-cybercrime-report-2016

Moro Visconti, R., & Morea, D. (2020). Healthcare digitalization and pay-for-performance incentives in smart hospital project financing. *International Journal of Environmental Research and Public Health, 17*(7), 2318. doi:10.3390/ijerph17072318 PMID:32235517

Mudrack, P. (2007). *Individual personality factors that affect normative beliefs about the rightness of corporate social responsibility.* Academic Press.

Mugarura, N., & Ssali, E. (2020). Intricacies of anti-money laundering and cyber-crimes regulation. *RT Journal.*

Muthuppalaniappan, M., & Stevenson, K. (2021). Healthcare cyber-attacks and the COVID-19 pandemic: An urgent threat to global health. *International Journal for Quality in Health Care, 33*, 1353–4505.

Nagra, J., & Collberg, C. (2009). *Surreptitious Software: Obfuscation, Watermarking, and Tamperproofing for Software Protection: Obfuscation, Watermarking, and Tamperproofing for Software Protection.* Pearson Education.

Nagy, J., Oláh, J., Erdei, E., Máté, D., & Popp, J. (2018). The role and impact of Industry 4.0 and the internet of things on the business strategy of the value chain—The case of Hungary. *Sustainability, 10*(10), 3491. doi:10.3390u10103491

Nakamoto, S. (2008). Bitcoin: A peer-to-peer electronic cash system. *Bitcoin.* https://bitcoin.org/bitcoin. pdf

Narayanan, A., Bonneau, J., Felten, E., Miller, A., & Goldfeder, S. (2016). *Bitcoin and cryptocurrency technologies: a comprehensive introduction.* Princeton University Press.

Nasdaq warns of market manipulation amid Coronavirus outbreak. (2020). Retrieved from https://www.nasdaq.com/articles/nasdaq-warns-of-market-manipulation-amid-coronavirus-outbreak-2020-03-23

Nasiri, S., Sadoughi, F., Tadayon, M. H., & Dehnad, A. (2019). Security requirements of Internet of Things-based healthcare system: A survey study. *Acta Informatica Medica, 27*(4), 253. doi:10.5455/aim.2019.27.253-258 PMID:32055092

Nazah, S., Huda, S., Abawajy, J., & Hassan, M. M. (2020). Evolution of Dark Web Threat Analysis and Detection: A Systematic Approach. *IEEE Access: Practical Innovations, Open Solutions, 8,* 171796–171819. doi:10.1109/ACCESS.2020.3024198

Nazaritehrani, A., & Mashali, B. (2020). Development of e-banking channels and market share in developing countries. *Financial Innovation, 6*(12), 12. Advance online publication. 10.118640854-020-0171-z

Nazi, K. M., Hogan, T. P., Wagner, T. H., McInnes, D. K., Smith, B. M., Haggstorm, D., Chumbler, N. R., Gifford, A. L., Charters, K. G., Saleem, J. J., Weingardt, K. R., Fischetti, L. F., & Weaver, F. M. (2010). Embracing a Health Services Research Perspective on Personal Health Records: Lessons Learned from the VA My Health*e*Vet System. *Journal of General Internal Medicine, 25*(1), 62–67. doi:10.100711606-009-1114-6 PMID:20077154

NCCS. (2018). *National Centre for Cyber Security.* https://www.nccs.pk

Netherlands Environmental Assessment Agency. (2016) *Cities in Europe: Facts and figures on cities and urban areas.* PBL Publishers. Retrieved from: https://ec.europa.eu/futurium/en/system/files/ged/pbl_2016_cities_in_europe_23231.pdf

Nguyen, K. T., Laurent, M., & Oualha, N. (2015). Survey on secure communication protocols for the Internet of Things. *Ad Hoc Networks, 32,* 17–31. doi:10.1016/j.adhoc.2015.01.006

Nigrin, D. J. (2014). When "Hacktivists" Target Your Hospital. *The New England Journal of Medicine, 371*(5), 393–395. doi:10.1056/NEJMp1407326 PMID:25075830

Nijboer, F., Morin, F., Carmien, S., Koene, R., Leon, E., & Hoffman, U. (2009). Affective brain-computer interfaces: Psychophysiological markers of emotion in healthy persons and in persons with amyotrophic lateral sclerosis. In *3rd International Conference on Affective Computing and Intelligent Interaction and Workshops.* IEEE. 10.1109/ACII.2009.5349479

Nixon, P. G., Koutrakou, V. N., & Rawal, R. (2009). *Understanding E-Government in Europe. Issues and Challenges.* Routledge Taylor & Group.

Nocamels. (2020). *Israel Is Number 1 Target For Hackers And Cybercriminals – Report.* Retrieved from https://nocamels.com/2020/12/israel-target-hackers-cybersecurity-cybercriminals/

Nollytech. (2019). *10 Advantages And Disadvantages of Electronic Banking.* https://nollytech.com/advantages-and-disadvantages-of-electronic-banking/

O'kane, P., Sezer, S., & McLaughlin, K. (2016). Detecting obfuscated malware using reduced opcode set and optimised runtime trace. *Security Informatics, 5*(1), 2. Advance online publication. doi:10.118613388-016-0027-2

OAIC. (2021b). *Tips to protect My Health Record.* Available from https://www.oaic.gov.au/privacy/health-information/my-health-record/tips-to-protect-your-my-health-record/

Office of Australian Information Commissioner (OAIC). (2021a). *Health Information Privacy.* Available from https://www.oaic.gov.au/privacy/health-information/

Offner, K., Sitnikova, E., Joiner, K., & MacIntyre, C. (2020). Towards understanding cybersecurity capability in Australian healthcare organisations: A systematic review of recent trends, threats and mitigation. *Intelligence and National Security, 35*(4), 556–585. doi:10.1080/02684527.2020.1752459

Ög˘ütçü, G., Testik, Ö. M., & Chouseinoglou, O. (2016). Analysis of personal information security behavior and awareness. *Computers & Security*, *56*, 83–93. doi:10.1016/j.cose.2015.10.002

Okot-Uma, R. (2000). Electronic Governance: Reinventing Good Governance. *Proceedings of African Computing and Telecommunications Summit.*

Omar, I. A., Jayaraman, R., Salah, K., Yaqoob, I., & Ellahham, S. (2020). Applications of blockchain technology in clinical trials: Review and open challenges. *Arabian Journal for Science and Engineering*, 1–15.

OMNI-SCI. (2021). *Data Science - A Complete Introduction.* OMNI-SCI. https://www.omnisci.com/learn/data-science

Orbach, M., & Hazani, G. (2020). *Israel's supply chain targeted in massive cyberattack.* Calcalist. Retrieved from https://www.calcalistech.com/ctech/articles/0,7340,L-3881337,00.html

Orshesky, C. M. (2003). Beyond technology – The human factor in business systems. *The Journal of Business Strategy*, *24*(4), 43–47. doi:10.1108/02756660310494872

Országos Katasztrófavédelemi Főigazgatóság. (2021). *A kritikus infrastruktúra* [The Critical Infrastructure]. Retrieved from https://regi.katasztrofavedelem.hu/index2.php?pageid=lrl_index

Ortega, B., Martinez, J., & Hoyos, M. J. M. (2007). An analysis of web navigability in Spanish internet banking. *Journal of Internet Banking and Commerce*, *12*(3), 1–8.

Overby, S. (2020). *What is digital transformation?* https://enterprisersproject.com/what-is-digitaltransformation

Paganini, P. (2020). *Tens of thousands Israeli websites defaced.* Security Affairs. Retrieved from https://securityaffairs.co/wordpress/103570/hacktivism/israeli-websites-defaced.html

Pakistan Today. (2018, November 2). *Pakistan's remittances may reach $22bn in FY19.* https://profit.pakistantoday.com.pk/2018/11/02/pakistans-remittances-may-reach- 22bn-in-fy19/

Panagariya, A. (2000). E-commerce, WTO, and developing countries. *World Economy*, *23*(8), 959–979. doi:10.1111/1467-9701.00313

Pandey, P., & Litoriya, R. (2020). Securing and authenticating healthcare records through blockchain technology. *Cryptologia*, *44*(4), 341–356. doi:10.1080/01611194.2019.1706060

Pan, Y., Ge, X., Fang, C., & Fan, Y. (2020). A Systematic Literature Review of Android Malware Detection Using Static Analysis. *IEEE Access: Practical Innovations, Open Solutions*, *8*, 116363–116379. doi:10.1109/ACCESS.2020.3002842

Papp-Váry, Á. (2019). *Országmárkázás [Country branding]* (Vol. 41). Akadémiai Kiadó.

Paquet-Clouston, M., Haslhofer, B., & Dupont, B. (2019). Ransomware payments in the Bitcoin ecosystem. *Journal of Cybersecurity*, *5*(1), tyz003. Advance online publication. doi:10.1093/cybsec/tyz003

Parisi, A. (2020). *Securing blockchain networks like Ethereum and Hyperledger Fabric* (1st ed.). Packt Publishing.

Park S., Specter M.A., Narula N., Rivest R. (2021). Going from bad to worse: from Internet voting to blockchain voting. *J. Cybersecur., 7.*

Parker, W. N. (1984). *Europe, America, and the wider world: Essays on the economic history of western capitalism.* Cambridge University Press.

Parviainen, P., Tihinen, M., Kääriäinen, J., & Teppola, S. (2017). Tackling the digitalization challenge: How to benefit from digitalization in practice. *International Journal of Information Systems and Project Management*, *5*, 63–77.

Pavithra, V., & Chandrasekaran, J. (2021). Developing Security Solutions for Telemedicine Applications: Medical Image Encryption and Watermarking. In *Research Anthology on Telemedicine Efficacy, Adoption, and Impact on Healthcare Delivery* (pp. 612-631). Retrieved from www.igi-global.com/chapter/developing-security-solutions-for-telemedicineapplications/

Pavlopoulos, J., Vrettaros, J., & Drigas, A. (2008). The Development of a Self-assessment System for the Learners Answers with the Use of GPNN. *Emerging Technologies and Information Systems for the Knowledge Society, First World Summit on the Knowledge Society, WSKS 2008, Athens, Greece, September 24-26, 2008. Proceedings.* 10.1007/978-3-540-87781-3_37

Pawson, R., Greenhalgh, T., Harvey, G., & Walshe, K. (2005). Realist review - A new method of systematic review designed for complex policy interventions. *Journal of Health Services Research & Policy, 10*(1), 21–34. doi:10.1258/1355819054308530 PMID:16053581

Paycale. (2021). *Salary for Skill in Israel: Cyber Security.* Retrieved from https://www.payscale.com/research/IL/Skill=Cyber_Security/Salary/Page-4

Pedersen, K., & Tjørnehøj, G. (2018). Successful E-government Transformation: Pressure, Support, Capabilities and the Freedom to use them. *The Electronic Journal of E-Government, 16*(2), 168–184.

Pedro, C. P., Ramalho, J. J. S., & Silva, J. V. (2018). The main determinants of banking crises in OECD countries. *Review of World Economics, 154*(1), 203–227. doi:10.100710290-017-0294-0

Pelletier, C., & Cloutier, L. M. (2019). *Challenges of Digital Transformation in SMEs: Exploration of IT-Related Perceptions in a Service Ecosystem. Hawaii International Conference on System Sciences, Maui,* HI. 10.24251/HICSS.2019.597

Peltier, T. R. (2005). Implementing an Information Security Awareness Program. *Information Systems Security, 14*(2), 37–49. doi:10.1201/1086/45241.14.2.20050501/88292.6

Perakslis, E. D. (2014). Cybersecurity in Health Care. *The New England Journal of Medicine, 371*(5), 395–397. doi:10.1056/NEJMp1404358 PMID:25075831

Pervane, T., & Gu, K. (2019). How Cities Should Prepare for Artificial Intelligence. Frontiers. August 07, 2019. Massachusetts Institute of Technology. *MIT Sloane Management Review.* Retrieved from: https://sloanreview.mit.edu/article/how-cities-should-prepare-for-artificial-intelligence/

Petticrew, M., & Roberts, H. (2006). *Systematic reviews in the social sciences: A practical guide.* doi:10.1002/9780470754887

Petticrew, M., & Roberts, H. (2008). *Systematic reviews in the social sciences: A practical guide.* John Wiley & Sons.

Phan, D. D. (2001). E-business management strategies: A business-to-business case study. *Information Systems Management, 18*(4), 61–69. doi:10.1201/1078/43198.18.4.20010901/31466.7

Phaneuf, A. (2021a, January 15). The disruptive trends & companies transforming digital banking services in 2021. *Business Insider.* https://www.businessinsider.com/digital-banking

Phaneuf, A. (2021b, January 15). The future of retail, mobile, online, and digital-only banking technology in 2021. *Business Insider.* https://www.businessinsider.com/future-of-banking-technology

Pilkington, M. (2017). Can blockchain improve healthcare management? Consumer medical electronics and the IoMT. *Consumer Medical Electronics and the IoMT.*

Pilkington, M. (2016). Blockchain technology: Principles and applications. In F. X. Olleros & M. Zhegu (Eds.), *Research handbook on digital transformations* (pp. 1–39). Edward Elgar. doi:10.4337/9781784717766.00019

Polasik, M., & Wisniewski, T. P. (2009). Empirical analysis of internet banking adoption in Poland. *International Journal of Bank Marketing, 27*(1), 32–52. doi:10.1108/02652320910928227

Ponemon-Institute. (2018). *Cost of a Data Breach Study: Global Overview*. IBM Security and Ponemon Institute.

Porter, M. E. (2001). The value chain and competitive advantage. *Understanding Business Processes, 2*, 50-66.

Pranggono, B., & Arabo, A. (2021). COVID-19 pandemic cybersecurity issues. *Internet Technology Letters, 4*(2), e247. doi:10.1002/itl2.247

PricewaterhouseCoopers. (2019). *Creating the smart cities of the future: A three-tier development model for digital transformation of citizen services*. PricewaterhouseCoopers. Retrieved from: https://www.pwc.com/gx/en/sustainability/assets/creating-the-smart-cities-of-the-future.pdf

Prince, J. D. (1904). Review: The code of Hammurabi. *The American Journal of Theology, 8*(3), 601–609. doi:10.1086/478479

Privacy Act. 1988 (Cth) part ii.6 (Austl.). (1988). https://www.legislation.gov.au/Details/C2014C00076

Queensland Health. (2017). *Digital Health Strategic Vision for Queensland 2026*. Retrieved from https://www.health.qld.gov.au/__data/assets/pdf_file/0016/645010/digital-health-strat-vision.pdf

Rabah, K. (2018). Convergence of AI, IoT, big data and blockchain: a review. *The Lake Institute Journal, 1*(1), 1-18.

Rabiu, I. D., Ladan, S., Usman, H. A., & Garba, M. (2019). Impact of e-banking on the operational efficiency of banks in Nigeria. *International Journal of Academic Research in Business & Social Sciences, 9*(2). Advance online publication. doi:10.6007/IJARBSS/v9-i2/5527

Rahi, S. (2017). Research design and methods: A systematic review of research paradigms, sampling issues, and instruments development. *International Journal of Economics & Management Sciences, 06*(6). Advance online publication. doi:10.4172/2162-6359.1000403

Ram, Y., Israel, I., & Baram, G. (2020). Cyberwar Between Iran and Israel Out in the Open. Yuval Ne'eman Workshop for Science, Technology and Security at Tel Aviv University.

Ramalingam, R., Khan, S., & Mohammed, S. (2016). The need for effective information security awareness practices in Oman higher educational institutions. *Symposium on Communication, Information Technology and Biotechnology: Current Trends and Future Scope, Sur College of Applied Sciences, Ministry of Higher Education, Sultanate of Oman*, 1-6.

Rathee, G., Sharma, A., Saini, H., Kumar, R., & Iqbal, R. (2019). A hybrid framework for multimedia data processing in IoT-healthcare using blockchain technology. *Multimedia Tools and Applications*, 1–23. doi:10.100711042-019-07835-3

Rathee, P. (2020). Introduction to Blockchain and IoT. In *Advanced Applications of Blockchain Technology* (pp. 1–14). Springer. doi:10.1007/978-981-13-8775-3_1

Ravenel, J. P. (2007). Effective operational security metrics. *The EDP Audit, Control, and Security Newsletter, 34*(6), 11–20.

Ravich, S. (2015). *Cyber-Enabled Economic Warfare: An Evolving Challenge*. Hudson Institute. Retrieved from: http://prognoz.eurasian-defence.ru/sites/default/files/source/2015.08cyberenabledeconomicwarfareanevolvingchallenge.pd

Ray, P. P., Dash, D., Salah, K., & Kumar, N. (2020). Blockchain for IoT-based healthcare: Background, consensus, platforms, and use cases. *IEEE Systems Journal*. Advance online publication. doi:10.1109/JSYST.2020.2963840

Raza, S., Wallgren, L., & Voigt, T. (2013). SVELTE: Real-time intrusion detection in the Internet of Things. *Ad Hoc Networks, 11*(8), 2661–2674. doi:10.1016/j.adhoc.2013.04.014

Razzaq, A., Hur, A., Ahmad, H. F., & Masood, M. (2013). Cyber security: Threats, reasons, challenges, methodologies and state of the art solutions for industrial applications. In *2013 IEEE Eleventh International Symposium on Autonomous Decentralized Systems (ISADS)* (pp. 1-6). IEEE. 10.1109/ISADS.2013.6513420

ReachOut Australia. (2021). *Disclosing personal information.* https://schools.au.reachout.com/articles/disclosing-personal-information

Rees, L. P., Deane, J. K., Rakes, T. R., & Baker, W. H. (2011). Decision support for cybersecurity risk planning. *Decision Support Systems*, *51*(3), 493–505. doi:10.1016/j.dss.2011.02.013

Reeves, A., Delfabbro, P., & Calic, D. (2021, January). Encouraging Employee Engagement with Cybersecurity: How to Tackle Cyber Fatigue. *SAGE Open*, *11*(1). Advance online publication. doi:10.1177/21582440211000049

Regan, C. M. (2020). *A federated deep autoencoder for detecting IoT cyber attacks* (Master's Thesis). Faculty of the Department of Computer Science, Kennesaw State University.

Regola, N., & Chawla, N. V. (2013). Storing and Using Health Data in a Virtual Private Cloud. *Journal of Medical Internet Research*, *15*(3), e63. doi:10.2196/jmir.2076 PMID:23485880

Restuccia, F., D'Oro, S., & Melodia, T. (2018). Securing the internet of things in the age of machine learning and software-defined networking. *IEEE Internet of Things Journal*, *5*(6), 4829–4842. doi:10.1109/JIOT.2018.2846040

Reuters. (2020). *Israel says it thwarted serious cyberattack on power station.* Retrieved from https://www.reuters.com/article/us-israel-cyber-powerstation/israel-says-it-thwarted-serious-cyber-attack-on-power-station-idUSKBN1ZS1SU

Rhode, M., Tuson, L., Burnap, P., & Jones, K. (2019). LAB to SOC: Robust Features for Dynamic Malware Detection. In *2019 49th Annual IEEE/IFIP International Conference on Dependable Systems and Networks – Industry Track* (pp. 13–16). 10.1109/DSN-Industry.2019.00010

Ribeiro, C., Leitold, H., Esposito, S., & Mitzam, D. (2018). STORK: A real, heterogeneous, large-scale eID management system. *International Journal of Information Security*, *17*(5), 569–585. doi:10.100710207-017-0385-x

Ricciardi, W., Pita Barros, P., Bourek, A., Brouwer, W., Kelsey, T., Lehtonen, L., Anastasy, C., Barros, P., Barry, M., Bourek, A., Brouwer, W., De Maeseneer, J., Kringos, D., Lehtonen, L., McKee, M., Murauskiene, L., Nuti, S., Ricciardi, W., Siciliani, L., & Wild, C. (2019). How to govern the digital transformation of health services. *European Journal of Public Health*, *29*(Supplement_3), 7–12. doi:10.1093/eurpub/ckz165 PMID:31738442

Riley, T. B. (2000). Electronic Governance and Electronic Democracy: Living and Working in the Wired World. Academic Press.

Robinson, M., Jones, K., Janicke, H., & Maglaras, L. (2018). An Introduction to Cyber Peacekeeping. *Journal of Network and Computer Applications*, *114*, 70–87. Advance online publication. doi:10.1016/j.jnca.2018.04.010

Roddy, A. L., & Holt, T. J. (2020). An Assessment of Hitmen and Contracted Violence Providers Operating Online. *Deviant Behavior*, 1–13. doi:10.1080/01639625.2020.1787763

Romanosky, S. (2016, December). Examining the costs and causes of cyber incidents. *Journal of Cybersecurity*, *2*(2), 121–135. doi:10.1093/cybsec/tyw001

Rose, K. J. (2017). Mobile Health: Telemedicine's Latest Wave but This Time It's for Real. In L. Menvielle, A. F. Audrain-Pontevia, & W. Menvielle (Eds.), *The Digitization of Healthcare.* Palgrave Macmillan. doi:10.1057/978-1-349-95173-4_9

Roundy, K. A., & Miller, B. P. (2010, September). Hybrid analysis and control of malware. In *International Workshop on Recent Advances in Intrusion Detection* (pp. 317-338). Springer. 10.1007/978-3-642-15512-3_17

Rouse, M. (2019). *ICT (Information and Communications technologies)*. https://searchcio.techtarget. com/definition/ICT-information-and-communications-technology-or-technologies

Rouse, M. (2019). *ICT (Information and Communications technologies)*. https://searchcio.techtarget.com/definition/ICT-information-and-communications-technology-or-technologies

Rowe, D. C., Lunt, B. M., & Ekstrom, J. J. (2011). *The Role of Cyber-Security in Information Technology Education*. SIGITE'11, West Point, NY, USA. .2047628 doi:10.1145/2047594

Russell, S., & Norvig, P. (2002). *Artificial intelligence: A modern approach*. Academic Press.

Russo, E., Sittig, D. F., Murphy, D. R., & Singh, H. (2018). Challenges in patient safety improvement research in the era of electronic health records. *Health Care, 4*(4), 285–290. PMID:27473472

Saarikko, T., Westergren, U. H., & Blomquist, T. (2020). Digital transformation: Five recommendations for the digitally conscious firm. *Business Horizons, 63*(6), 825–839. doi:10.1016/j.bushor.2020.07.005

Sadiq, N. (2020, October 26). Minimum wage. *The News International*. thenews.com.pk/print/734687-minimum-wage#:~:text=Like%20all%20other%20countries%2C%20Pakistan,social%20security%20and%20overtime%20pay

Saeed, I. A., Campus, J. B., Selamat, M. A., Ali, M., & Abuagoub, M. A. (2013). A survey on malware and malware detection systems. *International Journal of Computers and Applications, 67*(16), 25–31. doi:10.5120/11480-7108

Safaldin, M., Otair, M., & Abualigah, L. (2020). Improved binary gray wolf optimizer and SVM for intrusion detection system in wireless sensor networks. *Journal of Ambient Intelligence and Humanized Computing*, 1–18. doi:10.100712652-020-02228-z

Safa, N. S., Sookhak, M., Von Solms, R., Furnell, S., Ghani, N. A., & Herawan, T. (2015). Information security conscious care behaviour formation in organizations. *Computers & Security, 53*, 65–78. doi:10.1016/j.cose.2015.05.012

Sagduyu, Y. E., Shi, Y., & Erpek, T. (2019, June). IoT network security from the perspective of adversarial deep learning. *2019 16th Annual IEEE International Conference on Sensing, Communication, and Networking (SECON)*, 1-9. 10.1109/SAHCN.2019.8824956

Sagirlar, G., Carminati, B., & Ferrari, E. (2018, October). AutoBotCatcher: blockchain-based P2P botnet detection for the internet of things. In *2018 IEEE 4th International Conference on Collaboration and Internet Computing (CIC)* (pp. 1-8). IEEE.

Saint Yen, Y., Chen, Z. W., Guo, Y. R., & Chen, M. C. (2019). *Integration of Static and Dynamic Analysis for Malware Family Classification with Composite Neural Network*. Retrieved from https://arxiv.org/abs/1912.11249

Salam, A. (2020). Internet of Things for Sustainability: Perspectives in Privacy, Cybersecurity, and Future Trends. In *Internet of Things for Sustainable Community Development. Internet of Things (Technology, Communications and Computing)*. Springer. doi:10.1007/978-3-030-35291-2_10

Sallos, M. P., Garcia-Perez, A., Bedford, D., & Orlando, B. (2019). Strategy and organisational cybersecurity: A knowledge-problem perspective. *Journal of Intellectual Capital, 20*(4), 581–597. doi:10.1108/JIC-03-2019-0041

Sandhu, K. (2008). E-services acceptance model (E-SAM). In Advances in Computer and Information Sciences and Engineering (pp. 224–229). Springer. doi:10.1007/978-1-4020-8741-7_40

Sandhu, K. (2009). Measuring the performance of the electronic service acceptance model (E-SAM). *International Journal of Business Information Systems, 4*(5), 527–541. doi:10.1504/IJBIS.2009.025205

Sangal, A., & Verma, H. K. (2020). A Static Feature Selection-based Android Malware Detection Using Machine Learning Techniques. In *2020 International Conference on Smart Electronics and Communication (ICOSEC)* (pp. 48–51). 10.1109/ICOSEC49089.2020.9215355

Santos, I., Penya, Y. K., Devesa, J., & Bringas, P. G. (2009). N-grams-based File Signatures for Malware Detection. *ICEIS*, *9*(2), 317–320.

Sanzhez-Iborra, R., & Skarmeta, A. F. (2020). TinyML-Enabled Frugal Smart Objects: Challenges and Opportunuties. *IEEE Circuits and Systems Magazine*, *20*(3), 4–18. doi:10.1109/MCAS.2020.3005467

Sari, A. (2019). Turkish national cyber-firewall to mitigate countrywide cyber-attacks. *Computers & Electrical Engineering*, *73*, 128–144. doi:10.1016/j.compeleceng.2018.11.008

Sarkar, D. (2018). *Get Smarter with Data Science — Tackling Real Enterprise Challenges. Take your Data Science Projects from Zero to Production.* Towards Data Science. https://towardsdatascience.com/get-smarter-with-data-science-tackling-real-enterprise-challenges-67ee001f6097

SAS. (2021). *History of Big Data.* SAS. https://www.sas.com/en_us/insights/big-data/what-is-big-data.html

Saxena, K. (2005). Towards excellence in e-governance. *International Journal of Public Sector Management*, *18*(6), 498–513. doi:10.1108/09513550510616733

Sayar, C., & Wolfe, S. (2007). Internet banking market performance: Turkey versus the U.K. *International Journal of Bank Marketing*, *25*(3), 122–141. doi:10.1108/02652320710739841

Schallmo, D., Williams, C. A., & Boardman, L. (2018). Digital Transformation of Business Models-Best Practices, Enablers and Roadmap. *International Journal of Innovation Management*, *21*(8), 1–17.

Schenkel, M. T., Farmer, S., & Maslyn, J. M. (2019). Process improvement in SMEs: The impact of harmonious passion for entrepreneurship, employee creative self-efficacy, and time spent innovating. *Journal of Small Business Strategy*, *29*(1), 64–77.

Schmandt-Besserat, D. (1992). *Counting to cuneiform.* University of Texas Press.

Schmeelk, S., Yang, J., & Aho, A. (2015, April). Android malware static analysis techniques. In *Proceedings of the 10th annual cyber and information security research conference* (pp. 1-8). Academic Press.

Schmelzer, R. (2021). *Data science vs. MLI4P vs. AI: How they work together.* TechTarget. https://searchbusinessanalytics.techtarget.com/feature/Data-science-vs-machine-learning-vs-AI-How-they-work-together?track=NL-1816&ad=937375&asrc=EM_NLN_144787081&utm_medium=EM&utm_source=NLN&utm_campaign=20210114_An%20open%20source%20database%20comparison

Schneier, M., Schneier, M., & Bostelman, R. (2015). *Literature review of mobile robots for manufacturing.* US Department of Commerce, National Institute of Standards and Technology. doi:10.6028/NIST.IR.8022

Scholl, M. C. (2018). *Awareness in Information Security.12th International Multi-Conference on Society.* Cybernetics and Informatics.

Schulman, S. (2021). *The best for cyber: How much do you earn in the hottest professions in the field?* Calcalist. Retrieved from https://www.calcalist.co.il/internet/articles/0,7340,L-3902412,00.html

Schumacher, A. (2017). *Reinventing healthcare: Towards a global, blockchain-based precision medicine ecosystem.* Available from: https://www.researchgate.net/publication/317936859_Blockchain_Healthcare_-_2017_Strategy_Guide

Scupola, A., Anders Henten, A., & Hanne Westh Nicolajsen, H. (2009). E-Services: Characteristics, Scope and Conceptual Strengths. *International Journal of E-Services and Mobile Applications*, *1*(3), 1–16. Advance online publication. doi:10.4018/jesma.2009070101

Sebastien G., Anderhalden D. (2020). *Insurability of Critical Infrastructures.* . doi:10.1007/978-3-030-41826-7_3

Secret Tel Aviv. (2018). *Best Coding And Tech Schools In English In Tel Aviv.* Retrieved from https://www.secrettelaviv.com/magazine/blog/useful-info/best-coding-schools-in-english-in-tel-aviv

Seebacher, S., & Schüritz, R. (2017). Blockchain technology as an enabler of service systems: A structured literature review. *International Conference on Exploring Services Science*, 12–23. https://link.springer.com/chapter/10.1007/978-3-319-56925-3_2

Senarak, C. (2021). Port cybersecurity and threat: A structural model for prevention and policy development. *The Asian Journal of Shipping and Logistics, 37*(1), 20-36. doi:10.1016/j.ajsl.2020.05.001

Senge, P. M. (1995). *Learning organizations.* Gilmour Drummond Publishing.

Senol, M., & Karacuha, E. (2020). Creating and Implementing an Effective and Deterrent National Cyber Security Strategy. *Journal of Engineering (Stevenage, England).*

Seppänen, V., Penttinen, K., & Pulkkinen, M. (2018). Key Issues in Enterprise Architecture Adoption in the Public Sector. *The Electronic. Journal of E-Government, 16*(1), 46–58.

Seselja, E. (2021). *Cyber attack shuts down global meat processing giant JBS.* ABC Radio Brisbane.

Shabak. (2020). *Career in the Shin Bet.* Retrieved from https://www.shabak.gov.il/career/jobs/Pages/TechnologicalUnits.aspx?pk_campaign=quiz&pk_kwd=klali-3001#cbpf=*

Shad, M. (2019). Cyber Threat Landscape and Readiness Challenge of Pakistan. *Strategic Studies, 39*(1), 1-19. https://www.jstor.org/stable/10.2307/48544285

Shafiq, M., Tian, Z., Sun, Y., Du, X., & Guizani, M. (2020). Selection of effective machine learning algorithm and Bot-IoT attacks traffic identification for internet of things in smart city. *Future Generation Computer Systems, 107*, 433–442. doi:10.1016/j.future.2020.02.017

Shakeel, P. M., Baskar, S., Fouad, H., Manogaran, G., Saravanan, V., & Montenegro-Marin, C. E. (2020). Internet of things forensic data analysis using machine learning to identify roots of data scavenging. *Future Generation Computer Systems.*

Sharma, M., & Joshi, S. (2021). Barriers to blockchain adoption in health-care industry: an Indian perspective. *Journal of Global Operations and Strategic Sourcing.*

Sharma, R., & Purohit, M. (2018). Emerging Cyber Threats and the Challenges Associated with them. *International Research. Journal of Engineering Technology, 5*(2). https://www.irjet.net/archives/V5/i2/IRJET-V5I2127.pdf

Shaw, T., Hines, M., & Kielly-Carroll, C. (2017). *Impact of Digital Health on the Safety and Quality of Health Care.* Sydney: ACSQHC. Available from https://www.safetyandquality.gov.au/

Shea, S. (2021). Cybersecurity. *SearchSecurity.* https://searchsecurity.techtarget.com/definition/cybersecurity#:~:text=Cybersecurity%20is%20the%20protection%20of,centers%20and%20other%20computerized%20systems

Shillair, R., Cotten, S., Tsai, H.-Y. S., Alhabash, S., LaRose, R., & Rifon, N. (2015). *Online safety begins with you and me: Convincing Internet users to protect themselves.* Academic Press.

Shulman, E. (2020). *Iranian Hackers Test Israeli Cyber Mettle*. Mishpacha. Retrieved from https://mishpacha.com/iranian-hackers-test-israeli-cyber-mettle/

Sikander, M., & Khiyal, H. (2018). *Computational Models for Upgrading Traditional Agriculture*. Preston University. https://www.researchgate.net/publication/326080886

Simões, A. C., Soares, A. L., & Barros, A. C. (2020). Factors influencing the intention of managers to adopt collaborative robots (cobots) in manufacturing organizations. *Journal of Engineering and Technology Management, 57*, 101574. doi:10.1016/j.jengtecman.2020.101574

Simonin, J., Bertin, E., Traon, Y., Jezequel, J.-M., & Crespi, N. (2010). Business and Information System Alignment: A Formal Solution for Telecom Services. In *2010 Fifth International Conference on Software Engineering Advances*. IEEE. 10.1109/ICSEA.2010.49

Singh, A. K., Jaidhar, C. D., & Kumara, M. A. A. (2019). Experimental analysis of Android malware detection based on combinations of permissions and API-calls. *Journal of Computer Virology and Hacking Techniques, 15*(3), 209–218. doi:10.100711416-019-00332-z

Singh, P., & Singh, N. (2020). Blockchain With IoT and AI: A Review of Agriculture and Healthcare. *International Journal of Applied Evolutionary Computation, 11*(4), 13–27. doi:10.4018/IJAEC.2020100102

Singh, S., Cabraal, A., & Hermansson, G. (2006). What is your husband's name?: Sociological dimensions of internet banking authentication. In *Proceedings of the 18th Australia conference on Computer-Human Interaction: Design: Activities, Artefacts, and Environments*. ACM. 10.1145/1228175.1228217

Siponen, M. (2000). A conceptual foundation for organizational information security awareness. *Information Management & Computer Security, 8*(1), 31–41. doi:10.1108/09685220010371394

Sittig, D. F. (2002). Personal health records on the internet: A snapshot of the pioneers at the end of the 20th Century. *International Journal of Medical Informatics, 65*(1), 1–6. doi:10.1016/S1386-5056(01)00215-5 PMID:11904243

Sittig, D. F., Belmont, E., & Singh, H. (2018). Improving the safety of health information technology requires shared responsibility: It is time we all step up. *Health Care, 6*(1), 7–12. PMID:28716376

Smart Cities Information System. (2017). *The making of a smart city: Policy recommendations for decision makers at local regional, national and EU levels*. Smart Cities Information System. Retrieved from: https://smartcities-infosystem.eu/library/publications

Sohan, M. F., & Basalamah, A. (2020). A Systematic Literature Review and Quality Analysis of Javascript Malware Detection. *IEEE Access: Practical Innovations, Open Solutions, 8*, 190539–190552. doi:10.1109/ACCESS.2020.3031690

Solomon, S. (2019). *Israel cybersecurity sector hamstrung by shortage of labor, report says*. The Times of Israel. Retrieved from https://www.timesofisrael.com/israel-cybersecurity-sector-hamstrung-by-shortage-of-labor-report-says/

Solomon, S. (2020). *Program arms discharged fighters with cyberskills, wins IDF Chief of Staff award*. The Times of Israel. Retrieved from https://www.timesofisrael.com/progam-arms-discharged-fighters-with-cyberskills-wins-idf-chief-of-staff-award/

Sonicwall. (2020). 2021 SonicWall Cyber Threat Report. *2020 SonicWall*, 1–38. Retrieved from https://www.sonicwall.com/resources/2020-cyber-threat-report-pdf/

Soro, S. (2020, September). *TinyML for Ubiqutious Edge AI*. MITRE Technical Report.

Souri, A., & Hosseini, R. (2018). A state-of-the-art survey of malware detection approaches using data mining techniques. *Human-centric Computing and Information Sciences*, *8*(1), 1–22. doi:10.118613673-018-0125-x

Souza, P. V. de C., Guimarães, A. J., Rezende, T. S., Araujo, V. S., do Nascimento, L. A. F., & Batista, L. O. (2020). An Intelligent Hybrid Model for the Construction of Expert Systems in Malware Detection. In *2020 IEEE Conference on Evolving and Adaptive Intelligent Systems (EAIS)* (pp. 1–8). 10.1109/EAIS48028.2020.9122770

Srivastava, G., Parizi, R. M., & Dehghantanha, A. (2020). The future of blockchain technology in healthcare internet of things security. *Blockchain Cybersecurity, Trust and Privacy*, 161-184.

Srivastava, A., Jain, P., Hazela, B., Asthana, P., & Rizvi, S. W. A. (2021). Application of Fog Computing, Internet of Things, and Blockchain Technology in Healthcare Industry. In *Fog Computing for Healthcare 4.0 Environments* (pp. 563–591). Springer. doi:10.1007/978-3-030-46197-3_22

Stallings, W. (1996). IPv6: The new Internet protocol. *IEEE Communications Magazine*, *34*(7), 96–108. doi:10.1109/35.526895

Stamatellis, C., Papadopoulos, P., Pitropakis, N., Katsikas, S., & Buchanan, W. (2020). A privacy-preserving healthcare framework using Hyperledger Fabric. *Sensors (Basel)*, *20*(22), 1–14. doi:10.339020226587 PMID:33218022

Standards Australia. (2011). *Information security management in health using ISO/IEC 27002 (AS ISO 27799-2011)*. Techstreet Enterprise.

Suganthi, R., Balachandher, K. G., & Balachandran, S. (2001). Internet banking patronage: An empirical investigation of Malaysia. *Journal of Internet Banking and Commerce*, *6*(1).

Suh, B., & Han, I. (2002). Effect of trust on customer acceptance of internet banking. *Electronic Commerce Research and Applications*, *1*(3-4), 247–263. doi:10.1016/S1567-4223(02)00017-0

Suki, N. M. (2010). An empirical study of factors affecting internet banking adoption among Malaysian consumers. *Journal of Internet Banking and Commerce*, *15*(2), 2–11.

Sundgren, B. (2005). What is a public information system? *International Journal of Public Information Systems*, *1*(1), 81–99.

Sun, M., Li, X., Lui, J. C. S., Ma, R. T. B., & Liang, Z. (2017). Monet: A User-Oriented Behavior-Based Malware Variants Detection System for Android. *IEEE Transactions on Information Forensics and Security*, *12*(5), 1103–1112. doi:10.1109/TIFS.2016.2646641

Survicate. (2021). *Customer satisfaction: Why it's still important in 2021.* https://survicate.com/customer-satisfaction/importance-customer-satisfaction/

Symantec. (2009). *Symantec Internet Security Threat Report: Trends for 2008.* Symantec Corporation. Retrieved from http://eval.symantec.com/mktginfo/enterprise/white_papers/bwhitepaper_exec_summary_internet_security_threat__report_xiv_04-2009.en-us.pdf

Symantec. (2016). Internet security threat report. *Network Security*, *21*(2), 1–3. Retrieved from https://linkinghub.elsevier.com/retrieve/pii/S1353485805001947

Szor, P. (2005). *The Art of Computer Virus Research and Defense.* Addison Wesley Professional.

Tabansky, L. (2013). Critical Infrastructure Protection: Evolution of Israeli Policy. *International Journal of Cyber Warfare & Terrorism*, *3*(3), 80–87. doi:10.4018/ijcwt.2013070106

Taherdoost, H. (2016). *Electronic Service Technology; Concepts, Applications and Security* (1st ed.). OmniScriptum.

Taherdoost, H. (2018). Development of an adoption model to assess user acceptance of e-service technology: E-Service Technology Acceptance Model. *Behaviour & Information Technology*, *37*(2), 173–197. doi:10.1080/014492 9X.2018.1427793

Taherdoost, H. (2020a). Electronic Service Quality Measurement (eSQM); Development of a Survey Instrument to Measure the Quality of E-Service. *International Journal of Intelligent Engineering Informatics*, *7*(6), 491–528. doi:10.1504/ IJIEI.2019.104559

Taherdoost, H. (2020b). Evaluation of Customer Satisfaction in Digital Environment; Development of Survey Instrument. In K. Sandhu (Ed.), *Digital Transformation and Innovative Services for Business and Learning* (pp. 195–222). IGI Global. doi:10.4018/978-1-7998-5175-2.ch011

Taherdoost, H., & Hassan, A. (2020). Development of An E-Service Quality Model (eSQM) to Assess the Quality of E-Service. In R. C. Ho (Ed.), *Strategies and Tools for Managing Connected Customers* (pp. 177–207). IGI Global. doi:10.4018/978-1-5225-9697-4.ch011

Taherdoost, H., & Madanchian, M. (2020). Developing and Validating a Theoretical Model to Evaluate Customer Satisfaction of E-Services. In K. Sandhu (Ed.), *Digital Innovations for Customer Engagement, Management and Organizational Improvement* (pp. 46–65). IGI Global. doi:10.4018/978-1-7998-5171-4.ch003

Taherdoost, H., Sahibuddin, S., & Jalaliyoon, N. (2015). A Review Paper on E-Service; Technology Concepts. *Procedia Technology*, *19*, 1067–1074. doi:10.1016/j.protcy.2015.02.152

Tahsien, S. M., Karimipour, H., & Spachos, P. (2020). Machine learning based solutions for security of Internet of Things (IoT): A survey. *Journal of Network and Computer Applications*, *161*, 102630. doi:10.1016/j.jnca.2020.102630

Takeuchi, H., & Nonaka, I. (1995). *The knowledge-creating company: How Japanese companies create the dynamics of innovation*. Oxford University Press.

Tamr. (2014). *The Evolution of ETL*. Tamr. http://www.tamr.com/evolution-etl/

Tanwar, S., Tyagi, S., & Kumar, N. (2019). Security and Privacy of Electronic Health Records. London, UK: The Institution of Engineering and Technology.

Tanwar, S., Parekh, K., & Evans, R. (2020). Blockchain-based electronic healthcare record system for Healthcare 4.0 applications. *Journal of Information Security and Applications*, *50*, 102407. doi:10.1016/j.jisa.2019.102407

Tapscott, D., & Tapscott, A. (2017). How blockchain will change organizations. *MIT Sloan Management Review*, *58*(2), 10.

Ten, C. W., Manimaran, G., & Liu, C. C. (2010). Cybersecurity for critical infrastructures: Attack and defense modeling. *IEEE Transactions on Systems, Man, and Cybernetics. Part A, Systems and Humans*, *40*(4), 853–865. doi:10.1109/ TSMCA.2010.2048028

Teoh, C. S., & Mahmood, A. K. (2017, July). National cyber security strategies for digital economy. In *2017 International Conference on Research and Innovation in Information Systems (ICRIIS)* (pp. 1-6). IEEE. 10.1109/ICRIIS.2017.8002519

The Enterprisers Project. (2020). *What is digital transformation?* https://enterprisersproject.com/whatis-digital-transformation

The Express Tribune. (2018, November 10). *Remittances increase by 21% to $2 billion*. https://tribune.com.pk/ story/1844098/2-remittances-increase-21-2-billion/

The Financial Brand. (2018). *The four pillars of digital transformation in banking*. https://thefinancialbrand.com/71733/ four-pillars-of-digital-transformation-banking-strategy/

The Israel Institute for Biological Research. (2021). Retrieved from https://iibr.gov.il/Pages/Who-We-are.aspx

The Jerusalem Post. (2020). *Israel must use Intelligence to mitigate cyber attacks: official.* Retrieved from https://www.jpost.com/cybertech/israel-must-use-intelligence-to-mitigate-cyber-attacks-senior-official-632012

The Jerusalem Post. (2020). *Israel Police reports a staggering 8,377 cyberattacks for 2020.* Retrieved from https://www.jpost.com/jpost-tech/israel-police-reports-a-staggering-8377-cyberattacks-for-2020-653378

The Open Group. (2011). *Open Group Standard-TOGAF® Guide, Version 9.1.* The Open Group.

The Open Group. (2013b). *ArchiMate®.* Retrieved May 03, 2014, from https://www.opengroup.org/subjectareas/Entity/archimate

The State Comptroller and Ombudsman of Israel. (2019). *Matanyahu Englman. State Comptroller and Ombudsman of the State of Israel* Retrieved from https://www.mevaker.gov.il/En/About/mevakrim/Pages/Englman.aspx

The Times of Israel. (2020). *Israeli vaccine research centers reportedly among sites targeted by hackers.* Retrieved from https://www.timesofisrael.com/israeli-vaccine-research-centers-reportedly-among-sites-targeted-by-hackers/

Thuemmler, C., & Bai, C. (2017). Health 4.0: Application of industry 4.0 design principles in future asthma management. In C. Thuemmler & C. Bai (Eds.), *Health 4.0: How virtualization and big data are revolutionizing healthcare* (pp. 23–37). Springer International Publishing. doi:10.1007/978-3-319-47617-9_2

Tigre, P. B., & Dedrick, J. (2004). E-commerce in Brazil: Local adaptation of global technology. *Electronic Markets*, *14*(1), 36–47. doi:10.1080/1019678042000175289

Tilson, D., Lyytinen, K., & Sørensen, C. (2010). Digital Infrastructures: The Missing IS Research Agenda. *Information Systems Research*, *21*(4), 748–759. doi:10.1287/isre.1100.0318

TOGAF Modelling. (2015a). *Data dissemination view.* TOGAF Modelling. http://www.TOGAF-modelling.org/models/data-architecture-menu/data-dissemination-diagrams-menu.html

Trad, A., & Kalpić, D. (2020a). *Using Applied Mathematical Models for Business Transformation. Author Book.* IGI-Global. doi:10.4018/978-1-7998-1009-4

Trifunovic, D. (2020). *Elements of Critical Infrastructure Resilience. National security and the future.* Retrieved from https://www.researchgate.net/publication/347514909_Elements_of_Critical_Infrastructure_Resilience doi:10.37458/nstf.20.1-2.6

Trim, P. R. J., & Lee, Y.-i. (2019). The role of B2B marketers in increasing cyber security awareness and influencing behavioural change. *Industrial Marketing Management*, *83*, 224–238. doi:10.1016/j.indmarman.2019.04.003

Tripathi, G., Ahad, M. A., & Paiva, S. (2020, March). S2HS-A blockchain based approach for smart healthcare system. In Healthcare (Vol. 8, No. 1, p. 100391). Elsevier.

Trivedi, D., Zavarsky, P., & Butakov, S. (2016). Enhancing relational database security by metadata segregation. *Procedia Computer Science*, *94*, 453–458. doi:10.1016/j.procs.2016.08.070

Turing, A. M. (1950). Can a machine think. *Mind*, *59*(236), 433–460. doi:10.1093/mind/LIX.236.433

Ulas, D. (2019). Digital Transformation Process and SMEs. *Procedia Computer Science*, *158*, 662–671. doi:10.1016/j.procs.2019.09.101

Umamaheswaran, S., Lakshmanan, R., Vinothkumar, V., Arvind, K. S., & Nagarajan, S. (2019). New and robust composite micro structure descriptor (CMSD) for CBIR. *International Journal of Speech Technology*, 1–7. doi:10.100710772-019-09663-0

Universitat de València. (2018). *Connecting Regional and Local Administrations to Spanish eIDAS Node (eID4Spain)*. Retrieved from: https://lmtgroup.eu/eid4spain/

Uprety, A., & Rawat, D. B. (2020). *Reinforcement Learning for IoT Security: A Comprehensive Survey*. IEEE Internet of Things Journal.

Usman, M., Ahmed, I., Aslam, M. I., Khan, S., & Shah, U. A. (2017). SIT: A lightweight encryption algorithm for secure internet of things. *International Journal of Advanced Computer Science and Applications*, *8*(1).

Usman, N., Usman, S., Khan, F., Jan, M. A., Sajid, A., Alazab, M., & Watters, P. (2021). Intelligent Dynamic Malware Detection using Machine Learning in IP Reputation for Forensics Data Analytics. *Future Generation Computer Systems*, *118*, 124–141. doi:10.1016/j.future.2021.01.004

Valluripally, S., Sukheja, D., Ohri, K., & Singh, S. K. (2019, May). IoT Based Smart Luggage Monitor Alarm System. In *International Conference on Internet of Things and Connected Technologies* (pp. 294-302). Springer.

Varadharajan, V. (2018). *Cybersecurity and privacy issues surrounding My health records*. Retrieved from https://www.newcastle.edu.au/newsroom/research-and-innovation/my-health-record

Vardarlier, P. (2020). Digital transformation of human resource management: digital applications and strategic tools in HRM. In *Digital Business Strategies in Blockchain Ecosystems* (pp. 239–264). Springer. doi:10.1007/978-3-030-29739-8_11

Vella, A., Corne, D., & Murphy, C. (2009). *Hyper-heuristic decision tree induction*. Sch. of MACS, Heriot-Watt Univ.

Velliangiri, S., & Kasaraneni, K. K. (2020). Machine Learning and Deep Learning in Cyber Security for IoT. In *ICDSMLA 2019*. Springer.

Veneberg, R. (2014). *Combining enterprise architecture and operational data-to better support decision-making*. *University of Twente*. School of Management and Governance.

Verhoef, P. C., Broekhuizen, T., Bart, Y., Bhattacharya, A., Dong, J. Q., Fabian, N., & Haenlein, M. (2019). Digital transformation: A multidisciplinary reflection and research agenda. *Journal of Business Research*, *122*, 889–901. doi:10.1016/j.jbusres.2019.09.022

Vial, G. (2019). Understanding digital transformation: A review and a research agenda. *The Journal of Strategic Information Systems*, *28*(2), 118–144. doi:10.1016/j.jsis.2019.01.003

Victor, L. (2008). Systematic reviewing in the social sciences: Outcomes and explanation. *Enquire*, *1*(1), 32–46.

Vidal, E. (2021). *Israel's 2021 Cyber landscape: Which sector will the new unicorns emerge from?* Calcalistech. Retrieved from https://www.calcalistech.com/ctech/articles/0,7340,L-3892650,00.html

Vila, J. A. (2015). *Identifying and combating cyber-threats in the field of online banking*. Academic Press. https://www.sslshopper.com/what-is-ssl.html

Villalva, D. A. B., Onaolapo, J., Stringhini, G., & Musolesi, M. (2018). Under and over the surface: A comparison of the use of leaked account credentials in the Dark and Surface Web. *Crime Science*, *7*(1), 1–11. PMID:31984202

Vina, G. (2016). *Patients in limbo after cyber attack*. Retrieved from https://www.ft.com/content/1292d25c-a12a-11e6-891e-abe238dee8e2

Vinayakumar, R., Alazab, M., Soman, K. P., Poornachandran, P., & Venkatraman, S. (2019). Robust Intelligent Malware Detection Using Deep Learning. *IEEE Access: Practical Innovations, Open Solutions, 7*, 46717–46738. doi:10.1109/ACCESS.2019.2906934

Vondracek, F. W., Lerner, R. M., & Schulenberg, J. E. (2019). *Career development: A life-span developmental approach.* Routledge., doi:10.4324/9781315792705

Vrincianu, M., & Popa, L. A. (2010). Considerations regarding the security and protection of e-banking services consumers' interests. *Academy of Economic Studies, Bucharest, Romania, 12*, 28. https://core.ac.uk/download/pdf/6492899.pdf

Vu, L., Nguyen, Q. U., Nguyen, D. N., Hoang, D. T., & Dutkiewicz, E. (2020). Deep Transfer Learning for IoT Attack Detection. *IEEE Access : Practical Innovations, Open Solutions, 8*, 107335–107344.

Wagner, M., Rind, A., Thür, N., & Aigner, W. (2017). A knowledge-assisted visual malware analysis system: Design, validation, and reflection of KAMAS. *Computers & Security, 67*, 1–15. doi:10.1016/j.cose.2017.02.003

Waheed, N., He, X., & Usman, M. (2020). *Security & Privacy in IoT Using Machine Learning & Blockchain: Threats & Countermeasures.* arXiv preprint arXiv:2002.03488.

Walvin, J. (2011, February 17). Slavery and the building of Britain. *British Broadcasting Corporation.* http://www.bbc.co.uk/history/british/abolition/building_britain_gallery_02.shtml

Wang, H., Barriga, L., Vahidi, A., & Raza, S. (2019, November). Machine Learning for Security at the IoT Edge-A Feasibility Study. In *2019 IEEE 16th International Conference on Mobile Ad Hoc and Sensor Systems Workshops (MASSW)* (pp. 7-12). IEEE.

Wang, P., Yao, C., Zheng, Z., Sun, G., & Song, L. (2018). Joint task assignment, transmission, and computing resource allocation in multilayer mobile edge computing systems. *IEEE Internet of Things Journal, 6*(2), 2872–2884.

Wang, Q. (2014). Applicability of Jus in Bello in Cyber Space: Dilemmas and Challenges. *International Journal of Cyber Warfare & Terrorism, 4*(3), 43–62. doi:10.4018/ijcwt.2014070104

Warkentin, M., & Orgeron, C. (2020). Using the security triad to assess blockchain technology in public sector applications. *International Journal of Information Management, 52*, 1–8. doi:10.1016/j.ijinfomgt.2020.102090

Warren, M., & Hutchinson, W. (2000). Cyber attacks against supply chain management systems: A short note. *International Journal of Physical Distribution & Logistics Management, 30*(7/8), 710–716. doi:10.1108/09600030010346521

Watkins, B. (2014). The impact of cyber attacks on the private sector. Briefing Paper. *Association for International Affair, 12*, 1–11.

Webster, C. W. R., & Leleux, C. (2018). Smart governance: Opportunities for technologically-mediated citizen co-production. *Information Polity, 23*(1), 95–110. doi:10.3233/IP-170065

Weimann, G. (2005). Cyberterrorism: The sum of all fears? *Studies in Conflict and Terrorism, 28*(2), 129–149. doi:10.1080/10576100590905110

Whitman, M., & Mattord, H. (2011). *Principles of information security.* Nelson Education.

Wiese, L., Waage, T., & Brenner, M. (2020). CloudDBGuard: A framework for encrypted data storage in NoSQL wide column stores. *Data & Knowledge Engineering, 126*, 101732. doi:10.1016/j.datak.2019.101732

Wikipedia. (2021a). Artificial neural network. *Wikipedia, the free encyclopedia.* https://en.wikipedia.org/wiki/Artificial_neural_network

William, C. M., Chaturvedi, R., & Chakravarthy, K. (2020). Cybersecurity Risks in a Pandemic. *Journal of Medical Internet Research*, *22*(9), e23692. doi:10.2196/23692 PMID:32897869

Wood, S., Schwartz, E., Tuepker, A., Pres, N. A., Nazi, K. M., Turvery, C., & Nichol, W. P. (2013). Patient Experiences with Full Electronic Access to Health Records and Clinical Notes Through the My HealtheVet Personal Health Record Pilot: Qualitative Study. *Journal of Medical Internet Research*, *15*(3), e65. doi:10.2196/jmir.2356 PMID:23535584

WorldJute.Com. (2002). *Internet banking frauds*. http://www.worldjute.com/ebank1.html#:~:text=Internet%20Banking%20Fraud%20is%20a,through%20techniques%20such%20as%20phishing.

Wu, D., Ren, A., Zhang, W., Fan, F., Liu, P., Fu, X., & Terpenny, J. (2018). Cybersecurity for digital manufacturing. *Journal of Manufacturing Systems*, *48*, 3–12. doi:10.1016/j.jmsy.2018.03.006

Xiao, L., Wan, X., & Han, Z. (2017). PHY-layer authentication with multiple landmarks with reduced overhead. *IEEE Transactions on Wireless Communications*, *17*(3), 1676–1687. doi:10.1109/TWC.2017.2784431

Xiao, L., Wan, X., Lu, X., Zhang, Y., & Wu, D. (2018). IoT security techniques based on machine learning: How do IoT devices use AI to enhance security? *IEEE Signal Processing Magazine*, *35*(5), 41–49. doi:10.1109/MSP.2018.2825478

Xu, G., Yu, W., Chen, Z., Zhang, H., Moulema, P., Fu, X., & Lu, C. (2015). A cloud computing based system for cyber security management. International Journal of Parallel. *Emergent and Distributed Systems*, *30*(1), 29–45. doi:10.1080/17445760.2014.925110

Xu, L., Jiang, C., Wang, J., Yuan, J., & Ren, Y. (2014). Information security in big data: Privacy and data mining. *IEEE Access: Practical Innovations, Open Solutions*, *2*, 1149–1176. doi:10.1109/ACCESS.2014.2362522

Yaga, D., Mell, P., Roby, N., & Scarfone, K. (2019). *Blockchain technology overview*. doi:10.6028/NIST.IR.8202

Yang, F., Zhuang, Y., & Wang, J. (2017). Android Malware Detection Using Hybrid Analysis and Machine Learning Technique. In X. Sun, H.-C. Chao, X. You, & E. Bertino (Eds.), *Cloud Computing and Security* (pp. 565–575). Springer International Publishing. doi:10.1007/978-3-319-68542-7_48

Yar, M., & Steinmetz, K. F. (2019). Cybercrime and society. *Sage (Atlanta, Ga.)*.

Yavuz, F. Y. (2018). *Deep learning in cyber security for Internet of Things* (Master's Thesis). Graduate School of Natural and Applied Sciences, Istanbul Sehir University.

Yildiz, M. (2007). E-government research: Reviewing the literature, limitations, and ways forward. *Government Information Quarterly*, *24*(3), 646–665. doi:10.1016/j.giq.2007.01.002

Yi, P., Zhu, T., Zhang, Q., Wu, Y., & Pan, L. (2016). Puppet attack: A denial of service attack in advanced metering infrastructure network. *Journal of Network and Computer Applications*, *59*, 325–332. doi:10.1016/j.jnca.2015.04.015

Yiu, C. S., Grant, K., & Degar, D. (2007). Factors affecting the adoption of internet banking in Hong Kong, implications for the banking sector. *International Journal of Information Management*, *27*(5), 330–351. doi:10.1016/j.ijinfomgt.2007.03.002

Young, E. (2004). *Global Information Security Survey 2004*. Ernst & Young.

Yu, C. S., & Lo, Y. F. (2007). Factors encouraging people to adopt online banking and discouraging adopters to use online banking services. In *Proceeding of Business and Information, Tokyo, Japan: International Conference on Business and Information*.

Yuan, J., & Li, X. (2018). A reliable and lightweight trust computing mechanism for IoT edge devices based on multi-source feedback information fusion. *IEEE Access : Practical Innovations, Open Solutions*, *6*, 23626–23638.

YuSheng, K., & Ibrahim, M. (2019). Service innovation, service delivery, and customer satisfaction and loyalty in the banking sector of Ghana. *International Journal of Bank Marketing*, *37*(5), 1215–1233. doi:10.1108/IJBM-06-2018-0142

Zaccaria, A., Schmidt-Kessel, M., Schulze, R., & Gambino, A. M. (2019). *EU eIDAS Regulation: Regulation (EU) 910/2014 on electronic identification and trust services for electronic transactions in the internal market*. Beck C.H. Publisher.

Zaidi, E. (2021, March 3). Future of e-banking tied to digital inclusion of masses. *The News International*. https://www.thenews.com.pk/print/798127-future-of-e-banking-tied-to-digital-inclusion-of-masses

Zaied, A. N. (2012). Barriers to e-commerce adoption in Egyptian SMEs. *International Journal of Information Engineering and Electronic Business*, *4*(3), 9. doi:10.5815/ijieeb.2012.03.02

W. Zamojski, J. Mazurkiewicz, J. Sugier, T. Walkowiak, & J. Kacprzyk (Eds.). (2019). Engineering in Dependability of Computer Systems and Networks: *Proceedings of the Fourteenth International Conference on Dependability of Computer Systems DepCoS-RELCOMEX*, July 1–5, 2019, Brunów, Poland (Vol. 987). Springer.

Zaoui, F., & Souissi, N. (2020). Roadmap for digital transformation: A literature review. *Procedia Computer Science*, *175*, 621–628. doi:10.1016/j.procs.2020.07.090

Zeadally, S., Adi, E., Baig, Z., & Khan, I. A. (2020). Harnessing Artificial Intelligence Capabilities to Improve Cybersecurity. *IEEE Access : Practical Innovations, Open Solutions*, *8*, 23817–23837.

Zeadally, S., & Tsikerdekis, M. (2020). Securing Internet of Things (IoT) with machine learning. *International Journal of Communication Systems*, *33*(1), e4169.

Zezulka, F., Marcon, P., Bradac, Z., Arm, J., Benesl, T., & Vesely, I. (2018). Communication systems for industry 4.0 and the iiot. *IFAC-PapersOnLine*, *51*(6), 150–155. doi:10.1016/j.ifacol.2018.07.145

Zhang, P., Schmidt, D., White, J., & Lenz, G. (2018). Blockchain technology use cases in healthcare. In *Advances in Computers*. Elsevier.

Zhang, Q., Yang, L. T., Chen, Z., & Li, P. (2018). A survey on deep learning for big data. *Information Fusion*, *42*, 146–157.

Zhou, F., Goel, M., Desnoyers, P., & Sundaram, R. (2013). Scheduler vulnerabilities and coordinated attacks in cloud computing. *Journal of Computer Security*, *21*(4), 533–559. doi:10.3233/JCS-130474

Zhou, L., Varadharajan, V., & Gopinath, K. (2016). A Secure Role-Based Cloud Storage System for Encrypted Patient-Centric Health Records. *The Computer Journal*, *59*(11), 1593–1611. doi:10.1093/comjnl/bxw019

Zhou, Z., Chen, X., Zhang, Y., & Mumtaz, S. (2020). Blockchain-empowered secure spectrum sharing for 5G heterogeneous networks. *IEEE Network*, *34*(1), 24–31. doi:10.1109/MNET.001.1900188

Zizi, M. (2019). The Flaws and Dangers of Facial Recognition. *Security Today*. Retrieved from: https://securitytoday.com/articles/2019/03/01/the-flaws-and-dangers-of-facial-recognition.aspx

Zouave, E., Bruce, M., Colde, K., Jaitner, M., Rodhe, I., & Gustafsson, T. (2020). *Artificially intelligent cyberattacks*. Academic Press.

About the Contributors

Kamaljeet Sandhu is an active scholar, experienced & passionate about research in Digital Innovation & Strategy, Business Data Analytics, Digital Health, AI, IoT, Cryptocurrency, Blockchain, Cloud Computing, IT Startups, FinTech, Cybersecurity, Accounting, Corporate Governance & CSR, Supply Chain, ERP, SMEs, & Entrepreneurship. Editor of 4 Books & published internationally over 180 articles in peer-reviewed (refereed) journals, conferences, & book chapters. He earned his Ph.D. from Deakin University Melbourne campus, Australia. Having held multiple Leadership positions including Professor at the University of Northern British Columbia Canada, Senior Research Fellow at the University of South Australia, and other Senior Academic positions at: University of Wollongong, Charles Darwin University, Deakin University, & at the University of South Pacific, Fiji. As a Ph.D. Principal Supervisor (Advisor), has supervised & mentored several Ph.D. Research students to successful completion & students have successfully gained academic & research appointments at leading international universities & other organizations.

* * *

Fatimah Al Obaidan is student of Masters of Computer Science at Imam Abdulrahman Bin Faisal University, Dammam, KSA.

Shahid Alam is currently working as an assistant professor in the department of Computer Engineering at Adana Alparsalan Turkes Science and Technology University, Adana, Turkey. He received his PhD in Computer Science from University of Victoria, Canada in 2014. His research interests include software engineering, programming languages, and cyber security.

Alper Kamil Demir is currently working as an assistant professor in the department of Computer Engineering at Adana Alparsalan Turkes Science and Technology University. He received his BS degree from Hacettepe University, MS degree from University of Southern California, and PhD degree from Kocaeli University. Between 2009-2013, he worked at Huawei Telecommunications Inc. as a Senior Software and Research Engineer. He is interested in Computer Networks, Distributed Systems and Security in general.

Rebeca Díez-Somavilla is a PhD Teacher of Audiovisual Communication at UPV (Universitat Politècnica de València), Campus de Gandia. Co-director of the International Congress on Communication and Technology, #Comunica2. Researcher on online marketing, communication and social networks and technologies applied to education.

Mona Ebrahimi 's educational background includes a Master's Degree in Business Administration and a Bachelor's Degree in Industrial Engineering. After earning her degree, she soon entered the business world as a business analyst and planner to explore her lifelong passion for making improvements in the business processes of large organizations. In addition to her primary job functions after 6 years of experience in business, she realized that she is extremely obsessed with research and development. Her passion for research and development can be traced back to her prior researches to find gaps in different businesses and analyze them. So she joined the Hamta Group | Hamta Business Corporation to help different businesses make developments in their processes. Currently, she is involved with a range of multidisciplinary research projects in business management, cybersecurity management, digital transformation, information system, and performance management.

Esha Jain is faculty in the finance and accounting area with more than Fourteen years of work experience with Ph.D. and UGC-NET qualification. Currently, she is Finance faculty in the School of Management and Liberal Studies at The NorthCap University, Gurgaon. An awardee of 'Eminent Educationist Award', 'Asia Pacific Gold Star Award', 'Young Woman Educator and Scholar Award', 'Excellence Award 2017', she was also selected for "Rajiv Gandhi Education Excellence Award" and 'Bharat Vidya Shiromani Award'. She is the Resource Person for Various Faculty Development Programmes in the field of Academics, Research, and SPSS. She is also awarded 29 Honors and Awards, including 17 Best Research Paper Awards and a Dean Committee Choice Award in various International Conferences of repute. She has been invited by IIM Indore for review of 'Institutional Development Plans (IDPs)' under the World Bank-supported Madhya Pradesh Higher Education Quality Improvement Project (MPHEQIP) to be submitted to the Department of Higher Education, Government of Madhya Pradesh, and also took webinar sessions for Financial Management and Taxation Management (PG level) of Sikkim Manipal University Distance Learning Education. She has taken modules of Chartered Institute of Management Accountants (CIMA), London, UK, and certified by the Institute of Chartered Accountants of India (ICAI) for conducting 'Investor Awareness Programmes' in institutions and organizations. She has published seven patents with the Government of India and Two patents with the Government of Australia. More than 90 of her research papers are published in various International Journals (including Scopus and Web of Science) and Conference Proceedings of repute as well as authored two books, one is on 'Foreign Exchange Management' & another one is on 'Principles of Management with text and cases' under reputed Brands. She has also presented more than 80 research papers and cases at various national and international conferences as well as has chaired various National and International Seminars and Conferences as Session Chair, Keynote Speaker, and Panelist in Panel Discussions. She has also associated 12 various International Journals as Editorial Board Member, Academic Advisor, Research Paper Reviewer & Editor-in-Chief. She is also an External Examiner for evaluating Ph.D. Thesis for Jain University, Bengaluru, University of Madras, and the University of Pune. A Certified Technical Analyst (in Stock Market) from Government of NCT of Delhi and Government of India, and Amazon Trained E-commerce Specialist, she has also qualified a module of Financial Markets with Distinction organized by (NSE) National Stock Exchange of India. She has also achieved a Statement of Accomplishment with Distinction in the certification course on 'Personal and Family Financial Planning' from the University of Florida.

Giménez López Jose Luis. Assistant professor at the Higher Polytechnic School of Gandía, Polytechnic University of Valencia, Spain. He teaches in the Degree in Audiovisual Communication and the Degree in Interactive Technologies. Member of the Graphic Technologies Research Center. Expert in interactive environments, user experience and usability. He has participated in several national and international research projects on the use of technology in education. He has worked in different national and European R + D + I projects related to the use of technology in education. Researcher ID: K-6260-2014. ORCID: https://orcid.org/0000-0003-1762-3071. ID de autor de Scopus: 26656726900.

Jonika Lamba is a research scholar in the School of Management and Liberal Studies at The North-Cap University Gurugram, India.

Mitra Madanchian is a holder of a Ph.D. degree in the field of Business Management. She is passionate about business management and R&D and has done industrial practice in both SMEs and one of the Big Four (KPMG). With over 8 years of industry experience, she has established herself as an industry expert in the field of Business Management, and Research and Development. Beside her industrial experiences, she has an enthusiastic experience in academic research, in area of Business Management, Leadership, FinTech and IT Management. Her views in science have been published in reputable publishers such as Elsevier, IGI Global and MDPI. She has authored scientific articles in authentic peer-reviewed international journals and conferences proceeding, book chapters as well as book in the field of leadership. Currently, she is involved in several multidisciplinary research projects among which includes digital transformation, blockchain applications, customer satisfaction and business management.

Teresa Magal-Royo. PhD in Fine Arts, Associate Professor at the Graphic Engineering Department. Degree: Product Design Universitat Politécnica de Valencia, Spain. Post graduate in the Royal College of Art, London, England. Developing and coordinating projects related to the use of new technology in the field of education/Design and development of user-oriented interfaces/ Adaptation of graphic interfaces for viewing on mobile devices/ usability and accessibility in digital communication devices and in product design for business. Multimodal interfaces user oriented for ubiquitous devices. She has participated in several national and international research projects on the use of technology in education. http://www.upv.es/ficha-personal/tmagal. Researcher ID: K-6728-2014. ORCID: http://orcid.org/0000-0002-7640-6264. https://www.redalyc.org/autor.oa?id=31963.

Anita Medhekar is a senior lecturer in economics and holds a PhD from Deakin University, Australia. She has taught at undergraduate and post graduate levels in India, Indonesia and Australia. Currently, she is teaching at Central Queensland University, Rockhampton, Australia. Her research interests are in Applied Economics, Health Economics, International Trade, Development Economics, Public Finance, South-Asia, Tourism Economics, Economies of Asia-Pacific, Healthcare Supply Chain, Bilateral Trade and Development for Peace, Public Policy, and Public-Private Partnerships. She has numerous publications to her credit as refereed conference proceedings, book chapters, and journal articles.

Peadar O'Connor has worked in the telecommunications industry for more than 20 years, specialising in network design, geospatial intelligence, software development, and process automation. His recent postgraduate studies at Queensland University of Technology have focused on cyber security, with his final project centred on managing privacy and security in blockchain technologies.

Fahri Özsungur graduated from Ataturk University Faculty of Law, Hacettepe University Department of Family and Consumer Sciences PhD. and Aksaray University Department of Business Ph.D. He serves as a Higher Degrees by Research (HDR) Examiner /Ph.D. Examiner for the University of New England. He is a Eurostars Technical Expert (EUREKA Secretariat). He is affiliated with Mersin University Faculty of Economics and Administrative Sciences Department of Labor Economics and Industrial Relations, Adana Science and Technology University, Rotary International, Osmaniye Korkut Ata University, Çağ University, WEGATE- European Gateway for Women's Entrepreneurship, and Canadian Institute for International Law Expertise (CIFILE). He has 4 books, 9 book chapters, and more than 78 (4 SSCI/SCI/SCI-Expanded,10 ESCI) published articles and 18 international conference papers. He is the editor of 14 Journals (1 SSCI/SCI/SCI-Expanded), and the reviewer of 109 Journals (9 SSCI/SCI/SCI-Expanded, 26 ESCI).

Shailesh Palekar completed his PhD from the Queensland University of Technology, Brisbane. His research focuses on Social Media, IT disruption and innovation, and the impact of new emerging technologies on individuals and organizations.

Árpád Ferenc Papp-Váry is the dean of the Faculty of Tourism, Business and Communication at the Budapest Metropolitan University, Hungary. He is also the head of the Commerce and Marketing BSc programme and vocational programme, the Marketing MSc programme (running from 2019), and the Digital Marketing executive MBA postgraduate programme. At the same time he is research associate of the Urban Marketing and Geostrategy Centre of John von Neumann University, Kecskemét, Hungary. Besides university education, Árpád regularly holds training sessions and provides branding consultancy for cities, companies and professionals. He is serving as Vice President of the Hungarian Marketing Association. His teaching and research areas are country branding, city branding, personal branding, sports branding and branded entertainment. Árpád is the author of six books and several hundred publications, most of which are available online at www.papp-vary.hu.

Romil Rawat is currently working as Assistant Professor in Shri Vaishnav Vidyapeeth Vishwavidyalaya, Indore., India. He has completed MTech in 2015 and published several research paper attend many international and national conferences across world.

Tansif ur Rehman has a Ph.D. in European Studies. He has several publications and has over 20 years of teaching as well as 14 years of research experience.

José Rocha is an R&D&i Manager. PhD by the Polytechnic University of Valencia (UPV), Spain, 2011. Computer Engineer by the State University of Campinas (UNICAMP), Brazil. Researcher, professor and IT project manager specialised on Cloud Computing, Big Data, EDI integration, Semantic Web, Artificial Intelligence and R&D&i Project Management. He is an expert on software development and R&D Projects. As lecturer and researcher at the Polytechnic University of Valencia and at the Carlos III University of Madrid during 14 years, plus the years he had being working to the private sector, he had developed more than 32 R&D&i Projects funded by public entities (20 by the European Commission, 8 by the Spanish government, 3 by the Brazilian government), published more than 30 books and papers on international editorials and journals, participated in several scientific events and other important research activities like organising international conferences, coordinating EU consortium partners, being member of scientific associations and receiving awards and grants to carry out research projects in Spain, Brazil, Dublin and USA.

Saqib Saeed is an associate professor at the Computer Information System department at Imam Abdulrahman Bin Faisal University, Dammam, KSA. He has a Ph.D. in Information Systems from University of Siegen, Germany, and a Masters degree in Software Technology from Stuttgart University of Applied Sciences, Germany. He is also a certified software quality engineer from American Society of Quality. His research interests lie in the areas of human-centered computing, computer supported cooperative work, empirical software engineering and ICT4D. He has more than 80 publications to his credit.

Surabhi Singh is a student of Commerce at Amity University Jharkhand.

Szabolcs Szolnoki, as the Science and Technology Diplomat of Hungary in Tel-Aviv, focuses on projects of applied research, experimental development and startup cooperation. Mr. Szolnoki assists the interested companies in searching partners, the areas of cooperation and interest mainly are: life sciences, digital health, cybersecurity, mobility and autonomous vehicles, space-industry. At the same time he is an external research associate of the Urban Marketing and Geostrategy Centre of John von Neumann University, Kecskemét, Hungary. Mr. Szolnoki is the founder president of an NGO called Association for Innovative Initiatives. The Association has a special focus on improving the labour market situation by helping people to improve their employability potential and their entrepreneurial skills Mr. Szolnoki is a doctoral student at the University of Pécs, Insititute of Geography and Earth Sciences. Before his diplomatic service he assisted innovative Hungarian inventors in starting their businesses and entering domestic and foreign markets.

Hamed Taherdoost is an award-winning leader and R&D professional. He is the founder of Hamta Group and Sessional Faculty member of University Canada West. He holds PhD of Computer Science from Universiti Teknologi Malaysia. With over 20 years of experience in both industry and academic sectors, he has established himself as an industry leader in the field of Management of Technology and Information System.Throughout his career, he has been highly involved in development of several important projects in different industries. He has spent the last 8 years helping startups to grow by implementing new projects. To date, he has received some international awards including Rahnamafar Award, SEAB Award & Business Excellence Award for Business Leadership, and, finalist of Southeast Asian Startup Awards by Global Startup Awards. Apart from his experience in industry, he also has numerous achievements in the academic environment. He has been an active multidisciplinary researcher and R&D specialist involved in several academic and industrial research projects. He has been working with researchers from various disciplines and has been actively engaged in different research studies. His views on science and technology has been published in top-ranked scientific publishers such as Elsevier, Springer, Emerald, IEEE, IGI Global, Inderscience, Taylor and Francis and he has published over 130 scientific articles in authentic peer-reviewed international journals and conference proceedings, eight book chapters as well as seven books in the field of technology and research methodology. His research achievements also include winning several best paper awards and outstanding reviewer awards. He was lecturer in PNU and IAU Universities. Beside on lectureship positions, he was researcher at IAU for over 8 years, R&D Manager and Academic Program Manager of Research Club, Tablokar, MDTH and Hamta Academy, Malaysia, and is Advisory Board of Cambridge Scholars Publishing, UK, Scientific

Board of Nan Yang Academy of Sciences (NASS), Singapore, Research Advisor at Pinmo, Mentor at Publons Academy and Futurpreneur Canada. Moreover, he has served as editor of journal, book & proceedings for prestigious publishers, and has also organized and chaired numerous conferences and conference sessions respectively & has delivered speeches as chief guest & keynote speaker. Currently, he is Senior Member of IEEE, IASED, & IEDRC, Working group member of IFIP TC 11 - Information Security Management, and Member of CSIAC, ACT-IAC and many other professional bodies. Currently, he is involved in several multidisciplinary research projects among which includes studying innovation in information technology & cybersecurity, fintech, blockchain technology, people's behaviour and technology acceptance.

Shrikant Telang is an Assistant Professor in Shri Vaishnav Vidyapeeth Vishwavidyalaya, Indore, India.

Nagarajan Venkatachalam is a Senior Fellow of Higher Education Academy. His action design research projects explore how to generate social value with novel use of blockchain mechanism. His blockchain based student assessment ledger project won competitive funding from the Australian Council of Deans of ICT Learning and Teaching Academy in 2020. With his passion for teaching, he ensures his diverse learning communities at QUT develop 21st century skills through authentic assessments and impactful feedback procedures. He also consults with start-ups and social enterprises for developing digital capabilities based business models.

Index

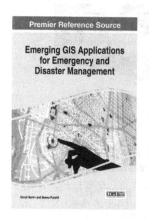

www.igi-global.com

Publisher of Peer-Reviewed, Timely, and
Innovative Academic Research Since 1988

IGI Global's Transformative Open Access (OA) Model:
How to Turn Your University Library's Database Acquisitions Into a Source of OA Funding

Well in advance of Plan S, IGI Global unveiled their OA Fee Waiver (Read & Publish) Initiative. Under this initiative, librarians who invest in IGI Global's InfoSci-Books and/or InfoSci-Journals databases will be able to subsidize their patrons' OA article processing charges (APCs) when their work is submitted and accepted (after the peer review process) into an IGI Global journal.

How Does it Work?

Step 1: **Library Invests in the InfoSci-Databases:** A library perpetually purchases or subscribes to the InfoSci-Books, InfoSci-Journals, or discipline/subject databases.

Step 2: **IGI Global Matches the Library Investment with OA Subsidies Fund:** IGI Global provides a fund to go towards subsidizing the OA APCs for the library's patrons.

Step 3: **Patron of the Library is Accepted into IGI Global Journal (After Peer Review):** When a patron's paper is accepted into an IGI Global journal, they option to have their paper published under a traditional publishing model or as OA.

Step 4: **IGI Global Will Deduct APC Cost from OA Subsidies Fund:** If the author decides to publish under OA, the OA APC fee will be deducted from the OA subsidies fund.

Step 5: **Author's Work Becomes Freely Available:** The patron's work will be freely available under CC BY copyright license, enabling them to share it freely with the academic community.

Note: This fund will be offered on an annual basis and will renew as the subscription is renewed for each year thereafter. IGI Global will manage the fund and award the APC waivers unless the librarian has a preference as to how the funds should be managed.

Hear From the Experts on This Initiative:

"I'm very happy to have been able to make one of my recent research contributions *freely available* along with having access to the *valuable resources* found within IGI Global's InfoSci-Journals database."

– Prof. Stuart Palmer,
Deakin University, Australia

"Receiving the support from IGI Global's OA Fee Waiver Initiative *encourages me to continue my research work without any hesitation*."

– Prof. Wenlong Liu, College of Economics and Management at Nanjing University of Aeronautics & Astronautics, China

For More Information, Scan the QR Code or Contact:
IGI Global's Digital Resources Team at eresources@igi-global.com.

Printed in the United States
by Baker & Taylor Publisher Services